Marketing

Larry J. Rosenberg

New York University

Marketing

Prentice-Hall, Inc.

Englewood Cliffs, New Jersey

To Janet

Library of Congress Cataloging in Publication Data

Rosenberg, Larry J
    Marketing.

    Includes bibliographical references and indexes.
    1. Marketing.   2. Marketing management.   I. Title.
HF5415.R578   658.8   76-54711
ISBN 0-13-556100-0

Printed in the United States of America

10 9 8 7 6 5 4 3 2 1

PRENTICE-HALL INTERNATIONAL, INC., *London*
PRENTICE-HALL OF AUSTRALIA, PTY. LTD., *Sydney*
PRENTICE-HALL OF CANADA, LTD., *Toronto*
PRENTICE-HALL OF INDIA PRIVATE LIMITED, *New Delhi*
PRENTICE-HALL OF JAPAN, INC., *Tokyo*
PRENTICE-HALL OF SOUTHEAST ASIA (PTE.) LTD., *Singapore*
WHITEHALL BOOKS LIMITED, *Wellington, New Zealand*

Cover photo by Gabe Palmer/The Image Bank
Part opening photos: Part 1, Hank Delespinasse/The Image Bank;
Part 2, Sepp Seitz/Magnum; Part 3, J. Paul Kirouac/A Good Thing Inc.,
Part 4, William Rivelli/The Image Bank; Part 5, Erich Hartmann/Magnum
Part 6, United Nations.
Table 25-2 is reprinted by permission of Holt, Rinehart and Winston. Copyright © 1971
by Holt, Rinehart and Winston, Inc.

Contents

Promotion

Distribution

Case Studies

Preface

During the mid-1970s marketing was faced with an unprecedented series of challenges. Suddenly, the environment seemed to explode. A variety of economic conditions combined with a host of social issues and a higher degree of political involvement in the marketplace. It is clear that these challenges will continue on well into the 1980s and beyond.

To be meaningful, an introductory marketing text must come to grips with this changing environment. It must combine an analysis of the basic marketing principles that have survived intact with a consideration of the changing assumptions, goals, and techniques that marketing needs to face this new era. These are the aims of this book, which has been written in order to provide a relevant and dynamic framework for future practitioners. Specifically, the book has these key features:

Three-dimensional approach. While the orientation of the book is primarily managerial (since that is the role most of its readers are preparing for), it also reflects the reality of the new era in marketing by recognizing the interplay of the three major participants in the marketing process: management, consumers, and society. In the past, the conventional marketing concept focused on the consumer point of view. The three-dimensional perspective of this book embraces larger social considerations as well.

Important new themes. This book integrates contemporary economic, political, and social themes of marketing with the durable fundamentals of marketing. And the role of marketing in nonprofit organizations is recognized throughout.

Future view. Changing conditions are a fact of marketing life, and current decisions must try to anticipate the future. This book points out the dynamics of change and gives glimpses of what marketing is likely to be like in the future.

Career consciousness. This book highlights many of the exciting career opportunities that exist in organizations practicing marketing. Glimpses are given throughout the book, and especially in the last chapter, of marketing careers that will be available to its readers.

Practical orientation. Stress is given to practical applications of the marketing concepts and techniques that are discussed. Numerous real-life examples of marketing practices are drawn from a wide variety of situations: products and services, consumer and industrial, profit-making and nonprofit, large and small organizations. The case studies that follow each part provide further insight into the implications of marketing theory in actual business situations.

High-impact learning. A great deal of effort has gone into making the book interesting both to read and to learn from. Each chapter opens with a list of key tasks that the reader should be able to accomplish by its completion. The text of each chapter begins with a vignette that offers a look at what will follow. Within chapters, practical examples of particular interest are boxed off from the text for emphasis. The book relies heavily on charts, graphs, and tables to make key concepts more learnable. Some of them are reproduced from important published sources; many of them were created for this book. Each chapter closes with a group of discussion questions designed to give the reader an opportunity to explore the marketing problems that have been discussed in the chapter.

Supplement for the Student. Accompanying the text is a Study Guide and Workbook. Each chapter of the study guide is keyed to a chapter of the text and provides a chapter outline, a list of key terms and concepts, and a group of self-tests. Answers to the self-tests appear in a marginal column next to the questions themselves, providing the student with immediate verification of responses.

ORGANIZATION OF THE TEXT

The book is divided into six parts.

Part 1, *Overview*, sets the stage for the discussion that follows. Marketing is described in both its organizational and its societal setting, and important economic, political, and social aspects of the marketing environment are introduced.

Part 2, *Analyzing the Marketplace*, begins with a description of the tools of planning and forecasting. It then considers the dimensions of market demand, competition, and market segmentation.

Part 3, *Buying Behavior*, considers consumer behavior and decision making as well as the behavior of organizations as customers.

Part 4, *Elements of Marketing Strategy*, presents an in-depth picture of the four basic elements of marketing strategy: product, pricing, promotion, and distribution. Three chapters are devoted to each element.

Part 5, *Carrying Out Marketing Strategy*, is devoted to the managerial processes involved in marketing information systems and marketing research, the implementation of marketing strategy, and the control of marketing performance.

Finally, Part 6, *Broadened Marketing Perspectives*, begins with a description of marketing management in the multinational arena. The final chapter challenges the reader to develop his or her own practical philosophy of marketing and reconsiders some of the broad social questions with which the book began. It also highlights many of the career opportunities that exist in the field of marketing today.

ACKNOWLEDGMENTS

In preparing this book, I have been fortunate to have the support and encouragement of many people. Some of them influenced my professional development; others worked directly with me on the text itself.

My earliest exposure to marketing took place during the ten years I spent as an employee in my parents' small business in Philadelphia. It is to William and Florence Rosenberg that I therefore express my gratitude for my first experience in marketing.

I also wish to thank the faculty members of The Ohio State University during my graduate education in the 1960s, especially Louis W. Stern, William R. Davidson, Robert Bartels, James F. Engel, Arthur Cullman, and the late Theodore N. Beckman.

My colleagues at New York University have helped me to expand my thinking on the nature of marketing and marketing education. This group includes Gerald J. Glasser, Arnold Corbin, John A. Czepiel, Barbara J. Coe, George J. Szybillo, James MacLachlan, Henry Assael, F. Robert Shoaf, Alfred Gross, Robert W. Shoemaker, and Russell M. Moore.

I gratefully acknowledge as well the inspiration of several professionals in New York whose philosophy of human relations I share: James Dix, Barry Heettner, Geoffrey Lindenauer, Theodora Hirshhorn, and Bea Langerman.

Several distinguished colleagues commented on various parts of the manuscript. I am happy to count among them:

Gary Armstrong, University of North Carolina, Chapel Hill
John W. Brown, Jr., Monroe Community College
M. Bixby Cooper, Michigan State University
Robert M. Fishco, Middlesex County College
Ronald E. Frank, University of Pennsylvania
Roy R. Grundy, College of DuPage
Franklin S. Houston, Temple University
R. W. Nason, University of Rhode Island
Leonard Kreitz, Rio Hondo College
Eric I. Kulp, Middlesex County College
William G. Panschar, Indiana University
Barbara A. Pletcher, California State University, Sacramento

A special note of acknowledgment is due Philip Kotler of Northwestern University. His intellectual contributions to the field are so pervasive as to make it impossible to write a modern marketing textbook without being in his debt.

The case studies used throughout this book are based on many diverse sources. Names of firms, people, cities, etc., have in most cases been disguised, but all of the cases are substantially based on actual marketing situations taken from consulting reports, published works, term projects, or personal experience. I am pleased to acknowledge my debt to Jerry D. Coffin, Stuart M. Herman, Steven M. Jasper, and Philip W. Sachs for permission to use certain sources. Special appreciation is extended to Terry Davidson, who opened the case files of the Urban Business Assistance Corporation to me. I also want to thank Bonnie Reece for her flair with case development.

I have indeed been fortunate to have Prentice-Hall as my publisher and to have had the pleasure of working with several talented members of its staff. Special recognition is due Judy Rothman, Claudia Wilson, Paul Atkinson,

Ruth Kugelman, Cecil Yarbrough, Wayne Spohr, Robert Nott, Florence Silverman, Carole Saltz, Susanna Lesan, and Nancy Myers. Thanks is also due to Robert Lamm, James McDonald, and Linda Pembrook.

Three special assistants have been both diligent and enthusiastic. I am grateful to Hugh Cannon and Dennis Sandler for their research work, and to Terri Glatz, whose superb editorial and secretarial assistance was evident throughout the manuscript.

Finally, I want to thank the many students in my classes at The Ohio State University and New York University. They have kept me thinking on my feet, developing my working notes and teaching concepts, and in touch with the times.

Larry M. Rosenberg

Marketing

Overview

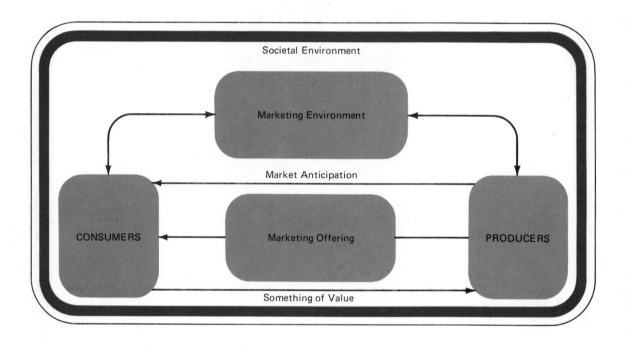

1

MARKETING IN ITS SOCIETAL SETTING

After completing this chapter, the reader should be able to:

1. Define the major participants in the marketing model and explain how they are related in the marketing process.

2. Explain how the marketing process is shaped by its economic, societal, and historical foundations.

3. Describe the nature of marketing in an organization in the production, sales, and marketing eras.

4. Update the marketing concept to account for its newer dimensions—societal, nonprofit, and a future orientation.

5. Identify the reasons why studying marketing may benefit his or her professional career.

MARKETING IS HAPPENING AROUND YOU

As a buyer and consumer of goods, services, and ideas, you are already a participant in the **marketing** process. This book will present marketing not only as the consumer sees it but also from a broader perspective. For example, we will examine marketing as society's way of fulfilling consumer needs, and as a process by which organizations satisfy the demands of specific groups of consumers. Let's look at a few examples of marketing in action and the essential points that underlie them.

A Reliable Chicken

"It takes a tough man to make a tender chicken," claims Frank Perdue. In recent years, his rural image and homespun style have become a fixture on eastern United States television screens. This promotional campaign has built an $80 million chicken empire. There are several key factors that have gone into Perdue's success story. These include his personal salesmanship in television and newspaper advertising and his promises of reliable, plump, top-quality poultry. Also important are his widely publicized money-back guarantee and the distinctive yellow coloring of Perdue chickens (due to extra feeding with marigold petals), which buyers have come to associate with quality chicken. Consumers have clearly responded to the Perdue image. Sales are booming, even though Perdue chickens have been priced from five to ten cents per pound higher than other brands.

The spectacular rise of Perdue, Inc. suggests the power of an effective marketing approach. Perdue chickens were not simply presented as another brand sold in supermarkets; rather the product became the object of a broad marketing approach. This included product development (plumper, yellower chickens), the producer's brand name, a distinctive advertising campaign, distribution of the product to selected supermarkets, and Frank Perdue's personal selling approach through advertising and his visits to supermarket managers. Marketing a product goes far beyond selling. It means putting many elements together to make an impact on consumers—here is a chicken they can trust.

From Snowmobiles to Mass Transit

For years, Bombardier, Ltd. dominated the snowmobile market. But in the early 1970s sales of snowmobiles began to drop, and Bombardier needed to find new areas of operation in order to survive. In 1974 the company entered the mass transit business with a $117.8 million contract to build 432 subway cars for the city of Montreal. This sale was Bombardier's first step in pursuing a mass transit market in Canada that is estimated at $6 billion over the next fifteen years.

Bombardier originally produced snowmobiles for a consumer market. The company then began making a new product (subway cars) for a new type of market (Canadian cities). A company's market orientation must change when it hopes to sell to industrial customers rather than to individuals. When a company sells its product to an industry, it may deal with far fewer customers and its dealings may be more indirect. But a large organization has many layers, and corporate decision making is a complex process. Marketing to such an organization must be aimed at this structure.

No Smoking, Please

Cigarette consumption has been on the rise in Sweden since 1920. In 1975 the government undertook a program to raise a nation of nonsmokers. The program consisted of antismoking education in maternity clinics and schools, increased restrictions on cigarette advertising, higher cigarette taxes, and prohibitions on smoking in public places. Sweden was especially concerned that children grow up in nonsmoking environments.

Marketing does not always involve the sale of a product with the goal of producing a profit. The Swedish program to reduce smoking is an example of a social cause that could benefit from a marketing approach. The government must first define a target population (possibly children and young adults). Then it must develop effective tools (such as public advertising and school programs) to reach them with its antismoking message.

The Pepski Generation

Pepsi Cola, the first American item produced in the Soviet Union, became an instant success. It was promoted as a prestige drink; one brochure recommended serving it in an ice bucket along with champagne. The key was the beverage's American mystique. "That makes it special for us, an exotic treat," declared a Russian newspaper editor.

Pepsi Cola may be an American product, but marketing is not an exclusively American phenomenon. It can occur in a socialist system such as that of the Soviet Union. Of course, brand names, advertising, and other marketing techniques must be permitted for marketing in socialist systems to resemble the sophisticated processes used in affluent capitalist nations.

The Smart Job Seeker

Polly Di Lauro, a marketing major, hoped to work as a buyer for a large downtown department store after her graduation from college. In anticipation of this goal, she had carefully selected her business courses and taken summer jobs in a boutique. During her senior year she visited the college placement service and obtained a list of stores registered with them. She then prepared her résumé, stressing her sales experience in summer jobs, her marketing major, and her hobbies and travel experiences. She also indicated her willingness to relocate if necessary. Polly mailed the résumé to those stores with training programs, reasoning that they would be the most likely prospects. She also contacted employment agencies that specialized in her field. Polly went out on several interviews, and was offered a trainee position in a city not far from her hometown.

Polly Di Lauro's job search benefited from a solid marketing approach. She gave careful and systematic thought to the needs of her desired employer. Then she figured out how best to develop her capabilities and to present them in light of those needs.

MARKETING DEFINED

The concept of marketing has been continually redefined in recent decades. As conditions in the marketplace have changed, so have our definitions of marketing. Marketing has been viewed as a process or set of activities that have to do with distribution, economics, management, decision making, and social roles.

In our study of marketing, we will use a definition that incorporates many ideas.

> *Marketing is a matching process, based on goals and capabilities, by which a producer provides a marketing mix (product, services, advertising, distribution, pricing, etc.) that meets consumer needs within the limits of society.*

Figure 1-1
MODEL OF THE
MARKETING PROCESS

This definition is illustrated by Figure 1-1.

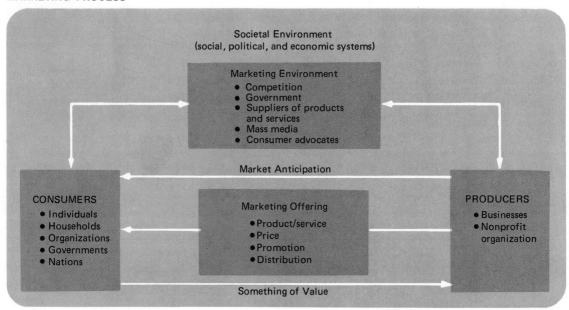

As we can see from the model, the marketing process brings together, or matches, two primary participants—producers and consumers. The term **producer** is used broadly. It can mean a manufacturer (of cameras or machine tools), a retailer (department store or florist), a service establishment (radio station or dry cleaner), or a nonprofit institution (university or hospital). The producer may be a single organization or it may be a coalition of firms, such as the network of manufacturers and dealers for Chevrolet cars.

Each producer has various reasons for being in existence, including the desire for profit, growth, and prestige. It might also provide a social service. Producers have different capabilities in making and marketing products. These include holding patents on products (the Polaroid camera), devising special advertising messages (Joe Namath selling men's cologne), having large financial resources, and employing skilled key personnel (a famous physician on a hospital staff).

The producer attempts **market anticipation**—finding out consumer wants and needs—either through educated guesses or formal market research. The consumer is then given a **market offering**, representing elements of the product or service and its price, promotion, and distribution. The **consumer** may be an individual, a household unit, an organization (General Motors buying steel for its cars from U. S. Steel), or a government. A **transaction** occurs when the consumer accepts the producer's market offering, and gives something of value in return, usually money.

The model also shows us that the marketing process involves more than producers and consumers. The environment within which marketing exists, including the government, competitors, the mass media, and consumer advocates, places competitive, legal, cost, and other constraints on the producer. It also alerts the consumer to other options. Producer, consumer, and the environment in which they operate—all function within a social, political, and economic system. This system is governed by certain "rules of the game," which are subject to change, sometimes without much notice.

The model presented in Figure 1-1 will be our primary frame of reference in this text. It allows us to view marketing as a managerial process, thus focusing attention on the objectives, resources, and performance of the producer. Yet the model also suggests that marketing can be successful only if societal dynamics are considered. Thus, we must understand the operations and roles of both producer and consumer and know how the marketing environment affects them. This will provide us with a full view of the marketing system at work.

The model is most descriptive of the work of business firms, since they are still the center of marketing knowledge and technique. However, the model may also be applied to nonprofit organizations. Although we will focus primarily on marketing in the United States, this model can also help us to understand marketing in other countries. Finally, it is important to remember that this model is dynamic. Forces and norms which affect marketing are bound to change in the future, and the model is constructed to incorporate such changes.

SOCIETAL FOUNDATIONS OF MARKETING

SEPARATION OF PRODUCERS AND CONSUMERS

William McInnes has observed the economic reality of a **market** and defined it as "the gap which separates producer and consumer."[1] Few people today make the goods they consume and perform the services they use. Producers and consumers are therefore *separated* and need to find one another in order to arrive at an *exchange*. Some force must bring together the producer and consumer in order for there to be a market relationship. This force is known as marketing. McInnes defines it as "any activity which actualizes the potential market relationship between the makers and users of economic goods and services."

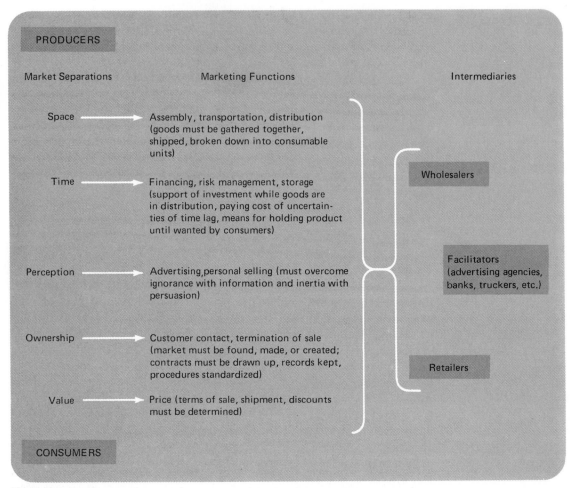

PRODUCERS

Market Separations	Marketing Functions	Intermediaries

Space ⟶ Assembly, transportation, distribution (goods must be gathered together, shipped, broken down into consumable units)

Time ⟶ Financing, risk management, storage (support of investment while goods are in distribution, paying cost of uncertainties of time lag, means for holding product until wanted by consumers)

Wholesalers

Perception ⟶ Advertising, personal selling (must overcome ignorance with information and inertia with persuasion)

Facilitators (advertising agencies, banks, truckers, etc.)

Ownership ⟶ Customer contact, termination of sale (market must be found, made, or created; contracts must be drawn up, records kept, procedures standardized)

Retailers

Value ⟶ Price (terms of sale, shipment, discounts must be determined)

CONSUMERS

Figure 1-2
ECONOMIC RATIONALE OF MARKETING

Based on William McInnes, "A Conceptual Approach to Marketing," in R. Cox, W. Alderson, and S. J. Shapiro, eds., *Theory in Marketing* (Homewood, Ill.: Irwin, 1964), pp. 51–67.

Separations between producers and consumers may take several forms, including the following:

1. spatial separation (physical separation);

2. separation in time (lapse between production and consumption);

3. perceptional separation (consumers' knowledge of and interest in product);

4. separation of ownership (legal title of ownership is held by producer or consumer);

5. separation of values (producers' costs measured against consumers' wants and ability to pay).

Because of these separations, various things must be done to bring consumers and goods or services together, as indicated in Figure 1-2. For example, *assembling* and *transportation* are necessary to eliminate spatial separation. Goods must be created in saleable units and shipped to the place of consumption. Advertising is important in breaking down perceptional separation. Through advertising, the consumer receives information about the product and is given greater incentive to make a purchase.

Some of these marketing functions are handled by specialist intermediaries—for example, railroads for transportation of goods, or market research companies to develop information on consumer interests. Many of these functions can be divided and shifted among producers, intermediaries, and consumers. Air conditioners, for example, may be advertised by both the manufacturer and the retailer. The consumer who goes grocery shopping most often brings the products home himself, and thereby takes on part of the transportation function.

MARKETING—A SOCIETAL PROCESS

In the previous section, we looked at marketing mainly in economic terms. Yet we must also understand how society shapes what happens in a market economy.

Robert Bartels observes that marketing takes place in all societies, but that the way in which it is carried on reflects the native culture.[2] Local psychological, geographic, economic, temporal, and informational conditions affect the marketing process. Both producers and consumers act out social roles according to the customs of the society; they do not simply function as economic units. Marketing is always a process of social interaction. It is subject to the behavioral norms and customs that dominate a particular society. Extending credit to customers indicates trust, as does the belief that a producer will stand behind his or her product or service.

Marketing is a societal activity designed to meet consumption needs for human existence. These include survival, pleasure, and the need for meaning. Marketing removes separations between producers and consumers and allows exchanges to take place. For this to happen, a variety of market interactions must be completed. Participants must play various economic and social roles; they must act as managers, employees, owners, consumers, financiers, competitors, intermediate customers, suppliers, government, and the community. The interactions between these individuals and organizations form a complex series of movements (or flows) that define the marketing process. All of these interactions are affected by the behavioral constraints of the society, including economic, legal, social, and ethical limitations.

Society sanctions the marketing process, and must evaluate and regulate its effectiveness. The various segments of society impose differing types of standards. Some are geared to achieve high levels of economic performance, while others direct the marketing process to reflect social responsibility and ecological concerns.

MARKETING IN DIFFERENT ECONOMIC SYSTEMS

There are three types of systems by which key economic questions affecting production, distribution of income, and consumption are decided. In reality, most economies are characterized by one of these systems, with aspects of the others mixed in. These systems determine who has the power in an economy and how it will be used. Marketing takes a different character under each.[3] The three systems are:

1. The **tradition-directed** system, in which basic economic problems are solved through ancient custom. Some developing societies today fit this description, such as Afghanistan, Uganda, and Bolivia.

2. The **command-directed** system, which uses central planning and top-down decision making. The Soviet Union and other socialist countries have dramatically enforced industrialization through this system.

3. The **market-directed** system, in which the forces of supply and demand determine production and compensation decisions. This is the basic system in the United States, although some government programs are command-directed.

In tradition-directed systems, industrial progress and marketing practices tend to be slowed down by ancient customs and practices. Government-directed systems give little or no consideration to the needs of private markets. Limitations on political freedom and personal choice are also part of this system. It is only when the system is market directed that marketing can contribute to the efficient use of economic resources and consumer satisfaction. The increasing complexity and rapid rate of change in the United States keeps the debate going on how much market direction is needed.

ECONOMIC GROWTH AND MARKETING'S ROLE

As Table 1-1 suggests, societies evolve through four basic economic stages: preindustrial, industrializing, industrial, and postindustrial. The character of marketing in each of these stages is shaped by the prevailing economic, political, and social conditions.

Certain African tribes are still in the **preindustrial stage**. They rely mainly on hunting and farming in order to survive. Some of the newly emerging nations in Asia and Africa can be considered industrializing societies. They are in the early stages of developing assembly-line production and more sophisticated distribution of goods. Many Western nations are already at the **industrial stage**. They produce a high output of goods, but must locate sufficient consumer markets in order to maintain economic growth.

No nation is fully in the **postindustrial stage**, although the United States comes closest. It can be said to be in the late industrial and the early postindustrial stages at the same time. The more affluent segments of American society have enough economic goods and security to be able to think about personal growth and the quality of life. For other Americans, however, inflation and unemployment persist as overwhelming problems. The marketing process must therefore cope with a variety of conditions.

In summary, marketing exists because producers and consumers are separated. As a result, marketing functions have to be performed and institutions have to be created to perform them. The societal setting and economic system in which marketing takes place influence how it is carried out. Knowing what stage of economic development a society is in provides information about how goods and services are brought to the consumer. An understanding of society and the economy contributes to an understanding of the success (or failure) of quadraphonic stereo in the United States or hybrid corn in India.

Table 1-1
THE CHARACTER OF MARKETING IN THE FOUR STAGES OF ECONOMIC SOCIETY

STAGE	DESCRIPTION	CHARACTER OF MARKETING
Preindustrial	Most people are engaged in hunting, herding, or farming, capital is scarce, and most human effort is devoted to meeting basic needs for food, clothing, and shelter.	Marketing is trading goods for other goods or money.
Industrializing	Producers attempt to increase productivity by increasing the amount of physical capital available and by improving work processes through product standardization and assembly-line production.	Marketing is bringing goods to concentrated urban populations through a distribution system consisting of countless small merchants who seek desired assortments for their local customers.
Industrial	Producers have achieved a high level of output; main problem is to generate sufficient demand. Increases in growth depend on expansion of consumer demand, and so does continued employment and income.	Marketing is generating sufficient demand, at given prices, for the output of a high-geared production system through the use of marketing research, product design, packaging, promotion, customer service, and sales analysis.
Postindustrial	Most citizens have lost their preoccupation with getting and spending and are searching for more freedom and time to develop as persons rather than as consumers. People grow less interested in the quantity of their goods and more interested in the quality of their lives.	Marketing is identifying advanced personal and social needs more precisely and developing offerings, information, and supply systems that will more efficiently satisfy these needs.

Adapted from Philip Kotler, "Defining the Limits of Marketing," in Boris W. Becker and Helmut Becker, eds., *Combined Proceedings of the 1972 Conferences of the American Marketing Association*, 1973, p. 49.

MARKETING ORIENTATION FOR ORGANIZATIONS

In this section, we will translate societal, economic, and historical explanations of marketing into their meaning for organizations—large or small, business or nonprofit. The main focus will be on large business firms, for within them marketing is most vivid and complex. We will explore how marketing has evolved into what can be called **managerial marketing**. We will also analyze more recent trends toward **societal marketing** and marketing within **nonprofit organizations**.

THE EMERGENCE OF MANAGERIAL MARKETING

A dramatic marketing revolution has been taking place within many American corporations in the twentieth century. Whereas business activity was once characterized by an emphasis on production, marketing has become the crucial concern today. Of course, this change did not take place overnight. Most firms began with a **production orientation**, then evolved to a **sales orientation**, and finally have arrived at a **marketing orientation**. The experiences of the Pillsbury Company provide an excellent and typical example of how a business shifts toward a marketing philosophy.[4]

Production Orientation

During its first fifty years of operation after its founding in the 1860s, the principal goal of the Pillsbury Company was production. "We manufacture flour" was the philosophy and the self-image of the firm. Management worked at increasing output and reducing production costs through scientific improvements. Sales concerns were secondary, because it was assumed that consumers would want to buy high-quality products. In other words, Pillsbury's flour would practically sell itself.

Sales Orientation

During the 1930s, the emphasis at Pillsbury shifted from production to sales. In addition to seeing themselves as manufacturers of flour, management began to realize that "We *sell* flour." The company created a commercial research department and for the first time began to study the needs, habits, and motivations of consumers.

Like Pillsbury, many firms shifted from a production orientation to a sales orientation during the 1930s. The basic economic problem for management was no longer a shortage of goods. Instead, many competing companies faced a shortage of consumers. Advertising, merchandising, and distribution became crucial in the competition for consumer dollars.

Marketing Orientation

After World War II, Pillsbury began moving from a sales orientation toward a marketing orientation. Instead of trying to sell whatever products the company was manufacturing, the company focused on determining which products (old or new) consumers really wanted. Market research and product development activities became more important, with the emphasis placed on the preferences and values of consumers. When it was learned that housewives wanted more finished products, such as ready-made desserts and biscuits, entirely new divisions were developed to meet these consumer needs.

The creation of a marketing department was essential to moving Pillsbury past a simple sales orientation. Marketing became the central management function at the company:

Marketing plans and executes the sale—all the way from the inception of the product idea, through its development and distribution, to the customer purchase.[5]

As similar transitions occurred in large firms across the nation, marketing became the dominant concern of business managers. Some economic experts suggested that all business decisions be made with marketing in mind. The customer orientation of marketing was increasingly viewed as essential to the success of any serious business.[6]

Of course, as was pointed out earlier, the American economic system is a market-directed system. In theory, the buying power of the consumer has always affected what products are created and sold, and by whom. But the marketing approach goes even further in stressing consumer participation in economic decisions. Previously, the consumer could act only in response to corporate decisions—by buying or not buying specific products. Today, consumer preferences have significant impact on the planning process in firms like Pillsbury.[7]

The marketing orientation came to be called the **marketing concept**. This concept will be analyzed in more detail and the extent of its use will be explained in Chapter 2.

In the 1970s, the marketing revolution went one step further. Marketing began to be the controlling philosophy of all corporate activities at firms like Pillsbury. Areas such as capital and financial planning, long-term volume, and profit goals were increasingly affected by marketing considerations. In the future, every aspect of corporate activity may focus on meeting the needs of consumers.[8]

Organizations that are experiencing success with nonmarketing orientations (production, sales, or financial) see little reason to change. Low profit levels, however, whether now or in the future, force most business firms to consider a marketing orientation. (See the accompanying story of the Crocker National Bank.)

SOCIETAL MARKETING

Because marketing has increasingly shaped the character of the American economy, critics have questioned its effects on society. John Kenneth Galbraith claims that the consumer is manipulated by large business interests.[9] Instead of reflecting the preferences of consumers, businesses shape and manage consumer demand through mind-probing research and expensive advertising, packaging, and the like.

The power of marketing is not as absolute as Galbraith argues. But marketing does have a significant impact on our society, and this troubles many observers. Some see the marketing concept as amoral, since the producer's total preoccupation with immediate consumer needs and wants can conflict with long-term needs of society as a whole.[10] The consumer may want throw-away packaging, but if businesses simply go on producing such products, our already polluted landscape can only get worse and worse.

Such dilemmas have led to new societal demands on the marketing system. Socially responsible marketing must balance three important considerations: consumer wants, company profits, and societal welfare.[11] Thus, in order to meet social responsibilities (and satisfy critics), the marketer must consider the effects of his operations on society as a whole.

The societal marketing concept aims at providing a higher level of consumer welfare. This includes satisfying the personal needs of consumers and at the same time considering the good of society and the environment. The product is seen not only as an item to be bought and consumed, but also as something that can affect the entire society. For example, Pillsbury is now emphasizing the nutritional value of its products.

Societal marketing is relatively new. Most corporations are only beginning to integrate this sense of social responsibility into their everyday activities. Chapter 4 will describe the increasing pressures on businesses to be socially responsible and will discuss what they can do about it.

MARKETING FOR NONPROFIT ORGANIZATIONS   Our attention thus far has focused on marketing as it is conducted by profit-seeking business firms. Yet marketing philosophy has become increasingly widespread among nonprofit institutions such as hospitals, colleges, labor

---

THE EVOLUTION OF MARKETING AT CROCKER NATIONAL BANK

In 1975, Judy Geller began work as a product manager for savings accounts at the Crocker National Bank's headquarters in San Francisco. Three years before that, the bank didn't even have a product manager. But that was before Thomas R. Wilcox came to Crocker as chief executive officer.

In a mere 15 months, Wilcox drastically restructured Crocker. Wilcox's main goal was to inject a modern, aggressive marketing orientation into bank operations. To achieve this, he reorganized or dismantled most of the bank's internal departments. Two-thirds of the senior executives were replaced, generally by managers with a strong marketing orientation.

The new marketing thrust was evident, as Judy Geller saw it, in what happened to the bank. Interest rates were raised to the legal maximum of 5 percent for passbook savings accounts. The bank stayed open evenings and Saturdays and provided free checking accounts for senior citizens. Two officers work solely with corporate clients on investments. Posters displayed around the bank showed Wilcox, who had announced each Crocker innovation on local television commercials. The emphasis was on improved personal service for customers. Judy Geller now takes part in an increasingly refined operation aimed at determining and meeting consumer savings needs.

Based on "Crocker's Tom Wilcox: Tough Management for a Stodgy Bank," *Business Week*, August 11, 1975, pp. 38–44.

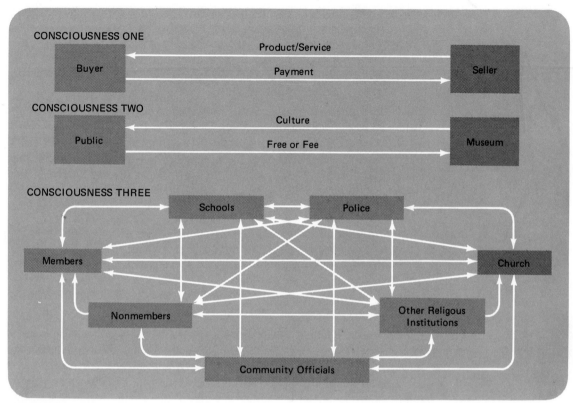

CONSCIOUSNESS ONE

Buyer ← Product/Service — Seller
Buyer — Payment → Seller

CONSCIOUSNESS TWO

Public ← Culture — Museum
Public — Free or Fee → Museum

CONSCIOUSNESS THREE

Schools · Police · Members · Church · Nonmembers · Other Religous Institutions · Community Officials

**Figure 1-3
STAGES OF THE
MARKETING CONCEPT
IN NONPROFIT
ORGANIZATIONS**

Based on Philip Kotler, "A
Generic Concept of Marketing,"
Journal of Marketing 36 (April
1972): 47–49.

[handwritten margin notes] Conscious II & I the same? Yes — very similar — profit & non-profit orgn marketing techniques very similar I & II

unions, and churches. An organization like Alcoholics Anonymous has a kind of "social product"; it helps alcoholics to stop drinking. This group might wish to improve its product through marketing techniques—more effective advertising, public education campaigns, or better allocation of resources. In this way, Alcoholics Anonymous could better service its "consumers."[12]

The marketing concept among nonprofit organizations has evolved in three basic stages,[13] which are illustrated in Figure 1-3. In Consciousness One, marketing is a business operation; the buyer always makes an explicit payment. In Consciousness Two, organization–client transactions are the marketing model. For example, the "seller" may be a museum that provides a product (cultural appreciation) to the general public. Or it might be a university that offers education to the "buyer," the student. A marketing transaction in Consciousness Two can require an explicit payment (a fixed or suggested fee to enter the museum), or it can be free of charge (a city park playground). In Consciousness Three, the concept is broadened even further to include the organization's transactions with all of its publics, not simply with its direct clients. Thus, a local church may have certain kinds of transactions with its members, but it will also interact with other individuals and organizations. These include other religious institutions, the schools, the police, community officials, and residents who do not belong to the church. Each of these interactions may be interpreted in marketing terms under Consciousness Three.

THE FUTURE OF MARKETING

It would be mistaken to assume that marketing will remain as it is today. Our society has changed drastically since World War II, and the rate of change seems to be accelerating. Alvin Toffler has written in *Future Shock* that an avalanche of change has become the norm in advanced technological society. The result is a kind of "future shock" for the many people unable to cope with this phenomenon. And, as Toffler notes, we have seen only the beginning of this era:

> *Reaching deep into our personal lives, the enormous changes ahead will transform traditional family structures and sexual attitudes. They will smash conventional relationships between old and young. They will overthrow our values with respect to money and success. They will alter work, play and education beyond recognition. And they will do all this in a context of spectacular, elegant, yet frightening scientific advance.*[14]

Obviously, if this is true, it has serious implications for marketing and all other business activities? Today's fundamental assumptions may become as outmoded as the horse and buggy. In fact, we have already learned that we do not have unlimited resources, that our technology can sometimes be harmful, and that our planet cannot indefinitely absorb our waste.[15]

The market economy itself is being challenged. Many experts have already called for some type of national economic planning. Arthur Schlesinger, Jr. has insisted that the unregulated marketplace cannot cope with such problems as massive unemployment, deteriorating mass transit, welfare, urban decay, and environmental protection. Rebutting critics of planning, he noted:

> *. . . it is hard to imagine a greater mess than the refusal to plan has got us into already—the worst inflation in a generation, the highest unemployment in 35 years, the worst decline in real output in nearly 40 years, the worst deficit in the balance of payments ever, the worst peacetime budgetary deficits ever, the worst energy shortages ever, the worst crises in municipal finance ever.*[16]

Although the situation has improved somewhat since the time Schlesinger was writing, the social, political, and economic atmosphere within which the marketplace must operate is forcing marketing professionals to reassess basic (and previously unquestioned) assumptions. It has been suggested that a "whole new marketing environment" exists today.[17] Part of this environment includes serious questioning of marketing orientation by organized consumer groups and by government regulators. Marketing experts must reexamine previous assumptions about competition, markets, and growth. Original and imaginative thinking is needed to meet the marketing problems of the future, problems that will barely resemble the problems of the past. It is the purpose of this book to provide you with a framework within which you can understand the future of marketing.

MARKETING'S IMPORTANCE TO YOU

You have seen that marketing has evolved to handle the important social and economic tasks of businesses and nonprofit institutions. At this point, you may be wondering, "What's in this for me? Why should I study marketing?" Here are some possible reasons:

1. *Marketing is a crucial part of our economy.* It affects the vitality and strength of the United States and the lives of all citizens. Marketing helped the GNP (gross national product) hit $1.4 trillion in 1974; 12.4 million firms practice it in one form or another. It is instrumental in shaping and delivering our economic standard of living, and affects the quality of life. Half of every dollar that consumers spend on a product represents the cost of marketing.

2. *Marketing can lead to career opportunities.* It is an important skill for students interested in product management, advertising, personal selling, financial planning, international business, retailing, and many other fields. At this time in your life, your career plans may seem only vaguely related—or totally unrelated—to marketing. But, in a rapidly changing society, you may find yourself shifting jobs when the opportunity exists. Marketing skills can be useful in a wide range of positions.

3. Even if you choose a nonmarketing position, *you will probably have to work with people involved in marketing.* If you work in accounting or operations research, financial analysis, or international accounts, a knowledge of marketing can help you do your job better. A double major—in one of these fields and marketing—may be a real asset to you in the years ahead.

4. *An understanding of marketing makes you a better consumer* (you know what business is trying to do to you). You will also be a better regulator (in case you work for a government agency or as a consumer advocate). If you are employed by a nonprofit organization, you may be a more effective representative. From almost any possible angle, having a marketing perspective will make you a better professional and citizen.

CONCLUSION

We have examined the foundations, the "big picture" of marketing. This is our starting point, because it keynotes the three major challenges of marketing within organizations:

1. *The challenge of satisfying consumers.* Since everything an organiza-

tion does affects consumers, every person in the firm must have at least some awareness of the marketing concept.

2. *The challenge of conserving and expanding organizational resources.* The lifeblood of all organizations, both business and nonprofit, is productivity —how well they use their resources. Only organizations with sufficient output can remain healthy and meet their obligations to the public.

3. *The challenge of maintaining standards of social responsibility while coping with other basic tasks.* This is the final test of any marketing performance. An organization that meets this challenge without forgetting the other two must make hard decisions. Can a business be socially responsible even at the risk of displeasing some customers? Should a business take the risk of educating customers to be socially responsible? Should an organization forgo some profits in order to act responsibly? To what degree can an organization afford to do so?

Of course, there is a difference between short-run and long-run profits. A focus on social responsibility removes the organization from its immediate interests. Instead, it takes the organization into greater participation with government, competitors, and consumer representatives to redefine and enhance the marketing system. In the future, successful marketing will have to balance these three challenges.

DISCUSSION QUESTIONS

1. Using the model of the marketing process given in Figure 1-1, describe the marketing of: a political candidate for the Senate, a community-wide charity drive, a large department store, an aircraft manufacturer, a country club, and a big-league football team.

2. Referring to this chapter's discussion of the societal foundations of marketing, support or refute this statement: "Our marketing system is necessary, important, and a result of the society and economy we have."

3. Recalling Pillsbury's evolution in marketing orientations—production, sales, and marketing—describe how the following industries have handled the same transitions: television, life insurance, tractors, synthetic fabrics, and hospitals.

4. As a result of recent government rulings permitting competition, the former monopoly AT&T has made some changes in the way it relates to its market. One of these has been to drop the term "subscriber" and use "customer" instead. What does this change tell you about AT&T's marketing orientation?

5. Referring to the discussion about the three stages of the marketing concept, diagram the "Consciousness Three" stage for a university. How can the university use marketing in its relationships with its several publics?

6. A decade from now, our society will have experienced such extreme changes that marketing as we know it (and as we have described it in this book) will be different in important ways. What can marketing organizations do to prepare themselves for this future environment. As someone who is probably anticipating a business career, how can you prepare yourself for it?

NOTES

1. This section is based largely on William Mc-Innes, "A Conceptual Approach to Marketing," in R. Cox, W. Alderson, and S. J. Shapiro, eds., *Theory in Marketing* (Homewood, Ill.: Irwin, 1964), pp. 51–67.

2. This section is based largely on Robert Bartels, "The General Theory of Marketing," *Journal of Marketing* 32 (January 1968): 29–33.

3. John F. Grashof and Alan P. Kelman, *Introduction to Macro-Marketing* (Columbus, Ohio: Grid, 1973), pp. 38–43.

4. Robert J. Keith, "The Marketing Revolution," *Journal of Marketing* 24 (January 1960): 35–38; and John F. Mee, "Marketing Dominated Economy," *Business Horizons* 7 (Fall 1964): 63–64.

5. Keith, p. 37.

6. John Douglas, "A Comparison of Management Theory with the Marketing Concept," *The Quarterly Review of Economics and Politics* 4 (Autumn 1964): 24–25.

7. Ibid., pp. 28–29.

8. Keith, p. 38.

9. John Kenneth Galbraith, *The New Industrial State* (Boston: Houghton Mifflin, 1967).

10. Frederick E. Webster, Jr., *Social Aspects of Marketing* (Englewood Cliffs, N.J.: Prentice-Hall, 1974), p. 12.

11. Philip Kotler, *Marketing Management: Analysis, Planning, and Control*, 2d ed. (Englewood Cliffs, N.J.: Prentice-Hall, 1972), p. 26.

12. Reed Moyer, *Macro Marketing: A Social Perspective* (New York: Wiley, 1972), pp. 9–10.

13. Philip Kotler, "A Generic Concept of Marketing," *Journal of Marketing* 36 (April 1972): 47–49.

14. Alvin Toffler, *Future Shock* (New York: Random House, 1970), p. 166.

15. John E. Sawyer, "As the World Turns," *New York Times*, December 30, 1974, p. 23.

16. Arthur Schlesinger, Jr., "Laissez-Faire, Planning, and Reality," *Wall Street Journal*, July 30, 1975, p. 10.

17. "A Marketing Man Takes Marketers to Task," *Business Week*, July 28, 1975, p. 42.

2

MANAGERIAL MARKETING IN THE ORGANIZATION

After completing this chapter, the reader should be able to:

1. Describe the nature and importance of the systems approach to analyzing marketing.

2. Relate the marketing concept to its organizational setting.

3. Explain the key characteristics of the marketing concept.

4. Diagram the major elements of the managerial marketing process.

5. Distinguish between organizational and marketing goals, and between organizational and marketing capabilities.

6. Identify the major participants in the uncontrollable external environment and the dimensions of the controllable marketing mix.

7. Describe the trends that are updating the marketing concept.

In Chapter 1 we examined marketing in its societal setting. Now we will analyze the role of marketing in the organization. To do so, let us first take a look at a hypothetical company, Circle Cycles.

CIRCLE CYCLES

The story of Circle Cycles began when Charlie Winters, a stockbroker, came to the conclusion that he'd had enough of "down markets." He decided to start a motorcycle dealership in a St. Louis suburb with Mike McFarlane, a retired motorcycle racer. Mike and Charlie wanted to make enough money to cover their salaries and give them at least a modest return on their investment for the first two years.

After assessing their strengths, Charlie and Mike were optimistic about their chances of success. First, they had the franchise for Benelli equipment, a good quality, moderately priced line. (Honda at that time dominated the St. Louis market.) Mike's reputation and Charlie's business background were further assets. The showroom also had a good location in a former A&P supermarket just off a major highway. Finally, if the success of Honda was any indication, there was a sizable population around St. Louis that enjoyed cycling as a leisure activity.

Looking for ways to attract potential customers, Charlie thought back to the principles he learned in his introductory marketing course in college. After analyzing the situation, he decided that Circle Cycles should present itself as *the* cycling center in the St. Louis area. It should be a place where the target customer could feel comfortable, have fun, and socialize. The showroom should offer information about cycling; it should be a place where cycling enthusiasts mix with and learn from other cyclists and experts; and it should offer the opportunity to buy equipment and obtain fast and reliable service.

To reinforce this desired image, Circle Cycles' celebrity Mike would be on hand and his trophies and special racing bicycle would be displayed. The service and repair capabilities of the center would be emphasized through a program of periodic cycle checkups. Public interest in cycling would be stimulated by special sales, publicity events, and information displays. The store's layout would include areas for cycle-inspired art and one-of-a-kind clothing and equipment. There would also be a coffee wagon to encourage conversation.

MARKETING MANAGEMENT DEFINED

Underlying all of Charlie's ideas and plans for Circle Cycles were three basic operational elements of the marketing concept:

    1. the business has to express a customer orientation;

2. all the people in the organization have to coordinate their activities in order to satisfy the customer;

3. profits come from satisfied customers.

Theoretically, at least, it is the customers' needs, not the organization's product, that should guide the organization's marketing program.

Having accepted this customer-oriented spirit of marketing, Charlie then went through the following series of steps in laying the actual groundwork for his business:

1. he determined his objectives;

2. he took stock of his capabilities (strengths and weaknesses);

3. he investigated his market;

4. he made himself aware of his competition;

5. he recognized those factors that would make his organization unique and identifiable;

6. he carried out his planned strategy;

7. he made plans to evaluate this strategy after a year.

In short, Charlie analyzed and developed the marketing management program his company needed. He "analyzed, planned, implemented, and established controls for programs designed to bring about desired exchanges with target audiences for the purpose of personal or mutual gain."[1]

THE SYSTEMS APPROACH TO MARKETING

As we have seen, Circle Cycles has a well-defined and limited product line, customer group, and competition. Nevertheless, there is more than one way of determining its marketing strategy. Consider, then, how much more complex the situation must be in a huge organization like Procter & Gamble or Sears, Roebuck. Such an organization must take into account many products, many levels of competition, and numerous markets, suppliers, and personnel. Moreover, constant changes, both inside and outside the organization, have repercussions for the company's products, competition, and customers. Developing a marketing strategy that accounts for all of these elements is the challenge that faces marketing decision makers. In order to do so, they must find an effective way of analyzing these elements and their interrelationships. The method used by business strategists today is known as the **systems approach.**

WHAT IS THE SYSTEMS APPROACH? The systems approach in marketing is an adaptation of the principles used by the military during World War II to plan attack and defense strategies. It has been defined as:

An inquiry to aid a decision maker choose a course or action by systematically investigating his proper objectives, comparing quantitatively where possible the costs, effectiveness, and risks associated with the alternative policies or strategies for achieving them, and formulating additional alternatives if those examined are found wanting.[2]

A model of the systems approach, based on the "black box" concept of the computer, is given in Figure 2-1. In this model, the **processor** administers the operation. **Inputs** of products or product ideas are thereby converted into **outputs.** (Outputs are the system's actual "offerings" and the messages it sends out about them.) The **objectives** direct the process, while **controls** monitor it. **Feedback** from both internal and external sources is the basis for further system change.

Figure 2-1
THE SYSTEMS
APPROACH

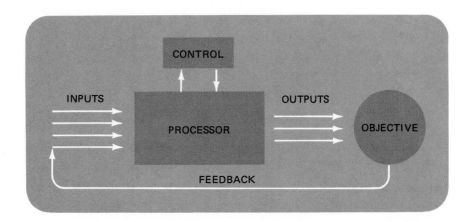

THE SYSTEMS APPROACH IN MARKETING

Unlike the closed and relatively limited environment of the computer, the environment of a marketing system is a large and open one with many inputs, outputs, and feedbacks. The marketing environment can be broken down into five basic layers, as illustrated in Figure 2-2. Each of the five layers in itself constitutes a system. The inner layers become the subsystems for the outer, more general layers, and outputs from one layer become inputs for the next.

The systems approach thus helps focus attention on issues that are broader than those usually contained in any single aspect of marketing. It also provides for the logical and orderly analysis of marketing activity by:

1. stressing marketing linkages both inside and outside the firm;
2. emphasizing the relationship of inputs to outputs;
3. highlighting changes in the environment;
4. providing an approach for control;
5. offering opportunities for innovation;
6. providing a means of measuring results.[3]

While the systems approach is particularly relevant to this chapter's analysis of managerial marketing in the organization, it is a concept we will also use later in our analysis of several of the systems contained in Figure 2-2 as well as of other activities.

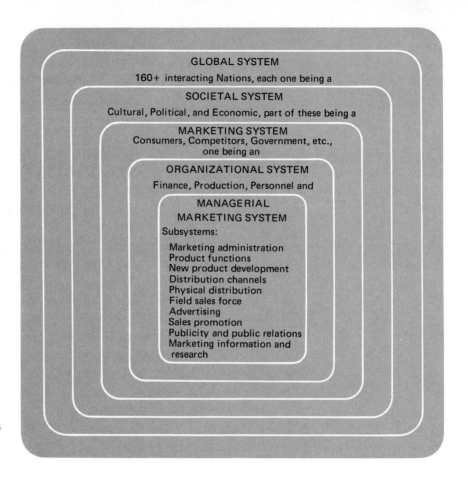

Figure 2-2
MARKETING SYSTEMS
AND THEIR
SUBSYSTEMS

Inside the figure:

GLOBAL SYSTEM
160+ interacting Nations, each one being a

SOCIETAL SYSTEM
Cultural, Political, and Economic, part of these being a

MARKETING SYSTEM
Consumers, Competitors, Government, etc.,
one being an

ORGANIZATIONAL SYSTEM
Finance, Production, Personnel and

MANAGERIAL
MARKETING SYSTEM
Subsystems:

Marketing administration
Product functions
New product development
Distribution channels
Physical distribution
Field sales force
Advertising
Sales promotion
Publicity and public relations
Marketing information and
  research

THE MARKETING CONCEPT OF THE ORGANIZATION

The marketing concept of an organization, as described in Chapter 1, is basically a matter of customer orientation. To be truly customer-oriented, an organization must not only understand and believe in the marketing concept, it must also put it into practice. It must adopt ways of operating that will help it to serve its customers more fully and effectively.[4]

TOP MANAGEMENT COMMITMENT

To be effective, an organization's commitment to the marketing concept must start with the head of the organization. This executive must have a thorough understanding of the concept and its application to the organization. What is more important, the executive must have adopted a marketing frame of mind. All decisions and judgments coming from the top in regard to objectives, direction, or specific procedures should reflect this state of mind.

This commitment to the marketing concept must be shared by key members of the executive staff as well. This unity of purpose and outlook will create a situation in which the key executives feel at home, no matter where they are in the company.[5] It will do much to prevent the "prima donna" syndrome, in which a particular person or unit within the organization perceives himself (or itself) as the heart of the company, with other persons or units performing only peripheral functions.

ORGANIZATION-WIDE COORDINATION

The increasing trend toward specialization within the units of large organizations (finance, product, data processing, personnel, etc.) is both good and bad for the marketing concept. On the positive side, specialization leads to efficiency and flexibility in meeting perceived customer needs. Each unit in the organization, theoretically at least, is engaged in doing what it is most qualified to do. On the negative side however, employees and management alike tend to identify with their particular unit and its problems, rather than with the organization and its goals as a whole. Some of the conflicts that may arise as a result are summarized in Table 2-1. With these differences in views, cooperation in achieving a marketing orientation may be hard to come by.

MAKING THE MARKETING CONCEPT WORK

Where there is a will to use the marketing concept, there will be a way to implement it. The particular method of implementation will vary with each organization's size, products, markets, management style, and so forth. However, here are several fundamental principles that operate in every organization:

1. customer orientation;
2. marketing organization (a chief marketing executive, integration of marketing functions, use of a marketing staff);
3. a profitable volume criterion.[6]

These principles also apply to nonprofit organizations. With the nonprofit organization, however, efficiency of resource usage replaces profit.

CUSTOMER ORIENTATION

Most organizations assume that they are customer oriented. In reality, however, an organization's own selling needs and production and/or distribution capabilities often come first. In order to be truly customer oriented, a company must introduce marketing considerations at the beginning rather than at the end of the production cycle. For example, in the General Electric Company the focus of one of its divisions was changed from a production orientation to a customer orientation. G. L. Phillips, chairman of the board, has described the changeover:

> . . . *Some of my associates laughed a few years ago when our Electric Fan and Blanket Department changed its name to the Home Care and Comfort Department. Now the management of that department is having the last laugh because this change in name triggered a change in the whole attitude of the department, from a factory or hardware orientation to a customer orientation. These astute business managers saw that they were not*

Table 2-1

SUMMARY OF ORGANIZATIONAL CONFLICTS BETWEEN MARKETING AND OTHER DEPARTMENTS

OTHER DEPARTMENTS	THEIR EMPHASIS	MARKETING EMPHASIS
Engineering	Long design lead time Functional features Few models Standard components	Short design lead time Sales features Many models Custom components
Purchasing	Standard parts Price of material Economical lot sizes Purchasing at infrequent intervals	Nonstandard parts Quality of material Large lot sizes to avoid stock-outs Immediate puchasing for customer needs
Production	Long production lead time Long runs with few models No model changes Standard orders Ease of fabrication Average quality control	Short production lead time Short runs with many models Frequent model changes Custom orders Aesthetic appearance Tight quality control
Inventory	Fast-moving items, narrow product line Economical levels of stock	Broad product line High levels of stock
Finance	Strict rationales for spending Hard and fast budgets Pricing to cover costs	Intuitive arguments for spending Flexible budgets to meet changing needs Pricing to further market development
Accounting	Standard transactions Few reports	Special terms and discounts Many reports
Credit	Full financial disclosures by customers Low credit risks Tough credit terms Tough collection procedures	Minimum credit examination of customers Medium credit risks Easy credit terms Easy collection procedures

From Philip Kotler, *Marketing Management: Analysis, Planning, and Control,* 3d ed. (Englewood Cliffs, N.J.: Prentice-Hall, 1976), p. 415.

in the business of producing and getting rid of fans or blankets. Rather, they are in the business of anticipating what the public would be interested in buying that will make the home more comfortable and easier to take care of. And they are not only selling more fans and blankets than ever, but an expanded line of products as well.[7]

MARKETING ORGANIZATION

Putting the marketing concept into practice depends upon a carefully thought out organizational structure. This structure will naturally vary from company to company. The most basic approach is to group the marketing organization's responsibilities by activities, products, services, location, time, or functions. Grouping by functions (sales, advertising, product management, and so on) is one of the more common approaches used by companies offering a variety of products or services.

No matter how an organization is structured, three components seem to be necessary for the marketing concept to work successfully: a chief marketing executive, integration of marketing functions, and a marketing staff.[8] Of course, smaller companies and nonprofit organizations do not have all of these management levels and staff specialists. However, the same activities should be performed by those people who deal with customer concerns.

Chief Marketing Executive

The chief marketing executive, whatever title this individual has, is responsible for translating the organization's commitment to the marketing concept into a workable program. In large measure, the success of the marketing program will depend upon the executive's influence at the top management level and participation in the decision-making process. This participation is especially vital in organizations where top-level management personnel do not have marketing backgrounds, most often the case in the electronics industry or nonprofit organizations.

Integration of Marketing Functions

A successful marketing effort also demands that those functions concerned with developing and moving goods and services to customers be coordinated under the chief marketing executive. Figures 2-3 and 2-4 illustrate typical changes that take place in a company when it is reorganized to implement the marketing concept. Before reorganization (Figure 2-3), there is little or no coordination of marketing functions except at the presidential level. Some functions, such as sales forecasting and product planning, may not even exist. Moreover, engineering and research and development have no direct relationship to marketing. After reorganization (Figure 2-4), all marketing functions are united under the chief marketing executive. These functions are organized into two major subgroups, operations and services.

Marketing Staff

A marketing organization such as that presented in Figure 2-4 means that the marketing staff must perform several vital new functions.

1. *Marketing research* helps the organization to be more geared to customers by providing intelligence concerning customer needs and wants. In this type of research, data are gathered concerning product and service design, competitive product advantage, demand curves, and so forth (see Chapter 23).

2. *Product management*, often called brand management, is the system by which responsibility for each product or product group is delegated to one person or team. The responsibilities of this job include coordination of the annual marketing program among the different departments in the organization—production, advertising, sales, public relations, and so forth (see Chapter 11).

3. *Product planning* includes screening new ideas, testing the new ideas

for feasibility, and planning a marketing program. The object here is not only to direct the organization toward profitable enterprises but to avoid potential disasters (see Chapter 11).

PROFITABLE VOLUME CRITERION

In marketing, more isn't always better. That is, a large volume of sales is not in and of itself a guarantee of high profits. The organization must determine its acceptable profit levels through an analysis of its products, customers, distribution methods, and sales territories. Under the marketing concept, it is *long-run* profits that should be sought. Because of large production or marketing expenses called for in launching a product, profits may be low or even nonexistent in the short run. Long-run profits are often used to measure the balance between customer satisfaction and the organization's financial efficiency.

HOW WIDESPREAD IS THE MARKETING CONCEPT?

Nowadays, nearly everyone in the business community is at least vaguely familiar with the marketing concept. The term pervades marketing literature and provides the general framework within which marketing management is taught. But to what extent has the marketing concept been accepted by United

Figure 2-3   COMPANY ORGANIZATION BEFORE MARKETING REORGANIZATION

From Hector Lazo and Arnold Corbin, *Management in Marketing: Text and Cases* (New York: McGraw-Hill, 1961), p. 118. Copyright 1961. Used with permission of McGraw-Hill Book Company.

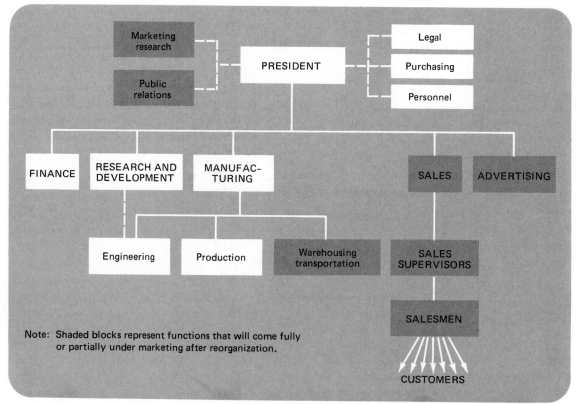

Figure 2-4 COMPANY ORGANIZATION AFTER MARKETING REORGANIZATION

From Hector Lazo and Arnold Corbin, *Management in Marketing: Text and Cases* (New York: McGraw-Hill, 1961), p. 119. Copyright 1961. Used with permission of McGraw-Hill Book Company.

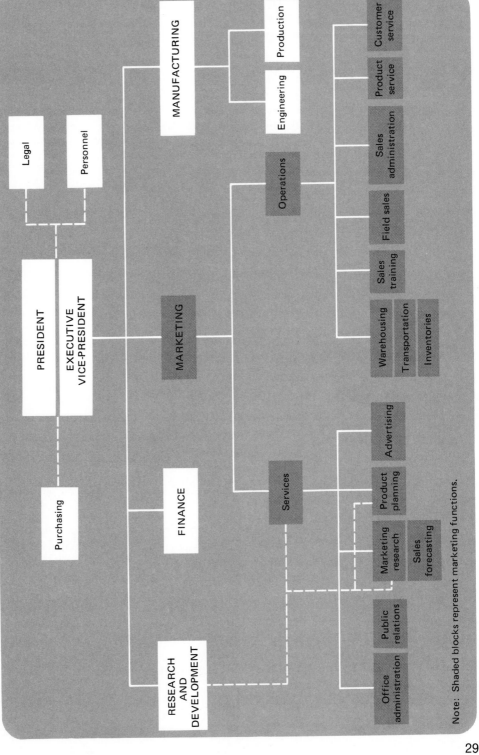

Note: Shaded blocks represent marketing functions.

29

States business firms? One survey of nearly 1,500 companies showed that:

1. consumer goods companies have tended to adopt and implement the marketing concept to a greater degree than industrial goods companies;

2. large companies have tended to adopt and implement the concept to a greater degree than have small- and medium-sized companies.[9]

Aside from the type and size of the business, the degree to which the marketing concept has been implemented is also determined to a large extent by the attitudes of the company's key executives. Another survey was taken of some 400 business executives and educators to determine their attitudes toward the marketing concept. According to this study, most respondents believed that:

1. the marketing concept is a powerful and workable idea;

2. it has influenced management philosophy in at least the larger American business firms;

3. it has contributed to the improvement of the organization and management of marketing activities;

4. the consumer has benefited in tangible ways from its implementation.[10]

On the other hand, the study also revealed that most firms have experienced only limited success in actually implementing the marketing concept.

An increasing number of nonprofit organizations, from the U.S. Army to the Cleveland Orchestra, are using more marketing techniques. However, one hesitates to conclude that many such organizations have embraced the marketing concept in full.

LIMITATIONS OF THE MARKETING CONCEPT IN PRACTICE

Why has the implementation of the marketing concept met with such uneven success? The fault does not seem to lie with the principles of the marketing concept, but rather with the organization's resistance to them. The key factors in the marketing concept's failure are mismanagement, internal dissension, increased costs, lack of suitable personnel, and the tendency to keep the status quo.[11]

Mismanagement

If a company is in the wrong business or badly managed, marketing is irrelevant. No amount of sales promotion or advertising will help a buggy whip manufacturer in the late 1970s. The U.S. Postal Service and many passenger railroads seem to be encountering this limitation.

Internal Dissension

When an organization transfers certain functions formerly under other departments to a newly created marketing unit, internal dissension often results. Some companies have put off or forsaken the needed reorganization altogether because of the disruptive effect it might have. Look again at what happens when the "other departments" in Table 2-1 win out.

Increased Costs

The addition of a marketing unit means an increase in an organization's outlay for salaries, benefits, and facilities. Research and consultation fees will also increase. These costs are a serious problem only when marketing fails to generate more in revenue.

Lack of Suitable Personnel

The search for marketing personnel has proven difficult and sometimes fruitless for many firms. One company president has even said, "Before we can use these techniques, we need a new generation of marketing management. The older group just wasn't and probably can't be educated up to it."[12] A person raised under a sales orientation may have a difficult time switching to a marketing orientation.

Adherence to the Status Quo

Marketing units have tended to provide those products and services for which a customer can see an immediate need. According to marketing's critics, this tendency has limited industry's desire and ability to experiment with new ideas that might have long-range benefit, such as the packaging of nutritious processed foods. We will elaborate on this social theme in Chapter 4.

In the face of these limitations, modern marketing has now begun to develop operational definitions for the marketing concept that will allow its implementation on a day-to-day basis. For instance, written marketing guidelines and marketing information help keep the sales person, controller, and consulting engineer on the marketing wavelength. The challenge to do so is becoming more urgent as business becomes increasingly complex and consumers become more demanding.

THE MANAGERIAL MARKETING PROCESS

Having just examined what marketing is *in* the organization, let us now explore what marketing does *for* an organization. The specific processes that take place when a firm develops a marketing strategy are illustrated in Figure 2-5. This diagram reflects the systems concept discussed earlier, in which output from one stage provides input for another. The stages involved are:

A. Defining the organization's mission and goals and from there its marketing objectives.

B. Defining the organization's capabilities and appraising its marketing capabilities. These capabilities will both determine and be determined by the organization's goals.

C. Developing a marketing opportunity analysis that will identify target markets, consumer segments within those markets, and the environment in which they exist.

D. Developing a marketing strategy that will create a differential advantage for the firm, in other words, defining the elements of unique strength that will be attractive to the potential customer. The specific methods of implementing the marketing strategy will be developed from this vision of special competence.

E. Putting the strategy into action. This means that all components of the marketing network have to work together. These components include the

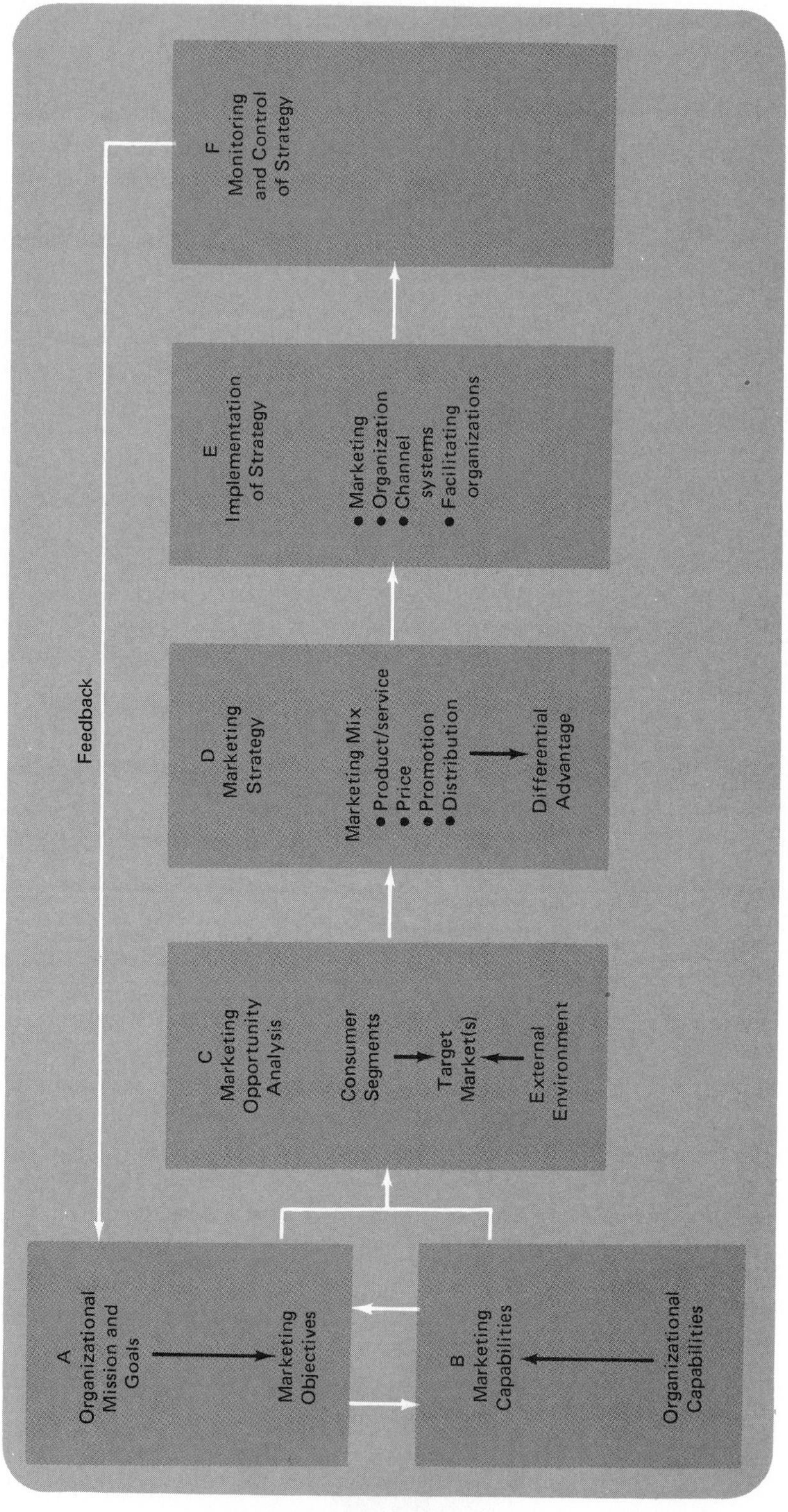

Figure 2-5 THE MANAGERIAL MARKETING PROCESS

A
Organizational Mission and Goals

Marketing Objectives

B
Marketing Capabilities

Organizational Capabilities

C
Marketing Opportunity Analysis

Consumer Segments

Target Market(s)

External Environment

D
Marketing Strategy

Marketing Mix
- Product/service
- Price
- Promotion
- Distribution

Differential Advantage

E
Implementation of Strategy

- Marketing Organization
- Channel systems
- Facilitating organizations

F
Monitoring and Control of Strategy

Feedback

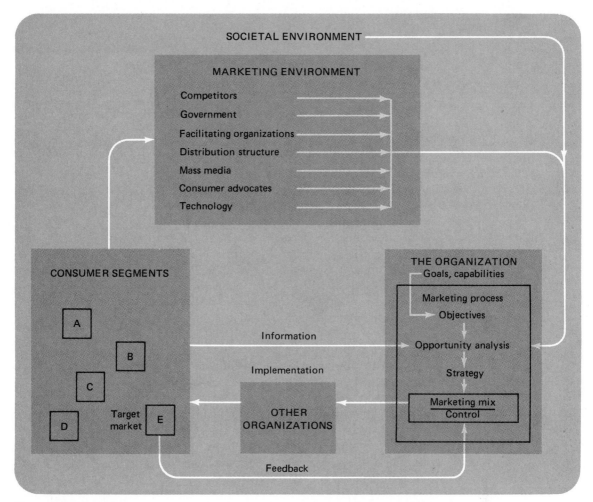

SOCIETAL ENVIRONMENT

MARKETING ENVIRONMENT

Competitors

Government

Facilitating organizations

Distribution structure

Mass media

Consumer advocates

Technology

CONSUMER SEGMENTS

A

B

C

D

Target
market   E

Information

Implementation

OTHER
ORGANIZATIONS

Feedback

THE ORGANIZATION
Goals, capabilities

Marketing process
Objectives

Opportunity analysis

Strategy

Marketing mix
Control

Figure 2-6
THE MANAGERIAL
MARKETING PROCESS
WITHIN ITS EXTERNAL
ENVIRONMENT

units in the organization, channel systems, and facilitating organizations.

F. Monitoring and controlling the strategy in order to guide and adjust the program and to evaluate its effectiveness. This evaluation is incorporated into the next round of planning.

The time span within which the process occurs will vary. It could be the short run (less than one year), the intermediate run (one to five years), or the long run (five, ten, or even more years). In addition, it must be remembered from Chapter 1 that this process does not exist in a vacuum. It relies on the societal environment, the immediate organizational environment, and especially the consumer. Figure 2-6 illustrates the relationship of the managerial marketing process to this external environment.

OBJECTIVES OF
THE MARKETING
PROCESS

If an organization is to develop a sense of direction and plan a supporting marketing program, it must first know what it wants to be and where it wants to go.[13] This includes defining its organizational mission, setting organizational goals, and establishing marketing objectives. Only after it knows where it wants to go can the organization decide how to get there.

I was ready to set the world on fire, ready to ride on the cloud nine that marketing promised back in 1958 when, shiny new business degree in hand, I was hired by a major electric utility in the Midwest. I was supposed to help the firm penetrate new markets, measure market potentials, and gather customer opinions about product performance, price levels, and other features.

At first, since the company was hesitant about becoming a superaggressive sales/marketing force, it introduced the marketing concept under the gentle guise of "merchandising." This didn't seem to work too well, however. Eventually, a formal marketing department, including sections for planning and research, was established. A lot of young M.B.A.'s were hired at this time. The company now had all the trappings of a marketing program. This was enough for sales to rise dramatically, but the resulting overload caused errors in service, orders, and billings. Normal operations, personnel, and procedures were disrupted. Sales started falling again.

Those of us in marketing realized that one of our major problems was to convince management that it must be truly customer oriented. In other words, that the marketing concept must be wholeheartedly adopted by the entire organization. At first, we thought that a few lectures from marketing professors would do the trick. But soon we found it was "business as usual," and the marketing department's influence sank even lower.

What we should have been doing, of course, was studying why things had fallen apart, what the company's direction should have been, and how best to implement the marketing concept. It was only the economic problems of the late 1960s and a series of adverse court decisions that finally forced the company into a full-scale re-evaluation of its marketing program.

Jeffrey Bowman's story is based on the marketing situation at an actual service corporation.

MARKETING MISCONCEPTIONS AND MISTAKES (as told by Jeffrey C. Bowman)

Organizational Mission and Goals

The organization's self-concept, its **organizational mission**, is determined in part by the way management thinks society will respond to the organization and in part by the way society does in fact respond. The mission usually takes the form of a broad qualitative definition of the organization. Such well-known corporate slogans as "serving man's need for knowledge," and "partners in progress around the world," are typical examples.

Although an organization's mission may be expressed in general terms, its goals are usually quite specific. They are often tied in with the survival or growth of the firm, a division, a product line or product, or with the enlargement of market size, or other marks of progress.

How does the organization arrive at these goals? One study shows that specific goals are formulated by studying the following areas:

1. material resources (industrial products such as plastics or natural resources such as gas);

2. manufactured objects;

3. events or activities (recreational or business activities that create needs);

4. specific types or categories of people (housewives, students, blue-collar workers);

5. specific parts of the body (cosmetics, sound equipment, and so on);

6. wants and needs for a specific type of product.[14]

After the goal has been established, quantitative dimensions can be defined. These include return on investment (net profit as a percentage of assets), sales growth, profit target, and market share.

Marketing Objectives The organization's corporate mission is fulfilled and its goals are achieved in large part through its **marketing objectives**. Essentially, these are statements that specify what is to be accomplished in regard to market segments and customer needs. They might include 25 percent of customers trying a new food product, delivery of executive jets to customers in eight weeks, selling 10 percent more foreign vacation packages each year at a travel agency. They are not ends in themselves, but serve as instruments for carrying out a total corporate policy. Figure 2-7 illustrates a general flow model of a marketing planning procedure that enables a company to:

1. define its objectives;

2. assign priorities to the objectives;

3. determine a time span within which they are to be accomplished.

The experience of the Koppers Company, a chemical and engineering firm, indicates how this procedure can be applied. In determining its objectives, the company takes into account the pursuit of growth markets, the size of the potential market share, flexibility in pricing, the importance of the product to its customers, and an analysis of profitability.[15]

ORGANIZATIONAL AND MARKETING CAPABILITIES Realistic planning demands that a company take stock of its **organizational and marketing capabilities**. A firm's organizational capabilities are determined by its present and anticipated physical and financial resources as well as by the talents and experience of its personnel. These capabilities can and do change. The management tries to make deliberate changes that are to the company's advantage.

An organization's success is based upon a combination of these capabilities:

1. its personnel (who innovate, analyze, plan, and implement);

2. its production process (in terms of the quality and cost of its products and/or services);

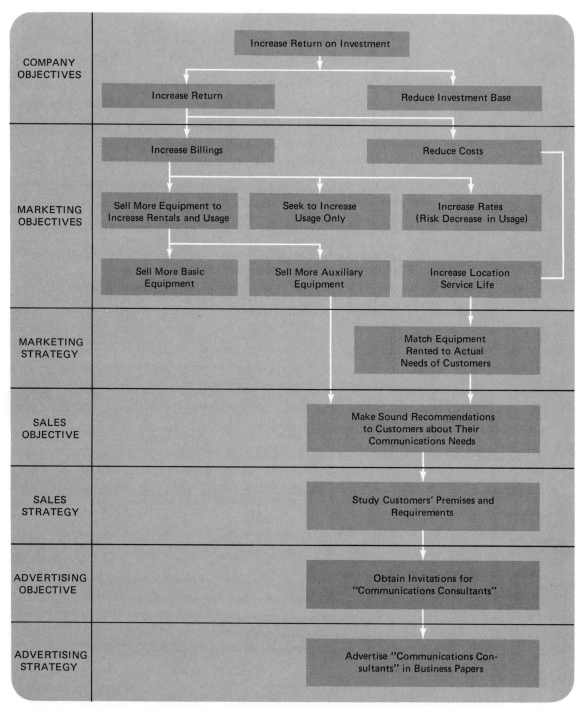

Figure 2-7   HIERARCHY OF OBJECTIVES FOR THE INTERSTATE TELEPHONE
COMPANY

Reprinted from Leon Winer, "Are You Really Planning Your Marketing?" *Journal of Marketing* 29 (January 1965): 3.
Published by the American Marketing Association.

3. its money and credit (which basically fuel the firm's operations and make possible the acquisition of other resources);

4. its research and development capabilities (which are often responsible for breakthroughs resulting in new or much better products or services);

5. its marketing capabilities (within the framework of the marketing concept).

An organization's marketing capabilities include those elements of the marketing program that the organization can use to its advantage. Such an element may be a Kodak instamatic camera; one of Procter & Gamble's aggressive sales forces covering supermarkets across the nation; the price-bidding system of an IBM submitting bids to a foreign government; or an award-winning advertising campaign for McDonald's fast-food chain. All of these elements together make up the marketing mix, which will be discussed later in the chapter.

MARKETING OPPORTUNITY ANALYSIS

Success, it is often said, depends mainly on brains and luck. If some firms or individuals seem long on luck, it is not so much that lucky opportunities land right on their doorstep, as that they seek and recognize them. The job of finding opportunities that have marketing potential cannot be approached in a casual or haphazard fashion. Some companies have "think tanks" to analyze future economic, technological, and societal opportunities. Some limit their investigation to specific marketing mission areas in their fields. Others investigate such general areas as innovative products, services, or channels of distribution, improved efficiency, creation of competitive differences, and establishment of new market niches.

Whatever form it takes, opportunity analysis requires that a firm have a clear sense of its own objectives and capabilities. It must also understand the external environment in which it exists and the customer segments in which it is interested. Procedures for identifying, appraising, and responding to opportunities must also be formulated.

Needs, Segments, Targets

One of the basic steps in conducting an opportunity analysis is to pinpoint the customer for whom the product is to be developed. That customer's needs and wants are then identified and evaluated. These needs and wants are influenced by a number of things and change frequently, due to alterations in life style and socioeconomic fluctuations.

Consumers with similar characteristics (education, income, life style, buying patterns, and the like) will tend to have distinctive needs and wants which they will express through distinctive patterns of consumption. Such groups of consumers, called **consumer segments**, are first spotted in the marketplace. The organization then selects **target markets** on which to concentrate its marketing efforts (see Chapter 7). In looking for new opportunities, a firm must look at consumers in the context of the environment that influences their behavior.

External Environment

Many clues to marketing opportunities can be found in the external environment of the marketplace in which the firm operates. This is also the environment in which potential consumer segments exist. It consists of many levels, as was illustrated in Figure 2-4. Let us examine some of the major elements that affect the evaluation of potential marketing opportunities.

Competitors. A firm has two types of competitors. The first type are direct rivals with competing products or services (such as the American Red Cross vs. the March of Dimes, or Kimberly-Clark's Kimbies vs. Procter & Gamble's Pampers). The second type are indirect rivals who offer alternative products for the same amount of money (such as recarpeting a house vs. taking a trip to Hawaii).

Government. At the federal, state, and local levels, government is charged with regulating marketing directly or indirectly. This regulation is most obvious in the areas of promoting competition, protecting consumers, and buying vast quantities of goods and services.

Facilitating Organizations. A firm's marketing capabilities depend in large measure on those whom it contracts to perform functions for it or provide products to it. These organizations include suppliers of raw materials, advertising agencies, finance companies, freight lines, public warehouses, and others.

Distribution Structure. The distribution structure consists of the whole network of wholesalers and retailers who move products or assist with services to consumers.

Mass Media. The mass media, especially through journalism and entertainment, help to mold public opinion. They also provide an outlet for the organization's own advertising messages.

Consumer Advocates. In recent years, several individuals and organizations have emerged to speak for the social and ecological interests of the consumer. Ralph Nader is the best known among them. These persons or groups are influential both in the marketplace and in government regulatory agencies.

Technology. How well science and technology can provide products that satisfy customers or processes for the production function is a major determinant of what or how much an organization can do.

Societal Environment. Included here are all the social, political, and economic systems that shape and contain the marketing system. These forces were once considered more or less remote from marketing operations, but this is no longer the case.

The external environment, including consumers, is considered to be noncontrollable by any single organization's marketing efforts. Even General Motors finally was pressured by this environment into marketing small cars (after years of resisting these lower-profit models). However, some degree of influence is clearly possessed by large firms, key industries, and by the nation's top 500 corporations. This influence is exerted through large-scale advertising and selling expenses, political lobbying and contributions, and holding a monopoly on a commodity in short supply.

Marketing Information

While most firms that are committed to the marketing concept do keep an eye on all these factors, many fail to assess them in a way that is really helpful to marketing opportunity analysis. They may pay only lip service to the collection and analysis of data related to future environmental changes. This task may be assigned to the marketing research department. However, with research priorities aimed at more "practical" problems, future-oriented inquiries receive scant attention in such departments.

The purpose of studying the environment for future opportunities is to help decision makers anticipate likely areas of change. It also enables them to analyze how changing interactions between elements in the environment will alter existing marketing situations. This "blue sky" approach is, unfortunately, often disconcerting to traditional planners and researchers. Their focus is on the more day-to-day operating decisions and quarterly or annual profit performance.

MARKETING STRATEGY

Once marketing opportunities have been identified, a **strategy** must be formulated for taking advantage of them. Strategy in the broadest sense, is a dynamic, action-oriented blueprint for accomplishing the organization's mission, goals, and objectives. Marketing strategy involves determining the level, mix, and allocation of the marketing effort over time.

The development and use of a marketing strategy can be relevant for nonprofit organizations as well. For them, the objective may be to increase influence, prestige, or popularity. The story of the two universities outlined in the accompanying box is an example of how marketing strategy can be used by such organizations.

The Marketing Mix

The development of a successful marketing strategy depends on the effective combination of those elements that make up what is called the **marketing mix**. These elements are the product (or service), price, promotion, and distribution.

Product/Service. This element includes the decisions relating to:

1. product planning (the product lines to be offered, the sales markets, and the research and development program for new products);

2. branding (selection of trademarks, use of individualized or family brands, sales under a private label, or unbranded sales);

3. packaging (formulation of package and label);

4. servicing (providing needed services to accompany the product).

Two private universities with about the same national rating decided at about the same time to adopt a similar objective. Each wanted to advance into the ranks of the top five private universities in the nation within ten years. One succeeded and one failed in meeting its objective. Why?

A TALE OF TWO UNIVERSITIES

The one that succeeded developed a well-formulated strategy to accomplish its goal. For each major department, the university hired a distinguished scholar who had a reputation for attracting money and other scholars. It started a research institute that would work closely with business firms. Its scholarship fund was increased to attract highly talented students, and it established a first-class development office and public relations department. Thus, the successful university identified each important market (students, faculty, government, business foundations) and developed a plan for becoming strong in each.

The other university did not develop a specific strategy. Instead, it haphazardly hired some good people, kept control over funds, and reminded its alumni of their obligation to be supportive. This university failed to achieve its objective because it did not do anything innovative that would have built public interest and respect. It also failed to allocate enough resources to the necessary marketing job.

Based on Philip Kotler, *Marketing for Nonprofit Organizations* (Englewood Cliffs, N.J.: Prentice-Hall, 1975), pp. 63–64.

Price. This element includes the decisions relating to:

1. price level and specific prices to adopt;

2. price policy (one price or varying prices, price maintenance, use of list prices);

3. price margins for the company and distribution channel members.

Promotion. This element includes the decisions relating to:

1. advertising (amount to spend, product and corporate image, mix of advertising to distribution channel members and to consumers);

2. personal selling (the extent of the personal selling effort, the selling approaches to be used);

3. sales promotions (the extent of special selling aids, such as contests, gifts, displays, which should be directed at or through the distribution channel);

4. publicity (company efforts to have mass media mention the company message favorably).

Distribution. This element includes the decisions relating to:

1. channels of distribution (channels to use between producer and consumer, degree of selectivity among wholesalers and retailers, efforts to gain their cooperation);

2. physical distribution (warehousing, transportation, and inventories).

These four elements are assumed to be the controllable variables, that is, the marketer decides what they should be. However, "controllable" is a relative term in this context. Such things as budget limitations, industry customs, and leadership by competitors greatly influence how much discretion an organization has in designing its marketing mix.

Effort and Allocation

Marketing effort has been defined as "the total amount of company input into the marketing process to stimulate sales."[16] A dollar value can be assigned to this effort by determining the investment made in each of the four factors of the marketing mix. The combined dollar value represents the level of the marketing effort at a given time. The effectiveness of that effort is harder to measure. Usually, it is judged by comparison with the competition or, negatively, by the success of a similar program that spent less money.

In addition to determining how much to invest in each element of the marketing mix, an organization may have to decide how to allocate its funds among many such mixes. This is the problem faced by organizations that produce more than one product or service, that sell to various markets, or that divide their efforts over several territories.

Differential Advantage

The success of any given marketing mix is in part measured by the differential advantage it provides. The **differential advantage** is the difference between the effectiveness of the company's marketing mix and that of its competitors in satisfying consumer wants. The objective, of course, is for the organization's marketing mix to have a greater impact in satisfying consumer wants than that of its competitors. In this way, the organization attempts to develop a preferred position with the consumer. The mix elements must be chosen and combined so that the organization sells more than does the competition (see Chapter 6).

IMPLEMENTATION AND CONTROL OF STRATEGY

Having established a marketing strategy, the marketing executive now puts it into action through research, planning, organization, and consideration of the strengths and weaknesses of personnel.

Two of the biggest implementation challenges facing the executive are motivation and coordination. To provide the best motivation, management may institute programs for employee recognition and offer clear-cut opportunities for advancement and financial rewards. Coodination of effort concerns not only the marketing unit itself, but other units within the organization, as well as distribution channels, and facilitating organizations. This means coordinating the work of finance, research and development, engineering, and others in the organization; wholesalers and retailers in distribution; and advertising agencies, credit-granting institutions, and delivery services, among other facilitating organizations.

A control system capable of monitoring the actual results of the marketing strategy and measuring them against the desired objectives is essential to effective marketing management. Such control allows the marketing executive to concentrate on the problem areas and to formulate alternative plans that are more likely to achieve the organization's objectives.

Information such as a control system takes two basic forms: data-based information about the company's operations and market, and feedback from the marketplace and the consumer. Such information must be relevant, complete, and timely. It must enable the marketing executive to identify a problem, formulate alternative solutions, and then choose a course of action.

The form such information takes should reflect the needs of the people who will use it. Statistical results will inform marketing managers about the current status of their product in the marketplace. Customer panels, market surveys, and advertising tests will clarify or identify changes in the needs and wants of customers.

UPDATING THE MARKETING CONCEPT

The growth of the marketing concept during the last twenty years has no doubt been enhanced by the affluence, prosperity, and unprecedented growth of the last two decades. But just as businesses have changed their orientation from production to consumer orientation, so too the marketing concept itself has changed. It appears that in the future, the trend toward organizational efficiency as well as societal pressures will play an important role in the evolution of marketing.

ORGANIZATIONAL EFFICIENCY

The increased pressure for organizational efficiency has led to the development of the concept of **total organizational planning**. According to this concept, most planning is done in a central, organization-wide department. Traditionally, planning has been delegated to one unit within the organization—usually marketing, finance, or production. As a result, planning has not taken into account the needs and capabilities of all units within the organization. According to one authority:

> *Fragmented management is not only incorrect; it is unrealistically oversimplified. The true complexity of management is brought into focus when interrelated functional problems are considered simultaneously. The selection of a channel of distribution without computing the effects of distribution (purchasing, transportation, and storage), production costs, and total net profits is an unrealistic travesty of planning.*[17]

The movement toward total organizational planning is also being accelerated by a growing emphasis on the financial function of organizations. Scarcity of money and credit has made efficiency in planning imperative. In addition, marketing itself may become only a secondary cause of corporate growth. Large conglomerates today may owe their expansion to financial rather than marketing moves. "Growth" has come to mean the acquisition of smaller companies, rather than the direct expansion of the organization's own marketing coverage. The decision to acquire another company may be grounded in financial considerations, but the marketing opportunity and strategy must be sound for that company to prosper in the long run.

The scarcity of energy, raw materials, and credit has also created a situation in which organizations are increasingly cautious about taking risks.

Finally, the computer, which has already had a major impact on the storage and retrieval of marketing information, is bound to become increasingly important and useful in marketing operations. The computer's potential has scarcely been tapped in the area of marketing decision making, where alternatives must be weighed under uncertain conditions. At the present time, the pace of computer technology is moving so rapidly that marketing people have not yet taken full advantage of it.

SOCIETAL MARKETING

As we saw in Chapter 1, the nature of marketing is influenced to a large extent by the society in which it is carried out. As societal norms and pressures change, so does marketing. One of the most influential of societal pressures today is the growing consumer movement.

Marketing has always been interested in the needs and wants of consumers. This interest was grounded in the theory that satisfying the consumer's desires was the surest way to make a profit. In the consumer movement, on the other hand, the satisfaction of the consumer is the goal rather than the means to an end. In addition, the interest of the consumer is now defined as *what is best* for him or her, rather than just *what will sell*. The pressure created by the consumer movement is leading to some reordering of priorities and basic changes in the marketing concept. There are three major changes:[18]

1. *The consumer gets more satisfaction for his money.* This means supplying more and better product information to the potential buyer and taking the "puffery" and deception out of advertising. Also, the producer takes more responsibility for the effects of the use of the product and any necessary servicing. Implied in this change of attitude is a positive business effort to advance product safety and environmental protection. Generally speaking, these concerns have been the result of the threat of governmental regulation or loss of sales through adverse publicity.

2. *The concept of the organization as a total operational system.* When this concept is put into practice, all company resources are channeled toward the goal of consumer and societal benefit. As a result, the problems of operating the company are given a lower priority.

3. *A redefinition of the role of profit.* Business is no longer carried out mainly for the sake of profit, but profits will result if consumers are satisfied. This is not to say that organizations should not make a profit, but that consumer interests must come first.

This new approach to marketing requires a substantial increase in feedback mechanisms. It will also require a greater degree of consultation among firms in an industry and even negotiation with competitors, government agencies, and consumers. Broadly stated, it will demand a greater amount of communication between consumer and producer. The organization that wants to improve its communication with consumers beyond what marketing has been able to do can create a **consumer affairs** unit. One company's experience with such a unit is summarized in the accompanying box.

Since many organizations have not gotten to first base in adopting even the marketing concept or implementing it effectively, they probably will not follow this societal direction. Even many of those firms that have accepted the marketing concept will resist these revisions. It is still rare to find top management, staff, and operational personnel all committed to the "newest" marketing concept.

THE SHOPPERS' FRIEND AT GIANT SUPERMARKETS

When Giant Foods, Inc., a regional supermarket chain, decided to strengthen its proconsumer actions by hiring Esther Peterson as consumer representative, some said it was like "inviting the cops to a burglary." Esther Peterson was no mere store representative and chief apologist to the consumer. As a former labor lobbyist and a militant consumer advocate, she would not stand for that. Instead, she and Giant have taken some major proconsumer steps. These include advocating and supplying recycled paper products and low and no-phosophate household detergents and launching a major toy safety campaign during the holiday season. They have also repackaged Giant's private label soft drinks and mixers in shatterproof bottles and have undertaken other reforms.

Giant has profited from customer goodwill because of these reforms, even though its financial profit has been somewhat modified because of conditions such as rising fuel and labor costs and galloping inflation. Still, its increasing share of the market indicates that Giant's proconsumerism is attracting consumer loyalty.

Based on "The Shoppers' Friend at Giant Supermarkets," *Business Week*, April 16, 1974, p. 38.

Giant Food, Inc.

CONCLUSION

Every organization that deals with customers is necessarily involved in marketing. The effectiveness of any marketing program, however, depends in large part upon the degree to which the organization as a whole has embraced a marketing orientation. Marketing must be a system for structuring all of the company's functions. Organizations that have accepted this view have found marketing to be instrumental in their survival, growth, and profitability.

There are, of course, situations in which a marketing emphasis may be irrelevant. Such situations include lack of competitors, the existence of only one customer (such as the government), or subsidies from government or organized crime. Nevertheless, our discussion in this chapter has been based on the idea that marketing is a normative concept, in other words, organizations should use the marketing concept as an organizing principle. The risks in not doing so are too great.

At its best, marketing serves as a means by which an organization can alert itself to changes in the environment. To ignore these changes, or simply to be unaware of them, may lead to disaster. As someone who has studied marketing, you will be able to tell how well marketing is working for the organization. You will be able to point out the dangers of the absence of marketing and the positive value of strengthening any marketing program that does exist. You will also be able to organize an effective marketing program.

As you read through the rest of this book, it will be helpful to organize your thoughts around the following general concerns of the marketing manager:
1. The basic marketing concepts and approaches to marketing analysis. This area concerns the consumer, the environment, and the marketing mix.
2. The nature of the marketing organization. This is the relationship of the marketing unit to the organization as a whole and to the environment in which it exists. The environment includes trade associations, distribution channels, community projects, and so on.
3. The social aspects of marketing. This area includes the question of how well marketing anticipates and reflects societal standards at any given time.

DISCUSSION QUESTIONS

1. It has been claimed that the systems approach applied to marketing is "the greatest thing since sliced bread." However, another source called it the "same old wine in a new bottle." What do you expect you will be able to do with the systems approach as you learn more about marketing?
2. What type of organizational conflicts would develop between the marketing department and (a) the engineering department of a microwave oven manufacturer, (b) the credit department of a department store, and (c) the production department of a chemical plant?
3. Within the first week of a job at a book publisher, how would you learn whether the marketing concept is present and working? How would you know if it were present and working in a chain of hardware stores? a community charity?
4. Run through the managerial marketing process for a food service (for institutions), a home study school, a drug counseling program, and a manufacturer of pollution control equipment.
5. What would be appropriate organizational goals and marketing objectives for an enclosed mall shopping center, a city–suburban bus line, a rock band,

and a mobile home producer? What marketing capabilities would be most critical in achieving those objectives?

6. What forces in the external environment are having the greatest impact on the way American automobiles are designed, promoted, and priced?

NOTES

1. Philip Kotler, *Marketing Management: Analysis, Planning, and Control,* 2d ed. (Englewood Cliffs, N.J.: Prentice-Hall, 1972), p. 13.
2. Lee Adler, "Systems Approach to Marketing," *Harvard Business Review* 45 (May–June 1967): 112.
3. Ibid., p. 114.
4. James H. Myers, "Marketing Organization and Administration," in Frederick D. Sturdivant et al., *Managerial Analysis in Marketing* (Glenview, Ill.: Scott, Foresman, 1970), p. 284.
5. Robert Sessions, "The Marketing Concept in Action," *47th National Conference Proceedings* (Chicago: American Marketing Association, 1964), p. 9.
6. This discussion is based largely on Myers, pp. 284–308.
7. Ibid., pp. 286–87.
8. This discussion is based largely on Myers, pp. 299–307.
9. Carlton McNamara, "The Present Status of the Marketing Concept," *Journal of Market-*
ing 36 (January 1972): 56–57.
10. Hiram Barksdale and Bill Darden, "Marketers' Attitudes toward the Marketing Concept," *Journal of Marketing* 35 (October 1971): 29.
11. This discussion is based largely on Myers, pp. 309–12.
12. Ibid., p. 311.
13. This discussion is based largely on Eugene Kelley and William Lazer, *Managerial Marketing: Policies, Strategies, and Decisions* (Homewood, Ill.: Irwin, 1973), pp. 55–58.
14. Harper W. Boyd, Jr. and Sidney J. Levy, "What Kind of Corporate Objectives?" *Journal of Marketing* 30 (October 1966): 54–58.
15. Otto Wheeley, "Marketing Philosophy" (Speech, 1973), pp. 7–17.
16. Kotler, 2d ed., p. 45.
17. W. I. Little, "The Integrated Management Approach to Planning," *Journal of Marketing* 31 (April 1967): 34.
18. Martin L. Bell and William Emory, "The Faltering Marketing Concept," *Journal of Marketing* 35 (October 1971): 41–42.

3

ECONOMIC CONDITIONS AND PUBLIC POLICY

After completing this chapter, the reader should be able to:

1. Describe the various forces in the economic environment—prosperity, recession, inflation, and scarcity.

2. State how these economic forces influence the marketing process.

3. Explain the rationale for and the legal foundations of the government's procompetition and proconsumer public policies toward marketing.

4. Apply these public policy directions to the conduct of marketing.

The headlines of the mid-1970s gave a bleak forecast of the economic weather ahead:

Inflation to Continue, May Get Worse
End to Energy Crisis: Would You Believe 1990?
Big Companies Put Brakes on Business Growth

Equally ominous were the reports of government action:

IBM Charged with Being "Too Big"
Government Clamps Down on Price Fixers
Congress Presses Down for More Consumer Protection

These headlines illustrate two major influences on the form and approach of marketing. The first is *economic issues*, such as inflation, recession, and material shortages. The second is *public policy* applied by the government to keep the business world honest and the consumer protected. This chapter will deal with the dynamics of these two influences and the way in which marketing organizations must adapt to them now and in the future.

THE ECONOMIC ENVIRONMENT

The United States has a reputation for having the biggest, soundest economy in the world. But in the mid-1970s it ran headlong into an era that has been described as turbulent, confusing, and crisis-ridden. In short, the signs of "hard times" were here again.

Economic forecasters looking ahead through the next decade or two are likely to find their crystal balls clouded by the recurring themes of material and energy shortages, rising costs, and up-and-down business cycles. There are no grounds for labeling the years ahead as "The Economic Dark Age" or "The End of Affluence," nevertheless, dramatic changes in economic conditions will present marketing managers with new challenges.

Traditionally, economic forces such as inflation and recession affect the *demand* aspect of the economy. In the mid-1970s, the *supply* side was threatened as a result of material and energy shortages. The strain put on business by these pressures was expressed by W. Michael Blumenthal, president of Bendix Corporation:

There are moments in our history when public affairs so overshadow our private concerns that it seems ... hardly to matter how we manage. ... Wherever we look we see inflation and governments too weak or discredited to deal effectively with it. Internationally, unemployment is on the rise and the oil squeeze is subjecting the economies and financial systems of the free world to intolerable strains.[1]

Other experts have an unshakable faith in America's ability to remain unaffected by these economic pressures. Still others, even more optimistic, feel that technological and political changes will soon launch us all toward an era of overabundance and prosperity.

Perhaps the only certainty is that it is impossible to be certain. Economic forces have a habit of interacting with each other—inflation with recession, scarcity with inflation. At the same time, social and consumer issues modify and are modified by the economic forces. Therein lies both the frustration and the fascination of economic analysis and prediction: the economy is a complex chain of action and reaction, all happening at once. The future will contain periods of economic prosperity and even some growth. However, the pace of rapid national and international change means that economic traumas will be mixed in with good times. The implications of these economic problems affect all aspects of marketing strategy and will be discussed in this chapter and throughout this book.

MARKETING UNDER DIFFERENT BUSINESS CONDITIONS

Throughout most of the 1950s and 1960s, organizations became accustomed to conditions of prosperity, growth, and healthy demand. They are now learning that the counterpoint to these conditions, inflation and recession, may be mild or serious, separate or simultaneous.

Prosperity

Prosperity may be measured in national, personal, and technological terms. Table 3-1 shows the economic growth of the United States in the past 25 years. The sizable increase in consumer goods and services is apparent.

During this same period, as may be expected in times of prosperity, personal income showed a significant rise. For example, between 1950 and 1973 the per capita income in the United States rose by 226 percent in dollars and cents and 70 percent in real terms.[2]

"I look upon it as a haven to which I can retreat and laugh at inflation, recession and shortages."

Wall Street Journal, October 3, 1975, p. 8. Reprinted by permission of the Wall Street Journal/Al Kaufman.

Table 3-1
**TWENTY-FIVE YEARS OF ECONOMIC GROWTH IN THE
UNITED STATES (in billions of dollars)**

	1950[a]	1975[b]	% CHANGE[c]
Durable consumer goods	31	125	310
Nondurable consumer goods	98	399	307
Consumer services	62	390	524
Investment goods and services	54	163	201
Net exports	2	9	417
Exports	14	143	939
Imports	12	134	1018
Government goods and services	38	332	775
	285	1418	398

[a] *Statistical Abstract of the United States* (Washington, D.C.: U.S. Department of Commerce, 1974), p. 374
[b] *Survey of Current Business* 55 (May 1975), p. 5.
[c] During the period, the rate of inflation was 127 percent.

Technological advances are also closely related to prosperity. New buying power creates new demands and new resources for development of technology. During those same 25 years of economic growth shown in Table 3-1, American consumers learned to take for granted such technology as color television, moon landings, freeze-dried coffee, computerized bank statements, electric blankets, and birth control pills.

Obviously, a prosperous society will exert an influence on marketing. Prosperity will affect marketing's approach to advertising, research, product development, and cultivation of mass markets. The reverse influence, marketing's effect on the life style of a prosperous society, is not as obvious. The central principle involved is the shift from an emphasis on production to an emphasis on consumption. David Potter writes:

> The culture must be reoriented to convert the producer's into a consumer's culture . . . and the society must be adjusted to a new set of drives and values of which consumption is paramount.[3]

Consumption, fostered and encouraged by marketing, leads to a greater emphasis on materialism—a characteristic commonly cited by critics of American society. But the desire to possess things is not necessarily immoral. William Lazer has pointed out that when a person's material circumstances improve, the individual is better able to recognize intrinsic values, his general tastes acquire a new dimension, his moral climate is enhanced, and his life is enriched by a greater appreciation of art and beauty.[4]

Lazer is not claiming, of course, that two cars in the garage will automatically lead to a wall of van Gogh and Rembrandt prints in the living room. The implication, however, is that marketing policies do have a moral dimension. The decision makers who formulate those policies today and in the future must become increasingly aware of the impact their actions have on society.

Recession Since the Depression of the 1930s, the economy has experienced several recessions. None of them, however, was as severe as the recession of the mid-1970s. The lesson, for some, was painful: recession can happen and it can hurt. Recession brings with it lower purchasing power, higher unemployment, and a general feeling among consumers of insecurity in their position now and in the future.

Another dimension of the recession of the mid-1970s lies in its long-range implications. After suffering through the low-demand period of the recession, the economy may have a lingering period of low growth for many years to come. The recession of the 1970s, with its low rate of growth, provided organizations with a basic training period for tackling the marketing challenges of the future. Some experts felt that the recession would lead to an important change in consumer buying patterns, notably the decline of buying to maintain or improve status and the "opulent facade." Other professionals were more conservative in their outlook. They saw the recession as only a temporary slowdown of growth and affluence. To Mark Worden of General Motors, it was only a sales problem that could be solved by simply getting back to basics and selling the country's way out of its economic troubles.[5]

The effect of a recession on individual companies may vary considerably. Luxury or fashion products may be hard hit. Other kinds of goods may actually show a sales increase; consumers do buy less cake but more bread. Producers of power tools may do well as more householders join the do-it-yourself ranks to save money. Other manufacturers survive by adapting product designs and selling techniques from luxury items and by using a sales theme that emphasizes such economies as low operating costs and easy maintenance.

Inflation When demand for goods and services grows faster than they can be supplied, prices go up and inflation occurs. Since the 1940s, inflation has been an almost constant feature of the American economy (see Figure 3-1). The rate of inflation, however, was always under 10 percent. It was not until the 1970s that double-digit inflation came onto the scene.

The immediate cause of this largely unforeseen inflation was a combination of events. These included the wheat crop failure in Russia, the drought in Africa, the devaluation of the U.S. dollar, and the Arab oil embargo. These events sent prices up and supplies down—a straight road to inflation. The long-term causes were ineffective government policies, mainly price controls that discouraged needed production and expansion. Efforts to minimize unemployment caused greater demand, leading to greater inflation.

Another cause of the inflation of the seventies was the emergence of new nations throughout the world, all with sudden demands for a better standard of living. Their governments simply were not ready to deal with the people's increased needs. Tremendous pressures were created for industries in these nations to increase production. Politically, these pressures were aimed at the governments in power, forcing too many of them to adopt inflationary policies in order to survive.

When a high rate of inflation becomes a reality, the whole structure of the economy is threatened. Business incentives and consumer confidence may be

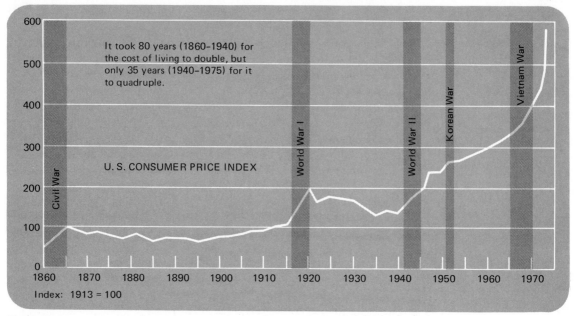

It took 80 years (1860-1940) for the cost of living to double, but only 35 years (1940-1975) for it to quadruple.

U. S. CONSUMER PRICE INDEX

Civil War

World War I

World War II

Korean War

Vietnam War

Index: 1913 = 100

Figure 3-1
THE PRICE PICTURE SINCE THE CIVIL WAR: A LONG DECLINE, THEN A FAST RISE

From "Is Inflation Dead?" *Business Week*, March 3, 1975, p. 48.

thrown into confusion as conventional market relationships no longer apply. Traditional economic cures for inflation, which lead to unemployment may no longer be acceptable to society. The almost inevitable result of rising prices in this situation is a planned economy with wage and price controls, such as the federal government imposed from 1971 to 1974. However, in some industries, the economic dislocations caused by controls resulted in higher prices to the consumer—the exact opposite of the intended effect.

Changes in consumer buying habits have also resulted from new conditions of inflation and scarcity. Some purchases have been eliminated altogether, others have been postponed. There is a general trend toward getting the most for one's money and an emphasis on utility—a "no-frills" mentality. Marketers must analyze the reasons for these changes in buying habits and attempt to predict which of the changes will be permanent. Emphasis on lower prices will appeal to those who must spend less out of economic necessity. Appeals to social conscience will be effective with those who feel it is everyone's duty to be less wasteful.

MARKETING UNDER SCARCITY CONDITIONS

In 1973, America found itself unexpectedly and frustratingly short of energy and materials. How could these shortages happen in peacetime? They were blamed on demands for a better life from a growing population, increased popular concern about the environment, and the deliberate holdback of raw materials by producing nations (especially Middle Eastern oil). The results were rising prices, rising unrest, and rising tempers. Production methods had to be changed. Marketing approach, too, was affected: Many companies with the right product found that the rules of the game had been suddenly changed.

Material Shortages

In the summer of 1973, meat became hard to get at any price. Poultry, dairy products, and sugar reached a scarcity that rivaled wartime shortages. Magazine and newspaper publishers had to scramble to find enough paper to print their products on. Motorists lined up for hours to fill their tanks with gasoline. Manufacturers searched frantically for new sources of raw materials.

It was soon evident that some shortages were going to persist and that people would have to adapt. New emphasis was placed on technology to develop more efficient production methods and ways to recycle materials. The period of rapid growth was over. In the new low-growth economy, production and marketing policy makers were forced to shift their production from quantity to quality. With materials in short supply (and expensive), consumers wanted products that would last. Manufacturers were also beating shortages by substituting more abundant materials. Food processors, for example, made more use of nonanimal protein sources and artificial sweeteners.

The interaction of supply and demand forces is illustrated by the shortage of metal lids for home canning, which became evident in the summer of 1975. The previous year, a tin shortage had cut supplies for these lids. Manufacturers increased production 30 percent for 1975. It wasn't enough. They had underestimated the increase in the market as more and more home gardeners tried to cut food costs by canning their own produce. In addition, panic buying by those who feared another shortage made lids even more scarce, and much home produce went to waste.

Energy Limitations The American economy runs on energy, particularly oil. Because it was always taken for granted that the oil supply was not only cheap but limitless, industry and consumers were understandably shaken by the energy crisis. The crisis

---

Until the 1973 fuel shortage, Toyo Kogyo Company of Japan had high hopes for its rotary-engine Mazda. The low pollution levels of such an engine made it a natural for the ecology-conscious population of the early 1970s. Moreover, it performed better than everybody else's piston engines and its few parts promised fewer repairs. This, combined with the publicized "humming" noise of the motor, seemed to guarantee the Mazda a large share of the market, both in the United States and in Japan.

MAZDA MEETS THE MILES-PER-GALLON MENACE

But just as things began to worsen on the energy front, the United States Environmental Protection Agency issued its report on Mazda's fuel consumption. According to EPA, Mazda got only 11 miles per gallon in city driving (this figure was later raised to 13). Despite Toyo Kogyo's protests that these figures were inaccurate (they claimed 17 to 21 mpg), Mazda sales in the United States declined dramatically. The company's figures showed a drop of 39 percent in the first five months of 1974. A simultaneous drop in the Japanese market spelled hard times ahead.

The right innovation (a rotary engine) at the right time (during concern for air pollution) had turned sour in the wrong time (during concern for gas mileage). Admitting defeat, all marketing efforts were switched to the Mazda Mizer (note the stingy mileage image)—the old piston engine model.

Based on Norman Pearlstine, "Mazda Maker Hopes to Revive Hummmm though Energy Crisis Has Slashed Sales," *Wall Street Journal*, June 11, 1974, p. 46.

Mazda Motors of America, Inc.

Marketing strategy is affected by resources and productive capacity. If both are adequate and marketing demand is increasing, conditions are present for growth strategy (position A in the figure shown below). This is clearly the situation in which marketing usually operates; it leads to the most profit. The energy crisis, by creating shortages, has forced many firms into position B, calling for a market retention strategy (serving present customers for the time being). When demand is declining, as in positions C and D, it is important to consider how long the decline will last. If it is likely to be permanent, diversification or a major realignment of strategy may be necessary. Marketing and material resources must be allocated to the most promising market targets.

AVAILABILITY OF RESOURCES: MARKETING WILL FIND A WAY

MARKET DEMAND	RESOURCES AND PRODUCTIVE CAPACITY	
	Adequate	Inadequate
Increasing	A. Growth strategy	B. Market retention strategy
Declining	C. Market building and/or diversification	D. Balancing and realignment strategies

From David W. Cravens, "Marketing Management in an Era of Shortages," *Business Horizons* 17 (February 1974): 80.

created more than a temporary shortage. Even after the Arab embargo on oil was lifted, prices remained at four times their early-1970s level. The days of low-cost energy were over. To survive economically, people had to make major changes in life style. The consumption-mad mentality and throw-away attitude had to be loaded into the big gas-guzzling cars and driven off into the sunset. Positive thinkers regarded the crisis less as a problem than as an opportunity. They saw it as an incentive to cut down on needless waste and return to quality. In the long run, energy limitations will make possible a happier, healthier environment for everyone.

Higher fuel prices shifted emphasis not only to smaller cars but to the development of more and better mass transit. Consumers were urged to save energy by persuasion (turn down your heat) and by law (slow down your car to 55 mph). "Recycling" became a household word. Marketing, caught in the middle between energy-conscious consumers and rising manufacturing costs, had to adapt to meet the situation. New attention was paid, both in manufacturing and marketing, to durability, low energy consumption, and ease of repair. Competition increased considerably as consumers adjusted their thinking and their budgets to fit new conditions of higher prices and scarcities.

MARKETING IMPLICATIONS OF ECONOMIC CONDITIONS

Some marketing management implications have been drawn for each of the economic conditions we have examined so far. Moreover, these economic conditions usually occur in combination with each other—shortages with inflation or inflation with recession. They affect virtually every aspect of the managerial marketing process as it was described in Chapter 2. The impact of the various economic conditions on this process is illustrated in Figure 3-2. The pressure points shown in this figure are the result of the nonprosperity economic forces. For marketers who have been used to several decades of economic growth and stability, these economic crises present new problems for which sound marketing solutions are still being found.

Marketing objectives become more difficult to attain when economic conditions turn sour. Marketing capabilities are also undercut, expecially when scarcities occur. Consumer segments are particularly sensitive to a troubled economy, as inflation and/or recession diminish both income and the confidence to purchase. In the external environment, competitors fight harder for the smaller economic opportunities. At the same time, government feels political pressure to increase its regulatory activities. Marketing strategy must undergo several types of adjustment to meet these conditions. Many of the chapters in this book (especially Chapters 11–22) are concerned with the elements of the marketing mix and how they are modified by adverse economic conditions. Under these conditions, implementation of strategy is tightened to allow fewer errors to occur. The control of strategy becomes more important as finances and sources of supply are threatened.

PUBLIC POLICY

The marketing environment exists within a vast complex of private and public law, combined with the pressures of public opinion and government economic policy. In general, laws and government controls work less quickly than the economic influences of a free market. Laws and regulations take time to implement; market systems may react immediately to economic pressures.

Politicians, understandably, want to return the economy to a healthy state without risking their jobs by subjecting it to a major shake-up. But times are changing. As Senator Gary Hart has pointed out:

> The nation cries out for leaders who will tell the hard truth ... that the economic pie is shrinking; that economic stimulation through weapon procurement is inherently inflationary; that a democracy cannot long survive with a tax system as inequitable as ours; that our "free enterprise" economy is being eaten alive by big enterprise while the government acquiesces; that the quality of life is more important than the quantity of goods consumed.[6]

The rest of this chapter provides a picture of public policy as determined

Figure 3-2   ECONOMIC CONDITIONS AFFECT MANAGERIAL MARKETING

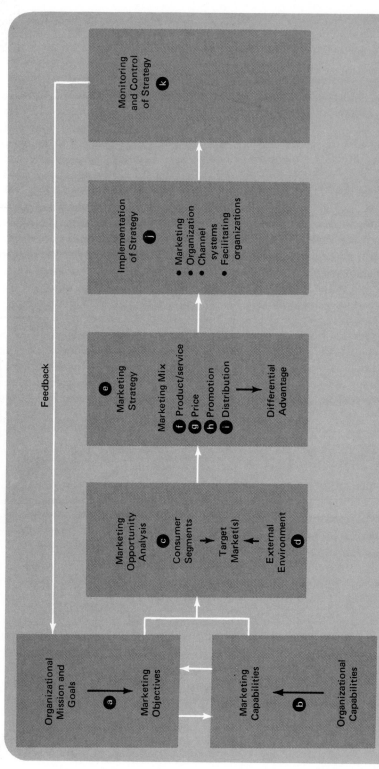

a Squeeze on sales growth, increase in costs, pinch in profits.
b Limited by any scarcities, ability to realize production efficiencies.
c Inflation and recession change consumer behavior, such as favoring store brands, switching of brands, seeking out discounts, buying do-it-yourself products, stressing durability in purchasing.
d Competition becomes more active, government undertakes more regulations.
e Adjustments to new business conditions and scarcity conditions.
f Pressure to streamline product lines, to simplify products.
g Pressure to increase prices.
h Sales force counsels and communicates the situation to customers, gathers more information, expedites orders. Advertising stresses certain products, educates customers to cope.
i Reduce support to distribution intermediaries, concentrate on certain distribution channels.
j Allocate scarce resources, pursue greater planning efficiency, shift marketing functions to other organizations.
k Closely monitor financial performance and sources of supply.

by government. The effect of public policy on managerial marketing is briefly discussed in this chapter. In addition, certain legal implications of marketing will be discussed throughout the book.

GOVERNMENT AND THE MARKETPLACE

Federal government forces regulating business include the president, Congress, the courts, and regulatory agencies such as the FTC. Traditionally, these forces have acted on marketing slowly and gradually. But today their pace is increasing. Government policy toward regulation is changing, as evidenced by new laws and by courts less and less influenced by precedent. In their interpretation of the law, the courts are respecting the aims of Congress for what has been called "the threefold blessings of material prosperity, political democracy and an ethical society."[7] Congress promotes material prosperity by its belief in the healthy competition of a free market, without regulation by price controls or public planning. The courts, in line with this thinking, have dealt to some extent with executives guilty of price fixing, bribery, and creating monopolies.

In addition to being committed to the goal of material prosperity, Congress has always believed that an open, competitive market is in keeping with a democratic society. The courts back this up with a growing concern for the protection of small businesses. Government exerts a determined effort to prevent the massive accumulation of corporate power that may be used for political influence as well as for the practice of unfair competition.

In an effort to create an ethical society, Congress has continuously attempted to establish ethical standards for the business community. The courts have responded by paying particular attention to a company's attempts to destroy competitors. An offender who has openly and knowingly flouted the rules of fair play may expect to be dealt with harshly.

Finally, public policy at the federal, state, and local levels has been procompetition and proconsumer.

GOVERNMENT IS PROCOMPETITION

The government regards competition as the major condition of healthy economic interaction. This belief assumes that there is a relationship between the structure of the market and how efficiently and productively the market performs. The government, moreover, views this relationship in terms that are ideal for vigorous price competition:

1. large numbers of buyers and sellers to react to market changes;
2. a market easy to get in and out of in response to new opportunities of supply and demand;
3. accurate information about market conditions available to all participants.

Public policy is based largely on this ideal model.

There is considerable disagreement, however, as to the validity of this approach. The relationship between market structure and performance can be influenced by other criteria: the efficiency with which the market can shift allocation of materials to meet changing demands; the ease with which a firm can enter an industry; the firm's technical efficiency and progress; and whether or not selling costs are high. Also, in the government's ideal model maximum profit is the only measure of performance. Other criteria, such as income distribution and employment levels, may make the effect of public policy more difficult to predict.

The government is aware of these limitations. This is evident in the formulation and wording of the antitrust laws. The first objective of these laws is to prevent private interests from interfering with open competition. To allow the courts enough leeway to adapt the laws to changing market conditions, Congress worded them in broad, general terms rather than with specific prohibitions. This gives the courts enough freedom in interpretation to apply the laws effectively to specific cases.

TYPES OF ANTITRUST LEGISLATION

Anyone with the power to make a marketing decision should be familiar with the antitrust laws and their implications for every stage of the marketing process. The major laws summarized in Figure 3-3, may be grouped in three categories; according to their preventive powers: present restraints, probable restraints, and unfair restraints.

Present Restraints

After the Civil War, the formation of cartels, trading associations, and pools created fears of price fixing and production control. The Sherman Antitrust Act was passed in 1890 to prevent such restraints. Section 1 of the act stipulated that any contract or conspiracy aimed at restraining trade is illegal; section 2 prohibits attempts to monopolize trade. The intention of the act was clear. The actual wording gave the courts plenty of discretion to apply it as they saw fit. At first, however, they saw fit to apply it in a generally ineffective manner through a tendency toward mild interpretation. Still, the teeth were there; only the bite was missing. This was supplied in the early 1900s, during the presidency of Theodore Roosevelt. Stringent enforcement of the Sherman Act became the rule. The number of suits filed against businesses increased greatly as the courts demonstrated their willingness to break up conspiracies and potential monopolies. Even with this strong action, it soon became clear that more legislation was needed to keep competition alive and fair.

Probable Restraints

To be convicted under the Sherman Act, an organization had to restrain trade or create a monopoly. The Clayton Act of 1914 extended coverage to include practices "where the effect . . . may be to substantially lessen competition or tend to create a monopoly." Proof of price restraint, conspiracy, or monopoly was no longer necessary. The probability of such was enough.

The Clayton Act spelled out four main areas of concern. Section 2 forbids sellers to discriminate in price between purchasers of commodities of like grade, quantity, and quality where such discrimination results in lessening of competition or tends to create a monopoly. Section 3 forbids a supplier to insist on an exclusive dealing arrangement or on "tying arrangements" under

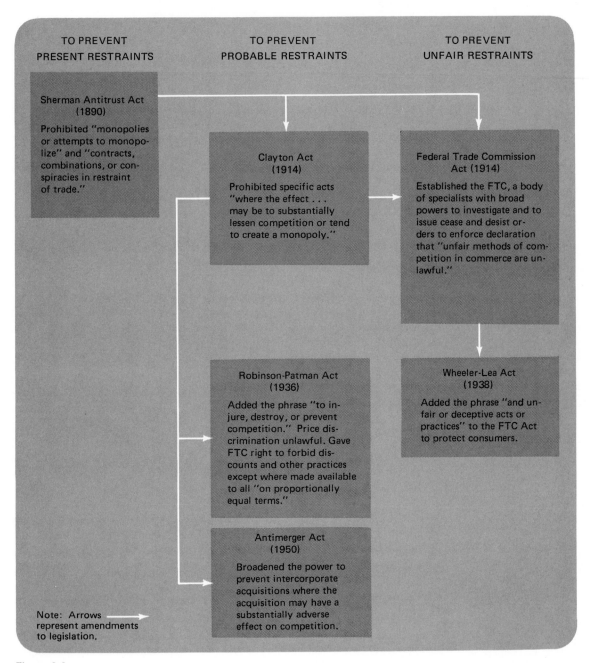

TO PREVENT PRESENT RESTRAINTS

Sherman Antitrust Act (1890)

Prohibited "monopolies or attempts to monopolize" and "contracts, combinations, or conspiracies in restraint of trade."

TO PREVENT PROBABLE RESTRAINTS

Clayton Act (1914)

Prohibited specific acts "where the effect . . . may be to substantially lessen competition or tend to create a monopoly."

TO PREVENT UNFAIR RESTRAINTS

Federal Trade Commission Act (1914)

Established the FTC, a body of specialists with broad powers to investigate and to issue cease and desist orders to enforce declaration that "unfair methods of competition in commerce are unlawful."

Robinson-Patman Act (1936)

Added the phrase "to injure, destroy, or prevent competition." Price discrimination unlawful. Gave FTC right to forbid discounts and other practices except where made available to all "on proportionally equal terms."

Wheeler-Lea Act (1938)

Added the phrase "and unfair or deceptive acts or practices" to the FTC Act to protect consumers.

Antimerger Act (1950)

Broadened the power to prevent intercorporate acquisitions where the acquisition may have a substantially adverse effect on competition.

Note: Arrows ⟶ represent amendments to legislation.

**Figure 3-3
MAJOR FEDERAL
ANTITRUST
LEGISLATION**

which a dealer, to get one product line, is forced to take others as well. Section 7 of the Clayton Act forbids corporations to acquire the stock of competitors when such action might lead to less competition or a monopoly. For the same reasons, section 8 forbids directors to sit on the boards of competing corporations.

Cases tried under the Clayton Act have had to deal with the vagueness of terms such as "substantially to lessen competition" or "tend to create a monopoly." As a result, such trials are usually complicated procedures with highly uncertain outcomes.

The Robinson-Patman Act of 1936 is an amendment to the Clayton Act. It relieves some of the ambiguity by the addition of the phrase "to injure, destroy or prevent competition." In other words, it is no longer necessary to lessen the competition "substantially" for an action to be unlawful. In addition, the Robinson-Patman Act defines price discrimination in more detail and prohibits indirect price discrimination by means of advertising allowances, brokerage fees, and special services.

The Antimerger Act of 1950, also an amendment to the Clayton Act, was designed to remove the threat posed by the concentration of big business through merger and acquisition. The act broadens the Clayton Act to include the prohibition of acquiring assets, as well as stock of competing firms, where the effect might be a threat to competition.

Unfair Restraints The Federal Trade Commission Act, passed in 1914 and amended in 1938, extended the Sherman and Clayton Acts. It legislated against "unfair or deceptive acts or practices." The significant difference between this and the other antitrust laws is that it outlaws all "unfair" practices, whether they interfere with competition or not. In addition, the FTC is given the power to define these practices and prosecute offenders. As in the case of the other antitrust laws, the wording of the Act was phrased in general terms to allow interpretation and clarification, case by case. Early attempts to apply the law in cases charging unfair practices against "consumers," however, were unsuccessful. It was held to pertain only to "competitors." This was changed by the Wheeler-Lea Act of 1938. Today, the FTC has jurisdiction over a wide variety of areas involving consumer protection.

ENFORCEMENT OF ANTITRUST LEGISLATION The sections of the antitrust laws dealing with enforcement are written in the same broad terms as the sections dealing with offenses. This language provides the same flexibility in handing out punishment as in defining the nature and extent of the transgression.

Enforcing Agents The responsibility for enforcing the laws rests with the Federal Trade Commission and the Justice Department. Private citizens and business firms can also institute civil antitrust proceedings. Under the Sherman Act, the Justice Department can bring charges that are civil, criminal, or both. The most common are civil suits in which a company, if guilty, is ordered to stop a particular trade-restraining practice or to take some specific action to break up a monopoly. The court order may take several forms, such as an order to break up a trade association, to grant patent licenses to competitors, or to sell controlling shares of stock.

The majority of antitrust suits are settled by consent decrees. In such proceedings, the defendant does not admit guilt but does agree to do as the court has suggested. This process can save time, legal fees, and embarrassment.

The FTC, in addition to instituting proceedings, tries to get companies to comply with the law voluntarily. It establishes guidelines of acceptable conduct for specific industries and make them readily available. Companies still in doubt can request the FTC's viewpoint on the legality of specific courses of action they may be planning. Guidelines for mergers in specific industries are also issued by the FTC.

Record of Enforcement The number of antitrust laws and the agencies created to enforce them may make it seem as though the antitrust forces always "get their man." In reality however, the antitrust record is an uneven one. The laws contain many loopholes that are regularly taken advantage of by business lawyers. The resources of regulatory agencies are often limited. Finally, the courts are generally lenient toward corporate violators of the law.

In general, antitrust has made some progress in moving against attempts to victimize the consumer through price fixing, market control, and out-and-out monopolies. A few well-publicized, heavy fines and prison sentences have made American industry aware that such practices are, to say the least, frowned upon.

On the other hand, the laws have been largely ineffective in preventing small groups of large companies from virtually controlling their market through a kind of group monopoly, or, more exactly, an oligopoly. As a result, 80 percent or more of the market in many industries is controlled by a small, powerful group. This is the case with steel, automobiles, petroleum, tobacco, and aluminum, among others. Antitrust seems powerless to reverse this fact of industrial life.

The inflation of the 1970s triggered a crackdown on price fixing. Rising

---

PRICE FIXING AND THE SMALL BUSINESSMAN

A midwestern supplier of shipping cartons, indicted for price fixing, expressed a view held by much of the business world:

These days, most businesses are looking for security. Protecting price levels is simply a matter of survival. Competitors have to be at least influenced by each other's prices. All I did wrong was talk to my competitors about it—we never even sat down and said, "Okay, let's all agree." Price wars can kill the small business—who wants that?

Asked if he was aware that he was breaking the law, he replied, "Price fixing is like breaking the speed limit. It's only illegal if you get caught."

He reflects the view that antitrust laws do not prevent price fixing. They just make offenders more cautious. "It's almost impossible to avoid price fixing," said another convicted offender. "My son, when he takes over the business, will probably have to face the same problems. I can't see the practice disappearing. All that will happen is people will get smarter and harder to catch."

Based on "Price-Fixing: Crackdown under Way," *Business Week*, June 2, 1975, pp. 42–48.

prices combined with rising costs have put a squeeze on profits. This makes the temptation to maintain prices by collusion irresistible to more and more executives in more and more industries.

Although small businesses feel threatened by strong government action against price fixing, big corporations are the main target of antitrust legislation. As far as the public is concerned, big companies are not necessarily socially responsible. Corporation executives are concerned with the form of the laws. They feel that antitrust laws drawn up almost a century ago may be outdated. Also these laws may be written in such vague language that honest enterprise is inhibited by not knowing what may and may not be legally done. Business leaders' anxiety is all the more understandable when you remember that, if the axe falls, they may end up in jail.

For the future, there are clear signs of increased legislative attack. New legislation and investigations of big industry are on the way, with stronger penalties likely. Movements are even under way for the prosecution of companies because of their size alone. IBM and AT&T stand accused of antitrust violations in cases that will take years to go through the courts.

Until recently, critics such as Ralph Nader have accused the government of "using current antitrust weapons like peashooters against dinosaurs."[8] If present trends continue, the peas may become more like poisoned darts.

EXCEPTIONS TO ANTITRUST LEGISLATION

Although the acknowledged purpose of antitrust laws is to encourage competition, there are exceptions that appear to do just the opposite. These exceptions to the antitrust laws can be neatly categorized: (1) regulated industries, (2) exempted industries, (3) licensing and other procedures, (4) subsidies, and (5) governmental purchases.[9]

Regulated industries are areas of near monopoly where competition has been replaced by government control of prices in the consumer's interest. In this category are public utilities, the phone company, water and natural gas companies, and in part, public transportation such as railroads and local bus service.

Exempted industries are more difficult to define. Exemptions may be complete and full, or partial and implied. They remove the competitive requirements from many areas of the economy including organized labor, agricultural cooperatives, insurance, and foreign trade.

Licensing and other procedures are mostly aimed at controlling public health and safety or preventing fraud and adulteration. They regulate such areas as the sale of alcoholic beverages, building codes and inspections, and the licensing of doctors, lawyers, and other professionals. Critics of many licensing programs maintain that they are too often perverted into a means to control, inhibit, and prevent competition rather than protect the public.

Subsidies are even more controversial. Ostensibly meant to support and protect vital industries, government subsidies have been paid to railroads, agricultural and maritime industries, airlines, small businesses, and educational institutions. Another major area is federal funding of state or municipal projects. A fundamental measure of a politician's worth is how much money he or she can wring out of Washington to pay for local sewers, airports, highways, or recreation centers.

Government purchases account for a significant portion of the total market. Most government contracts are filled on a competitive basis, often with sealed bids. Defense contracts, however, are usually an exception. The development of new weapons requires research and testing in strict confidence over a period that sometimes may run into years. Such conditions do not fit with the normal rules of competition, so normal marketing rules generally do not apply. For companies who want government contracts, the government bureaucracy has specific procedures to be followed, complicated regulations to be observed, committees to be convinced. Although the competition for these contracts may be fierce, the ability to maneuver through the intricate maze of government bureaucracy may require more political than marketing expertise.

GOVERNMENT IS PROCONSUMER

In spite of some antitrust sanctions against industrial giants, both government and consumer have come to accept big business and industrial concentration as not only here but here to stay. Nonetheless, accepting a situation does not mean ignoring all its aspects. In the last decade, the government has shown increasing concern for the consumer's welfare. It has provided safety standards for drugs and automobiles, health warnings on cigarette packages, disclosure of the true interest rate in credit transactions, and similar safeguards designed to protect all but the most gullible consumer. "Let the seller beware" has replaced the centuries-old tradition of "let the buyer beware."

WAVES OF CONSUMER LEGISLATION

Federal legislation in the area of consumer protection has occurred in three main waves. The first took place just before World War I and protected consumers against unsafe and adulterated food and drugs. The second wave followed the Great Depression. The earlier food and drug legislation was significantly strengthened at this time. The Wheeler-Lea Act was also added to the FTC Act to protect consumers against deceptive advertising.

The third and most active wave took place in the consumerism era of the 1960s. President John F. Kennedy officially involved the presidency with a message to Congress on the rights of consumers in 1962. Backed by political interest and by champions such as Ralph Nader, consumerism became a cause. A generous crop of legislation has since followed (see Wave III, high gear, Table 3-2) to protect consumers from drug abuse, unsafe cars and toys, hazardous cigarettes, and unwholesome poultry, among other things.

The agencies charged with enforcing these regulations, such as the Federal Trade Commission and the Food and Drug Administration, are under increasing scrutiny of both government and consumer representatives. The basic challenge is whether these agencies have the necessary understanding of consumer needs and the ability to do something about them. One criticism is that the commissions tend to consider consumer choice only in economic

Table 3-2
IMPORTANT PROCONSUMER LEGISLATION

Wave I	
1906	Food and Drugs Act of 1906
1914	Federal Trade Commission Act
Wave II	
1938	Federal Food, Drug, and Cosmetic Act of 1938
	Wheeler-Lea Amendment
1939	Wool Products Labeling Act
Wave III (low gear)	
1953	Flammable Fabrics Act
1958	Automobile Information Disclosure Act
1959	Textile Fiber Products Identification Act
1960	Federal Hazardous Substances Labeling Act
	Color Additives Amendment
1962	Kefauver-Harris Drug Amendments
Wave III (high gear)	
1965	Drug Abuse Control Amendments
	Fair Packaging and Labeling Act
1966	National Traffic and Motor Vehicle Safety Act
	Child Safety Act
	Cigarette Labeling Act
1967	Wholesome Meat Act
	National Commission on Product Safety Act
1968	Consumer Credit Protecting Act
	Wholesome Poultry Products Act
	Hazardous Radiation Act
1969	Child Protection and Toy Safety Act of 1969
	Public Health Smoking Cigarette Act of 1969
1970	Fair Credit Reporting Act
	Council on Environmental Quality
1971	Federal Boat Safety Act
1972	Consumer Product Safety Act
1974	Motor Vehicle Information and Cost Savings Act
	Magnuson-Moss Warranty—Federal Trade Commission Act
	Transportation Safety Act of 1974

terms. Since the consumer is influenced by subjective criteria as well as economics, effective protection must be based on a clearer understanding of his or her motives (see Chapters 8 and 9).

Changing marketing patterns have been influential in cases tried under consumer protection legislation. For example, the courts have held that since today's consumer has less opportunity to inspect and test merchandise before buying, the manufacturer must accept more liability for product performance.

MARKETING IMPLICATIONS OF PUBLIC POLICY

In order for legal and ethical standards of marketing to be established, society must define by law those practices that are considered antisocial or anti-competitive.[10] Once this is done, marketing managers must be made aware of the ways in which these laws limit their freedom to make decisions. At present, some marketing practices are clearly illegal under existing laws, court rulings, and regulatory agency actions. Other practices are open to interpretation as to their legality. The job of this chapter is not to make a lawyer of everyone studying marketing, but to make marketers more sensitive to those areas in which questions of legality may arise.

The effect of public policy on managerial marketing is shown in Figure 3-4. Certain marketing objectives may be constrained if they smack of achieving monopoly or fixed market share. The ability to compete may be limited when a firm is very large and its actions invite government attention. Consumer segments must be looked at in terms of their needs and the standards of protection established by government policies. The structure of competing firms in the external environment must permit active competition to take place. Marketing strategy in general, and each of the specific marketing mix elements in particular, are subject to numerous legal prohibitions. (Many of these legal questions will be discussed in later chapters.) There are two principles that are always operative, however. Strategy must be implemented independently by each firm, not in collusion with its competitors. Control of strategy requires close attention to any changes in public policy.

THE ECONOMIC AND PUBLIC POLICY ENVIRONMENTS OF THE FUTURE

Without the aid of a crystal ball, we will now attempt a preview of future economic and public policy environments.

In the economic sphere, there are two schools of thought on how the United States can best get out of the economic turbulence of the 1970s. One group sees economic planning at the national level as the inevitable solution. When imbalances become apparent, specific actions would be taken to correct the situation. These actions might include price and supply controls, tax breaks, incentives, and so forth. The other group favors a free market, based on the assumption that a rise in price will force consumers to use a product more sparingly, thereby stabilizing the economy. This group feels that a free market would encourage industry to find cheaper alternatives to fuel and to develop a more productive technology.

The actual solution may lie between the two. There is already a noticeable trend toward some form of coordinated national planning. This coordination of effort may lead us to an increase in productivity and a more efficient use of our natural resources.

When economic conditions get tough, antitrust enforcement gets tougher.

Figure 3-4 PUBLIC POLICY AFFECTS MANAGERIAL MARKETING

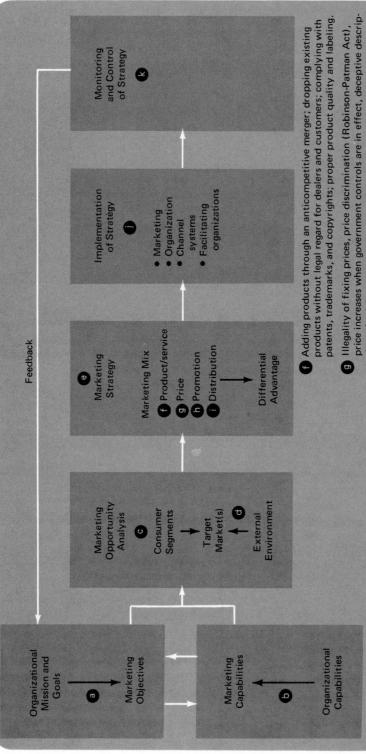

a Rate of growth and share of market in its own industry and in other industries (Sherman Act, Clayton Act).

b Size of business relative to competitors.

c Level of consumer sophistication, effect of safety and health hazards, amount and kind of information received.

d Level of economic concentration, effect of acquisition or actions on competition, ease of entry by prospective competitors, rate of technological advances.

e Illegal to pursue too large a share of the market through unfair marketing practices.

f Adding products through an anticompetitive merger; dropping existing products without legal regard for dealers and customers; complying with patents, trademarks, and copyrights; proper product quality and labeling.

g Illegality of fixing prices, price discrimination (Robinson-Patman Act), price increases when government controls are in effect, deceptive description of pricing terms.

h Illegality of false and misleading advertising, bait advertising (where products exist in small quantities, if at all), promotional allowances and services on proportionally unequal terms (Robinson-Patman Act).

i Illegality of practices that foreclose access to distribution channel members, such as exclusive dealing arrangements, exclusive territorial distributorships, and tying agreements.

j Collusive relations among competitors, such as price fixing, dividing up markets, agreeing on various customers, and excluding new competitors.

k Watch for changing laws, court rulings, regulations, the political mood, competitive responses.

Antitrust action is an odd mixture of renewed government faith in the magic power of competition to keep the economy vigorous and a recognition of the need for more government pressure to bring this about. Consumers, frustrated by rising prices, respond favorably to invigorated antitrust enforcement. For corporations that violate the law, stronger attacks and stiffer penalties lie ahead.

Paralleling the drift toward coordinated planning is a trend toward a more centralized approach to antitrust legislation. Both moves will require the increased gathering of relevant information to facilitate federal monitoring. A related trend is the increasing recognition that social values have a place in national economic and public policy. Such values as consumer health and clean air are explored in Chapter 4.

Throughout the marketplace, an air of uncertainty remains. Current policy is, typically, hard to grasp and future policy hard to predict. Large corporations live with the uneasy possibility that, if they compete too successfully, they will eventually be branded as having an unfair advantage. Management must keep a constant and alert eye on the market environment and hope to recognize the clues that indicate they are competing unfairly.

The consumer, recently arrived as a group with rights and collective influence, is here to stay and be heard. The government is listening with increased sensitivity. The result should be more laws and administrative rulings, more vigorously enforced by government agencies. Big business may contribute to the election campaigns, but consumers cast the votes.

There are two steps the marketing executive can take to deal with future consumer legislation. The first is to obtain legal advice on how existing legislation may affect his or her business. If the lawyer is not sure how this legislation is interpreted or applied, the company may appeal to the courts for a ruling. The second step is to anticipate the trends of public policy and gear the company's marketing approach accordingly.

STATE AND LOCAL GOVERNMENTS ARE INVOLVED, TOO

While federal laws apply only to *inter*state commerce, state and local laws regulate all competition *within* the state. There are state laws controlling minimum prices, Sunday selling, restraint of trade, and consumer protection. Some overlap with federal laws is inevitable, as is some conflict. What is good for Alabama or Michigan may not be deemed good for the country as a whole.

The most striking local trend is the growing awareness of the need for consumer complaint offices. Between 1969 and 1974, the number of state, county, and city consumer affairs agencies increased nationally from sixteen to nearly twenty.

California, for example, launched an energetic attack on TV repair fraud, following it up with a similar bill to protect consumers against unscrupulous auto repair shops. Auto repair dealers are required to register with the state, paying a fee that is used to finance the investigation of consumer complaints and the inspection of repair shops. Offenders are punished severely with up to $1,000 in fines and six months in jail. Other states are considering—or have already passed—similar legislation.

CONCLUSION

Although we have looked at economic and public policy separately, marketing is interested in the relationship between the two. We are at a stage where private enterprise is being increasingly watched by the public. Another kind of economic system seems to be emerging, although its precise form is hard to predict. It is certain, however, that national economic fluctuations, international economic changes, and social developments at home will improve the system—including consumers, government, and marketing organizations.

What can someone in marketing do to help keep his or her organization on top of the wave?

1. Keep a critical eye on the economic and political environments to see what is happening and watch for signs of what is likely to happen.

2. Study the decision process and the relationship of government, pressure groups, and public opinion.

3. Know where the balance of power lies among these groups.

4. Develop a marketing program that combines the company's private interests with the public good. The hard part may be to arrive at an adequate definition of what the public good is. Even harder may be the decision to favor the public good when there is a conflict between the two.

5. Don't automatically fight the pace of change in the environment. Tradition and past success formulas may become outdated faster than yesterday's *Wall Street Journal*. Ability to adapt will be a saving grace.

DISCUSSION QUESTIONS

1. What are the positive consequences of high-cost energy and resource scarcities for society? For marketing management?

2. How should an appliance manufacturer react when energy limitations, inflation, and recession, all occur at the same time?

3. Is the economic turmoil and uncertainty so great that business needs some central form of national economic planning? What would be the advantages and disadvantages for marketing?

4. Which parts of the antitrust laws name the marketing practices that are absolutely off-limits to large corporations? What are today's "gray areas" in antitrust enforcement?

5. How can a large firm avoid the temptations of violating the antitrust laws through price fixing? A small firm?

6. Which aspects of the managerial marketing process (Chapter 2) must be followed in response to recent proconsumer federal legislation for a drug manufacturer, a toy manufacturer, and a bank's consumer loan department?

NOTES

1. W. Michael Blumenthal, *Bendix Corporation Annual Report, 1974*, p. 3.

2. U.S. Bureau of the Census, Statistical Abstract of the United States (Washington, D.C.:

U.S. Government Printing Office, 1974), p. 376.

3. David M. Potter, *People of Plenty* (Chicago: University of Chicago Press, 1954), p. 173.

4. William Lazer, "Toward Scientific Marketing," *1963 Proceedings of the Winter Conference* (Chicago: American Marketing Association, 1964), p. 135.

5. Mack W. Worden, "Marketers Must Sell America Out of Its Economic Troubles," *Marketing News*, December 1, 1974, p. 7.

6. Gary Hart, "Free Lunch Is Over," *New York Times*, April 21, 1975, p. 29.

7. Jerrold G. Van Cise, *The Federal Antitrust Laws* (Washington, D.C.: American Enterprise Institute for Public Policy Research, 1965), p. 16.

8. Quoted in "Is John Sherman's Antitrust Obsolete?" *Business Week*, March 23, 1974, p. 47.

9. E. T. Grether, *Marketing and Public Policy* (Englewood Cliffs, N.J.: Prentice-Hall, 1966), pp. 11–17.

10. Philip Kotler, *Marketing Management: Analysis, Planning, and Control*, 2d ed. (Englewood Cliffs, N.J.: Prentice-Hall, 1972), pp. 824–26.

4

SOCIALLY RESPONSIBLE MARKETING

After completing this chapter, the reader should be able to:

1. Describe the emerging viewpoints regarding the social responsibility of marketing.

2. Distinguish among the major social responsibility directions—consumerism, ecology, and disadvantaged consumers.

3. Evaluate the different responses an organization may make to consumerism.

4. Describe the several levels of standards relevant for marketing decision making.

5. Develop consumerism programs and consumer affairs organizational changes.

6. Assess the potential of industry-wide self-regulation.

One of the major forces in the societal environment that affects marketing is the issue of social responsibility. The meaning of this complex and growing issue, and what marketing management should do about it, is the central concern of this chapter.

GETTING A FAIR HEARING

Newsweek—Lawrence McIntosh

In 1973 Americans spent $150 million on hearing aids.[1] Senator Charles Percy of Illinois, who himself wears a hearing aid, felt that this figure was much too high. He charged that dealers were making "immoral" profits by purchasing instruments for $70 to $150 and selling them for $400. In addition, Percy claimed that high-pressure dealers unloaded these devices on people who did not need them. He cited a study in which 42 percent of elderly volunteers were sold hearing aids when they had perfectly good hearing. As a result of these findings, Percy asked the Federal Trade Commission and the Food and Drug Administration to investigate the hearing aid industry.

Retailers responded angrily to Percy's charges. An industry spokesperson insisted that the 250 percent retail markup covers the cost of service for the life of the hearing aid. He denied that the industry includes "fly-by-nights" and "scoundrels," and questioned Percy's political motivations in making such charges. Despite these denials, the FTC and the Department of Health, Education and Welfare began studies of the hearing care problem.

HERE WE GO AGAIN

The dynamics of overpricing have become familiar in the last decade. A national opinion leader such as Percy easily gains publicity when he raises questions about a relatively new and unregulated industry. When such issues as the consumer's right to fair prices, ethical sales practices, and government supervision come into play, the industry responds by defending the status quo on economic grounds, denying unethical practices, and questioning the political motivations of the accuser. Government agencies then launch studies which nearly always lead to new regulations.

Marketing is being "played" today as a "new ball game" with an emerging set of new rules. If a business or industry is not aware of its social responsibilities, certain social forces will make them aware and insist upon changes.

In Chapter 3 we discussed two major influences on the marketing environment: economic conditions and public policy. In this chapter we will analyze the **societal environment** of marketing, the social forces that are shaping marketing practices today, and the future marketing structure. Economic, political, and social forces are combined in the marketing environment. One set of forces can support another (developing fuel-saving automobiles helps in the fight against air pollution) or interfere with another (the sale of safety equipment is

71

"Let's not tell them our medicine man determined smoking is hazardous to health. Why screw up the economy?"

Reprinted with permission from the June 9, 1975 issue of *Advertising Age*. Copyright 1975 by Crain Communications.

hindered by inflated prices). Next, this chapter will provide marketing management implications of consumerism, the force that has the most immediate and extensive impact on marketing. Progressive organizations have already responded to this force; further responses should be seriously considered by other conservative organizations.

THE SOCIAL RESPONSIBILITY DIMENSION

The crucial dilemma of marketing has been summed up by David Finn, who notes, "the free enterprise system does provide many unique benefits for our society, but it has also gotten us into a lot of trouble."[2] The marketing system is structured to produce and deliver products that make life comfortable for the consumer and provide profit for the investor. Yet some are critical of the effects this production and consumption have on society. On society's agenda, and therefore of concern to business, are such issues as using up resources (food, oil), polluting the environment (automobile emissions, phosphates in detergents), and dangers to consumer health and safety (cigarettes, unsafe toys). Also of concern is the issue of the exploitation of consumer groups, such as the poor and the elderly.

One consequence of this awareness must be a more sophisticated concept of legal and social responsibility for American business. Christopher Stone has suggested that legal restraints on corporations are ineffective, since a corporation cannot be jailed and fines are often seen as insignificant.[3] With so many issues where the law will not work, corporate social responsibility is needed. In cases where the use of a product may result in harm (for example, possible genetic damage from a food additive), the manufacturer must make changes.

Of course, social responsibility is not only the duty of large corporations. Nonprofit organizations must also think of overall social welfare. And the individual public citizen cannot afford to be irresponsible. Pollution of a river may result largely from industrial dumping, but the person who throws in his picnic garbage does not help any. Thus, we can define **social responsibility** as the obligations and accountability to society of individuals and organizations above and beyond their primary functions and interests. Increasingly accepted beliefs about social responsibility and their impact on marketing are shown in Table 4-1.

Social responsibility has been brought about by certain social forces (external pressures) and the nature of organizations today (internal pressures). The major external pressures include:

1. *Public opinion.* The post-Watergate era has seen a growing public distrust of business leaders and of business in general. In a 1975 Gallup poll,

Table 4-1
CONSENSUS ON SOCIAL RESPONSIBILITY AND THE MARKETING RESPONSE

SOCIAL RESPONSIBILITY PROPOSITIONS	MARKETING RESPONSE
1. Social responsibility arises from social power. The interests of society as a whole must be protected.	1. Environmental or health consequences of new products.
2. Business must operate as a two-way open system. It must be open to societal feedback; its operations must be open to full public disclosure.	2. Full disclosure of installment debt charges; comparative price shopping of grocery prices; disclosure on labels of product-use hazards.
3. Before business chooses to proceed with marketing a product, the social costs and benefits must be calculated and weighed.	3. Environmental degradation by automobiles; side effects of new drugs.
4. Social costs must be priced into products. The consumer (user) must pay for the effects of his or her consumption.	4. Auto safety equipment; electric bills covering pollution controls; vitamins in cereals.
5. Corporations as citizens have responsibilities beyond social costs. They must be concerned about social welfare in areas of their competence.	5. Nutrition education; low-cost ghetto housing.

Adapted from Keith Davis, "Five Propositions for Social Responsibility," *Business Horizons* 18 (June 1975): 19–24.

citizens expressed less confidence in big business than in any other major American institution.[4] Younger and better educated groups (the nation's future leadership) were the most antibusiness. Many members of these groups belong to what has been called the "new class" of professionals in the work force.[5] These people, employed as social workers, teachers, journalists, and other noncorporate personnel, tend to make more idealistic demands on the business community.

2. *Consumers.* The "new consumer," having achieved the goals of security and survival, is now seeking to fulfill "postindustrial" goals. These are non-material goals and include finding meaning and purpose in life, a close sense of community, social justice, and participation in decision making. Moreover, today's consumers are becoming increasingly impatient, translating their wants and desires into a list of presumed rights.[6] Thus, the consumer may feel that he or she has a right to a low-priced store in the neighborhood, a right to know the exact contents of a breakfast cereal, and a right to a car that will hardly ever need repairs. These rising expectations contribute to increased consumer pressure on business.

3. *Consumer advocates.* In the last decade, a wide variety of consumer advocates has emerged as a force to be reckoned with. These advocates have been notably successful in gaining media exposure and political support, especially Ralph Nader. One difficulty confronting these advocates is the question: "Who really represents the interest of the consumer?" Many other participants in the political system—including corporate leaders and politicians—also claim to have the welfare of the consumer at heart. Indeed, the "consumer interest" itself is difficult to define. Part of this task is being performed by a number of independent specialists.

4. *Government.* The government is an important force in the societal environment of marketing. As we saw in Chapter 3, a series of proconsumer bills has been passed by Congress and state legislatures. At the same time, government has been getting tougher in regulating business, particularly on the federal level. The FTC, for example, has begun setting broad guidelines for industry—a change from its previous policy of case-by-case consideration of complaints. As consumer advocates have pointed out, continued inaction by business leaders will result only in more government action to protect consumer rights.

At the same time that these external forces having been operating, the following developments have been taking place within organizations:

1. *Business is becoming more bureaucratic.* Leading corporations seem to have become huge, unwieldy bureaucracies that are unresponsive to consumer needs and complaints. Decisions seem to be made by an anonymous few executives. Many employees feel no sense of responsibility toward consumers.

2. *Emphasis is placed on efficiency.* The dominant value in the "new professionalism" of business executives is efficiency. The resulting focus on scientific expertise tends to exclude an interest in human values and moral questions. The marketing information and decision-making systems may be so elaborate that they may exclude "soft" issues such as respect for consumer complaints.

3. *There is an unwillingness to give in to public pressure.* The public has demanded that corporations behave as do other social and political institutions. All too often, corporations react only in defense of their economic interests and are insensitive to social values and ethical issues. The price for this insensitivity is a loss of trust and confidence on the part of the American people.[7]

THE ECOLOGICAL ENVIRONMENT

In a sense, ecology is the broadest social issue that marketing must deal with today. At stake are the preservation and survival of our entire ecological system. Some environmentalists have offered grim "doomsday warnings" if certain marketing and production trends continue.

One recent example is the effect that aerosol sprays may be having on the earth's ozone layer. It is claimed that the fluorocarbon propellants used in most spray cans eventually reach the stratosphere and destroy much of the earth's protective ozone covering. This may lead to more ultraviolet radiation reaching the planet and to a serious rise in skin cancer. If unlimited industrial growth means the production of more and more aerosol spray cans causing more and more skin cancer, is this growth justifiable in the name of prosperity and profit? Of course not, but the harmful effect of aerosols has not yet been positively proven. The broader issue, however, is that increased consumption poses a serious threat to our already polluted environment.

There are some indications that the American public is accepting a new conservation ethic. A 1975 report by the National Academy of Sciences suggested that consumers may adopt a modified life style that uses less energy and natural resources.[8] This may be essential for survival because pollution is an inevitable by-product of our high-consumption economic system. If we continue to increase our levels of production to meet this high consumption level, we can expect the pollution problem to become much more serious. Rising soft drink and beer consumption levels leave a lot of containers lying around, as well as using precious resources and creating a waste-disposal problem.

George Fisk points to a need for "responsible consumption."[9] He notes that few business leaders understand the ecological consequences of marketing decisions. In his view, we must develop specific concepts of responsible consumption—or preventing pollution and using resources efficiently. The problem is of international dimensions; it cannot be solved in any one nation independently of others. One element in responsible consumption is clearly the individual consumer, who must reduce his or her need to consume certain products (large automobiles and detergents). There must be a reduction in the drive for production as well, and a world-wide notion of "zero energy growth," if we are to avoid ecological disaster.[10]

At the same time, it is clear that ecological problems cannot be solved solely by individual firms or citizens. Individual actions such as recycling bottles or using less gasoline will not in themselves be enough. We need a system of marketing priorities and production processes that reflects socioecological priorities. This means evaluating a product (such as the automobile) in terms of its full social, economic, and ecological implications.

In one sense, this poses serious problems for business. It may mean drastic redefining of traditional marketing assumptions. But greater public awareness of socioecological needs also offers new opportunities and profitable (and socially useful) business activity. These include the development of improved energy-conversion systems; the creation of efficient, inexpensive, and energy-saving mass transit forms; and the stimulation of effective recycling processes.[11] Such areas offer fertile ground for businesses interested in preserving our environment while prospering economically.

CONSUMERISM

The term **consumerism** emerged in the mid-1960s. It was first coined by businessmen who saw the consumer movement as another "ism" just as threatening as socialism and communism.

Actually, the history of consumers in the social protest movement began long before the activism of the 1960s in the United States. Protests actually started in the underdeveloped nations of the world, focusing on people's needs for adequate food, clothing, and housing. The present American consumer movement is, in reality, a third wave of consumerism. The first occurred in the early 1900s; the second coincided with the Depression years.

Consumerism has been defined as a social force designed to protect the consumer by organizing legal, moral, and economic pressures on business.[12] Philip Kotler describes it more specifically as a social movement seeking to increase the powers and rights of buyers in relation to sellers.[13] As Figure 4-1

Figure 4-1   BALANCE OF POWER IN THE MARKETPLACE
Based on Philip Kotler, "What Consumerism Means for Marketers," *Harvard Business Review* 50 (May-June 1972): 48–57.

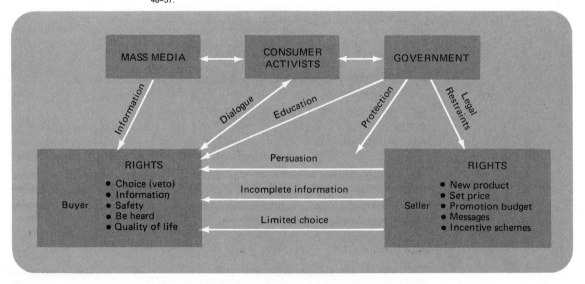

suggests, the marketplace can be analyzed in terms of a balance of power. After examining these traditional rights of buyers and sellers, the conclusion is that the balance of power presently lies with the seller. Consumerism is society's attempt to redress this imbalance.

This definition raises serious questions about the basis of the marketing concept. Daniel Yankelovich puts the question squarely: "Can the market economy through the free play of competition respond to the legitimate demands of the public, or is there an inherent defect in the market mechanism that has to be corrected by political means?"[14] Similarly, Peter Drucker observes that consumerism challenges four critical assumptions of the marketing concept:

1. Consumers really know their needs.

2. Business really cares about those needs and knows how to find out about them.

3. Business provides useful information that clearly matches product to need.

4. Products and services really deliver what consumers expect and business promises.[15]

There are varying explanations for the energy and emotion behind the consumer movement. Some critics believe that Americans are frustrated by the depersonalization of all of modern life. Business may be serving as a lightning rod for such discontent, since all citizens have frequent contact with market institutions. Others have pictured the marketplace as the "last refuge" of the middle class. The breakdown of business performance may be the final, intolerable letdown for these consumers.

Consumerism has included demands for four principal types of protection measures:

1. labeling requirements and/or supplementary information, including advertising, from the seller or manufacturer;

2. issuance of information about products and services by government agencies or quasipublic agencies;

3. regulation of the structure of business organizations, for example, antitrust actions;

4. control of the nature of offerings, prices, and the production process.[16]

Across the country, consumers and their advocates have fought for legislation covering all of these areas.

DISADVANTAGED CONSUMERS

Until now, we have referred to consumers as a general group, without making any distinctions. This term usually refers to those who are enjoying the benefits of affluence, the middle and upper classes. However, we must recognize that many people do not share in this affluence, or are in some other way **disadvantaged consumers** in the marketplace. Low-income citizens, the elderly, children, and women all face particular problems as consumers.

**Low-Income
Consumers**

Consumer protection is most essential for Americans with low incomes. The poor cannot afford to waste their limited resources on defective cars, unhealthy foods, or shoddy household goods. Low-income citizens badly need to make the most of their money, but they are severely hampered by inadequate education. The poor lack information and skills that are vital to making the best consumer purchases and "deals" within the marketing system.

Low-income consumers in particular are often victims of high prices. They may pay more than middle-class citizens for the same goods and services. There are three principal causes of this imbalance:

1. Low-income consumers have less access to public or private transportation and thus have fewer shopping options outside their neighborhoods.
2. Merchants in low-income areas have relatively high operating costs, which affect pricing.
3. The poor often must rely on credit buying in small neighborhood stores. The costs of such credit are considerable.[17]

It seems clear that low-income citizens need effective consumer education programs. The poor can greatly benefit from instruction in buying techniques and in means of recourse against unfair practices. However, as necessary as it is, consumer education is not sufficient in itself. Solutions to the poor consumer's problems depend upon change in business and politics. Large, efficient retailers are badly needed in ghetto areas. Credit must be made available at fairer rates in major department stores. Such reforms, tied in with increased consumer awareness, will give the low-income citizen a more realistic chance at making effective use of his or her dollar.[18]

**The Elderly, Children,
and Women**

Many senior citizens are severely disadvantaged by their limited resources and even more limited mobility. The elderly are especially vulnerable to deception and fraud because of their health care needs. The costs of medical attention are sky-rocketing, yet senior citizens have disproportionate needs for the services of doctors and dentists.[19]

Children are especially susceptible to manipulative advertising techniques. As Dean Burch, chairman of the Federal Communications Commission, commented:

> . . . in the case of advertising directed to children, the standards of what is false and deceptive must be judged in light of the crucial fact that the audience is so unsophisticated, so young and trusting.[20]

The National Advertising Review Board has voiced similar concerns. In a 1974 report, it cautioned that all advertising should be "child-proofed." All media messages should be understood and evaluated in terms of their potential impact on children.[21]

Women consumers have been the victims of discriminatory banking practices and sexist advertising. Banks have a sad history of treating women as "second-class citizens." It is difficult for a woman, no matter how secure her job and income, to receive a loan or mortgage in her own name, to start a business, or even to obtain a credit card. Such discrimination is indirectly promoted by sexist advertising stereotypes. Women are typically presented as mothers, housewives, or sex objects. They are rarely seen as professionals, business leaders, or serious, independent thinkers. The contemporary feminist movement has strongly challenged these practices and demanded that women be treated with equality, dignity, and respect.

MARKETING IMPLICATIONS OF CONSUMERISM

At first, marketing reacted reluctantly if at all to the rapidly evolving "rules of the game." But this has changed in recent years. The harried decision maker in the cartoon below recognizes the new layers of considerations, complexity, and pressure that are becoming a part of marketing decision making. To meet these pressures, organizations must develop different sets of goals, plan new strategies, and restructure their internal organizations.

The problem is most acute for large organizations, whether Exxon, Bank of America, or Indiana University. However, smaller firms—a baking company in Charleston, S.C., or a furniture dealer in Toronto—also face more and more social responsibility decisions.

WHAT ARE THE ALTERNATIVES?

Organizations have responded in a variety of ways to the pressure of consumerism. They have ignored it, resisted it, profited by it, adapted to it voluntarily, adopted self-regulation, and accepted the government way. Let us examine some of the reasons for these various responses.

I made the decision!! Now I only have to check it with the legal department, Ralph Nader, the TV Code, the FTC, the FDA, our consumer advisory board, the Urban League, and my two teenage daughters.

1. *Ignore it.* Some organizations simply ignore the consumer movement. Essentially, they are hoping that it will go away—but it will not. This response virtually ensures government action to control marketing.

2. *Resist it.* Large and powerful industries have sometimes been successful in resisting consumer demands. In many cases, their lobbying efforts have prevented the passage of regulatory legislation. But this is a delaying tactic, not an answer.[22] Government will eventually be forced to satisfy consumers. In a confrontation with government's overwhelming legislative and taxing powers, business can only fight a losing battle and alienate the public at the same time.

3. *Profit by it.* To respond to consumer pressure by creating new means of profit is the most acceptable alternative for business. Yankelovich argues that the real conflict is not between marketing and government regulation, but between concern about short-run sales and profits vs. the need for long-run security.[23] He notes that IBM has effectively "built customers" by risking immediate profits in order to meet important consumer needs. The result is that many satisfied customers stay with IBM product systems time after time— even when competing systems are cheaper and better.

4. *Adapt to it voluntarily.* Voluntary action is one means of meeting consumer demands and, at the same time, heading off government regulation. For this option, it does not matter whether the action will increase profit or costs. But there are risks in committing corporate resources to social goals. Without a secure financial base and enlightened executive leadership, a business would find bold voluntary action to be financially dangerous.

5. *Adopt self-regulation.* Business has to police itself if it wishes to retain public support. One way to do this is through industry-wide self-regulation. The movie industry, for example, adopted its own rating system in order to prevent government from doing the job and to bolster the confidence of the public. The limits of self-regulation are discussed later in this chapter.

6. *Accept the government way.* Government regulation of business has increased on all levels (federal, state, and local) in response to consumer demands. Business has traditionally resisted government regulation, fearing higher taxes, expanded government power, and the process of change itself.[24] Yet, as Drucker observes, regulation may be a prerequisite for rather than an alternative to competition. A universal standard that applies to all firms can create equal burdens and opportunities for everyone. Without such a standard, irresponsible and opportunistic companies may attempt to drive competitors out of business.[25] For example, had not automobile antipollution equipment been required of all manufacturers, those who installed it voluntarily would have lost sales to those who did not, due to the resulting rise in prices.

One possibility is for government to work with business in a kind of "partnership." Business will not make a maximum effort to resolve social problems unless such ventures are made profitable. Government can help to increase chances for profit by subsidizing risky projects with direct grants or with tax incentives.

ACCEPTING HIGHER MARKETING STANDARDS

Figure 4-2 illustrates three distinct levels of marketing standards and shows how candy marketing is influenced by them. In **conventional marketing** there is competition and product differentiation. Marketing research, promotion, and other techniques are used to maximize sales, profits, brand share, and loyalty to the firm or to its products. Quantitative tools and resources are used to measure consumer satisfaction and to resolve complaints.

LEVEL 1	Conventional Marketing	Candy produced and advertised for "great taste" and "high energy." Rising sales mean consumers are satisfied.
LEVEL 2	Consumer Affairs	To reduce dissatisfaction due to tooth decay, advertising can explain (in cartoon form) how toothbrush and dental floss fight decay.
LEVEL 3	Social Responsibility	Dental educators want to limit sweets (sugar) in a child's diet. Management considers changing ingredients, promoting reduced consumption, or switching from candy to other food products.

Figure 4-2
LEVELS OF STANDARDS IN MARKETING

Consumer affairs marketing reinforces consumer rights, measures good will, and makes the goals of the firm compatible with consumer desires. **Social responsibility marketing**, on the other hand, goes much further. It focuses on the quality of the marketing system, taking into account such factors as consumer health and welfare and the ecological consequences of consumption. It helps business assess and deal with the impact of marketing practices on the social order.

This expanded conception of marketing incorporates social responsibility goals into the decision-making framework of business. The managers of a firm would, of course, consider immediate objectives such as profit and return on investment, but the expanded marketing concept would make consumer satisfaction and social benefit explicit goals. In addition, decision makers would consider the impact of a marketing transaction on third parties not directly involved, such as nonconsumers of the product or future generations of consumers.

CONSUMERISM PROGRAMS

Many firms have launched programs to make consumers' needs and social goals a part of their everyday business. Alexander's Markets, a California food chain, has taken measures to promote ecological awareness. Products are marked with ecological pluses and minuses, and the phosphate content of all detergents is posted. Green and white "ecology-preferred" labels are attached to such items as soft drinks in returnable bottles.[26]

Table 4-2 summarizes the results of a study of business attitudes toward consumer-oriented programs. From a list of sixteen programs designed to deal with consumer issues, 3,418 executives selected the three most constructive programs. The highest-rated programs were those where efforts were made to upgrade product quality and performance standards.

The following examples illustrate ways in which two firms developed consumer consciousness and established high-standard consumer programs.

Consumer Manufacturer—Eastman Kodak. Kodak's product design keeps the inexperienced photographer in mind. The company attempts to anticipate all problems so that customers can avoid mistakes and not lose important pictures. Quality and safety in design and rigorous testing are essential in building consumer satisfaction.

Kodak also has many specific programs and services aimed at helping consumers. The company advertises that it will assist customers with photographic problems and answers 100,000 such letters per year. All Kodak products come with a clearly stated warranty. Kodak stresses prompt repair work: its eight national service centers generally return equipment within three to five days.

Retailer—J. C. Penney Company, Inc. J. C. Penney has developed nonpromotional and noncommercial consumer education materials for over 40 years. Currently, it sponsors *Forum*, a magazine for professional educators; *Buying Guides*, product information leaflets for consumers; and multimedia teaching aids for schools on consumer-related subjects. Penney also runs various educational programs in schools and universities.

A staff of 60 engineers, chemists, technicians, and mathematicians tests merchandise quality. The Product Safety Committee makes safety checks on a wide variety of Penney products, most of which carry Penney's private brand. Some 120 Penney staff members work with buyers and suppliers to ensure high-quality production standards. Penny also maintains a Customer Relations Department that keeps management informed about trends in consumer dissatisfaction.

NEW ORGANIZATIONAL DEVELOPMENTS

Certain types of changes take place in an organization when it tries to respond to consumer demands. This response usually takes place in three stages, spanning a six- to eight-year period.[27] At first, *the chief executive speaks out on consumer issues.* He or she informs all managers of the need for an updated company policy. But there are no clear directives, and busy, profit-oriented managers tend to ignore consumerism issues.

In the second stage, *a specialist is appointed to take charge of organizational efforts at change.* (This specialist may be called a consumer affairs director.) He or she views the problem in technical terms and begins to compile information on company activities. But operating managers do not fully

Table 4-2
THE SCORE CARD OF CONSTRUCTIVE CONSUMER PROGRAMS

CONSUMER PROGRAM	ALL RESPONDENTS	RESPONDENTS' INDUSTRY							
		CONSUMER DURABLE PRODUCTS MANUFACTURERS	CONSUMER NONDURABLE PRODUCTS MANUFACTURERS	INDUSTRIAL PRODUCTS MANUFACTURERS	ADVERTISING, MEDIA, PUBLISHING	BANKING, INVESTMENT, INSURANCE	GOVERNMENT	PERSONAL CONSUMER SERVICES	RETAIL OR WHOLESALE TRADE
Upgrading product quality and performance standards	51%	55%	54%	60%	32%	36%	45%	61%	42%
Establishing industry product standards	26	29	29	33	11	13	28	22	23
Increasing research commitments to better identify consumer wants and needs	24	13	30	11	13	17	22	14	35
Modifying products for greater safety, ease of use, and repair	23	36	21	35	14	7	31	9	20
Making postsale follow-up calls on consumers	22	13	10	29	19	24	8	22	16
Supporting industry self-regulation efforts (e.g., Better Business Bureau)	20	14	21	12	30	29	17	31	20
Making advertisements more informative	19	10	16	9	48	38	11	23	24
Developing owners' manuals on product use, care, and safety	16	27	8	29	9	2	15	4	17
Creating new organizational positions to deal with consumer affairs	15	12	16	8	8	21	22	16	15
Providing more informative product labeling	14	16	36	10	16	8	8	5	25

Note: These figures are derived from aggregate responses to the question: Considering your own industry, please check the three programs you consider most constructive in responding to consumerist pressures. Ratings are included for only the ten most frequently mentioned programs among the sixteen listed in the questionnaire. Categories where industry action is high (30 percent or above) are in color.
From Stephen A. Greyser and Steven L. Diamond, "Business Is Adapting to Consumerism," *Harvard Business Review* 52 (September–October 1974): 57.

cooperate with the new executive, partly because he or she has no real leverage with them.

The final stage begins when top executives realize that neither policy statements nor special departments are enough to bring about internal change. New institutional policy is set down from above, and *all managers are expected to integrate these priorities into their day-to-day business*. They may receive special training, and their performance may be evaluated and rewarded (or penalized) based on their compliance.

Consumer Participation

One complex issue for the firm is how to bring consumers into the decision-making process of marketing. In some nonprofit organizations, such as hospitals, client participation is being used. Under the conventional marketing concept, as outlined in Chapters 1 and 2, consumers were given an elevated, but indirect and passive role. Marketing research supposedly "consulted" consumers before, during, and after key decisions. But this process clearly did not make executives aware of the changing consumer mood. The result was a communications gap and a breakdown in the marketing process.

One way to help bridge this gap is to allow a designated group of consumers to deal directly with decision makers through a **consumer advisory board**. The Stop & Shop Companies in Boston did exactly this.[28] The Consumer Board of Directors is comprised of 25 women, representing Boston shoppers. They hold monthly meetings with seventeen members of the food chain's high-level management. The women set the agenda for the meetings by submitting questions, complaints, and suggestions for new programs. The advisory board brings consumer concerns about shopping and pollution to the attention of the firm's managers. A number of significant changes in company operations have resulted from these meetings.

Consumer Affairs Unit

The **consumer affairs unit** is a company department that specializes in communications with the consumer. Traditionally, the marketing unit was the chief consumer specialist. Now, however, this job is shared by the consumer affairs unit, whose specific responsibilities and degree of power and influence vary widely from company to company.

A 1973 survey of leading American manufacturers in the United States revealed that approximately one-third of the 500 respondents had a consumer affairs unit.[29] Some were large, newly created departments; others were small customer-service departments that were merely modified versions of previously existing units. Most of the respondents saw the purpose of the consumer affairs unit as improving relations and communications with consumers, and making companies more responsive to the valid needs and grievances of consumers. Most thought the units had the solid backing of senior management.

Although the size and influence of these units may vary, their activities generally involve the handling of customer complaints and queries and the dissemination of information on the purchase and use of products or services sold by the company. They also serve as an internal consumer ombudsman and a liaison with consumer-interest organizations outside the company.

There are many indications that the majority of organizations are accepting the idea of consumer activism. As with the marketing concept itself, however, the problem lies in what organizations do about it. All too often, for example, the consumer affairs unit is just a public relations unit with a facelift. To be really meaningful, the head of the consumer affairs unit must not simply protect management from consumer complaints. He or she must analyze sources of trouble and correct them, which means being listened to by other members of the organization.

THE CORPORATE COMMITMENT TO CONSUMERS

In order to commit itself to serious action on consumer issues, an organization must first overcome certain difficulties.[30] There must be recognition that treating surface symptoms will not be enough; the fundamental problems of marketing must be addressed. However, it is not always easy to understand underlying social issues. This is especially true for large business firms. Usually market research concerns itself with analyzing consumer behavior in the face of competitive alternatives. Rarely does it look beyond the symptoms to uncover real consumer needs and feelings of discontent.

In order to plan socially responsible marketing strategy, the organization must analyze the internal and external systems relevant to the firm's consumer commitment. Figure 4-3 suggests an approach to this analysis. Evaluating the social issue is the most difficult—and yet the most necessary—part of analysis. Consider, for example, the debate over the use of aerosol spray cans that was referred to earlier. These cans are attractive and popular with consumers, yet they may pose potential threats to health, safety, and the environment. When such conflicts emerge, it is the social pressures (see the bottom of Figure 4-3) that are most often felt by business. Only through this type of systematic analysis can an organization balance consumer commitment, profit needs, and social responsibility in its decision-making process.

An organization's commitment to consumers may be assessed by measuring the impact of its actions on consumers. One way to do this is to conduct a **consumer affairs audit**, which may be defined as a systematic and standardized evaluation of the effectiveness and efficiency of a company's formal and informal communication with its customers. The audit evaluates a firm's goals, programs, communication, and organization in terms of consumer needs and demands. Figure 4-4 shows how an organization would gear itself to conduct such an audit.

The audit generally begins with an inventory of existing efforts to increase consumer welfare. The objectives, legal requirements, and associated costs of any consumer-oriented programs (such as a complaint-handling office) will come under scrutiny. In its next step, the audit focuses on how consumer problems and needs are being researched. The purpose is to define problems and to develop relevant information for improvement.

An important aspect of the consumer affairs audit involves comparisons between an organization's consumer program and organization- or industry-wide standards. The organization's goals and performance can be compared

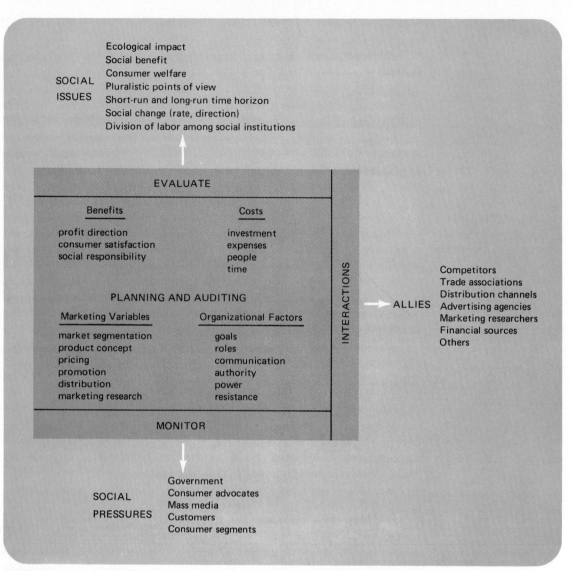

SOCIAL ISSUES
- Ecological impact
- Social benefit
- Consumer welfare
- Pluralistic points of view
- Short-run and long-run time horizon
- Social change (rate, direction)
- Division of labor among social institutions

EVALUATE

Benefits
- profit direction
- consumer satisfaction
- social responsibility

Costs
- investment
- expenses
- people
- time

PLANNING AND AUDITING

Marketing Variables
- market segmentation
- product concept
- pricing
- promotion
- distribution
- marketing research

Organizational Factors
- goals
- roles
- communication
- authority
- power
- resistance

MONITOR

INTERACTIONS

ALLIES
- Competitors
- Trade associations
- Distribution channels
- Advertising agencies
- Marketing researchers
- Financial sources
- Others

SOCIAL PRESSURES
- Government
- Consumer advocates
- Mass media
- Customers
- Consumer segments

Figure 4-3
MARKETING SYSTEMS
ANALYSIS TO
DETERMINE SOCIAL
RESPONSIBILITY

with those of competitors and with government or trade association norms. Finally, the audit can include some monitoring of consumer pressure groups such as attitude surveys of members and data collection on the public statements of consumer lobbyists.[31]

OVERVIEW OF
SOCIALLY
RESPONSIBLE
MARKETING

Several of the implications of social responsibility for marketing management have been described so far in this chapter. These implications are having an increasing impact on the way an organization practices marketing. As a result, the relationship of social issues to marketing practices will be emphasized throughout this book. Figure 4-5 puts into perspective how completely social responsibility affects the managerial marketing process.

Figure 4-4 HOW AN ORGANIZATION CONDUCTS A CONSUMER AFFAIRS AUDIT

From Larry J. Rosenberg, John A. Czepiel, and Lewis C. Cohan, "Auditing Corporate Consumer Affairs," *California Management Review*, forthcoming.

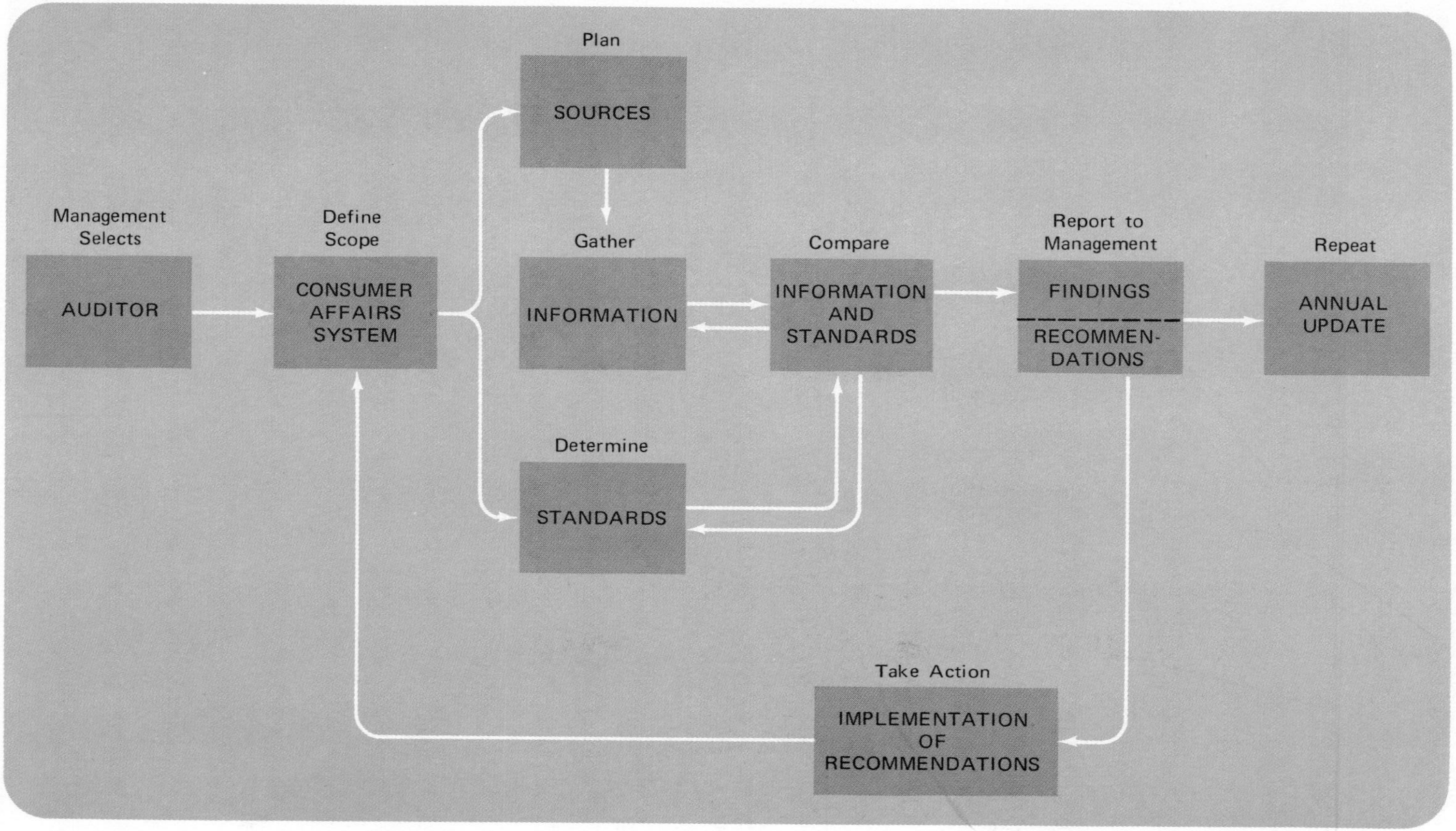

Figure 4-5   SOCIAL RESPONSIBILITY AFFECTS THE MANAGERIAL MARKETING PROCESS

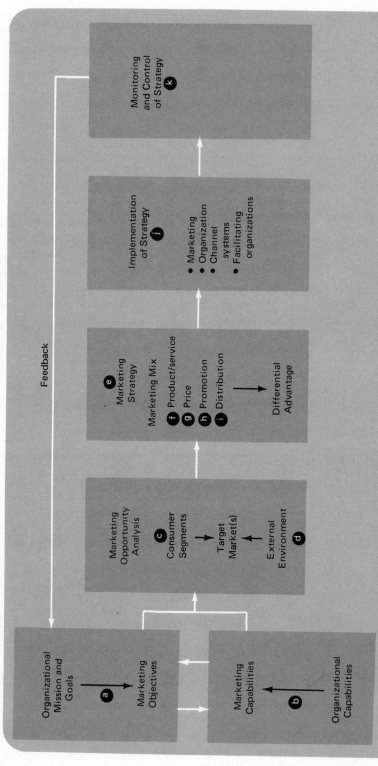

a Long-run consumer welfare, social benefits, ecological impact.

b Consumer-sensitive research, representation of consumer viewpoint, long-run planning and forecasting.

c Consumer activism, ecological consciousness, concern for quality of life.

d Public opinion, consumer advocates, mass media, government trade association interaction regarding the ecological environment, consumerism, disadvantaged consumer groups.

e Commitment to a consumer orientation, new consumerism programs.

f Safe product design, safe packaging, higher quality, less pollution, ingredient labeling, improved warranty.

g Fair pricing, truth-in-lending, unit pricing, absorbed ecological costs.

h Advertising—more complete and accurate information, higher taste levels. Sales force—more responsive to social and ethical issues.

i Complaint handling throughout distribution channel, repair service, guarantees, delivery standards.

j Committees on social and ecological issues, consumer affairs department, consumer advisory boards, role of trade association.

k Environmental scanning, consumer affairs audit.

Although marketing objectives will continue to be profit- and sales-oriented, they must be balanced by consumer, social, and ecological objectives. An organization's understanding of consumer issues and the extent to which it can anticipate environmental changes will become vital marketing assets. Social pressures will reshape all of the marketing mix variables. Strategy implementation will require the creation of new departments, which must be coordinated within the organization and with other organizations. Strategy control will involve increased attention to the changing social environment.

INDUSTRY-WIDE MARKETING RESPONSE TO CONSUMERISM

This section will examine the response of existing trade associations and special industry-wide groups, such as the Better Business Bureau and the Chamber of Commerce, to consumer issues. The key question is how well industry-wide organizations can serve as central institutions in promoting consumer and social sensitivity.

FORMS OF SELF-REGULATION

Historically, trade associations have played a largely defensive role in consumer issues. Their main activity has been to lobby against legislative change. Today, however, individual firms are looking to their associations for leadership in four critical areas of consumer concern:

1. coordinating and disseminating research (for example, on consumer, social, and government topics);
2. consumer and dealer education;
3. development of industry-wide standards, especially regarding product standardization and certification;
4. handling of complaints.[32]

One such effort that has achieved notable success is the Association of Home Appliance Manufacturers (AHAM), which was created in 1966 by the major appliance manufacturers. AHAM deals with a wide spectrum of inter-related consumer issues, including complaints, product testing, consumer information, and formulation of standards. In 1970 AHAM joined with two other industry groups to establish the Major Appliance Consumer Action Panel (MACAP), an independent panel of consumer-oriented specialists from fields outside the appliance industry. This panel responds to complaints, initiates needed services and innovations, conducts research to better understand industry patterns, and develops minimum consumer performance standards for the appliance industry.[33]

LIMITS OF SELF-REGULATION

While self-regulation is desirable in many respects, it also raises many serious problems. Companies in a particular industry may choose not to join in cooperative industry-wide policing, thus preventing effective self-regulation.

In fact, an entire industry has the option *not* to regulate itself, or to provide meager funding so that regulation is not very effective.

There are other problems as well.[34] Often the standards developed by the association are weak, due to the lack of a consensus among its members. The association may also lack adequate powers of enforcement. Yet, if the standards are actually tough and meaningful, they may place smaller firms at a severe competitive disadvantage. Finally, self-regulation means that the industry may define its own problem areas, thus ignoring critical issues or deciding that difficult social problems (such as pollution) are beyond the scope of its responsibility.

Irving Kristol observes that the spirit of the "corporate clubhouse" may deter effective self-regulation. He points to a spirit of "clubbiness" among corporate executives that makes collective self-discipline almost impossible.[35]

The legal difficulties of meaningful self-regulation are explained by Louis L. Stern.[36] Industry-wide collective action—such as a boycott against an offending association member—constitutes an illegal restraint of trade under the Sherman Antitrust Act (see Chapter 3). Stern argues that removal of this legal barrier is essential to serious self-regulation. If this step is accompanied by a legal requirement that all industry-wide regulations be periodically approved by the FTC, an atmosphere for effective voluntary action may be possible. Stern also presents a "softer" proposal for self-regulation, in which trade associations would prosecute offenses under existing law.

EVALUATION OF CONSUMERISM

Consumerism has been part of the marketing environment since the early 1960s. During this time, many members of the marketing community have embraced the spirit and substance of consumerism. There are two basic points of view as to how seriously business practice has changed as a result of the consumer movement:

1. A study by the United States Senate was intended to compile a "good guys" list of proconsumer corporate projects.[37] But of 300 manufacturers invited to reply to the survey, only 181 answered. Did the other 119 firms not have anything positive to say about their own work, or did their bureaucracies simply swallow up the government request?

A 1973 survey by Frederick E. Webster, Jr., indicated dismal proconsumer performance by business.[38] Webster concluded that "planned, coordinated programs of response to consumerism are the exception, not the rule. More common are defensive, isolated responses to specific problems." He also found a far-reaching ignorance of the basic nature of consumerism, with a disturbing number of businessmen who thought of consumerism as "something to be resisted and openly attacked." If you refer to Table 4-2, you will see that the number of industries implementing consumer programs is not all that impressive.

2. On the other hand, Greyser and Diamond have pointed to a broad corporate acceptance of consumerism.[39] In their 1974 survey, seven out of ten respondents saw it as an opportunity for marketers, while only one out of ten

saw it as a threat. To most of the executives, consumerism was an ally and a means through which greater profits could be achieved. Greyser and Diamond conclude that "what executives are telling us is that *consumerism is good for the consumer and good for business.*" Most executives did admit, however, that the quality of products and repair services, sensitivity to consumer complaints, and truthfulness in advertising could all be improved.

How do we reconcile these conflicting findings? Or is there really a conflict? Perhaps the question here is similar to asking whether a bottle is half empty or half full. It is clear that business has responded significantly to consumerism. Since the early 1960s, the marketing response has been dramatic. Yet we must ask whether this change—this heightened consumer commitment —has been fully integrated into the decision-making system of organizations. Business managers are still concerned with the basic goals of profits, sales, economic growth, and keeping their jobs. Takas grimly admits that: "In the conceptual framework of today's marketer, the consumer is at best a target, or an adversary to be conquered; at worst he is putty to be manipulated."[40]

CONSUMERISM IN THE FUTURE

Consumerism has become a basic part of marketing. It is not a superficial movement demanding "frills," but a basic expression of consumer rights and social sensitivity. While the economic turmoil of the 1970s (energy crisis, inflation, and recession) may have slowed the growth of a social and consumer consciousness, there is no doubt that the trend is vigorous and is here to stay. For example, every year Ralph Nader presents a consumer agenda for the future. Included in the 1975 agenda were proposals for legislation to remove procedural barriers to class action suits to make federal officials personally accountable for failure to enforce the law.[41] It took roughly seven years for major consumer proposals of the 1960s to become federal legislation; thus, we may see such ideas instituted in the early 1980s.

Marketing will remain vulnerable to consumer pressure. The consumer movement is most effective when the following conditions exist:

1. There is gradually declining confidence in management's intentions and capacity to perform.

2. Management's perception of problems is out of step with the public's expectations.

3. The problem cannot be solved by the efforts of an individual firm (safety shortcomings, advertising clutter, pollution from nonreturnable bottles).

4. Public attention is focused through a sensational disclosure which indiscriminately affects all members of an industry.

The reforms undertaken in the last few years have made this atmosphere possible. Thus, marketing will probably continue to face serious conflicts with consumers.

Kotler sees consumerism as dynamic and becoming broader in scope.[42] He and Keith Davis both forecast that the consumer movement will endure, that it will not be a fleeting social craze.[43] Kotler believes that the long-run impact of the consumer movement will be beneficial. He points to four consumerist arguments:

1. Consumerism will lead to buyers having more information and thus becoming more efficient. This may lead to more purchasing power and sales.

2. Limitations on promotional expenditures such as games and trading stamps may lead to lower prices.

3. Consumerism will bring about a reduced demand for high cost social goods and will lead to a higher quality environment.

4. Consumerism will reduce the number of unsafe and unhealthy products on the market.[44]

However, as business becomes more concerned with social responsibility goals, costs will rise. In many cases, higher prices for consumer goods will result.

CONCLUSION

The pressures of social responsibility have altered the traditional social contract of business. In the past, the desirability of economic growth was virtually unquestioned. Business had almost free rein to pursue its economic goals. Today, however, social goals are being balanced with economic ones. The public is demanding that marketing concern itself with the quality of life.

Most of the rest of this book is devoted to the kind of marketing that will increase productivity for the organization as a whole, as well as its marketing function. Given the present state of knowledge and technology, the question concerning productivity is "How well can it be done?" Social responsibility introduces a whole new set of rules, many of which are in dispute, ill-defined, or still emerging. Socially responsible organizations pose the question, "Should it be done?"

One way to end this cleavage is to combine the productivity and responsibility concepts into the organizational posture of **social responsiveness**. This means being in touch, anticipating, and reacting to the forces of society, while at the same time functioning according to productivity guidelines.

It is time to ask the question, "What could you, as an employee, do about making your job, department, or even company practice socially responsible marketing?" Of course, any answers must take into account the efficiency and profit requirements of the enterprise. Here are some *pro*responsibility thoughts to consider:

1. Know what top executives in your organization have said about social responsibility. Their statements may be useful in approaching other employees.

2. Seek allies wherever possible. Find people who think and feel as you do. They may be higher executives, peers in your department, or others.

3. Do your homework on all social-marketing issues. Clarify the marketing and social impact of all complex decisions.

4. Ask relevant questions. Find out what others think about the social and marketing consequences of current practices and proposed changes.

5. Look for the long-run profit impact of a social-marketing issue. This is not always possible, but when it is, the information should be pursued.

DISCUSSION QUESTIONS

1. Social responsibility has been called the "new frontier" of marketing decisions. As you see them, what are the major guidelines to help the marketer plan strategy in the short run? In the long run?

2. In what direction is the balance of power between marketers and consumers now weighted? (Consider these industries—automobiles, nursing homes, processed food, and supermarkets.) Can consumerism make a meaningful difference in correcting any imbalance favoring marketers?

3. How much is the marketing system to blame for the disadvantages experienced by some groups of consumers? How can business help solve these problems?

4. Describe possible "higher marketing standards" that could be applied in the following: children's clothing industry, bank loans, a department store, and an adoption agency.

5. What consumerism programs would be appropriate for an airline? Describe the role of a consumer affairs department for that airline. Set up a consumer advisory board for it.

6. Design a consumer affairs audit to be conducted annually by a large gasoline marketer.

7. Community resistance to the opening of fast-food outlets such as McDonald's and Burger King has been increasing in city neighborhoods and suburban areas. After over a decade of vast expansion of such outlets and popularity with consumers, these organizations are accused of disrupting the quality of life with their location policy and mass-merchandising formula. Conduct an assessment of the "social issues" involved and cost-benefit analysis considerations for a fast-food organization.

8. The Pharmaceutical Manufacturers Association is seeking a role in the prescription drug industry in response to consumerism pressures. What programs and policies would you recommend? What position regarding enforcement among its membership would you propose?

NOTES

1. "Getting a Hearing," *Newsweek*, June 24, 1974, p. 68.
2. David Finn, "The Business of Businessmen Is Not Just Business," *New York Times*, July 28, 1975, p. 27.
3. Christopher D. Stone, *Where the Law Ends* (New York: Harper & Row, 1975).
4. George Gallup, "Big Business Has Black Eye with American Public," *Gallup Poll*, July 13, 1975, pp. 3–4.
5. Irving Kristol, "Business and 'The New Class,'" *New York Times*, May 19, 1975, p. 8.
6. Daniel Yankelovich, "Priorities in the Age of Consumerism," *Proceedings of the American Bankers Association, 1973, National Marketing Conference*. Reprinted in Leonard L. Berry and James S. Hensel, eds., *Marketing and the Social Environment: A Readings Text.* (New York: Petrocelli Books, 1973), pp. 194–95.
7. Irving Kristol, "The Corporation and the Dinosaur," *Wall Street Journal*, February 14, 1974, p. 20.
8. "Solving Shortages: Shift Life Style, Lower Demand," *Advertising Age*, February 24, 1975, p. 160.

9. George Fisk, "Criteria for a Theory of Responsible Consumption," *Journal of Marketing* 37 (April 1973): 34.

10. James P. Gannon, "Getting Off the Treadmill," *Wall Street Journal*, April 12, 1974, p. 6.

11. Hazel Henderson, "Redeploying Market Resources toward New Priorities: The New 'Consumer Demand,'" in William Lazer and Eugene J. Kelley, eds., *Social Marketing: Perspectives and Viewpoints* (Homewood, Ill.: Irwin, 1973), pp. 253–55.

12. D. W. Cravens and G. E. Hills, "Consumerism: A Perspective for Business," *Business Horizons* 13 (August 1970): 24.

13. Philip Kotler, "What Consumerism Means for Marketers," *Harvard Business Review* 50 (May–June 1972): 49.

14. Yankelovich, p. 200.

15. Peter F. Drucker, "The Shame of Marketing," *Marketing Communications*, August 1960, p. 60.

16. Francis E. Brown, "Consumer Protection: Who Needs It and How Much?" *Wharton Quarterly* (Fall 1972), 72–73.

17. Frederick E. Webster, Jr., *Social Aspects of Marketing* (Englewood Cliffs, N.J.: Prentice-Hall, 1974), pp. 23–24.

18. Leonard L. Berry, "The Low-Income Marketing System: An Overview," *Journal of Retailing* 48 (Summer 1972): 58–62.

19. Brown, p. 73.

20. Dean Burch, *Wall Street Journal*, February 16, 1971, p. 22.

21. "Euell Gibbons and Safety," *Advertising Age*, July 14, 1975, p. 14.

22. Andrew Takas, "Societal Marketing: A Businessman's Perspective," *Journal of Marketing* 38 (October 1974): 6.

23. Yankelovich, p. 202.

24. Theodore Levitt, "Why Business Always Loses," *Harvard Business Review* 46 (March–April 1968): 83–84.

25. Peter F. Drucker, "Business and the Quality of Life," in Peter F. Drucker, ed., *Preparing Tomorrow's Business Leaders Today* (Englewood Cliffs, N.J.: Prentice-Hall, 1969), pp. 82–83.

26. "Eating for Ecology," *Business Week*, February 27, 1971, p. 116.

27. Robert W. Ackerman, "How Companies Respond to Social Demands," *Harvard Business Review* 51 (July–August 1973): 92–94.

28. "The Stop & Shop Consumer Board of Directors," Harvard Business School case 571-058 M525, pp. 1, 9.

29. E. Patrick McGuire, *The Consumer Affairs Department: Organization and Functions* (New York: The Conference Board, 1973), p. 4.

30. David A. Aaker and George S. Day, "Corporate Responses to Consumerism Pressures," *Harvard Business Review* 50 (November–December 1972): 117–18.

31. George S. Day, "The Role of the Consumer in the Corporate Social Audit," in Meinholf Dierkes and Raymond Bauer, eds., *Corporate Social Accounting* (New York: Praeger, 1973), pp. 118–25.

32. Aaker and Day, pp. 120–21.

33. *Fulfilling Consumer Rights* (Washington, D.C.: Chamber of Commerce of the United States, 1972), p. 25.

34. Aaker and Day, pp. 122–23.

35. Irving Kristol, "Ethics and the Corporation," *Wall Street Journal*, April 16, 1975, p. 18.

36. Louis L. Stern, "Consumer Protection vs. Self-regulation," *Journal of Marketing* 35 (July 1971): 49, 51–52.

37. U.S. Senate Commerce Committee, Consumer Subcommittee, *Initiatives in Corporate Responsibility* (Washington D.C.: U.S. Government Printing Office, 1972), p. 1.

38. Frederick E. Webster, Jr., "Does Business Misunderstand Consumerism?" *Harvard Business Review* 51 (September–October 1973): 89–91.

39. Stephen A. Greyser and Steven L. Diamond, "Business Is Adapting to Consumerism," *Harvard Business Review* 52 (September–October 1974): 58.

40. Takas, p. 3.

41. Frances Cerra, "Consumer Agenda Offered by Nader," *New York Times*, February 1, 1975, p. 52.

42. "A Marketing Man Takes Marketers to Task," *Business Week*, July 28, 1975, p. 43.

43. Kotler, p. 52; Keith Davis, "Five Propositions for Social Responsibility," *Business Horizons* 18 (June 1975): 24.

44. Kotler, p. 53.

WILLIAM PARKER & SON, INC.

William Parker & Son is a medium-sized manufacturer of women's apparel. Located in Cincinnati, the firm concentrates on moderate- to high-priced dresses and separates sold under the Park Place label. Although the company's growth in sales had slowed somewhat during the recent recession, it had always shown a profit until 1975, when it lost nearly $225,000 on sales of $18 million.

Bill Parker founded the company in 1934 and ran it singlehandedly for years. In 1970 Parker's youngest son, Stewart, joined the firm after he finished college. By 1976 Stewart had become vice-president; however, the elder Parker continued to serve as president and maintained active control of management. Bill Parker's concept of how the garment industry operated was very traditional, but Stewart thought that the results of 1975 indicated the need for some changes in management style.

Old Days of Fashion

When Stewart tried to talk his father out of making any major style changes for the company's fall lines, Bill Parker argued, "I always change the styles in the fall. I look at the European designers' offerings and I see what *Women's Wear Daily* is playing up in a big way. They always have a lot of sketches of the things they think will be hot numbers. Then I pick out the things I like best—the things I know we can make well—and that's what we sell."

"But, Dad," Stewart replied, "the designers aren't always right. Look at the midi. They said that was the only acceptable style in 1970, and you went along in a big way. Boy, did we get burned! We had inventory backlogs and retailer returns for months. That was a great introduction to women's ready-to-wear for me."

"Well, it just took a little longer than usual for that to catch on," his father answered. "We had to promote it harder, push it a little more."

"That's just my point. It took five years for longer hemlines to be accepted. Fashion is evolutionary now, not revolutionary."

"It's a nice theory, son," the elder Parker said, "but if you don't change the styles, women won't have any reason to buy new clothes. And that puts us out of business faster than a style that's slow to catch on."

Stewart tried to explain to his father that he thought women were tired of having a particular fashion look forced upon them. He believed that women wanted a variety of styles in their wardrobes, partly because their lives had more variety to them. In Stewart's opinion, women would buy new clothes to go with their new activities, even if styles did not change.

But Bill Parker simply held fast. "Since 1934, I've concentrated on a few styles, a narrow line that I could manage. It will take more than one year of bad luck to make me change my mind."

New Management Trends

The failure rate for companies in the apparel trade ran between 4 and 5 percent each year. As a hedge against this high risk, many companies had begun to adopt a marketing approach to fashion and to institute sounder management practices. Stewart wondered whether the success of these examples might influence his father in any way.

Carlo Pollard, for instance, offered enough styles in its various division to catch women in any fashion mood. This variety had been achieved through internal growth and by acquisition. Pollard also had expanded its operations through backward integration. By owning its own textile plants, Pollard was able to maintain complete product control from fiber to finished product. In addition, it was less vulnerable to fabric shortages than companies dependent upon outside suppliers.

A Merger?   As Bill Parker was considering which styles to adopt for the fall line, something happened to divert his attention. He was contacted by the owner of a company that manufactured sportswear for men and women. The owner wanted to discuss the possibility of a merger between the two companies. This man, only a few years older than Bill Parker, had no children interested in the garment business. He was concerned about the future of his company if anything happened to him.

Bill Parker, afraid he would be unable to work with another entrepreneur, was inclined to turn the man down on the spot. Furthermore, he did not want to be saddled with the management of a business he couldn't understand if the other man died or retired. Parker thought that sportswear was a highly seasonal business (summer only), and he had never followed men's fashions very closely, even for his personal wardrobe. However, he decided to talk over the offer with his son before making a final decision.

Questions   1. How would you convince Bill Parker that he should adopt a marketing approach?
2. What changes in goals, strategy, and organization would have to occur to make William Parker & Son, Inc., "marketing oriented"?
3. Should William Parker & Son go ahead with the merger?

NATIONAL TELEPHONE & TECHNOLOGY

In mid-1973, Arthur Hughes and Susan Jamison were asked by their boss, S. L. Hoyt, marketing director at National Telephone and Technology, to begin developing a marketing plan for the giant utility for the coming year. Although the marketing department had been a part of NTT for a number of years, recent events had increased its importance to the corporation. Several adverse decisions by the Federal Communications Commission had changed the nature of the telephone industry from monopolistic to competitive. Hughes and Jamison, who had been marketing majors in college, had been hired as assistants to Hoyt to help the company respond to this change.

In order to develop some perspective on where the company was and ought to be going, the two assistants tried to piece together the history of marketing at NTT. After digging through files and interviewing older employees, they met to compare notes.

HUGHES: Did you realize that there wasn't anything resembling marketing around here until 1958? And then they called it "merchandising" so they wouldn't offend anybody.

JAMISON: Yeah, the production department was in its glory trying to keep up with demand for basic service. The operating companies certainly weren't going out of their way to be very helpful to subscribers.

production

HUGHES: It was really a big step forward when they brought in a vice president of marketing and a formal marketing program in 1959. Look at this.

The first long-range marketing program consisted of a slogan ("Marketing is an attitude that recognizes that only through complete customer satisfaction can maximum profit be realized") and a four-point plan for the operating companies:

"plan here was here but no backbone to enforce it"

1. to establish a straight-line sales force—to sell to business markets;

2. to establish marketing research;

3. to create a product-planning organization; and

4. to educate management employees as to what the marketing concept was and how to apply it.

JAMISON: From what I have heard, that may have looked good on paper, but it never worked out in practice. The sales force did such a good selling job that the plant and billing departments couldn't cope. Everything ran behind schedule. So the sales force was reorganized and went back to taking orders and doing public relations work.

HUGHES: Same thing happened to market research. They hired a bunch of bright guys but never gave them any direction or tried to understand the language of research techniques. By 1964, there were only a few of them left and they were all at corporate headquarters. Product planners had it even worse. Production ignored their input right from the start and continued to make what it wanted—with long manufacturing and delivery schedules unchanged.

JAMISON: The education goal fizzled too. They tried to do it all in a week-long training program for all managers. That was promptly followed by everyone going back to business as usual. They actually considered doing away with marketing in the 1960s.

HUGHES: Then disaster struck! Earnings declined.

JAMISON: Right. At the same time that service was deteriorating, the utility commissions started to tie rate increases to service levels again. Then came competition in the market for communications and equipment. The last few years have really shaken up the company.

HUGHES: So here we are, Fred. This time NTT says it really wants a marketing orientation, and they hired us to prove it.

JAMISON: With that background, we've got our work cut out for us.

Questions
1. Why has marketing been so difficult at NTT?
2. What marketing goals would be appropriate for NTT?
3. Can you suggest any new marketing strategies that would help NTT achieve these goals?

ALL-VEND FOODS, INC.

In mid-1975, the Antitrust Division of the Justice Department brought suit against seven Illinois vending machine operators, some of their top executives, and the local trade association on charges of price-fixing. This case fit perfectly the profile of price-fixers the government had developed. The number of firms in the industry was small, concentration was high, and the product was basically a commodity.

The legal basis for the suit was the Sherman Act of 1890, which reads in part, "Every contract, combination, or conspiracy, in restraint of trade or commerce is hereby declared to be illegal. . . ." Conspiracies among competitors to fix prices are considered "per se violations." When Jerry Dermot, vice-president of All-Vend Foods, Inc., first learned that his company had been indicted, he believed that the charges were unfounded.

Coffee Price Rise

All-Vend Foods was caught in a profit squeeze during 1970 and 1971. The recession cut into sales volume and inflation pushed up costs for labor and supplies. Coffee was a good example of an item that produced little or no profit at the then-current price of 15 cents a cup. However, Dermot was afraid to raise the price of coffee to a more profitable level for fear of losing business to other vendors who maintained the lower price.

Dermot regularly attended meetings of the Illinois Automatic Merchandising Council. Talk at informal sessions following these meetings frequently centered on the profit squeeze in which most companies were caught. Some members discussed which product prices could be increased to cover higher expenses. Most agreed that the coffee price was one that could and should be raised, but each was afraid to be the first to do it. Finally a few members decided to raise the price of coffee to 25 cents, and Dermot found out about it.

Because no formal agreement had been signed, Dermot did not believe that a conspiracy was involved. Since his boss, the president of All-Vend Foods, was distrustful of lawyers, Dermot did not bother to seek a legal opinion. Instead he raised All-Vend's coffee price to 25 cents and congratulated himself for helping the company's profit picture. All-Vend's price boost took place about the same time as those of its competitors, and it was on the basis of the timing that the Justice Department brought suit.

The Phoenix Bakeries Case

As Jerry Dermot was thinking about his company's defense, he remembered that an old friend of his had been involved in a similar situation. Anxious to obtain advice, he called his friend Oliver McIntyre, who had been general sales manager of Bronson's Bread Company in Minneapolis until 1972, when he resigned and became a government witness in a price-fixing case against Bronson's and four other bakeries in Minneapolis.

McIntyre explained over the telephone that his case had been a clear-cut conspiracy. In order to cut out discounts and to increase prices, top executives of the bakeries met weekly in local motels to divide up the market among all competitors. At these secret meetings they shared figures and decided which accounts to keep and which to give up. Although McIntyre had been granted immunity in exchange for his testimony, other executives received fines and some were given jail sentences.

Dermot thought that attendance at occasional trade association meetings was considerably different from attendance at covert meetings in various motels. He was, therefore, surprised to learn that in 30 percent of the cases brought by the government, industry association meetings were the settings for price-fixing discussions.

Questions
1. Do you think the Council members violated the Sherman Act's price-fixing prohibition?
2. If the Justice Department wins the case, what could All-Vend Foods do to prevent this situation in the future?

KELTON PHARMACEUTICAL COMPANY

In May 1976, a national television audience watched the Senate subcommittee on health investigate Food and Drug Administration (FDA) charges that Kelton Pharmaceutical Company had manipulated research on two of its drugs. The company, which formerly maintained a low profile with the public, was badly shaken by this challenge to its integrity.

Moreover, the problem did not go away when the hearings ended. The findings of the Senate committee were handed over to the Justice Department for possible criminal indictments. In addition, the FDA reopened its investigation of all research data filed by Kelton since 1969.

Questionable Research

The drugs involved in the Senate hearings were two of Kelton's best sellers, Promycin and Nysone. Promycin was an anesthetic; Nysone was an antibiotic.

Kelton's problem began in 1973, when an article in the *Journal of the National Cancer Institute* questioned the validity of its research on Nysone. This article, and five separate studies conducted subsequently, reported an increased risk of cancer in mice that had received the drug. These findings put the FDA in a rather embarrassing position, since it had approved the drug's usage based on its review of the initial data. Consequently, early in 1975 the FDA assigned one of its investigators, Dr. Clifford S. Schutjer, to ascertain why the cancer risk was not disclosed in Kelton's own research.

Schutjer testified to the Senate subcommittee that Kelton was uncooperative during his investigation. He claimed that the company could not produce "an organized collection of observations" on which the report had been based.

The company was charged with mishandling and distorting test data on Nysone. A similar charge was lodged regarding Promycin. The FDA claimed that there was a cancer risk apparent in the raw data for this drug, and that a synopsis of the data filed by Kelton in February of 1976 failed to mention this risk. In response to these charges, the company admitted that the data were not well organized and that there were "clerical errors." The company denied, however, that any of the data had been manipulated.

Company and Industry Background

For many years, the drug industry suffered from a lack of public understanding. As a consequence, there was a flood of criticism about safety, efficacy, and industry profits. There was also regulation. The much-publicized investigation of the industry led by Senator Estes Kefauver was followed in 1962 by a law requring extensive new testing to verify drug efflcacy. In more recent years the Federal Trade Commission issued new guidelines that restricted claims made in drug advertising; and the Department of Health, Education and Welfare set rules that limited federal health care payments to the lowest price at which a drug could be purchased.

Over the fifteen years prior to Kelton's trouble, many drug companies became more aggressive in their public relations efforts. They attempted to develop a positive image rather than wait to react to negative information. Kelton was not among these companies. Under Robert V. Kelton's leadership (1938–1968), the company limited its communications efforts to promoting its drugs to the medical community through the use of detail salespeople and journal advertising.

Even after Kelton's son Keith took over, the company did not seek formal contacts with the press, politicians, or the general public. Although half of the company stock was publicly held, Kelton considered itself a family company that had little contact with the investment community.

Under Keith Kelton the company concentrated on expanding into other health-related fields. Acquisitions added medical instruments and hospital supplies to the company's product line. Sales and net income nearly doubled between 1969 and 1975 to $542 million and $61.8 million respectively. With 24 percent return on stockholders' equity, the company had been one of the most profitable in the drug industry.

Although drugs had become a less important element in Kelton's overall financial picture, they still contributed about 45 percent of sales and 65 percent of profits. Moreover, in 1975 Nysone and Promycin (along with a related drug) together accounted for about 18 percent of company sales. Keith Kelton was concerned about the negative impact on sales which the bad publicity of the hearings was likely to bring. In fact, a number of physicians, pharmacists, and consumers had spoken to him about their "shaken trust" in the company. By August of 1976, the company's stock price fell severely apparently in anticipation of a sales decline. If Kelton was to improve its corporate image and recover from the adverse publicity of the hearings, Keith Kelton knew that some changes would have to be made. Consequently, he appointed an in-house task force, reporting directly to him, to study the problem and to recommend ways in which the company could become more socially responsible.

Questions

1. What circumstance in society and in the Kelton organization caused the crisis to happen?
2. What should the Kelton task force recommend to establish the company as a leading socially responsible marketer?

Analyzing the Marketplace

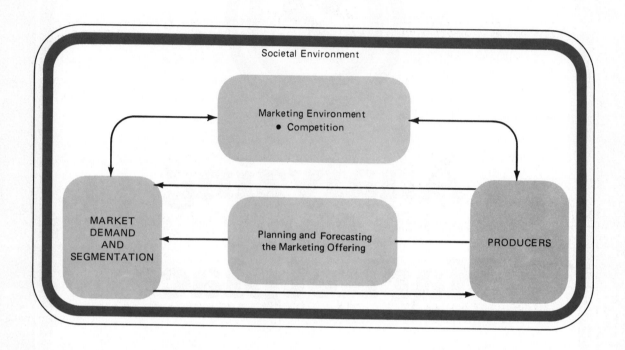

5

PLANNING AND FORECASTING IN MARKETING

After completing this chapter, the reader should be able to:

1. State the reasons for a systems approach to planning marketing activities.

2. Distinguish among types of planning—long-range, short-term, product, and venture.

3. Explain the major components of marketing planning—situation analysis, objectives, and strategy and actions programs.

4. Characterize the pressures on effective planning in the 1970s.

5. Identify the basic types of demand measures and forecasts—economic, market, and sales.

6. Describe the methods of sales forecasting in terms of their appropriate applications.

Until now, we have been discussing marketing from the outside in and from the inside out. From this perspective, we've been able to look at the external marketplace and the internal marketing strategy of an organization. Now it is time to look closely at the processes that link what goes on outside in the marketplace with strategy inside the organization. Two vital links are **planning** and **forecasting**.

WHAT WILL HAPPEN NEXT?

In the latter part of the 1960s there was talk about the development of an all-plastic car within the next decade.[1] Naturally, this caused concern in the steel industry, since automobile manufacturers are one of its major markets. Let's take a look at how the industry's fourth largest producer, Republic Steel, responded to this challenge.

The first step Republic took was to keep careful records about the use of materials other than steel in cars. In the beginning its research showed that there was a growing increase in the use of plastics, not just for upholstery and other noncritical interior parts, but for fender extensions, fan shrouds, special hoods, and fender liners as well. But then something happened to the competitive situation. The nation turned its attention to safety as a major objective, and the safety provided by steel gained new prominence. More steel was added to cars in the form of protective guard rails, roof liners, and stronger bumpers.

While the steel industry was congratulating itself on the fairly rapid increase in steel usage per car (some 200 lbs. per automobile), the trend toward compact cars was developing. These small cars, which use some 1,000 lbs. less steel per unit than standard cars, increased in sales from 20 percent to 40 percent of cars sold from 1969 to 1974. But again an offsetting factor appeared. While small cars were a growing percent of the total, so were small trucks and recreational vehicles, which use more steel than a standard car.

TODAY'S DECISIONS FOR THE FUTURE

The changes confronting Republic Steel demonstrate what can and will be happening in most industries—an increasingly rapid succession of twists and turns in their marketing environment. Any organization that hopes to prosper or even survive will have to look beyond its day-to-day operations to how things will be in one year, in five years, or longer. Marketing forecasting, a subject we will discuss later in this chapter, will help industry to determine the "probable course of events." Marketing planning can help a firm make those events work to its advantage by anticipating them and responding with strategy. Or, when those events are beyond the organization's control, planning can help the firm adjust its marketing strategy to meet new expectations. The positions of the planning and forecasting processes in the managerial marketing system are shown in Figure 5-1.

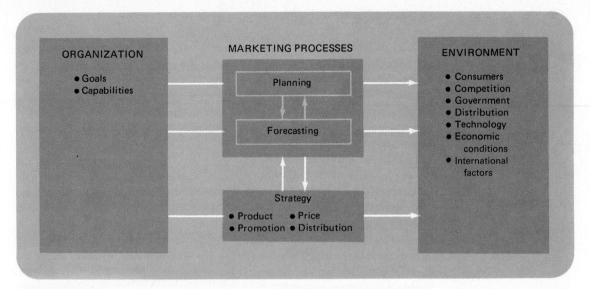

Figure 5-1
PLANNING AND
FORECASTING IN A
MARKETING
PERSPECTIVE

Most organizations that have adopted the marketing concept as part of their philosophy of management have accepted the need for planning as part of that concept. Planning helps an organization search for logical goals and for logical ways of achieving those goals in the marketplace. People engaged in planning need to focus not only on the organization's objectives, but on the customer's level of satisfaction and the impact of competitors, government, technology, and so forth.

The economy and society in general are becoming increasingly complex, and changing conditions are becoming part of our normal operating environment. Executives are recognizing the need to plan, not so much to help them make future decisions, but to help them see *the future implications of today's decisions*. And, more and more, they are being forced to make decisions that will have implications for the future. Should a successful faded-jeans boutique located near the campus open a suburban branch? Should Iran Air add more flights between the United States and Teheran? Should a city parks department lay out a bicycle path through a large park? These decisions involve future risk, and planning allows executives to understand the risks they are actually taking. Rather than provoking them to eliminate or cut down on the risk, planning helps them to better evaluate the need to take such risks.

Although planning is only one part of the whole managerial marketing process discussed in Chapter 2, it is crucial to the development of a consumer-oriented, integrated marketing strategy. In our earlier discussion, the focus was on **strategic planning**—the development of a general strategy for designing a system of marketing orientation for the organization. First, this chapter will focus on the importance of marketing planning and how it can be made to work.

PLANNING MARKETING STRATEGY

The importance of planning marketing strategy in today's complex environment is becoming more and more evident. Planning and planners are moving steadily from the fringes of the operation to a central position in many organizations. The whole management process is now structured around planning, and, in fact, it has become one of the guiding systems of an organization. In conjunction with the information systems (to be covered in Chapter 23), the planning system is being used to make possible the productive and dynamic functioning of the organization's other systems. It involves the flow of funds, the management–authority–responsibility system, and the material supply–production–distribution system.

Certainly some organizations have succeeded without a formal planning system because of an outstanding leader, a management team, or just plain luck. However, the prospects for an organization's rapid initial growth and continued ability to survive over the long run seem to be strengthened by a formal planning system.

"Formal" does not mean rigid or inflexible. On the contrary, a planning system must be flexible enough to fit the needs and characteristics of an organization's structure, people, products, and procedures. Nonetheless, it has been shown that most organizations have certain fundamental planning elements in common regardless of their differences.[2] These common elements are simplicity and systematization.

Simplicity assures that no special training, obscure or unavailable information, or disruption of existing procedures will be called for in the preparation of the plan. **Systematization** involves interrelated procedures, policies, and time schedules. These are all designed to cut down on the time and effort required in the planning and thereby to make the advantages of planning obvious. Systematization also enhances sound decision making by assuring the consideration, organization, and coordination of all important factors. It also stimulates the creative processes of the planners.[3]

Planning itself may be considered like a system (as was discussed in Chapter 2). To be effective, this system must incorporate a number of specific ingredients, which are illustrated in Figure 5-2.

APPROACHES TO ORGANIZATIONAL PLANNING

Just as the degree to which organizations have used marketing planning varies widely, so too do the approaches they take toward that planning.[4] To be effective, the way an organization plans should reflect the organization's objectives. Recognizing its importance, management may give responsibility for planning to:

1. functional executives, such as managers of the advertising, sales, pricing, sales promotion, and marketing research divisions of the marketing department;
2. a planning group staff;
3. everyone who has a part in marketing, including members of outside organizations;
4. product (or brand) managers.

Once primary responsibility has been assigned, an organization may choose one of the following approaches to planning:[5]

1. *Top-down.* In this frequently used approach, a few people close to the

Figure 5-2 THE MARKETING PLANNING SYSTEM

Based on John M. Brion, *Corporate Marketing Planning* (New York: Wiley, 1967), pp. 35–38.

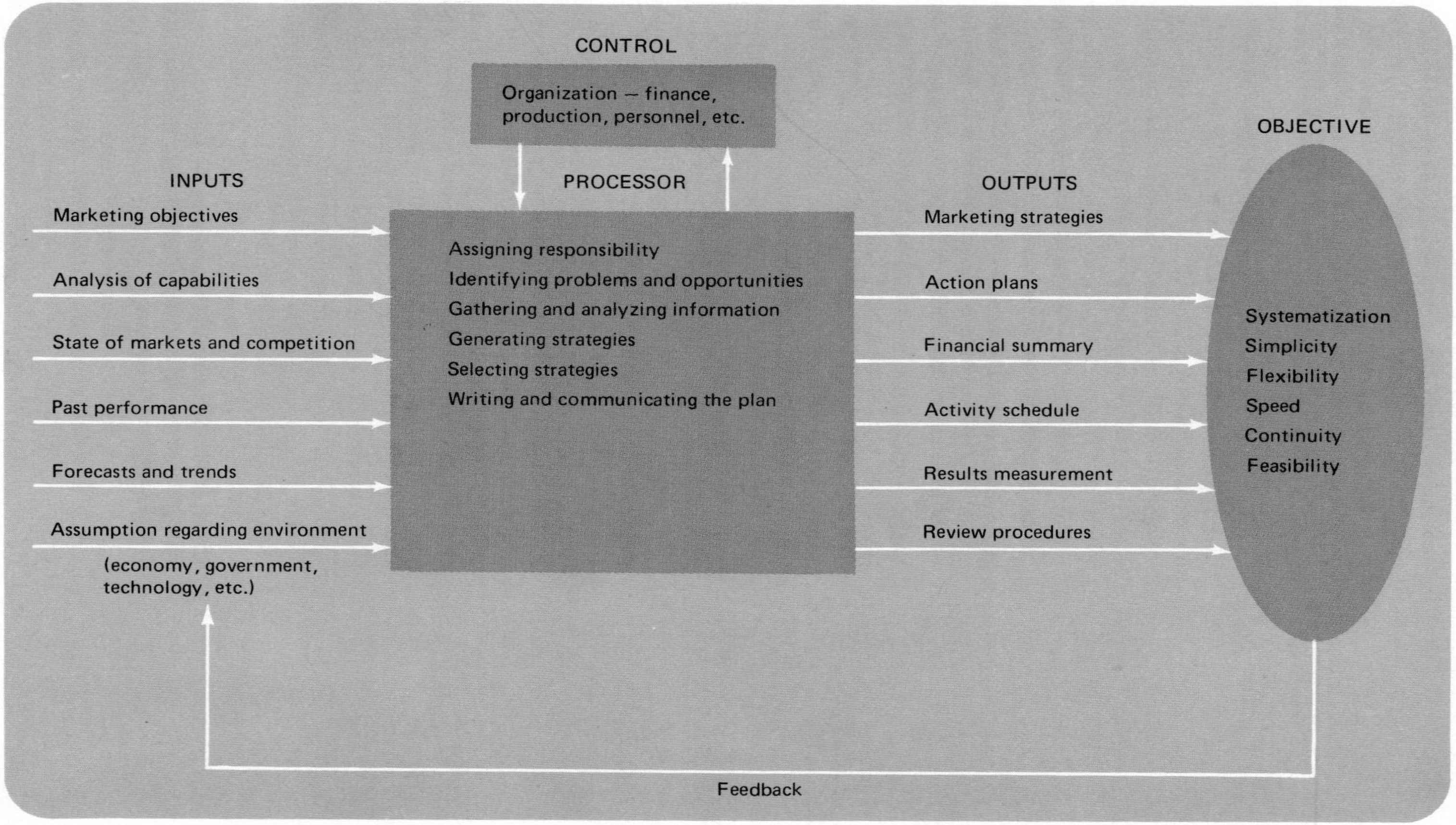

INPUTS

Marketing objectives

Analysis of capabilities

State of markets and competition

Past performance

Forecasts and trends

Assumption regarding environment (economy, government, technology, etc.)

CONTROL

Organization — finance, production, personnel, etc.

PROCESSOR

Assigning responsibility

Identifying problems and opportunities

Gathering and analyzing information

Generating strategies

Selecting strategies

Writing and communicating the plan

OUTPUTS

Marketing strategies

Action plans

Financial summary

Activity schedule

Results measurement

Review procedures

OBJECTIVE

Systematization

Simplicity

Flexibility

Speed

Continuity

Feasibility

Feedback

person in charge do most of the planning. Many marketing heads feel that the complexity and importance of marketing planning demand highly centralized direction and control. They also feel that lower-level personnel are not in a position to see the "forest for the trees." However, some studies show that the more top-down the process, the more likely it is that the plans will be inaccurate.

2. *Bottom-up*. In this approach, judgments by lower-level personnel are reviewed and adjusted at higher levels. These judgments form the basis for forecasts, performance goals, and budgets for the various units and personnel involved. The basis of this approach is the principle that those who have to carry out a plan should help make it. This is, in fact, supported by findings that when subordinates help to set their own goals, they tend to deliver what they promise. Although they are in the minority, companies using this approach are mainly found in the industrial products or service areas, such as insurance, where the field sales force can closely influence marketing results.

3. *Goals down-plans up*. Here, top management sets goals after taking a broad look at the organization's opportunities and requirements. The various units of the company then develop plans for achieving these goals. After approval by top management, these make up the official company plan. While this approach, quite prevalent in large companies, does take planning from the bottom up, corporate management often controls the allocation of resources among the units of a company. This, in effect, keeps centralized authority at the corporate level. At General Electric, for example, planning is carried out simultaneously, but with a different perspective, at corporate headquarters and in its 43 strategic business units. These units, essentially decentralized businesses, plan according to their needs, but planning and resource allocation are done at the corporate level.

TYPES OF PLANNING
Planning needs vary because future problems of various organizations differ. What types of energy sources other than oil should Mobil Oil develop by the end of the next decade? How much inventory should the Neiman-Marcus department store in Dallas have on hand for next season? Can the YM-YWCA intensify marketing efforts for existing products—its gym and pool facilities? Should Salton, the appliance maker, introduce a new product—the $14.95 hot pizza keeper? As a result of these different needs, planning takes four basic forms: long-range, short-range, product, and venture.[6] Most successful organizations recognize that these types are related (as illustrated in Figure 5-3) and may use all of them at one time or another.

1. *Long-range planning*. In this type, generally formulated by top management, basic objectives and strategy are developed to guide future company efforts. Long-range planning provides a framework within which other company plans are prepared. Generally, whether it is a two-, five-, or ten-year plan, it is more of a broad-gauge business plan than a function marketing one.

2. *Annual (short-range) planning*. This type is used to establish special goals and plans for the organization and its specific units. In principle, it is developed in the context of the company's long-range plans and reflects a

progressive implementation of those plans. Short-range planning should not be an overreaction to results of previous years. While "short-range" usually means annual, it can signify a shorter period, such as a season in the fashion industry.

3. *Product planning.* This type is used to establish both long-range and short-range plans for a particular product in the company's line. Most short-range marketing plans are written for each product line or service in such a way that every plan can stand on its own. At the same time, the plans must be related to the unit's total marketing plan and should take into account the product's recent history, its stage in the profit cycle, the economic outlook, competitors' plans, and so forth. Product planning is generally done by the product manager.

4. *Venture planning.* This type is used to guide companies in developing new products, entering new markets, and making acquisitions of other companies. This approach is being used more frequently as firms face a rapidly changing environment and intense competitive pressures. Usually directed by a special department, committee, or venture team, one of several approaches may be used in venture planning to estimate the value of a venture at any particular stage of its development.

COMPONENTS OF PLANNING

At some point in the beginning of the planning process—generally, the earlier the better—an organization should ask itself three questions:[7]

Where are we now?
Where do we want to go?
How do we get there?

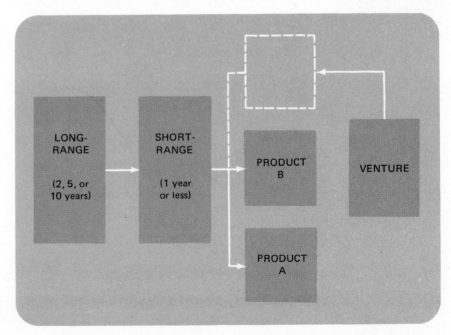

Figure 5-3
RELATIONSHIP AMONG
PLANNING TYPES

The typical marketing plan reflects these three concerns and includes, in addition to other supporting information, a situation analysis, marketing objectives, and strategy or action programs. (Examples of each of these are provided in the accompanying boxes.) While these are mainly used for short-range planning (see Figure 5-4), they can generally be applied to the long-range, product, and venture types of planning as well.

Situation Analysis (Where Are We Now?)

The planning process usually begins with a review of the current market situation. In this review:

1. The product's sales trends in units and dollars for the past several years are studied. Sales figures are often charted in relationship to competitors' and/or industry sales and to past profit and/or expense patterns for the product.

2. Comparisons of previous performance with past forecasts for the product sales and profit are made to determine whether any obstacles could have been foreseen or avoided.

3. Market situation and competitive environment are often considered together in the marketing plan. These include future changes in demand, the identification of trends within market segments, changes in customer attitudes or purchasing behavior, and recent or anticipated actions by the competition.

4. An evaluation is made of problems and opportunities of market factors and product factors, such as technology or cost, that may hinder or support profitable sales growth. This evaluation is often the basis of situation analysis and bears most directly on the action programs called for in the planning period.

Figure 5-4
OUTLINE FOR EACH ACTION PROGRAM IN DIVISIONAL PLANS

From David S. Hopkins, *The Short-Term Marketing Plan* (New York: The Conference Board, 1972), p. 65.

OBJECTIVE	A brief statement of program's purpose.
TARGET	The key target toward which the program is directed. The target is a measurable attainment to be reached within a specific time.
BACKGROUND	a) Relation of program to established unit, group or corporate goals and strategies. b) Relation of program to current operations. c) Relation of program to external conditions — market, competition, nature of industry, etc.
DESCRIPTION	a) Outline of the program and how it will be carried out. b) Timetable of actions and assignment of responsibilities. c) Discussion of criteria used in planning the program, major assumptions, areas involving judgement, and factors which could affect the program's success.
FINANCIAL SCHEDULE	a) Pro forma profit and loss statements for specific action program. b) Investment schedule for capital requirements. c) Cash flow schedule.
CONTROL	a) Timetable. b) Procedures for interim measurement and review of program.

The year 1971 will be one of consolidation and continued change. The Astro-liner, our new Pacific routes, and a forthcoming merger are reshaping American. Our changed posture in 1971 is illustrated by the following points:

AMERICAN AIRLINES MARKETING PLAN: SITUATION ANALYSIS

1. American's route miles will have more than doubled to 62,831 in one year because of our Caribbean and Pacific routes.

2. Personal/pleasure travel volume will surpass business travel volume for the first time in our history.

3. Wide-bodied aircraft will become the backbone of our fleet, accounting for over 27 percent of our available seat miles by the end of the year. Americans will therefore enjoy the advantage of domestic wide-body dominance during this period.

4. For the first time since 1949, American will begin a new year showing an annual loss on its income statement.

5. Domestic industry traffic is forecast to grow less than 2 percent in 1971. American's prospects for 1971 should be better than those of the rest of the industry mainly because of new domestic and international markets.

6. The severity of the industry's economic distress will lead our competitors to concentrate on American's long-haul segments—which have greater profit potential for them—using wide-bodies as the main selling tool.

Based on excerpts from the annual marketing plan of American Airlines, Inc., in David S. Hopkins, *The Short-Term Marketing Plan* (New York: The Conference Board, 1972), pp. 82–83.

5. Planning assumptions and constraints are provided for. These may be outside the company (such as economic conditions, government regulations, and social trends) or inside (plant capacity, financial or personnel limitations, and management standards for the investment return rate of new products).

This information enables planners to gain comprehensive knowledge of the economics of business and the trends of the marketplace. Such knowledge in turn helps planners to recognize areas where the company can develop an advantage, and where it might be vulnerable.

Marketing Objectives (Where Do We Want to Go?) Establishing marketing objectives is generally considered the most important step in formalized planning. Without this step, planning procedures would have no practical purpose, says one executive. "If you don't know where you want to go, any road will take you there."[8]

Serving as the framework for the marketing objectives are the organization's overall goals, previously discussed in Chapter 2. Within this framework, management often requires planners to restate or define the primary goal for the organization's division (the complete garden-care line) or product (the

The economic slowdown of the past year has dampened what might otherwise be a most optimistic outlook for 1971. Assuming that recovery will be gradual, and recognizing that we have a demanding and immediate need for short-term profitability, key objectives of our 1971 strategy will be:

**AMERICAN
AIRLINES
MARKETING PLAN:
OBJECTIVES**

1. To provide greater marketing efficiency than American has ever had before.

2. To improve and stress the reliability of American's product.

3. To ensure that American's Astroliners provide the best air transportation service in the industry and to communicate this fact to the public.

4. To expand American's participation in the personal/pleasure travel market.

5. To strengthen American's leadership in the commercial travel market.

(Specific financial objectives were not reported because of their confidentiality.)

Based on excerpts from the annual marketing plan of American Airlines, Inc., in David S. Hopkins, *The Short-Term Marketing Plan* (New York: The Conference Board, 1972), p. 84.

budget pleasure-boat engine). This is necessary in order to gain a clear understanding of the division or product's potential for expansion and change. The marketing objectives, once defined, give precise direction to the fulfillment of that primary goal.

Key objectives in many plans are stated in specific and measurable terms such as sales volume or share of market. A sales volume objective is based on the sales forecast, an aspect of planning to be discussed in detail later in this chapter. Some companies simply use a forecast as their sales volume objective. Others differentiate the forecast (the *expected* future outcome) from the objective of the *desired* results.

The process of drawing up a list of marketing objectives may begin with broad statements of strategy for the whole marketing operation. However, when it comes to planning for such marketing subfunctions or activities as field sales or advertising, the objectives for sales and pricing are usually stated in specific and measurable terms.

Strategy and Action Programs (How Do We Get There?)

Strategy and action programs are the plan of action or marching orders for getting where the organization wants to go. Even in plans where the situation analysis or objectives are covered lightly, it is common practice to be specific about strategies.

While strategy and action programs are often treated as a single subject within a plan, some organizations insist on separating them. They maintain that this makes the planner concentrate first on strategy, without being bogged down in the details of how it is to be carried out.[9]

The strategy part of a formal written plan is usually a single statement in broad general terms, sometimes showing specifically how objectives are to be gained. A well-phrased strategy statement might read, for example:

The market share of Product Y is to be increased from 6% to 8% within twelve months by (a) developing an attractive and functional package; (b) directing increased advertising package to reach the top 200 users; (c) redesigning product to improve appearance at no cost increase.[10]

No matter how well thought out a strategy is, however, organizations should generally have several alternative strategies ready. These strategies are contingency plans that prepare an organization to react to unanticipated but likely changes in any part of the environment—consumer, competitive, economic.

An action program describes the actual steps by which the strategy will be put into practice and objectives accomplished during the planning period. It often gives the priority for each step and the time span in months or quarters for carrying it out. Generally, the effort called for in the action program is believed sufficient to reach the objectives.

Service and product reliability will permeate our promotional efforts in developing preference for the Astroliner and strengthening our posture in the business and pleasure travel markets. By the same token, our Astroliner preference effort is a key element in our product design, as well as being a major point in our marketing campaign.

AMERICAN AIRLINES MARKETING PLAN: STRATEGY AND ACTION PROGRAM

1. Improving our product reliability will involve going back to the basics of good airline operation—high-quality service and on-time dependability. Market research tells us that we will gain customer preference by the efficiency and consistency of our service just as much, if not more than, the the quantity of service.

2. To expedite handling of phone sales conversations, we will test a new reference material retrieval device.

3. Among the new services for the embarking passenger is a new baggage identification tag.

4. On any routes where Astroliners are scheduled, Reservations Salesmen will feature the aircraft and recommend the customer's use of it. The Astroliner will be described as our prestige service—not just another flight on the segment.

5. Advertising, Sales Promotion, and Passenger Sales have joined together in a comprehensive vacation program entitled "The Endless Summer." A booklet distributed through advertising, direct mail, and direct sales will describe all our major vacation destinations.

6. A Vacation Card Club Newsletter will be mailed quarterly to American's Vacation Card holders suggesting tour programs.

7. To gain preference among selected groups of travel-prone prospects, American will develop special tours designed to appeal uniquely to certain markets.

Based on excerpts from the annual marketing plan of American Airlines, Inc., in David S. Hopkins, *The Short-Term Marketing Plan* (New York: The Conference Board, 1972), pp. 85–88.

LONG-RANGE PLANNING

Long-range planning was rated as the second toughest problem by a group of 94 marketing executives (market segmentation was the first).[11] It was also the one problem most often included on the respondents' lists of marketing problems.

It is easy to see just how hard long-range planning can be when one considers all the complexities involved. First of all, it requires coordinated planning in all functions and units of an organization. Every unit that will contribute to the marketing effort should give prime consideration to market and customer preferences in its planning and decision making.

Adding to the complexity of long-range planning is the constantly expanding span of time for which plans are being demanded. Some major corporations are looking ahead not just 5 years, but up to 25 or more years. Sears, Roebuck, for example, was estimating in 1965 how many stores it would be operating in the year 2000, and the management and physical distribution systems it would need by then.

Of course, as the demand for more sophisticated long-range plans has grown, so has the technology available to marketing planners. Such technological advances are particularly important in data processing systems, physical distribution concepts and facilities, and communication networks. The degree to which firms use and will continue to use these depends largely on the degree of accuracy they require of their plans.

MARKETING PLANNING IN PRACTICE

These reasons for planning a marketing strategy are persuasive, but to what extent has the marketing world actually accepted planning? The answer depends upon whom you talk to, what type of business the person is in, and what figures you go by. Generally, however, there seems to be more verbal support for planning than actual implementation, as is evidenced by a number of surveys.

A survey of 162 United States and Canadian firms found that reliance on formal short-range plans was widespread among all kinds of marketing operations.[12] However, marketing executives in a few very large companies and a number of small ones reported that they did not prepare written marketing reports.

In fifty industrial firms, a study of planning practices and results indicated that the planning approach which consumer companies used to good effect has yielded disappointing results.[13] In practice, industrial marketing planning did not work well because of differences in industrial context, overstructuring of the planning system, and failure to recognize alternative strategies.

Still another picture emerged from a survey of 346 corporations.[14] Of this group, 73 percent were either using or developing a corporate planning model. Most of the users said that their chief reason for using planning models was to enable the company to explore more alternatives in its planning. Another marketing observer has reported that only about 10 percent of all American companies, including most large corporations, have written marketing plans.[15]

The factors determining the degree of accuracy in long-range planning were examined in a large-scale study in the late 1960s.[16] This study found that accuracy tended to be greater in those companies that:

1. felt that an important purpose of planning was to provide a frame of reference for the operating budget;

2. had their top executives participate in planning, while encouraging subordinates to set their own goals;

3. used rigorous discipline in linking the plan to the budget, either by permitting no changes or by requiring a complete explanation of any changes.

The study found that the degree of forecasting accuracy was highest for the one or two years ahead, but decreased for the years following. Also, accuracy tended to be higher in large companies than in small ones, and lower in highly competitive industries.

THE CHALLENGE OF PLANNING IN THE 1980s

The headlines of the 1970s reflected an economic future and energy crisis that were about as consistent as a yo-yo.[17] (Refer to our discussion in Chapters 3 and 4). As a result of these rapidly changing characteristics, accurate planning has become more vital than ever, but also more difficult. The organizations likely to do the best in this increasingly unpredictable environment are those that are willing to adapt most quickly to some new styles of planning. These new styles differ most from older planning styles in flexibility and speed.

The demand for **flexibility** is causing some organizations to develop a whole battery of contingency plans and alternate scenarios instead of a single corporate plan with one or two variations. "We shoot for alternative plans that can deal with either/or eventualities," says the planning executive of one giant business. "This is a substantial change in planning style because we used to feel comfortable enough about the center line to plan to it . . . and adjust to discrepancies," says another.[18]

The need for **speed** is causing companies to review and revise plans more frequently to keep them in line with changing conditions. Plans are being updated quarterly or even weekly, instead of annually, and "dynamic plans" are being developed that may look ahead two years but are reviewed monthly. At Ralston Purina Company, for example, a 1 percent change in the price of a prime commodity kicks off a change in the company's cost models, and the whole marketing plan may change accordingly.

One of the major effects of decreased predictability and the need for faster reactions in the planning area is that contingency plans are flourishing. A survey of 346 corporations showed that those who were using or developing a corporate planning model were doing so in order to be able to explore more alternatives and plans.[19] There is a noticeable trend for corporate planners to be cautious; organizations appear to be less willing to take risks on investments, and planners are less secure about basing future plans on past or even present statistics.

Thus, the need is arising for new and more sophisticated planning methods and information based on the risks and uncertainties facing the business world today. The following section will explore the pivotal planning component—forecasting.

FORECASTING THE MARKET

The chicken-and-egg analogy seems to apply to the order of conducting the planning and forecasting processes. Some executives would say forecasting is just another step in the planning system. Others would say planning comes after and is largely a result of forecasting. This gives a clue to the importance of forecasting in the planning process. To one senior marketing person, it is the most important piece of data presented to management. To another, it is the basic financial course of planning efforts.[20]

The sales forecast is really an extension of market segmentation, which will be discussed in Chapter 7. While segmentation defines a market by identifying its relevant dimensions, forecasting quantitatively measures that market. It is basically an organization's estimate of future demands for and sales of its product(s) or service(s).

As with planning, there are many ways to approach forecasting, as well as the several related financial, production, and inventory decisions that must be made. Whatever method is chosen, however, the first step in preparing usable forecasts is for the manager and the forecaster to clarify the following items:[21]

1. *The purpose of the forecast*—how it will be used. While a gross estimate of the market is enough to determine whether to enter a business, a much more accurate estimate would be necessary for budgeting purposes.

2. *The dynamics and components of the system* for which the forecast is being made. This clarifies the relationship of such interacting variables as distribution, sales, and production systems. For example, when Corning Glass Works identifies how these elements are related for its color television tube, it is recognizing the appropriateness of different means of forecasting.

3. *To what degree the past is important in estimating the future.* Organizations vary in the degree to which they may be affected by new products, new competitive strategies, or other significant changes in the system. As the similarity between the actual past and the anticipated future diminishes, different forecasting methods would be used.

Once these items have been clarified, it is easier to determine the forecast requirements in terms of accuracy, power, components, and time framework. The next step is to identify the scope of different forecasting types.

BASIC TYPES OF FORECASTS

Forecasts are generally made for three levels of activity: economic, market, and sales. There are two basic factors in each of these sectors: the **potential** (total possible activity) and the **forecast** (estimated probable activity). These two related factors influence and interact with each other at the levels of activity within the market and sales sectors, as is indicated in Figure 5-5.

Economic Forecasting

Because of the increasing influence of national and world economic currents, organizations are finding that forecasting the economic and business climate is an important step in preparing a good sales forecast. Analyses of fiscal and monetary policy, consumer spending, and stock market prices can help to forecast turning points in business cycles and to assess the magnitude of rising or declining business activity. Other important indicators are the trend in corporate profits, the unemployment rate, and the wholesale and consumer price indexes.

How economic activity affects sales forecasting can be seen by Firestone Tire and Rubber Company's estimation of the demand for tires in the future.[22] The demand for tires for the "original equipment market" relies heavily on general business conditions as they influence new car and truck sales. In contrast, the estimate of future sales for the "replacement market" is directly related to the number of vehicles in operation that are two years old or more.

But whether a company is selling tires or tricycles, the economic indicators cited above are subject to more fluctuations than ever before, and even the best economic forecasts may be out of date shortly after they are made.

Market Forecasting

In evaluating its opportunities, a firm next estimates **market** (or **industry**) **demand**. As will be discussed in Chapter 6, there are a number of elements that make up demand. "The market demand for a *product* is the *total volume* that would be bought by a *defined customer group* in a *defined geographical area* in a *defined time period* in a *defined marketing environment* under a *defined marketing program*."[23] This concept of market demand is one of the sharpest thorns in the forecaster's side since it is so hard to pin down. But the forecaster's first step in pinning it down is to establish two figures:[24]

Figure 5-5
INFLUENCE AMONG
FORECASTING TYPES

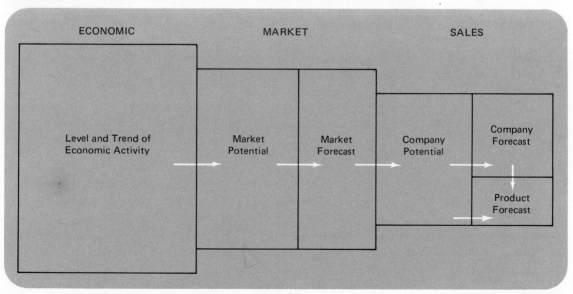

1. **market potential**, or the highest possible level of market demand in a given environment, where further increases in marketing effort would have little effect in stimulating further demand;

2. **market forecast**, or the expected level of industry market demand that will probably occur for the expected level of industry marketing effort and the given environment. The relationships between market potential and market forecast are illustrated in Figure 5-6.

Sales Forecasting

A **sales forecast** should offer a company a prediction of how many sales of a given product can be made under a given marketing plan. This prediction is based on the interrelationship between a number of sales-related elements, as illustrated in Figure 5-7.

As with previously discussed types of forecasting, potential and demand are two important factors determining the forecast.

Sales demand, also called **company demand**, is the company's share of the market demand. Like market demand, it is not a single number, but a function (hence, the curved line) that is subject to all the determinants of market demand, plus additional influences on the market share (especially competitive marketing efforts). The most popular view is that a company's market share will be directly proportional to the amount of marketing effort it makes.

Sales potential is that portion of the market potential that a firm can reasonably expect to achieve. A firm may not want to aim for 100 percent of potential sales, as desirable as that achievement may appear outwardly.[25] The company

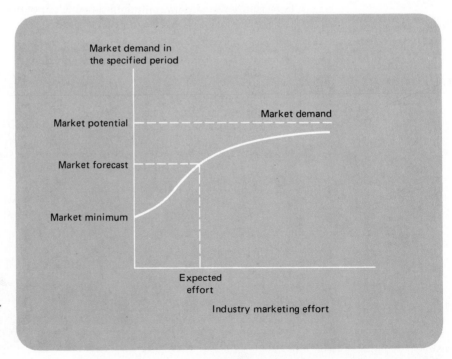

Figure 5-6
MARKET (INDUSTRY)
DEMAND

From Philip Kotler, *Marketing Management: Analysis, Planning, and Control,* 3d ed. (Englewood Cliffs, N.J.: Prentice-Hall, 1976), p. 121. Copyright © 1976. Reprinted by permission of Prentice-Hall, Inc.

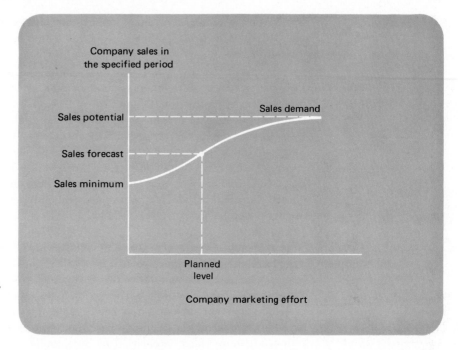

Figure 5-7
SALES (COMPANY)
DEMAND

From Philip Kotler, *Marketing Management: Analysis, Planning, and Control*, 2d ed. (Englewood Cliffs, N.J.: Prentice-Hall, 1972), p. 202. Copyright © 1972. Reprinted by permission of Prentice-Hall, Inc.

may have certain limitations that would make 100 percent unprofitable, as for example, limited distribution capabilities. So, in establishing its sales forecast, the company must take into consideration all internal and external factors. These must then be combined with market potential estimates and the anticipated effects of the chosen strategies. The firm can then proceed to offer a prediction of how many sales of a given product can be made under a given plan of marketing action.

There is good reason to discuss the sales forecast last, because it actually depends on the other two types. To clarify their interrelationship, we need to understand planning and forecasting in terms of which causes the other. A company can think of forecasting in two basic ways.[26] When forecasting is seen as an estimate of national economic activity or of market demand in a **nonexpansible** market (such as steel in a recession), plans for marketing action and sales can indeed be based on forecasting in the sequence:

Forecasting ⟶ Planning

But when a company thinks of forecasting as the level of marketing demand in an **expansible** market (such as digital watches), or the level of sales, then the sequence must be:

Planning ⟶ Forecasting

This is necessary because, as we have already seen, the amount and composition of marketing action often determine the sales forecast. In other words, the sales forecast depends, among other things, on the planned marketing activity of the firm.

METHODS OF FORECASTING

Forecasting may require that economic, market, and, ultimately, the key sales forecasts be determined in different ways. The available methods vary in technique, application to a particular problem, and degree of accuracy. The one thing they tend to have in common is the room they allow for sound managerial judgment and creative thinking in collecting and interpreting data.

Few firms rely on only one forecasting method. They have instead found that a combination of several of the methods discussed below is not only most effective for their particular circumstances, but also provides them with a series of checks and balances.

The Opinion Approach

This approach relies on the views of well-informed experts, either a group of outside people, or company-related personnel. Outside experts who prepare forecasts for the general economy or for specific industries are often sought out by firms. They can provide an outside assessment of future demand or a probabilistic event such as a new health technology for hospitals or a change in the price of oil for plastics producers. Another source of expert opinion about estimated future sales, often used by automobile companies, is distributors and dealers.

The **expert opinion approach** offers the advantages of an information-gathering method that is relatively quick and economical. It also gives access to different points of view and provides a viable alternative when basic data are sparse or lacking. There are disadvantages, however. Among other things, opinions are generally less satisfactory than hard facts; responsibility is dispersed, and good and bad estimates are given equal weight; the results are usually more reliable for aggregate forecasting than for developing reliable breakdowns by territory, customer group, and product.

In addition, the opinions of distributors, like those of salespersons, may be pessimistic or optimistic because of a recent sales setback or success. Moreover, such individuals may be unaware of broader economic developments. Their perspective concerning future business conditions may be too narrow and they may not have given the necessary time or attention to careful estimating.

A **sales force composite approach** is generally subject to adjustment by a firm. Some of the reservations cited above pertaining to distributors' opinions apply here also. In addition, sales personnel may supply biased estimates to gain some immediate advantage. Furthermore, as one manufacturer said, the sales personnel "do not have the data in the field to clearly identify how much market opportunity exists in their areas . . . and we have far better information here at headquarters. Consequently, they have to work intuitively and may set unrealistic goals for themselves."[27]

Despite these disadvantages, many companies feel it is worthwhile to try to override salesperson bias because of the advantages of this approach. First, the salesperson's closeness to the customer may provide more knowledge and better insight into developing market trends. When the salesperson participates in forecasting, he or she has a greater incentive to achieve derived sales quotas. Finally, "grassroots" forecasting can result in estimates broken down by product, territory, customer, and salesperson.

Since forecasting aims at anticipating what buyers are likely to do, it might seem that the opinions of the potential buyers themselves would provide the most reliable answers. However, experience has shown that a **consumer survey approach** is really practical only when the potential buyer market is small and the cost of reaching it effectively is low. Customers must have clear intentions of buying, must carry out their original intentions, and must be willing to disclose their intentions. Because of these limitations, such an approach is of value primarily for industrial products, consumer durables, product purchases where advanced planning is required, and new products where past data do not exist.

The Mathematical Approach

As an alternative to opinion surveys, some firms prepare their forecasts using statistical or mathematical formulas.[28]

The **time series projection** method relies on statistical analysis of past sales data to determine long-term growth patterns, cyclical fluctuations, seasonal variations and irregular movements, and estimations of their future effects. The underlying logic to this approach is that past data are an expression of enduring causal relations that can be uncovered through quantitative analysis. This method has been particularly valuable to companies with a large number of items in their product lines, such as a drug company with some 200 different items to forecast.

Regardless of the number of items involved, time series of past sales of a product can be analyzed in terms of four major components:

1. *Trend* (*T*), the result of basic developments in population, capital formation, and technology;

2. *Cycle* (*C*), which exists when the time series has a wavelike movement of sales of a fairly constant amplitude and periodicity;

3. *Season* (*S*), the consistent pattern of sales movement within the year, whether it be by season or any recurrent hourly, weekly, or quarterly sales pattern;

4. *Erratic events* (*E*), such as strikes, blizzards, fads, riots, fires, or other disturbances which tend to obscure the more systematic components.

According to one model of time series analysis, the above components interact with the original sales series (*Y*) in the formula

$$Y = f(T,C,S,E)$$

In this case *T* is stated in absolute values and *C*, *S*, and *E* are stated as percentages. This formula assumes that the seasonal and cyclical effects are proportional to the trend level of sales. But it does not take into account the effect of marketing plans which must be built into the final forecast. The impact of possible erratic forces can be conveyed by preparing optimistic, pessimistic, and most likely forecasts. By looking at the size of the forecast error band, management can judge how much confidence to put into the "most likely" forecast.

Since time series analysis treats past and future sales as a function of time, rather than of any real demand factors, it is an approach that will not work when the underlying demand factors are not stable. In such cases, it is more desirable to determine the direct relationship between sales and real demand factors using **statistical demand analysis**.

This is an attempt to discover the most important factors affecting the sales of any product, in the hopes that they will explain a significant amount about the variations in sales. In addition to gaining a better understanding of factors affecting or associated with changes in sales, some firms have uncovered relationships having useful predictive value in their forecasting procedures. The factors most commonly analyzed are prices, income, population and promotion. The basic formula used for statistical demand analysis is

$$Y = f(X_1, X_2, \ldots, X_n)$$

Sales represents the dependent variable Y, and sales variations are expressed as a result of variation in a number of independent demand variables represented by X_1, X_2, and so on.

Market Test Approach

In cases where the use of buyers' or experts' opinions are limited because of cost, availability, or reliability of information, the direct **market test approach** may be preferable. This is particularly useful with a new product or an established product in a new distribution channel.

The basis of this approach is to introduce a product and examine its reception in a specifically selected and limited market. This market represents "typical" demographics, effective buying income, trade distribution, competition, and media. Selection of a representative market is one of the big problems of this approach. When test areas are chosen improperly, the results can be erroneous, and it is time consuming and expensive to retest. Nonetheless, the obvious advantage of test marketing is that the results are obtained under actual buying conditions. Where a short-run forecast of likely buyer response is desired, for example, a small-scale market test is usually ideal. Test marketing will be discussed in more detail in Chapter 11.

MARKETING FORECASTING IN PRACTICE

In trying to determine why firms rely on forecasting approach A over B, the answers indicate that companies may use different techniques to deal with different kinds of forecasting problems.[29] A drug manufacturer, for example, uses a time series approach for its regular product forecasts, while for new products, it may rely on outside expert opinion forecasting.

A survey of 161 companies has shown that there is a difference of opinion as to preference for the various forecasting methods. A firm's preference is often related to whether its markets are primarily industrial or consumer. Of those firms whose products are sold mainly to consumers, three out of four place heavy or moderate emphasis on the expert opinion method. While many industrial product manufacturers also like this method, most use it in combination with the sales force composite method to check and reconcile the salespersons' appraisals against top managements' perspective. Service companies also rely both on sales forces and, especially, the expert opinion method.

For most users, the time series projection is the quantitative or objective method most used. The mathematical models, ranging from simple linear regression to complex econometric models, have gained greatest acceptance in the service firms surveyed. Other types of firms are experimenting with them as well, and about a third are making moderate use of them.

Finally, the buyer opinion approach (polling a sampling of current or potential users) is used mainly by firms that manufacture industrial products.

HOW ACCURATE ARE FORECASTS?

Considering the importance of forecasting in the planning process of most firms, and considering the fairly wide choice of forecasting methods, it would seem a safe guess that sales forecasting produces fairly accurate results. When asked this question, some of the 161 executives surveyed said that they were dissatisfied and were always trying to improve their forecasts.[30] An overwhelming majority, however, expressed general satisfaction with the usefulness and accuracy of their companies' sales forecast. Others gave a qualified "yes," saying that overall accuracy was acceptable, but that there were often serious errors in individual product or service items.

Most executives reported that on their main product line, the rate of error has been fairly consistent or has been improving. Chance is also reduced in many companies through the use of frequent update procedures with a self-correcting mechanism that helps to reduce error.

Most executives would welcome more accurate forecasting because it would lead to tighter controls, a higher degree of confidence, and savings to the company ranging from thousands to millions of dollars per year. Boeing Aircraft's experience in the later 1960s shows just how high the rate of return can be on forecast accuracy. In the mid-1960s its forecasters were predicting the growth of domestic air travel and the consequent replacement of small planes by larger ones on the same route system layout. What actually happened was a rapid increase in city-pair nonstops that avoided many of the crowded airports and offered direct service. Boeing had to switch from one forecast to the other. Fortunately for Boeing and the economy of its home base, Seattle, it responded in time by improving its smaller aircraft, the 727. A higher level of orders resulted.[31]

There is obviously more than luck involved in improving the accuracy of forecasting. Sometimes it is a matter of collecting better data while retaining the same method. Other times, the present method must be supplemented or replaced with a more elaborate or different one. Basically, accurate forecasting is a matter of retaining a critical eye and being flexible.

LONG-RANGE FORECASTING

Given the uncertainties and fluctuations of today's business market, forecasting even next week's estimated sales of a company's product may sometimes seem like a bit of crystal-ball gazing.[32] Yet there are companies that are not

Government and large corporations in the 1970s have a need to know what 1985 will be like. To give them a likely answer, Project Aware has been developed by a tiny but prestigious think tank called the Institute for the Future. It is sponsored by Du Pont, Scott Paper, Lever Brothers, and Monsanto at a three-year cost of $120,000 apiece. Using a technique known as Delphi Forecasting, which was developed at the Rand Corporation, Project Aware projects future trends by relying on a panel of experts who answer elaborate questionnaires. The panel's answers are summarized and the questions are repeated until the "oracles" agree on the shape of future trends.

DELPHI FORECASTING FOR A VIEW OF THE FUTURE

The Delphi method gained wide attention in 1964 when Rand used it to forecast such technological events as a manned lunar landing by 1970, but it is only one of several exotic methods used in future research. Others feature the sort of scenario made famous by Herman Kahn of the Hudson Institute, or the complex mathematical models developed at MIT as a basis for the chilling forecasts in D. H. Meadows et al., *The Limits to Growth* (Washington, D.C.: Potomac Associates, 1974).

Here's how the Institute for the Future sees 1985:

Event	Percent Probability
Many chemical pesticides phased out	95%
National health insurance enacted	90
Spending on environmental quality exceeds 6% of GNP	90
Insect hormones widely used as pesticides	80
Community review of factory locations	80
Substantial understanding of baldness and skin wrinkling	40
A modest (3%) value-added tax passed	40
Wide use of computers in elementary schools	25
Development of cold vaccines	20
Autos banned in central areas of at least seven cities	20
Breeder reactors banned for safety reasons	20

Based on "A Think Tank That Helps Companies Plan," *Business Week*, August 25, 1973, pp. 70–71.

only thinking two, five, and ten years into the future, but that have a resident "futurist" on staff who contemplates such matters as how woman's changing role will affect the family in the year 2000. These matters do not always pertain directly to the products of companies such as Shell Oil, Gillette, or General Electric that employ futurists. But there is obviously something to be gained, for companies are increasingly hiring economists or futurists trained in marketing research.

Of what value is this crystal-ball gazing? One researcher feels it helps companies ward off future shock or brace themselves for the crises that have been catching them off guard in recent years. These crises include the energy shortage, inflation, and the environmental outcry. To plan without such futuristic thinking, he continues, is like "looking at birthrates without considering birth control pills."[33]

There can be serious penalties for organizations that are not sensitive to the shadow of future trends. Long-range forecasting certainly would have indicated to the automobile industry the growing demand for safety features. It was not until the threat of government regulation, however, that the industry started doing something about self-regulation. At that point, their actions were subject to closer and more extensive scrutiny than they might have been earlier.

CONCLUSION

Marketing plans do not just happen. They evolve because there is a great deal of planning and analysis of organization needs and resources; also they are a response to the needs, demands, and resources of the marketplace, and the prospects for the future. In an era when the future is so uncertain, plans, whether short- or long-range, are difficult to make, but necessary for survival and prosperity.

The necessity of making plans—whether to determine strategy about pricing, promotion, distribution, or the product itself—and the challenges facing today's planners have together given rise to ever more sophisticated planning and forecasting systems and methods.

Even the marketing executive who does not directly participate in planning or forecasting should have a solid acquaintance with some of these methods and approaches, for they influence not only the product or service itself, but practically all aspects of the organization producing that product or service. Even nonmarketing executives will be linked to these processes by providing input data or by using the results.

DISCUSSION QUESTIONS

1. How would you convince each of these organizations that it needs a formal marketing planning system: a group practice of dentists, a city zoo, an importer of Far Eastern gift items, and a pretzel baker?
2. What might be some key questions to be asked in long-range, annual, product, and venture planning for Holiday Inns, Walt Disney Productions, and Champion Home Builders?
3. Construct the major consideration and any known data for the marketing planning (situation analysis, marketing objectives, and strategy and action programs) for your state's business development office, your area's largest commercial bank, and your favorite fast-food chain.
4. One marketing executive recently stated: "My company is finding that the rules and assumptions we have used for planning for the past twenty years don't always work in the 1970s." What factors account for the change? What recent developments and trends make you optimistic or pessimistic about corporate planning accuracy in the 1980s?
5. Identify the major factors that an automobile manufacturer might use to estimate its market potential and its sales forecast.
6. Which sales forecasting method(s) would you recommend for a burglar alarm producer, a contact lens dealer, and a political candidate for the House of Representatives? Explain your choices.

NOTES

1. E. Bradley Jones, "The Competition," in Earl L. Bailey, ed., *Tomorrow's Marketing* (New York: The Conference Board, 1974), pp. 17–18.

2. "Corporate Planning: Piercing Future Fog in the Executive Suite," *Business Week*, April 28, 1975, p. 46.

3. John Brion, *Corporate Marketing Planning* (New York: Wiley, 1967), p. 35.

4. Leon Winer, "Are You Really Planning Your Marketing?" *Journal of Marketing* 29 (January 1965): 7.

5. Richard Vancil, "The Accuracy of Long-Range Planning," *Harvard Business Review* 48 (September–October 1970): 100.

6. Philip Kotler, *Marketing Management: Analysis, Planning, and Control*, 2d ed. (Englewood Cliffs, N.J.: Prentice-Hall, 1972), pp. 364–65.

7. This section is based largely on David S. Hopkins, *The Short-Term Marketing Plan* (New York: The Conference Board, 1972), pp. 11–15.

8. Ibid., p. 13.

9. Ibid., p. 15.

10. Ibid.

11. "What's Bothering Marketing Chiefs Most? Segmenting," *Advertising Age*, June 4, 1973, p. 77.

12. Ibid., pp. 3–4.

13. B. Charles Ames, "Marketing Planning for Industrial Products," *Harvard Business Review* 46 (September–October 1968): 11.

14. "Corporate Planning," p. 48.

15. Walter O. Stack, "Flexible Market Plans Come from Flexible Marketers," *Marketing News*, August 1, 1974, p. 3.

16. Vancil, p. 100.

17. This section is based largely on "Corporate Planning," pp. 45–48.

18. Ibid., p. 45.

19. Ibid., p. 48.

20. Stanley J. PoKempner and Earl L. Bailey, *Sales Forecasting Practices: An Appraisal* (New York: The Conference Board, 1970), p. 1.

21. John C. Chambers, Satinder K. Mullick, and Donald D. Smith, "How to Choose the Right Forecasting Technique," *Harvard Business Review* 49 (July–August 1971): 46–49.

22. "The Marketing of Rubber Tires and Tubes," Firestone Tire and Rubber Company information sheet, 1972.

23. Kotler, 2d ed., p. 118.

24. Ibid., p. 121.

25. Mark E. Stern, *Marketing Planning: A Systems Approach* (New York: McGraw-Hill, 1966), p. 37.

26. Kotler, 2d ed., p. 202.

27. PoKempner and Bailey, p. 11.

28. This section is based largely on Philip Kotler, *Marketing Management: Analysis, Planning, and Control*, 3d ed. (Englewood Cliffs, N.J.: Prentice-Hall, 1976), pp. 134–37; and PoKempner and Bailey, pp. 17–20.

29. PoKempner and Bailey, p. 10.

30. Ibid., pp. 26–35.

31. John E. Steiner, "The Market for Commercial Aeroplanes," presentation to the World Aerospace Conference, San Francisco, October 16, 1974, p. 11.

32. Liz Roman Gallese, "More Companies Use 'Futurists' to Discern What Is Lying Ahead," *Wall Street Journal*, March 31, 1975, p. 1.

33. Ibid.

6

MARKET DEMAND AND COMPETITION

After completing this chapter, the reader should be able to:

1. Contrast the economic and marketing approaches to examining market demand.

2. Distinguish between economist–government and marketing views of competition.

3. Point out the nature of competition within different market structures and the current character of competition.

4. Evaluate the several ways of competing for differential advantage.

5. Describe how a philosophy of competition is selected and how an analysis of competition is conducted.

Chapter 5 introduced you to the concepts of marketing planning and forecasting. In this chapter, we will examine two of the most important areas to be planned and forecasted—**market demand** and **competition**.

READING THE TIME

Wittnauer, Inc.

The statistics on sales of digital watches in the United States form a devastating graph.[1] In 1973 fewer than 200,000 of these watches were bought by Americans. In 1974 that figure jumped to roughly 650,000. Projections for 1975 indicated that 2.2 million digital watches would be sold in the United States. And there were estimates that the U.S. figure might reach 10 million by 1977 and that the worldwide figure might hit 50 million units by the year 1980.

While sales were going up, prices were going down. The 1975 average cost of $90 for a digital watch was roughly half of the 1974 figure. A number of new lines had come out in the $30 to $70 price range. By the end of the decade, most digital watches will probably cost less than $20.

But declining prices and the faddish digital dials were not the only reasons for increased demand. Digital watches are more than fifty times as accurate as mechanical timepieces; they generally lose or gain only a minute per year. Consumers find digital watches convenient since they do not require constant winding. Their tiny batteries need replacement only once a year.

The development of the digitals shook up the entire watch market, both in the United States and throughout the world. The leading competitors in the United States were the semiconductor manufacturers (such as Texas Instruments) rather than the traditional watch companies (such as Bulova Watch Company). In fact, the traditional watch companies generally resisted the trend toward digitals. As newcomers in this field, not bound by traditional marketing practices, the semiconductor manufacturers engaged in price wars, and seriously lowered profit margins. As a result, they angered the traditional watch retailers.

On the international scene, the Swiss and the Japanese were just beginning to enter the digital market. Previously, they had dismissed digitals as simply an American fad. Now, however, the threat of the low-priced United States models forced them into the market. As the fight for lower prices and higher sales becomes more intense, some companies will certainly be driven out of the business.

MARKETING, DEMAND, AND COMPETITION

This brief case study of digital watches presents some of the key dynamics of the marketing environment. From this example, we can see that the marketer must be particularly aware of consumer demand and competition.

An organization's marketing specialists should be experts on demand analysis—although all major decision makers must grasp the significance of this factor. In the case of digital watches, the goal was to stimulate demand. Some watch manufacturers were going after the whole market, while others were zeroing in on a specific segment (by taking a fashion approach or offering a specific price line).

The other dimension that marketers must consider is competition. Should an organization meet its competitors head-on with similar products aimed at the same parts of the market? Or should it prepare a unique offering and pursue a particular market segment? The answer to these questions is provided by the organization's competitive strategy.

Clearly, these two dimensions are interrelated. The presence of high consumer demand attracts more and more competitors. The presence of vigorous competition forces intensified marketing efforts as firms vie for consumer dollars.

This chapter begins with a discussion of the basic elements of demand and the relationship of demand to marketing. We will treat this critical variable again, and in more detail, in Chapters 7–10. The second half of this chapter describes competition, its nature, and its impact on marketing.

DIMENSIONS OF MARKET DEMAND

A single consumer, whether an organization or a member of an individual household, seeks to fulfill certain needs and wants through the exchange process of marketing. Taken as a whole, these consumers make up markets—assuming that firms recognize them as such and pursue them with offerings. Taking a concept from economics, we can say that demand is what markets have for an organization's products. If you have taken a course in economics, you will be familiar with demand curves and what they mean to a firm. Here we will examine the marketing notion of demand as well as marketing's complex process of anticipating and responding to demand.

ECONOMIC VIEW OF DEMAND

To understand what demand is all about one must know how economists think.[2] In a private enterprise economy, the customer theoretically directs production by the way his or her money is spent. Thus, consumer demand is a crucial element of the business system.

Demand can be defined as the schedule of amounts of any product that buyers will purchase at different prices during some stated time period. We can better understand this definition by examining Figures 6-1a and 6-1b. Figure 6-1a presents an average individual consumer's hypothetical demand for wine. It shows how many fifths of wine that consumer will buy each month at each price shown. Thus, at a price of $2 per fifth, two fifths of wine will be bought per month. At a price of $1 per fifth, five fifths will be bought per month. Figure 6-1b represents the aggregate demand for wine in the United States, the sum of the demand curves for all the individual consumers in this country. The price per gallon indicated in this figure is the average selling price of all

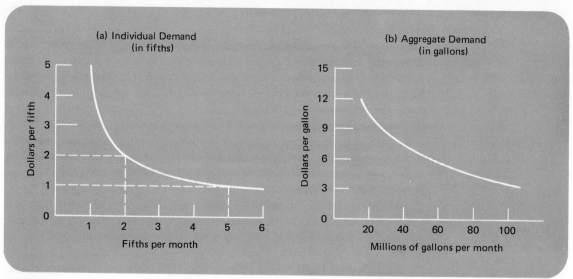

(a) Individual Demand
(in fifths)

(b) Aggregate Demand
(in gallons)

Figure 6-1
HYPOTHETICAL
DEMAND FOR WINE
IN THE UNITED
STATES

wines in the market. Of course, individual wine producers, such as Gallo, would be interested in the demand curves for their own particular brands.

The slope of these demand curves illustrates the obvious. If the price of wine is low, you will probably buy more wine than if the price is high. If you can suddenly buy for $10 the same amount of wine that you previously bought for $25, you may decide to take advantage of the bargain. Also, if the price of wine becomes low enough, you may be able to afford wine with most dinners rather than soda or coffee.

In our economic system, demand curves can reflect consumer preferences among many possible products. If Joan O'Reilly spends $5 on an Elton John album rather than on wine, this suggests a preference for one product over another. Producers keep an eye on consumer demand through research studies

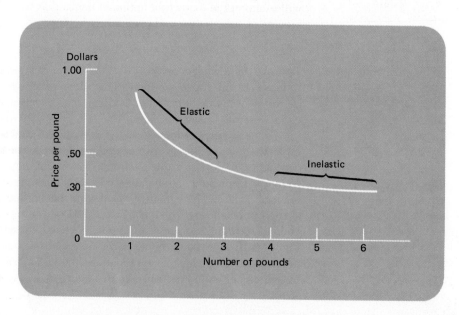

Figure 6-2
HYPOTHETICAL
AGGREGATE DEMAND
FOR SUGAR

and through observation of sales. This information helps them determine what products the consumers want.

A large wine store chain will be especially interested in the total market demand for various wines in its territory. Many factors influence this collective demand. If the area is sparsely populated, wine sales may tend to be low. If the local culture favors drinking beer or hard liquor, an impact will be made on wine sales. If the territory has many wealthy families, it may show a high level of sales of the most expensive and exotic wines. If the costs for competing beverages are unusually high, customers may turn to wine. Finally, of course, if the cost of wines tends to be prohibitively high, sales may drop even if other factors are favorable.

One additional factor that must be considered is the **elasticity of demand**, which is illustrated in Figure 6-2. Suppose the price of sugar rises from 30 cents to 50 cents per pound. If you buy only five or six pounds a year, this price rise will probably seem insignificant. If you and other consumers buy as much sugar at the new price as at the old one, we can say that the demand for sugar is **inelastic** over this price range. Of course, if the price were to rise from 30 cents to $1 per pound, consumers might well decide to ration their use of sugar, causing a considerable drop in sales. The demand for sugar would then be called **elastic** over this greater price range.

The concept of demand elasticity is especially useful in marketing. It helps predict the effects on the total revenue from a product when the price changes. In the first example of sugar, the small price rise did not substantially affect sales. Thus, when demand is inelastic, a price rise will lead to higher revenue and a cut in price will lead to a loss in revenue. But, when demand is elastic (as in the second sugar example), the situation is quite different. In this case, a rise in prices can actually lead to a loss in revenue.

Suppose that your local grocery store sold 1000 pounds of sugar at the standard neighborhood price of 30 cents per pound. The store's revenue on sugar would be $300. But what if the owner decided to raise the price of sugar to $1 per pound? Angry customers might decide to stop buying sugar at the store. They might even decide to avoid the store entirely. If this caused purchases to fall to only 200 pounds of sugar at the higher price, the store's revenue on sugar would then be only $200. Thus, increasing the price would decrease the revenue from the product, as is illustrated in Figure 6-3.

These considerations about demand constitute an economic view of the subject. But, for our purposes, this view is only a starting point. Its emphasis on price is useful, but the economic view of demand assumes that many important marketing factors will remain constant. These factors include product features, promotion, and distribution, as well as social, economic, and political forces. The economic view does not recognize the types and extent of power that marketers use to shape and change consumer demand. In the following sections, we will expand upon the economic view of demand to take these other factors into account.

Figure 6-3
WHEN THE DEMAND FOR SUGAR IS ELASTIC

$300 in revenue

1000 lbs. @ 30¢/lb.

$200 in revenue

$100 revenue lost

200 lbs. @ $1.00/lb.

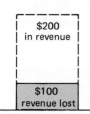

Knoass

MARKETING VIEW OF DEMAND

To analyze demand we must go beyond the notions of economists. Market demand includes all persons or organizations who buy or may be induced to buy a product, service, or idea. It is both an "actual" and "potential" concept.

Market demand can be seen as a simple formula:

$$M = P_1 \times P_2 \times P_3$$

M stands for **market demand**; it equals the interaction of three major forces:

P_1 stands for **population patterns**, which represent the people or organizations who are buying, showing who they are and where they are located. These are called demographic variables.

P_2 stands for **purchasing power**, or the ability to buy, based on income, credit, assets, and economic confidence.

P_3 stands for **purchasing propensity**, or life-style patterns, involving preferences to buy in a certain way. It includes taste and attitudes, psychological and sociological factors. These and other behavioral dynamics will be examined in Chapters 8 and 9 for individuals and households, and in Chapter 10 for organizations. Here, we will be concerned with certain life-style factors that strongly suggest patterns of and preferences for consumption.

Clearly, then, if any of the *P*s change or are limited, the demand potential will be affected accordingly. Population may shift from city to suburbs; income may drop due to recession; tastes may change. Analysis of the market must therefore:

1. identify the specific forces within these three *P* categories that are at work in any marketing situation;
2. discover the nature and magnitude of each force;
3. suggest the trends for the future.

This is the specialty of market research activities (see Chapter 23).

The market variables should be related to the sales that an organization can expect (more babies, more diaper sales), and to the market responsiveness of specific marketing strategy variables (salespersons contacting mothers-to-be may generate more sales than a price decrease would). When one examines these marketing variables it may not be possible to find a single or a few definitive causes for increase or decrease of sales (even "suburban population up, therefore lawnmower sales up" is not true if contract gardening services are doing well). The task of identifying such causes is difficult because:

1. the relationship between the market and how the firm responds to the market may be complex;
2. the market variables are interrelated;
3. everything is subject to change (some convenience foods have been victims of inflation–recession).

In order to understand the major components of market demand, market analysis can be viewed as a triangle: population patterns, purchasing power, and purchasing propensity (see Figure 6-4). In looking at factors that underlie market demand, we are trying to get a clear picture of the extent of the market analysis. For the sake of consistency, consumer marketing concepts and examples will be described.

Figure 6-4
THE MARKET
ANALYSIS TRIANGLE

In an important sense, marketing may be viewed as demand management. The marketing manager has the task of regulating the level, timing, and character of demand for various products. The challenge for a marketer is to try to adjust the actual market conditions to the type and level of demand his or her organization wants. Sizing up demand accurately is important because it provides the foundation for marketing strategy. For each demand situation, specific kinds of marketing action are needed, as indicated in the following table:

DEMAND STATE	FORMAL NAME AND DEFINITION OF MARKETING TASK	EXAMPLE
Negative demand	Conversional marketing (cause demand to rise from a negative to a positive level by overcoming consumer resistance)	Creating a job program for ex-convicts
No demand	Stimulational marketing (creating demand where none previously existed)	Building an artificial lake to stimulate interest in boats in a lakeless community
Latent demand	Developmental marketing (creating a product or service to fulfill an already existing need)	Creating a good-tasting, no-tar cigarette
Faltering demand	Remarketing (revitalizing a declining market by reconsidering the target market, product features, and current marketing program)	AMTRAK's overhaul of its railroad equipment in order to attract new customers
Irregular demand	Synchromarketing (trying to coordinate the movements of supply and demand)	Charging half-fare for mass transit during non-rush hours
Full demand	Maintenance marketing (control of marketing strategy to maintain ideal level of demand)	IBM preserving its current market share
Overfull demand	Demarketing (attempts to discourage customers)	Charging high tolls on bridges in order to discourage use of automobiles
Unwholesome demand	Countermarketing (attempts to eliminate demand altogether)	Antidrug abuse campaigns

Based on Philip Kotler, "The Major Tasks of Marketing Management," *Journal of Marketing* 37 (October 1973): 42–49.

Population Patterns   Abundant data are available on population, thanks to census surveys and breakdowns of the census findings by governmental and private researchers. Population statistics help to determine the size of demand, and they suggest market need and life styles as well. Population data mainly tell us *who* and *how many* comprise various markets. Such data may also provide some information on *how* they purchase. Population data describe both the broad American market and the particular market of a given organization (such as all teenagers in the St. Louis metropolitan area).

There are four key dimensions of population:

1. *Size.* The population of the United States will increase by roughly 70 million people—a 42 percent rise—in the 30-year period from 1955 to 1985.[3] By 1985 there may be twice as many households as in 1955.

2. *Birthrate and family size.* The decline in the birthrate continues, but it will probably level off in the 1980s.[4] "Zero population growth" will remain a distant possibility, because the increase in women of childbearing age in the 1980s will offset lower birthrates. Philip Hauser believes that it will be 60 or 70 years before our population growth ends.

3. *Age distribution.* In 1972 the median age of all Americans was 28.1 years.[5] By the year 2000, this figure will rise to 34 years, a dramatic increase. The age group from 25 to 39 years will show the highest level of population increase. There will be a corresponding drop in the under-25 population,

THE ELDERLY AS A SPECIAL MARKET

Americans are retiring earlier and living longer. Census statistics indicate that the over-65 age group is expanding faster than the under-65 group. This means that the elderly are becoming a larger and more important force in the American economy. Their market value exceeds $60 billion.

Yet senior citizens are one of the most neglected and discontented groups in our society. About one-fourth live below the government poverty level and many others are hit hard by continuing inflation. Yet economic difficulties are hardly the only problem of the elderly. Senior citizens are rarely treated with respect and dignity and find it almost impossible to participate in work or other societal institutions in a meaningful way.

Only recently has business begun to recognize the particular needs and feelings of elderly Americans. For example, the U.S. Foods Corporation of Houston has started a shop-by-phone grocery and drug service. The president of U.S. Foods, William Rogers, notes that elderly people do not want to be thought of as helpless. His corporation tries to meet their needs.

Focusing on the elderly can be a profitable business. Colonial Penn Group handles the travel and insurance needs of senior citizens. It keeps a close liaison with organizations such as the American Association of Retired Persons and the National Retired Teachers Association. Colonial Penn has developed a $100 million business and is expanding at a rate of 15 to 20 percent each year.

Rising political awareness and militancy among senior citizen groups (such as the Gray Panthers) mean that the elderly will no longer sit by quietly and be ignored. If marketers take heed of these changes, they may be able to service a growing and lucrative market.

Based on "The Power of the Aging in the Marketplace," *Business Week,* November 20, 1971, pp. 52–58.

a group which in the 1960s had come to account for almost half the people in the United States.

4. *Geographic dispersion*. The suburban population of the United States will jump from 70 million in 1970 to 110 million in 1980.[6] There will be increasingly fewer people living in farm areas and in the nation's largest cities. The South and West will continue to gain in their share of the national population. (More and more Americans seem to like year-round sunshine.)

The mobility of the American people will be even more evident in the future. Today, some 20 percent of all Americans change their residence in any given year. In newer communities, the houses look alike and the atmosphere is bland. It doesn't matter if your neighbors come from Philadelphia or Forest City, Iowa; they'll probably move in a year anyway.

Purchasing Power   Purchasing power is the economic dimension of market potential. It helps explain consumers' ability (and willingness) to buy. The following economic and attitude factors determine purchasing power:

1. *Income*. Individual and family real (after inflation is deducted) income will rise dramatically over the next decade. An annual growth rate of over 45 percent is projected. Disposable (after taxes) income will also increase; consumer spending may double between 1975 and 1990.[7] These statistics suggest a similar growth of discretionary income—the income available after necessities have been taken care of by an individual or family.

Engel's laws are useful in predicting spending patterns in periods of changing income.[8] Ernst Engel, a German statistician of the 1850s, observed that higher family income levels led to greater spending in all important consumer categories. Yet while the percentage of income spent on clothing, transportation, recreation, health, and education tended to increase, the percentage spent on housing remained constant and the percentage spent on food declined. The recent recession and inflation with its lower real income levels, caused the percentages to go the other way.

2. *Credit*. Credit represents the amount of money that a person can borrow. By 1974 outstanding consumer credit in the United States, excluding home mortgages, exceeded $177 billion, or nearly $5,000 per household.[9] The availability and cost of credit have a significant impact on marketing.

3. *Assets*. Consumers hold two types of assets. **Liquid assets** include savings bonds and money in savings and checking accounts. **Physical assets** include consumer goods such as television sets and automobiles. In recent years, total consumer assets have been on the increase. This may make consumers more secure financially, and better able to invest in new clothes, vacations, or housing.

4. *Consumer confidence*. The above three factors are objective elements of purchasing power. But the economic ability to buy may not count for anything if consumers are not *willing* to buy. George Katona sees the short-run and long-run confidence of consumers as the key to the level of consumer spending.[10] If people believe that inflation, unemployment, and recession are about to become more severe, they may be inclined to reduce their spending and concentrate on saving. It also works the other way.

**Purchasing
Propensity**

Life-style factors tell us how and why consumers behave. For the moment, we will not be greatly concerned with *why* consumers behave as they do. That question will be explored in Chapters 8 and 9.

Changes in the life styles of Americans have been significantly shaped by economic factors (see Chapter 3). Generally, patterns of consumer spending have remained relatively stable. Yet even small changes can have an important impact on business. The economic recession of the mid-1970s led to reduced use of electricity in homes, restricted purchases of clothing and gifts, and more home-cooked meals. In the future, life styles will become even more diverse. There will be more of a "singles culture," more working mothers and child-rearing fathers, and more alternatives to conventional family arrangements.[11]

As our social and economic patterns change, marketers study corresponding changes in life-style factors. These include:

1. *Family life cycle.* Most American households go through a series of six life-cycle stages:

1. Young, single individuals living away from home.
2. Young married couples with no children.
3. Young married couples with dependent children.
4. Older married couples with dependent children.
5. Older married couples with no children living at home.
6. Older single and widowed adults.[12]

Obviously, the finances and need patterns of households will vary in each of these stages. To take advantage of these changes, some insurance companies have instituted the "life-cycle" policy. Such a policy increases or decreases in face value and premiums over a person's lifetime, depending upon the individual's needs at any particular time.

2. *Women's role.* Women are entering the labor force in unprecedented numbers.[13] By the mid-1980s, they will represent almost 40 percent of all workers. There will be a noticeable increase in married women aged 35 to 44 working outside of their homes. At the same time, the division of labor inside the home will also be changing. Increasingly, as feminist consciousness has spread, women have challenged the assumption that cooking, cleaning, and childrearing are women's work.

3. *Education.* The percentage of Americans who have attended college is steadily rising.[14] In 1965, less than 20 percent had attended classes or received a degree; by 1985, the figure will pass 30 percent. Enrollment in major colleges and universities is declining, but community colleges as well as training and technical schools have made impressive gains.

4. *Occupations.* Related to the changes in educational patterns are changes in occupational expectations. It is clear that a growing number of Americans aspire toward high-status positions in professional and managerial fields. As the educational attainments of Americans continue to increase, this trend will become more pronounced.

COMPETITION AND MARKETING STRATEGY

Our economy is characterized by vigorous competition, and this is not likely to change in the future. Changing population trends, economic development, and scientific and technological advances will all necessitate new marketing strategies. Companies will compete to be among the successful survivors as these changes occur. Even increasing government regulation and some form of national economic planning will not fundamentally alter this situation. In the era ahead, nonprofit organizations will also get caught up in the competition for scarce dollar income and customers.

The study of demand is based on the need to select a market opportunity, one that an organization's marketing strategy should cultivate over the long run. This decision-making process means simultaneously pursuing demand and outmaneuvering competitors. A solid and innovative growth strategy has been considered essential for maintaining a satisfactory level of profit. However, in the economic and social environment of the future, the use of a balanced stategy for survival may become the norm.

DIFFERENT MEANINGS OF COMPETITION

We got an overall feel for competition in the public policy sense when we looked at antitrust policy in Chapter 3. In this section, we will compare the diverse views of competition held by economists and government officials on one side, and marketers on the other.[15]

Economists see consumer welfare as the main goal of competition. They compare actual market conditions with a model of "perfect competition," representing maximum freedom for consumers. Economists are particularly concerned that buyers have a wide range of marketing choices and sufficient information and capital to make satisfactory purchases.

Government officials have many concerns similar to those of economists. Antitrust policy represents a search for a workable definition of competition. In recent years, antitrust laws have tried mainly to prevent monopolies from emerging. Government tends to assume that a high level of competition will lead to a healthy economy.

Marketers, naturally, have a different perspective. The business executive views competition as "whatever he has to do to get sales away from his rivals and whatever they do to take sales away from him." For business, models of perfect competition seem irrelevant. The main goal of the competitive process is the welfare of one's own business enterprise. It is assumed that consumers will also gain from the competition, but this is not the overriding concern of any one firm or industry.

An example of the business version of competition can be seen in the battle over cash register sales. National Cash Register Company and Litton Industries have long been the dominant firms in this field. But technological advances have made the NCR and Litton machines somewhat obsolete. Industrial giants such as IBM and RCA are eyeing the growing market for computerized register systems. Meanwhile, Litton and more than ten other companies are already developing new electronic machines.[16]

MARKET STRUCTURE A **market** consists of the buyers and sellers of particular goods and services who deal with each other. **Structure** is a set arrangement of the interdependent parts that make up an organization. **Market structure** has been defined as "the economically significant features of a market which affect the behavior of firms in the industry supplying the market."[17]

Successful decision making in the competitive world of business requires a sophisticated awareness of market structure. Three primary elements are of vital interest to business executives:

1. *Degree of concentration.* This refers to the number of sellers and buyers in an industry, and the degree to which a few large firms dominate the field. In the auto industry, for example, the top four producers control 80 percent of the market. Generally speaking, such a high concentration ratio may imply limited competition. But an industry with many small firms may be sick and regressive, while an industry with a few active, highly competitive firms may be dynamic.[18]

2. *Character and importance of product differentiation.* This is the extent to which buyers of a specific product have preferences among the competitive choices offered by sellers. If all brands of toothpaste seem alike to consumers, advertising appeals are largely irrelevant.

3. *Conditions of entry for new sellers.* If costs or other considerations make it extremely difficult for a new seller to enter an industry, then the established firms have a significant competitive advantage.

In order to better understand market structure, we will again look at the economists' view of competition.[19]

Perfect Competition In a purely competitive market, there are a large number of small sellers. No one competitor does all pricing or supply. It is relatively easy for new firms to enter the field. Each firm can sell its products at the normal market price and each decides how much to produce.

The nearest thing to perfect competition in the United States is found in the farm sector of agriculture. A large number of sellers compete; product differentiation is limited; and sellers face few entry barriers. A few sellers cannot significantly shape the market price of goods.

Monopoly If an industry is a monopoly, there is only one seller. Since no competition exists, the seller can set his own price. It is difficult for competitors to enter the industry.

Many of our public utilities, such as electricity, telephone, and gas, are legally regulated monopolies. Historically, the rationale for these monopolies has been that the costs of competing in these fields are prohibitive and that competition would lead to inefficient service. But consumer advocates have challenged the claims of public utilities monopolies. Representative Richard Ottinger of New York has attacked the American Telephone and Telegraph Company for suppressing cost-saving improvements.[20] He claims that AT&T lobbied to limit or prevent the use of satellite communications, which could drastically reduce the price of international telephone calls.

Monopolistic Competition Monopolistic competition reflects two types of market behavior simultaneously. "Competition" means that there are many sellers, and it is relatively easy for new firms to enter the market. The "monopoly" side is the differences among products, with the seller having some control over pricing. For example, one firm may attempt to increase its market share by introducing a new product or by cutting prices. There is little sense of interdependence among firms because of the large number of competitors.

The retailing industry is an example of monopolistic competition. There are many competitors, and the several largest retailers control only a small percentage of the business. If one retailer cuts or raises prices, or institutes a new service, it will not necessarily lead to similar or retaliatory action by other firms.

Oligopoly In an oligopolistic industry, a few large firms determine their own prices. Product differentiation is low, and the conditions of entry are difficult. The crucial factor is the interdependence of competitors. With a few large firms sharing control of the market, each is constantly aware of the actions of the others. If Quaker Oats introduces a new type of natural cereal, Ralston will be forced to make some sort of retaliatory move.

As a result, the leaders of the oligopolistic industries tend to coordinate their prices. In this way, each firm trades some of its freedom of pricing for a greater degree of market security. Often a large firm will announce a price hike and its competitors will quickly follow suit. This can represent informal agreement—or illegal collusion—depending on the circumstances (remember our discussion earlier, in Chapter 3).

THE CHARACTER OF COMPETITION TODAY The structural models of competition described in the previous section all date from the industrial period of the nineteenth century. Competition as practiced by the industrial model emphasized price and homogeneous products. These were based on a scarcity of resources, growth through production of goods, competition within an industry, and the regulating capacity of self-interest of firms in the marketplace. Today's business competition is different.

Nonprice Competition In traditional economic theory, pricing is the key element in competition. Figure 6-5 indicates, however, that the attitudes of business management conflict with traditional economic doctrine. As the study of 485 executives showed, pricing is overshadowed by several forms of nonprice competition.[21] Techniques such as discounts, trade-ins, coupons, packaging differences, and fictitious list prices reduce the importance of rational price information. This reinforces consumer preferences based on nonprice considerations such as style, convenience features, brand names, personal buying assistance, and advertising image.

There are many reasons for the importance of nonprice elements in the competitive strategy of business. American consumers are relatively affluent and in many cases can afford to spend extra money to obtain a high-quality or

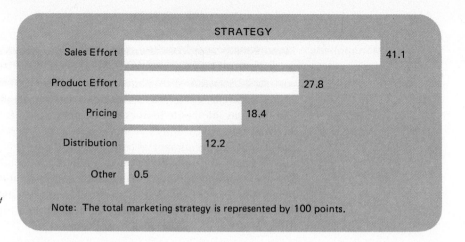

STRATEGY

Sales Effort	41.1
Product Effort	27.8
Pricing	18.4
Distribution	12.2
Other	0.5

Note: The total marketing strategy is represented by 100 points.

Figure 6-5
PERCEIVED
IMPORTANCE OF
THE MAJOR FACETS
OF MARKETING

From John G. Udell, "The Perceived Importance of the Elements of Strategy," *Journal of Marketing* 32 (January 1968): 35. Published by the American Marketing Association.

high-status product. The appearance of many complex products has created a need among buyers for substantial marketing information. Also, since most American industries are oligopolies, one firm usually cannot underprice another and competitors turn to other means of winning a larger share of the market.

Conditions of Affluence

American industries are, in most instances, not meeting the basic survival needs of the human species. Most firms are competing to meet needs that could only exist in an affluent society. Thus, firms typically do not produce food, clothing, and shelter, but create new types of food, clothing, and shelter. Furthermore, in recent years one of the fastest growing markets has been catering to people's desire for personal development: physical, intellectual, cultural, social, and moral.[22]

Economic trends in the 1970s have undercut some of the unbridled affluence of the last two decades. Nevertheless, the economy still has the capability to create varied goods and services, as well as the means to acquire these products.

Generic Competition

Generic competition occurs when a variety of products all can satisfy the same basic need. For example, a car maker is competing against other car makers in selling a means of transportation to the consumer. In terms of generic competition, car makers are not each other's only rivals. There are also the train, the bus, the plane, the subway, even the bicycle.

In the same sense, if a person has a certain amount of discretionary income and wants to spend it on some form of personal pleasure, he or she might take a vacation in Bermuda, buy a speedboat, purchase new rugs or furniture, or devote a summer to study in Europe. Each of these alternatives—and each of the industries behind them—is in generic competition with the other.

When *Look Magazine* folded in 1971, one might have assumed that this failure would benefit its most obvious competitor, *Life*. But roughly one year later, *Life* also was forced to end publication. *Look* did not die because of the competition from its immediate rival in the field of mass-circulation pictorial magazines. *Look* and *Life* both folded because of competition from more spe-

140

cialized magazines like *Penthouse* and *Cosmopolitan*, which affected all mass-circulation pictorials, as well as from the other mass medium, television.[23]

Competition among Systems

Increasingly, today, we can define competition as more than one firm rivaling others. The emphasis now is on one system of firms against a competing system. International Harvester and its network for distributing tractors compete against Deere and its dealer network. In bicycle production, the Schwinn organization with its independent distributors and dealers is vying with the Sears, Roebuck chain and its (anonymous) contracted producer of Sears private-branded bicycles. This type of competition also affects merchandise credit systems. The Bank-Americard and the retailers it services compete with department stores that have their own charge systems.

Consumerism and Ecology

The consumerism and ecology movements have a double impact on the competitive process:

1. As was described in Chapter 4, higher standards are being imposed on marketers. Some companies, such as American Motors and Whirlpool, have responded to consumer complaints with genuine reforms.[24] Each company links higher sales to its proconsumer program.

2. Competition has a new meaning beyond statistics about sales, profits, and market share. Companies wish to contribute to the broader public interest and to build an image of social responsibility. Thus, Citibank in New York City publishes a four-page newsletter offering money management advice to middle- and low-income consumers.[25] Some 160,000 copies are distributed each month in over 400 metropolitan area supermarkets.

COMPETITION FOR DIFFERENTIAL ADVANTAGE

When we discussed the managerial marketing process in Chapter 2, we suggested that firms need aggressive and effective marketing strategies to create a differential advantage not based on price. The purpose of such marketing activity is not to establish a monopoly but simply to maintain a satisfactory competitive position.

A differential advantage is the preferential competitive position that a firm holds based on differences between its product or marketing functions and those of its rivals. Some companies have gained a differential advantage through improving the product: Xerox developed a better copying machine; Avis provided cleaner cars and more personal attention than Hertz. Some organizations have improved their position through other marketing efforts. For example, Adelphi University teaches some graduate business courses in special Long Island Railroad cars during rush hours. Or, an endorsement by the right football hero can benefit nearly any product's image.

Differential advantage is always more than a competitive strategy; it is also clearly related to demand. The search for differential advantage has various forms, depending on the industry.[26] An established automobile line suffers if a competitor improves body style, performance, and gas mileage at the demand of consumers. Physicians will prescribe the manufacturer's drugs that are most effective and cause the least side effects.

The concept of differential advantage applies not only to corporate giants, but also to small firms. The technique of distribution offers hope for the small firm that needs a differential advantage. Timex has been successful in selling its low-priced watches in drug stores and discount shops. Avon developed a door-to-door method for selling cosmetics. Each firm gained a significant competitive advantage through unusual distribution methods. Now these two companies are no longer small.

Innovative and Imitative Competition

The major thrust of competition over the years has been in **innovations** made possible by new technology geared to satisfy demands. The computer, frozen foods, and birth control pills are all examples of such innovations. The quest for innovation is an essential part of marketing. A company that hangs on to the familiar, tried-and-true products and operations runs the risk of being overtaken by competitors' advances.[27]

The oil industry has been particularly affected by innovations. Each time the industry became satisfied with its products, competitive substitutes emerged that made them obsolete. Even in recent years, with all of the obvious ecological problems accompanying the use of gasoline, oil companies have not made active attempts to research fuel cells, batteries, solar power plants, and other alternatives to present energy forms.[28]

Innovation is not the only strategy for competitive growth. **Imitation** is another popular option.[29] Being first with an innovation is not so important; adopting the innovation is. IBM entered the computer field as an imitator and RCA entered the television industry as an imitator. Both have become leaders in their respective categories.

Often small firms rather than large businesses develop the innovation—motels, drive-in movies, paperback books, and so forth. Large firms may be afraid to take a risk by introducing an innovation that is different from their existing formula for success. This will be clearly seen in our discussion of distribution, retailing, and wholesaling (in Chapter 21). Innovations such as supermarkets, discount houses, and vending machines have been started by newcomers to the field.

The broad notion of innovation can include a technological application, market segmentation, or distribution arrangement that achieves some competitive advantages. Table 6-1 presents examples of different types of innovative marketing strategies.

Marketing Mix Adjustment

It is a bit of an oversimplification to say that firms build on one type of marketing innovation as their sole differential advantage. Usually, a differential advantage is the total marketing mix adjusted so that the consumer receives a unique package of attributes relative to competitors' offerings.

The competition between Procter & Gamble and the Scott Paper Company illustrates this point. Procter & Gamble, the nation's largest advertiser, has challenged Scott's dominance over the household paper-products field. The key element in the Procter & Gamble surge was money. In 1970 Procter & Gamble spent $13.5 million advertising its paper products. While Scott was spending $1.6 million to advertise three lines of its tissue products, Procter

& Gamble spent $2 million on Charmin alone. This advertising bombardment was backed up with an aggressive sales force and with significant upgrading of paper products. As a result, Procter & Gamble has taken over the disposable-diaper market.

Table 6-1
PICK AN INNOVATIVE MARKETING STRATEGY

MARKETING STRATEGY	DEFINITION	EXAMPLE
The end run	Producer defines his own area of competition, rather than accepting his competitor's definition	Sherwin-Williams considers itself in the decorating business, not the paint business
Domination	Concentration of effort in one area so as to "own" it	Advertising on radio only, so audience identifies the product with radio
Market segmentation	Concentration on a segment of a market that will yield a disproportionately high profit	Revlon has geared its entire approach to appeal to beauty-conscious American women
Market stretching	Redefining a business to create new markets	Dow Chemical now sells food wraps, oven cleaners, and Christmas tree decorations
Multibrand entries	Creating new brands to "compete" with one's own product	Bristol Myers has created four different brands of deodorant
Brand extension	Using same brand name for several related products	Dristan now refers to cold tablets, nasal spray, and cough medicine
Product change	Introducing new product or packaging, or varying existing product or packaging	Helena Rubinstein introduced a shampoo that is also a color rinse
Overseas expansion	Making use of foreign market potential	Colgate-Palmolive's foreign sales account for over half of its total sales
Distribution breakthroughs	Enlarging markets by using different distribution methods	Helene Curtis has acquired a new line to tap the door-to door market
Merger and acquisition	Diversification by combining with other companies	Coca-Cola has merged with Minute Maid and Duncan Coffee
Iconoclasm	Using unconventional marketing strategies that are contrary to custom for the product involved	Carling Breweries uses several local advertising agencies, rather than a national agency, to take advantage of local market variations

Based on Lee Adler, "A New Orientation for Plotting Marketing Strategy," *Business Horizons* 7 (Winter 1964): 41–49.

Nonprofit organizations are also concerned with differential advantages. A group like the March of Dimes is, in a sense, competing against other charitable organizations for donations. One March of Dimes organization, in an effort to find a differential advantage, conducted a study using various appeals. These appeals were currently used by the organization, or had been used in the past, or possibly would be used in the future.

WHAT MAKES THEM GIVE?

Twenty-four themes in three categories were rated in terms of their *distinctiveness, interest,* and *believability.* The majority of the themes did not score high in interest and distinctiveness. The themes that dealt with positive and active giving—and with the results of giving—seemed to be most effective.

Marketing strategy and technique were thus used by a nonprofit organization in order to establish a differential advantage for its fund-raising efforts.

Based on William A. Mindak and H. Malcolm Bybee, "Marketing's Application to Fund-Raising," *Journal of Marketing* 35 (July 1971): 15–17.

Making marketing adjustments often means differentiating as many aspects as possible of the marketing mix. Thus, when John Y. Brown, Jr.—the man who built Kentucky Fried Chicken into an empire—entered the hamburger business, he did so by building a total marketing package.[30] He paid a reported $1 million for the rights to Miami's popular "Ollieburger" and sent movable Ollie's Trollies with this burger to street corners in the Midwest and South. And he has integrated the trolley concept into still another purchase: the 53-store Lum's Miami food chain.

Any important element in the marketing mix has both a cost and a response linked to it.[31] Thus, if a shirt manufacturer upgrades the quality of his product, there will be a cost (the cost of implementing the change) and a response (the change in revenue that results from the change in quality). Marketers must gauge whether the cost is likely to yield a significant response.

Yet there are other considerations beyond these. Some competitive actions may pay better than others. Relative attractiveness can be judged in three ways. The *temporal dimension* represents the length of time during which a certain payoff will prevail. *Creative distinctiveness* takes into account the ease or difficulty of imitating a marketing mix. The *likelihood of reprisal* reflects the probability that competitors will attempt to retaliate against the firm's innovations. The most attractive marketing payoff is one that will prevail over a long period of time, that is difficult to imitate, and that will not lead to retaliation.[32]

COMPETITION ANALYSIS

Firms might be more profitable if marketers made great use of marketing resources to evaluate the potentials of a particular market. In this approach, known as **intensive marketing**, planning is begun on an individual market level, rather than on the national, state, or even local level.[33] Such an approach allows marketers to take into account the individual differences of each market and formulate their plan accordingly. This avoids the dangers of making generalizations that do not fit a particular situation. For example, the department store that must fight the many large stores for a share of the fashion market in Houston may find instead that it is able to dominate several small stores in El Paso.

One way to implement this approach is the **intensive competitive marketing audit**. This is an in-depth study of the marketing activities carried on by an organization and its competitors. Such an audit enables marketers to analyze exactly what is going on in a particular market and to determine how best to take advantage of profit opportunities. Moreover, the orientation of this audit is competitive. Marketers compare their own strengths and weaknesses with those of the competition. In this way they can accentuate their positive marketing actions and, if possible, eliminate the negative actions. A suggested format for such an audit is shown in Figure 6-6.

Figure 6-6
FORMAT FOR THE INTENSIVE COMPETITIVE MARKETING AUDIT

Adapted from Frank Rothman, "Intensive Competitive Marketing," *Journal of Marketing* 28 (July 1964): 14. Published by the American Marketing Association.

MARKETING FACTOR	THIS COMPANY	COMPETITOR A	COMPETITOR B	COMPETITOR C
1. Company image, reputation				
2. Products: claims, advantages, limitations				
3. Market, sales trends				
4. Consumer behavior				
5. Middlemen relationships				
6. Advertising				
7. Sales promotion				
8. Merchandising				
9. Packaging				
10. Personal selling				
11. Prices				
12. Physical distribution				
13. Compliance with legislative restrictions				
14. New product developments				
15. Effectiveness of marketing management and other personnel; internal organization				
16. Mergers, acquisitions				

The typical reaction of business executives to an innovative competitive challenge generally takes place in four stages, as follows:

LET'S PRETEND IT ISN'T THERE

1. *Blindness.* In the first stage, wishful thinking prevails. The executive holds on to the idea that nothing has changed, and immerses himself or herself in day-to-day business. When unpleasant facts about competitors come to light, the executive colors them in a way that makes the threat seem unreal.

2. *Attempts to destroy the new competitor.* This can take the form of trying to cut off the competitor's source of supply, or the company may promote restrictive legislation that would drive the competitor out of the industry.

3. *Direct confrontation and overcompensation.* When destructive tactics do not work, the executive may try to fight the competitor directly. If A cuts prices, B will cut prices even further. If A offers a new service, B will offer three new services.

4. *Adjustment and adaptation.* Eventually—but better sooner than later—the executive may learn to live with the existence of the competitor. The realization comes that the competitor can no longer be ignored and cannot be driven out of business. Thus, the executive must carefully evaluate the new conditions of competition and must develop a new marketing strategy to deal with the altered competitive picture.

Based on Alfred Gross, "Adapting to Competitive Change," *MSU Business Topics* 18 (Winter 1970): 14-22.

CONCLUSION

This chapter has focused on two aspects of the marketing environment that must be very close to home for the successful marketer. Demand is the lifeblood of marketing efforts. Competition can make it possible or impossible for the marketer to satisfy the demand of a sufficient number of consumers.

Market demand, market segments, and consumer behavior are all important parts of any marketing decision. Therefore, we will devote four more chapters (Chapters 7–10) to giving you a solid grounding in market and behavior analysis. You will need this understanding to deal creatively with the marketing strategy topics: product, price, promotion, and distribution. Be aware of the conflicts between consumer preference and behavior on one hand, and social demands on the other. The not-so-careful marketer will be caught in the middle, like auto manufacturers and soft drink bottlers. In both these industries, good competition turns out to be poor social responsibility. Auto manufacturers preferred higher-profit big cars that pollute more and consume more gasoline. Bottlers favored no-deposit, no-return containers that create litter and waste resources.

The marketer must always be conscious of competition. After answering the question, "Is the product right for consumers?" the marketer must consider the competition. Sizing up the presence or absence of competition, the strengths and weaknesses of rivals, the advantages and disadvantages of his or her marketing mix as opposed to theirs—these are important marketing tasks.

"Is the way we are competing in violation of the antitrust laws?" Examine the legal implications. "Will our marketing strategy give us a solid differential advantage over our competition?" This is a crucial question for marketing decision makers. The marketer must keep one eye on the consumers, the other on the competitors. And a few other eyes, those of co-workers, on the rest of the marketing environment.

DISCUSSION QUESTIONS

1. Of what benefit can a discussion of the economist's view be for understanding the market demand for state-operated campgrounds, airline travel for business purposes, and plumbing equipment?
2. What are the important elements (and their interaction in the marketing analysis) of the demand for mutual funds, three-year bachelor's degrees, and kitchen remodeling?
3. What is the current state of market demand for these products: downtown parking, billiard and pool halls, employment service for ex-convicts, wall-to-wall carpeting, and litter on highways? What type of marketing strategy would be recommended for each of these situations?
4. How would a government economist and the director of marketing view competition differently for branded prescription drugs, dry breakfast cereals, television broadcasting, and gasoline stations?
5. What type of competitive market structure best describes these industries: barber shops, coal mining, computers, universities, and intracity bus lines? Which modern characteristics of competition are causing each of these products to be inappropriately described by the market structure model?
6. What types of differential advantage would you recommend for a new competitor in these industries: motels, vitamins, labor unions, and photocopiers?
7. Select a specific department store in a given city (where you go to school or have lived), name its major competition, and conduct an intensive competitive marketing audit for your selected store and its competition.

NOTES

1. Isadore Barmash, "Upsurge in Digital Watches," *New York Times*, July 20, 1975, sec. 3, p. 1; "A Digital Watch for the Mass Market," *Business Week*, September 28, 1974, p. 38; "Digital Watches: Bringing Watchmaking Back to the U.S.," *Business Week*, October 27, 1975, pp. 78–91.
2. This section is based largely on George L. Bach, *Economics: An Introduction to Analysis and Policy*, 7th ed. (Englewood Cliffs, N.J.: Prentice-Hall, 1971), pp. 308–20.
3. Herbert Zeltner, *Advertising Age*, July 14, 1975, pp. 1, 40.
4. Ibid., p. 40; "Sociologists See Shifts in Living and Buying Habits," *Advertising Age*, July 14, 1975, p. 22.
5. "The Burgeoning Benefits of a Lower Birth Rate," *Business Week*, December 15, 1973, p. 22; Zeltner, pp. 1, 40–41.
6. William Lazer et al., "Consumer Environments and Life Styles of the 70's," *MSU Business Topics* 20 (Spring 1972): 11–12.

7. Lazer et al., pp. 8–9; Lindsay H. Clark, Jr., "Living with Inflation," *Wall Street Journal*, November 28, 1973, p. 27.

8. Philip Kotler, *Marketing Management: Analysis, Planning, and Control*, 2d ed. (Englewood Cliffs, N.J.: Prentice-Hall, 1972), p. 63.

9. U.S. Bureau of the Census, *Statistical Abstract of the United States* (Washington, D.C.: U.S. Government Printing Office, 1974), pp. 39, 461.

10. "Why Consumers Buy—or Hoard," *Business Week*, February 13, 1971, p. 54.

11. "Study Sees Only Small Shift in Consumer Buying," *Advertising Age*, May 12, 1975, p. 60; Zeltner, p. 41.

12. William D. Wells and George Gubar, "The Life Cycle Concept in Marketing Research," *Journal of Marketing Research* 3 (November 1966): 362.

13. Zeltner, p. 41; Lazer et al., p. 13.

14. Zeltner, p. 40.

15. This section is based largely on Joel Dean, "Competition—Inside and Out," *Harvard Business Review* 33 (November–December 1954): 68.

16. "The Battle of the Cash Registers," *Business Week*, April 10, 1971, p. 67.

17. Louis W. Stern and John R. Grabner, Jr., *Competition in the Marketplace* (Glenview, Ill.: Scott, Foresman, 1970), pp. 11–13.

18. Kotler, *Marketing Management*, 2d ed., p. 249.

19. This section is based largely on Stern and Grabner, pp. 33–46.

20. Richard L. Ottinger, "MaBellOpoly," *New York Times*, April 19, 1975, p. 31.

21. Jon G. Udell, "The Perceived Importance of the Elements of Strategy," *Journal of Marketing* 32 (January 1968): 35–36.

22. William Lazer, "Competition, Innovation and Marketing Management," in Lee E. Preston, ed., *Social Issues in Marketing* (Glenview, Ill.: Scott, Foresman, 1968), p. 133.

23. "What Finally Crippled the Cowles Empire," *Business Week*, September 25, 1971, p. 122.

24. Ronald G. Shafer, "Some of Consumerism's 'Good Guys,'" *Wall Street Journal*, December 5, 1972, p. 22.

25. "Bank Offers Help, but Not Money," *New York Times*, July 13, 1975, p. 13.

26. Wroe Alderson, *Dynamic Marketing Behavior: A Functionalist Theory of Marketing* (Homewood, Ill.: Irwin, 1965), p. 205.

27. Theodore Levitt, "Innovative Imitation," *Harvard Business Review* 44 (September–October 1966): 64.

28. Theodore Levitt, "Marketing Myopia," *Harvard Business Review* 53 (September–October 1975): 34, 44.

29. Levitt, "Innovative Imitation," pp. 63, 69.

30. "From Colonel Sanders to General Glickenhaus," *Business Week*, November 9, 1974, pp. 138–39.

31. Ronald R. Gist, *Marketing and Society* (Hinsdale, Ill.: Dryden Press, 1974), pp. 252–53.

32. Ibid., pp. 253–54.

33. Frank Rothman, "Intensive Competitive Marketing," *Journal of Marketing* 28 (July 1964): 14–17.

7

MARKET SEGMENTATION

After completing this chapter, the reader should be able to:

1. Explain the meaning and importance of market segmentation as a strategy of market analysis for consumer-oriented organizations.

2. Evaluate the different bases for segmenting markets—geographic, demographic, psychographic, and others.

3. Compare market segmentation to related types of strategies—product differentiation, market integration, market positioning, and market orchestration.

4. Distinguish among the alternative market targeting strategies—undifferentiated, differentiated, and concentrated.

5. Assess market segmentation as a tool in terms of management and social performance.

As we have already noted, all marketing efforts to be successful must be consumer oriented. The first step in establishing a consumer orientation is to determine just who the consumer is, what he or she wants, and how those wants can be fulfilled. Identifying the potential consumer will be the subject of this chapter.

BEYOND SUN AND SAND

United Press International

You might think that convincing people to vacation in the United States Virgin Islands would be the easiest job in the world. But the Virgin Islands must compete with hundreds of warm-weather resorts for vacation dollars. With a smaller marketing budget than other Caribbean islands, how can the Virgin Islands best lure consumers?

In planning its marketing strategy, their ad agency, Grey Advertising, made use of **market segmentation**.[1] The first thing that Grey did was to define the market itself by taking a survey of people who were in the habit of traveling during their vacations. The agency wanted to find out which travelers were most likely to be interested in an island trip. They found out such people tended to be better educated than other travelers, were more likely to be professionals with higher incomes, and generally lived in metropolitan areas.

Next, Grey wanted to know why these people were willing to spend the money for such a trip. The survey results showed that high on the list of reasons were "good weather" and "good beaches." In contrast, "good duty-free shopping" was low on the list. Yet duty-free shopping was what the people surveyed associated with the Virgin Islands. They were not aware that the Virgin Islands had the superior weather and beaches they were seeking.

Now that Grey knew who the most likely island travelers were, they could place their ads with the TV programs, magazines, and newspapers most likely to reach these people. And knowing what the travelers wanted, they could emphasize the Virgin Islands' wonderful weather and beaches.

MARKET SEGMENTS AND SEGMENTATION

The campaign to sell the Virgin Islands was successful because the advertisers first identified their **target market segment**. Once they knew who were the most likely tourists, they could devise the proper marketing strategy, or marketing mix, that would appeal to these people. Formally defined, "market segmentation is the subdividing of a market into homogeneous subsets of customers, where any subset may conceivably be selected as a market target to be reached with a distinct marketing mix."[2]

The basic premise of market segmentation is the identification of consumer needs. This consumer orientation makes marketing segmentation a vital part of the modern marketing process. One survey of marketing managers revealed that "problems in recognizing, defining, understanding, and segmenting markets" was the most important problem they had to deal with.[3] These managers felt that accurate identification of market targets was the basis of all successful marketing strategies. With the high cost of production, distribution, and promotion, accurate market segmentation has become increasingly important.

The process of market segmentation is illustrated in Figure 7-1. From this figure, we can see that it has three main parts: consumers, competitors, and capabilities. The process identifies many segments of consumers, offers one or a few of them a choice of products or services, and devises a strategy (or marketing mix) that will prove superior to that of the competition.

In Chapter 6, we discussed product differentiation, which creates a demand for an available product by using marketing strategy to distinguish it from the competition. Segmentation, on the other hand recognizes subgroups who already have certain demands and then creates products to suit those demands.[4] Differentiation and segmentation may be used at the same time, but usually the pendulum swings back and forth from one to the other as market conditions change.

Figure 7-1   MARKET SEGMENTATION IN THE MARKETING MODEL

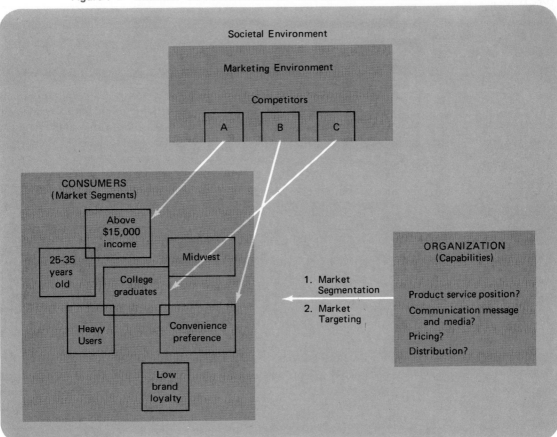

In this chapter, we will focus mainly on how segmentation is applied to consumer goods and services. Market segmentation, as it is used when the customers are organizations, will be covered in Chapter 10.

MARKET SEGMENTATION OVERVIEW

All companies, whether they are aware of it or not, have some sort of consumer model in mind when they plan a marketing strategy. The model may be researched and formal, or it may be based on casual observations. Generally, consumer models can be divided into three basic types.[5] The first model assumes that all consumers are *similar*, and that one product will satisfy everyone. The second assumes they are *different*, and that no one product will do. The third, more rational, model assumes that there are differences *and* similarities. In this case, the general consumer group is divided into smaller groups, or segments, with similar needs and wants. Marketing programs are then matched to each segment.

WHAT ARE THE ADVANTAGES OF SEGMENTING MARKETS?

Broadly speaking, market segmentation simply reflects reality. It recognizes that different consumers have different needs, which in turn influence market demand. Furthermore, analysis of these differences may reveal consumer needs that are not now being met. Filling these needs may result in profit and growth. Market segmentation offers the following specific advantages:

1. A segmentation perspective leads to a more precise definition of the market in terms of consumer needs. Segmentation thus improves management's understanding of the consumer and, more importantly, *why* he or she buys.

2. Management, once it understands consumer needs, is in a much better position to direct marketing programs that will satisfy these needs and hence will parallel the demands of the market. Systematic planning for future markets is thus encouraged.

3. A continuous program of market segmentation strengthens management's capabilities in meeting changing market demands.

4. Management is better able to assess competitive strengths and weaknesses. Of greatest importance, it can identify those segments where competition is thoroughly entrenched. This will save the company resources by foregoing a pitched battle with locked-in competition, where there is little real hope of market gain.

5. Segmentation leads to a more efficient allocation of marketing resources. For example, product and advertising appeals can be more easily coordinated. Media plans can be developed to minimize waste through excess exposure. This can result in a sharper brand image, and target consumers will recognize and distinguish products and promotional appeals directed at them.

6. Segmentation leads to a more precise setting of market objectives. Targets are defined operationally, and performance can later be evaluated against these standards. Segmentation analysis generates such critical questions as these: Should we add another brand? Should the advertising campaign be changed? Is the price still right?[6]

THE ROLE OF SEGMENTATION IN DETERMINING MARKETING STRATEGY

Segmentation is a deliberate, planned program. It improves products and profits in the six ways listed above. Sometimes, however, it has happened accidentally. A firm notices that a product appeals to a certain small segment and directs its marketing to this segment.

At times, however, a market may prove to be unsegmentable. That is the case when the needs of a large group of people are met by a single product. In such a situation, the large group cannot be separated into smaller target markets that will support a variety of offerings.

Although segmentation is a cornerstone of most marketing strategy, the opportunities it offers are not always fully recognized by organizations. Currently, there are two basic approaches to the segmentation process:[7]

1. *Market segmentation to marketing mix.* In this approach, the company assumes certain things about a segment, then prepares a marketing mix based on those assumptions. For example, certain things are known about the ever-growing singles population.[8] Compared to the rest of the population, singles tend to be more affluent, mobile, and self-concerned. They are oriented toward immediate enjoyment rather than long-term concerns and are clothes- and appearance-conscious. In general, they have active life styles and leisure pursuits. With this in mind, an auto manufacturer, for example, would appeal to this market by stressing sportiness and options such as stereo and tape decks.

2. *Marketing mix to market segmentation to revised marketing mix.* In this approach, the company already has a product. The buyers of that general type of product are studied to see if there are differences between buyers of the different product versions. From this information, the company decides which segment of customers will buy its product. On the basis of this information the marketer selects a target market and may revise the product and create new, related marketing strategy.

HOW ARE SEGMENTS SELECTED?

In order to evaluate the way segments are described, we should examine the four criteria by which they are selected. The better a **segment base** satisfies all four, the better it serves as a foundation for effective marketing strategy.

Measurability

The market characteristics on which the segment is based should be able to be measured. The population of a city, the over-65 age group, and college graduates are concrete measures. Some information is not easily measurable, however. For instance, it is often difficult to measure the status and quality a customer looks for in a product, while it is usually easier to know that a purchase was made because it was considered economical.

Size The segment has to be large enough to make the marketing effort worthwhile. There must be enough potential buyers with enough dollars to cover the costs of producing and marketing the product and to gain sufficient profits.

Reachability Reachability means that the segment must be accessible to the marketing efforts of the organization. Buyers must be exposed to the product through the media and the places where they do their shopping. Some segments have characteristics that are not suitable to this purpose. For instance, highly persuasible people—those who will buy easily—characteristically have low self-esteem. However, grouping by low self-esteem does not produce a unique segment that may be appealed to through a particular promotion or distribution strategy.

Market Responsiveness A clearly defined segment should react to changes in any of the elements of the marketing mix. For instance, if segments are determined by reaction to pricing, the potential customers interested in economy will buy less if a product's price is raised. But segments not interested in price will not react to a higher price.

BASES FOR MARKET SEGMENTATION

We can see by now that the concepts of segmentation are indeed useful in marketing. The key question, though, is which concepts are useful to the project at hand. Daniel Yankelovich warns that the first job of a marketing director "should be to muster all probable segmentation and *then* choose the most meaningful ones to work with."[9]

From Figure 7-2, we can see that there are two general approaches to iden-

Figure 7-2   APPROACHES TO MARKET SEGMENTATION

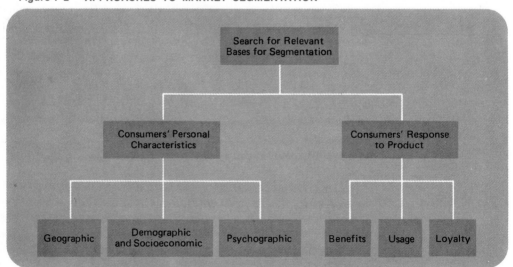

tifying market segments. These are to define segments by **consumer charac-teristics** or by **consumer response**. It is impossible to say that one is absolutely better than the other; the better one is the one that suits the particular market-ing situation. It is often necessary to use both approaches. In this way, the available information is both people-related (where they live, socioeconomic class, personality factors) and product-related (how consumers use and benefit from the product, their product loyalty).

While six different bases are examined, notice how in the analysis of seg-mentation data one base can lead to another. For example, a geographic base (the suburbs) may be spotted that leads to a demographic profile (ethnic groups). Or, based on demographics (age groups), psychographic information (attitude toward saving electricity) is generated.

CONSUMER CHARACTERISTICS APPROACH

The most commonly used bases for the consumer characteristics approach are geographic, demographic and socioeconomic, and psychographic. These bases describe consumers in terms of where they live, who they are, and how they think. We will consider them in the order in which they entered the segmenta-tion repertoire.

Geographic Characteristics

Grouping potential customers by **geographic** location is the oldest form of market segmentation. In the past, when communications and distribution methods were limited, a marketer would concentrate his efforts on a small area. Today, geographic segmentation involves, among other things, the use of local advertising media and the division of the sales force by territories. Rural and urban markets may also be divided and other territorial subdivisions may exist within larger geographic areas. Of course, consumers do not always stay where they are; geographic mobility is so high in the United States that it has become an important base for market segmentation.

It has been found that individuals who have undergone a recent long-distance move are above average in purchasing power and in potential pur-chasing power.[10] They are important customers for major household products and are subject to brand, store, and product switching after the move. These characteristics make these individuals important customers—important enough that marketers should consider them when making their marketing strategy decisions.

Demographic and Socioeconomic Characteristics

Demographic and **socioeconomic** segmentation includes such variables as age, sex, family size, income, occupation, education, family life cycle, religion, nationality, and social class. Demographic segmentation is the most popular of the consumer characteristics approaches.

The major value of demography seems to be in distinguishing users of a product from nonusers. The very existence of a certain age group, occupational category, or religious group may in itself guarantee at least a potential market for certain products.

Demographics has, for example, provided us with much information concerning those born in the post-World War II baby boom.[11] Now in their thirties, this group spends $600 to $1,200 on audio equipment. In contrast, those persons now 18 to 25 years old spend only $200 to $600 on such equipment. Marketers of audio equipment would be wise to direct their efforts at the war-baby group.

Although demography can help predict the likely purchasers of a product or service, it tells us nothing about which brand a buyer will choose. One manufacturer may make several brands, but he cannot predict by demography alone which brand will be most popular.

Social class has also been used to determine segmentation, with evidence that it has some bearing on store choice and life style.[12] Like demographics, social class seems to have little bearing on brand choice. In addition, the differences in social classes, as far as marketing is concerned, are probably decreasing with exposure to mass media.

Psychographic Characteristics

Grouping according to **psychographic** characteristics is the newest of the consumer characteristics approaches. Psychographic characteristics have been defined to include personality factors such as aggression, anxiety, masculinity and femininity; community involvement; leisure activities; nutrition or convenience orientation for foods; concern about germs; and safety values.[13]

As is the case with demographics, connections between personality traits and buying habits are not always clear. Even when personality makes a difference, it is difficult to know how this should affect marketing strategy. For instance, a study of housewives' personalities showed that certain groupings could be made according to existing differences (see Figure 7-3). Though personality differences would cause the housewife to buy a certain type of product, they did not cause her to choose one product brand over another.

Life-style analysis is an important part of psychographic studies. There are three basic relationships between life style and marketing data:

1. Two or three life-style segments account for 60 percent of the consumers using the brand. This is a very significant amount.

2. A number of segments have heavy users of the product, while a few segments do not.

3. There are different attitudes about the product among the groups, but not much difference in consumption patterns among them.[14]

All in all, psychographic or personality factors seem to be no more useful than demographic characteristics for market segmentation.

CONSUMER RESPONSE APPROACH

The consumer response approach concerns itself with differences in behavior. It is concerned with discovering why consumers buy a product, rather than describing the type of consumer who will buy. In order to do so it must investigate benefits response, usage response, and loyalty response as bases for segmentation.

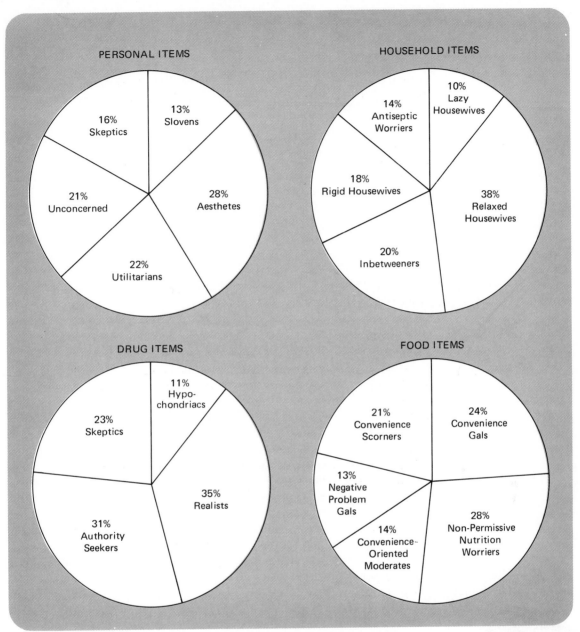

PERSONAL ITEMS

- 13% Slovens
- 16% Skeptics
- 21% Unconcerned
- 28% Aesthetes
- 22% Utilitarians

HOUSEHOLD ITEMS

- 14% Antiseptic Worriers
- 10% Lazy Housewives
- 18% Rigid Housewives
- 38% Relaxed Housewives
- 20% Inbetweeners

DRUG ITEMS

- 11% Hypo-chondriacs
- 23% Skeptics
- 35% Realists
- 31% Authority Seekers

FOOD ITEMS

- 21% Convenience Scorners
- 24% Convenience Gals
- 13% Negative Problem Gals
- 14% Convenience-Oriented Moderates
- 28% Non-Permissive Nutrition Worriers

Figure 7-3   SEGMENTATION FOR FOUR PRODUCT CLASSES

From Ruth Ziff, "Psychographics for Market Segmentation," *Journal of Advertising Research* 11 (April 1971): 6. Reprinted from the Journal of Advertising Research, by permission of the Journal of Advertising Research.

Benefits Response   In the **benefits response** approach, individuals are grouped according to the benefits they seek in a particular product. (Benefits may be defined as economy, durability, status, and so forth.) This form of segmentation is based on the assumption that people buy a product mainly for its benefits. Experience has shown that this is true.[15]

Table 7-1
TOOTHPASTE MARKET SEGMENT DESCRIPTION

	THE SENSORY SEGMENT	THE SOCIABLES	THE WORRIERS	THE INDEPENDENT SEGMENT
Principal benefit sought	Flavor, product appearance	Brightness of teeth	Decay prevention	Price
Demographic strengths	Children	Teens, young people	Large families	Men
Special behavioral characteristics	Users of spearmint-flavored toothpaste	Smokers	Heavy users	Heavy users
Brands disproportionately favored	Colgate, Stripe	Macleans, Plus White, Ultra Brite	Crest	Brands on sale
Personality characteristics	High self-involvement	High sociability	High hypochon-driasis	High autonomy
Life-style characteristics	Hedonistic	Active	Conservative	Value oriented

From Russell I. Haley, "Benefit Segmentation: A Decision-Oriented Research Tool," *Journal of Marketing,* 32 (July 1972): 33. Published by the American Marketing Association.

Once consumers have been segmented according to the benefits they seek, each segment can be analyzed in terms of demography, personality, and so forth. A better understanding of each segment can then be arrived at, and better marketing strategies can be designed.

Russell Haley has investigated the benefits people want from toothpaste (see Table 7-1).[16] From this research, he was able to segment the market according to certain personality characteristics. Such information would be invaluable in planning advertising and packaging.

A new benefits response has recently emerged.[17] If the researcher can identify that segment which is truly interested in ecology, the fact is useful in marketing. For instance, that buyer will be willing to give up super-clean clothes for a detergent that is less polluting.

It must not be assumed, however, that benefits response can always be related to demographic and psychographic segmentation. This possible lack of correlation should be considered before a costly research project is begun.

Usage Response Another form of the consumer response approach is **usage response,** or segmentation according to volume. In this approach, buyers of a product are classified as heavy, medium, light, and nonusers. Then, as with benefits response, the marketer tries to determine if there are any demographic or psychographic differences in the groups. Of course, the marketer is more interested in heavy users, because they buy four to ten times as much as light product users.

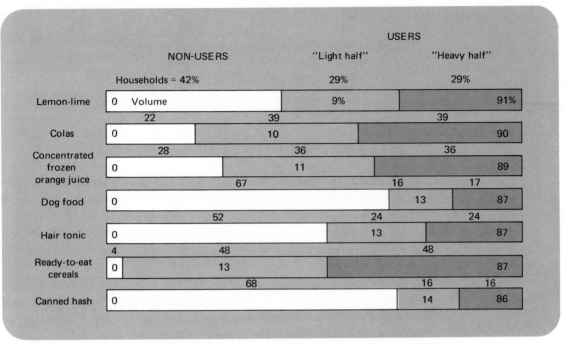

Figure 7-4   **ANNUAL PURCHASE CONCENTRATION IN SEVEN PRODUCT CATEGORIES**

Source: *Chicago Tribune Consumer Panel,* special analyses of 1962 data. Adapted from Dik Warren Twedt, "How Important to Marketing Strategy Is the 'Heavy User'?" *Journal of Marketing* 28 (January 1964): 72. Published by American Marketing Association.

From a study of nonusers, light users, and heavy users, Figure 7-4 summarizes the results of seven product categories. You can see that the number of heavy users may be small, but the proportion of the product they consume is very large.

Usage response alone, like other categories, does not give us all the marketing information we need. For instance, all heavy users do not buy the same brand, and they will not all respond to the same kind of advertising.

Loyalty Response The final consumer response approach we will consider is **loyalty response**. For instance, a consumer may rent cars only from Avis or purchase all major appliances from Sears, Roebuck.

Every marketer has hard-core loyals, soft-core loyals, and switchers.[18] The hard-core loyals are not necessarily heavy users, though. The marketers would be wise to find out what distinguishing characteristics the hard-core loyals have so that more of them may be acquired.

Brand loyalty is not always easy to measure. A buyer may appear to be a hard-core loyal, while the real reason for loyalty is that there are no other acceptable brands available. Or those that seem to be switchers may have been forced to switch because their store changed brands.

MARKET SEGMENTATION ANALYSIS We have seen that there are limitations to each of the segmentation bases discussed above. Therefore, the best approach in planning a successful marketing campaign seems to be to take a broader perspective. A research study must be concerned, of course, with all the implications segmentation has for marketing strategies. Therefore, a sequence of several measures and methods should be undertaken to make segmentation more useful to marketing.

How does the researcher improve the analysis for selecting a market segment and relating it to marketing strategy? Three steps will help ensure that the proper measures are taken:

1. Start with a small sample of consumers to explore possible segment characteristics.

2. Proceed carefully with other, larger samples, involving management at each stage. But warn management that these first findings are not conclusive and that no findings are to be accepted yet.

3. Use several measures to collect data regarding different potential segmentation bases. Do not make preconceived assumptions as to which segments will be most valuable in the end.[19]

Following these guidelines will yield certain advantages. Individual segmentation approaches have limitations, but the use of several methods can produce a more objective picture of the market. Management is given time to take needed action between each phase. Other parts of the organizaton will provide experts who may be able to offer advice in their special areas—R&D, production, and finance. However, if other members of management are involved in each step, they will be better able to understand the data and their implications.

THE CONTRIBUTION OF USAGE RESPONSE

The National Foundation of the March of Dimes is well known for its annual fund-raising drive. The concepts of marketing had not been used in identifying its donors (or, in our terms, heavy users), although there had been contacts with business and industry, a mother's march, and special teenage and school programs.

It was known that the "heavy user" concept was widely accepted in marketing practices. This led to the thought that maybe the concept could be used for fund raising. It was felt that the best general segment of donors was parents, who make up 48.5 percent of the population. A more realistic estimate was that 31.4 percent of the population comprised the prime campaign target (young married with no children, married with youngest child under six, married with child six and over).

Other evidence that segmentation might help was obtained from direct-mail contributions. They showed that certain geographic sections contribute more heavily than others.

It therefore seemed very probable that segmentation of the heavy users or donors, rather than merely aiming the campaign at the entire population, would be a huge advantage in planning a successful March of Dimes.

Based on William A. Mindak and H. Malcolm Bybee, "Marketing's Application to Fund Raising," *Journal of Marketing* 35 (July 1971): 14–15.

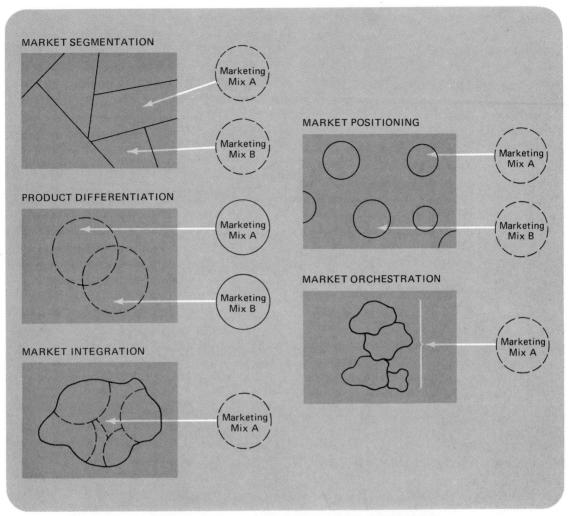

Figure 7-5 MARKET SEGMENTATION AND RELATED APPROACHES

SEGMENTATION-RELATED STRATEGIES

While market segmentation is the cornerstone of much of marketing strategy, there are also other strategic approaches closely related to segmentation. These approaches are product differentiation, market positioning, market integration, and market orchestration (shown in Figure 7-5).

PRODUCT DIFFERENTIATION

In **product differentiation,** a marketer promotes the real or supposed difference between his product and the competition. Advertising, packaging, and selling location are crucial in establishing these differences in the buyer's mind. By contrast, market segmentation recognizes the diversity of consumer demands in the market, and the product is adapted to these demands. This approach depends on the existence of a real difference or uniqueness in the product.

161

A strategy selection chart, such as that illustrated in Figure 7-6, helps a marketer determine whether his product is best suited for differentiation, segmentation, or both.[20] In Figure 7-6, the Xs represent rocking chairs, the Os, flyswatters. Each product is evaluated in terms of six key factors. Most Xs fall in the range of segmentation, while most Os are in the range of differentiation. Therefore, the manufacturers of rocking chairs should favor a segmentation approach, while the flyswatters would do best with differentiation.

Although differentiation and segmentation may seem to be contrary approaches, both may be used at the same time. For instance, if segmentation is used to market a certain product, the subsegments may become so small that the marketer needs something unique to make his product more desirable than a similar product. A little imagination can go a long way in making a packaging or advertising message or selling technique with a different twist that will appeal to the buyers.

Figure 7-6
STRATEGY SELECTION CHART

From R. William Kotrba, "The Strategy Selection Chart," *Journal of Marketing* 30 (July 1966): 25. Published by the American Marketing Association.

APPLY PRODUCT DIFFERENTIATION Strategy emphasis should be on promoting product differences	STRATEGY SELECTION FACTORS	APPLY MARKET SEGMENTATION Strategy emphasis should be on satisfying market variations
MARKET FACTORS		
Narrow	**Size of Market** — O at 3, X at 6 (scale 1–10)	Broad
High	**Consumer Sensitivity to Product Differences** — O at 4, X at 5 (scale 1–10)	Low
PRODUCT FACTORS		
Introduction Stage	**Product Life Cycle** — O at 6, X at 8 (scale 1–10)	Saturation Stage
Commodity	**Type of Product** — O at 3, X at 8 (scale 1–10)	Distinct Item
COMPETITIVE FACTORS		
Few	**Number of Competitors** — X at 5, O at 6 (scale 1–10)	Many
Differentiation Policy	**Typical Competitor Strategies** — O at 1, X at 8 (scale 1–10)	Segmentation Policy

MARKET **Market positioning** is a strategy through which an organization studies the
POSITIONING market to find a segment that is under-served by other firms. A product or service is then created for that segment.[21] Also, marketing strategy is the base of
the product's market position—especially promotion, distribution, and pricing. These elements may be modified even when no change is made in the
actual product. Market positioning may be narrowly referred to as "product
positioning" (see Figure 7-2). This strategy can be used for products, for institutions such as hospitals, or even for political candidates.

One cruise line used market positioning to increase its sales. Instead of
advertising its cruises as a special form of transportation, it offered trips for
special-interest groups, such as gourmets, classical music buffs, singles, and
even nudists.[22] Thus, special-interest segments were appealed to with special-
interest services.

An extension of positioning is repositioning an already existing product.
For example, Du Pont introduced Teflon-coated cookware with the message
that cooking fats would no longer be needed, reducing cholesterol levels.
This message created only moderate demand, so Teflon was repositioned by
using the message that it made pots and pans easier to clean. Sales skyrocketed
as a result.

MARKET Market integration is the converse of market segmentation. Where market
INTEGRATION segmentation seeks to satisfy the diverse wants of today's relatively affluent
buyers, market integration seeks to broaden the market so that a product can
compete over a wider market.[23] To achieve market integration, research seeks
consumer characteristics that are basic to widely different market groups. For
example, the need for a high-nutrition snack may be found among teenagers,
busy executives, and the active elderly. A snack food might be designed to
appeal to the on-the-go, energy-pickup dimension of these different demo-
graphic/life-style segments. This contrasts with the segmentation approach of
creating a special snack formula and marketing strategy for each of the three
segments.

Market integration may become even more important with the recent
shift in the economic situation of many Americans. Marketers should keep in
mind that people may be more willing to trade some particular demand of
theirs for a savings.

MARKET If an organization wants to deliver the same product or service to more than one
ORCHESTRATION segment, it is faced with the problem of **market orchestration**.[24] It must first
decide which market segments are to be included. Then it must decide which
parts of those segments it will serve (the target market range). Orchestration is
easier if the market segments are compatible with each other. Finally, the
organization must decide which percentage of the segment is to be included
in the target market range.

This is a particularly delicate problem for organizations whose customers
are actually face-to-face with each other, as, for example, with department
stores, restaurants, and universities. Certain hotels do not want disruptive in-

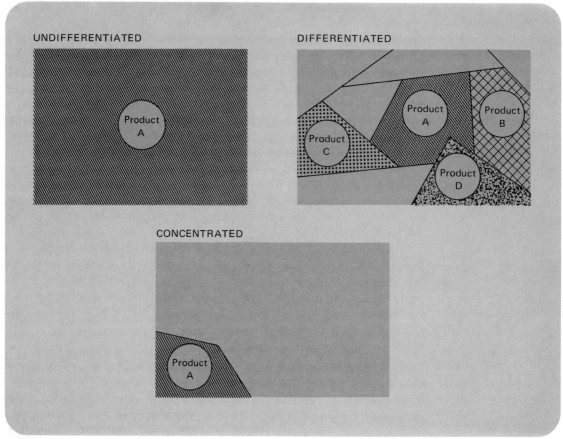

Figure 7-7
ALTERNATIVE MARKET
SEGMENTATION STRA-
TEGIES

dividuals for customers. High prices, signs, and turning them away often help demarket these customers. For instance, a fancy, high-priced restaurant may have a sign saying "Jacket and tie required by gentlemen." When a barefoot person in a tank shirt walks in, the management will ask the customer to leave. (That person has been demarketed.)

MARKET TARGETING STRATEGIES

As the earliest sellers learned, customers are very different, which means they can always be segmented. A company can plan its marketing around these differences or it can ignore them. Three strategies can be used to select the market target(s) from among the market segments, as illustrated in Figure 7-7:[25]

1. *undifferentiated* marketing, in which one marketing mix is used for the entire market;

2. *differentiated* marketing, with a different marketing mix for each segment;

3. *concentrated* marketing, putting all marketing efforts into one or a few segments.

UNDIFFERENTIATED
STRATEGY

Undifferentiated strategy treats the market as one target, focusing on how the customers' needs are alike rather than how they are different. Its product has the broadest possible appeal and uses mass advertising. For example, Coca-Cola for years used the same bottle, the same flavor, and the same slogan ("The Pause That Refreshes") all over the world. This strategy saves money by minimizing production, inventory, transportation, and marketing research costs.

However, this kind of strategy may result in hypercompetition. That is, several firms in an industry try to serve the same large segment, while neglecting the smaller segments. In past years, for example, all American cars were large, and the competition was fierce. Those wanting smaller cars bought from foreign manufacturers. Now, of course, many people are interested in economy because of rising fuel prices, so that the market is crowded with look-alike small cars from every manufacturer.

This heavy competition may make the large segment less profitable. This is called majority fallacy—the largest market segment makes the best business sense.[26] This may be true in the short run; but over the long run, market opportunities for specific segments make the undifferentiated target market vulnerable.

DIFFERENTIATED
STRATEGY

Using a **differentiated** strategy, an organization aims at all or many market segments, with different products or programs for each segment. In this way, the company hopes to achieve higher sales and greater customer identifications with the company. It also hopes for increased customer loyalty and the resulting repeat purchases. For example, Coca-Cola now comes in cans and bottles of varying sizes to suit the needs of the customer. It occasionally changes its advertising slogans and also makes a diet drink, Tab. When it was first marketed, Tab was strongly identified with Coca-Cola so that those loyal to "Coke" would try it.

Differentiated marketing usually results in higher sales than undifferentiated marketing. But it lacks one advantage of undifferentiated marketing—low production and marketing costs. For this reason, differentiated marketing can be profitable only if the resulting sales increase is greater than the cost increase. Because this often happens, many companies have adopted a differentiated strategy.

CONCENTRATED
STRATEGY

Concentrated strategy aims for one or a small number of segments, rather than all or most segments, as with differentiated and undifferentiated strategies. There are several advantages of concentration: the company knows and can serve its market better; costs are saved because there are large runs of fewer products; advertising and distribution have more impact.

A good example of the use of concentrated strategy is the case of Fisher-Price Toys.[27] Where other toy companies aim for more segments by producing games, toys, hobbies, and recreational equipment for many age groups, Fisher-Price has stuck with toys for preschoolers only. Advertising is aimed only at young mothers, rather than children, with an image of making safe, scientific

Most mass transit systems are designed to provide service for one large segment of the population. A differentiated strategy for marketing mass transit could create more users from smaller segments. The main competition of mass transit is the private automobile, so ways must be found to make mass transit more attractive than a car.

A typical segmenting of a city population would show that there are five big potential customer groups. These are manager/professional, clerical, inner city, elderly, and suburban housewife.

The manager/professional group, which often comes from the suburbs, could be offered service during peak hours at a fixed price. The benefits over an automobile would be speed and the opportunity to work while in transit. The clerical group would be interested in the same services, with emphasis on cost-saving—no maintenance, no parking fees for cars.

Inner-city residents should be offered access to several employment destinations away from the inner city, and a reduced fare, since they have a lower income.

The elderly and the suburban housewife should be offered special destinations. For example, clinics and business sections would be served for the elderly, and shopping areas for the housewife. Small vans and buses could accomplish this well.

Based on Norman Kangun and William A. Staples, "Selling Urban Transit," *Business Horizons* 18 (February 1975): 62–66.

toys. This concentrated marketing strategy has led them to enormous success, greater than many of the toy companies that differentiated.

But there are some risks involved in concentration. Because the company is serving a smaller market with a smaller number of products, it faces the possibility of a changing demand as well as the competition of other companies. The Volkswagen "beetle" finally lost its niche when other foreign cars became established in the small-car field. Because of these risks, profits can dip suddenly after a great soaring. This is less likely to happen when the company goes after a greater portion of the market.

SELECTING
A STRATEGY

Sometimes it is obvious that an organization must go with a particular market targeting strategy: differentiated, undifferentiated, or concentrated. Sometimes, however, there is a choice. Generally, five factors determine that choice: company resources, product homogeneity, product stage in the life cycle, market homogeneity, and competitive marketing strategies.[28] All of these should be considered before a marketing strategy is chosen.

Available company resources affect an organization's ability to purchase a certain strategy. Large financial and marketing resources are needed to follow undifferentiated and differentiated strategies. Limited resources make the concentrated strategy a more logical choice.

Product homogeneity refers to the degree to which a product is likely to retain the same characteristics. Fruit and natural gas, for instance, are not likely to change, while clothing and automobiles are subject to change more often. An undifferentiated strategy would be better for fruit, and differentiation or concentration would be better for changeables.

Product stage in the life cycle also affects strategy (see Chapter 11). If a new product is being manufactured, undifferentiated or concentrated marketing will best help to create a demand for it. But when the product is at a mature stage of its life cycle and has saturated the market, it is time for differentiation.

Market homogeneity refers to the degree to which consumers have the same needs and wants. If all are alike, segmentation would be a waste of time and the undifferentiated strategy would be best. Where consumers have more diverse needs, differentiation or concentration are best.

Competitive marketing strategies are those being used by the competition. If the competition is serving several segments, a company would be foolish to practice undifferentiated marketing. But if the competitor is serving a mass market, the company might profit by segmentation.

EVALUATION OF MARKET SEGMENTATION

Two types of controversies surround the concept of market segmentation. These controversies concern its use as a management tool and its social implications.

SEGMENTATION AS A MANAGEMENT TOOL

After segmentation became a popular instrument for marketing, it began to cause some grumblings among marketers who felt that it wasn't all it was cracked up to be. They maintained that segmentation had been oversold. In 1974, Joel P. Baumwoll interviewed 25 key research people to see just how successful segmentation had been.[29] The conclusion was that while the researchers were successful, the studies they conducted were often less successful. Baumwoll reminded firms that segmentation is basically a marketing strategy; research is only part of it. Furthermore, segmentation can succeed only when a marketing mix is developed to satisfy the potential customers.

Sometimes segmentation is not used properly. There are three ways in which segmentation may be misapplied:[30]

1. *Pursuing the wrong segment.* If a product is successful with a certain segment, promoting it to another segment may not work. It may be best to promote another brand to the other segment. Also, a low-growth economy offers fewer positioning opportunities as conditions blur and combine formerly distinct market segments.[31]

2. *Oversegmentation.* This occurs when a product is too specialized. For instance, some deodorants were aimed at women and others were aimed at men. But both sexes were using the same deodorants; the product had been oversegmented according to sex. As a result, the "family" deodorant concept was born.

3. *Overconcentration.* Sometimes a company concentrates so much on one segment that it neglects another segment that could be profitable. For instance, beer has been promoted as a young man's drink and the industry has lost many older beer drinkers.

In managing the market segmentation strategy, three major problems may arise:[32]

1. *Improper perspective regarding its use.* Marketers may not want to use segmentation because they do not realize its value. No product in the world can appeal to everyone. Marketers must realize that a certain product attracts a certain person and that promotion can heighten this effect. But the marketer must have realistic expectations about what segmentation can and cannot do.

2. *Inadequate planning and implementation.* If the proper up-front planning does not take place before a research project begins, and if the proper method of marketing strategy is not chosen, segmentation cannot possibly be implemented successfully.

3. *Incomplete follow-through.* After the research study, the researcher should have a hand in the marketing strategies that develop from the research. Otherwise, unwarranted interpretations of the data will lead to inappropriate strategies.

SOCIAL IMPLICATIONS

In theory, a situation in which all organizations effectively practiced market segmentation would result in the whole range of consumer needs and wants being satisfied. Important needs and wants would create profit opportunities or lead to publicly sponsored programs. However, segmentation doesn't quite work that way. There are frequent consumer accusations that certain segments are missed by marketers. In other words, they feel they have a legitimate desire for some product that does not exist. For instance, some consumers complain that a simple one- or two-speed blender is not available. They feel that the available blenders, with several speeds and a higher price, are being forced on them. It is doubtful that the blender manufacturers are being immoral or unethical, because most consumers do want more complex blenders. However, it may take time for market segmentation to convince blender manufacturers that a market does exist for the simpler, lower priced model.[33]

While this example does not represent a serious social flaw, the absence of adequate numbers of supermarkets in ghetto areas, as discussed in Chapter 4, does contribute to a social problem. Though this absence can be "cost justified" by firms, another view is that they should take a risk and accept greater social responsibility. This is also true when there is not an adequate "ecology alternative" for certain products that might pollute or create excessive litter. Thus the market invites more government initiative to correct these situations.

There are other accusations that marketers exploit the individual in a target market. A marketer aggressively trying to take a part of the market from a competitor may raise his prices. The consumer must be made to believe that the price difference is worth paying because of the product's value. Of course, a higher price is often justified because the product may work better, be made from better materials, or cost more to produce. But it may be unethical to increase price because a consumer segment thinks the product is better. This policy either promotes inflation or takes advantage of a vulnerable group of consumers. An example of such a questionable practice is selling high-priced investment land to the elderly, who may eventually discover that the land is far from being a paradise. Also, higher costs are created when a firm segments the entire population or makes as many segments as possible (as was analyzed in our discussion of differentiated strategy). Finally, oversegmentation uses more natural resources than necessary by creating more products than really may be needed. Such resources could otherwise be put to more productive uses.

CONCLUSION

We have seen that market segmentation is a foundation for market analysis in consumer-oriented organizations. In the following chapters we will examine consumer behavior and its implications for marketing strategy. As we examine the behavorial dynamics of individuals, households, and organizations, we should think of segmentation as an important goal of any knowledge that we uncover about consumer behavior. What you have learned about market segmentation also provides a foundation for the planning of the marketing mix, a procedure that will be the subject of the major part of this book.

DISCUSSION QUESTIONS

1. Gillette dominates the men's blade and razor market. What types of market segments might you consider capturing to win some of Gillette's huge market share? Given the much smaller budgets your firm has to support marketing efforts, what marketing mixes might be appropriate for these segments?

2. A marketing expert once remarked, "*Youth* needs a new definition. The 1970s promise to be the decade when youth becomes a state of mind and overflows all traditional age boundaries." How would you redefine the youth market in terms of these segmentation characteristics—geographic, psychographic, benefit, usage, and loyalty?

3. Show how each of these strategies relates to market segmentation for the product specified:
   a. product differentiation for a merchandise catalogue;
   b. market integration for bottled spring water;
   c. market positioning for a funeral home;
   d. market orchestration for a savings bank.

4. You are advising a manufacturer of leisure activity equipment who has the capability to market these product lines: equipment for skiing, bowling, golf, scuba diving, tennis, camping, and hunting. Compose a plan that outlines the segmentation strategies of undifferentiated, differentiated, and concentration marketing.

5. It has been said that market segmentation is one of the greatest market research techniques developed since marketing began. Why then are many marketing strategies that are based on it less than successful? What recommendations would you have for a movie maker who is using market segmentation for the first time?

6. Explain why you agree or disagree with the following statement: "As far as market segmentation works, it is fine for groups of consumers. But I'm not so sure that it is responsive to the best interests of society."

NOTES

1. Grey Advertising Inc., *Grey Matter* 46 (April 1975): 3–4.
2. Philip Kotler, *Marketing Management: Analysis, Planning, and Control,* 2d ed. (Englewood Cliffs, N.J.: Prentice-Hall, 1972), p. 166.
3. Charles N. Waldo, "What's Bothering Marketing Chiefs Most? Segmenting," *Advertising Age,* June 4, 1973, p. 77.
4. Wendell R. Smith, "Product Differentiation and Market Segmentation as Alternative Marketing Strategies," *Journal of Marketing* 21 (July 1956): 5.
5. James F. Engel, Harry F. Fiorillo, and Murray A. Cayley, *Market Segmentation: Concepts and Applications* (New York: Holt, Rinehart and Winston, 1972), p. 4.
6. Ibid, pp. 2–3.
7. John C. Bieda and Harold H. Kassarjian, "An Overview of Market Segmentation," *June 1969 Conference Proceedings* (Chicago: American Marketing Association, 1970), p. 249.
8. Grey Advertising Inc., *Grey Matter* 45 (January 1974): 3–4.
9. Daniel Yankelovich, "New Criteria for Market Segmentation," *Harvard Business Review* 42 (March-April 1964): 84.
10. Alan R. Andreasen, "Geographic Mobility and Market Segmentation," *Journal of Marketing Research* 3 (November 1966): 347.
11. Jim McCullough, "Grown-up Youth Market Returning to Hi-fi Dealers with Lots of Money," *Merchandising Week,* November 30, 1974, p. 1.
12. Bieda and Kassarjian, p. 251.
13. Ruth Ziff, "Psychographics for Market Segmentation," *Journal of Advertising Research* 11 (April 1971): 3.
14. Joseph T. Plummer, "The Concept and Application of Life Style Segmentation," *Journal of Marketing* 38 (January 1974): 35.
15. Russell I. Haley, "Benefit Segmentation: A Decision-Oriented Research Tool," *Journal of Marketing* 32 (July 1968): 31.
16. Ibid., p. 32.
17. Kotler, 2d ed., p. 175.
18. Ibid., p. 177.
19. T. P. Hustad, C. S. Mayer, and T. W. Whipple, "Segmentation Research Works If . . .," *1974 Combined Proceedings* (Chicago: American Marketing Association, 1975), p. 23.
20. R. William Kotrba, "The Strategy Selection Chart," *Journal of Marketing* 30 (July 1966): 24–25.
21. Philip Kotler, *Marketing for Nonprofit Organizations* (Englewood Cliffs, N.J.: Prentice-Hall, 1975), p. 110.
22. *Grey Matter* 46, p. 4.
23. Alvin C. Achenbaum, "To Do Is Not Necessarily to Know," *1974 Combined Proceedings* (Chicago: American Marketing Association, 1975), p. 12.
24. Kotler, *Nonprofit Organizations,* pp. 114, 119–20.
25. Kotler, *Marketing Management,* 2d ed., p. 182.
26. Alfred A. Kuehn and Ralph L. Day, "Strategy of Product Quality," *Harvard Business Review* 40 (November–December 1962): 102.
27. "How Fisher-Price Sells All Those Toys," *Business Week,* March 3, 1973, pp. 40–41.
28. Kotrba, pp. 22–25.
29. Joel P. Baumwoll, "Segmentation Research— The Baker vs. The Cookie Maker," *1974 Combined Proceedings* (Chicago: American Marketing Association, 1975), p. 15.
30. Lee Adler, "A New Orientation for Plotting Marketing Strategy," *Business Horizons* 7 (Winter 1964): 43.
31. "Conference Board Exec Urges Aggressive Moves to Boost Market Shares," *Advertising Age,* May 19, 1975, p. 4.
32. Fred Posner, "Let's Put the Bloom Back into the Segmentation Rose," *Marketing Review* 30 (December 1974): 10–11.
33. Engel et al., p. 460.

CASE STUDIES

DRAMBOL-TRIVETT COMPANY

Company Background
Drambol-Trivett, based in Dallas, Texas, entered the advanced-technology electronics industry in 1949 as a maker of scientific instruments. Drambol was the innovator; Trivett was the businessman. The company was an immediate success, primarily because it concentrated on developing products so sophisticated that they could command a premium price. Over the years the company used its position of leadership in scientific instruments to diversify into other electronic products. In 1974, Drambol-Trivett brought in Roger Whitney, a marketing consultant, to help them plan for the coming year.

"We built this company's reputation by trying to be best and by trying to be first," said Drambol. "When we got started we turned out several new products each year. Every one of them was so advanced that it had no competition for a couple of years."

"That gave us plenty of time to recover our investment in research and development before we had to worry about price cutting," said Trivett.

"But," added Drambol, "this business isn't as simple as it used to be. Products now use exotic semiconductors and sophisticated computer programs. You have to spend heavily on R&D to keep up."

"There are a lot more companies today that know how to manage technological change," sighed Trivett, "and that have been willing to spend on R&D. Even if a company doesn't innovate, it can duplicate. That long lead time for the innovator no longer exists. New products may have only a few months before a competing product hits the market. Moreover, companies have broadened their product lines. Instead of being complementary specialists, they are now competitors. And, as Howard mentioned, a lot of that competition is based on price."

Present Situation
At this point Roger Whitney interrupted the dialogue. "I'm beginning to get a feel for the nature of the industry. Can you tell me something about what the situation in the company is now and why you called me in?"

The chairman responded, "Only recently have we begun to see the financial problems this growth has created. As sales grew, our inventories grew even faster, in anticipation of a continued boom. Accounts receivable have been growing too. Unfortunately, we have not been able to finance this growth out of profits, because of price cuts. So now we have had to borrow from the banks, and I can see the need for more short-term debt by the end of this year. It could go as high as $12 million. We may have to consider long-term debt. Either way, the interest charges are going to be high."

"We've had some failures in technology too," declared Drambol. "In the rush to cash in on the economic boom and boost sales, we've tried to enter new markets with products that were not fully developed or with prices that were based on manufacturing improvements that we were never able to achieve. Some of those troubles have been caused by the large number of new employees we've taken on."

171

Whitney again interrupted the conversation to ask whether there had been any successes to balance the problems brought on during the last two years.

"Sure," replied Drambol. "Just this year we introduced an oscilloscope that we think is better than anything else on the market right now. [Note: An oscilloscope is an instrument used to visualize electronic signals on a cathode ray tube.] Our scope uses a semiconductor 'computer-on-a-chip,' which enables it to provide data that formerly required additional instruments."

"I hope you can see the dilemma we're in," said Trivett. "Products at the low end of the price range and me-too products that are price competitive build market share, but they don't contribute much to profits. Without those profits we can't afford the R&D necessary to turn out the new products we'll need when the coming recession is over. Besides, research is what gives Howard his thrills."

"You two have given me a pretty good overview of how the company operates. Enough to get started, at least." Whitney concluded, "I'll probably want to look at your financial records and talk to some of your product managers as I work. I should have some preliminary plans ready in the next week or two."

Questions
1. Prepare a short-run marketing plan for Drambol-Trivett that includes the situation analysis, marketing objectives, and strategy and action program.
2. Do the same for the long-run period of five years.

REED PRODUCTS COMPANY

"Well, I can't understand why you are so determined to change it, Mo," argued Ted Balkowski, Jr., as he stood in Maureen Jones Kovacs's office one afternoon in 1975. "I think you're just being stubborn." Balkowski and Kovacs were members of the Reed Products Company account team at the advertising firm of CC&R (Chicago), and they were discussing the possibility of a change in the company's slogan.

Changes in the marketplace and in Reed Products itself prompted the discussion, which was centered on the company's long-used slogan "We are in business for your baby." Mr. Balkowski and Ms. Kovacs were on opposite sides of the issue, Mr. Balkowski feeling strongly that it would be a mistake to drop the slogan.

End of the Baby Boom
Reed Products was founded by Ralph C. Reed in 1936 to market strained fruits for babies. By 1975 the Lincoln, Nebraska, company was the leader in the business, with 210 varieties of food for infants, "juniors," and toddlers in its line. Company sales went up every year until 1973, when they slipped 3 percent; they rose slightly in 1974 to $246 million.

Reed's competitors in the 1960s were Babytime, Weiler, and Phillips. All of these companies had had financial problems in the early 1970s. The post-World War II baby boom peaked in 1962, when there were 4.3 million births. By 1973, the figure had dropped to 3.1 million.

When the impact of the shrinking market size was felt, Babytime and Weiler cut prices to keep volume high enough to maintain distribution for their brands. At that time (1969) Reed had a 57 percent share of the market, Babytime and Weiler split 32 percent, Phillips 5 percent, and the remainder was private label. Reed decided it could live with a 1¢-per-jar price differential as long as it put extra money into coupons and trade merchandising. When the spread, however, got as high as 3¢ or 4¢ on each jar in some large cities, Reed's total market share dropped to 52 percent. When that happened the company retaliated, lowering its prices to within 1¢ or 1½¢ of the competition.

Then the federal government imposed price controls, and all three companies got caught with discount-level prices. The companies ended the price war in 1973 after the controls were lifted. As a result of that war, however, Phillips got out of the baby-food business completely and Universal Corp. sold its Babytime division. In terms of market share, Reed ended up with about 63 percent.

The Current Controversy

The argument between Ms. Kovacs and Mr. Balkowski centered on the appropriateness of "We are in business for your baby" for a company that was trying to appeal to the adult market.

KOVACS: The whole thing has to go. We will never be able to penetrate the adult market effectively as long as the name Reed conjures up the image of that chubby-cheeked cherub. We need something new that just connotes good things to eat, or a name you can trust.

BALKOWSKI: Listen Reed has tried to crack the adult market, and it hasn't worked. The "Enjoy Reed Again" campaign that we tested in four cities didn't generate much action. I don't think it is possible to sell baby food as a dessert or snack to adults.

KOVACS: Well, Ted, that's your opinion. I think we can. Besides, that's not the real problem. The real problem is that the company shouldn't be so dependent on one product. We need new food products—single-serving foods for adults, peanut butter, catsup.

BALKOWSKI: Reed will be up against some tough competition with ideas like those. Skippy, Peter Pan, and Jif spent nearly $10 million advertising peanut butter last year. With catsup, it would run into Heinz, Hunt-Wesson, and Del Monte. I'd much rather stick with what Reed knows best. Babies *are* its specialty, and that market is where the name Reed really means something. It would be better to concentrate on developing new baby products that meet the needs of today's families.

KOVACS: There you are—back with the same old slogan and baby face.

BALKOWSKI: That's right, Mo. I don't want to throw away something that represents 85 percent of the sales and even more of the profits.

KOVACS: But those sales will drop right along with the birthrate.

BALKOWSKI: That's where you and I disagree.

Questions

1. What demand factors are contracting the baby products market?
2. What should Reed do about it in terms of future market analysis and marketing strategy planning?

YOUR HOME IMPROVEMENTS CENTER

Do-It-Yourself Surge

As the owners of Your Home Improvements Center, the only full-fledged home improvement store in Santa Ana, California, Paul and Judy Paulson were in a perfect position to take advantage of the growth in the do-it-yourself market in the mid-1970s. Many retailers attributed this growth to consumer concern about the energy crisis and to inflation. In order to conserve on heating fuels, home owners were adding insulation, storm windows, and carpeting to their houses. Families that curtailed their automobile vacation plans because of the gasoline shortage were adding pools and patios so that they could enjoy a vacation at home.

Still others were making their own home improvements because of tight money and high mortgage rates. Rather than moving to a bigger or newer house, these people were modernizing kitchens or bathrooms, finishing basement playrooms, or adding a whole new room or wing. As labor rates soared, home owners were tackling many of these projects themselves. A trade magazine provided a profile of the typical customer:

> *He's 35 years old and makes around $15,000 a year. He has the skill to perform his own work. We're giving him an opportunity to be proud of his personal achievement, to prove his masculinity. In today's world, a man has a hard time proving his masculinity, but not in a home improvement store. When he buys something here and takes it home, he shows that he's the head of the family. We're selling masculine pride and feminine fulfillment.*

While the Paulsons agreed with the part of the industry report that claimed that the customers had the skills needed to do the work, they also knew that many customers needed help with their projects. Both the Paulsons and their sales help were very knowledgeable about most phases of home improvement work, and they also stocked booklets and other printed information.

Competition

The total construction and building materials supply business was one of the largest industries in America, second only to food in dollar sales. As such, it attracted the attention of a number of retailers who were interested in participating in industry growth. Thus, after nearly a decade of having an exclusive on the do-it-yourself market, Your Home Improvements Center was suddenly faced with competition from two large chain operations that would offer discount prices and to utilize aggressive merchandising techniques and computerized inventory control systems.

While the Paulsons knew that they could not match these methods, they believed that they could develop a marketing strategy that would enable them to stay in business. They thought they could identify some distinct customer groups that would remain loyal to Your Home Improvements Center in spite of the new competition and find a way to appeal to them.

Questions

1. What bases for market segmentation can you identify for Your Home Improvements Center?
2. What market segmentation strategy would you propose?

Buying Behavior

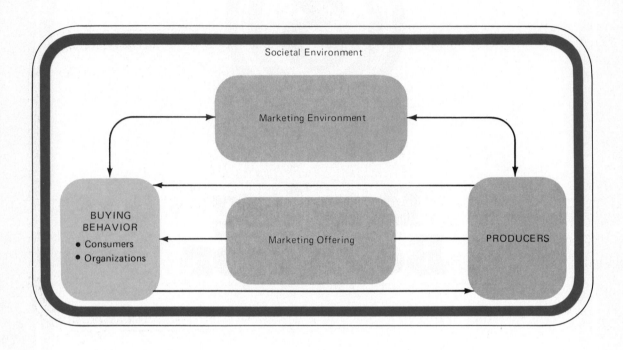

8

DYNAMICS OF CONSUMER BEHAVIOR

After completing this chapter, the reader should be able to:

1. Provide the rationale for studying consumer behavior in depth.

2. See the complexity of consumer behavior and the difficulty of identifying its mainsprings.

3. Explain the dynamics of the consumer behavior processes—individual, social, and sociocultural.

4. Describe possible marketing strategy implications suggested by the consumer behavior processes.

Anyone could understand and predict market behavior if only it didn't involve human beings. If every individual could be relied upon to act consistently and predictably at all times, marketing would be much easier. Fortunately, consumers don't act that way. The same idiosyncracies, rationalizations, and social influences that make life itself so interesting make consumer behavior a necessary and challenging field to explore.

WHAT'S WRONG WITH MY DIET SODA?

Coca-Cola, Inc.

Some years ago, David Stander conducted a classic experiment which illustrates the enigma of the normal consumer.[1] A group of housewives were asked to compare the taste of Coca-Cola (which they all said they liked) to a new "Diet Coke." They agreed that it tasted "awful with a bitter aftertaste." In fact, what they were drinking was regular Coke—the same soda they had reacted to with enthusiasm moments before.

The ability of the housewives to fool their own taste buds came mostly from their experience with early diet drinks. These drinks really did have a questionable taste followed by an aftertaste not to be discussed in polite company. This impression persisted; the housewives expected the same result and, in effect, persuaded themselves that they found it. An additional negative factor was supplied by the experimenters when they described the diet drink as being recommended by doctors, "especially if you're fat." Few women would jump at an opportunity to identify with such an image.

WHY STUDY CONSUMER BEHAVIOR?

Today's diet drink manufacturers have learned their lesson: witness the slim, beautiful models in the TV commercials who drink diet soda to stay young, thin, and dynamic. Compare that with the image of a housewife struggling to get rid of fat.

The starting point for studying consumer behavior is the same as the marketing concept described in Chapter 2: the idea of looking at the product from the consumer's point of view. Instead of trying to give your customers what *you* think they need, find out what *they* want (subject, of course, to some of the social responsibility constraints discussed in Chapter 4).

Consumer behavior has been defined as "the acts of individuals directly involved in obtaining and using economic goods and services, including the decision processes that precede and determine these acts."[2] Note that the actual purchase is only one part of the decision process (as will be discussed in Chapter 9). In studying consumer behavior, we have to consider not only what people buy but other factors such as where, how often, and under what conditions the purchase is made.

Another important consideration is that the consumer (the one who actually uses the product) may not be the same person as the purchasing agent (the one who actually buys the product). For example, a mother may be the purchasing agent for breakfast cereals consumed by her children. Market research usually concentrates on the purchasing agent; an accurate consumer behavior study should also include the influence of the purchaser's family on the buying decision.

In the first half of Chapter 6, we discussed market demand. In that discussion, market behavior was related to the combination of variables of population trends, purchasing power, and the tendency to consume in certain ways. These variables generate consumption patterns that can be researched and related to marketing strategy. But to get closer to understanding the causes of market behavior, it is necessary to probe consumer behavior in terms of individuals and households. Because few products are truly custom made (few customers can afford it), the dynamics of buyer behavior can be summed up to give a clearer picture of market behavior, especially market segments.

In Chapter 7, we looked at "market segmentation" as a way to pinpoint market demand for particular products. Segmentation, however, has limitations in studying consumer behavior because it does not provide for a cause-and-effect relationship. It is possible to isolate groups of yogurt-eaters or museum-goers, but simply grouping them tells only what they do, not why they do it. The understanding of the "why" of consumer behavior is essential to an understanding of the managerial and societal marketing processes. We need to look at what consumer needs are, how these needs are formed, and how they relate to marketing activity.

In practice, keeping in touch with consumer behavior and motivation is not easy. This is partly due to the tendency of marketers to regard their products as a combination of ingredients rather than as a means to the satisfaction of needs. Also, shifting social values and attitudes may drastically affect consumer habits. The movie industry, for example, nearly went under in the early years of television until moviemakers discovered the opportunities presented by changing social attitudes toward sex and human values.

The need for understanding consumer behavior is dramatized by the introduction of technological breakthroughs (computers, frozen foods) and new concepts (franchising, TV commercials), and the huge capital investments involved. For example, of the more than 6,000 new grocery products introduced each year, an estimated 80 percent fail to reach the goals set for them, mainly because they were not suited to consumers' needs.

This chapter and Chapter 9 treat the consumer behavior of individuals and households. Situations in which organizations are the buyers will be covered in Chapter 10.

APPROACHES TO CONSUMER BEHAVIOR

Consumer behavior responds so continuously to so many stimuli that it is virtually impossible to nail it down at any specific moment. The objective of marketing people, then, is not to discover the exact causes of consumer behavior; it is to see how close they can come. Many a marketing "expert" has based his or her strategy on a version of rational consumer action, only to be plunged into a marketing disaster by unforeseen consumer complexities. This does not mean that consumer behavior cannot or should not be studied. It does mean that the results are no more infallible than the consumers from whom they were taken.

WHAT CAUSES CONSUMER BEHAVIOR?

The complexities of studying and analyzing consumer behavior are demonstrated by the "black box" analogy illustrated in Figure 8-1. The black box represents the process that goes on in the consumer's mind, hidden from the researcher or analyst. The stimulus (a sales pitch or advertisement, for example) produces a response which might be a sale, a refusal, or a request for more information. The relationship between the stimulus and the response is governed by what goes on in the black box area of the consumer's head. Since we cannot directly observe what needs, motives, and cultural or social pressures affect the response, the best we can do is draw inferences based on what took place.

An example is the current trend in coffee drinking among young people.[3] In spite of a substantial exposure to different product forms (ground, instant, decaffeinated), advertising, and promotion (the stimuli), the response of a growing number of young Americans is to drink less and less coffee. The problem for the marketing analyst is to figure out what is going on inside the collective black box of young people's minds that yields this response. One theory is that young people prefer a quick, cold drink. An alternative view is that young people regard coffee's image as too "straight." In England, for example, where establishment members drink tea, young people are drinking more instant coffee than ever. A third supposition is that young people are turned off by coffee simply because they don't like the taste.

The significance of this example is not that one supposition is right and the others wrong. The point is that inference is involved in all three theories. Indeed, one must always infer to some degree the causes of consumer be-

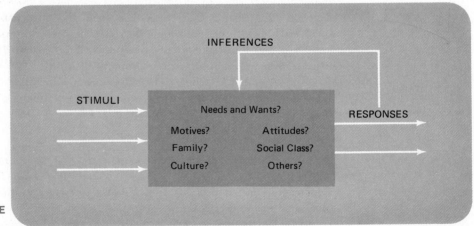

Figure 8-1
CONSUMER
BEHAVIOR:
WHAT IS IN THE
BLACK BOX?

havior. One of the prime objectives of the researcher is to reduce the amount of supposition and inference to a minimum. The more a study is based on concrete evidence, the more confidence can be placed in the conclusions.

It is apparent that the behavioral sciences, including economics, sociology, psychology, and even anthropology, are playing an increasingly important role in modern marketing concepts. The full-fledged application of these disciplines to marketing problems, however, is still in the exploratory stage. (Compared to the physical sciences, the behavioral sciences themselves are considered to be in a primitive stage of development.) Managements are extremely selective both in approach to consumer research and in the reliance they place on results. Some are highly suspicious. Most marketing executives, on the other hand, are finding that in a highly competitive market they can use all the help they can get.

NATURE OF CONSUMER RATIONALITY

In classical economic theory, the consumer always makes rational buying decisions. That's where the trouble starts. What is rational? **Economic rationality** refers to the consideration of objective criteria: price, size, ease of use, durability, and so on. In other words, it refers to characteristics that can be measured and evaluated by criteria other than personal opinion or preference. Subjective criteria refers to personal motives such as prestige, beauty, and ego gratification. According to the economic view, these are irrational.

In **behavioral rationality**, both criteria apply. It is accepted that rationality is purposeful behavior carried out to achieve goals that one feels are in his or her own best interests. Thus, if a man buys a sports car not only for driving to work but also because it makes him feel young and virile, he may be said to be making a rational decision. In any marketing situation, the consumer has a reason (or reasons) for his response. To an outside observer (such as an economist or a lawyer), many of the consumer's decisions will seem irrational. To the consumer, his actions are always rational.

The influence of society on consumer behavior has grown in the 1970s with emphasis on health, ecology, and energy conservation. (The impact of these societal forces was discussed in Chapter 4.) This has fostered a new interest in **societal rationality**, which is concerned with needs and responses outside the narrow range of economic rationality and the personal gratification approach of behavioral rationality. Societal rationality looks at issues in which the individual's behavior as a consumer may have adverse effects on his or her own long-run welfare and on society as a whole. Pollution control, banning of throwaway containers, and no-smoking sections on airplanes are examples of restrictions limiting the actions of the individual for the general good of all.

OVERVIEW MODEL OF CONSUMER BEHAVIOR

The overview model presented in Figure 8-2 shows the structure by which we will be examining the major dynamics of consumer behavior. The diagram indicates three sets of processes that influence consumer decisions: sociocultural, social, and individual.

Sociocultural processes refer to the influences of the consumer's broad

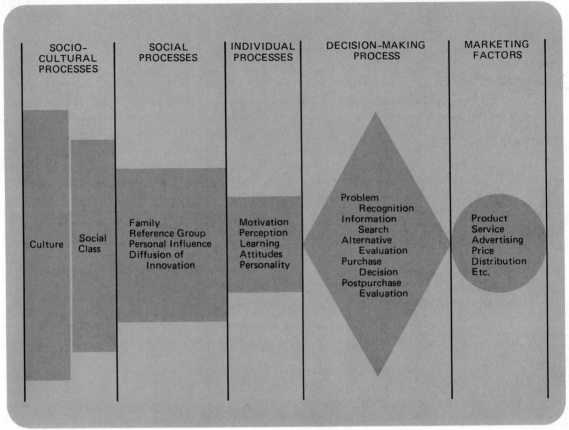

SOCIO-CULTURAL PROCESSES	SOCIAL PROCESSES	INDIVIDUAL PROCESSES	DECISION-MAKING PROCESS	MARKETING FACTORS
Culture Social Class	Family Reference Group Personal Influence Diffusion of Innovation	Motivation Perception Learning Attitudes Personality	Problem Recognition Information Search Alternative Evaluation Purchase Decision Postpurchase Evaluation	Product Service Advertising Price Distribution Etc.

Figure 8-2   OVERVIEW MODEL OF CONSUMER BEHAVIOR

Adapted from Harold H. Kassarjian and Thomas S. Robertson, *Perspectives in Consumer Behavior* (Glenview, Ill.: Scott, Foresman, 1968), p. 4. Copyright © 1968 by Scott, Foresman and Company. Reprinted by permission of the publisher.

cultural and social group. Americans, for example, may share attributes and beliefs that are significantly different from those of other cultures. Within America, a person with a working-class background will have attitudes and interests different from the upper class of his own country.

Social processes, as distinct from social class or culture, refer to the influences of the consumer's immediate social environment. Included in this category are family, friends, and business acquaintances. The influence of this group may be considerable. Sometimes it is direct: a family may demand certain standards of behavior and values. Often, however, the influence is indirect. An individual consumer tends to structure his actions within the accepted bounds of the group's behavior patterns to gain group approval.

Individual processes are based on the reasonably safe assumption that everyone is different. In spite of common cultural, social, economic, and geographical backgrounds, consumers are still capable of reacting individually. This could be due to a number of personal factors such as personality, motivation, and self-image.

Of course, these three categories do not exist apart from one another. They not only work all at once on the consumer's behavior, they influence each other. An individual's motivation and attitudes, for example, may be largely shaped by culture, social class, and family. These dynamics are also at work when the consumer goes through the **decision-making process** (examined in Chapter 9). An organization controls the set of marketing factors it uses to induce consumers to act a certain way (usually to buy its product).

From examining the dynamics in the model and their influence on consumer behavior one gains information that applies to marketing. First, do these dynamics explain how and why consumers behave in certain ways? Second, from this knowledge, is it possible to predict how consumers will behave? (For instance, it would be useful to be able to predict consumer reaction to new products, price rises, and advertising campaigns.) Third, is it possible to go from explaining and predicting to controlling consumer behavior through marketing efforts? Can we use this knowledge of consumer behavior, for example, to virtually ensure that consumers will try a new herbal shampoo or take their children to an amusement park?

INDIVIDUAL PROCESSES OF CONSUMER BEHAVIOR

The individual processes of consumer behavior include motivation, perception, learning, attitudes, and personality.

MOTIVATION   **Motivation** has a direct cause-and-effect relationship with behavior. Unfortunately for marketing planners looking for an easy answer, it is a complex, multilevel relationship. Motivation ranges from straightforward need fulfillment (I eat because I'm hungry) to subconscious ego gratification (I overeat because I'm lonely).

Basically, motivation is physiological and psychological. **Physiological motives** include basic biological drives such as the need for water, oxygen, food, and sleep. **Psychological motives** result from the social environment—the need for love, security, and approval.

Abraham Maslow developed a theory of human motivation based on five sets of basic needs: physiological, safety, belongingness and love, esteem, and self-actualization.[4] The order is important. Maslow felt that as each need is fulfilled, another higher need arises.

This is demonstrated in Figure 8-3, which is based on Maslow's theory. It shows how the number and variety of wants increase as the individual develops. In other words, not until the individual has satisfied physiological needs will he or she be strongly motivated to meet needs for safety. The physiological needs are relevant to marketers because they are closely related to what the product does—winter coats that keep the body warm, cars that transport, and hospitals that heal. The safety needs are relevant because they indicate a desire for security in the form of insurance, real estate, or birth control pills.

Marketers use the next level, the love needs, in more subtle ways. The product design and advertisements for everything from toothpaste to sports cars often promise love and affection. Marriage and parenthood, traditional love-fullfillment institutions, are linked to a diverse range of products in many advertisements.

If the Corvette promises love (and some sex as well), the Lincoln Continental promises esteem. The self-esteem level is concerned with the desire for prestige, self-respect, and a feeling of importance or usefulness to society. For many people, a college degree helps fill this need.

Once the need for self-esteem has been satisfied, the need for self-actualization can develop. Self-actualization is concerned with creative and spiritual fulfillment, with increased awareness, the pursuit of knowledge and experience as an integral part of living rather than as a means to the acquisition of power or prestige. Today, more people than ever are striving to reach this level. Marketing has helped in some efforts to facilitate self-actualization, for example, cultural programs, transcendental meditation, and human relations training.

It can readily be seen that marketing encompasses the full range of needs. The big problems with motivations are finding out what they are and how they influence behavior.

What, for example, were the motivations behind the craze to wear T-shirts bearing commercial brand names or trademarks that gripped the student population in the mid-1970s? Students from every socioeconomic group, of both sexes, gladly became human billboards for Budweiser, Honda, and innumer-

Figure 8-3
THE RELATIONSHIP AMONG NEEDS IN MASLOW'S THEORY OF MOTIVATION

Adapted from David Krech, Richard S. Crutchfield, and Egerton L. Ballachey, *Individual in Society* (New York: McGraw-Hill, 1962), p. 77. Copyright 1962. Used with permission of McGraw-Hill Book Company.

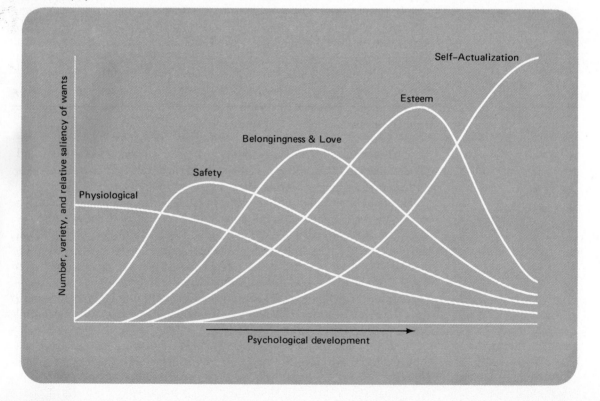

able other commercial enterprises. Many promoters searched for their psychological motives but only came up with theories about status symbols and macho images. No one seems to know for sure.

Marketing Implications　Interest in the "why" of consumer behavior reached a peak in the late 1950s with motivation research. Led by Ernest Dichter, the motivation researchers brought Sigmund Freud into the marketplace. Through depth interviews and psychoanalytical interpretation (sometimes questionable), they attempted to enter the world of symbolism and subconscious motivation. Here they found, for example, that blond women in automobile advertisements represent mistresses while brunettes are associated with wives.

One major problem with motivational research was that results meant little until interpreted by a trained psychologist. Even then, psychologists often interpreted the same material differently. Eventually, motivational research earned its place as a part of traditional marketing research. With some modification, it is still contributing to product development and advertising creativity.

PERCEPTION　Perception, from a marketing viewpoint, is the process by which a mental impression is formed from the stimuli within the consumer's field of awareness. The consumer gives significant meaning to what is observed. Because this meaning depends on personal experience, memories, beliefs, fantasies, and so on, no two people will have the same impression from any given observation. How, then, can we understand or define perception?

Let us approach the problem of understanding perception by defining four principles:[5]

1. Perception is *selective*. An individual cannot possibly perceive all stimulus objects within a perceptual field; therefore he or she perceives selectively.

2. Perception is *organized*. Perceptions have meanings for the individual; they do not represent a "buzzing, blooming confusion."

3. Perception depends upon *stimulus factors*. The nature of the physical stimulus itself, of course, helps determine perception. Whether a magazine advertisement is in color or black and white, a full page or a half, affects perception of the message. Stimulus factors which encourage perception include contrasts, intensity, frequency, and movement.

4. Perception depends upon *personal factors*. What the individual brings to the situation governs perception—the ability to see or hear the message; needs, moods, memory, experiences, and values—all these modify message reception. The individual who views himself as a playboy is more likely to perceive an ad for stereo equipment than one for an electric saw. The person's needs at a moment in time are also determinants of perceptual selectivity. The thirsty man is more likely to perceive a beer commercial (especially during a long football game). And, of course, because of past experiences, the individual has formed product preferences, making him more likely to see some ads than others.

Perhaps the most significant aspect of perception from a marketing viewpoint is that it is selective. The average consumer is "exposed" to 1,500 advertisements a day but consciously perceives only about 75 of them, of which only 12 are likely to have any effect on behavior. The individual consumer perceives a product in terms of its *brand image* resulting from experience with the product and any promotion or advertising. Cheap Jeans, for example, which advertise low price and big selection have a different brand image from Christian Dior slacks. To the average consumer, even the word "slacks" denotes a different socioeconomic and age group than "jeans." Yet these qualities which contribute to the brand image do not apply to the products but to their consumers. Product name, package design, and consumer experience with past performance all contribute to the consumer's perceptual evaluation.

Product price has special significance. Consumers often equate price with quality (the "you always get what you pay for" school of thought). André Gabor and C. W. J. Granger have put forth the interesting hypothesis that a consumer who is buying has two price limits in mind—an upper limit and a lower limit.[6] Anything over the higher figure is too expensive; anything under the lower must be of poor quality. The price perception is only part of the total brand image, however. To be maintained, the advertising, packaging, and retail outlets must reflect the same level of quality.

Another related factor is the concept of **perceived risk**. Consumers are engaged in taking risks in the sense that what the consumer does results in consequences that cannot accurately be foreseen, and some of the consequences of his behavior are likely to be unpleasant. Raymond Bauer contends that consumers attempt to minimize risk by making decisions based on their perceived analysis of the situation.[7] Donald Cox divided perceived risk into *functional* (related to product performance) and *psychosocial* (related to image and self-concept).[8] Scouring pads, for example, rate high on functional risk (will it really work?) and low on psychosocial (nobody will judge me by my scouring pads). Perfume may be low in functional risk, but high in psychosocial. Consumers can reduce risk through a variety of means such as gathering information about the product, buying small quantities to test, and simply not expecting too much of the product.

Psychologists tell us that there is learning in all human behavior. What is learning? Bernard Berelson and Gary Steiner define it as "all changes in behavior that result from previous behavior in similar situations."[9] The main conflicts arise when we try to discover *how* learning works. The most important theory from a marketing standpoint (since almost all research and marketing philosophy are based on it) is the **stimulus-response approach**. The stimulus-response school holds that learning is what takes place when a link is established between a particular stimulus and a particular response. Pavlov's dogs were the subjects of the classic experiment—they learned to salivate to the stimulus of the bell. Rats running mazes, drivers stopping for red lights, audiences applauding a performance are all examples of stimulus-response learning.

John Dollard and Neal Miller formulatèd the stimulus–response relation-

Movie film projects at the rate of 24 frames per second. Obviously, the human eye cannot perceive each frame individually. Supposing, then, you took out one or two frames of a feature film and replaced them with a frame containing the words "Drink Coke" or "Eat Popcorn." Although the message would flash on the screen, moviegoers would not be able to see it consciously. Would they react to it subconsciously?

In the 1950s, somebody (there is some question about who) tried it in a movie theater and reported significant increases in Coke and popcorn sales. Subliminal (below the level of conscious perception) advertising was born.

Initial reactions were mainly feelings of apprehension. People became afraid of brainwashing, mind control, and hordes of consumers all enthusiastically buying without knowing why. Others, in a more positive outlook, thought the technique could be used for endless good by flashing messages such as "God is love" or "Support Little League baseball" on the screen.

The controversy lost a lot of momentum when scientists could not substantiate the original results and repeat experiments failed to produce any results at all. Interest in the subject dropped.

In the 1970s, Wilson Bryan Key picked up this theme again with his book *Subliminal Seduction*. According to Key, we are all being insidiously manipulated by publishers and advertisers who are hiding messages in print ads, magazines, and TV commercials. Key claims, for example, that the letters s-e-x are cleverly concealed in everything from Playboy centerfolds to, of all places, Lincoln's beard on the $5 bill. Does this mean that the United States Treasury is trying to persuade us subconsciously that inflation can be fun?

Even if Uncle Sam were this diabolical, the persuasion wouldn't work, according to James Engel and others. There is little evidence that subliminal perception actually registers on the mind of the subperceiver. Furthermore, tests have shown that our subconscious minds are just as selective as our conscious minds, so we probably wouldn't eat more popcorn anyway.

Based on James F. Engel, David T. Kollat, and Roger D. Blackwell, *Consumer Behavior*, 2d ed. (New York: Holt, Rinehart and Winston, 1973), pp. 223–24; and Lynn Sharpe, "Subliminal Communication: Insidious Advertising," *Encore*, December 1974, pp. 39–40.

ship in more sophisticated terms by breaking it down into drive, cue, response, and reinforcement.[10] Drive refers to the individual's inner need which calls for action: hunger, fatigue, fear, insecurity, and so on. A cue is a stimulus in the environment related to the drive. If hunger is the drive, for example, a spaghetti commercial could be the cue. The response is what the individual does in reaction to the cue. Getting something to eat is the obvious example. Reinforcement is the strengthening of the cue-response relationship and is directly related to the degree of satisfaction the response brings to the original drive. If a response is reinforced regularly, the result is habit formation.

It all seems simple and straightforward until you consider the possible alternative response. Our hungry consumer watching the spaghetti commercial may react in several ways. The most direct response would be to go to the kitchen or out to an Italian restaurant and have some spaghetti. Or if the commercial simply focuses attention on hunger need, it may result in the consumption of a ham on rye or a yogurt and granola. If the consumer is on a diet, the commercial may have a negative effect: the consumer may respond by changing channels in an effort to forget about food.

Regardless of the immediate response, the consumer may respond further several days later when shopping. Remembering how appealing the spaghetti looked in the commercial, he or she may look for it in the supermarket. At this point, another intriguing element comes in. The consumer may notice that the store's private brand of spaghetti is five cents cheaper than the brand advertised on television. This may act as a cue to his drive for economy; the response may be to buy the store brand—unless the commercial convinced him that his needs would be better satisfied by paying the extra cost of the advertised brand. Anticipating and dealing with such chains of stimulus-response relationships is one of the most absorbing elements of marketing.

Marketing Implications

"Try it—you'll like it." This Alka-Seltzer slogan of the early 1970s just about summarizes the relationship between consumer learning and **brand loyalty**. Most purchases are based on past experience. If an experience with a particular product was satisfying, the consumer's response is likely to be a repeat purchase. If not, or if a competing product seems to offer even more satisfaction, the consumer may change brands.

The tendency for consumers to minimize risk and develop brand loyalty works to the advantage of established brands. A new entry into the market must break a habitual response—never an easy task. Free sampling, cents-off coupons, and introductory offers are attempts to break the habit of loyalty to competitors' brands and establish a pattern of loyalty to the new brand. The trick is to follow the new response with an acceptable reward in order to increase the probability of the response being repeated. This can be a tough job if the market leader is well established. This is also the reason why successful brands tend to adopt more conservative strategy; as many a football coach would say, "You don't fool around with a winner." On the other hand, as conditions change, even successful marketers must adapt. After staying with the same basic design for over 20 years, Volkswagen took a look at the stylish new competition for the mushrooming small car market of the 1970s and decided it was time for a change. Exit the Bug, enter the Rabbit.

Many of the Rabbit purchasers will be former Bug owners who will transfer their learned response from one VW product to another. This tendency is known as generalization and can apply not only to similar products such as two cars but to different products made by the same manufacturer. If Aunt Jemima makes good pancakes, her syrup must be at least worth a try. If you depend on your Dunlop tennis racquet, you can depend on Dunlop balls.

The hitch is that the theory doesn't always work. Consumers are also capable of discrimination, which means they can respond selectively to related stimuli. Some may love their Dunlop racquet but use only Wilson balls.

Most companies want consumers to discriminate toward their product, to perceive it as a desirable brand rather than just another toaster, political candidate, or rent-a-car. Obviously, the more the product differs from its competitors the more likely the organization is to achieve this goal.

Advertising plays the major role in providing consumers with cues about the product and the product's performance. A central concern is how long these cues are retained and what value repetition has in increasing retention. The conclusions from some psychological experiments dealing with retention and forgetting are as follows:

1. Forgetting is greatest immediately following learning; thereafter, it declines to a stable level.

2. Retention increases with repetition.

3. More meaningful or more vivid material is better retained than less meaningful or less vivid material.

4. The more completely material is initially learned, the greater is retention.

5. Material presented first (primacy) or last (recency) is better retained than material presented in the middle.[11]

Repeated advertising messages seem to stand a better chance of being retained if they are spread out over a period of time rather than concentrated within a short span. The scheduling decision, however, may depend on the product being advertised. Long-term, continuous advertising is generally considered best for established products. However, new products may need the impact of concentrated messages in order to reach consumer awareness.

ATTITUDES David Krech and Richard Crutchfield define attitude as "an enduring organization of motivational, emotional, perceptual, and cognitive processes with respect to some aspect of the individual's world."[12]

Social psychologists dwell on attitudes, and with justification. Attitudes govern the response to a stimulus and lead to behavior, usually to action. By definition, an attitude cannot be neutral; to have an attitude means to be involved, to be fired-up, ready for action. Attitudes immediately state, or at least imply, a person's position for or against, friendly or hostile, as surely as a basketball fan makes known his attitude toward the two teams on the court.

It is possible to have a belief without an attitude. You can believe there are two teams playing without caring who wins. You cannot, however, have an attitude without a belief. Indeed, most consumer behavior theorists feel that belief is one of the three main components of attitude. These components are:

1. The cognitive component is what the individual believes about the object. It includes not only the beliefs about the characteristics of the object, but also evaluations. The object is thought to be good or bad, moral or immoral, necessary or unnecessary.

2. The affective component is the individual's emotional reaction to the object. "Your perfume turns me on" and "This airline is for the birds" are examples, admittedly extreme.

3. The conative component is the behavioral part of an attitude, the readiness to respond with action. If the attitude is negative, the response may range from ignoring the object–stimulus to aggressively attacking it. A positive at-

BEHAVIOR CAN CHANGE BEFORE ATTITUDES

titude may result in praise or, hopefully for the marketer, the purchase of a product.

Each of these attitude components will vary according to the situation and the person. Obviously, everyone does not have an overwhelming good-bad, love-hate, destroy-worship attitude toward every product in the supermarket. Attitudes may range from indifference to passion, with many complexities along the way.

Attitudes, good and bad, are learned. They do not spring full grown from some mysterious inner source. Experience teaches us to love or hate classical music, to love or hate our neighbor. Our most influential teacher of attitudes is almost certainly our family. Later on, our peer group influences us by offering acceptance in return for sharing their attitudes.

Attitudes do not function in isolation. They interact with perception, thinking, feeling, reasoning. By selecting from the constant bombardment of stimuli we organize our world in an attempt to maintain our sanity and search for meaning in our environment.

Marketing Implications   The success of a product in the market is directly related to the company's ability to understand, predict, and influence consumer attitudes. Depending on how the product is doing, the marketer may want to:

1. confirm existing attitudes (if the product is doing well);
2. change existing attitudes (if the product is not doing well);
3. create new attitudes (introduce a new product).[13]

Confirming attitudes is the easiest course; you simply remind consumers why they like your product and why they should continue to do so. Changing attitudes is a much more difficult task. In fact, it sometimes makes more marketing sense to phase out support for a product that has run into negative consumer attitudes. You can then concentrate on creating positive attitudes for a new product. In support of this approach is the fact that it is more difficult to convert faithful users of other brands than it is to capture new entrants into the market. There are, of course, consumers who are "brand-hoppers" by nature. It takes nerve to kill off an ailing product in favor of an unproven alternative but the rewards if the new product is successful can make the risk worthwhile.

To the marketer, the most important instrument of attitude change is advertising. That it works, all are agreed. But what makes it work most effectively —in what way, with whom, and through what media—is still being tested and only part of the results are in. Take, for example, those irritating commercials showing us housewives with clogged-up drains, sinuses, or digestive systems. Do they really sell their respective products? The answer is self-evident—if they didn't sell, they wouldn't be on the air. There is some comforting evidence, however, that such commercials sell in spite of, rather than because of, their obnoxious character.

Attitude change comes from other sources besides advertising. A major influence is a change in the social environment the consumer belongs to or wishes to join. The mass media, by exposing people to new fashions, ideas, and values, exert an influence on their attitudes.

Carl Hovland and Walter Weiss did a classic study of the source effect.[14] They gave the same information to two groups, crediting the information to a reputable source with one group and a disreputable source with the other. At first, the reputable source had significantly more influence on attitudes, but as time went on this influence declined, while the other group showed an increase. Eventually, there was no difference. The conclusion is that, as time passes, the source of information becomes less important than the content.

Do scare techniques work ("Use this product or terrible things will happen to you")? According to one study, showing the results of poor dental care was *less* effective than mild persuasion in getting subjects to take care of their teeth.[15] Another study, however, reported that the contaminated tuna scare of the 1960s almost destroyed the tuna industry.[16] One explanation for this apparent discrepancy is that in the first instance, the subjects had to respond actively by taking better care of their teeth. In the second study, they responded passively by simply not eating tuna.

PERSONALITY

Psychologists tend to disagree over definitions of **personality**. As marketers, this need not worry us. Our concern is more with the essence of personality and with the reasonable assumption that an individual's personality makes him respond consistently to similar stimuli. Personality traits can include degrees of dominance, adventuresomeness, sociability, and responsibility.

Discussing personality inevitably leads to Sigmund Freud. Freud divided human personality into the psycho-trinity of id, ego, and superego. The way these three work together is the personality basis for behavior.

1. *Id.* This is the source—the animal instincts and cravings that demand immediate gratification; our basic drives.

2. *Superego.* The priest and policeman of our inner selves. Big Mommy, Big Daddy, the Searcher for higher planes of moralistic perfection. The stage

is set for the inevitable conflict between the high-minded superego and the earthy id.

    3. *Ego.* The referee between the superego and the id; the ego's job is to make them work together. The ego makes the plans and decisions and dictates the action. There are, of course, many variations in ego work-patterns, which accounts for the rich diversity in people's personality and behavior patterns.

    Just as many early disciples of Freud broke away to form their own theories of personality, later researchers looked for different motivations in buying behavior. Karen Horney's belief that much personality development is motivated by a striving for security, for example, is reflected in the many advertising platforms today offering social success and security in return for using the right toothpaste or deodorant. An individual's self-image is another motivating force that has been studied by research to show that we all buy certain products to express how we feel about ourselves. The man behind the wheel of a speedboat sees himself as the type who belongs there.

Marketing Implications   The most common characteristic of personality and consumer behavior tests seems to be the lack of certainty in their conclusions. Much of this may be due to variables in the personality testing methods used. Relationships do exist between personality and purchasing motivations, but the link seems to be either simplistically obvious or extremely thin. There is little surprise, for instance, in the finding that sports car owners tend to be more active and sociable than owners of standard four-door sedans. Other less-than-startling results showed that conservative consumers are less likely to experiment with new products or brands.

    On the other hand, an extensive study failed to show any positive relationship between personality and brand preferences of coffee, tea, or beer. Several tests have been conducted to find what makes a Chevrolet owner different from a Ford owner, with results best described as inconclusive.

    The aim here is not to put down such efforts as a waste of time and money. They are neither. Not only are many tests successful in their stated objectives but even unsuccessful attempts result in useful findings on methods and approaches to personality research and its relationship to consumer behavior.

SOCIAL PROCESSES OF CONSUMER BEHAVIOR

The social processes include family, reference group, personal influence, and diffusion of innovation.

FAMILY   Most consumers belong to a family group and are therefore subject to its influence in establishing buying patterns. The family is a major influence in shaping consumption patterns and determining decision-making roles.

    The impact of the family on the formation of values, attitudes, and purchasing habits has been considerable. For example, many of the brands in a new housewife's kitchen are those favored by her mother. However, the dramatic social changes experienced by recent generations, along with the power of the mass media, have reduced the power of the family's influence.

Each family member has defined areas of purchasing influence based on his or her product knowledge and use. Children, for example, might influence the choice of breakfast cereal, toothpaste, dog food, and their own clothes. Their opinions will not be considered in the family choice of carpeting, car tires, or coffee. Everyone may have a say in a major purchase such as the family car. Ultimately, either the father or the mother will make the final decision.

Marketing Implications

Marketing organizations are aware that not all households are headed by a married couple. They are also aware that 46 million households are, and that they control 80 percent of consumer income. It is noteworthy that the family does influence consumer behavior. The person making the purchase may be acting on some family member's judgment, on a joint judgment, or even against his or her own judgment. Most products and most brands are chosen and purchased by the woman of the family. Her decisions are more or less influenced by the children and her husband, the degree of influence depending on the product and on the individual family structure Most decisions are made jointly by husband and wife, although one or the other tends to dominate, as in most husband and wife relationships (see Table 8-1).

Table 8-1 confirms that most purchases in this representative group of product categories are made by the wife. The study was sponsored by a group of five magazines in order to measure the importance of male and female readership in the categories chosen. One criticism of the study was the lack of consideration for the influence of children. Peanut butter brand selection, for example, may be more dependent on children than on husbands.

Table 8-1
WHO MAKES THE BUYING DECISIONS?
RELATIVE PURCHASE INFLUENCE: HUSBANDS AND WIVES (% INFLUENCE)

	PURCHASED BY		DIRECT INFLUENCE				INDIRECT INFLUENCE			
			PRODUCT		BRAND		PRODUCT		BRAND	
	W	H	W	H	W	H	W	H	W	H
Cold (unsweetened) cereal	84	16	74	26	71	29	65	35	67	33
Packaged lunch meat	73	27	60	40	64	36	56	44	57	43
Peanut butter	81	19	70	30	74	26	65	35	68	32
Bar soap	85	15	65	35	64	36	60	40	61	39
Headache remedies	67	33	67	33	67	33	64	36	65	35
Dog food (dry)	76	24	60	40	59	41	60	40	61	39
Fast-food-chain hamburgers	68	32	55	45	55	45	53	47	52	48
Catsup	75	25	68	32	68	32	60	40	62	38
Freeze-dried coffee	68	32	57	43	62	38	56	44	59	41

SOURCE: "Purchase Influence Measures of Husband/Wife Influence on Buying Decisions," Haley, Overholser & Associates Inc., New Canaan, Conn., January, 1975. Percentages reflect relative purchase activity, direct and indirect influence of husbands and wives in the sample. Adapted from *Advertising Age,* March 17, 1975, p. 52.

Family purchase patterns change both in product category and buying decision as the family grows older. (The concept of the family life cycle was introduced in Chapter 6.) Young couples with children, for example, not only buy more furniture and toys, but tend to confer more in making decisions. As the family grows older, the responsibility for the purchase of individual products rests more and more on one member or another. The influence of the family members may still be there, but it is understood rather than stated.

REFERENCE GROUPS

We all need someone we can lean on, and **reference groups** are the social, economic, or professional groups an individual uses to evaluate his or her opinions and beliefs. Reference groups may vary in size from one person to an entire profession or political party. The individual may turn to the reference group in whole or in part, for confirmation or, in some cases, for the self-assurance that he is acting in opposition to their views.

Tamotsu Shibutani divided reference groups into three classifications.[17]

1. *Groups that serve as comparison points.* Our own status varies according to the group with which we compare ourselves. We may feel poor compared to those richer than ourselves or rich compared to those poorer than ourselves.

2. *Groups to which a person aspires.* The outsider, trying to get in, imitates the status symbols and buying behavior of the group to which he or she aspires to belong. This could be a higher social group or a cult group such as hippies, the jet set, revolutionaries, or advertising's own Beautiful People.

3. *Groups whose perspectives are assumed by the individual.* An individual may also adopt the views of a group without wanting to belong to it. We

Table 8-2
REFERENCE-GROUP INFLUENCE ON PRODUCT DECISIONS

BRAND OR TYPE	WEAK– PRODUCT	STRONG+
STRONG+	Clothing Furniture Magazines Refrigerator (type) Toilet soap	Cars Cigarettes Beer (premium vs. regular) Drugs
WEAK–	Soap Canned peaches Laundry soap Refrigerator (brand) Radios	Air conditioners Instant coffee TV (black and white)

SOURCE: Foundation for Research on Human Behavior, *Group Influence in Marketing and Public Relations* (Ann Arbor, Mich.: The Foundation, 1956), p. 8. From James F. Engel, David T. Kollat, and Roger D. Blackwell, *Consumer Behavior,* 2d ed. (New York: Holt, Rinehart and Winston, 1973), p. 174. Copyright © 1968, 1973 by Holt, Rinehart and Winston, Inc. Reprinted by permission of The Dryden Press.

may, for example, adopt the opinions and outlook of pop stars or famous artists without dreaming of achieving their popularity or talent. Conversely, a member of a minority group may adopt the values and perspectives of the very majority he or she dislikes.

Marketing Implications   According to Francis Bourne, a particular product must be conspicuous to come under the strong influence of reference groups. Table 8-2, which shows the results of his study on the influence of friendship reference groups, supports this conclusion. Choices of highly visible products such as beer and cars are more strongly influenced than products such as canned peaches and refrigerators. Bourne's analysis applies to product influence and/or strong brand (or type of product) influence.

Products may move from category to category in response to fashion, time, or technological advance. Radios, for example, are shown as being only weakly influenced by friendship groups. This study was done in the 1950s, before transistors, stereo, and AM/FM became choice considerations, so radios today may well belong to a more strongly influenced category.

Advertising campaigns can also create an influence, making a particular product or brand the "in thing," at least temporarily.

PERSONAL INFLUENCE   **Personal influence** is a more accurate term for the better known phrase "word-of-mouth advertising." By any name, it has always been popular with advertisers, partly because it is effective but mostly because it is free. The problem has always been to discover how to set it in motion and to avoid its being negative.

In the 1950s, Elihu Katz and Paul Lazarsfeld did some studies on the flow of mass communications and the part people played in it. Their major finding was the **two-step flow thesis**, which stated that the mass media first influence opinion leaders who, in turn, communicate what they read and hear to companions whom they influence.[18] Charles King supported this theory with a study showing the error in the belief that fashion popularity "trickled down" through the upper to the lower levels of society.[19] He suggested that "trickle across" would be more accurate.

Who are these opinion leaders, the trend setters that tell the rest of us what is in fashion? Leaders are found at all levels of society (the points from which the influence "trickles across"). The more sociable they are, the greater their market influence. Being married increases the possibility of a woman's being a leader, and the bigger her family, the bigger her influence. Above-average exposure to media in the particular sphere of influence in question also helps.

An opinion leader for fashion, however, is not necessarily an opinion leader in another area, such as food. Leadership is a quality related to a specific product or interest rather than a generalized attribute possessed by some people and not by others.

Marketing Implications   The more conspicuous a product is, the more likely it is that the purchaser was influenced by other people in making the decision to buy. The car you drive, for example, is more likely to reflect this influence than the hairblower you use. Products such as toiletries and food come into the category of products easily tested by the consumer. When we can readily try things for ourselves, we are less likely to depend on the opinions of others.

In choosing products with a high degree of perceived risk, consumers want all the help they can get in order to minimize that risk. Products in this category include medicines, holiday resorts, and major appliances.

Assuming you have a product ripe and ready for the market, how do you take advantage of its personal influence? The obvious method is to reach the opinion leaders, tell them about it and let them influence the others. The theory is fine, the problem is how to do it. First, you have to find the opinion leaders; second, you have to persuade them to like your product; third, you have to pay in some way for the influence. As Thomas Robertson has suggested, the estimated cost of selling a product through opinion leaders is usually greater than the cost of running a conventional advertising campaign and letting personal influence run its natural course.[20]

With the right kind of product, such as a swimming pool or encyclopedia, you can try to create your own opinion leaders by giving selected consumers a special deal in return for showing your product off to the neighbors. Another example in this category is party-plan selling where selected housewives demonstrate kitchenware or potted plants to their friends.

The most logical and sensible way to exploit the personal influence process is to study the characteristics of opinion leaders, find out what media may reach them, and tailor a promotional program for them.

There are, of course, many noninfluential people who may want to know more about your product. This information seeking can be as important as information giving. As a result, reaching this noninfluential group may be as important as reaching the opinion leaders.

Advertising can sometimes be as effective as personal influence when it creates the impression that all the best people are using your product and therefore everyone can feel safe by joining them. Testimonials fall into this category. Their effectiveness depends upon the extent to which the product is subject to personal influence and on the presenter's qualifications as a product expert. A Frenchman recommending wines and O. J. Simpson endorsing footballs would be acceptable; the reverse would be much less influential.

Direct mail offers a method of using media to select potential opinion leaders. They may be narrowed down in a variety of ways, such as by geographic region, occupation, age group, and income level. Often, mailing lists can be purchased according to these dimensions (as politicians well know).

Salespersons may act as opinion leaders with their customers, especially if they sell multiple brands and can be assumed to have some unbiased knowledge of them. Drugstore sales clerks, for example, are called on by many of their customers to recommend best brands for cold remedies and the like.

DIFFUSION OF INNOVATION **Diffusion of innovation**, for marketing purposes, may be translated roughly as "launching a new product." More accurately, it is the process by which

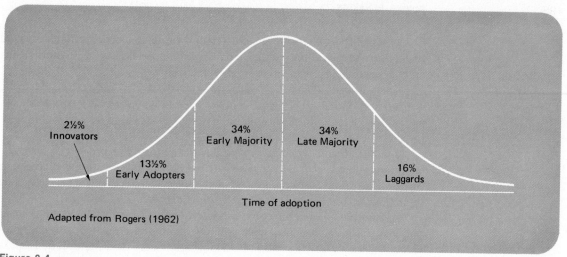

2½%
Innovators

13½%
Early Adopters

34%
Early Majority

34%
Late Majority

16%
Laggards

Time of adoption

Adapted from Rogers (1962)

Figure 8-4
GENERALIZED NON-CUMULATIVE DIFFUSION PATTERN

From Thomas S. Robertson, *Consumer Behavior* (Glenview, Ill.: Scott, Foresman, 1970), p. 131. Copyright © 1970 by Scott, Foresman and Company. Reproduced by permission of the publisher.

new goods or services are introduced to consumers. Since not everyone adopts a new product at the same time, there is considerable interest among marketers over who the early adopters are, and why.

The generalized diffusion pattern shown in Figure 8-4 has been found by Everett Rogers to approximate a normal distribution relationship between the number of adopters and their behavior over time.[21] The division between innovators, early adopters, early majority, late majority, and laggards is arbitrary and will not necessarily apply to all product innovations. Innovators, for example, are often defined by researchers as the first 10 percent of the product's adopters.

Diffusion, in order to be examined, must be assumed to take place within the boundaries of a social system. This may be defined broadly as the market segment as a whole. It is more useful, however, to consider the consumer's friendship group as his social system since friends communicate with each other. Consequently, the influence of the innovators and early adopters within this group may be assumed to be more direct.

The **degree of newness** of a product is determined by its effect upon established patterns of consumption. New products may range from true innovations (air travel, computers) to major innovations (electric toothbrushes, car leasing) to minor innovations (cranberry juice, free checking accounts). Most products that marketers deal with are in the minor innovation category (see Chapter 11).

How quickly and completely a product is accepted depends, in general, on how consumers perceive it. Rogers proposed a set of influential product characteristics including relative advantage, compatibility, divisibility, and communicability.[22]

Relative advantage is the degree to which the new product will be better than the old. Adding mint to bath soap was not significant; adding fluoride to toothpaste was.

Compatibility refers to how the new product relates to existing ways of doing things. The more the consumer has to adapt to new methods or change old habits, the slower the product is likely to diffuse.

197

Divisibility is the extent to which a new product may be tried on a limited scale. Introductory samples and small sizes are examples of attempts to increase consumer acceptance through divisibility.

Communicability is the degree to which new products are likely to be noticed and discussed among consumers. Clothes, particularly new fashions, are high in communicability; a new medication for athlete's foot is likely to be low.

The other main decision in the diffusion of innovation process is **consumer adoption**. What makes a consumer an innovator, an early buyer? Here are some of the important characteristics discovered by consumer research, and their relationship between early and late adopters.[23]

Among demographic factors, innovators have a higher income and occupational status and are somewhat younger and better educated than noninnovators. In their communication behavior, innovators read more; television is not strongly correlated either way. In social interaction, innovators tend to be more active within both friendship and organizational groups. Innovators are also found to be more ready to take risks, to perceive of themselves as innovators, to have favorable attitudes toward new products, and not be afraid to try them.

The social dimension of new product diffusion is how the product has become known through personal influence. This dimension produces what is known as the interaction effect. There is also a sociocultural dimension to consider. The values and norms of a culture have an effect on the diffusion rate of a new product.

Marketing Implications

An understanding of the processes at work in diffusion can lead to a more efficient promotion of a new product. Marketers emphasize the product attributes most likely to appeal to consumers. If the product has a strong relative advantage, this should be featured in the promotion. The availability of small sizes for sampling is also important, as is an opportunity to experience a service on a trial basis. If the product requires a major adaptation on the consumer's part, promotion should emphasize explanation and education.

Marketing research can also establish a profile of the consumer most likely to adopt the new product. Advertising and promotion can then be aimed at reaching this influential segment of the market first. Later, strategies may be changed to concentrate influence on late adopters. If special effort is made to reach and convince the opinion leaders, the adoption rate may be accelerated throughout the social system. This effect will depend on how conspicuous the product is and how susceptible it is to word-of-mouth communication.

Marketers must also consider the sociocultural characteristics of their target area, particularly if foreign markets are contemplated. Many a marketing failure can be traced to the assumption that consumers in other countries will react the same as consumers in America. What sells out in New Haven may bomb in New Delhi.

The place of innovation diffusion in marketing is related to an understanding of the dynamics of product life cycle (Chapter 11), especially the early stages of a new product.

SOCIOCULTURAL PROCESSES OF CONSUMER BEHAVIOR

Although consumers are all individuals, they are also members of larger social groups. The sociocultural processes that influence consumer behavior as a result include social class and culture.

SOCIAL CLASS   Everyone is born into a family that belongs to a **social class**. In tradition-bound societies, class is the main determinant of an individual's future position in that society. Defining a particular social class in the United States is difficult because the classes themselves have no absolute boundary. Many marketers, rather than struggle with identifying families of equal social prestige, prefer to rely on more easily identified characteristics such as income level. Similar incomes, however, do not always lead to similar purchasing habits and selections.

How, then, can social class be identified? Education and occupation are two available indicators. While not infallible, these probably are the most accurate way to pinpoint social class, especially when used together. Source of income and dwelling area are also useful characteristics.

The United States tends toward an open-class system, allowing individuals to move up (or down) to a different social class. Moving down is, unfortunately, easier than moving up, particularly in situations where race and lack of education are factors. Education is the number one doorway to a higher social class.

Determining social class categories has always been a sticky problem. Table 8-3 shows one of the more acceptable breakdowns. The social groups of most interest to marketers are the middle and lower classes. Together they make up most of the population. In addition, the influence of middle-class attitudes and values spreads upward into families with incomes high enough to theoretically put them in a higher social classification.

Each social class has families who are referred to in marketing terms as "overprivileged" and "underprivileged" consumers. This grouping is based on income. A lawyer and a college professor, for example, may belong to the same social class. If the lawyer has an above-average income (for that class), he is considered overprivileged. His academic peer, on the other hand, may sacrifice income for intellectual pursuit and be classified as economically underprivileged. Unskilled laborers, social workers, and graduate students tend to be underprivileged. Factory foremen, union leaders, and top surgeons tend to be overprivileged.

Richard Coleman claims that members of both of these groups in every social class have consumption patterns that differ significantly from the rest of their social peers.[24] Overprivileged consumers in every social class are the first on the block with new or expensive innovations such as color television, home air conditioning, and aluminum tennis racquets. Equally true for all classes is the tendency of underprivileged consumers to lead the trend toward economy purchases such as small cars. The important distinction is that these consumers are high income or low income in relation to their social group rather than in relation to the country as a whole.

Table 8-3
SOCIAL CLASS HIERARCHY—WARNER

CLASS	DEFINITION	PERCENTAGE
Upper-upper	Aristocracy, "old family," inherited wealth	1.4
Lower-upper	Similar to upper-upper in income, occupation, and costly homes, but newer, lacking distinguished ancestry	1.6
Upper-middle	Professionals and substantial businessmen, civic leaders but not "society"	10.2
Lower-middle	Small businessmen, white collar workers, smaller homes, "good common people"	28.1
Upper-lower	Semiskilled workers, lower incomes, less desirable homes, "poor but hardworking people"	32.6
Lower-lower	Semiskilled and unskilled, worst homes, often on relief, low incomes, "level below the common man"	25.2
Unclassified		0.9
	Total	100.0

From James H. Myers and William H. Reynolds, *Consumer Behavior and Marketing Management* (Boston: Houghton Mifflin, 1967), p. 210. Based on the study by W. L. Warner and P. S. Lunt, *The Social Life of a Modern Community* (New Haven, Conn.: Yale University Press, 1941).

Marketing Implications   Although there are some products, such as crystal sherry decanters, which are linked principally to one social class, this is the exception rather than the rule. Even so, different social classes follow different life styles and thus form a basis for market segmentation. Robertson suggests that in formulating a marketing program for a social class, a marketer should answer three questions.[25]

1. *Is the product almost exclusively bound to a given social-class level?* If so, the marketing strategy can be specifically aimed to reach and appeal to that particular class. Rawhide work gloves and hand-sewn calfskin gloves will require different advertising appeals, media selection, and retail outlets to reach their class-separated potential buyers.

2. *Is the product consumed in greater proportions at a given social-class level?* William Wells and others found that upper-middle-class households with a more than average number of children tend to be heavy users of toothpaste, cold cereal, peanut butter, and frankfurters.[26] Lower on the social scale they found the heavy users of canned goods such as pork and beans, beef stew, and spaghetti.

3. *If the product is consumed across all social-class levels, what social-class segmentation possibilities exist?* All classes buy cameras but different classes tend to buy different types and to concentrate in different price ranges. A Pinto driver usually comes from a different class than a

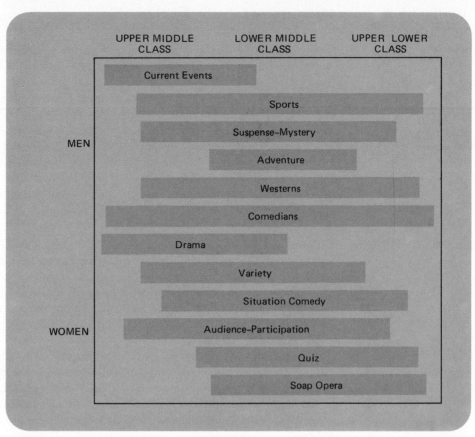

	UPPER MIDDLE CLASS	LOWER MIDDLE CLASS	UPPER LOWER CLASS

MEN

- Current Events
- Sports
- Suspense–Mystery
- Adventure
- Westerns
- Comedians
- Drama
- Variety
- Situation Comedy
- Audience–Participation
- Quiz
- Soap Opera

WOMEN

Figure 8-5
PROGRAM SELECTION BY SOCIAL CLASS AND SEX

From Peter D. Bennett and Harold H. Kassarjian, *Consumer Behavior* (Englewood Cliffs, N.J.: Prentice-Hall, 1972), p. 121. © 1972. Reprinted by permission of Prentice-Hall, Inc., Englewood Cliffs, New Jersey.

Cadillac driver. One manufacturer may have a whole range of grades for his product from standard to "super premium deluxe" in an attempt to broaden the product's social-class appeal.

Social classes also tend to segregate themselves in their selection of retail outlets. For clothing shoppers, a fashionable specialty store and a discount house may be further apart than a few city blocks.

Media audiences in general may show some social-class leaning. On the average, magazines are more likely to have a higher social class appeal than television. AM radio is typically more middle-class than FM radio. Time of day can also be important. Because the working class starts work earlier, you can catch them with AM radio from 6:00 to 7:30 a.m. From then until 9:00 a.m. the middle class is likely to be awake and listening.

Media content is a major determinant of which social class is likely to be watching, listening, or reading. A typical newspaper reader from the working class may start with the sports page, then read the comics. The middle- and upper-class reader will more likely look first at the news of the day and possibly the editorial page. A classical music program on FM radio may reach a socially higher audience than an AM hockey broadcast.

Television programming, as shown in Figure 8-5, shows differences as well, although most categories cover quite a wide range of viewers. Particular program content may sometimes concentrate viewership more within one class.

Research has shown that each social group has its particular consumption patterns and therefore segmented marketing approaches should be successful. However, social-class segmentation is not always relevant. Sometimes other criteria, such as age or sex, may be more appropriate. The benefits to be gained by social-class segmentation for undifferentiated products may cost more than they are worth. Social-class segments would be more effectively used with other variables such as stage in the family life cycle and ethnic group.

CULTURE   **Culture** has been described as a concept that "includes a set of *learned* beliefs, values, attitudes, habits, and forms of behavior that are *shared* by a society and are *transmitted* from generation to generation within that society."[27]

Culture may be continental, such as the European culture, the African culture, the Asian culture. In the next division are the national cultures: the Italian, the Nigerian, the Cambodian, each with distinctive characteristics and traditions.

If we divide still further, we can identify subcultures. Within the American culture are subcultures based on national origin (Polish-American, Mexican-American), on religion (Catholic, Jewish), and on race (black, oriental).

It is a common mistake to regard culture as a defined, static list of characteristics, beliefs, and traditions which are of value to a particular group or nationality. Culture is alive, moving, changing. It reacts to pressures from inside and from outside itself. Resistance to these pressures often causes conflict between members of the culture and other cultures, and between the young and the old within the culture. This has been especially true of America's most prominent subcultures which are based on race or original immigrant status.

Cultural change may result from technological advances, such as new farming methods that make traditional methods obsolete. Education and travel can have profound effects on culture as more and more young people experience life in other countries and adopt new values. Advances such as the birth control pill result in a whole restructuring of moral values which, in turn, affects censorship, entertainment, and advertising.

Much of the fashionable popularity of products or ideas reflect not cultural change but temporary fascinations. The trick is to spot the long-term trend behind the fad. Miniskirts and tight jeans may come and go but the trend toward sexual frankness and honesty will probably continue, with significant cultural meaning. The interest in women's liberation may die down but the long-term cultural trend will continue toward equality and male–female relationships on new terms.

Marketing   Marketing in the 1970s has been paying increasing attention to ethnic sub-
Implications   cultures. Strategies and advertising campaigns have been aimed at specific groups such as Spanish speakers and blacks. Success has been varied. Where

it falls down most often is in the failure to realize that the black or Chicano or Irish-American market is not one group with one common level of needs and desires. Each of these groups is varied in terms of age, income, and social class.

The middle-class black American has been particularly hard to categorize. Through mass media he or she has been conditioned, like the white American, to desire a certain standard of living that, too often, is beyond his or her economic means and limited by discrimination. Some marketers see the black consumer as a challenge; others react by rejecting this particular market as not worth the efforts of market segmentation.

Reaching different subcultures within a society calls for a close study of media in general and outlets within each media in particular. Radio, for example, is said to be a major medium for blacks in general, with certain stations showing an above-average number of black listeners.

Ethnic cultures are speaking out more and more against advertising that offends them. After ignoring requests from Chicano groups, the Frito-Lay Company finally responded to legal action and removed the "Frito Bandito" character from their corn chip advertising. Polish-American groups have also gone to court to have ethnic humor banned from advertising.

Obviously, companies planning to market in foreign countries or nonprofit organizations planning public service projects must take cultural differences into account. This applies not only to national characteristics but to the cultural patterns of the potential consumer segment within the country. We will explore this type of analysis further in Chapter 25.

CONCLUSION

The field of consumer behavior is complex, involving an interplay of individual, social, and sociocultural processes. A mountain of explanations and data from the behavioral sciences and consumer research has told us a lot about it. However, some of the present findings about consumer behavior are tenuous; others are downright contradictory. Because the understanding of consumer behavior is so crucial to the development of sound marketing strategy, the search for explanations will go on.

For the ambitious marketer, the dynamics of consumer behavior provide a challenge. The exploration of consumer patterns brings the considerable benefit of understanding market behavior in depth. We will continue our exploration of buyer behavior in the next chapter, paying special attention to the consumer decision-making process.

DISCUSSION QUESTIONS

1. As a marketing executive with a national airline, you must choose between spending $500,000 on more crew training (especially for flight attendants) or on new Balenciaga-designed uniforms. In what way can knowledge of consumer behavior help you reach a decision?

2. Using your knowledge of consumer behavior, give some explanations of why a student (like yourself) would purchase a particular kind of typewriter? How would you go about determining which explanations are the most accurate?

3. Describe how the three views of consumer rationality—economic, behavioral, and societal—would apply to a study of consumer behavior in cigarette smoking, snowmobiling, and family planning.

4. Of all the dynamics of consumer behavior described in this chapter, which three processes do you think are most useful for understanding why consumers behave as they do? Explain why. Which are the two least useful? Explain why.

5. You have been requested by an environmental activist organization to design a comprehensive marketing program to discourage consumers from contributing to pollution. Assuming you would accept this assignment, what findings from consumer behavior topics would be valuable to you? What are some types of strategy implications that you can base upon them?

6. Describe how these consumer behavior processes would be relevant to an understanding of:

a. consumer attitudes toward a blood bank;

b. diffusion of innovation for digital watches;

c. reference groups for a "faded denim" clothing boutique;

d. families for a telephone answering service;

e. social class for an indoor tennis club;

f. perception of a new high-protein soy drink;

g. a state-wide referendum on banning aerosol cans.

NOTES

1. David M. Stander, "Testing New Product Ideas in an 'Archie Bunker' World," *Marketing News*, November 15, 1973, p. 1.

2. James F. Engel, David T. Kollat, and Roger D. Blackwell, *Consumer Behavior,* 2d ed. (New York: Holt, Rinehart and Winston, 1973), p. 5.

3. Barry Newman, "Troubles Are Brewing for Coffee Concerns as Youths Shun Drink," *Wall Street Journal*, December 3, 1970, pp. 1, 29.

4. Abraham H. Maslow, "A Theory of Human Motivation," *Psychological Review* 50 (1943): 370–96.

5. Thomas S. Robertson, *Consumer Behavior* (Glenview, Ill.: Scott, Foresman, 1970), pp. 15–16.

6. André Gabor and C. W. J. Granger, "Price as an Indicator of Quality: Report on an Enquiry," *Economica* 33 (February 1966): 43–47.

7. Raymond A. Bauer, "Consumer Behavior as Risk Taking," *Proceedings of the American Marketing Association* (Chicago: American Marketing Association, 1960), pp. 389–98.

8. Donald F. Cox, ed., *Risk Taking and Information Handling in Consumer Behavior* (Cambridge, Mass.: Division of Research, Graduate School of Business Administration, Harvard University, 1967).

9. Bernard Berelson and Gary A. Steiner, *Human Behavior* (New York: Harcourt, Brace and World, 1964).

10. John Dollard and Neal E. Miller, *Personality and Psychotherapy* (New York: McGraw-Hill, 1950).

11. Robertson, pp. 28–29.

12. David Krech and Richard S. Crutchfield,

Theory and Problems of Social Psychology (New York: McGraw-Hill, 1948), p. 152.

13. Robertson, p. 45.
14. Carl I. Hovland and Walter Weiss, "The Influence of Source Credibility on Communications Effectiveness," *Public Opinion Quarterly* 15 (Winter 1951–52): 635–50.
15. Irving L. Janis and Seymour Feshbach, "Effects of Fear-Arousing Communications," *Journal of Abnormal and Social Psychology* 48 (January 1953): 78–92.
16. John R. Stuteville, "Psychic Defenses against High Fear Appeals: A Key Marketing Variable," *Journal of Marketing* 34 (April 1970): 39–45.
17. Tamotsu Shibutani, "Reference Groups as Perspectives," *American Journal of Sociology* 60 (May 1955): 562–69.
18. Elihu Katz, "The Two-Step Flow of Communication: An Up-to-Date Report on an Hypothesis," *Public Opinion Quarterly* 21 (Spring 1957): 61–78.
19. Charles W. King, "Fashion Adoption: A Rebuttal to the 'Trickle Down' Theory," in *Proceedings of the American Marketing Association* (Chicago: American Marketing Association, 1964), pp. 108–25.
20. Robertson, p. 91.
21. Everett M. Rogers, *Diffusion of Innovations* (New York: Free Press, 1962).
22. Ibid.
23. Thomas S. Robertson, *Innovation and the Consumer* (New York: Holt, Rinehart and Winston, 1971).
24. Richard P. Coleman, "The Significance of Social Stratification in Selling," in *Proceedings of the American Marketing Association* (Chicago: American Marketing Association, 1960), pp. 171–84.
25. Robertson, *Consumer Behavior*, pp. 125–26.
26. William D. Wells, Seymour Banks, and Douglas Tigert, "Order in the Data," in *Proceedings of the American Marketing Association* (Chicago: American Marketing Association, 1967), pp. 263–66.
27. Peter D. Bennett and Harold H. Kassarjian, *Consumer Behavior* (Englewood Cliffs, N.J.: Prentice-Hall, 1972), p. 123.

9

CONSUMER DECISION MAKING

After completing this chapter, the reader should be able to:

1. Tell what consumer decision making adds to an understanding of consumer behavior.

2. Explain the nature of the stages in the consumer decision-making process—problem recognition, information search, alternative evaluation, purchase decision, and postpurchase evaluation.

3. Describe the marketing implications that are suggested by the stages in the consumer decision-making process.

4. Point out the value of a comprehensive model of consumer behavior.

5. Evaluate the current state of consumer behavior knowledge, theory, and research techniques, from managerial and social perspectives.

In Chapter 8 we examined the factors that influence consumer behavior. For marketers, the most important behavior on the part of a consumer is the process of deciding whether to buy or not to buy. In this chapter, we will analyze the process of **consumer decision making** and how marketing can influence it.

CHUCK'S DREAM MACHINE

In July following commencement, recent college graduate Chuck Zegar bought a Cougar. At first, this might be considered a simple consumer decision. Chuck realized that he needed a car; he looked around at what was available, and bought a Cougar. But in reality, a vast array of economic and social forces affected Chuck's ultimate decision.

Chuck was in the position of many new college graduates who have just begun working (in Chuck's case, as a management trainee in a Pittsburgh department store). He didn't have much money, he didn't own a car, and he envied his friends who did. In time, he decided that he was uncomfortable "bumming" rides from his friends and was being inconvenienced by the inadequate mass transit system in his town. A new car would give him status and prestige. Also, its later trade-in value was money in the bank.

Ford Motor Company

Chuck preferred small cars because they saved money on gas and because they were easier to handle and park. He made a careful survey of various possibilities, including the Maverick, Cougar, Mustang, Gremlin, Charger, and Pinto (he wanted to get an American car). He spoke to friends and neighbors with small cars and evaluated each model in terms of safety, comfort, cost, upkeep, and appearance. After carefully studying *Consumer Reports* recommendations, he settled on a Cougar convertible in the "hottest" red color available. Months later, except that it had a rattle in a door, Chuck was delighted with his dream-come-true machine.

Chuck Zegar, as a typical consumer, can be viewed as a problem solver within the marketing system. He solves a problem (his need for transportation) by deciding on a plan of action (buying a new Cougar) that meets his subjective wants (a red convertible). He went through a series of mental action steps before and even after making the "I'll take it" decision. This decision-making process is affected by many variables, including:

1. influential people (family, friends, and neighbors);

2. sources of information (*Consumer Reports,* government mileage studies);

3. evaluative criteria (style, price, safety factors, and fuel economy);

4. marketing factors (advertising, auto dealers, financing plans).

In Chapter 8 we examined the dynamics of consumer behavior. Its central issue is the consumer's ability to make an effective purchase. Some consumers attempt to know as much as they can about various alternatives, as Chuck did when he consulted *Consumer Reports.* Nevertheless, most consumer decisions are very much affected by emotional preferences. Logic is often bent when subjective feelings (or media-suggested stereotypes) are aroused. Remember the Perdue chicken success story from Chapter 1? Consumers who decide that supermarket chickens are somehow "better" if they look particularly yellow in color, may discard cost comparison and even their own sense of taste (all chicken tastes more or less the same) to satisfy this feeling.

Figure 9-1 presents the model of consumer behavior that we are using as the basis for Chapters 8 and 9. Here we will focus on five basic stages in the consumer decision-making process:[1]

1. *Problem recognition.* A consumer may have a problem or need but not recognize it. Nothing will happen until he or she becomes aware of the problem. Chuck may have used the bus and accepted rides from friends for a year before he realized that he wanted a car of his own.

2. *Search for information.* Once a consumer understands that he has a problem, he will search for information that will help him resolve the problem. If he needs a car, he will make an *internal* search. During this search he will think about what kind of car he needs, how much he can afford to pay, whether he knows a car dealer who will give him a "break," and so forth. He will also conduct an *external* search by consulting friends, neighbors, relatives, car dealers, and garage mechanics.

3. *Evaluation of information.* This depends in good part on the results of the information search. If the consumer has not developed adequate or correct information, his or her evaluation process will clearly suffer. But effective evaluation also requires a sophisticated analysis that few consumers are able or willing to do. If Chuck doesn't understand the workings of all cars, it may be difficult for him to evaluate the strengths and weaknesses of various models.

4. *Purchase decision.* Here the facts and realities of evaluation are balanced, often against the consumer's subjective feelings. Every bit of evidence may point to the Pinto as the superior choice for Chuck, but if his friends think that a Cougar has more status, he may discard logic and go with his emotions.

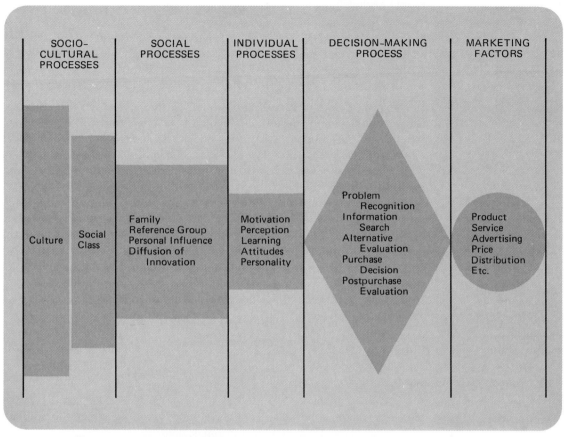

Figure 9-1   OVERVIEW MODEL OF CONSUMER BEHAVIOR

Adapted from Harold H. Kassarjian and Thomas S. Robertson, *Perspectives in Consumer Behavior* (Glenview Ill.: Scott, Foresman, 1968), p. 4. Copyright © 1968 by Scott, Foresman and Company. Reprinted by permission of the publisher.

5. *Postpurchase evaluation.* Feedback on the decision may be seen as coming "too late," but actually it helps the consumer make a better decision in his or her next purchase. If Chuck eventually discovers that his Cougar burns a surprisingly high amount of gas, he will at least "know better" the next time he looks for a car.

A knowledge of the consumer decision-making process is quite useful for marketers. It helps them define target markets and prepare effective appeals to consumers. The better a marketer understands what the consumer weighs in making a purchase, the more he or she can tailor the marketing mix to the preferences and desires of the consumer.

In a socially responsible marketplace, consumers will be able to make the most effective decisions possible. Marketers are under more pressure to do their part to make this ideal a reality. If they do not provide adequate information and services to help consumers make the best decisions, then the coalition of government, mass media, and consumer advocates will force this task on marketers anyway (as we saw in Chapter 4).

Other types of nonmarket situations also can be viewed as decision-making processes. Examples are the use of birth control and the choice of a birth control method; the decision to go on to graduate school in business administration and the choice of a school; and the extent of use of health-care facilities.

THE CONSUMER AND DECISION MAKING

The consumer does not have an easy time in the marketing system. Life in late twentieth-century America is complex, as is coping with the constant activities of consumption. The consumer must constantly make decisions about purchasing, despite a variety of handicaps, including lack of capital, insufficient information about products, many alternative products, time pressures, and little training.

One way that consumers can deal with this problem is by planning. Every consumer decision involves the selection of a specific course of action (such as buying a new Cougar) from among various alternatives. Planning means making decisions in anticipation of needs or problems. Thus consumer decision planning is basically the recognition of a problem and choice of a solution.[2]

Consumer planning helps the consumer in three principal ways:

1. It forces the consumer to think logically and develop realistic goals.

2. It encourages the consumer to focus on the most serious or persistent buying problems.

3. It helps the consumer organize decision making and set meaningful priorities.

Most consumers, unfortunately, either do not plan rationally at all or are not efficient at planning. Although consumers differ in how well they plan and execute decisions to buy, the act of decision making is common to all.[3]

There are four important types of **market-related decisions** that consumers must make:

1. *What to buy.* This involves choice of product and brand, price, product quality, and service choice.

2. *Where to buy.* Next to "what to buy," this is the most important decision. Products, prices, and services vary in different locations (downtown or in the suburbs) and in different stores (department stores versus discount houses).

3. *When to buy.* Grocery stores have sales on certain days; department stores may have inventory clearances in off-peak months. Thus, consumer options vary during different time periods. "When to buy" also involves "what time of day." Crowds may be particularly bad in certain stores in the middle of the day.

4. *How to buy.* This includes how far a consumer will travel to make a purchase, how much time will be allowed for browsing, and whether the consumer will attempt to bargain with store-owners (if permitted), as well as other choices.

CONSUMER DECISION STAGES AND MARKETING

Earlier we briefly described the five stages of consumer decision making: problem recognition, information search, alternative evaluation, purchase decision, and postpurchase evaluation. In this section, we will discuss these stages in greater detail and analyze the marketing implications for each.[4]

One important point must be underscored. These five steps represent a model of typical consumer behavior. But every consumer does not follow this model perfectly. For many routine purchases, the decision is almost automatic (think of your favorite brand of candy). In these cases, the five stages are cut short. Consumers operate intuitively and may not even be aware that they are performing all of these tasks. Thus, the model is not exact, but it is useful in studying consumer behavior.

PROBLEM RECOGNITION
The consumer's first step in entering the market is the recognition that he or she has a **problem**—a need is not being satisfied. The consumer is unsure of how to satisfy this need. (If the solution is fairly certain, there is no real problem.) Consumer problems can involve a broad range of market factors, including products, brands, stores, services, and prices. C. Glenn Walters notes that problem recognition is "essentially a mental process in which memory, experience, learning, perception, and forgetting function together, bringing the problem to the consciousness."

There are many different sources of consumer problems. Among the most important are:

Assortment Deficiency. The consumer must determine what he or she has in inventory, evaluate the extent of any deficiencies, and decide what product preference he will make. The assortment includes the range of goods and services (such as food, toiletries, housing, transportation, entertainment, and so forth) that an individual or family needs in order to live. When the refrigerator looks empty, an assortment deficiency exists.

New or Different Information. The knowledge of a new product, brand, service, or store might possibly cause the consumer to reexamine his present purchasing habits.

Expanded Desires. The individual may suddenly find that he or she wants more products or better services (especially after learning that a friend has them).

Expanded Means. If the individual's material conditions change (for instance from a raise in salary), he or she may become dissatisfied with the products and services currently available.

Changed Expectations. Advertising, status pressures, or changed family structure can all affect a person's desires and perceptions of his or her needs.

Once the consumer recognizes that a problem exists, he or she has a number of basic choices. He or she can ignore the problem, postpone action until a later time, or attempt to find a solution. In any event, whatever the consumer chooses to do (or not to do), problem recognition has altered his or her awareness.

**Marketing
Implications**
Marketing researchers measure problem recognition through the use of **purchase-intention scales**.[5] The accuracy of these scales is significantly affected by the length of the forecast period. (This is the length of time between the decision to purchase and the actual purchase.) If the period of anticipation is long, it is more likely that the intervening environmental changes will affect the purchase. Thus, these scales will be most useful when there is little time lag.

Information about purchase intentions can be used in a variety of ways by marketers. **Purchase-probability scales** help to identify promotional targets and to direct promotional efforts. Analyzing purchase intentions over time is useful in determining the effectiveness of marketing programs. Also, marketers can actually develop **problem recognition sets**.[6] For example, if we know that bride-to-be Anne Fredericks has recently bought Lenox china, we can develop certain priority patterns that may suggest her future purchases (related to tableware and small appliances). Through techniques like these, marketers can gain important insights from research data concerning problem recognition and purchase intentions.

**INFORMATION
SEARCH**
The search for product-related information is a vital activity for consumers. An informed consumer may be able to get the equivalent product for a lower price, or may be able to get a better product for the same price. Of course, this search process has its costs, both financial and psychological. It is a time-consuming process which can be expensive and draining.[7]

The prime sources of information for consumers are personal experience, reference groups, and businesses or professionals. Personal experience is an internal source that includes the consumer's previous problems, solutions, and level of satisfaction. Reference group sources may be family members, friends, work associates, or other members of the community whose opinions are considered relevant.

Business sources are generally the mass media, personal salespeople (door-to-door or telephone), and retail stores. Advertising is a key marketing technique for passing along information to the consumer. Brands, prices, sales, product features, locations, and store names are transmitted through advertising.[8] Insurance and cosmetics are often sold by personal salespeople. Retail stores also provide information for the consumer, but comparison shopping is often confusing and tiring. Professional sources include physicians, lawyers, clergy, social workers, government officials, and others.

Five important factors affect the consumer's search for information:

1. *Experience.* If a consumer already knows enough about a purchase, a search will be unnecessary. A person with years of experience and interest in house plants will not need to spend hours or days figuring out whether a particular store's offerings are a "good buy."

2. *Availability of information without search.* The consumer will usually try to avoid a physical search whenever possible. If the local supermarket advertises fruit and vegetable bargains in the newspaper, the consumer can avoid the arduous task of going from store to store and writing down prices.

3. *Satisfaction derived from search.* Sometimes, the search process is convenient and enjoyable. It may also be unpleasant and tiresome. Some consumers enjoy spending an hour wandering around a clothing store. Others want to leave after ten minutes and order from a catalog next time.

4. *Perceived consequence of search.* If a search may have important consequences, the consumer will be more likely to invest time and energy. This could be the case if the consumer believes it could lead to a substantial monetary savings, a higher quality product, or less chance of product dissatisfaction. Think of that "right" suit or outfit for job interviews or dentist known for painless drilling.

5. *Value placed on the product.* Some products are more valuable to the consumer than others, either because they have high financial value or they satisfy important consumer needs. Most people will spend more time shopping for a color television than they will shopping for new linen. But a science fiction enthusiast may spend more time searching for interesting new books that cost $3 each than for other, more expensive items.

Marketing Implications

An organization in a particular field may decide that it must adapt its marketing system to the information-seeking behavior of consumers. If this occurs, the organization will generally take four critical factors into account.[9]

Percentage of the target market engaging in search. If postrecession vacationers are engaging in a search, travel agencies may want to focus on search behavior.

2. *Percentage of the target market using each type of information source.* If most shoe buyers who seek information check window advertisements in stores, and very few consult newspaper advertisements or consumer magazines, then companies can easily determine how to tailor marketing campaigns.

3. *Relative importance of information sources.* If surveys suggest that the decisive information source in consumer purchases of various cold remedies is the recommendations of local pharmacists, rather than television advertising, there might be a redirection of promotional budgets.

4. *Family role structures associated with information seeking.* Firms are interested in which family members seek information in various consumer fields. Who conducts the search when the family needs a new vacuum cleaner? When the family needs a new stereo? Related to this are efforts to determine who the important opinion leaders are in a community.

ALTERNATIVE EVALUATION

An effective search for information is pointless unless the consumer makes use of the information found to evaluate alternatives. In order to do so, the consumer must (1) systematize information, (2) establish decision criteria, (3) determine the type of alternatives, and (4) compare alternatives.

The first step is to organize the data into a form that is useful for evaluation. A consumer does this when he or she tears out "Sale" advertisements for citizen-band radios from the newspaper and compares them. At a more complex level, organizing data can involve making charts and graphs of important statistics.

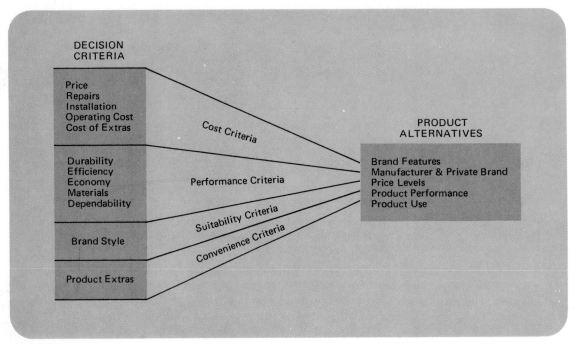

Figure 9-2

DECISION CRITERIA USED IN PRODUCT COMPARISON

Reproduced with permission from C. Glenn Walters, *Consumer Behavior: Theory and Practice*, rev. ed. (Homewood, Ill.: Irwin, 1974), p. 551.

Next comes the establishment of decision criteria. Typically, consumer criteria are developed from within the individual himself, from the input (or pressure) of reference groups, and from the influence of marketing sources. People are making increasing use of objective sources, such as *Consumer Reports*, consumer advice in newspapers and on television, and government "how-to-buy" publications.

While the criteria used by each consumer vary, there are four basic groupings: cost, performance, suitability, and convenience. Figure 9-2 presents a model of decision criteria and their impact on product alternatives.

Studies of consumer behavior suggest certain patterns in consumer purchasing criteria. Generally, consumers tend to employ more than one criterion when making a decision. A consumer may rent a car from Jerry's Junction Auto Rental because it is cheaper than Hertz or Avis, while still having an acceptable performance record. Most consumers seem to rely on a very small number of criteria in selecting a product. It is often assumed that cost is the critical variable in a decision, but there is evidence that this factor may be somewhat overrated. For example, a consumer may prefer a brand of superior quality, even when its price is higher than some competitors.

Once the consumer has decided upon the criteria for decision making, he or she can survey the available alternatives. These can include:

1. product alternatives (what brand to buy; what price level);

2. store alternatives (what area of town to buy in; what particular store);

3. method-of-purchase alternatives (whether to pay cash or charge; whether to have merchandise delivered or to carry it home).

POSTPURCHASE EVALUATION

Postpurchase evaluation is the final stage in the consumer's decision-making process. It may be an informal evaluation, for example, telling your friend that your new freezer doesn't work properly. It may involve some formal evaluation technique, such as a record of your new car's gas mileage. These evaluations are always based on new information—mainly on your own experiences with the product after you have taken ownership. In some cases, the opinions of family or friends may become a significant part of the postpurchase evaluation process. If everyone tells you that your new dining room set seems overpriced, these opinions are bound to affect your satisfaction with the transaction.

Postpurchase evaluation can be a helpful educational process. The consumer gains knowledge and experience about a product and a particular brand and also about the general problems of functioning within the marketing system. If serious evaluations of buying strategy and technique are made, he or she will probably become a more efficient consumer and make better buys in the future.

Table 9-1
TYPICAL CONSUMER DECISIONS

PRODUCT DECISIONS	STORE DECISIONS	METHOD-OF-PURCHASE DECISIONS
1. *Brand decisions.* Manufacturer's brands vs. private brands. Most consumers prefer manufacturer's brands; some choose private brands due to lower prices and trust in retailers.	1. *Choice of store.* Affected by location, price lines, assortment, services, personnel, atmosphere.	1. *Use of telephone.* Telephone shopping increasing; convenient for many consumers.
2. *Price and deal decisions.* Attitude toward price varies by product. Affected by "deals" such as coupons and reduced-price-off products.	2. *Display and shelf decisions.* End-aisle displays can boost sales of some products. Consumers prefer products at eye-level or waist-high.	2. *Attitudes toward time and distance.* Most consumers won't travel more than one-half mile for frequently purchased goods or one mile for high-priced goods.
3. *Impulse decisions.* Involves frequently purchased items more than large-ticket items. Affects store design—candy and magazines placed at check-out counters.	3. *Consumer reactions to store layout.* Certain layout areas have greatest traffic flow and popularity. Fashion displays placed in front locations in department stores.	3. *Multiple-shopping decisions.* In same trip, consumers will buy hardware and drugs; or clothing, food, and personal items; or furniture, records, and clothing.

Reproduced with permission from C. Glenn Walters, *Consumer Behavior: Theory and Practice,* rev. ed. (Homewood, Ill.: Irwin, 1974), pp. 554–58.

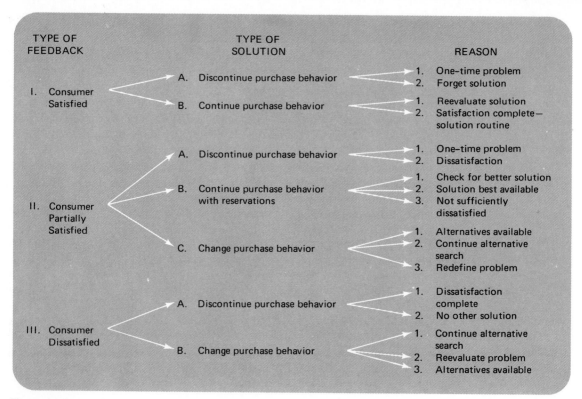

TYPE OF FEEDBACK	TYPE OF SOLUTION	REASON
I. Consumer Satisfied	A. Discontinue purchase behavior	1. One-time problem 2. Forget solution
	B. Continue purchase behavior	1. Reevaluate solution 2. Satisfaction complete—solution routine
II. Consumer Partially Satisfied	A. Discontinue purchase behavior	1. One-time problem 2. Dissatisfaction
	B. Continue purchase behavior with reservations	1. Check for better solution 2. Solution best available 3. Not sufficiently dissatisfied
	C. Change purchase behavior	1. Alternatives available 2. Continue alternative search 3. Redefine problem
III. Consumer Dissatisfied	A. Discontinue purchase behavior	1. Dissatisfaction complete 2. No other solution
	B. Change purchase behavior	1. Continue alternative search 2. Reevaluate problem 3. Alternatives available

Figure 9-3
ADJUSTMENT IN CONSUMER MARKET DECISIONS

Reproduced with permission from C. Glenn Walters, *Consumer Behavior: Theory and Practice*, rev. ed. (Homewood, Ill.: Irwin, 1974), p. 561.

Figure 9-3 presents a variety of adjustments in consumer market decisions that may arise from postpurchase evaluation. These adjustments differ depending on whether the consumer is satisfied, partially satisfied, or unsatisfied by the original purchase decision. Consumer adjustments generally depend on three factors: the amount of new information; the type of feedback—satisfaction or dissatisfaction; and the mental reaction of the consumer.

As we saw in Chapter 4, the activist consumer movement of the last decade has, in part, been a response to widespread consumer dissatisfaction with purchase decisions. Figure 9-3 lists buying another of the "alternatives available" as one consumer adjustment when dissatisfaction exists. Another alternative has been to question and reexamine many practices of the marketing system. The consumerism movement has flourished because many consumers have concluded that unsatisfactory purchase decisions have not been their own fault, but reflect unfair practices or mediocre performance by industry.

Marketing Implications

Organizations are shortsighted when they consider a transaction closed once a consumer has purchased their product. If the buyer has difficulties with a microwave oven's installation, instructions, and use, these difficulties will certainly lead to a negative postpurchase evaluation. Or if an airline does not prepare relevant promotional literature, it may miss the opportunity to sell such companion services as car rental and hotel reservations. Finally, if a small college does not attempt to aid a freshman in financing his or her education, a favorable decision to enroll may turn sour when it is time to pay the bursar. For these reasons, marketing strategy emphasizes a vision of the **total purchase act** and all its relevant consequences.

Some organizations have experimented with follow-up letters to buyers or with other advertising strategies tailored to consumers who have already purchased their product. These efforts are intended to reinforce favorable postpurchase evaluations. However, the effectiveness of these tactics is not clearcut. If the consumer is using a product and is dissatisfied, promotional efforts of this sort could actually backfire.[12]

A COMPREHENSIVE CONSUMER BEHAVIOR MODEL

In the last 20 years, a number of consumer behavior models have been developed. Each is an effort to describe the key variables operating in consumer behavior dynamics, and to picture the interaction of these variables. Some models are focused on an important consumer dynamic (brand-switching, attitude change, diffusion of innovation). Others are comprehensive and include nearly all of the processes of consumer behavior (particularly problem solving and information processing).

The process of consumer behavior is intricate. As a result, any effective model must describe a wide variety of inputs. Indeed, it must encompass most of the concepts covered in this and the preceding chapter. It must do more than list variables; it must explain how these forces are integrated in the decision-making behavior of consumers.[13]

If the model is to be useful, it must be clear, precise, and comprehensive. This type of consumer model gives an overall picture of what we know about consumer behavior and suggests the kinds of data that would be useful in consumer research. Eventually, the computer simulation of consumer models will permit more certainty in predicting outcomes of consumer behavior. The "consumer" in these models would be "Mr. or Ms. Average" in the target market segment.

THE HOWARD-SHETH MODEL

Figure 9-4 illustrates the Howard-Sheth model of consumer behavior, one of the most sophisticated that has yet been developed. The Howard-Sheth model has also been the focus of research suggesting that several of its key parts are valid.

The inputs on the left of the model represent significant, symbolic, and social stimuli. These include the effects that business and environment have on the consumer. When the consumer becomes aware of one of these factors, a condition of stimulus ambiguity results. At this point, the consumer searches for more information. This information is processed through an interaction with the consumer's perceptual bias, including attitudes and motives in his memory.

New information can lead to changes in motives, choice criteria, brand comprehension, and purchase intentions. Ultimately, this affects the final purchase decision. Once the decision has been made, the information then becomes data feedback. It may result in satisfaction and an understanding of the qualities of a certain brand. It will also have an impact on attitudes, intention, and attention.

Figure 9-4 HOWARD-SHETH MODEL OF CONSUMER BEHAVIOR

From John A. Howard and Jagdish N. Sheth, *The Theory of Buyer Behavior* (New York; Wiley, 1969), p. 30.

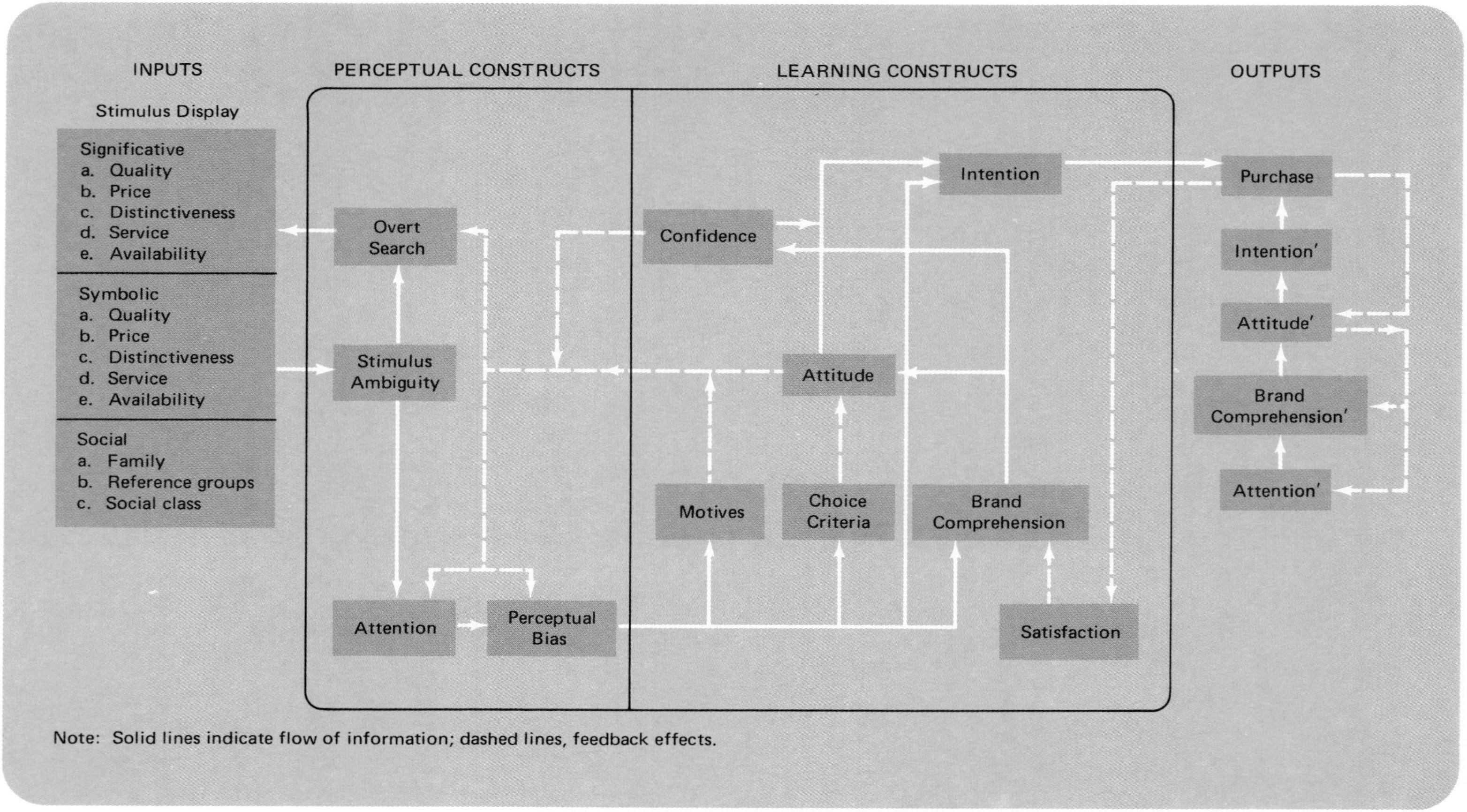

INPUTS

Stimulus Display

Significative
a. Quality
b. Price
c. Distinctiveness
d. Service
e. Availability

Symbolic
a. Quality
b. Price
c. Distinctiveness
d. Service
e. Availability

Social
a. Family
b. Reference groups
c. Social class

PERCEPTUAL CONSTRUCTS

Overt Search

Stimulus Ambiguity

Attention

Perceptual Bias

LEARNING CONSTRUCTS

Confidence

Intention

Attitude

Motives

Choice Criteria

Brand Comprehension

Satisfaction

OUTPUTS

Purchase

Intention'

Attitude'

Brand Comprehension'

Attention'

Note: Solid lines indicate flow of information; dashed lines, feedback effects.

John A. Howard has suggested that the model can be applied, with some alterations, to three separate types of buying situations. These situations are extensive problem solving, limited problem solving, and automatic response behavior.[14] **Extensive problem solving** refers to situations where a buyer seeks a product that is both important and expensive, but is hampered by limited knowledge. In this situation, the buyer is an active information seeker with few previous purchase experiences. **Limited problem solving** occurs when the buyer has had some experience purchasing the product in question. There is a high likelihood of the buyer staying with his or her previous buying pattern, but it is possible that new stimuli and information will lead to a different conclusion. **Automatic response behavior** means that the buyer's habits are quite fixed and unlikely to change. The decision is barely thought out; the buyer knows the product is needed and instinctively chooses his or her traditional brand.

The Howard-Sheth model is complicated and somewhat confusing and has been criticized on a number of key points. These include its failure to explain adequately the interaction of inputs, stimulus ambiguity, and perceptual bias, and its neglect of variables such as needs, communications, and the decision processes. Nevertheless, most of the academic commentary on the model stresses its value in clarifying our understanding of consumer behavior.

EVALUATION OF CONSUMER BEHAVIOR

In Chapter 8 we mentioned that our discussion of the study of consumer behavior would be concerned with whether this study can enable marketers to explain, predict, or control consumer behavior. Now, since these two chapters have examined consumer behavior, we can ask to what degree current approaches to consumer behavior have reached these three goals (all of which are of great interest to marketing management).

We shall first assess the explanation and prediction goals from a management point of view. The control of consumer behavior is important to consumers as well as to management, and will be examined in a social context.

MANAGEMENT VIEWPOINT Table 9-2 presents an evaluation of the study of consumer behavior. It focuses on various goals of this study, including those of explanation, prediction, and control, which were introduced in Chapter 8.

We are perhaps closest to the goal of **explanation**, but more advances are necessary. Extensive knowledge has been accumulated in the last few decades and marketing research methods are constantly being improved. The market segmentation approach, for example, permits a fine-tuned examination of the general behavior of people and their reactions to specific products.

There are two principal requirements which relate to explanation goals. There must be explanatory relevance; in other words, there must be a logical reason to believe that the specified consumer behavior will occur as described. Also, expectations must be open to *testing* (through market research) to verify their accuracy.[15]

Table 9-2

ASSESSING THE STUDY OF CONSUMER BEHAVIOR

EXPLANATION GOALS	PREDICTION GOALS	CONTROL GOALS
ACHIEVEMENTS		
Extensive knowledge Marketing research methods Market segmentation strategy	Historical relationships Probabilistic models	Monopolistic power Conditioning process Control over disadvantaged consumers
CONSTRAINTS		
Limitations of behavioral concepts and techniques Incomplete information and theories	Complexity of behavior Lack of reliable models Translating psychoanalytic techniques into laws of market behavior	Marketing inefficiencies Sophisticated consumers Competition New technology Government Consumer advocates Mass media Education Religion

There are significant limitations to our ability to explain consumer behavior. Primarily, we are constrained by the primitive nature of behavioral science concepts and techniques—what they mean and how they are measured. The behavioral sciences have been modeled on the physical sciences, but they are not nearly as precise or reliable. Their predictions retain a significant margin of error, which casts doubt over the adequacy of any resulting explanation.

Also, much of the necessary data for accurate explanations are still missing. We can only wonder how much information is stored in the files of one corporation or another (and therefore cannot be printed in this book). As long as our data are incomplete, we can hardly be certain that our explanations of consumer behavior are valid.

In conclusion, we seem to have a reasonable grasp of what is happening with consumers and why. (Of course, it is easier to be correct after the fact.) The insights of Chapter 8 and this chapter can assist us in determining how consumers act and how marketers can respond.

As for the goal of **prediction**, we are by no means there. Predictions can be formulated by analyzing past behavior that resulted from the use of a given marketing strategy. We have techniques and models that enable us to estimate how likely it is that consumers will respond in a similar manner in the future.

Most attempts to predict consumer behavior have not been particularly successful. The key problem here is that, as we saw in Chapter 8, consumer behavior simply does not follow set patterns. Consumers Jackson and O'Hara may both be looking for a new washer-dryer set, but may behave in totally different ways. Or, consumer Vitelli may be looking for a living room rug in June, and for a bedroom rug in September, and may handle each situation in · a totally different way.

An additional problem in the area of prediction goals involves the use of psychological techniques to predict consumer behavior.[16] In many cases, business has tried to convert theories of psychoanalysis into laws of market behavior. But many of these theories have never been scientifically proven, and their conversion into psychological "truths" of consumer decision making has only produced dubious results. It is not at all clear that the theories of Freud, Adler, and Jung are actually helpful in explaining why a consumer buys Tide detergent instead of Cold Power.

Consumer behavior is much more complex than many of these theories suggest. Furthermore, the patterns of motivation and behavior of consumers can change over time. While the direction of change may be anticipated, the precise reaction still defies exact prediction.

SOCIAL VIEWPOINT **Control** means the capacity to change or manipulate the consumer by the use of marketing strategy. It may be based on prediction, but, as we saw above, prediction is hardly foolproof. Control may also be based on the sheer power to modify behavior so that consumers do what marketers want them to.

The question is, do marketers actually control consumer behavior? One side of the argument holds that marketing is strong and consumers are relatively weak and defenseless. This charge was forcefully expressed by former Federal Communications Commissioner Nicholas Johnson:

> *Our entire consumer-manipulating economy is based on a dishonest, destructive exploitation of human emotions and motivations. Television teaches—with continuous, air-hammer effectiveness—the dangerous and debilitative lie that the solution to all life's problems and nagging anxieties can be found in a product, preferably one that is applied to the skin or taken into the body. It has so distorted and demeaned the role of women as to make it almost impossible for either men or women to relate to each other in other than a sex-object, manipulative way. It has educated our children to go for the quick solution, to grow impatient and disinterested in developing skills and solutions requiring discipline and training. And it has urged us all to seek "better living through chemistry."*[17]

The basis for marketers' control over consumers, according to critics, is the manipulation of people's deepest feelings and fears—all in the name of building profits. In this view, the vaunted "free will" of American consumers is a myth and a hoax. The advertising bombardment of people's anxieties—which includes attempts at subliminal communication—has effectively created a "free will" that is determined by marketers themselves.[18]

Furthermore, there are plenty of "success stories" about business which seem somewhat chilling. Marketers seem able to get consumers to do exactly what they want, even when it means overcoming old behavior patterns and developing entirely new habits.

Of course, there is another side to the argument. Marketers claim that they are merely doing their job; they recognize the power and wishes of consumers and simply adapt their products to the situation. Philip Kotler notes that the wants of the consumer are shaped not only by Madison Avenue, but also by family, friends, work associates, the government, the church, and so forth.[19] He argues that it is much easier for marketers to respond to real needs of consumers than it is to artificially "create" needs.

It has also been argued that consumers are too busy, tired, and preoccupied with their daily routines to fully come to terms with what they ultimately "want." When one appliance company surveyed women on possible improvements, the answers involved very limited changes: prettier ovens, dials moved to different places, extra burners on top of stoves.[20] Not one woman asked for a self-cleaning oven. But when the company proposed this possibility in a series of follow-up interviews, the women were ecstatic. Did the company "create" this need? Or was it always there, below the surface? It is argued that many times consumers cannot identify something which they actually want until presented with a concrete alternative, which is the task of marketing.

Marketers insist that, rather than manipulating the consumer, they are only discovering his or her needs and putting together a satisfactory marketing mix. For example, many American pet owners show a high degree of anthropomorphism—a tendency to attribute human traits to their house pets. Pet food manufacturers have responded to this tendency with new lines of gourmet foods, including "beef burgundy in gravy" for dogs and shrimp- and tuna-flavored "sea dinners" for cats.[21] Also, one line of Laddie Boy dog food advertisements now depicts dogs' heads shown atop human bodies. Their slogans put across messages such as "Laddie Boy—dogs just can't resist it. After all, they're only human." Marketers argue that they are merely satisfying the needs of pet owners by providing gourmet food lines.

Are marketers getting away with controlling their relationships with consumers? There is plenty of evidence that they can't. Recall, from Figure 9-2, the qualifications of most modern consumers, the dynamics of competition, and the parade of new technology. These and the other factors in the environment (consumer advocates, mass media, and so forth) educate the consumer and update rules of the game.

It is a fact that, despite all of their supposed power, marketers can register dismal failures. General Motors had its Corvair, DuPont its Corfam, RCA its computers, and Kellogg's its cereal with dehydrated bananas.

The debate on marketers' power over consumers tends to center on the needs and wants that are the standards for consumers' decisions. Clearly, these emerge from the surrounding culture, of which marketing efforts are only one part. But to what extent do marketing efforts simply mirror consumer wants and needs, and to what extent does marketing influence these desires? And, for whose benefit are these efforts being made—the marketer's, the consumer's, or society's? Or all of the above? These are still the critical questions.

It is obvious that, marketing must, in large part, adapt to consumer preferences. Yet advertising in particular has real power to concentrate on particular motivations of the consumer. This power is at the center of advertising's ability to reinforce, reshape, or amplify certain wants and needs of the buying public.

CONCLUSION

The importance of a consumer orientation, with societal constraints, has been stressed in all chapters so far. The discussion of consumer behavior in Chapters 8 and 9 has exposed you to much of what we know about "how" and "why" consumers act as they do. These behavioral and decision making perspectives should prove useful in the design of any market research (covered further in Chapter 23) and in the planning of marketing strategy (the largest part of this book, Chapters 11 to 22).

While these two chapters (8 and 9) may give you an uncomfortable feeling that consumers have few secrets from marketers who have studied them, there does seem to be a natural check. Marketers don't know everything about what makes consumers tick and never will. Moreover, in our society, there are enough people and institutions that will see to it that no one organization or industry can control consumers, at least not for long.

Knowing about consumer behavior does provide marketers with power. Therefore, they have a social responsibility to use that power constructively, to be sensitive and responsive to consumers and society, and not to abuse their privileged position.

DISCUSSION QUESTIONS

1. Describe what might be happening in each of the stages of the consumer decision-making process as each of these consumer segments decides on the following purchases:
   a. elderly couples on a retirement village in New Mexico;
   b. vacationing couples on an automobile rental in Canada;
   c. up-and-coming junior executives on business suits;
   d. new-in-town families on a physician;
   e. overweight, middle-aged persons on a diet plan.
2. What would be the major sources of information used by consumers for these purchase decisions: real estate, a movie camera, a college, a Rocky Mountain ski vacation?
3. At what stages in the consumer decision-making process for an electronic calculator would these marketing efforts have the most potential impact on the consumer: advertising, personal selling, and price reduction?
4. The Federal Trade Commission wants to assure the consumer's right to be informed. A staff member has learned about the consumer decision-making process and the pressures that marketing can exert at various points to induce the consumer to purchase. What types of FTC policy implications are generated by understanding the process which might be subject to abuse or deception?

5. Trace these products through the Howard-Sheth model of consumer behavior: a Bic pen, a life insurance policy, a motorcycle, a hamburger supplement (the primary ingredient of which is seaweed).

6. A former government official once noted, "Advertisements for over-the-counter medicines may be a contributing factor in drug abuse problems in the United States." Discuss your point of view.

NOTES

1. Marcus Alexis and Charles Z. Wilson, *Organizational Decision-Making* (Englewood Cliffs, N.J.: Prentice-Hall, 1967), p. 75.

2. C. Glenn Walters, *Consumer Behavior: Theory and Practice* (Homewood, Ill.: Irwin, 1974), p. 453

3. Ibid., 454.

4. Unless otherwise indicated, this section is largely based on Walters, pp. 531–62.

5. James F. Engel, David T. Kollat, and Roger D. Blackwell, *Consumer Behavior*, 2d ed. (New York: Holt, Rinehart and Winston, 1973), p. 361.

6. Ibid., pp. 366–70.

7. Eugene J. Kelley, "The Importance of Convenience in Consumer Purchasing," *Journal of Marketing* 23 (July 1958): 32–38.

8. Leo Bogart, B. Stuart Tolley, and Frank Orenstein, "What One Little Ad Can Do," *Journal of Advertising Research* 10 (August 1970): 3–13.

9. Engel et al., 2d ed., pp. 422–24.

10. George Katona and Eva Mueller, "A Study of Purchasing Decisions," in Lincoln Clark, ed., *Consumer Behavior: The Dynamics of Consumer Reaction* (New York: New York University Press, 1955), p. 48; William P. Dommermuth, "The Shopping Matrix and Marketing Strategy," *Journal of Marketing Research* 2 (May 1965): 128–32.

11. James F. Engel, David T. Kollat, and Roger D. Blackwell, *Consumer Behavior* (New York: Holt, Rinehart and Winston, 1968), pp. 438–40.

12. Ibid.

13. Walters, pp. 56–57.

14. John A. Howard, *Marketing Management: Analysis and Planning*, rev. ed. (Homewood, Ill.: Irwin, 1963), pp. 35–38.

15. Engel et al., 2d ed., pp. 647–48.

16. William A. Yoell, "The Abuse of Psychology by Marketing Men," *Marketing/Communications* 298 (August 1970): 42, 44.

17. Nicholas Johnson, "Dear Vice President Agnew," *New York Times*, Oct. 11, 1970, p. D17.

18. Lynn Sharpe, "Subliminal Communications: Insidious Advertising," *Encore*, December 1974, p. 40.

19. Philip Kotler, *Marketing Management: Analysis, Planning, and Control*, 2d ed. (Englewood Cliffs, N.J.: Prentice-Hall, 1972), p. 166.

20. David M. Stander, "Testing New Product Ideas in an 'Archie Bunker' World," *Marketing News*, November 15, 1973, p. 4.

21. David P. Garino, "Sales of Pet Food Boom as Ads Emphasize Human Traits and Push 'Gourmet' Treats," *Wall Street Journal*, April 19, 1971, p. 36.

10

ORGANIZATIONAL CUSTOMER BEHAVIOR

After completing this chapter, the reader should be able to:

1. Distinguish organizational demand from consumer demand.

2. Explain the relationships among the variables that influence organizational buying behavior—individual, social, organizational, and environmental.

3. Relate the variables that influence organizational buying behavior to the steps in the organizational buying decision process.

4. Draw marketing management implications from the concepts of buy-grid, buying situations, buying center, and organizational market segmentation.

Chapters 8 and 9 explored buying behavior on the part of consumers—individuals and households. This chapter will focus on the buying behavior of **organizational customers**. While there are similarities between these two types of behavior, the differences between them are outstanding.

THE HOSPITAL MARKET IS ALIVE AND WELL

As of 1974, there were some 7,200 hospitals in the United States.[1] Most of them buy products and services independently from small distributors or manufacturers. Some government hospitals participate in federal, state, or local purchasing arrangements.

Major hospital needs fall into the following areas:

1. *Improved patient care.* New life-saving products include automatic monitoring devices and warning systems.

2. *Saving of time and labor.* The nurse's nonmedical chores can be eased by new equipment. Patients will be able to regulate bed position, heat, drapes, and television.

3. *Speedier communications and movement.* Products such as two-way radios and conveyor belt systems can improve the functioning of hospitals.

4. *The new hotel wings.* These will be "self-care" centers for patients. Outside contractors will take charge of meals, laundry, and other services.

Hospital purchasing involves a variety of officials. Professionals, including department heads, nursing directors, and dietitians, select the equipment. In many hospitals, a purchasing agent handles the actual buying process. But, in nine out of ten hospitals, the administrator carries final responsibility for such decisions.

ORGANIZATIONS AS CUSTOMERS

Hospitals are typical organizational customers. As such, their buying process is complex. It must take into account an intricate set of rules and procedures, clearance with various supervisors, budget pressures, and multiple buying decisions. The implication here for marketers is clear. They must pinpoint the needs of their hospital customers in a very different context from those of consumers or families. For example, marketers should approach hospital buyers with logical, well-documented appeals that include proof of product quality and the availability of fast, reliable service and repair.

Buying is a universal activity for all formal organizations. Business firms, governmental agencies, colleges, churches and synagogues, and political parties must all purchase essential goods and services in order to perform their normal tasks. A supermarket must buy paper bags so that customers can carry

home their food. Western Michigan University needs seating for its lecture halls. A religious institution may require cleaning services to maintain a neat and orderly atmosphere.

Thus, organizations, like individual consumers and families, must constantly buy goods and services in order to function. But organizational buying is a complex process rather than a single act. It generally occurs over a long period of time and requires a significant amount of information as well as the services of many people.

Organizational buying behavior is actually one type of problem solving. Some member of the organization first realizes that there is a need for a certain product or service. He or she then initiates the internal procedure for purchasing that product or service. The seller's marketing manager must understand how the buying process is used in solving problems. This awareness can help the marketer to design effective strategies for organizational customers.

The understanding of consumer behavior we gained in Chapters 8 and 9 can give us insight into organizational buying behavior, since there are similarities. In each situation, human decision makers are purchasing products or services. But, of course, there are important differences in the roles of organizational and consumer buyers. The consumer buyer is often interested in satisfying personal needs and rarely has formal training in the buying role. The industrial buyer must satisfy the needs of the firm and must operate on the basis of objective criteria. He or she usually is trained as a buyer, for the purchases made must lead to performance for a library or profit for a radio station.

In this chapter, we will focus on organizational buying in general, rather than simply discussing industrial buying (by profit-making firms). This is because the essential workings of the buying process are similar for industrial firms and other types of large organizations. The purposes of the organizations may be different, but they follow similar purchasing processes.

ORGANIZATIONAL DEMAND

In order to understand **organizational demand**, we will first try to get a feel for the types of organizations that are potential customers. We will study the characteristics that differentiate them from individual consumers and develop an analytical approach specifically geared to organizations.

**SCOPE OF
ORGANIZATIONAL
DEMAND**

Under the broad heading of industrial customers, we can include many kinds of businesses, institutions, and governmental units. Businesses may include manufacturers, construction firms, commercial establishments, transportation companies, service companies (motels, golf courses), and professional groups (lawyers, dentists).

Table 10-1 presents the scope (ten categories of organizations) and size (number of units and employees) of organizational demand for the year 1973. Services, many of them nonprofit, are broken down in detail in order to emphasize their diverse makeup. In this table, the term **units**, when used to refer to a nonmanufacturing business, is defined as a single establishment or group of similar establishments under one control. Thus, if a particular nonmanufacturing firm has five establishments in the same county, all selling the same products, they will be counted as one unit (such as a chain of dry-cleaning outlets).

The reporting units for manufacturing organizations are classified on the basis of establishments. An **establishment** is an economic unit engaged in a distinctive activity, for example, a mine, a factory, or a store.

Table 10-1 gives us an idea of the size of organizational demand. By comparing the number of units with the number of employees for each category, we can see a significant difference between categories. For example, there are over three times as many retail units as there are manufacturing units (1,000,000 vs. 300,000). But each manufacturing unit represents an average of 66 employees, compared with 12 in the retail category.

Governmental units have increasingly demanded industrial goods, as a result of heavy expenditures for national defense and the expansion of government services into new areas (such as child care, narcotics addiction treatment, and medical care for the aged).[2] The governmental units making such demands include federal, state, and local departments; administrative units such as school systems; autonomous agencies such as the Tennessee Valley Authority.

**CHARACTERISTICS
OF
ORGANIZATIONAL
DEMAND**

The study of organizational buying patterns is valuable for marketers in three ways: it suggests which marketing factors are most important in this type of decision making; it assists in the analysis of market information; it enables firms to make more accurate predictions about market response and marketing strategies.

The market demand of organizations is different from the consumer market in the following ways:[3]

1. *The organizational market has a derived demand.* The demand for industrial goods and services does not exist as an independent force. It is actually derived from the demand for consumer goods and services, and from the demand for goods and services supplied to the government. DuPont sells its synthetic fibers only because mills have orders for study clothing from consumer outlets.

2. *The organizational market has fewer buyers.* Numerically, consumer goods have the greater market by far. Millions of individuals or families may

Table 10-1
SCOPE AND SIZE OF ORGANIZATIONAL DEMAND

TYPE OF ORGANIZATION	UNITS	EMPLOYEES	EMPLOYEES PER UNIT
1. Agricultural services, forestry, fisheries	35,057	225,341	6
2. Mining	22,087	602,236	27
3. Contract construction	350,730	3,731,774	11
4. Manufacturing	298,918	19,768,681	66
5. Transportation, public utilities	134,569	4,018,043	30
6. Wholesale trade	291,837	4,224,245	14
7. Retail trade	1,056,311	12,378,033	12
8. Finance, insurance, real estate	341,043	4,137,997	12
9. Services (partial list)	967,457	10,178,178	11
Hotels, lodging places	52,327	898,638	17
Personal services	163,479	909,415	6
Miscellaneous business services	105,426	1,856,903	18
Auto repair services, garages	76,841	435,549	6
Miscellaneous repair services	40,798	222,642	5
Motion pictures	11,506	190,137	17
Amusement, recreation	38,492	494,019	13
Medical, health services	231,495	3,425,013	15
Legal services	73,885	298,218	4
Educational services	39,577	1,012,312	26
Museums, botanical gardens, zoos	912	21,266	23
Nonprofit membership organizations	132,719	1,312,704	10
10. Government (federal, states, and local)	78,336	13,657,000	174

SOURCE: U.S. Department of Commerce, *County Business Patterns 1973*, p. 12.

purchase Dial soap. But a specialized industrial product may have a potential market of fewer than 1,000 organizations, such as atomic power plants.

3. *The organizational market is more concentrated.* Over half of the manufacturing firms in the United States are in seven major states: New York, California, Pennsylvania, Illinois, Ohio, New Jersey, and Michigan.[4] Of the more than 3,000 counties in the country, roughly 15 (less than 1 percent) contain some 23 percent of the national work force.

4. *The organizational market must respond to a fluctuating demand.* The effects of periods of recession or economic growth cause rapid swings in the accumulation or depletion of inventories. The ups and downs in the demand for housing cause headaches for construction firms and appliance manufacturers.

5. *The organizational market has a greater flow of dollars.* Although conventional wisdom suggests the opposite, more dollars actually change hands

in sales to industrial buyers than in sales to consumers. This is because many exchanges take place in the production-consumption process before a finished product is sold to a consumer by a retailer. The total value of these exchanges exceeds the retail sales price of the product.

We are now ready to state a few general differences between organizational and consumer buyer behavior.[5] These generalizations will be considered in more detail later in this chapter.

1. *Organizational buying is rational.* Whereas consumers often buy in line with their whims, moods, or personal feelings, the industrial buyer is guided by budgetary considerations and established policies. The choice of a supplier is based on objective factors, such as quality, service, and price. Thus, the organizational decision process rests on rational considerations. Organizations may base their buying on techniques of **value analysis**—a thorough inquiry into the performance of an item in relation to its price.

2. *Organizational buying involves large volume purchases.* The individual consumer or family often makes small purchases—one electric light bulb, one automobile, two television sets. The industrial buyer more typically purchases large quantities of a product or service. For example, United Airlines needs a vast amount of food to serve to its passengers in any given year.

3. *Many individuals are involved in the buying process.* Rarely in the industrial buying field is one individual solely responsible for the purchase of products or services. Instead, many individuals, departments, and organizational needs may be integrated into the organizational buying process.

4. *Evaluation of purchases is very specific.* Determinations of criteria and results of product performance can be much more precise in the organizational market. The consumer, by contrast, generally settles for a more general product performance evaluation. In part, this is because the individual's "sample" is small and the consumer can rarely conduct testing or research.

5. *Service and leasing–renting are more important.* Industrial marketing requires more service both before and after a sale is made than does consumer marketing. Often equipment is leased or rented (rather than purchased) by the industrial buyer—an option that exists less frequently for the consumer. These differences have been narrowed as consumerism and a less possessive life style have emphasized services and product renting.

DYNAMICS OF ORGANIZATIONAL CUSTOMER BEHAVIOR

Paralleling our discussion of consumer buying behavior in Chapters 8 and 9, we shall look at several buying dynamics of the organizations, and also at their decision-making processes.

OVERVIEW MODEL OF ORGANIZATIONAL BUYER BEHAVIOR
Figure 10-1 presents an overview model of organizational buyer behavior. The fundamental assumption underlying this model is that organizational buying must be understood as a decision-making system. Individuals interact within (and outside of) the organization, and the organization itself is in-

Figure 10-1 OVERVIEW MODEL OF ORGANIZATIONAL BUYER BEHAVIOR

Adapted from Frederick E. Webster, Jr. and Yoran Wind, "A General Model for Understanding Organizational Buying Behavior," *Journal of Marketing* 36 (April 1972): 15. Published by the American Marketing Association.

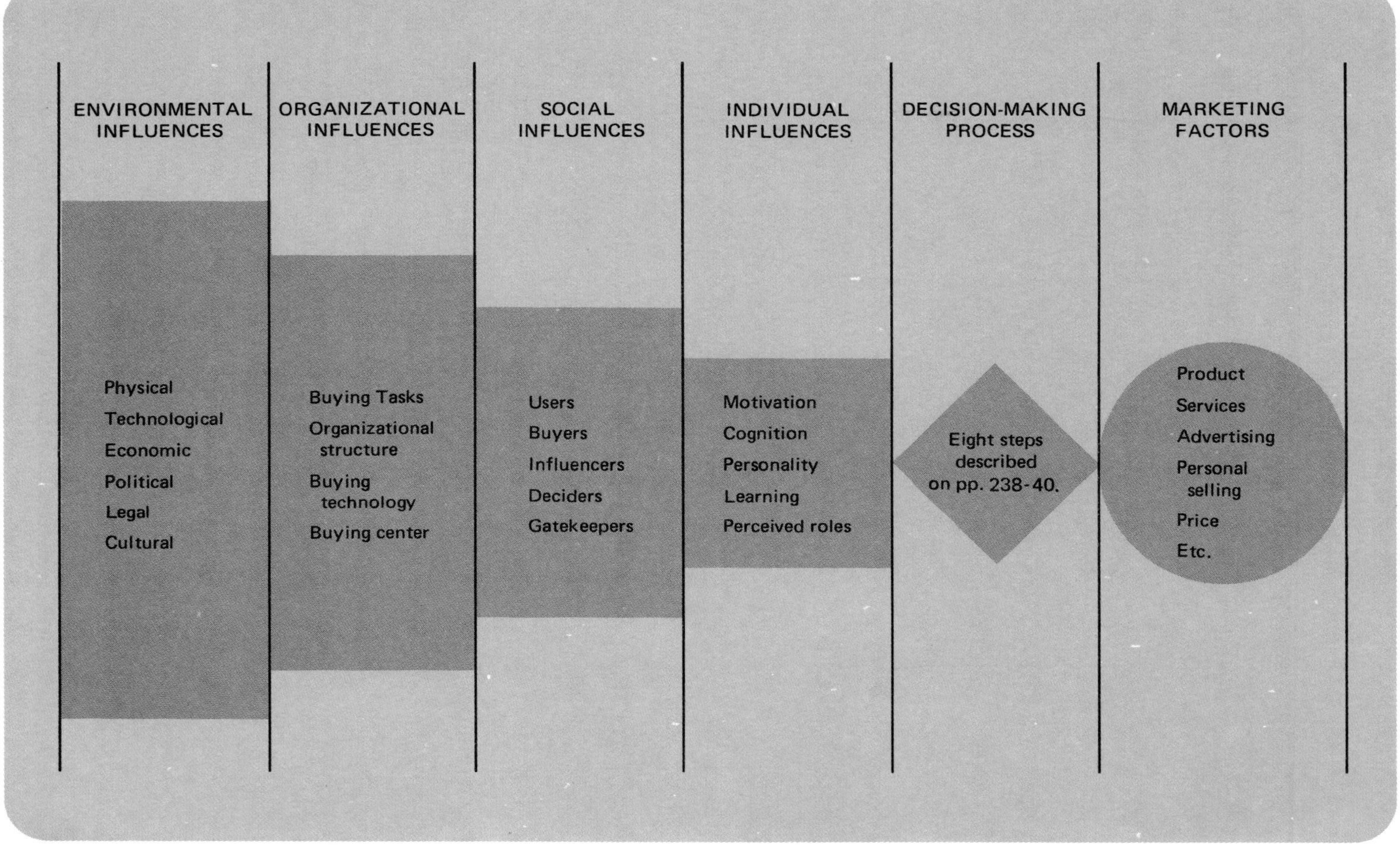

ENVIRONMENTAL INFLUENCES	ORGANIZATIONAL INFLUENCES	SOCIAL INFLUENCES	INDIVIDUAL INFLUENCES	DECISION-MAKING PROCESS	MARKETING FACTORS
Physical	Buying Tasks	Users	Motivation	Eight steps described on pp. 238-40.	Product
Technological	Organizational structure	Buyers	Cognition		Services
Economic	Buying technology	Influencers	Personality		Advertising
Political	Buying center	Deciders	Learning		Personal selling
Legal		Gatekeepers	Perceived roles		Price
Cultural					Etc.

233

fluenced by environmental forces. Four important types of variables affect the decision-making process: the individual, social, organizational, and environmental variables.[6]

Individual influences are an important part of the buying process. Whatever the social, organizational, and environmental forces and pressures, some individual or individuals must make decisions if a product or service is to be purchased. The individual buyer's motivation, cognition, personality, learning, and perceived roles are all relevant elements of the organizational buying decision. If a buyer has a conservative streak and favors the "old reliable" product, new competitors may face a severe disadvantage whatever their strengths.

Social (or interpersonal) **influences** are also an essential ingredient in the buying behavior of organizations. The buying center—the members of the organization involved in the buying process—includes five key roles. Some members are formally responsible as buyers of goods and services; some members are the users of these purchases. Influencers provide information and criteria that assist the buying process. Deciders choose among various alternatives, and gatekeepers control the entry of information and materials into the buying center. The ways in which members of the organization perform these various roles (sometimes more than one at a time) affect the eventual buying decisions.

Organizational factors in the buying process represent the degree to which the goals and resources of the organization influence (or restrict) the buying process. Four sets of variables interact as part of these organizational forces:

1. the organization's tasks—the work it must complete to reach its goals;
2. the organization's structure—its subsystems of communication, authority, status, rewards, and work flow;
3. technology—the management and information systems that help the organization to perform its buying and its other functions;
4. the people who comprise the buying center of the organization.

Finally, in addition to individual, social, and organizational forces, there are **environmental factors** which contribute to the buying process. These environmental influences are physical, technological, economic, political, legal, and cultural. They come from a wide variety of outside groups, including business firms, government, unions, consumer groups, and professional associations. Environmental factors define the climate in which an organization conducts its business—and the limits of the freedom with which it does so.

As Figure 10-1 suggests, these four sets of dynamics interact to influence the organization's decision-making process. In addition, the marketing efforts of sellers provide input and may influence the process. Let us examine the four major influences on organizational buyer behavior in more detail.

INDIVIDUAL INFLUENCES   At the center of the organizational buying process is the individual. The organizational buyer is both similar to and yet different from the individual consumer. Like the consumer, the individual buyer's behavior is affected by three important factors:

1. his or her personality, motivation, cognitive structure, and learning process;

2. how he or she interacts with and is influenced by the environment;

3. how he or she makes decisions.

At the same time, the individual buyer for an organization is also subject to forces which are unknown to the consumer. The goals of the organization, the members and structure of the organization, and the information sources available to him, all place the organizational buyer in a much more complex and delicate position than the individual consumer.

The organizational buyer can be said to have both task motives and non-task motives. The buyer's general **task motives** involve purchasing "the right quality in the right quantity at the right price for delivery at the right time from the right source."[7] The individual buyer's task-related motives are his or her desire to fulfill these responsibilities and duties.

The more personal, **nontask motives** usually include the buyer's desire for achievement or for risk reduction. The buyer wants personal advancement and recognition within the organization, industry, or profession. He or she also wants to reduce risk and uncertainty, since an unfortunate purchase decision can have serious consequences for the organization and for the individual as well. Often a buyer will preserve a long-time pattern of purchase decisions out of fear of experimenting with new suppliers or products.

As one observer put it, ". . . considering the relative risks and rewards to the individual, is it surprising that . . . an impulse buyer at home becomes super cautious at the office?"[8]

SOCIAL INFLUENCES
The social or interpersonal influences in the buying decision process involve three sets of variables.[9] These are the roles in the **buying center**, the interpersonal interactions between persons in the buying center and "outsiders" (such as salespeople for suppliers), and the dynamics of the group as a whole. As mentioned earlier, there are five principal categories of actors in these interactions: users, influencers, buyers, deciders, and gatekeepers.

Users may influence the buying decision in a positive way (when workers in a department suggest using a new product that will reduce costs), or in a negative way (when workers refuse to work with the materials of a particular supplier). Sometimes users exert influence as individuals; sometimes they do so as a group.

Influencers generally help to shape criteria for buying or provide useful information for decision making. In the complex world of modern business, technical experts and research and development personnel often influence buying decisions.

Buyers have formal authority for contacting suppliers and negotiating business transactions. Their latitude may be wide, or it may be severely restricted by criteria developed by technical experts. Buyers often exert influence in decision making by having the power to choose the supplier for a job or to develop a list of suitable suppliers. This may be a difficult task if many factors (such as price and quality of materials) are left to the judgment of buyers.

Lloyd Konrad is a buyer for Walker Manufacturing Company, a subsidiary of Tenneco, Inc. He joined the company in 1952 and is now a vice-president. Konrad oversees the purchase of nearly fifty items, but his prime concern is steel. Walker buys more than 100,000 tons of steel each year, which accounts for roughly one-third of the company's purchasing budget.

PROFILE OF A PURCHASING AGENT

Experienced buyers like Konrad have an important effect on the welfare of their firms. As one business person notes, buyers are "on the very leading edge of business activity" because of their early perceptions about coming economic trends. Especially during times of spiraling or declining business activity, the buyers out in the field may be among the first to spot the coming change.

Buying is, of course, a complicated process played for high stakes. A purchasing manager may be in competition with 1,000 other customers to beat a price increase. The idea is to get the largest amount of goods at the lowest possible prices, which sometimes means stockpiling a material like steel just before a price increase takes effect.

Buyers like Lloyd must also weigh the benefits and costs of long- and short-range purchasing decisions. In 1975, he passed up a deal in which he could have bought steel from foreign mills at an unusually low cost. But the savings were not sufficient to offset an anticipated problem that might result. He expects that steel shortages will recur over the next decade and that the steel market will be very tight at times. He does not wish to jeopardize long-standing relationships with normal domestic suppliers.

Based on Eric Morgenthaler, "How Lloyd Konrad, a Purchasing Agent, Wheels for Good Deals," *Wall Street Journal*, October 7, 1975, pp. 1, 10.

Deciders have final say over buying decisions. The buyer may in some cases be the decider as well, but the buyer may also be a lower official who carries out the decision of the more powerful decider. Of course, formal decision-making power does not always lead to effective control over decisions. If the university's head librarian recommends a book security system that only one firm produces, the administrator with ultimate authority for the purchase may have little choice in the matter.

Gatekeepers, who may be either purchasing agents or salespersons, control the flow of information into the firm. There is hidden power in this function, for if the available information includes only a few limited alternatives, the final decision obviously must fall within these boundaries. The president of the company cannot opt for an experimental product if lower officials never bring the product to the attention of the buying center.

ORGANIZATIONAL INFLUENCES

The key organizational influences that affect decision making in the buying process are tasks, structure, technology, and people.

Buying tasks can be broken down according to four dimensions:

1. *The organizational purpose served.* Is a product being bought to increase production, to be resold at a profit, or for some other reason?

2. *The nature of demand.* Does demand come from within the organization itself or from outside forces? Are there seasonal and/or cyclical fluctuations?

3. *The extent of programming.* To what extent has the decision-making process become routine?

4. *The degree of decentralization.* How much buying power has been delegated to specific officials and departments? How much has remained in the hands of a small central authority?

The **organizational structure** consists of five basic subsystems: communication, authority, status, rewards, and work flow.

The communications subsystem is responsible for four essential tasks.

1. It gathers information for the buying center about buying problems, evaluation criteria, and sources of supply.

2. It analyzes the way in which commands and instructions are processed within the buying decision-making system.

3. It evaluates the pattern of influence and persuasion that shapes the nature of the buying process.

4. It integrates and coordinates the various operations of the buying center.

The authority subsystem determines which actors in the buying process can set goals and evaluate performance. It defines who can make decisions and who can reward (or penalize) decisions.

The status subsystem defines the formal hierarchy and the informal power structure of the organization. It pinpoints the officials with authority and responsibility, both in theory and practice.

The rewards subsystem defines the payoffs for organizational actors within the buying process. It is here that the personal, nontask goals of an individual tie into the task objectives of the firm.

The work-flow subsystem manages the smooth processing of buying suggestions and decisions. It is that element in the buying system which keeps things moving in a steady and appropriate direction.

Buying technology is another important organizational influence. Obviously, if the Ford Motor Company begins making a new type of car and finds that an essential step in production cannot be completed with the existing technology, the results can be disastrous. Thus, the firm's technological capacity shapes its buying decisions. To complete production of the automobile, Ford will have to purchase new machinery.

The organization's tasks, structure, technology, and individual actors combine to form the unique "personality" of the firm as an organizational customer. If a marketing strategist wishes to influence a firm's buying patterns, he or she must take all of these factors into account.

ENVIRONMENTAL INFLUENCES

Environmental influences have a number of noticeable effects on the buying process. They define the availability of goods and services and create the general business conditions in which purchases take place. In addition, environmental influences (especially cultural, social, legal, and political forces) have an impact on values and norms that shape relationships among people and among organizations. Finally, a variety of environmental forces affect the flow of information into the firm's buying center.

Because of the recent energy crisis, shortages of supplies have significantly influenced the buying behavior of business firms. If a company cannot purchase the materials it needs for its products, its survival may be jeopardized. Business firms are reacting to this grim prospect in a number of ways. Some have beefed up their purchasing departments so that more buyers are out in the market searching for supplies. Increasingly, firms are responding to the demands of vendors that they make long-range commitments to buy; in a "seller's market" there may be no choice. Another buying approach—of dubious integrity—is ordering more than the firm needs from a number of different vendors in order to be certain of adequate supplies.

THE ORGANIZATIONAL DECISION-MAKING PROCESS

In Chapter 9, we looked at the consumer decision-making process. It will now seem simple compared to the organizational decision-making process.[10] This process, also called the **procurement process**, is a sequence of eight distinct activities. These eight phases may in some cases occur simultaneously; however, the general rule is that they take place in the following order:

1. *Anticipation or recognition of a problem (or need).* This is the first phase in organizational buying. Someone within the organization recognizes that there is a problem (or an outsider points it out). In this step there is also the recognition of a potential solution to the problem, that is, to make a purchase to fulfill a certain need.

Many situations can lead to the recognition of a need. The inventory for an important item may fall to a low level, requiring new purchases. A piece of machinery may break down or wear out, thus necessitating a replacement. Or the organization may decide upon a totally new line of products that requires different types of materials and technology. In each case, some company official must become aware that the firm needs something and that a realistic solution is possible.

2. *Determination of the characteristics and quantity of the needed item.* If the item is a simple and common one, this phase of decision making will be fairly routine. The department that will use the product makes an estimate of its needs and decides which brands of the product are satisfactory. If a technical item is required, the procedure will be slightly more complicated. The using department may have to develop a set of criteria for the item, outlining in detail exactly what attributes it must have. Mistakes or carelessness here will almost certainly lead to buying errors, sometimes of a costly nature.

3. *Description of the characteristics and quantity of the needed item.* It is not enough for the using department to prepare an accurate picture of the item that is needed. The description of this item must be communicated in a detailed and precise manner. If a technical expert in the using department understands exactly what is needed, but a field buyer misreads the instructions, then the accuracy of the original information is irrelevant. A clear and comprehensible description is essential for later stages of the organization buying process.

Marketers have an important opportunity to plug into a firm's buying needs

The nation's largest set of business customers, the government market, consists of all governments (federal, state, and local) that purchase or rent goods. As of 1974, governments purchased $277 billion worth of products and services, or 21 percent of America's gross national product. Of this $277 billion, some 65 percent is accounted for by federal government purchases.

Government spending on the federal level is handled by a wide variety of agencies. Military buying is carried out largely by the Defense Department through the Defense Supply Agency and the Army, Navy, and Air Force departments. Civilian buying is more diversified, although many agencies purchase supplies through the Bureau of Federal Supply of the General Services Administration, which acts as a kind of intermediary for federal purchases.

Government buying practices differ from those of most industries because of the many detailed statutory requirements for public spending. There is an enormous amount of paperwork; often many levels of clearance are necessary before a simple item like sponge mops can be ordered.

There are two important types of government buying procedures. With open-bid buying, qualified suppliers can submit bids for materials that the government wishes to purchase or for services that must be provided by an outside vendor. Generally, the government agency in charge of the bidding must award the contract on a winner-take-all basis to the firm that submits the lowest bid.

The other buying procedure is negotiated-contract buying. In this situation, a government agency will directly negotiate a contract for a project with one or a few firms. There is no open or competitive bidding. The government usually uses negotiated contracts when a project is large and complex and research and development costs are high. If the supplier seems to be making an unfair profit, the contract may be subject to review and renegotiation.

Based on Richard M. Hill, Ralph S. Alexander, and James S. Cross, *Industrial Marketing* (Homewood, Ill.: Irwin, 1975), p. 75; and Philip Kotler, *Marketing Management: Planning, Analysis, and Control*, 3d ed. (Englewood Cliffs, N.J.: Prentice-Hall, 1976), pp. 112–15.

during this phase of decision making. If a supplier anticipates a need of a frequent (or potential) client, he or she may be able to work with the officials in the buying center of the firm who develop specifications for purchase. To do so, the marketer must understand how the buying firm gathers information and draws up specifications.

4. *Search for and qualification of potential sources.* Once the firm has a clear vision of what kind of item it needs to purchase, it begins a search for potential suppliers. If the purchase situation is a familiar one, then a reliable and trusted vendor may be immediately consulted. But if the item is new to the firm's inventory—or if the stakes of the purchase are high and the possible consequences of failure are grave—there may be an extensive search and evaluation process.

5. *Acquisition and analysis of proposals.* Once a buyer has developed a list of potential suppliers, he or she may want to see specific proposals from each company. Sometimes this is a simple process, requiring little more than consulting a catalogue or making a few phone calls. If, however, the product is

unusual or the deal is complex, the buyer may request detailed written proposals from each potential vendor.

In many buying situations—especially when the buying firm does not require a great deal of information—phases 4 and 5 take place simultaneously. When the organization has minimal information, phase 5 becomes more distinct from the search for qualified sellers.

6. *Evaluation of proposals and selection of suppliers.* During this phase, important members of the buying center study the various proposals and may negotiate changes with vendors. Eventually, one or more proposals will be accepted and the others discarded. After the selections are made there may be further negotiations about details in the agreement, including prices, terms, and deliveries.

A critical legal problem in organizational buying is reciprocity, which can be defined as favoring a supplier who is also a customer or potential customer for the buyer's products. This practice is commonly used in industry. Reciprocity can inhibit good purchasing decisions by introducing an element of bias into the buying process. It can also undermine the morale of both the supplier and the sales staff. Each would prefer to believe that a deal is being completed because of the quality of their products and work, rather than because of an inbred reciprocal relationship.

In some cases, reciprocal arrangements may be illegal. The Federal Trade Commission and certain federal court decisions have outlawed such relationships under certain circumstances. The acceptance of gifts by members of the buying center is an ethical problem for organizations. In some circumstances, it is socially difficult for a purchasing agent to refuse inexpensive gifts or free meals from a supplier. Yet the line between harmless gestures and more significant favors, entertainment, and even bribes is sometimes unclear. The seller cannot be hurt if influential buying personnel feel some sort of personal obligation to him. Thus, even small gifts can corrupt the buying process.

7. *Selection of an order routine.* During this phase, the buyer gives an order to a vendor. The order is processed, shipped out, received, inspected, and paid for. A number of internal activities must be conducted during this phase, including status reports to the using department and inventory management.

Some observers might consider these activities to be part of the post-purchase delivery process and therefore irrelevant to the study of buying behavior. But from the important point of view of the using department, these functions are an instrumental part of the buying process. Until goods are actually delivered, a deal is still theoretical in the eyes of the users.

8. *Performance feedback and evaluation.* After the purchase has been completed, and the items are in use within the company, an evaluation process begins. Both the product and the vendor are the subjects of this study. It is in the interest of every firm to learn from its mistakes or successes.

Feedback is crucial to the evaluation process. It may come formally as reports from using departments. Or it may travel informally, by word of mouth from one official to another. In some circumstances, there will be a formal system for developing feedback, including internal research, questionnaires, and so forth.

IMPLICATIONS FOR MARKETING

The organizational buying model is useful for marketers who wish to understand typical buying behavior. It helps a marketer to know what information is needed, what marketing strategy is appropriate, and the role of market segmentation.

RELEVANT INFORMATION FOR MARKETING DECISIONS

The marketers need information on four important aspects of organizational buying:[11]

1. the identity of the buying center;
2. the nature of the buying decision-making process;
3. the buying situation (new task, modified rebuy, or straight rebuy);
4. the environmental, organizational, interpersonal, and individual factors that affect the buying process.

The marketing strategist will use this information to answer four critical questions:

1. What market segment(s) should the firm pursue?
2. How should the firm handle questions of products, price, promotion, and distribution?
3. How should marketing operations be organized, planned, implemented, and controlled?
4. What marketing research efforts are necessary?

Marketing strategy must focus on the **buying center** of an organization, the individuals who determine what products and services will be purchased. Marketers attempt to identify the important members of the buying center and to understand their degrees of power within the firm's hierarchy. The information flow among these officials is a significant concern of marketers since it often suggests the power relationships within the firm. Marketers must sometimes approach lower officers in the hierarchy in the hopes that they will pass information along to their superiors.

One study of 2,400 respondents from a wide range of industries determined that engineering and research personnel are important in all three phases of management.[12] These phases consist of initiating the purchase project, determining the kind of material, and deciding on the make or supplier. Administrative officers mainly initiate buying projects, while purchasing agents are mainly responsible for actual purchase decisions and choice of suppliers.

Marketers have a particular interest in the role of the salesperson in the buying process. Often the salesperson plays a key initiating role, determining and demonstrating the need for a new product or service. Many industrial buyers regard salespeople as a valuable source of new product information. The flow of information into an organization is a critical concern of marketing and the salesperson is often instrumental in creating this flow. While out in the field, the salesperson may discover something new and relay that knowledge to the home office.

In every **buying situation** there are three important and interrelated factors:[13]

1. the newness of the problem and relevant buying experience of decision makers;

2. the information needs of the buying center;

3. the number of new alternatives that exist in the decision-making process.

Buying situations can be divided into three basic categories—the new task, the modified rebuy, and the straight rebuy.[14] The buygrid conceptual framework illustrated in Table 10-2 builds a model of the buying situation out of these three **buyclasses** and the eight phases of the buying process described earlier. It should be noted that the most complex buying problems occur in the upper left portion of the table, where a new task is in its initial phase of problem recognition. A modified rebuy is not as difficult for most firms, and a straight rebuy is usually a very routine matter.

Figure 10-2 illustrates the way in which the decision-making process varies with each buyclass. Each situation requires marketing to create a specific set of selling procedures.

In **new-task buying**, the organization must face a new need or problem. Buyers have little experience in this task and need a great deal of information. In this situation, the reputation of the supplier is a most crucial factor, since buyers have limited knowledge of the field they are entering. It is not time to "take a chance" on an unknown supplier.

Table 10-2
THE BUYGRID FRAMEWORK FOR INDUSTRIAL BUYING SITUATIONS

BUYPHASES	BUYCLASSES		
	NEW TASK	MODIFIED REBUY	STRAIGHT REBUY
1. Anticipation or recognition of a problem (need) and a general solution			
2. Determination of characteristics and quantity of needed item			
3. Description of characteristics and quantity of needed item			
4. Search for and qualification of potential sources			
5. Acquisition and analysis of proposals			
6. Evaluation of proposals and selection of supplier(s)			
7. Selection of an order routine			
8. Performance feedback and evaluation			

From Patrick J. Robinson, Charles W. Faris, and Yoram Wind, *Industrial Buying and Creative Marketing* (Boston: Allyn & Bacon, 1967), p. 14.

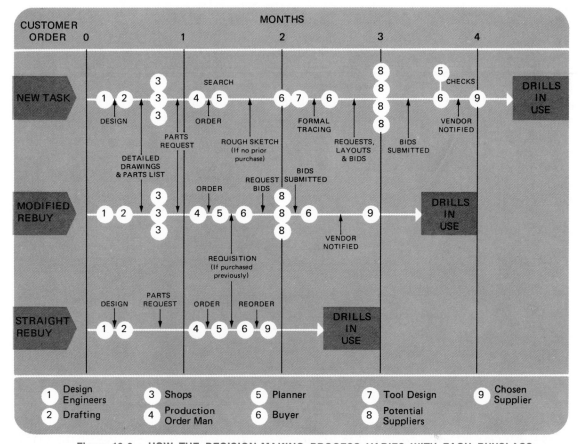

Figure 10-2   HOW THE DECISION-MAKING PROCESS VARIES WITH EACH BUYCLASS

Until the buyer (6) begins his search for a supplier, the three types of buying situations are essentially the same, as these critical-path diagrams demonstrate. From that point on, however, the process of purchasing a product, in this case a special drill, varies markedly. A new task may entail policy questions and special studies, while a straight rebuy is nearly automatic.

From "All Eyes Are on the Buyer," *Sales Management* 99 (October 15, 1967): 73. Reprinted by permission of Sales Management, The Marketing Magazine. Copyright 1967.

A **straight rebuy** can often be handled in a routine manner by the purchasing department. There is little interest in new information or in pursuing sales from new suppliers. The firm will usually continue with a long-time, reliable vendor and a proven, traditional product. Marketers wishing to change this pattern have a difficult task; they must convince buying center members that they are somehow missing out on a real advance.

The **modified rebuy** usually occurs when buyers want to save money, get better service, or find a slightly more efficient product. Here buyers need information on new products, particularly, how they compare with the traditional choice. Marketers can gain new clients if they develop effective and helpful presentations.

As a first step in analyzing organizational demand, we will classify the industrial market. The chief tool used in this classification is the Standard Industrial Classification System, or SIC, a numerical system set up by the government (see below). In this system, the national economy is divided into 20 major industry groups. Each group is subdivided into 150 industry groups; then into detailed four-digit sub-subgroups. Thus, SIC 28 represents chemicals, SIC 283 represents drugs, and SIC 2834 represents pharmaceutical preparations.

Through use of the SIC, a firm can come close to determining its industrial markets. The firm will primarily be interested in the *composition* of its market, including the industries that can make use of its product, the number of plants in each industry, and the relative market value (in dollars) of each industry. Market researchers will then examine these factors in great detail, to judge which industries will be most likely to purchase the firm's product and how they should be approached by marketing campaigns.

It should be noted that it is not always easy to apply the SIC system to specific marketing data. However, the system is generally reliable.

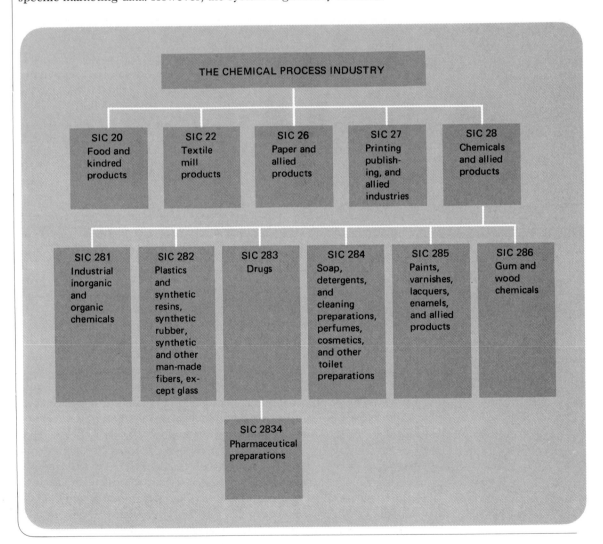

MARKET SEGMENTATION   Chapter 7 described segmentation of consumer markets. There are three parallel but different means of classifying organizations:[15]

1. *General organizational characteristics.* These include type of business (the SIC classifications), geographical location, and size of operation (sales, assets, number of employees). Typically, the geographical location and end use of the industrial product are stressed.

2. *Specific response.* Other possible bases for segmentation include the degree of source loyalty, the nature of the buying center, and the specific buying situation. The attitudes and preferences of buying center personnel toward suppliers and the determinants of the buying situation may also be used.

3. *Decision-making unit.* Markets can also be segmented by internal characteristics within the firm—such as the age, education, professional affiliation, personality, and attitudes of key decision makers and units.

CONCLUSION

As we have seen in this chapter, the buying behavior of organizations has both important similarities to and differences from the buying behavior of individual consumers. Organizational buying is a complex process which is affected by many individual, social, organizational, and environmental influences.

The key personnel in the organizational buying decisions comprise the buying center. Within the buying center, the decision-making process that leads to a purchase is a complex eight-stage operation. This process is, in good part, a function of the various influences on buying behavior. Organizational buying patterns also vary depending on whether the purchase in question is a new task, a straight rebuy, or a modified rebuy.

Marketing strategists find it extremely helpful to understand the internal workings and external pressures which shape the buying behavior of organizations. This includes understanding individuals—learning who the key figures in a firm's purchase decision making are, how they fit into the firm's hierarchy, and how the internal flow of information proceeds. Through analysis of these factors, marketers can more easily determine how to design the proper marketing strategy.

DISCUSSION QUESTIONS

1. What should a producer of pool tables know about the market demand of resorts with game rooms as compared to that of private households with basement recreation rooms? What should the New Orleans Hilton know about the market demand of organizations holding conventions and conferences as compared to that of vacationing families?

2. What are the similarities and differences between a family purchasing a suburban house and a New England textile mill searching for a new location in the Southeast? Where appropriate, analyze these two situations according the individual, social, organizational, and environmental dynamics.

3. Assume you are the purchasing agent for a mining company that regularly places orders for steel rods to be used in the manufacture of mine roof bolts. Describe how your job differs when steel rods are in short supply from when they are in plentiful supply.

4. Mattel, Inc., a toy manufacturer, wants to switch to another supplier of plastic. Valley National Bank of Arizona is seeking a new maintenance contract. What might each of their decision-making processes look like? Explain how suppliers might get each of these accounts.

5. As a marketer of mayonnaise to restaurants and cafeterias, how might your marketing strategy differ as you approached market segments in each of the buyclasses—new task, modified rebuy, and straight rebuy?

6. How might the Honeywell computer division identify the members of the buying center of commercial banks, state lotteries, and small food processors? What differences in marketing strategy would be appropriate for these three market segments?

NOTES

1. Peter Hilton, *Keeping Old Products New* (Englewood Cliffs, N.J.: Prentice-Hall, 1967), pp. 49–50.
2. Richard M. Hill, Ralph S. Alexander, and James S. Cross, *Industrial Marketing*, 4th ed. (Homewood, Ill.: Irwin, 1975), p. 61.
3. These points are based largely on George Risley, "Industrial Marketing," in Albert Wesley Frey, ed., *Marketing Handbook*, 2d ed. (New York: Ronald Press, 1965), p. 27:11; and Industrial Marketing Committee Review Board, "Fundamental Differences between Industrial and Consumer Marketing," *Journal of Marketing* 19 (October 1954): 153.
4. Hill et al., p. 64; and Philip Kotler, *Marketing Management: Analysis, Planning, and Control*, 3d ed. (Englewood Cliffs, N.J.: Prentice-Hall, 1976), p. 99.
5. These points are based largely on Hill et al., p. 54; Risley, p. 21; and Industrial Marketing Committee, p. 154.
6. The discussion of these points is based largely on Frederick E. Webster, Jr., and Yoram Wind, *Organizational Buying Behavior* (Englewood Cliffs, N.J.: Prentice-Hall, 1972), pp. 78–80, 88–89; and Webster and Wind, "A General Model of Understanding Organizational Behavior," *Journal of Marketing* 36 (April 1972): 13–19.
7. Webster and Wind, "General Model," p. 19.
8. W. C. Howard, "Selling Industrial Products," Norton Company speech, 1973, pp. 1–4.
9. Webster and Wind, "General Model," p. 17.
10. This section is based largely on Patrick J. Robinson, Charles W. Faris, and Yoram Wind, *Industrial Buying and Creative Marketing* (Boston: Allyn & Bacon, 1967), pp. 13–18.
11. Webster and Wind, *Organizational Buying*, p. 110.
12. Research Department, *Scientific American*, "How Industry Buys—1970" (New York, 1969), p. 4.
13. Webster and Wind, *Organizational Buying*, p. 115.
14. Robinson et al., pp. 12–14.
15. Webster and Wind, *Organizational Buying*, pp. 118–19.

CASE STUDIES

COUNTRIBANK OF KANSAS CITY

In January 1975 the Countribank of Kansas City, Missouri, commissioned a study of the affects of inflation and recession on the demand for commercial bank services by consumers. When Janet A. Marlow and Eugene Spivey, both vice presidents of the bank, met to discuss the report a few months later, they discovered that each had a different interpretation of the results. Spivey opened the meeting.

"You certainly look rather cheerful for a woman who is supposed to discuss money problems. You must have read a different report from the one that I received."

"On the contrary, Eugene," replied Marlow, "I have the very same report. And I'm terribly excited about the opportunities that I think are implied by this study."

"Opportunities?" questioned Spivey. "For what? According to this study, money problems dominate the concerns of adult family members in Kansas City, and you know what that means. When people are worried about money they do not rush to the bank for car loans or home mortgages."

"Money problems have forced some families to make major changes in their life styles," Marlow agreed, "but for most of them inflation has merely brought about a period of accommodation and adjustment. I think that Countribank ought to adjust its marketing program accordingly. For instance, we might offer new special savings plans—different rates of interest, lower initial deposit requirements, automatic deduction from checking accounts."

Spivey looked puzzled. "Why do we need special savings plans? According to this study, families are committed to saving in spite of inflation."

"True," responded Marlow, "but look at the reasons why they save—they are mostly negative ones. When hard times are over they might stop saving. I'd rather see families save *for* something, like the down payment on a house. That would be good business for the bank. The report also indicates that more than 60 percent of the families admit to having made some unwise financial decision recently. Countribank could offer a counseling service on money management or offer a course on money management taught by our own personnel."

"Hold it!" interjected Spivey. "Financial counseling is a sensitive issue. These people may admit to having made a bad decision, but in general they think that they are doing a good job of managing their money. We would only antagonize them if we suggested that they needed help."

Marlow had a ready response. "Even those who wouldn't admit that they needed counseling might read a newsletter that included helpful hints and stories about how other families are coping. Or we might offer a workbook to teach and to encourage budgeting."

Spivey shook his head. "This has always been a conservative bank. I see no need to change that image just because of some bad times. This research shows me that people's basic attitudes and values have not changed. These adjustments are merely temporary."

"These hard times may be temporary," said Marlow, "but, if we could teach our customers good financial habits now when the pressure is on, we would reap the benefits when the economy improves.

1. 35 percent of the families are afraid that investments/savings are losing value due to inflation.

2. Most think that they are doing a good job of managing their money.

3. 46 percent of the families consider themselves "spenders" and 48 percent consider themselves "savers."

4. More than 50 percent managed to put money into savings banks.

5. Savings are regarded as a protection against emergencies, hard times, and old age.

6. 87 percent reject the idea that there is no longer any point in saving.

7. One way many families are meeting hard times is by having the wife go to work, either full time (26 percent) or part-time (15 percent).

8. In about four out of ten households financial decisions are made by both husband and wife. In the remaining families, the husband is about twice as likely as the wife to be the sole decision maker.

9. 63 percent admitted to making some unwise financial decisions in the past year.

10. Families in Kansas City are split over budgeting—49 percent have a budget, while 49 percent do not. People who budget and those who don't hold very different views about the benefits of budgeting.

VIEWS OF BUDGETING

	Budgeters	Nonbudgeters
Only way to keep track of money	53%	18%
Inflation makes it impossible	46	46
Keeps me from overspending	45	16
Only way to get ahead financially	42	17
Best way to build up savings account	36	15
Doesn't work in emergencies	23	37
Can do as well without it	12	37
More trouble than it's worth	10	34
Not enough willpower	9	20

11. Most families report changes in their spending patterns this year. They are spending more on insurance, utilities, car repairs and gasoline, meat, and canned and frozen foods. They are cutting back on expenditures for movies, hobbies, entertaining, clothing, and cookies and candies.

Questions

1. What concepts of consumer behavior would provide further insights into the consumer research findings?
2. Which of the two Countribank vice presidents has the stronger argument?
3. Assuming Marlow's "opportunity analysis" viewpoint is favored by the president of the bank (whose family owns 63 percent of Countribank's common stock), what marketing mix recommendations would you make?

MEXICAN NATIONAL POPULATION COUNCIL

Dr. Juan Orozco sat dejectedly in his office on the 19th floor of one of Mexico City's new high-rise office buildings. As general coordinator of the Mexican National Population Council, Dr. Orozco has to review and to approve the Council's plans to expand its birth control program.

Background

The population growth rate in Mexico during the 1960–1970 decade rose to 3.43 percent a year, one of the highest in the world. In the view of the government, this growth rate jeopardized further improvements in the standard of living and threatened to create cities of unmanageable size.

The country's population of 58 million was projected to reach 100 million before 1990. Implicit in this rapid growth was a coincidental growth in the need for health care, schooling, and other public services. To slow this population boom before it became a burden on the economy, the National Population Council (NPC) began in 1973 to suggest voluntary limitations on family size. This was considered a radical move in a country that was heavily Roman Catholic.

A major cause of the population explosion was a decline in the death rate, especially among newborns, at a time when the fertility rate remained high. For example, a 1964 study found that women in Mexico City averaged 3.27 live births during their child-bearing years. This rate was higher than in seven other large Latin American cities, and the fertility rate in rural Mexico was higher still. According to research gathered by the NPC, high fertility rates were generally associated with a high degree of illiteracy, a large rural population, and a low rate of employment among women.

The NPC Program

During the two years in which the NPC had been campaigning for a reduction in family size, its theme had progressed from "Let's make ourselves fewer to live better" (Phase One) to "The small family lives better" (Phase Two). The success of the program was measured in terms of numbers of women actively enrolled in family-planning programs. By the end of Phase Two, 1.5 million women were participating in one of the NPC programs. While this figure represented only 11 percent of the approximately 13.5 million Mexican women of child-bearing age, it was considerably higher than the 250,000 participants at the end of the previous year. Dr. Orozco knew that the NPC would be unable to reach all of these women with the funding available to it at the present time. Such a goal would require an increase in resources of about 20 percent a year until 1980.

The Council's program consisted of counseling and clinical work that were offered through existing government-related clinics and mother-child care centers. Birth control pills were paid for by the government. There was no opposition to family planning by the existing health-care bureaucracy or the Roman Catholic Church.

Problems with Population Control

Although many families that were interviewed for NPC studies seemed interested in limiting family size, there appeared to be great reluctance to do anything about it, especially in the smaller cities. Moreover, attitudes toward family planning were not changing rapidly among farm workers or the urban poor. Those with more education were more likely to accept the idea. Given the small number of people who attended lectures at the free clinics, it appeared to NPC members that many families were not yet interested in gathering information on the subject.

Dr. Orozco wondered whether this attitude was due at least in part to a lack of communication between spouses. In one NPC study, women were quoted as saying that they did not want more children but that their husbands did not accept that idea. This same study indicated that many men in the same village would like to stop having children because it was too expensive. Critics contended that to overcome this opposition and misinformation the government would have to become more aggressive. Yet Dr. Orozco knew that assertiveness could also lead to problems. One of his case study folders contained the story of a very enthusiastic doctor who decided that all of the women in the neighborhood served by his clinic should have a cancer check-up. He told these women that they had to have the check-up in order to register their children for school. When the husbands found out, they became angry, refused to let their wives go to the clinic, and registered their children at another school.

The National Population Council recognized that it might need help in overcoming opposition to its programs and fear of its clinics. It maintained, therefore, a folder with information about influential people who were sympathetic to its cause. Dr. Orozco read several records in this folder. The first described Reverend Juan Martinez, a Roman Catholic priest in Tlaxcala, a city east of Mexico City. Father Martinez was known to meet with groups of parents in his parish to discuss children, education, and family planning. At these meetings he emphasized individual choice and responsibility so that parishioners would learn to make decisions independently of the church.

A very different report described Garcia Jimenez, the 53-year-old "herb doctor" in a town south of the capital. Señor Jimenez claimed that many women consulted him without embarrassment about their problems. He offered herbs for "sexual disability," for stomach discomfort, for "bruises internal and external," for preparing contraceptive mixes, and for inducing abortion.

After struggling through a wide assortment of reports, Dr. Orozco was not sure that the National Population Council was ready to proceed with Phase Three of its program. He decided to seek the advice of a marketing consultant to learn whether the NPC was on the right track.

Questions

1. Which dynamics of consumer behavior would help Dr. Orozco analyze the market for birth control?
2. What marketing implications could Dr. Orozco draw from the decision-making process of consumers in the market?
3. What market segments can be identified? Which market targeting strategy would you recommend?
4. What elements of a marketing plan would you recommend to Dr. Orozco, especially a promotional strategy?

Elements of Marketing Strategy

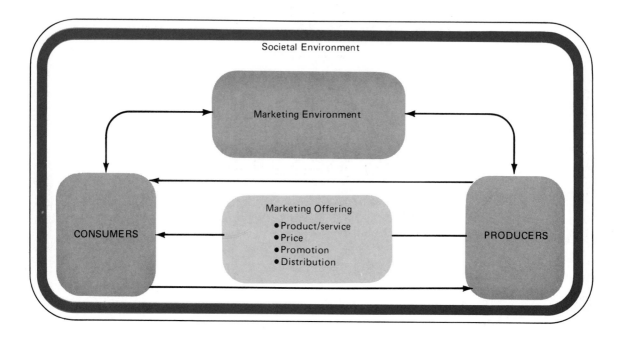

Although consumers perceive the marketing mix as a total marketing offering, from the organization's point of view it has four distinct strategy elements: product, price, promotion, and distribution.

- The *product* or service (Chapters 11–13) is at the heart of the marketing mix. No matter what its category or its characteristics, its relevance is based on how consumers view its functions and value.

- Every product must have a *price* (Chapters 14–16), a monetary value in terms of what consumers are willing to exchange for it.

- The product-price mix is the focus of *promotion* efforts (Chapters 17–19), which communicates the existence and attributes of the product and its marketer to consumers and tries to get them to make a decision to buy it.

- Product, price, and promotion together are *distributed* (Chapters 20–22), are made physically available to consumers through the combined efforts of the producer, intermediaries, and other facilitating organizations.

These elements of the marketing mix are analyzed in detail in Part 4.

Product

PRODUCT CONCEPT AND STRATEGY

After completing this chapter, the reader should be able to:

1. Identify the relevant dimensions of a product—managerial, consumer, and societal.

2. Show the relationship between organizational goals and product mix.

3. Explain the product management process as it relates to the product life cycle.

4. Describe the constraints affecting new product introduction—internal and external.

5. Apply the six-stage product planning process.

6. Point out the nature of product modification strategy and product abandonment strategy.

7. Evaluate the different organizational approaches to new product planning and the functioning of the product management system.

The heart of the marketing mix is the product (or service). The modern marketing concept is continually broadening the definition of the term **product**. Once we understand what a product is, we will be in a better position to make it part of a marketing strategy and to manage it.

THE UP-IN-THE-AIR SERVICE

American Airlines.

A classic example of a modern product concept can be found in the case of a service provided by American Airlines.[1] Looking for new ways to keep its expensive airplanes busy from midnight to dawn, American approached the Raytheon Corporation as a potential customer for air cargo. At the time, Raytheon's Distributor Products Division was operating from five warehouses supplied from a single factory warehouse near Boston.

After intensive study of the operation, American came up with a proposal to eliminate all five warehouses. American would pick up the daily orders at the Boston factory each night and transport them by air cargo to fourteen locations all over the country. From these points they would be immediately delivered to distributors by truck.

But American didn't stop there. Working with Friden Company and Western Union, they designed a computerized ordering system complete with inventory control and production scheduling. The result was a proposal that was so complete in every detail that Raytheon's decision to convert to air cargo was almost automatic.

THE PRODUCT— CORE OF THE MARKETING MIX

At first glance, the product (or in this case, service) being sold by American Airlines would seem to be "air cargo." What American was really selling was a solution to a problem in the form of a system. Although the system was built around air cargo, what Raytheon needed was not actually air cargo but a smooth, competitive, economical way to distribute their products. And that is what American provided. By going outside their usual field, passenger transport, into air cargo, and working out the details of a computerized ordering system, they actually created a concept that the customer saw as meeting a need.

In any organization, the product is at the center of the marketing operation. For this reason, the formulation of product strategy involves nonmarketing executives (top management, R&D, and production) as well as marketing executives. The goal is to match the product to the needs of the consumers. The organization's competitive edge is fundamentally tied to the efficiency of achieving this goal.

Howard J. Morgens, chairman of Procter & Gamble, gives the credit for his company's success to the practice of providing products that satisfy the consumer's wants. "The only way you can succeed in this business is with a good product," he says. "You can't do it with advertising. If you haven't got the product, the surest way to go broke is to pour money behind it."[2]

Morgens has a point. When the product is right for the market, there are other benefits as well. Less expenditure on promotion is required; extra sales force enthusiasm is generated (nobody loves a winner more than a salesperson); more flexibility and independence in pricing and distribution are possible. Where competitive products are basically similar, promotional activity may still work, but the cost becomes more expensive in relation to the results.

For the marketer, the most important meaning of product is what it means to the consumer. Toothpaste may be a product to the manufacturer, but to the consumer it means the hope of whiter teeth or fewer cavities or sex appeal. That hope is what the consumer buys, not toothpaste. The consumer buys beauty and hope, not mascara and skin cleanser; the organization buys problem solving and time for creativity, not computer systems. In short, the consumer buys what Theodore Levitt neatly described as "the expectations of benefits."[3]

What the producer sees as the consumer benefits may differ from what the consumer sees. In a marketing situation, the consumer's viewpoint is the most relevant. For example, a small casket company marketed a simple pine box as an inexpensive alternative to the usual ornate caskets. Only two were sold for funerals. Fortunately for the company, however, consumers saw other benefits and bought the product to use as bookcases, liquor cabinets, and coffee tables.

The casket manufacturer saw his caskets in terms of product offering. The consumers saw them in terms of marketing offering. The **product offering** is the physical object or service being provided (can openers, landscape gardening, car rentals). The **marketing offering** is the "expectations of benefits" plus the other elements that go along with the product offering (fast and easy access to the can's contents, the pride and prestige of a beautiful garden, the convenience of a rented car). To provide these benefits, other elements are added to create the total product concept. These elements might be technical advice and service for a switchboard system, the Good Housekeeping seal on an oven cleaner package, and a money-back-guarantee against rain on a vacation.

The large number of products or services within all but the smallest organizations requires that we differentiate between product item, product line, and product mix. A **product item** is a specific product. A **product line** is a group of related products. A **product mix** is the full range of products offered. For example, General Motor's Chevette is a product item; GM cars are a product line; GM cars, trucks, air conditioners, appliances, and all the other GM products form a product mix.

It is important to note that our concept of "product" in this chapter includes not only physical products but services and ideas as well. Many nonprofit organizations have a problem defining their product because it is more elusive than commercial goods or services. Such groups have a clearly defined mission but multiple ways of working toward that mission with a product mix. The Cancer Society, for example, is dedicated to fighting cancer but has many routes to follow, such as research, treatment, public information, prevention and detection programs, and so forth.

THREE-DIMENSIONAL PRODUCT CONCEPT

The product concept includes certain explicit, implicit, and external characteristics.[4] The three-dimensional model is shown in Figure 11–1. **Explicit characteristics**, to a large extent, may be objectively observed and are managed by the producing organization. They include physical construction of the product, packaging, brand name, and the like.

Implicit characteristics are more consumer centered and include such subjective qualities as symbolism, perception, and satisfaction.

Figure 11-1   THE THREE-DIMENSIONAL MODEL OF PRODUCT CONCEPT

Based on Jerome B. Kernan, "Product Planning and Control," in Frederick D. Sturdivant, et al., *Managerial Analysis in Marketing* (Glenview, Ill.: Scott, Foresman, 1970) pp. 328–33.

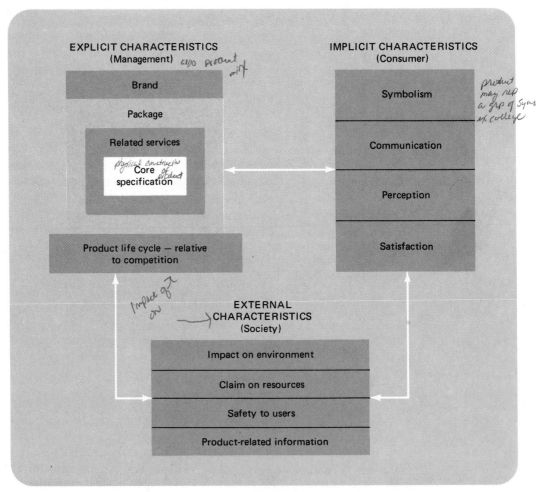

The third dimension, society, is **external**; however, it affects the product concept. Society is concerned with the impact of the explicit characteristics on the environment and social structure. Society also affects the relationship between the implicit view of the product and how product use alters the individual's welfare and society as a whole.

THE MANAGERIAL DIMENSION

From the managerial viewpoint, a product has certain explicit characteristics, such as appearance, construction, and relation to other products in the manufacturer's product mix. These characteristics add up to the **total product offering** when considered in relationship to competitive products.

There are five aspects to the managerial dimension:

1. *Core specifications.* A physical product has basic properties such as shape, size, materials, and color. The core specifications define _what_ the product is: goods (dog food, fertilizer, shampoo), a service (dry cleaning), or an idea (hire the handicapped).

2. *Related services.* With many products comes a stated or implied understanding that certain services are part of the selling agreement and therefore part of the product. Such services may include installation, repair service, or operator training. Computers are a prime example. New car warranties also come under the heading of related services.

3. *Package and brand.* Packaging may be an important part of the product, even a leading feature, as in aerosol dispensers. The more difficult it is to actually distinguish among products such as different gasolines, beers, aspirins, and facial tissues, the more important brand name and packaging become as part of the product. We will discuss these features in greater detail in Chapter 12.

4. *Product mix.* Both seller and buyer view a particular product in relation to the other products from the same seller. The seller makes product design and distribution decisions in a way calculated to create a market position that relates well with other products in the line. The buyer transfers product characteristics from other products by the same seller. For example, if a consumer considers General Electric products to be well constructed, he or she is likely to regard a new GE product in the same way.

5. *Product life cycle.* The sales of a typical product follow a general time pattern: there is a starting period of slow growth; faster growth follows; then comes a period of gradually slower growth, leading to a sales peak; finally there is a period of decline. Although the time taken for the cycle varies considerably, most products follow this general trend. Both seller and buyer define the product in part by its position on the time line. Sometimes, early stages of development are seen as a product advantage (new and improved), sometimes middle stages (established and proven), and this may be true even in the final stage (close-out sale bargains). The product life cycle is discussed on pages 263–65.

THE CONSUMER DIMENSION

Every consumer views a product somewhat uniquely. This brings us back to the concept stressed in Chapter 2 and again in Chapter 8, that the successful marketer must learn to see the product from the consumer's point of view.

There are four aspects to the consumer dimension:

1. *Symbolism.* To the consumer, every product symbolizes its function; its meaning comes from its purpose. Since one product may have different meanings for different consumers as well as several meanings for an individual consumer, a product is actually a group of symbols. For example, going to college may symbolize credentials for a career, the opportunity to obtain a well-rounded education, a way to meet a spouse, a fun-filled social life, and getting away from home.

2. *Communication.* Rice Krispies is not the only product that talks to consumers. Every product is a number of symbols, each communicating information. The exact nature of the information represents an interaction between the product's characteristics and the consumer's personality, background, and culture. Management's task—and it is not easy—is to discover the most profitable message and then fashion the product to convey it.

3. *Perception.* Most marketers would agree that consumer perception of a product is critical to its success or failure. Unfortunately, there is little understanding and agreement as to how consumer perception works—which cues will be perceived and what meaning will be given to them. A relevant product is one that is perceived by the consumer in the way the marketer intends. But what makes a product relevant? Chapters 8, 9, and 10 suggested a wide range of possibilities, including price, group influence, and the consumer's life style and self-concept, among others. The problem for the marketer is to discover which criteria are relevant in the consumer's perception of a particular product.

4. *Evaluation.* A product is evaluated by the consumer after he or she has experienced it in some way (in shopping, at a friend's house, after consuming it). The important concern for marketing managers is whether that evaluation is favorable and why. Since a favorable evaluation depends on the degree of satisfaction produced by the product, it becomes necessary to come up with some criteria to determine satisfaction. One widely accepted suggestion is to consider the relationship between the anticipated reward of a product and the effort necessary to reach it. The effort includes elements such as how much the product costs, how good it looks, how long it lasts, how hard it is to find, and so on.

THE SOCIETAL DIMENSION

Until the 1970s, it was always considered the consumer's right to use whatever product he or she pleased as long as its use did not have too adverse an effect on people. Since then, society has begun to change many rules of the game. Today's marketers must consider a number of external characteristics of their products.

Sometimes the societal dimension conflicts with the managerial and consumer dimensions. For example, cigarettes have a health warning on the label (which does not please the manufacturers at all). There are also "no smoking" areas in elevators, classrooms, and airplanes, which is frustrating to many smokers. The following are a few external product characteristics:

"This medicine will probably do you no good, but it has no side effects."

1. *Impact on environment, society, and consumer welfare.* Society has developed a moral concern for the effect of some products on users and nonusers. Pressures have been increasing for a higher nutrition level in food products and for package warnings concerning the use or abuse of many drug products. The concern for others is reflected in ecological awareness and consumer behavior preferences, which, in turn, find their way back to product design and production. Nonpolluting packaging, less-polluting automobiles, and airplane noise restrictions are some results.

2. *Claim on resources.* Shortages of materials and the energy crisis focused people's attention on diminishing resources. The result has been new efforts to conserve materials and energy by redesigning products and cutting out many frills. Many electrical products are now promoted on an economy-in-use theme, extending the concern for shortages from the manufacturing process to the product's energy consumption.

Some organizations, fearing an increasingly great materials shortage, are shifting from providing products to providing services. It has been suggested that the automobile industry, which now plans for product obsolescence every five years, should instead design cars for the long term. Automobile manufacturers should also promote a service industry to refurbish and restyle cars.[5]

3. *Safety to users.* Public concern over many potentially harmful products has resulted in product redesign and many new safety regulations. Consumer protest has brought about safer cars, cans, appliances, new fire-resistant fabrics for children's sleepwear—the list goes on and on. In industry many new systems have been developed for handling dangerous chemicals. Product recalls and improved warranty protection have become standard.

4. *Product-related information.* An increase in the amount of information provided to the consumer through labeling, consumer programs, and packaging

regulations makes it more difficult for products to be sold on implied rather than real benefits. Nutritional information on food packaging is an example. For the conscientious marketer, however, the more information the consumer has about the product, the better. Consumers who know what they are buying (from listed product ingredients), how to use a product (from explicit directions), and how to take care of it (instructions on proper maintenance) are more likely to be truly satisfied with the product.

5. *Government regulations.* Local, state, and federal laws ultimately institutionalize the external dimensions of products. Restrictions on the composition and packaging of many products are increasing. This will lead to more product standardization and conformity, making the marketer's task of differentiating a product from its competitors more and more challenging.

ORGANIZATIONS AND PRODUCT STRATEGY

Organizations exist to supply products and services to consumers. Their success in doing this may be measured in terms of sales growth, sales stability, profits, and social value. Each is closely related to the organization's product mix, which leads to the principle that the right mix will produce the right results.

Complications occur in two areas: in determining the best, most realistic objectives; and in coping with the fact that those objectives (even if they are right) are not going to remain fixed. Marketing conditions are constantly changing. So too, marketing goals and ways of meeting these goals need periodic (if not constant) reassessment and revision. A corporation must keep its product mix flexible if it is to reach its objectives. One ultimate question keeps marketing executives on their nervous toes: How do you really know you have the best objectives and the best product mix to meet them? The bad news is that you never completely do; the good news is that neither does anyone else. As with many aspects of marketing, you can only come as close as you can with the information and expertise you have available.

ORGANIZATIONAL GOALS

Four major goals—sales growth, sales stability, profits, and social value—govern the construction of the product mix. It follows, therefore, that the efficiency with which the product mix is chosen will determine which goals are realized and to what degree they are achieved. The marketing objectives and, in turn, the product objectives, are also influenced by these four goals.

1. *Sales growth.* The company that remains stagnant in its sales may soon find itself falling behind as markets expand or standing in a dangerously inflexible position as new competitors and new products enter the field. Growth may be attempted in two ways: by increasing sales of existing products or by changing the product mix in order to develop new markets. Either way, the organization must have the capacity to grow. This is determined by the product mix. Without the right products, promotion is likely to produce more groans than growth.

The basic relationship between product mix and sales growth is shown in Figure 11-2. **Growth vector components** are the strategies an organization may choose in order to achieve sales growth.[6] As the matrix shows, there are four possibilities, depending on the relationship between the product mix and the mission (consumer needs which can be satisfied).

While sales growth is directly determined by the product mix, the opposite influence may equally apply: the product mix may be decided by the degree of sales growth that is wanted. A company with ambitious growth targets, for example, will be more likely to take a chance on adding a new, untested, but promising product to its mix.

Sales growth in a low-growth economy poses special problems. Many companies in the United States have responded by diversifying in what are, for them, extreme new market directions. Sometimes the present and the new markets are related: a carpet manufacturer begins to make furniture; a cereal company brings out a line of dog foods. Sometimes they are unrelated: sewing machines and filmstrips; tobacco companies and almost anything. Sometimes the results are promising, sometimes they are disastrous.

2. *Sales stability.* Sales stability is important not only for the marketing manager's peace of mind but for the health of the organization. Stable sales allow for more efficient production and supply planning. Often sales fluctuations are, of course, unavoidable. One objective, then, of a good product mix is to balance total sales as much as possible, so that when one product is in a slump, another is selling above average. On other occasions, instability may be temporary and acceptable, such as during the planning of a major product design change or when entering a new market.

Figure 11-2   FOUR WAYS TO SALES GROWTH

Adapted from Jerome B. Kernan, "Product Planning and Control," in Frederick D. Sturdivant et al., *Managerial Analysis in Marketing* (Glenview, Ill.: Scott, Foresman, 1970), p. 335

PRODUCT / MISSION	PRESENT	NEW
PRESENT	*Market Penetration* (Increasing market share for present products in existing uses)	*Product Development* (Existing customer needs are approached with new—or highly modified—products)
NEW	*Market Development* (New uses for the present product mix)	*Diversification* (New products are acquired or developed in order to satisfy new customer needs)

3. *Profits.* Profits are still the primary measure of a company's success. The potential profits are determined by the product mix. Usually, some of a company's line of products are much more profitable than others, although this is hard to measure accurately because of overhead costs common to all of the firm's products. Unprofitable or less profitable items are not necessarily candidates for extinction, however. They may be performing a valuable role in helping to sell the company's more profitable lines. They may also be easy sellers and good sales insurance against an unforeseen failure of a profitable line.

Material and energy shortages can also play havoc with efforts to achieve the most profitable product mix. Companies are forced to re-examine their product lines and evaluate them in the light of the most profitable way to use the materials available. Often, this means cutting special products aimed at small market segments in favor of big volume sellers.

Although firms usually try to plan their product mix to achieve maximum profits, there are circumstances that call for a different policy. Companies fearing government intervention, for example, may think it wise to show a comfortable yet not large profit.

4. *Social value.* This includes those goals for which no sales or profit yardstick is appropriate. Nonprofit organizations justify their services (and maybe even products) because society or some part of it feels that their "product mix" provides benefits. Hospitals promote health, museums fulfill cultural desires, and public parks furnish opportunities for recreation. Of course, their costs have to be covered by government, foundations, assorted wealthy persons, or user fees.

Business firms may evaluate some of their products according to social value. Most railroads keep their passenger lines because the government says they must, not because these lines produce a profit (they do not). Other social value products reflect the corporation's social responsibility. The company that produces low-cost wall material for remodeling ghetto dwellings may benefit by building good will, although profits may be very low or even nonexistent. Of course, a product that starts out contributing only to social values may eventually be a profit winner.

PRODUCT MIX   The three dimensions by which a product mix may be described are width, depth, and consistency. **Width** refers to how many different product lines the company has. Wrigley, for example, has only one product line, chewing gum, in its product mix. Colgate-Palmolive, on the other hand, sells everything from razor blades to hockey sticks in addition to household lines of detergents, window cleaners, and toothpastes. The **depth** of the product mix refers to the number of items within each product line. Wrigley sells a full range of chewing gums in order to appeal to as many tastes in the market as possible. The **consistency** refers to the relationship between the company's various product lines, in terms of common use, distribution outlets, or other characteristics. Toothpaste, deodorant, and shaving cream have an obvious relationship; shampoos and hockey sticks do not.

These three dimensions—width, depth, and consistency—should be considered in putting together the best items, lines, and market opportunities. Increasing the width of the product mix sometimes means altering product policy at the product item level—deciding what products to add, modify, or drop. The depth dimension involves product line policy—what parts of existing lines should the marketer increase or shorten. Consistency is related to product mix decisions—what markets should the marketer enter or expand.

Since markets are not static, regular review is needed to determine if the product mix is achieving maximum sales growth, sales stability, and profits. One way to evaluate the product mix is to compare each product for sales growth, market share, and profitability.

PRODUCT LIFE CYCLE The **product life cycle (PLC)** refers to a product's sales growth from its beginning to its peak, followed by a decline and its eventual withdrawal from the market. The forces affecting the life cycle—consumer demands, competition, government rulings—are basically beyond the control of the company and the influence of the company's marketing efforts. This PLC relationship is shown in Figure 11-3. Profits are almost nonexistent in the introductory stage because of heavy promotional and introduction costs. During its growth stage profits improve substantially, reaching a peak as the product approaches the maturity stage of its life cycle. In the saturation stage, the sales curve passes its peak as the product reaches its full potential among buyers. From then on it's downhill for both sales and profits until the zero point is reached.

"If you're having a downtrend, certainly more diversification would seem to be indicated."

Courtesy of *The Wall Street Journal*

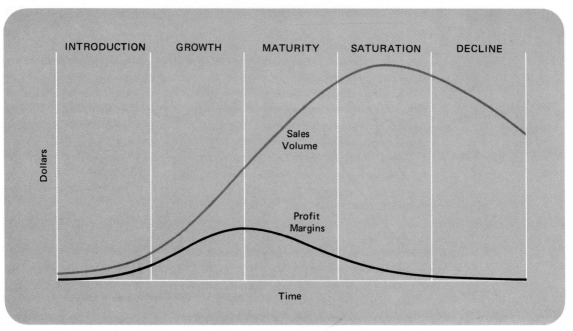

| INTRODUCTION | GROWTH | MATURITY | SATURATION | DECLINE |

Sales
Volume

Profit
Margins

Dollars

Time

Figure 11-3   **BASIC LIFE CYCLE OF PRODUCTS**

Note: Some versions of the product life cycle drop the saturation stage and make it part of the maturity stage.

Adapted from Eugene J. Kelley, *Marketing Planning and Competitive Strategy* (Englewood Cliffs, N.J.: Prentice-Hall, Inc., 1972), p. 85. The original source is the Management Research Department, Booz, Allen & Hamilton, Inc.

There are, of course, exceptions to the life cycle shown in Figure 11-3. One of the most common exceptions occurs when there is a second peak in sales. This may be caused by such things as promotional effort when the first sales decline begins, an important modification of the basic product, expanded distribution, or the discovery of a major new use for the product. Demand then springs back again, as was the case with coal when oil prices skyrocketed in the mid-1970s.

Marketing theory behind the life-cycle curve is closely related to the diffusion of innovation discussed in Chapter 8. A new product entering the market must overcome existing purchase patterns. The innovative consumers adopt it first, followed in increasing numbers by other sectors of the market. If new customers like the product, the sales curve rises higher and faster until it levels off as the proportion of new buyers to regular users decreases. If competition enters the market, the time needed to reach this peak may be shortened. Eventually, the sales of the product decline as new products and ideas replace it.

The concept of PLC will vary in its application depending on whether we are considering a **product class** (such as automobiles), a **product form** (such as compact cars), or a **brand** (such as the Honda Civic). Product classes have the longest life, encompassing many changes of product form. The life of brands shows the greatest variation. Brands may evolve through several product form changes (the Hoover vacuum cleaner is an example). Or, brands may come and go quickly within one product form cycle, never to be heard from again.

A special kind of PLC is called a **fad.** Fads hit fast, peak fast, and fade fast. Some items that seem to be fads at the outset (frisbees, waterbeds, negative heel shoes) make the grade and continue to grow well past the fad stage. Some, such as yo-yos and hula hoops, make a comeback every ten years or so, but most fads are over after a few months. Their appeal to consumers is shown in the increasingly large number of product categories they have appeared in. The obvious secret of marketing a fad is to hit fast at the right time with the right product.

The PLC concept has limited value as a method of forecasting because of the many variables involved in individual product characteristics, market reactions, and time periods. It can be used as a planning aid in anticipating marketing strategies stage by stage. A product can also be compared to similar or related products in the past to estimate how well it is doing in the market. Manufacturers of color television sets could use the PLC experience they had with the original black-and-white sets.

The PLC concept is not without its critics.[7] They argue that the variation among product forms in a product class and among brands in a product form is too great for the concept to be a reliable guide for planning. Marketing support may be withdrawn from a brand that management feels is in the decline stage. That action itself guarantees that the brand will decline. Thus, the idea that the PLC is inevitable may close management's eyes to the possibility of creating a marketing strategy that will revive brand sales. Also, the PLC concept stresses new product introductions (many of which fail) at the expense of established brands that may still have a lot of life left in them. To avoid the PLC blinders, management should use a marketing information system to keep track of consumer patterns. This will be discussed in Chapter 23.

New products represent money invested now in the hope of profits later. According to the PLC concept, management's goal is to shorten the expensive introductory stage and keep the profitable growth and maturity stages going as long as possible. This is accomplished through three **product strategies**: by adding new products, modifying present products, and abandoning old products.

We will now discuss these three product strategies in greater detail. Of course, the PLC can also be influenced by the other marketing strategy elements—price, promotion, and distribution.

PRODUCT INTRODUCTION STRATEGY

New products are critical to the long-run survival of the organization. They also involve a high degree of risk. We will therefore concentrate a good deal of attention on **new product planning.**

Table 11-1
WAYS IN WHICH A PRODUCT CAN BE "NEW"

ATTRIBUTES MAKING INTRODUCTION EASIER	ATTRIBUTES MAKING INTRODUCTION MORE DIFFICULT	ATTRIBUTES GOING EITHER WAY
New cost or price, if lower	New methods of use (unless simpler)	New appearance or other sensed difference
New convenience in use	Unfamiliar patterns of use	Different services
New performance, if believable	Unfamiliar benefit	New market
New availability		
Conspicuous-consumption possibilities	Costliness of possible error in use	
Easy credibility of benefits		

Based on Chester R. Wasson, "What Is 'New' About a New Product?" *Journal of Marketing* 25 (July 1960): 54.

WHAT IS A "NEW" PRODUCT?

Consumers are so bombarded with advertising claims of "all-new" products and ideas (not to mention "revolutionary breakthroughs") that they may be permitted some skepticism. In most cases, new ingredients, flavors, features, or product size result in what can be called a new product; in few cases are they truly innovations.

Strictly speaking, a new product is one that serves an entirely new function or is a major improvement in an existing function. Ball-point pens, the first instant coffee, Xerox reproduction, television, and the Polaroid camera were all new consumer products. If you try to think of more, you may realize that they do not come along every day. It is more common for technological breakthroughs, from computers to lasers, to be industrial products.

The real test of newness is what a product does for the consumer. Table 11-1 shows consumer-related attributes that can make the introduction of a new product easier or harder to achieve. In today's market, consumers have been conditioned to expect new products. Companies without the capacity or the inclination to produce them are risking eventual market failure. Corporations must either create or acquire new products to achieve long-term stability. In this chapter, we will speak of products that are being marketed for the first time by a company as "new," even though they may not be new to the market.

FORCES AFFECTING PRODUCT INTRODUCTION

Every year, $15 billion is spent on creating and launching new products. Over 100,000 patent applications are filed each year; less than 3 percent ever lead to profit-making products. In the grocery field, companies average three new products each year.

The introduction of new products requires dealing with forces both inside and outside the company. The internal forces are:

1. *The large number of ideas needed.* As shown in Figure 11-4, about 58 ideas are needed initially to produce one successful new product. About 46 of these ideas fail to pass the initial screening for technical feasibility. Of the 12 remaining, 5 are eliminated for lack of profit potential, 4 do not survive the product-development stage, and 2 more fail during test marketing, leaving 1 new product worthy of market introduction.

2. *The short product planning time available.* Marketing timetables are becoming shorter and shorter. This is due, in part, to potential shortages of materials and the danger of basing production on a material that may be hard to find when a manufacturer needs it most. Also, managements are exerting pressure to shorten the time between investment in new products and profit returns. Many experts feel that this is a mistake, that longer times are needed to complete market research, prepare production, and reduce risks in new product development.

3. *The large capital investment needed.* The costs of launching new products began climbing with inflation, and they are still going up. This has, understandably, made managements more cautious as they confront mounting break-even points. Money is being concentrated on genuinely innovative products; at the same time, more attention is being given to repositioning existing brands to meet new market opportunities as an alternative to developing new products.

4. *The high rate of product failure.* In a marketplace of product failures, it is no wonder marketing managers tend to stick to tried-and-true ideas. One

Figure 11-4   MORTALITY OF NEW PRODUCT IDEAS

From Jerome B. Kernan, "Product Planning and Control," in Frederick D. Sturdivant et al., *Managerial Analysis in Marketing* (Glenview, Ill.: Scott, Foresman, 1970), p. 349. The original source is Booz, Allen & Hamilton, Inc.

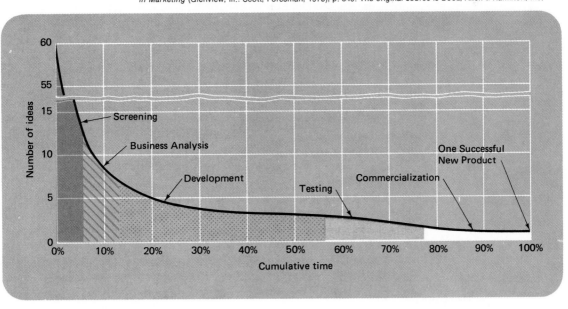

survey of 125 companies showed that the median percentage of new products not living up to expectations was around 20 percent for companies in general and 40 percent for consumer products in particular.[8]

5. *The short product life cycle.* During the last ten years, the average life of grocery products has shortened from three years to one. Competition, too, is becoming stronger; the more successful the product, the sooner the imitations are launched against it.

6. *The small size of market targets.* Another effect of hard competition is to break the market into smaller segments. Companies are often opting for a big chunk of a small market, instead of trying to be everybody's favorite. This may lead to smaller sales and smaller profits, which are hopefully offset by a longer product life.

In addition to considerations within the company, there are external forces affecting the introduction of new products:

1. *Scarcity of real innovations.* While the pessimistic observation that "innovation is dead" may be too harsh, there is little doubt that minor new products are most common. Few real innovations are being developed. Some people blame the scarcity on management for being overcautious in the face of uncertainties caused by such problems as inflation, recession, and shortages. Others claim that the government is restricting American industry until it has lost the will to innovate.

2. *Social constraints.* Consumer groups and other public voices are raised more and more against products that do not show adequate regard for consumer safety and ecological protection. This can result in government intervention, as when pollution control standards were set for the automobile industry.

3. *Economic restraints.* Because of material shortages and uncertainties, rising production costs, and the shifting of market emphasis from small to large, the cost of launching a new product is increasing at a rate that alarms many companies. If a product fails to live up to expectations, the added investment makes the decision to dump it all the more painful.

THE PRODUCT PLANNING PROCESS

Practically speaking, a company has to come up with new products to survive; consumers demand it. To discover how to carry out this risky business with a minimum of trauma, Booz, Allen & Hamilton, Inc., studied the problem and came up with a step-by-step procedure in the evolution of a new product: (1) exploration, (2) screening, (3) business analysis, (4) development, (5) testing, and (6) commercialization.[9] At each stage, a decision must be made to continue, abandon, or collect more information before deciding to go ahead with the product.

An alternative possibility to this planning process is the decision to acquire existing products from other companies. The product is either licensed for production or purchased outright by a company. In other cases, the other company itself is acquired.

New products are born from **ideas**. It follows, then, that the more ideas a company gathers, the better its chances for successful new products. Ideas may come from outside the company: competitor's products, consumers, scientists,

Philip Kotler has suggested a way of classifying new product opportunities, using the dimensions of immediate satisfaction and long-run consumer interests.

THE SOCIAL SIDE OF NEW PRODUCT OPPORTUNITIES

Desirable products combine high immediate satisfaction and high long-run benefit. Tasty, nutritious breakfast food is an example. **Pleasing products**, such as cigarettes, give high immediate satisfaction but may hurt consumer interests in the long run. **Salutary products**, such as low phosphate detergent, have low immediate appeal but long-run benefits. **Deficient products** have neither immediate appeal nor long-run benefits. Their chances are so slim that they are best forgotten; the effort and cost of producing them are not worth the potential reward.

Greatest opportunities lie in developing desirable products such as new foods, textiles, appliances, and building materials. Their immediate appeal helps initial sales, and their long-term benefits help to increase and sustain profits.

Pleasing and salutary products also present considerable opportunity and challenge. With pleasing products, the challenge is to provide some long-run benefits without reducing the immediate appeal of the product. The challenge for salutary products is the reverse: to make them initially attractive without reducing the long-run consumer benefits.

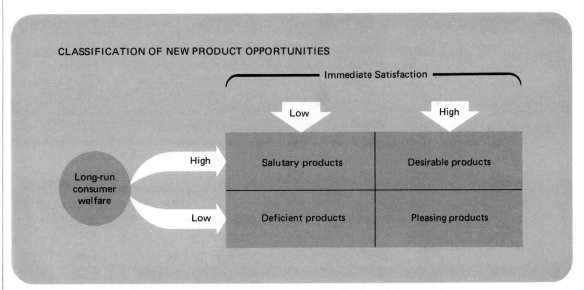

CLASSIFICATION OF NEW PRODUCT OPPORTUNITIES

Based on Philip Kotler, "What Consumerism Means for Marketers," *Harvard Business Review* 50 (May–June 1972): 55–56.

technicians. Or they may originate inside the company: salespeople, brand managers, research staff.

More and more companies are realizing the value of organized "idea-spawning" sessions involving company experts from every area of operation.

The result is usually a large volume of ideas, mostly mediocre, with a few gems scattered through. To recognize the gems takes skill.

New ideas may come from unexpected sources. Monsanto, in developing a synthetic ribbon, had the wild idea that it might make a substitute for grass. They designed a padded base and a drainage system; the brand name is Astroturf.

Many ideas come from consumer research. Studies have revealed that most housewives agree that their family should eat a good breakfast. They have also showed that not many of them do. This creates a conflict for the housewife. Unable to resolve it, most housewives prefer the peaceful period after the family has gone to work or school to the hectic atmosphere at breakfast. This leads to two product ideas: one to lessen the breakfast conflict and one to reinforce the pleasant period following the family exit.[10]

Idea Search Screening

Once the first stage has generated a large number of good ideas, the job of the remaining stages is to cut them all down again. **Screening** is the first of these stages, and, consequently, the one where most pruning is done. Ideas are shot down for lack of potential profit, too much risk, too great a development cost, too little consumer interest. This is the stage where management saves the most money by weeding out unfeasible ideas before capital is invested in them. Even those ideas that do survive the screening must be ranked, because few companies have the resources to turn all their good ideas into products.

Some companies use what they call the **protocept testing method**. This means that they test consumer response to a rough sample of the product even before a prototype exists, just to get an idea of the market reaction.

Evaluation Techniques. The "evaluation matrix" is one method of comparing ideas by assigning them a number on an evaluation scale. It involves a two-part analysis. First, the various spheres of company performance are ranked and weighted in relation to the overall future success of the company. This ranking serves as a guideline to determine the competitive advantage the new product may offer. Second, values are assigned to rate the degree of product compatibility in relation to these spheres of performance. This reflects the way the product fits in with the company as a whole. The following hypothetical example illustrates the application of the matrix.[11]

A large manufacturer of a wide line of photographic equipment is considering adding a Citizens Band (CB) radio to its product line. Preliminary market studies are promising.

In the company there are six operational or functional spheres that have a direct effect on company performance and success. In addition, there are two nonoperational spheres (the last two listed in Table 11-2) that must also be considered. This is a relatively common breakdown.

In translating the product idea into actual competitive advantages, the company must consider its areas of major strength to see if the product will fit in with the company's success pattern. Since this company has good marketing and promotional strength, a product price advantage is not a necessity.

Table 11-2
EVALUATION MATRIX—PRODUCT FIT

SPHERE OF PERFORMANCE	(A) RELATIVE WEIGHT	(B) PRODUCT COMPATIBILITY VALUES											(C) A × B
		0	.1	.2	.3	.4	.5	.6	.7	.8	.9	1.0	
Company personality and goodwill	.20							x					.120
Marketing	.20										x		.180
Research and development	.20								x				.140
Personnel	.15							x					.090
Finance	.10										x		.090
Production	.05									x			.040
Location and facilities	.05				x								.015
Purchasing and supply	.05										x		.045
Total	1.00												.720˙

*Rating Scale: 0-.40, poor; .41-.75, fair; .76-1.0, good. Present minimum acceptance rate: .70.
From Barry M. Richman, "A Rating Scale for Product Innovation," *Business Horizons* 5 (Summer 1962): 43.

In order for the CB radio to capitalize on the organization's reputation and image, the company feels that the product should be of high quality, innovative style, durability, good performance, and have a competitive guarantee.

The results of the evaluation in Table 11-2 show a net figure of .720 out of a maximum of 1.0, which places the product high up in the "fair" category in terms of compatibility with the company as a whole. The cutoff level is, of course, an individual company decision that may change with market conditions or company position. If several new products are being considered, the company may simply choose the items with the highest ratings.

The minimum cutoff is best determined by comparing actual results to what had been anticipated. The matrix as a tool thus gains in value and accuracy according to the amount of experience a company has in using it.

Profitability, while not directly measured by the matrix, can be related to it simply because the products with the best chance of success are the ones most likely to turn a good profit. The matrix should help to provide a more realistic profit estimate than evaluation by the common method. With this technique, the company establishes an arbitrary profit target without the necessary information to judge the product's capability of reaching that goal.

Increasing attention is being paid to a product's impact on society. This has hurt the SST jet and the snowmobile, for example. Therefore, an evaluation method should recognize this new market reality.[12] A checklist can be designed to include such factors as environmental/production compatibility, environmental/user compatibility (in use and after use), recycling potential, and social and moral impact.

Business Analysis   The next stage in the development of a new product is to undertake a business analysis. This analysis tells what the economic consequences of the product will be for the company as a whole. Forecasting and demand analysis (which were discussed in Chapter 5) play an important role in this process. All estimated costs (including those of marketing and those related to social and environmental impact) must be matched against estimated revenue. Only those products that have profit potential will survive this stage. Moreover, business analysis continues throughout the development of the product, as new information becomes available.

Product Development   Until this stage, the product is only an idea. Now the company gets down to brass tacks or silver hooks or whatever is called for by the idea specifications. **Product development** is where the big financial risk begins. Products must be manufactured, at least to the prototype stage, and then tested. Occasionally, a product is eliminated at this stage if it is technically unfeasible. Even service development (establishing a prototype) may necessitate a large investment, such as when facilities must be constructed and labor hired.

   The product is designed in accordance with consumer tests undertaken to find out what the product's market consists of and what product characteristics the market prefers. The main objective is to discover if the product idea is technically possible and will be commercially attractive. This means not only prototype development and testing but also branding and packaging.

Test Market   Although the new product has usually been tested in the development stage, it is not until the **test market** stage that it is tested under actual market conditions. The goal of the test market is to validate and extend the results obtained from prototype testing and early consumer research. It is a minilaunch, a last check against the financially high risk of a marketwide introduction.

   Test marketing is generally done by consumer companies rather than industrial firms. (Industrial firms usually try out new products with selected customers or obtain general reactions by having their salespeople demonstrate products on their calls.) Not all consumer companies, however, believe in test marketing. Some companies, in highly competitive businesses such as fashion, feel that the risk of tipping your hand is greater than that of jumping straight into the market. Failing to test, however, carries risks other than the possibility of investment loss. Dealers and distributors may lose faith in a company that launches a failure. The company's other lines may also suffer by association.

   Those who do test market must make critical decisions, such as how many markets to test in, how long the test should run, what information it should collect, and how the results should be interpreted. Packaging, pricing, promotional approaches, and distribution strategies can also be tested.

   Picking the right town to run a test in can be a real problem. The essence of the task is usually to find "Average Town, U.S.A.," with typical demographics, income, media options, and distribution channels. Once discovered and proven suitable, certain towns tend to be used again and again. The list in the margin shows most of the industry favorites. Consumers in these areas may be deciding right now what products you will be able to buy next year. The trend has always been to stay away from very large markets because of high cost and very small markets because of atypical results. That attitude is changing. Products are now being test marketed in areas as large as Chicago to save time and concentrate effort. At the other extreme, cities of 50,000 population or even less are being used to save money.

To further reduce testing costs, fewer variables of pricing, advertising approaches, and packaging are being tested. The length of time spent on testing is shrinking as well. Restrictions such as these make the actual choice of test market all the more critical. Management, still seeking typical demographics and maximum security, is willing to make more compromises in order to control costs. The final selection of a test market is determined by the product, the marketing objective, the degree of risk involved, and the budget for the project.

Competition must also be considered in the choice of test market. Rival companies have been known to flood the area with free samples of their own product simply to invalidate a competitor's test market results.

Sometimes, even when you win, you lose: of all the consumer products that fail in the United States each year, a full 90 percent had successful test results! If nothing else, this points up the need for more accurate testing and analysis of results.

Commercialization   Let us say the product has tested well, modifications have been made, and the other marketing mix elements have been programmed. Now comes the moment of truth: the decision to go ahead with **commercialization** of the product. Such big money is at stake that the investment up to now seems small in comparison. The necessary factory equipment may have to be installed and put into operation for mass production. The sales force may need special training. Huge sums may be needed for advertising and promotion. (It costs an estimated $10 million in advertising and promotion alone to launch a new detergent, for example.)

Because of the huge capital investment, most companies enter the battlefield one market at a time, starting with the most promising one. If that lives up to expectations, the next most promising market is entered. The rate of market expansion may depend on a number of factors, including initial sales results, competitive activity, and investment funds available. Usually the company limits its expansion to minimize its loss in case of market failure.

Although successful new products are challenged by competitive products at a faster and faster rate, there are still advantages in being first in the market. The usual reward is a larger market share than later competitors. The obvious disadvantages of being first are that a company has to assume the expense of preparing the market and risk the failure of the idea after good test market results. Disaster can strike in two ways: if the product is not ready for the market, or if the market is not ready for the product. Early attempts at instant tea are an example of a product that was not ready (the taste was bland, to say the most); disposable paper underwear is an example of a product that the market is not ready for yet.

Even patents are becoming less of a guarantee of protection from competitors. Imitators are getting around them with a speed that is alarming to the innovators.

In some cases, competition is welcomed. If a great deal of consumer education is needed, competitors share the cost through their advertising. This can increase the total market substantially, with the innovators getting a major share of it. (IBM still holds 70 percent of the computer market.)

Following the introduction of the new product, the marketing manager watches nervously for signs of a healthy repurchase rate. Without it, the product is in trouble, particularly if it is a consumer item. It runs the risk of losing its space on the supermarket shelves, which could lead to its early demise.

PRODUCT PROBLEMS AND FAILURES

Not all products or services are high risk. Take "Rent-A-Drunk," for example, a business started by a British pub owner on the theory that a drunk is an essential ingredient at a party. His raw materials (drunks) were plentiful and inexpensive, as were his rental fees of $3 a night plus all the liquor the rented drunk could drink. Business, however, fell flat on its face (figuratively, if not literally), presumably because the supply of drunks at most parties already vastly exceeded the demand. Renting out drunks, however, is one thing; million dollar products are another. When they fall on their face, it hurts. For a small company, a huge loss can be fatal.

Why, after screening, analysis, development, and test marketing, do exciting new products flop with consumers? Through common sense, hindsight, or research an answer can usually be found. Most often, a failure is due to a management lapse or oversight during the basic planning stages. This happens to the biggest and the best companies.

Bristol-Myers had what seemed like a great idea: a combination analgesic-antacid tablet that a person could take anywhere, since, as the advertising proclaimed, "It works without water." Clinical tests showed a clear superiority over the competition in effectiveness. The product's sales effectiveness, however, was so bad that it proved to be more of a headache than a cure, and it quickly suffered symptoms of early withdrawal from the market. The reason for this was that the idea of pain relief without water went against everything consumers believed; to them, pain relief is always associated *with* water.

To be fair to Bristol-Myers, almost every big company has had similar failures. Dropouts include Campbell's Red Kettle Soups, Colgate's Cue toothpaste, Gillette's Nine Flags men's cologne, and Hunt's Flavored Ketchups. (Not to mention the Edsel, which Ford executives do as seldom as possible.)

Even with careful planning and attention to detail at every stage, market failures occur. There are, of course, a variety of complex reasons for this, including subtle changes in the market or unexpected new products from the competition. Sometimes management does not have enough confidence in its new idea to give it a fair chance. However, the leading cause of new product failure is just the opposite: overenthusiasm. Management, after triumphantly solving all the knotty problems of bringing a new idea to life in the market, forgets the simple truth that the consumers are hardly ever as excited about the new product as they are.

Are You in a Popular Test Market Town?

Albany-Schenectady-Troy
Atlanta
Buffalo
Cleveland
Columbus
Dallas-Fort Worth
Dayton
Denver
Des Moines
Fort Wayne
Fresno
Grand Rapids-Kalamazoo
Houston
Indianapolis
Jacksonville
Kansas City
Milwaukee
Minneapolis-St. Paul
Oklahoma City
Omaha
Peoria
Phoenix
Portland
Quad cities: Rock Island and Moline, III.; Davenport and Bettendorf, Iowa
Rochester
Rockford
Sacramento
St. Louis
Salt Lake City
San Diego
Seattle
Spokane
Syracuse

From Sally Scanlon, "Test Marketing: Is the Chemistry Changing?" *Sales Management*, April 16, 1973, pp. 33-34.

Companies even cause consumer aloofness in a number of ways. They bring out products that are too costly, or too complicated, or so different that the consumer has no frame of reference by which to judge them. Sometimes a product with excellent potential fails because the company rates it so highly that they cut back on promotion. Instead of selling itself, as the company hopes, the product flops because consumers are not educated about it.

Much new product failure can be laid at the door of the marketing research department. Often, initial research is either inadequately done or bungled in the interpretation. Many times, an eager management may rationalize or even ignore discouraging results. Another common fault is to devote too little time to research in order to get to the market as soon as possible.

The chief causes of market failure can be summed up as lack of sound market appraisal, product problems and defects, inadequate marketing support, and the failure to estimate competitive reaction correctly. All of these reasons lead to the conclusion that the fault for new product failure usually lies within the control of the company itself.

FURTHER PRODUCT LIFE-CYCLE STRATEGIES

At any one time, most products are in the maturity stage of their life cycle, but marketing environments change; if products do not adapt to meet those changes, they may die. Products may be modified by changing either the item itself or the marketing mix of which it is a part.

Stimulating new sales or attracting new users by modifying the product is called a **product relaunch**. Early versions of products tend to be largely functional. As time passes, more sophisticated or more simple versions appear with characteristics that were not present in the first model.

When modification seems unlikely to pump new life into a fading product, the alternative may be to abandon it. Often this is, to a marketer, like betraying an old friend or lover. However, for better or for worse (till dying sales do us part), it has to be done. And, like all phases of marketing, there are more efficient and less efficient ways of going about it.

PRODUCT MODIFICATION STRATEGY There are countless ways to modify a product. It can be called "new and improved" even after a small change. Generally, **product modifications** can be grouped into four categories: functional changes, quality changes, style changes, and socioecological changes.

1. *Functional changes.* This means making a product work better or answer new needs: self-cleaning ovens, sewing machines that change stitch at the push of a button, banks that take their loan applications over the phone. The right change, consistent with the company's market experience, can produce a big jump in product sales. The catch is that really significant functional changes are likely to be expensive to carry out and, if successful, are likely to be adopted so quickly by the competition that the market advantage may be lost before the investment is recovered.

2. *Quality changes.* By changing the materials from which a product is

made or by changing the performance level of a service, the quality can be moved up or down. Moving the quality up means making the product more attractive to its present market or positioning it in a new, more sophisticated market. Moving the quality down is intended to either lower the price or broaden the appeal.

3. *Style changes.* In today's cultural atmosphere, where modernity and style have high value, changes in appearance are an obvious way to modify a product. The automobile industry is the classic example of one that creates new styles every year, although the concept of last year's model being less desirable has now spread to everything from clocks to tennis rackets.

Style changes are always difficult to evaluate, since their acceptance depends on the subjective opinion of consumers. The more radical the change, the more "love it or leave it" the reaction is likely to be, thus increasing both the risk and the possible gain.

4. *Socioecological changes.* Changes to improve product safety may be carried out to increase consumer receptiveness in response to government pressure, or because of the social awareness of the company. These modifications may be for the sake of product safety (tractors, child-proof drug bottles) or ecological impact (auto pollution devices, biodegradable detergents).

Modification strategy may call for an across-the-board change, including functional, quality, and style features all at once. This plan is often followed to reduce risk. The theory is that modifications that may turn out to be unpopular will be offset by those that meet consumer approval. The main objective is to lure new buyers with the modified product without losing existing buyers who may like the product just the way it is. Changes are often made gradually to achieve this objective.

PRODUCT ABANDONMENT STRATEGY

Many companies follow the mistaken philosophy that as long as a product is making even a modest profit, it is worth hanging on to. This is not necessarily so. The marginal product may be tying up company resources that could well be invested in more profitable items. Market opportunities may be being missed; valuable raw materials may be being squandered; company morale, customer confidence, and the company image may be suffering. This situation has its parallel in the nonprofit organization that seeks social value goals. For example, a church-supported counseling center maintains separate programs for family therapy and adolescent drug abusers. While both are somewhat successful in attracting clients, the facilities and the staff are being taxed severely.

It is equally demoralizing, however, to drop products from the line overnight. **Product abandonment** requires a system in order to be carried out efficiently. Criteria against which product performance is judged might include: actual sales volume, deviation from sales forecast, market share, profit contribution, and social value.

The most common reason given for product abandonment is a poor forecast for future sales and for return on investment.[13] Greater competition for supermarket shelf space adds to the trend. Fast-moving lines naturally get the best space, making marginal products more and more insignificant. Although product trimming means a lower level of choice for the consumer, it can also mean a slowing of inflationary costs as line simplification results in the elimination of many product variation costs.

A company must first decide how often products are to be reviewed. Sometimes a periodic assessment works most efficiently; in other situations, an almost continuous evaluation is best.

Who should conduct the product abandonment review? The decision group should be clearly defined. Obviously the decision group must have the relevant information on which to base its verdict. This should involve more than figures for sales, profits, and market potential. Corporate objectives, original sales targets, and future sales projections must also be considered.

Once a product is selected for the ax, a definite procedure should be followed for phasing it gently out of the market and, hopefully, phasing a new product in. For the counseling center just described, dropping the drug program may permit resources to be more effectively used in the family program. In this instance, the center may make arrangements for another community agency to pick up the drug program.

One of the biggest problems with product abandonment is the reluctance of the decision makers to face the inevitable. Arguments are put forward that the setback is temporary and happy days are just around the corner; that a few modifications (sometimes costly ones) are all the product needs; that it is important to maintain the faith of salespeople and consumers in the product mix as a whole.

Companies, however, are learning. One of the trends that developed from the market shake-up of the 1970s was "deproliferation," the trimming of product lines to eliminate models, options, and products that have minimal effects on overall company profits and market coverage. Companies have realized that they do not have to be all things to all consumers.

The ethics of product elimination are also somewhat overlooked: providing service and spare parts after the product dies, informing customers of what is coming in advance, the effect that sudden withdrawal may have on the market community. The increasingly influential voice of the consumer may make such disregard unadvisable, to say the least. Class-action lawsuits over product withdrawal are already in the courts.

PRODUCT ORGANIZATION

Essentially, the departments of the organization dealing with the product must be structured to perform two major functions: to generate new products and to manage existing products.

NEW PRODUCT MANAGEMENT   Unfortunately, many of the obstacles between a new product idea and the marketplace come from within the organization. The usual complaints are that the cost will be too high; it will take too long to research; the personnel is not available; most new products fail anyway. Cautious executives, not wanting to be identified with a failure, will withhold approval until the last minute when success looks certain and they can grab part of the credit.

New product management requires an early marriage between marketing and product research. Too many companies develop their new products separately and then present them to the marketing department to sell. They overlook the fact that choosing areas that need new ideas and selecting ideas to be developed further are marketing decisions and therefore should involve marketing people. The research should be in problem solving rather than simply information gathering.

In actually structuring new product-planning responsibility, there are several organizational forms possible:

1. *Venture team.* Many big companies now entrust new product development to a special team made up of experts from the various departments of the organization. Usually, they are given a fairly free hand in terms of deadlines and working procedures. The main ingredients of a successful venture team are expertise and enthusiasm. Their objectives are strongly market-oriented rather than product-oriented.

2. *New product department.* Venture teams are likely to be disbanded or changed with each project; new product departments are a more permanent part of the corporation structure. The department is usually given the responsibility for developing, screening, and testing new products up to the point of commercialization.

3. *New product committee.* This group, made up of top management representatives from various departments, is charged not with developing products but with reviewing new product proposals and ideas. The main function of these people is to act as a check; they tend toward conservatism and are regarded more with frustration than enthusiasm by those engaged in actually developing the products.

4. *New product manager.* Also called product planners, new product managers theoretically have the expertise and continuity that committees lack. However, they tend to be weak on authority and organizational power to guide new products through their various stages. Their role is more one of integration and coordination than execution.

PRODUCT MANAGEMENT

Company marketing and sales activity for a particular product or product line is usually the responsibility of the **product manager**, also called the brand manager. The job involves working with marketing, sales, production, and other advertising managers to make sure the product gets what it needs. This executive must also interact with the consumers, distributors, sales force, advertising agencies, product development groups, and marketing research departments. Such executives are often positioned as "president" of their own little companies, middle-management coordinators with broad decision-making powers. In other organizations, the product manager has less power and makes recommendations to higher-ups rather than decisions.

Procter & Gamble pioneered much of the early structural work in estab-

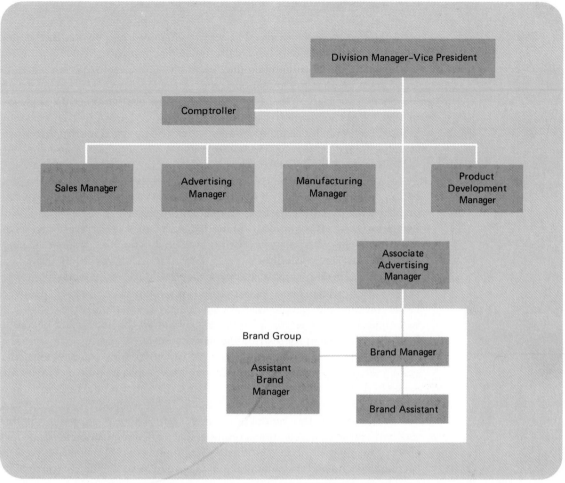

Figure 11-5 **CONVENTIONAL PRODUCT MANAGEMENT SYSTEM—PROCTER & GAMBLE MODEL**

From "The Brand Manager: No Longer King," *Business Week*, June 9, 1973, p. 58.

lishing the brand manager concept. Their system, shown in Figure 11-5, makes one manager responsible for every function of his product. Other systems break responsibility down into functions such as distribution, planning, advertising, and merchandising.

Product managers, however, should stop thinking of themselves as "risk-taking entrepreneurs," according to Stephen Dietz.[14] Instead, they should concentrate on what they do best: market interpretations and reinterpretations. As an example, Dietz points to Quaker Natural Cereal, which was marketed in spite of research results showing that "natural" foods were considered faddist and unappetizing. Quaker reinterpreted the market by reasoning that a natural cereal could appeal to a wide market if it tasted good. Following this reasoning, they launched a successful product.

While the 1970s have shown a trend toward increased importance of the product manager, there have been signs of a new approach to managing products. Pepsico was one of the first major companies to abandon the product manager system in favor of a specialized function approach. Separate managers specialize in advertising, promotion, planning, and other marketing functions, and work with all company brands.

Some experts feel that brand managers are not equipped to deal with trends toward segmented markets and increasing pressure from consumer groups, environmentalists, and government regulators. Conditioned to exist on sales figures alone, they must now consider social dynamics and deal with shorter product life cycles.

Many product managers tend to have all the responsibility for their product but no authority to control it. In other words, they get the credit for its success or blame for its failure, but are dependent on other executives and departments to carry out their plans. Many big companies are trying to overcome these problems with a more flexible system, giving the product manager access to company specialists.

Many companies are segmenting responsibility to coincide with their segmented markets. These new positions are often called *market managers*. Heinz, for example, has moved from one brand manager for bottled ketchup to two—one in the grocery division for distribution to consumers and one in the food service division for distribution to restaurants.

Kodak gave up the product manager system as long ago as 1965. Their system is now structured around markets and distribution channels with separate divisions such as business systems, consumer products, international operations, and professional customers.

Supporters of the product manager system, however, point out that emphasis on sales and earnings requires that someone must be held accountable at the product level. In other words, somebody still has to be sure the product does not get lost among the many products in the mix, because of the investment it represents. There is a risk in spreading such responsibility among the advertising, sales, and market planning departments, as is done at Pepsico, or among customer groups, as is the case at Kodak.

The future may well lie somewhere between the two positions. Product managers will still have important functions, but will have far less power than they did in their heyday.

CONCLUSION

The product is the justification for a marketing organization's existence; it is the core of the marketing mix, the fundamental factor that largely decides what business the organization is in.

The normal product follows a life cycle that starts with its introduction, followed by a period of growth to maturity, then market saturation, and finally a period of decline to the end of its cycle.

For convenience, this chapter has focused on product management across the product mix, and on each product item over the course of its life cycle. Product strategy, however, is not the only consideration for marketing success over the product life cycle. Market segmentation (Chapter 7), and ways in which the same product can be tailored to different market segments at once or over a period of time, must also be considered. The other marketing mix elements of price, promotion, and distribution must also be adjusted to keep the life cycle healthy for as long as possible.

The alert marketing executive must be constantly aware of the changing relationship between product and market and between product and other factors in the marketing mix. Because of the large economic investment that each product represents, top executives and financial managers should also have a compelling interest in product strategy.

DISCUSSION QUESTIONS

1. How would consumers, management, and society view the relevant definition of these products: commercial banks, charities, automobile tires, and children's clothing?
2. What product strategy guidelines would you recommend to these organizations desiring to emphasize these goals:
   a. Levi Strauss, apparel (especially jeans)—profit goal;
   b. Fabregas & Company, apartment rental agents, San Diego, Cal.—sales growth;
   c. Carrier Air Conditioning—sales stability;
   d. NBC—social value.
3. In what stage of the product life cycle are each of these products: Astroturf artificial grass covering; data processing rentals; railroad travel; and trading stamps. What "product strategy" would be appropriate for each of these products when it enters the next stage of the life cycle?
4. Describe the major considerations for evaluating the risk of these specific product introductions for these organizations:
   a. A hand-propelled riding toy—Marx Toy Company;
   b. Nonwoven face masks for protection against hazardous dusts—Minnesota Mining & Manufacturing Company;
   c. Fried chicken—McDonald's restaurants;
   d. A magazine specializing in college sports coverage—a small Ames, Iowa, publishing house.
5. What might be the nature of the six stages in the product planning process for these products: airline service between two points currently not served; a detection system to prevent book thefts from libraries; and a downtown business school's weekend MBA program in a suburban location.
6. How might these products, which are in the maturity stage of the product life cycle, be modified: laundromats, popcorn, accounting–bookkeeping services for physicians, and museums.
7. After keeping it for 30 years in the product mix, the Wurlitzer Company is considering what to do with the jukebox. Sales have slid gradually since 1970, and profits are low but have held steady for several years. For a decade, Wurlitzer's market share has varied between 20 and 40 percent of

the jukebox market, but is much smaller as a percentage of other electronic music systems operated by the management. Several executives feel that the Wurlitzer jukebox is an excellent product and that the next nostalgia craze should improve business once again. How would you go about deciding if the jukebox should be dropped from the product mix?

8. What might be an appropriate product organization for both new product development and existing product management for these type of firms: a scientific instruments manufacturer, a university student union, an electric utility, and a hotel chain.

NOTES

1. Theodore Levitt, *Marketing for Business Growth* (New York: McGraw-Hill, 1974), pp. 13–14.
2. "How Morgens Makes P&G No. 1," *Business Week*, July 21, 1973, p. 49.
3. Levitt, p. 8.
4. The following discussion of explicit and implicit characteristics is based largely on Jerome B. Kernan, "Problem Planning and Control," in Frederick D. Sturdivant et al., *Managerial Analysis in Marketing* (Glenview, Ill.: Scott, Foresman, 1970), pp. 328–33.
5. "The Squeeze on Product Mix," *Business Week*, January 5, 1974, p. 55.
6. H. I. Ansoff, *Corporate Strategy* (New York: McGraw-Hill, 1965).
7. Nariman H. Dhalla and Sonia Yuspeh, "Forget the Product Life Cycle Concept!" *Harvard Business Review* 54 (January–February 1976): 102–12.
8. David S. Hopkins and Earl Bailey, "New Product Pressures," *The Conference Board Record*, June 1971, pp. 16–24.
9. Booz, Allen & Hamilton, *Management of New Products*, 1968.
10. Harold Reed, "New Products in the 1970s," American Management Association chapter conference, New York, January 22, 1970.
11. Barry M. Richman, "A Rating Scale for Product Innovation," *Business Horizons* 5 (Summer 1962): 39–44.
12. Dale L. Varble, "Social and Environmental Considerations in New Product Development," *Journal of Marketing* 36 (October 1972): 13.
13. R. T. Hise and M. A. McGinnis, "Product Elimination: Practices, Policies, and Ethics," *Business Horizons* 19 (June 1975): 29.
14. Stephen Dietz, "Product Managers: Are Those Great Ideas Really Great?" Marketing Management Conference, American Marketing Association, Chicago, March 13, 1974.

12

PRODUCT-RELATED STRATEGIES

After completing this chapter, the reader should be able to:

1. Identify the benefits of branding for consumers, marketers, and society.

2. Explain the strategy of product branding.

3. Identify the benefits of packaging for consumers, marketers, and society.

4. Describe the strategy of packaging.

5. Contrast and compare the product-related policies of quality and safety, support service, credit, warranty, and after-sale service.

The physical product or service seldom stands alone when it is presented to the potential consumer. In this chapter we will consider the various elements, such as branding and packaging, that surround the product or service.

SUPERSTORES AND STEAM IRONS

A dramatic new marketing center has appeared in certain North American cities: the superstore.[1] The average supermarket contains almost 18,000 square feet of selling space, but America's new "superstores" average 30,000 square feet. Chicago's four Grand Bazaar stores range from 68,200 to 89,000 square feet, while the Hyper-Marché Laval in Montreal has 180,000 square feet of shopping space and some 40 checkout counters. A superstore is much more diversified than a supermarket, with garden items, clothing, boutique items, bakery products, and many household goods.

The superstore creates an entirely new mode of marketing communication with consumers. There is a much larger supply and display of each item than in the typical supermarket (the consumer may face a 60-foot aisle of paper toweling eight feet high), and the store makes available a much wider mixture of goods and services. The experience of shopping in this environment will clearly be a departure from traditional supermarket patterns.

As a result, industry is taking greater interest in packaging communications research. Marketers and package designers must coordinate their efforts in an attempt to discover how consumer buying behavior will be altered by the new superstore environment. It seems clear that new packaging approaches will be necessary. In the opinion of one market researcher, "Packages which function at the new points of purchase will be those which communicate and relate to the consumers' rapidly changing life styles."

On February 13, 1969, Mr. Michael J. Espok of Irwin, Pennsylvania, bought a General Electric steam iron for his wife.[2] He made the purchase at a local K-Mart discount store, which had marked the iron down from $11.97 to $8.97. But, after only one week of use, the iron developed a leak and spotted the Espoks' clothing.

Mrs. Espok first called a GE service center, and was told to take the iron back to the K-Mart store. But K-Mart would not accept the iron, claiming that it had been sold more than ten days before and thus was not their responsibility. The K-Mart representative suggested that Mrs. Espok send the defective iron back to GE, which she did. Four weeks went by before she received a replacement in the mail.

Mr. and Mrs. Espok were angered by the incident. They felt that K-Mart should have accepted responsibility for the defective iron and replaced it.

(A store official explained that there was a misunderstanding, and that there should have been an exchange.) Furthermore, the Espoks resented the one-month delay before GE managed to send a new iron.

But the GE service representative was much more fatalistic about the nature of the defective iron. "It's a cheap line of iron. People expect too much from them."

The two cases just described may at first seem totally unrelated. But in each, marketers must seriously consider important product-related factors. The first passage, on packaging, looks at a concrete dimension of the product, practically inseparable from the product itself, and its role as a communicator of persuasion and information in the presale stage. The new environment of the superstore will have a dramatic impact on the consumer, and thus on the product itself. A product that sells effectively in small neighborhood grocery stores or normal-sized supermarkets—in part due to its packaging—may be overlooked in the giant superstore.

The second case concerns warranty and service policies that are in force after the sale (although they provide presale information or a reason for purchasing). Here the issues are the lack of a clear warranty and the confusion between manufacturer (GE) and retailer (K-Mart) on after-sale responsibility. Consumers like the Espoks may not be anxious to buy a General Electric iron at K-Mart stores unless both companies can avoid "passing the buck" when a product proves to be defective.

The above two strategies can be said to "surround the product," in terms of the producer's activities and, more important, the consumer's perceptions. They are different aspects of the total product offering, whether a physical product, service, or idea. This concept of the **total product offering** was introduced in Chapter 11 and will be explored in greater depth in this chapter.

As Figure 12-1 illustrates, most products or services are marketed with a specific brand and in a specific package. The quality and safety of the product are insured by the guarantee, the warranty, and the after-sale service. Product support service is educational, while credit service eases the financial commitment of the consumer and facilitates the purchase. All of these important product-related strategies will be examined in this chapter.

The product-related strategies discussed in this chapter apply mainly to physical consumer products (breakfast cereal, speedboats). However, in a marketing era, the elements of the total product offering are increasingly relevant to industrial products (computers, machine tools) and nonprofit services (health care, education).

BRANDING STRATEGY

From the point of view of the consumer, a brand name is part of product identification. The brand name has become a central focus in arranging a marketing mix, because all marketing efforts come together (in the mind of the consumer and in the organization's planning) in a brand name. As we saw in Chapter 1, Frank Perdue has built a virtual empire by developing a unique and highly personalized marketing effort—all keyed to the reputation of the Perdue brand name on chickens.

In formulating strategy for branding, marketers must resolve three important questions. Should they use brand names on products? Should the brand names be those of their firms (the manufacturers) or those of the various distributors? Should their own brands go under one name, a few names, or many individual names?

THE LANGUAGE OF BRANDING

But what, exactly, is a brand? **A brand** can be defined as "a name, term, sign, symbol, or design, or a combination of them which is intended to identify the goods or services of one seller or group of sellers and to differentiate them from those of competitors." **A brand name** is "that part of a brand which can be vocalized—the utterable."[3] Some well-known brand names are Chevrolet, Colgate, Budweiser, Green Giant, Avis Rent-A-Car, Revlon, Holiday Inn, Exxon, Disneyland, BankAmericard, UCLA, and the March of Dimes.

A **brand mark** is the part of a brand that people can recognize but cannot say in words. This includes symbols, designs, or distinctive coloring or lettering. Well-known brand marks include the Metro-Goldwyn-Mayer lion, McDonald's Golden Arches, Prudential Insurance's "Rock of Gibraltar" symbol, and NBC's N.

A **trade name** is the actual legal name of a company. It may help to identify its products in the market, but it does not refer to any specific products of the company. For example, the Minnesota Mining and Manufacturing Com-

Figure 12-1   MAJOR PRODUCT-RELATED POLICIES

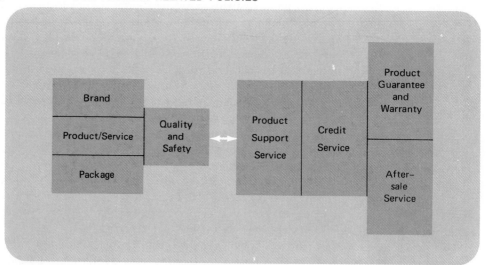

pany produces Scotch brand and 3M brand tapes. "Minnesota Mining and Manufacturing Company" is the trade name; "Scotch" and "3M" are the registered trademarks.

A **trademark** is "a brand or part of a brand that is given legal protection because it is capable of exclusive appropriation."[4] It is a legal term and concept that allows a seller to gain sole rights over a particular brand name or brand mark. Thus, Minnesota Mining and Manufacturing has exclusive control over the brand names Scotch tape and 3M tape. No competitor can manufacture tape and put it out on the market as "Scotch tape" without the consent of Minnesota Mining and Manufacturing.

A **manufacturer's brand** is one that is owned and controlled by a firm whose primary economic activity is production. An example is the Swanson brand of frozen dinners, owned by the Campbell Soup Company, whose main work is production. A **distributor's brand**, by contrast, is one that is owned and controlled by a firm whose primary activity is distribution, not production. An example is the Kenmore refrigerator, whose owner, Sears, Roebuck, has a primary commitment to distribution.

THREE DIMENSIONS OF BRANDING

Branding can be seen from three points of view—those of the consumer, the marketer, and society. The consumer and the marketer must both benefit from branding, or it serves no purpose; to this end, society imposes limits or rules on how brands can be used.

The Consumer's Viewpoint

Branding is an important information source in consumer decision making. Consumers receive four specific benefits from brands:[5]

1. *Brands may mean "better."* The consumer will often pay extra costs in order to purchase a brand name product that he or she associates with high quality and dependability. Studies indicate that blacks and other ethnic groups, the elderly, and young adults all show preferences for status-label brands.

2. *Brands may ensure security.* Related to the desire for status is the desire of consumers to purchase a brand that they can trust. When budgets tighten because of inflation, recession, and unemployment, people cannot afford to gamble on untested and uncertain products. They want brands that they know will be good every time. One instructor has said about Levi's, "There is an inherent, identifiable quality in Levi's which defines them as staple, secure, and symbolic of our culture."[6]

3. *Brands may aid innovation.* The appearance of a new brand informs consumers in a dramatic way of a product innovation. The arrival of important new product types, such as DuPont's cookware coating (Teflon), Gillette's double razor blade (Trac II), and Standard Brand's egg substitute (Egg Beaters) were keynoted by their brand names. All too often, however, a creative brand name is given to a new product that is similar to its competitors or reflects only a minor modification (or none at all).

4. *Brands permit freedom of choice.* Consumers interested in a soft drink can purchase Coca-Cola or Pepsi-Cola or Dr. Pepper or various brands of

The trademark "Levi's" is one of the six most famous trademarks in the world. It is registered in the United States and over 130 other nations. Each week, more than a million garments are stamped in some way with the "Levi's" trademark.

LEVI'S WANTS IT JUST RIGHT

Because competitors are always anxious to copy or absorb a successful trademark, Levi Strauss and Company has designed stringent rules to protect the trademark "Levi's." It is always spelled with a capital "L" and an apostrophe preceding the "s." A small ® mark always appears with it to note that the trademark is officially registered in the federal government's Patent Office.

One problem that Levi Strauss and Company has faced is confusion over use of the term "Levi's." Often people refer to any pair of blue jeans as "Levi's," even when they are made by another company. But, actually, the "Levi's" trademark applies to many of the company's products, including blue jeans, flare pants, and sportswear.

Based on *Trademark*, a fact sheet from Levi Strauss and Company, undated.

orange, cherry, grape, root beer, and so forth. Or they can purchase milk, juice, beer, or wine instead. Within each category of products, the existence of brands offers consumers a choice.

The Marketer's Viewpoint

Almost all major American marketers use brand names in selling their products. The brand name or trademark appeals to the marketer because it helps buyers and distributors identify and handle the product. In addition, it helps promote a unique image and character for the product that may allow for price differentiation. Because of these possibilities, branding must be understood in the context of market segmentation, product differentiation (Chapter 7), and promotional strategy (Chapters 18 to 20).

The marketer gains four major advantages through the use of branding:[7]

1. *Market control.* Branding can assist an organization in cornering a significant share of the market for its product.

2. *Pricing independence.* Consumers will often buy well-established brands even when their prices are higher than those of less-publicized competitors.

3. *New product introduction.* A new product is more favorably received both by consumers and by dealers if it is linked to a respected brand name.

4. *Promotional advantage.* When a brand name is firmly fixed in the public mind and is received with trust, promotional campaigns can become more effective and less expensive.

Society's Viewpoint

Branding touches on three general areas of social concern:

1. *A guide to quality.* Brand advertising for many generic products (such as prescription drugs, milk, detergents, and gasoline) may be a sound guide to quality identification or an economic "ripoff." An example occurred when United Brands attempted (and failed) to market a Chiquita brand lettuce—

specially packaged and promoted—at a 30 to 50 percent premium. As former Federal Trade Commissioner Mayo Thomson observed, "Making an expensive brand name product out of something that has previously sold in a low cost 'commodity' market is, in my view, a practice that is plainly incompatible with the maintenance of an effective market economy."[8]

2. *Protection of trademarks.* A trademark is one of the most precious assets that a firm has. If it is not registered with the U.S. Patent Office, it is fair game for any competitor. If the trademark is not continually identified as an exclusive branding device and becomes popular as the generic name of a product, the name can fall into the public domain and become available to all sellers. "Shredded wheat" and "aspirin" were once trademarks; now they are broadly used generic names. The Coke and Xerox people constantly fight to prevent this from happening to their brands.

3. *Consumer meaning.* A landmark federal court decision has established that promotion and branding can create economic value for a product. In a case involving the Federal Trade Commission and the Borden Company, the courts sanctioned Borden's charging a higher price for a brand name evaporated milk than for a private label of similar grade and quality.[9] In effect, a manufacturer can sell the same product with a brand name at a higher price—*if* it can be demonstrated that a significant segment of the public will pay more because the product is a certain brand.

BRAND SELECTION STRATEGY

Several different branding policies are used in the marketing strategy. Some of the alternatives are: Should there be a brand name on the product or should it just be sold unmarked to someone else (another producer or a distributor)? What kind of brand name should be on the product? Should there be a manufacturer-controlled brand and a distributor-controlled brand for the identical or similar version of a product?

Philip Kotler distinguishes four basic brand name strategies.[10] These are individual brand names, a blanket family name for all products, separate family names for all products, and a company trade name combined with individual product names.

The **individual brand name** strategy has been used by companies such as Procter & Gamble, which manufactures Tide, Bold, Dash, Cheer, Gain, Oxydol, and Duz. With this strategy, the company does not put all its eggs in one basket. If one specific product does not sell or proves to be inferior, the reputation of the entire company will not necessarily suffer. The firm can search for a winning name for each of its products and can introduce a variety of lines of a single product class. Each of these lines would then appeal to a different market segment and carry a different name and price.

The **blanket family name** is carried by all products of companies such as General Electric and Heinz. If the entire line of products has a good reputation, each product can benefit from the general approval. Advertising for any product will benefit all products that carry the family name. Furthermore, a well-established family name is a vital advantage in promoting a new product or product line.

Some companies follow a branding strategy of using **separate family names** for all products. Sears produces Kenmore appliances, Kerrybrook women's clothing lines, and Homart home installations. The main marketing advantage here is that the firm avoids confusion. Each line of products has its own distinct name and image.

The final branding strategy is linking a company trade name to **individual product names**. Kellogg's puts out Kellogg's Rice Krispies, Kellogg's Raisin Bran, and other cereals with the Kellogg's trade name and distinct product names. In this way, consumers are presented with a name that combines the general reputation of the company with the specific image of the product. The combined strategy is also useful in advertising for the trade and for individual consumers at the same time.

Before deciding to brand a particular product, a marketer will need to see that certain conditions are fulfilled. There must be a strong consumer demand for the product and clear evidence that this demand is not temporary. There must be a way to differentiate the product from competing goods—a differentiation that can be strengthened through branding. Finally, retailers must be willing to distribute the new brand.

We have already outlined the four basic strategies for branding products. But there are two additional strategies that deserve examination: brand-extension strategy and multibrand strategy.

Brand-extension strategy means using an established brand name to develop product modifications or new products. Thus, we hear of Arrid Deodorant, then Arrid Extra-Dry, then Arrid Double-X. A brand may be extended by new package sizes, flavors, or models. Or the manufacturer may present entirely new product lines based on the original brand name. When Quaker Oats Cap'n Crunch cereal became a success, it spun off into Cap'n Crunch ice cream bars and T-shirts.

When a company employs **multibrand strategy**, it places two or more of its brands in competition with each other. This technique was originated by Procter & Gamble when it introduced Cheer detergent as a competitor for its already successful Tide. Tide sales dropped slightly, but the combined sales of Cheer and Tide exceeded the previous level reached by Tide alone. Multibrand strategy allows for marketing appeals in the same field aimed at varying segments of the market. Thus, an auto manufacturer can produce one car with elaborate luxury conveniences, another with the highest quality safety features, and a third for the driver concerned with getting the best gasoline mileage. This strategy suggests another way of looking at the differentiated market segmentation strategy, as was mentioned in Chapter 7.

Should a manufacturer offer **private brands**? Most manufacturers of branded items prefer to avoid private-label business. While they may be tempted to get into such projects in order to maintain full plant operations at all times, the long-term dangers seem to outweigh the potential benefits. It often proves wiser to concentrate on new product development and strong marketing campaigns for brand name products.

But some producers find it difficult to turn down the big orders that an increasing number of major wholesalers and retailers have contracted for.

These distributors want to concentrate on selling products manufactured by others under their own brand names. In this way, a firm like A & P can avoid the developmental and promotional costs of the manufacturer and gain more control over pricing. Often it can sell its own brand name product at a lower price than the manufacturer's brand name, and still make a higher profit.

CRITERIA FOR A GOOD BRAND

There are many possible sources for a brand name. A marketer may use initials from the trade name (IBM), numbers (66 on gasoline), historical or mythological characters (Atlas tires), or distinctive combinations of common words (Head and Shoulders shampoo). The manufacturer may also coin his own name (Yuban or Kodak).

There are five key criteria in determining a desirable brand name:[11]

1. *It should bring to mind the product's benefits.* When consumers think of Wash 'n' Dry, they instantly picture what the product does.

2. *It should suggest product qualities.* Burger King, Budget Rent-a-Car, and Sea-and-Ski all are effective names in suggesting specific qualities of products.

3. *It should be easy to pronounce, recognize, and remember.* Short, snappy names like Bic, Tang, and L'Eggs are particularly vivid.

4. *It should be distinctive.* A good brand name has an easily visualized image, such as London Fog, Ocean Spray, and Whirlpool.

5. *It should be suitable for international export.* The name must be one that foreigners can pronounce, and it should not have unclear meanings in other languages. Sony and Exxon meet these criteria.

BATTLE OF THE BRANDS

The "battle of the brands" refers to the competition between **manufacturers' brands** and **distributors' brands**. Actually, there are three types of brands competing for consumer dollars: the manufacturer's advertised brand; the distributor's advertised brand (often controlled by giant retailers); and the traditional "private brand." But private brands have little advertising and consumer recognition, and are seldom able to compete effectively with manufacturers' or distributors' brands.[12]

Distributors' brands enjoy some distinct advantages in comparison with manufacturers' brands. A retailer such as Safeway supermarkets can develop high quality brands and can sell them at a lower price than most manufacturers' brands. Safeway can give its own brands an unusual amount of display space as well as the most desirable store locations. These are significant advantages during a time of limited shelf space in retail stores.

The emergence of these distributors' brands has had dramatic effects on the sales of some products. In the tire industry, the share of the market held by traditional leaders such as Goodyear, Firestone, and Goodrich has fallen from 42 to 32 percent in the last decade. Among retail department and discount stores, Sears, Woolworth, and Korvette's have all reported that distributors' and private brands have taken increasing amounts of business away from manufacturers' labels. Some observers predict that this trend will continue, and that giant retailers will attempt to build up their own brands until they account for 30 percent of all store sales.[13]

Of course, manufacturers' brands still retain some noteworthy advantages in this economic competition. As mentioned earlier, well-known brands have a particular appeal for consumers. In addition, studies suggest that manufacturers' brands may produce greater profits for the retailer.[14] And there is evidence that manufacturers' brands continue to hold their own in many product areas despite vigorous competition from the brands of giant retailers.

Thus, the future of the battle of the brands remains unclear. E. B. Weiss observes that "the manufacturer's presold brand and the presold brand of wholesalers and retailers are becoming virtually indistinguishable."[15] He predicts that the consumers of the future will purchase the brands that they respect and trust most—regardless of whether they are put out by a manufacturer, a wholesaler, or a retailer.

PACKAGING STRATEGY

The **package** is one of marketing's most vital selling tools. Many products have a distinct image in the consumer's mind through their packaging—for example, the Coke bottle. The package attracts the attention of a buyer, communicates relevant sales information, and presents an attractive visual appeal. Intelligent and creative packaging can mean the difference between the success or failure of a product.

A new package for a product can keynote a new marketing campaign. The aerosol can totally reshaped the marketing of shaving cream and whipped topping. The fliptop can was the focus of a revised marketing strategy for soft drink and beer products. When the package is drastically changed, it can, in effect, mean the creation of a "new" product.

THE LANGUAGE OF PACKAGING

Primary packaging refers to the product's immediate container. In some cases, the primary package will hold the product until the consumer is at home and ready to use it. In other situations, the primary package is retained throughout the entire life of the product (a toothpaste tube, or a cardboard box for detergent).

Secondary packaging is the additional layers of protection that are removed when the product arrives home or is ready for use. For example, a tube of toothpaste usually comes in a cardboard box. When the consumer takes the product into the bathroom, he or she will probably dispose of the secondary package (the box) but retain the primary package (the tube of toothpaste).

Shipping packaging refers to further packaging components necessary for storage, identification, or transportation. Thus, the manufacturer of the toothpaste tubes may ship them to retailers in cases of 500 boxes, each containing a tube of toothpaste. The retailer may remove the outer case, or may use it for storage if shelf space is limited.

Labeling helps to identify the product. It may be a permanent part of the primary package (the brand name on the tube of toothpaste), or it may appear in the form of added tags, bands, or stickers (Ten Cents Off!).

THREE DIMENSIONS OF PACKAGING

The impact of packaging can be examined from three particular points of view—those of the consumer, the marketer, and society. A package cannot really be successful unless it satisfies all three.

The Consumer's Viewpoint

The consumer usually views the package as an integral part of the total product offering. Here's what he gets from the packaging itself:

1. *Identification.* The information on the package may answer many of the consumer's questions about the product. These include the brand name (discussed in the previous section), product contents and ingredients, instructions for use, various uses of the product, safety warnings or limitations of product use, and a guarantee or warranty. The name and address of the producer or distributor may also be provided. Finally, promotional messages in words and graphic design (including coupons or special offers) may be part of the package.

2. *Convenience.* This takes many forms: ease of carrying (a handle on a gallon jug of wine), protection (unbreakable plastic bottles, styrofoam encasements for televisions), use (decorative facial tissue dispenser), reuse (jelly jars that become drinking glasses), disposal (throw-away bottles), or maximum possible selection (taking one or two beer cans out of a six-pack rather than buying all or none).

3. *Prestige.* The materials and design (esthetic values) of the packaging communicate the status of the product, especially for cosmetics, gourmet foods, and jewelry. Consumers expect most high quality and expensive products to be found in elaborate, costly packages, and they expect low-cost products to be found in simple packages. If the package does not suit the product, consumers may become disenchanted.

The Marketer's Viewpoint

Manufacturers have four primary packaging concerns: product protection, economy, convenience, and promotion.[16]

Product protection affects both the consumer and the retailer. If its package is not adequate, a product can leak, spill, or spoil. Consumers will often change brands immediately if these defects in packaging become apparent. Retailers are interested in the protective elements of packaging because of the high incidence of shoplifting. If a product's package makes it easy to steal, retailers may ultimately choose a safer brand.

A desirable package must also be economical for the marketer. In 1975, the Ruffino winemaking firm eliminated the famous straw encasement for Chianti bottles because the cost of the straw covering had risen from 7 cents to 55 cents in seven years. The materials of a package must perform well and present an attractive image, but the costs cannot be prohibitive.

Convenience of packaging is also an important selling point for marketers. This includes the shape, size, ease of opening, and disposability of the package.

Finally, as discussed earlier, the package is a valuable promotional device in marketing. One West Coast industrial products manufacturer switched from a drab box costing 21 cents to a multicolored box that cost more than four times as much. The company's sales jumped by 20 percent!

Society's Viewpoint

There are various aspects of society's view of packaging:

1. *Information.* One of the most crucial social issues affecting food packaging is nutrition-labeling standards. In 1975, the Food and Drug Administration's twelve-part set of standards (most of them voluntary) covering such labeling went into effect. These standards required that all food products that advertise and promote nutritional value must clearly list relevant nutritional information on their labels. Consumers have been lobbying not only for nutrition labeling, but also for open dating (how fresh is the product?), unit pricing (showing the cost of the item by a standard measure rather than by the package), grade labeling (a way to rate the quality of some consumer goods), and percentage labeling (how much beef is in beef stew?).

2. *Excessive packaging.* Critics of packaging, some of whom are consumerists, have attacked excessive packaging, which they claim leads to skyrocketing food costs. Industry response has been to point out that a package must often perform a variety of functions. For example, a coffee container must be able to preserve aroma and prevent undue moisture from seeping in. It must also be durable and efficient for storage on a supermarket shelf.

3. *Pollution.* Pollution control has become a critical and highly controversial issue in packaging. William N. Gunn vividly describes the problem:

> As public concern with consumerism and ecology becomes more intense, waste packaging becomes more aggravating. Broken bottles, crushed cartons, and bent cans litter our streets and choke our municipal dumps and incinerators. To many people waste packaging has come to represent the most sinister aspects of marketing-minded, growth-oriented U.S. corporations.[17]

4. *Resource scarcity.* It is difficult to separate the issue of pollution control from that of resource scarcity. The same precious natural resources that are being wasted on nonreturnable containers later contribute to litter and pollution problems. In 1970, the glass industry produced 52 million gross of nonreturnable soft drink containers and 51 million gross of nonreturnable beer containers.[18] The United States and the world as a whole cannot sustain these consumption patterns forever.

5. *Energy limitations.* Among the many resources being wasted, our energy sources are the most critical. This issue touches directly on packaging techniques. Studies indicate that throwaway bottles use more than three times the energy of returnable bottles, while cans use 2.7 times the energy of returnable bottles.[19] The efficient, energy-saving, returnable bottle is the one that business is most anxious to do away with. The result can only be to worsen the energy crisis.

6. *Waste disposal.* R. Bruce Holmgren has reported that of the total solid waste we produce, perhaps 40 percent is made up of packaging.[20] This is certainly a statistic that marketers involved in packaging, and consumer critics of packaging, must examine soberly.

PLANNING PACKAGING STRATEGY

The first critical task in developing a package is to arrive at a **packaging concept**.[21] This is essentially a vision of the principal functions of the package. Is it designed to suggest important information about the product, to introduce an impressive visual element, or to protect the product more efficiently than the competitors' packages? Once the packaging concept is clear, decisions can be made about size, shape, color, text, and brand mark. A harmonious presentation must be developed; all elements of the package must fit into an integrated whole. Finally, after these steps have been completed, various tests are conducted, including engineering tests, visual tests, dealer tests, and consumer tests.

Planning and testing are essential because packaging impact cannot be taken for granted. Surveys indicate that customers may not notice up to 80 percent of nationally advertised brands of some products on supermarket shelves.[22] There are sharp variations in brand visibility on shelves, ranging from 41 to 89 percent among brand users, and from 15 to 82 percent among nonusers. With packaging impact so uncertain, careful planning and research are vital if a firm is to develop the most effective presentation.

CRITERIA FOR A GOOD PACKAGE

According to one concise model, a good package is:

Economical—to manufacture, to fill, to move.
Functional—in transit, in stores, at home.
Communicative—of brand, of product, of usage.
Attractive—in color, in design, in graphic impact.[23]

To the above we must add two more contemporary considerations: social and ecological criteria. The marketing manager may have to reduce immediate consumer convenience in order to meet the long-range needs of the society as a whole.

Companies have instituted various measures to reduce waste in packaging.[24] These include cutting down on materials in packaging, replacing scarce materials with more common substances, and recycling containers such as corrugated boxes. Packaging arrangements have also been changed so that more materials will fit into a single container, or eliminated for certain products where packaging is not essential.

OTHER PRODUCT-RELATED STRATEGIES

There are several product-related strategies that can be used in different combinations. We will focus on some of the major ones that can be added to the total product offering in order to meet market requirements and to help distinguish the product from competing products.

PRODUCT QUALITY AND SAFETY

The National Commission on Product Safety has estimated that 20 million Americans are injured each year by consumer products.[25] Therefore, the goals of product **quality** and **safety** have become an important focus of consumer legislation. Agencies such as the Food and Drug Administration and the Federal Trade Commission have taken action to more closely regulate consumer goods such as cigarettes, food, detergents, health care products, and soft drinks. In certain instances, the agencies have required manufacturers to recall unsafe products, for example, automobiles, canned soups, and drugs.

In 1973, one government–business group issued a report on product performance and servicing.[26] It noted that consumers are dissatisfied with the performance and servicing of most consumer goods. Among the recommendations of the report were:

1. Manufacturers should maintain and enforce up-to-date, written policies and procedures on product quality and reliability.

2. Manufacturers should promote the development and use of corporate product standards.

3. Wherever appropriate, manufacturers should promote the development of mechanisms for providing consumers with performance information on consumer durables, such as refrigerators.

4. Retailers should encourage their sales personnel to stress the importance to the buyer of proper product use and care, as outlined in the manufacturer's manual for owners.

PRODUCT SUPPORT SERVICE

For consumers, **product support service** includes such aids as interior decorating in a furniture store, a short course on how to use a foreign camera, or advice from a travel agent on what to do in Morocco. Installation services are especially important in the sale of certain consumer goods, such as heaters and air conditioners. Manufacturers may establish procedures for training retail sales personnel in correct installation techniques. Most consumer goods do not need to be installed, but in the electrical and mechanical fields this is a vital service.

In industrial sales, educational services are particularly significant. The supplier may have to educate the buyer to the advantages and uses of a new product. If the sale is made, the supplier may then be expected to train the buying firm's personnel in the workings of the product (such as a computer).

CREDIT SERVICE "Buy now, pay later" is what **credit service** is all about. Manufacturers often grant credit to distributors, dealers, and direct buyers. Also, retailers and service businesses may make credit one of their services. This allows the customer to purchase goods while promising to pay for them at an agreed-upon date in the future.

Marketers usually grant credit to customers for the following reasons:

1. Many buyers will not be able to make purchases unless credit is available.

2. Through credit selling, the marketer can build up a permanent and stable clientele.

3. Competitors generally offer credit, so the marketer can't afford not to.

4. For manufacturers, credit negotiations often mean advance orders, thus enabling them to avoid fluctuations in production.

The most important factors affecting the specific credit policy of a firm are:[27]

1. *Nature of the product and market.* If the product has a wide margin of profit, it may be worth taking a greater risk with credit arrangements. If the product is unique and there is little competition, the marketer can impose tighter credit terms.

2. *Needs of customers for credit accommodations.* Credit policy must focus on the needs of buyers. A long-term client with a heavy buying pattern will generally receive more favorable credit terms than an occasional buyer.

3. *Financial situation of the marketer.* The marketer must decide how much capital can be tied up in credit arrangements.

4. *Pressure of competition.* When competitors offer attractive credit terms, a marketer may be forced to match or surpass their offers. If credit is generally tight in an industry, a marketer in that industry may be able to dictate the terms for any agreements.

A retail or service firm may choose to have its own charge account plan, or may use a bank card plan (Master Charge, BankAmericard) or a universal card system (American Express, Diners Club, Carte Blanche). Credit is being extended by an increasing number of nonprofit organizations, such as hospitals, universities, museums, and charities.

PRODUCT GUARANTEE AND WARRANTY Heightened consumer consciousness in the last decade has led to a new concern for product guarantees and warranties. The **guarantee** is the general policy of the manufacturer concerning responsibility for defective products. The **warranty** specifies the exact terms under which the manufacturer will take

During your first year of ownership, all parts of the appliance which we find are defective in materials or workmanship will be repaired or replaced by Whirlpool free of charge, and we will pay any labor charges.

During the first five years of ownership, all parts of the sealed refrigeration system, which consists of the compressor, condenser, evaporator and connecting tubing, which we find defective in materials or workmanship will be repaired or replaced at *no cost* to you, and we will pay the labor charges.

This protection is yours as the original purchaser for your home use, and requires that all service be performed by a service organization authorized to service Whirlpool products. Naturally, it does not cover damage by accident, misuse, fire, flood, or acts of God. But it does cover you wherever you live in the United States . . . even if you move.

Whirlpool Corporation

"THANKS FOR BUYING OUR APPLIANCE, NOW TAKE A LOOK AT YOUR WARRANTY"

some sort of action. Because of consumer pressure, the warranty has become both a selling point and a means of product differentiation in some industries.

Some manufacturers' guarantees carry very broad promises; they may offer the consumer "general or complete satisfaction" with the product. Others are much more specific; the manufacturer may guarantee the materials or workmanship for a six-month period. Generally, a guarantee will include a commitment either to replace a defective product or part, to refund the consumer's payment, or to remedy whatever defects exist.

In 1972, a government–business committee issued a report on product warranties.[28] Included in the report's recommendations were the following:

1. Product warranties should be effective for a period sufficient to allow any hidden defects to surface.

2. Product warranties should be transferable to subsequent owners during the period of coverage.

3. Manufacturers should provide clear, complete, and simple product and warranty literature for use by sales personnel and by consumers.

4. Warrantors should systematically and periodically review warranty service policies and programs to eliminate unnecessary constraints inhibiting good service. Similarly, positive incentives should be adopted to encourage more effective warranty service.

5. Warrantors should regularly review warranty policies on compensation to servicing agencies to insure that they adequately cover all reasonable expenses.

Three years later, a Congressional study of corporate warranty policies concluded that "all too often the warranties shroud and effectively cover up the obligations of the seller."[29] Congress passed this legislation in response to continuous consumer protests about warranty policies. The law dictates that warranties shall "fully and conspicuously disclose in simple and readily under-stood language the terms and conditions" of all warranties. It compels manu-facturers to replace or make refunds for any product that they cannot repair after a "reasonable" number of attempts.

In addition to their use as an important promotional tool, warranties are becoming part of price competition. For example, in recent years television manufacturers have begun to *shorten* warranty periods as a means of keeping their prices down. In 1975, both RCA and Zenith cut back significantly on the warranty times for certain new television models. This was intended to offset rising costs for labor and parts (such as glass tubes).

AFTER-SALE SERVICE   **After-sale service** has become an important part of a marketing transaction. Frederick Webster has pointed out that the consumer is probably dissatisfied with the quality of after-sale service and installation as often as with the products themselves.[30] This dissatisfaction has fueled the fires of the con-sumerist challenge to business practices.

It is becoming clear that the obligations of the seller to the buyer no longer end when the sale is completed. Under the new marketing realities, the seller bears some responsibility for the satisfactory functioning of the product. The auto industry is one example of a seller that has become widely distrusted because it has not given enough attention to these after-sale responsibilities. IBM, on the other hand, is an example of a firm that has built a solid reputa-tion for marketing a total package of computer services, including high quality, professional after-sale servicing.

Marketers who wish to respond to this problem may do so in a number of ways. One is to upgrade the efficiency and reliability of dealer-provided service through training programs. Another is to develop company-owned service centers to repair consumer goods, as is done by many makers of electric shavers. A final alternative is to place greater emphasis on better product design. In most industries, this means more testing, research, and quality control. Upgrading product design may also necessitate a search for simple and durable products that consumers themselves can repair without help from skilled personnel.

A government–business group offered a number of recommendations on after-sale activities in its 1973 report.[31] Among these were:

1. Manufacturers, trade associations, and educators should take steps to improve service personnel job status.

2. Service personnel job prerequisites should be based on training and experience that reflect the actual skills and aptitudes required.

3. Manufacturers and trade associations should expand efforts to assist vocational education programs to assure that training is directly related to future job openings.

4. Manufacturers and trade associations should place high priority on the expansion of quality service personnel training programs.

CONCLUSION

Product-related strategies have become an important marketing concern. Among the most significant are branding, packaging, product quality and safety, product support service, credit service, product guarantee and warranty, and after-sale service. Underlying all of these marketing concerns is the notion of a total product offering. Marketers have come to realize that they do not simply sell a product, they sell a complex product offering.

When consumers buy a product, they are actually buying the marketer's offering of all of these features in one package. This understanding is a vital part of marketing because it makes the sales process more intricate. A marketer may be successful with a product or service because of its quality, because of a brilliant trademark campaign, because of a generous credit policy, or because of a strong reputation for warranties and servicing. A marketer may be successful because of the right combination of all of these for the target market. It is important to have a good product to sell, but it is even better to have an excellent and complete product offering.

DISCUSSION QUESTIONS

1. Identify the major product-related strategies for an automobile, an airline, and life insurance.
2. Explain why marketing strategy and the marketing mix as we know them would be less complete and important without branding.
3. What branding strategy might be most appropriate for these marketing situations:
   a. a new safety helmet marketed by an industrial equipment manufacturer;
   b. a peanut butter substitute marketed by a drug manufacturer;
   c. a colorful plastic carrying case for toys marketed by a quality luggage manufacturer;
   d. a chain of fast-food restaurants opened by a major hotel-motel franchiser?
4. How can packaging be made an even more strategic part of the marketing mix of cosmetics, dry plant food, hot health-food cereals, and low-energy light bulbs?
5. How would you evaluate the suitability of each of these packaging concepts:
   a. stand-up corrugated containers for shipping garments on hangers;
   b. a cardboard box for kitty litter that becomes an outdoor birdhouse;
   c. ground coffee in a plastic bag;
   d. a pagoda-shaped can for a new line of fancy Chinese foods?
6. What considerations would be important in determining the product-related strategies for these products:
   a. the quality of a car battery;
   b. installation service for a rustic wood fence;
   c. credit service for an electronically controlled garage door;
   d. warranty for sunshine on a Carribean island during certain months;
   e. after-sale repair service for an imported sewing machine?

NOTES

1. "New Superstores Change Packaging, Increase Research Needs," *Marketing News*, October 10, 1975, pp. 1, 4.
2. "Many People Complain the Quality of Products Is Deteriorating Rapidly," *Wall Street Journal*, June 26, 1969, p. 15.
3. Philip Kotler, *Marketing Management: Planning, Analysis, and Control*, 3d ed. (Englewood Cliffs, N.J.: Prentice-Hall, 1976), p. 190.
4. Ibid., p. 191.
5. Grey Advertising Inc., *Grey Matter* 45 (June 1974): 3.
6. Levi Strauss and Co., *1974 Annual Report*, p. 4.
7. Robert I. Goldberg, "Packaging," in Albert Wesley Frey, ed., *Marketing Handbook*, 2d ed. (New York: Ronald Press, 1965), pp. 6:37–38.
8. "Branding and Nutrition," *Advertising Age*, June 24, 1974, p. 16.
9. *The Borden Co. v. FTC* 381 F. 2d. 175 (5th Cir. 1967), in Morris L. Mayer, Joseph B. Mason, and Einar A. Orbeck, "The Borden Case—A Legal Basis for Private Brand Price Discrimination," *MSU Business Topics* 18 (Winter 1970): 56–61.
10. This section is based largely on Kotler, 3d ed., pp. 193–96.
11. Ibid., p. 216; Goldberg, p. 6:39.
12. E. B. Weiss, "Private Label? No, It's Now 'Presold'—Wave of Future," *Advertising Age*, September 30, 1974, p. 27.
13. Ibid., p. 27; *Wall Street Journal*, February 1, 1974, p. 1; *Business Week*, August 17, 1974, p. 54.
14. *Business Week*, October 5, 1974, p. 100; Grey Advertising, pp. 3–4.
15. Weiss, p. 68.
16. Kotler, 3d. ed., p. 216.
17. William N. Gunn, "Packages and the Environmental Challenge," *Harvard Business Review* 50 (July–August 1972): 103.
18. Carl D. McDaniel, Jr., "The Social Costs of Disposable Packaging," *Business Horizons* 14 (February 1971): 46.
19. R. Bruce Holmgren, "Product Packaging in an Age of Scarce Resources," *Journal of Contemporary Business* 4 (Winter 1975): 20.
20. Ibid., p. 80.
21. Kotler, 3d ed., p. 217.
22. "Packaging Impact Test Finds Many Brands Are Not Noticed on Supermarket Shelves," *Marketing News*, October 10, 1975, pp. 1, 4.
23. Goldberg, p. 6:3.
24. Holmgren, p. 76.
25. Frederick E. Webster, Jr., *Social Aspects of Marketing* (Englewood Cliffs, N.J.: Prentice-Hall, 1974), pp. 64–65.
26. *Product Performance and Servicing*, Report of the Sub-Council on Performance and Service of the National Business Council for Consumer Affairs, September 1973, pp. iv–vi.
27. Webster, p. 68.
28. *Product Warranties*, Report of the Sub-Council on Warranties and Guarantees of the National Business Council for Consumer Affairs, December 1972, pp. iv–v.
29. John E. Moss, "Buyers Still Get the Short End of Warranties," *Business and Society Review* 13 (Spring 1975): 80.
30. Webster, p. 68.
31. *Product Performance and Servicing*, pp. v–vi.

13

PRODUCT CLASSIFICATION AND MARKETING STRATEGY

After completing this chapter, the reader should be able to:

1. Provide a rationale for classifying products to determine marketing strategy.

2. Distinguish between the types of consumer goods—convenience, shopping, and specialty.

3. Explain the basis for the classification of industrial goods—foundation, entering, and facilitating.

4. Describe the different approaches to classifying services—buyer, seller, and regulation.

5. Discuss how product classification schemes are used to determine marketing strategy.

6. Evaluate product strategy in terms of managerial and societal performance.

Chapters 11 and 12 discussed product strategy and product-related strategies. This chapter provides a bridge between different types of products and the other elements of marketing strategy.

THE TECHNOCRATIC HAMBURGER

William E. Frost

If there is a secret to McDonald's rise to fame and continuing growth, it is the carefully controlled operation of each McDonald's outlet to provide a fast, dependably uniform product in an equally dependable atmosphere of cleanliness and efficient service.[1] McDonald's achieves this goal by careful technological control of every phase of the marketing operation.

In other words, discretion may be the better part of valor, but it can play havoc with a cheeseburger. If an employee can choose how to prepare the product, the result can be good or bad. McDonald's eliminates the risk by eliminating the choice; there is only one way to make a hamburger at McDonald's and that is McDonald's way. Raw patties are carefully measured and prepacked. Similar control is exercised over all of the outlet's products. French fryers are just big enough to keep a good supply flowing, not big enough to allow huge batches to sit and get soggy. Wrappings are color coded to denote their contents. Garbage cans in the parking lot are so numerous and conspicuous that only the most dedicated litterbug could avoid them.

THE PRODUCT CLASSIFICATION CHALLENGE

McDonald's has taken what is normally a people-oriented service operation and translated it into a manufacturing process. It is, in effect, a machine that produces a highly standardized, perfected product with a minimum of input by unskilled attendants—a machine that can be operated only in the way it was designed to work.

The point is that *the type of product and the marketing strategy are interrelated.* The initial impetus could start with either one. In this case, McDonald's is marketing a service in a certain way in order to give the buyer value through product standardization. Consider also the marketers of industrial products who sold the kitchen equipment to McDonald's. Their marketing was also based on customer needs, their product concept, and their marketing strategy. This strategy, in turn, was related to McDonald's use of the equipment in carrying out its own strategy.

In any examination of marketing techniques, the temptation is to categorize approaches into *kinds* of marketing. The implication is that food, computers, and travel service are very different products requiring very different marketing approaches. It is the overriding assumption of this book that these different products are similar enough for generalized marketing concepts and techniques to be equally applied. Having stated that assumption, however, we are going to put it aside in this chapter and approach different types of products separately.

In actual practice, of course, marketing is too complex and changing, too creative and innovative a subject to permit concise classification schemes with specialized marketing strategy for each product class. But given the large variety of products being marketed today, classification will help us conduct a systematic analysis of product planning, price setting, distribution channel selection, promotional campaigns, and other aspects of marketing strategy.

The major product classifications are those of goods and services. **Goods** are products whose value lies in their tangible form, while **services** are the performance of an act. Buyers are classified as consumer and industrial. Often, the same product fits into both of these groups—typewriters, tape recorders, and car rentals may have both industrial and consumer uses.

CLASSIFYING CONSUMER GOODS

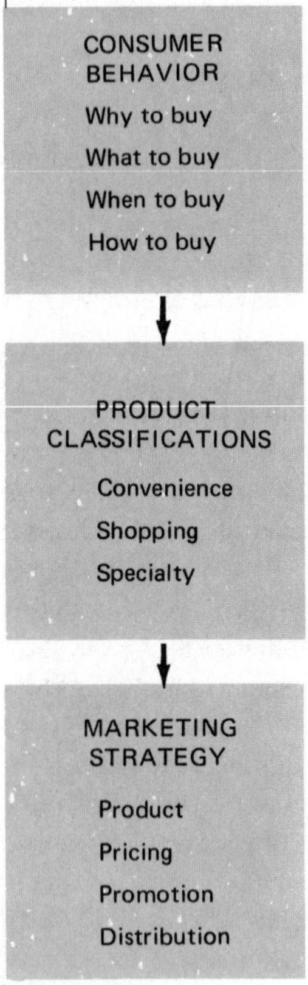

CONSUMER BEHAVIOR

Why to buy

What to buy

When to buy

How to buy

PRODUCT CLASSIFICATIONS

Convenience

Shopping

Specialty

MARKETING STRATEGY

Product

Pricing

Promotion

Distribution

Figure 13-1
THE PRODUCT
CLASSIFICATION
SEQUENCE

There is nothing new about attempting to devise a classification scheme into which products ranging from hominy grits to holiday homes may be fit without undue strain. One widely accepted solution is to distinguish three categories on the basis of the rate of consumption. These are **durable goods**, such as carpeting, washing machines, cars; **nondurable goods**, such as soap, food, gasoline; and **services**, such as haircuts, drycleaning, automobile repairs.

A second classification scheme also distinguishes three categories, but bases them not on the product's characteristics but on the buying behavior of the consumers:[2]

Convenience goods: *Those consumers' goods which the customer usually purchases frequently, immediately, and with the minimum of effort (soap, gasoline, most food products).*

Shopping goods: *Those consumers' goods which the customer, in the process of selection and purchase, characteristically compares on such bases as suitability, quality, price, and style (furniture, major appliances, used cars).*

Specialty goods: *Those consumers' goods with unique characteristics and/or brand identification for which a significant group of buyers are habitually willing to make a special purchasing effort (cameras, stereo equipment, special-occasion clothing).*

The purpose of this classification scheme is to provide a framework for developing marketing strategies based on consumer buying behavior and choice of distribution outlets. This approach takes into account the consumer's tendency to continue to shop around for any particular product as long as he or she feels that the additional effort of making comparisons will be sufficiently rewarded with additional satisfactions. This means that a product can be regarded as a convenience good only if consumers consider it as such. Likewise, a shopping good is a shopping good only if enough consumers are willing to make an effort to comparison shop for it. Specialty goods are also defined by the fact that they are available in relatively few outlets, and the consumer must make a special effort to locate and buy them. These three categories are based on the assumption that consumers perceive them as part of their immediate and relevant needs over a period of time.

Figure 13-1 shows the relationship of consumer behavior to product classifications based on that behavior. This relationship is one basis for determining marketing strategy.

CONVENIENCE GOODS

Convenience goods are usually purchased frequently and with a minimum of comparison and evaluation by the consumer, the gain from such deliberation not being considered worth the effort involved. Examples are drugs, newspapers, and most grocery and household products.

Retail outlets selling convenience goods (supermarkets, drugstores) tend to sell a relatively small volume of each of a large number of items. For this reason, the wholesaler becomes an important part of the distribution system. Manufacturers cannot normally afford to deal directly with so many retailers unless they are marketing a large line of products that can add up to a worthwhile order.

Because consumers normally buy and use convenience goods frequently, they are reasonably well informed about the product characteristics. This means that the retail sales staff becomes less important. Self-service is an ideal selling method for convenience goods.

SHOPPING GOODS

Shopping goods are purchased only after the consumer has made a search and compared suitability, style, price, or quality. The degree to which the consumer is willing to search and compare depends on the potential reward he or she may expect to gain from the product. There is, in other words, a variable degree of qualification involved. Women's clothing is an example. The more expensive or the more critical the style of a particular article of clothing, the more the consumer may be willing to search in different outlets for the desired item. At the other end of the scale, many cheaper articles (aprons, pantyhose) are not shopping goods at all, but simple convenience goods. The buyer's budget may also affect the product category; the well-to-do housewife may buy caviar on impulse, while her less affluent counterpart is shopping around for good value in canned tuna.

In times of inflation or recession (or both, as in the mid-1970s) expensive shopping goods may show a sales decline. Exceptions may be goods fulfilling new needs or presenting new solutions to problems. Examples are microwave ovens and freezers, which have done well (because they save energy) during a time when the appliance field in general was showing a lag.

SPECIALTY GOODS

When a consumer insists on a particular brand or model to the extent that he or she will make considerable effort to find it, even though substitutes are more readily accessible, that item becomes a specialty good.

Shopping goods tend to be sold in a number of large stores, often located in downtown high traffic areas or in large suburban shopping centers. Specialty goods, however, may be available in only a limited number of outlets. This is no problem to the manufacturer because consumers tend to seek out the product. Specialty goods are also most likely to be sold directly by the manufacturer to a few retailers rather than through wholesalers.

Most specialty goods are high priced. There are exceptions; many consumers will go to considerable lengths to get a particular brand of cheesecake or seafood from a particular region. At the expensive end of the scale, home computers are on the market for prices ranging up into the thousands of dollars. Cordless telephones are also on their way to the home market.

MARKETING IMPLICATIONS OF GOODS CATEGORIES

A manufacturer may understandably have difficulty in deciding to which classification his product belongs. Since the system is based on consumer buying habits, one product may be classified differently for different buyers. For example, an umbrella may be an impulse purchase for one consumer (especially on a rainy day), putting it into the convenience category. Another may shop around for the same item, searching for a suitable price, style, or color. A third may go to considerable lengths to find a particular umbrella, styled and signed by a French designer, which makes it, for that consumer, a specialty good. This classification flexibility is illustrated in Figure 13-2.

Even within classifications there may be considerable variation. One consumer, shopping for a particular item, may visit seven different outlets, while another consumer may limit the search to whatever brands are available in one outlet. It is possible for marketers to position a particular product to some extent by limiting distribution to selected outlets; here, the marketer is trying to create a specialty good. Or marketers may go to great lengths to make a product available and familiar to the public in the hope of positioning it as a convenience item. (Timex did this with its low-priced, mass-distributed watches.)

One study of 205 consumers concluded that the consumer product-classification scheme can be helpful as a market segmentation tool.[3] This classification is illustrated using razor blades as an example in Figure 13-3a and automobile tires in Figure 13-3b. Consumers "not in market" are current nonusers. "Unsought good" consumers are users who are not making product decisions at this time. The size of the segments can be measured for convenience, shopping, and specialty goods. While a marketing strategy can be directed at each of these segments, it will probably be more effective for products about which consumers are in greater agreement.

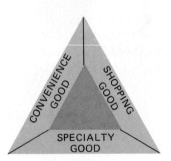

Figure 13-2
PRODUCTS CAN SHIFT IN THE CLASSIFICATION SYSTEM

CLASSIFYING INDUSTRIAL GOODS

In the industrial market, it is not particularly helpful to base the classification of goods on customers' buying behavior. As was discussed in Chapter 10, organizations are more systematic in their "shopping" behavior, and are often

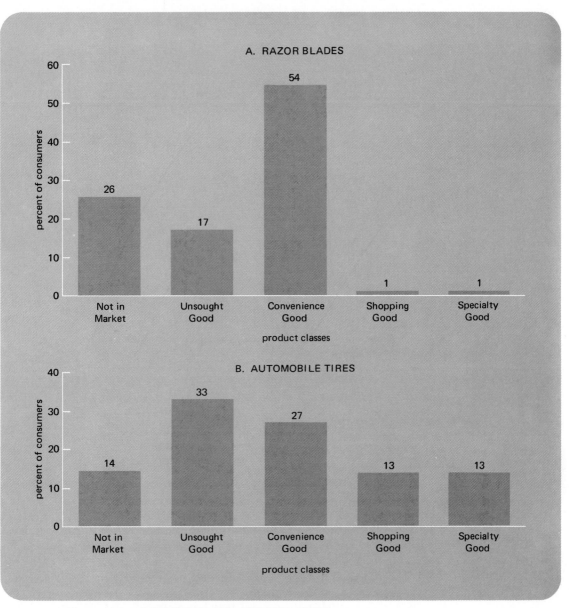

Figure 13-3   CONSUMERS PER PRODUCT CLASS

From Barnett Greenberg and Danny Bellenger, "The Classification of Consumer Goods: An Empirical Study," Georgia State University, School of Business Administration, research monograph no. 56 (1975), pp. 21, 24.

sought out by sellers. Therefore, the classification of goods outlined earlier (based on consumer behavior) does not apply.

A more useful classification is one based on the relationship of the goods to the organization's production process and cost structure. "Organization" can refer to a manufacturer producing plastic garden hoses, a campus theater producing live entertainment, and a hospital producing health care. This production-process breakdown is illustrated in Figure 13-4. This classifica-

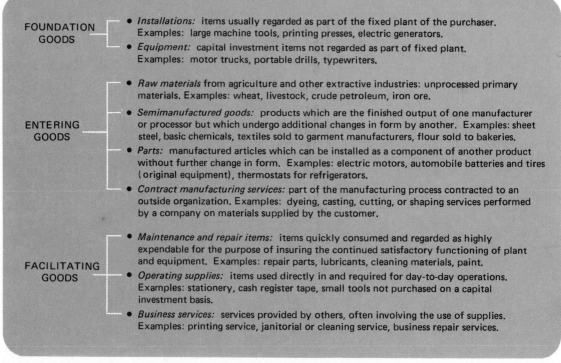

Figure 13-4   CLASSIFICATION OF INDUSTRIAL GOODS

Adapted from Theodore N. Beckman, William R. Davidson, and W. Wayne Talarzyk, *Marketing*, 9th ed. (New York: Ronald Press, 1973), pp. 154–55. Copyright © 1973 the Ronald Press Co., New York.

tion refers to industrial services, which are treated more fully in the following section.

Foundation goods are the manufacturing machines that make production possible. They are used to perform the production process rather than becoming part of the product.

The normal practice is to distinguish two types of foundation goods: installations and accessory equipment. Installations are the major equipment—the boilers, milling machines, turbines, or drill presses that are directly used in manufacturing the product. In a restaurant, for example, the kitchen equipment—ovens, griddles, refrigerators—would be part of the installation.

Accessory equipment is made up of shorter lived capital items not used in the actual manufacturing process. They include such items as typewriters, cash registers, delivery trucks, and calculators.

Foundation goods are "used up" over a course of years, during which a part is usually charged off as depreciation. They are, in other words, a long-term investment. Occasionally, foundation goods become obsolete before they wear out. For example, when solar energy facilities become feasible power sources, many conventional power plants may become out of date and prohibitively expensive to operate in comparison.

ENTERING GOODS

Entering goods are the ingredients or components of a product, the parts that go into the product itself. They may be divided into raw materials and fabricating materials.

Raw materials are goods that have been processed only enough to make handling convenient and safe; they enter the manufacturing process basically in their natural state. They originate either from agriculture or from industries such as mining and lumbering. Examples are cotton, iron ore, crude oil, and most farm produce.

Fabricating materials undergo some degree of initial processing before they enter the product manufacturing process. This may be a relatively basic step such as changing iron ore into pig iron or wheat into flour. In other cases, an ingredient may be completely prefabricated, such as an automobile tire or an electric motor for a home appliance.

The more sophisticated or complicated a product is, the more likely it is to contain both raw and fabricating materials. Computers and calculators, for example, use basic materials such as silicon crystal, glass, and metals. They also use integrated circuits, which are often manufactured by an outside company and supplied as fabricated material.

FACILITATING GOODS

Facilitating goods are the operating supplies that are used up in the operation of the firm but do not become part of the product. They are usually budgeted as expenses (rather than capital expenditures) and have a short life. The purpose of such goods is to keep the foundation goods functioning properly and to help in the handling and supply of the entering goods. Examples are lubrication oil, saw blades, order forms, labels, and protective clothing.

Facilitating goods are easily confused with the accessory equipment subcategory of foundation goods. One differentiating characteristic is that facilitating goods are usually consumed as supplies, while accessory equipment is a capital cost consumed and depreciated over time. An office copying machine is accessory equipment; the special paper it uses is a facilitating good.

CLASSIFYING SERVICES

The average consumer spends more than one-third of his or her disposable income on service rather than goods. Although this percentage has gone down in the past two decades, there is some evidence that it is now increasing. Furthermore, over half the labor force is employed by service organizations (industrial, government, health, education, and so forth). As we enter the postindustrial age, the service sector will grow even larger.

ARE SERVICES DIFFERENT FROM GOODS?

Can you tell the difference between a haircut and a hot dog? Unfortunately, it's not always that easy to distinguish a service from a good. For example, is electricity a product or a service? If a travel agent sells you a ticket, is it a product or is he or she providing a service? What is a plastic credit card?

Most services require goods of some kind, and most goods involve related services—which doesn't make the problem of classification any easier. *Who owns the goods*, however, provides a clue. It is now possible, for example, to rent entire furnishings for your home. This is obviously a rental service, in which you use the goods (the furniture) rather than own them. In other words, wherever a tangible product changes ownership, it is a good; where it is rented, it is a service. Leasing an office coffee machine is a service; a bought coffee maker is a good. Although the producer of a service usually markets it (IBM does the leasing for its own computers), sometimes an intermediary, such as a travel agent or insurance broker, does the marketing.

Just to reintroduce a little complication, more and more products include service commitments in the purchase price, and most services involve some supporting goods. Car rentals, tuba lessons, and the telephone are obvious examples. You pay for the calls, but Ma Bell owns your phone.

Figure 13-5 shows the differing relationships between production and consumption for products and services. Services are consumed as they are produced. They require a capacity to provide; products require an inventory.

Having shown how basically different goods and services are, we now examine the reasoning that says they are basically the same.

To start with, the argument that it is difficult to standardize the quality of a service may be met head on with our example of McDonald's fast-food service—an industry built on dependable uniformity.

Are services more likely to be fashioned individually to suit individual customers? Perhaps. Haircuts are hardly mass produced. But hot dogs may be made in a variety of individual combinations of mustard, relish, and ketchup.

Figure 13-5   **BUYER–SELLER INTERACTION: GOODS AND SERVICES**

Reprinted from John M. Rathmell, *Marketing in the Service Sector.* © 1974 by Winthrop Publishers, Inc. Reprinted by permission.

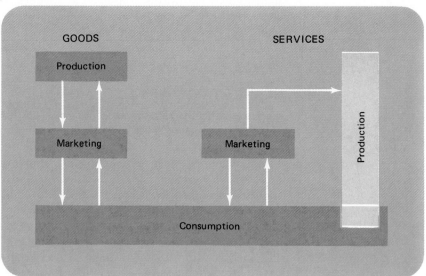

Automobiles come in enough styles, sizes, and choice of options to provide as much individuality as a package tour of Europe.

Products can be tried out and tested; services cannot. Or can they? You can't test-drive a bank, but you can judge the type of service it provides by the attitude of its officers or the experiences of your friends who bank there.

Similar examples may be found, pro and con, for both viewpoints—that products and services are alike or not alike. Because there is merit in both viewpoints, we will deal with the dilemma by using both approaches.

WAYS TO CLASSIFY SERVICES

There are several approaches to the classification of services, but the following three seem to have the most clarity and value:[4]

1. *By buyer.* Services are bought by two major classifications of buyer: individual (or household) and industry. Personal and recreational services purchased by individuals include everything from tennis lessons to fortune telling. Many services may be purchased by individuals or households: insurance, electricity, house painting.

Industry, which in this context includes agriculture, mining, and government, may use an even wider range of services than individuals. Some industrial services have as their function the smooth, economical performance of the manufacturing and marketing operation: transportation, maintenance, training. Other services are used at the administrative level: consulting services, advertising agencies, legal advisers.

2. *By seller.* Classifying services by the seller creates three major groups. The first group makes up the majority: service organizations owned by private individuals or groups who share the profits and suffer the losses. The second group of services are also privately owned and sell their services, but not for profit. Private schools, symphony orchestras, and museums are examples. The third group is made up of companies owned by the public but managed by the government: public utilities, state parks, and some ventures, such as Amtrak, which are jointly owned and run by the government and private industry.

3. *By form of regulation.* Services may be categorized by the extent to which they are controlled by public regulations. Some services, such as electric utilities, financial services, and communications, are subject to much more extensive controls than are normally found with goods. A second class of services is regulated to roughly the same degree as most goods; hotels, theaters, and travel agencies belong to this group. A third group is largely unregulated by any public body. Most repair services, business consulting, and other professional services fall into this category. Many professional practitioners, such as lawyers and doctors, are controlled by regulations laid down by their own professional group. This practice has no legal counterpart in the marketing of goods, although, as discussed in Chapter 5, there are voluntary trade associations in most industries.

Another classification approach is to separate industrial from consumer services. Industrial services include everything from machine repair to the work done by advertising agencies. Consumer services are equally varied, ranging from emptying clogged drains to filling swimming pools.

The "convenience, shopping, and specialty" categories applied to goods may also be applied to services. Convenience services, such as newspaper delivery and car washing, are low priced and require a minimum of skill. In general, consumers are less apt to go shopping for services than for goods. Examples of shopping services might be automobile repairs, travel agencies, and savings banks. Specialty services, on the other hand, may be relatively more common than specialty goods. Many consumers will go well out of their way to see specific entertainers, ski at a particular resort, or have their hair styled at a favorite salon.

Industrial services are mostly purchased on a shopping service basis: examples are advertising, insurance, and anything purchased on a specification-bid basis.

MARKETING STRATEGY FOR SERVICES

Services, like goods, may be viewed as need satisfiers with the same social and psychological considerations. The classification schemes we have been considering for services can be partially applied to marketing processes. Although some formulation of marketing strategy on the basis of these schemes is possible, compromise between the generality of the classification and the specific nature of the service is necessary.

What is needed is a grouping of consumer or industrial offerings that differentiates not just on the basis of service characteristics but includes market characteristics of services as well.[5] Consumers may feel less secure about the services of a dentist or a travel agent than they feel about using a product they own (or even rent). Also, some services received during a crisis, such as fire insurance or funeral benefits, provide little basis for evaluation and comparison. Therefore, the following relationship is suggested:

offer characteristics + market characteristics = marketing strategy

The life cycle of a service may be another market characteristic to be analyzed, along with the offer characteristics. Specific guidelines for relating service classification to marketing strategy remain to be developed.

BRIDGES TO MARKETING STRATEGY

The goal of product classification is to gain insight into the development of marketing strategy. By necessity, this insight has to be based on generalizations both of product classifications and of marketing strategy. In this section, we will relate several product classification schemes to marketing strategy implications and generalizations. Of course, innovations and creativity always produce enough exceptions to keep the practice of marketing in a dynamic and varied state. But to understand and appreciate these variations it is first necessary to grasp the basic structures involved in the planning of marketing strategy.

THE COLOR GOODS THEORY

The color goods theory was created by Leo V. Aspinwall, based on a product classification system with five characteristics that he felt were critical in the formulation of marketing strategy.[6] The theory sets up a continuous scale (rather than product classes) and defines the criteria for placing any product on the scale. Since many products conform to the system, it allows some prediction as to how a product should be marketed.

The five characteristics selected by Aspinwall are:

1. *Replacement rate.* The rate at which a good is purchased and consumed by users to provide the satisfaction a consumer expects from the product.

2. *Gross margin.* The money sum, which is the difference between what is paid in cost and the final realized sale price.

3. *Adjustment.* Services that are applied to goods in order to meet the exact needs of the consumer.

4. *Time of consumption.* The measured time during which people get what they want from a good. This characteristic is related to the replacement rate, since goods with a short consumption time are likely to have a high rate of replacement.

5. *Searching time.* The measure of average time and distance from the retail store.

Figure 13-6 is based on a relative rating of these five characteristics. Aspinwall chose colors to show three categories of goods. *Red goods* have a high replacement rate and a low gross margin, adjustment, time of consumption, and searching time. Most food products belong to this group. *Orange goods* have a medium score on all five characteristics. Men's suits would be an example. *Yellow goods* have a low replacement rate and score high on the other four characteristics (refrigerators, for example).

Line *AB* in Figure 13-6 has a value of 63, which represents the sum of its characteristics on a scale of 0 to 100. This means, in effect, that a product on this line has 63 percent yellow characteristics and 37 percent red. In marketing terms, this might be ladies' ready-to-wear dresses sold through department stores and shipped directly from the factory to these stores in larger cities.

Line *CD*, near the red end of the scale, has a yellow characteristic value of 15 and a red value of 85. This could be a soap product sold mainly through wide wholesale distribution.

Product position on the scale is not static. Most products fall into the yellow classification when they are first introduced and then move toward the red end of the scale as the replacement rate increases.

FIVE PRODUCT GROUPS

Gordon E. Miracle lists nine product characteristics (see Table 13-1) as the basis of his formula for defining marketing strategy.[7] He divides products into five groups, also arbitrarily as Aspinwall did with his color groups. To define the groups, Miracle includes examples, which are also shown in Table 13-1.

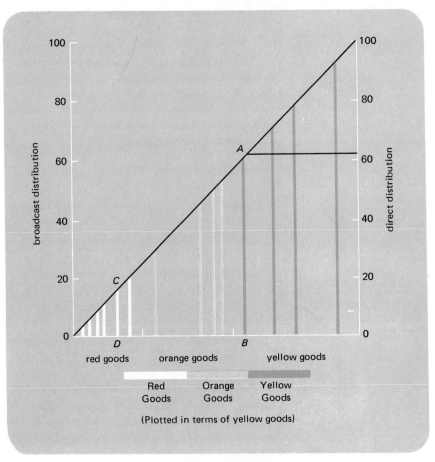

Figure 13-6   SCHEMATIC ARRAY OF A FEW SELECTED GOODS

Reproduced with permission from Leo V. Aspinwall, "The Characteristics of Goods Theory," in William Lazer and Eugene J. Kelley, eds., *Managerial Marketing: Perspectives and Viewpoints,* rev. ed. (Homewood, Ill.: Irwin, 1962), p. 635.

By studying the product characteristics, the approximate nature of a suitable marketing mix can be predicted. In practical terms, other limitations, such as budget restrictions, may apply. The theory can also be used as a check; if, for example, plans for a new product do not fit the theory, a close review may be called for.

General marketing directions may be found for each group. Group I should have relatively little investment in product development, since a standard version is suitable for most customers. Considerable effort should be put into increasing distribution to make the product readily available. Consumer advertising should be heavy; products in this group are generally presold by advertising.

At the other extreme, products in Group V are more often sold by salespeople rather than advertising. They are more apt to be custom built and sold directly by manufacturer to consumer. Pricing is more important; an individually negotiated price may be the basis of the sale.

Products falling in Groups II, III, and IV are governed by modifications of the two extremes.

Table 13-1
PRODUCT CHARACTERISTICS FOR FIVE PRODUCT GROUPS

PRODUCT CHARACTERISTIC	GROUP I	GROUP II	GROUP III	GROUP IV	GROUP V
Unit value	Very low	Low	Medium to high	High	Very high
Significance of each purchase to consumer	Very low	Low	Medium	High	Very high
Time and effort spent in purchase	Very low	Low	Medium	High	Very high
Rate of technological and fashion change	Very low	Low	Medium	High	Very high
Technical complexity	Very low	Low	Medium to high	High	Very high
Consumer need for service	Very low	Low	Medium	High	Very high
Frequency of purchase	Very high	Medium to high	Low	Low	Very low
Rapidity of consumption	Very high	Medium to high	Low	Low	Very low
Extent of usage	Very high	High	Medium to high	Low to medium	Very low

Group I: Examples are cigarettes, candy bars, razor blades, soft drinks. *Group II:* Examples are dry groceries, proprietary pharmaceuticals, small hardware items, industrial operating supplies. *Group III:* Examples are radio and television sets, major household appliances, women's suits, tires and inner tubes, major sporting and athletic equipment. *Group IV:* Examples are high quality cameras, heavy farm machinery, passenger automobiles, high quality household furniture. *Group V:* Examples are electronic office equipment, electric generators, steam turbines, specialized machine tools.

From Gordon E. Miracle, "Product Characteristics and Marketing Strategy," *Journal of Marketing* 29 (January 1965): 20. Reprinted from *Journal of Marketing,* published by the American Marketing Association.

CONSUMER GOODS AND RETAIL STRATEGY

The third bridge to marketing strategy is based on a three-by-three matrix created by Louis P. Bucklin.[8] This matrix is illustrated in Table 13-2. The matrix cross-classifies the three product types—convenience goods, shopping goods, and specialty goods—with the three retail outlet types.

The table shows the probable consumer behavior for a given product in any given outlet. Theoretically, there are nine possibilities for each product. In actual practice, only three or four of the cells are likely to apply to any one product; the remaining empty cells would indicate that no consumers purchase the product by those methods. For example, Kodak film might be regarded by different consumers as a convenience, shopping, or specialty item and purchased in all three types of outlet. A Nikon camera, on the other hand, would hardly be considered a convenience purchase.

The planning of retail strategy using the matrix has three steps. The first is to classify the potential customers for the product, using the nine categories to define the principal market segments. The second step is to determine an effective marketing strategy designed to appeal to each of these segments. The final step is to select the most promising segment and the strategy most likely to reach it effectively. In this way, the retailer can isolate the important market segments and assess the probability of success in selling to them with the appropriate strategy.

Table 13-2
THE PRODUCT–PATRONAGE MATRIX

PATRONAGE	PRODUCT		
	CONVENIENCE GOODS	SHOPPING GOODS	SPECIALTY GOODS
Convenience Store	Consumer prefers to buy the most readily available brand of product at the most accessible store.	Consumer selects purchase from among assortment carried by the most accessible store.	Consumer purchases favored brand from the most accessible store which has the item in stock.
Shopping Store	Consumer is indifferent to the brand of product, but shops among different stores in order to secure better retail service and/or lower retail price.	Consumer makes comparisons among both retail controlled factors and factors associated with the product (brand).	Consumer has strong preference with respect to the brand of the product, but shops in a number of stores in order to secure the best retail service and/or price for this brand.
Specialty Store	Consumer prefers to trade at a specific store, but is indifferent to the brand of product purchased.	Consumer prefers to trade at a certain store, but is uncertain of which product to buy and examines assortment for best purchase.	Consumer has both a preference for a particular store and a specific brand.

Based on Louis P. Bucklin, "Retail Strategy and the Classification of Consumer Goods," *Journal of Marketing* 27 (January 1963): 53–54. Reprinted from *Journal of Marketing*, published by the American Marketing Association.

EVALUATION OF PRODUCT STRATEGY

We have discussed product concepts, strategy, and management (Chapter 11), product-related strategies (Chapter 12), and product classification schemes, including the major dimensions of product strategy and its links to marketing strategy (this chapter). Now let's stare boldly at the real, outside world and see who has been paying attention. How effectively are product decisions being made? Are they being made in the best interests of the organization? Are society's best interests being considered?

MANAGERIAL VIEWPOINT
Only the most cynical of critics would deny that marketing, in combination with research and development and production, has made possible an impressive array of new products and services closely matched to consumer demand. The result has been a substantial contribution to the standard of living, healthy competition in the marketplace, and general economic growth.

However, only the most enthusiastic supporters could claim that marketing management skill with product strategy has given the best possible consumer satisfaction. Nor has it been as economical as organizations might want.

The failure rate for new products still lies between 10 and 90 percent, depending upon which study is quoted. That's a lot of money and effort down the drain. More important, marketers continue to have the courage to try— many experts feel it is better to have launched products and lost than never to have launched them at all.

There is, however, no avoiding the Big Question: How is it, after ten to twenty years of developing new, sophisticated, computerized marketing and research techniques, no significant gain has been made in the success ratio of new products? If marketers are getting smarter, why aren't they getting better?

Some marketers feel that the situation is a "stand-off," since both the competition and the consumers are getting smarter. Others see it as a "turn-off," with consumers numb from being barraged with so many new products. Then there is the "widening gulf" theory, which says that consumers behave so independently that marketers do not understand what they want any more. Others blame government regulations and consumerism for preventing marketers from discovering and responding to consumer needs.

As yet, the answers are not all in. But the challenge for organizations to market more consumer-oriented products still remains fully to be met.

SOCIETAL VIEWPOINT   We know that ample goods and services are available with a capacity to satisfy consumers and to make positive contributions to their standard of living. Society, however, is posing some tough questions about the impact of goods and services.

Consumer groups and representatives are focusing more attention on just what a product really is—what the consumer pays for. Marshall Efron, on public television, demonstrated that Morton's frozen lemon cream pie contained monosodium phosphate, whey solids, guar gum, and other ingredients, but no eggs, no cream, and no lemons.[9] He also pointed out that paying five times as much for Bayer aspirin as for Brand X does get you more for your money: "A nicely printed cardboard box, a sheet of instructions, and a special bottle that has the name Bayer on the cap. Also, the cotton in the Bayer bottle is milder than the cotton in the Brand-X bottle." In response, Bayer could claim that its product quality control surpasses that of many competing brands.

Many critics feel that in spite of the flood of new products, consumers are not getting their fair share of true innovations. Many companies are following the safe line by adapting and improving existing products. Product planning is concerned mainly with existing resources and products rather than with looking ahead to future markets. Innovations do exist, of course, but society's standards are higher than ever today. The supersonic airplane, aerosol spray cans, large automobiles, and cigarette smoking are getting rougher and rougher receptions. Socioeconomic forces, such as population crowding and material scarcities, must be considered. Developers of new products must take into account the long-term impact of their innovations on the interests of mankind.

"I was just wondering, Edith, why his food is 100% beef, and our hamburger is 25% soybeans."

Joseph Serrano/*The Wall Street Journal*, July 10, 1975.

CONCLUSION

Because so many different types of products exist, attempts have been made to classify them and relate those classifications to marketing strategy. The simplest product classification is goods and services, which may then be divided into consumer goods and services and industrial goods and services.

Consumer goods may be categorized on the basis of the buying habits of consumers as convenience goods, shopping goods, and specialty goods. This allows the development of marketing strategies based on consumer buying habits and choice of distribution outlets.

Industrial goods are more usefully classified on the basis of the relationship of the goods to the organization's production process: foundation goods, entering goods, and facilitating goods.

Services may be classified on the basis of buyer, seller, or the form of regulation to which they are subject. Like goods, services may be divided between industry and consumer, and into convenience, shopping, and specialty categories.

The goal of product classification is to gain insight into the development of marketing strategy. By the color goods theory of Aspinwall or Miracle's five product groups, product characteristics may be examined in order to group products with similar marketing requirements. This provides a basis for prediction or a check on the applicability of present product and marketing strategy.

Marketers must evaluate product strategy today from both the managerial viewpoint and the societal viewpoint. Increasing the social awareness of both consumers and marketers makes this consideration essential.

DISCUSSION QUESTIONS

1. What benefits can marketing strategists obtain from designing a product classification scheme? What are the limitations of all such schemes?
2. Identify the following consumer products as primarily convenience, shopping, or specialty goods: digital wristwatch, diet foods restaurant, bottled water, and color television. Explain how each product might be classified in a second (or third) category.
3. Identify the following industrial products as primarily foundation, entering, or facilitating goods:
   a. electrical wall outlets for a construction contractor;
   b. cotton balls for a physician's office;
   c. offshore drilling equipment for an oil producer;
   d. a window-cleaning service for an art museum.
4. How helpful is it for marketing strategists to use different product classification schemes for consumer services and for consumer goods? (Answer with reference to these consumer services: laundromats, savings banks, gyms for business executives, and birth control counseling.)
5. Compare the managerial marketing implications of the three consumer goods schemes of Aspinwall, Miracle, and Bucklin. Which do you feel is the most insightful?
6. Comment on this statement: "Product strategy success would be greater if all social pressures were relaxed. Then profits would be higher and all of society would be better off."

NOTES

1. Theodore Levitt, *Marketing for Business Growth* (New York: McGraw-Hill, 1974), pp. 55–58.
2. Definitions Committee, American Marketing Association, *Marketing Definitions* (Chicago: American Marketing Association, 1960), pp. 11–22.
3. Barnett Greenberg and Danny Bellenger, "The Classification of Consumer Goods: An Empirical Study," Georgia State University, School of Business Administration, research monograph no. 56 (1975), pp. 36–41.
4. This section is based largely on John M. Rathmell, *Marketing in the Service Sector* (Cambridge, Mass.: Winthrop, 1974), pp. 6–17.
5. R. G. Wyckham, P. T. Fitzroy, and G. D. Mandry, "Marketing of Services: An Evaluation of the Theory," *European Journal of Marketing* 9 (1975), 59–66.
6. Leo V. Aspinwall, "The Characteristics of Goods Theory," in William Lazer and Eugene J. Kelley, eds., *Managerial Marketing: Perspectives and Viewpoints*, rev. ed. (Homewood, Ill.: Irwin, 1962), pp. 633–43.
7. Gordon E. Miracle, "Product Characteristics and Marketing Strategy," *Journal of Marketing* 29 (January 1965): 18–24.
8. Louis P. Bucklin, "Retail Strategy and the Classification of Consumer Goods," *Journal of Marketing* 27 (January 1963): 50–55.
9. "Who Took the Lemons Out of Mom's Pie?" *Business Week*, February 6, 1971, p. 23.

CASE STUDIES

SUPERCLEAN, INC.

"We've got a problem on our hands," said Albert Hollebrands, president of Superclean, Inc. Hollebrands was speaking to a small group of associates gathered in the conference room at 8:00 A.M. on Friday, January 13, 1969. Included in the group were Marie McCray, director of marketing; Dennis Carlson, advertising manager; Dan Albetta, controller; and Alan Steinhaus, assistant to the president.

History and Crisis Superclean, Inc., was founded in 1922 and soon became the major producer of household liquid bleach, its only product. In 1967, the Supreme Court upheld a ruling by the Federal Trade Commission that the acquisition of Superclean by Costa, Margan Company in the early 1960s violated the antimerger laws. Costa, Margan was ordered to divest itself of Superclean, a process that was completed early in January of 1968. As of that date, Superclean was a publicly owned company with shares traded on the American Stock Exchange. It depended on one product—Superclean, a chlorine bleach—for all of its sales and profits.

After everyone was settled around the table, Hollebrands continued his opening remarks. "As you all know, during the last year the major detergent makers have introduced a collection of enzyme laundry products. Each has had some form of sampling and heavy expenditures for introductory advertising. Even worse, each has claimed that it can remove stains and that chlorine bleach is no longer necessary. Our sales are now off sharply."

"I don't understand," said Albetta. "I thought the reports from our lab indicated that, except in certain applications, enzymes didn't work very well. I thought those products were *not* substitutes for chlorine bleach."

"That's what we all thought," added McCray. "I believed that the impact on our sales would be moderate and temporary. But now it looks as if we can't count on that. What do you think we should do under these circumstances?"

Proposed Solutions Carlson was the first to respond. "For one thing, we should increase our advertising expenditures. We may be making the same number of impressions now as we were six months ago, but that is a smaller proportion of the total in the laundry products category. We're getting lost in the deluge."

After a moment's thought, Hollebrands spoke. "I'm not sure that we can afford to cut into our profits any more than the sales decline is already doing."

"I couldn't agree with you more," declared Albetta, in his usual role of financial worrier. "If sales are down, we probably ought to cut advertising expenditures to keep our advertising-to-sales ratio fairly constant."

"Now, Dan," said Hollebrands, "don't you think that stopping our advertising or even cutting back might be an overreaction? Superclean has always had solid, consistent advertising. If we cut back, it may seem as if we are conceding the battle."

Steinhaus entered the conversation at this point. "I think we should maintain our media advertising at its planned level. It occurs to me, though, that we might change the thrust of our copy. Why not tell the housewife about the poor performance of enzymes?"

"It seems to me," mused McCray, "that another alternative is to fight fire with fire. I'm not saying we should abandon Superclean, but it is a mature product. Perhaps we ought to market an enzyme product of our own."

"Why, Marie," Hollebrands responded, "it sounds as if you don't believe the reports of our own lab. Besides, our research and development capability is pretty minimal. I don't know if they could formulate a new product in a reasonable amount of time."

"Perhaps we ought to do something about that deficiency," continued McCray. "If we could develop a whole line of nonfood household products, we wouldn't be so vulnerable to competitive efforts in one area."

Carlson joined in the spirit of this suggestion. "I agree that we ought to broaden our product line, but don't you think it would be easier to buy an established company rather than to try to develop products of our own?"

"With what money would we buy another company?" mumbled Albetta.

Steinhaus ignored this remark. "We could diversify our customer segments from there. We ought to be able to market those new food and nonfood products to the food service industry as well as to households."

"Before we do anything," said Hollebrands, cutting off this line of discussion, "we'd better have some agreement on the fundamental goals and objectives for the company. Then maybe things will fall into place."

Questions
1. In the short run (1970 to 1971), what should Superclean do about marketing its liquid bleach?
2. In the long run (the next ten years), what should Superclean do with its product mix?
3. What marketing capabilities would Superclean have to change in order to handle the product mix you recommend in question 2?

MONTGOMERY WARD

Interoffice Memorandum

TO: Carol Fudin, Manager
Hosiery Department
FROM: Jason R. Alexander, Project Director
Corporate Research Department
SUBJECT: *New Pantyhose Package and Product Study*
DATE: January 20, 1976

In conjunction with the planned introduction of a new pantyhose by the hosiery department, corporate research conducted a consumer opinion survey of the proposed package and product. This new product is called Super Natural Pantyhose, and it will be marketed as a moderate support pantyhose. As such, it is intended to compete with L'eggs' Sheer Energy and Sears' Legtricity, not with old-line support stockings such as Supp-hose. The concept of moderate support involves downplaying the use of the word "support" in favor of the notion of "all-day massage" for the active, attractive woman.

Methodology   Because of the speed with which the hosiery department wanted to get the product into production, the study was a one-day-only test in Milford, Connecticut. The test was made up of three parts: a study of our package, a comparative package study, and a product wear test. A total of 218 adult women participated in the test; all usually wore pantyhose.

In the first part of the study, individual respondents were given a sample of the study, participants were shown three packages (Wards Super Natural, questionnaire designed to elicit reactions to this package. In the second part of the study, participants were shown three packages (Ward's Super Natural, L'eggs Sheer Energy, and Sears' Legtricity) and asked to fill out a second questionnaire covering comparative qualities of these packages. Finally, respondents were given a pair of unmarked pantyhose (Super Natural) in the size they selected from a size chart based on a height/weight grid. They were asked to wear these pantyhose while they participated in a series of tests which involved walking, sitting, standing, and trying on clothes. At the end of these tests (minimum elapsed time: one hour), the women were given a self-administered questionnaire which asked for their reactions to the pantyhose they were wearing.

Results   *Demographics.* The women who participated in this study ranged in age from 16 to 60, with three-quarters in the 25 to 54 age group. More than half of the group listed their family income as $10,000 to $20,000 annually, while another 37 percent said they earned over $20,000. More than half of those interviewed said they were housewives. An additional quarter had white collar jobs, and the remainder were either students or blue collar workers.

Height of Respondents		*Weight of Respondents*	
Under 5'3"	26%	Under 110 lb.	8%
5'3"–5'6"	55	110–150 lb.	71
Over 5'6"	19	Over 150 lb.	21

Package Study—One Way. Mock-ups of the proposed Super Natural package were produced by the package design department. This package is a blue and silver box with a clear dome top. There is a picture on two sides of the box, a size chart, and some descriptive copy. Positive comments made by respondents concerned the color of the box, the ease of reading the size chart, the overall attractiveness of the box, the informativeness of the package, and the clear top, which permitted visibility of the hosiery color.

Some 44 percent of the respondents made no negative comments about the package. Others, however, thought that the box was too large or too bulky (13 percent), that the picture did not make sense (10 percent), that the pantyhose were not clearly visible (7 percent), or that the word "pantyhose" was too small (6 percent).

After reading the descriptive copy on the package, 43 percent of the women said that the product inside was probably support hose, even though the word "support" does not appear in the copy. Sheerness and comfort were also mentioned frequently. Just over half of the respondents thought the package looked like the package of a high-priced pantyhose, while just under half thought the product would have an average price.

Package Study—Comparative. The three packages shown to consumers had the brand names on them (Sheer Energy, Legtricity, and Super Natural) without the related manufacturer's or retailers' names. Each is considered to be a non-traditional pantyhose package—Sheer Energy is packaged in a silver-colored plastic egg; Legtricity is packaged to look like a light bulb.

When asked which package they liked best, respondents preferred Super Natural (39 percent) by a small margin over Sheer Energy (33 percent). The major reason given for preferring Super Natural was that the color and texture of the hosiery could be seen. Those who chose Sheer Energy cited its appeal, its small size and shape, and its reusable container. Among the women who preferred the Legtricity package (28 percent), the main reasons given were its small size and shape, the ability to see the product inside and the whole concept.

When declaring which package they liked least, the smallest percentage (23 percent) chose Super Natural. The most frequently mentioned reason for disliking it was its bulkiness.

In comparing specific package features, Super Natural was selected by the highest percentage of women for "shows product well," "easiest to read," "gives full information," "size chart is easy to use," and "overall appearance." Super Natural was chosen by the fewest number of participants for having the best package shape.

Product Wear Test. More than 40 percent of the participants indicated that the pantyhose were comfortable. In fact, some 60 percent said that they preferred the test hose to their usual brand. Other frequently mentioned positive comments about the product were that it fit well and that it gave support.

The negative comments made most often about the test hose were aesthetic in nature; specifically, that the color was not good (23 percent) or that the pantyhose should be more sheer (17 percent). A few women also complained about poor fit—overall shortness or shortness of crotch.

In reacting to specific product qualities, women gave the highest rating to the way the pantyhose feel on the leg (56 percent very good) and the worst rating to color (29 percent very poor).

Carol, I think you should be pleased by these test results. I hope you find them helpful in deciding how to market Super Natural and how, if at all, to modify the product or package. Please let me know if there are any supporting details that you need.

Questions

1. From the description of the marketing research study, what would you say is Wards new product strategy?
2. What is Wards packaging strategy and brand name strategy?
3. Based on the research findings, what modifications should Carol Fudin make in the product and package?

SHARON, OHIO

Michael K. Wilder was immersed in an intense learning experience. Wilder, a former Boston real estate consultant, had just been chosen by a major oil corporation to manage its subsidiary, which ran Sharon, Ohio, a "New Town" near Cleveland. Although Wilder had had experience with a New Town in Arizona, he was spending his first week on the job reading reports and meeting with people connected with Sharon in an attempt to discover why the project was not succeeding.

Background

Sharon began in the 1960s as the idea of Charles Finch, a Cleveland real estate entrepreneur. It was a New Town, a self-contained city with employment and housing for 75,000 residents located twenty miles from Cleveland. When completed, Sharon's master plan called for six separate villages with residents living in clusters of buildings. The villages would contain recreational and cultural facilities and would be surrounded by open spaces. Most homes in Sharon were modern row-style town houses.

This trend toward planned communities was strongly endorsed by many architects, urban planners, and government officials. They looked upon this new concept as a way to save space and construction materials as well as a way to conserve energy. In addition, New Towns were seen as a method of moving people away from metropolitan areas that were already overcrowded and polluted. Finally, many communities, including Sharon, aimed toward the social ideal of mixing high-income families with lower-income families so that they could learn to live together.

Under Finch's leadership, Sharon was successful in attracting industry to the community. By the mid-1970s, seven plants were located in Sharon and eight more were on the way. However, few of the people who were employed in these plants lived in Sharon. Because of the emphasis on community facilities and architectural innovation, town houses in Sharon were fairly expensive. Most were in the $45,000 to $60,000 price range, well above the level affordable by factory workers earning $12,000 to $15,000 per year. (A real estate rule of thumb states that people can afford a home worth two to two-and-a-half times their annual income.)

Thus, Sharon had to look for prospective home buyers among people employed in Cleveland. The problems of a long commute, poor roads along the way, and lack of public transportation made this a difficult task. Finch and his salespeople sold only 550 homes in three years, which put house construction about a year and a half behind schedule.

With sales going so slowly, Finch found it difficult to keep up the interest payments on loans of $12 million from an oil corporation and $24 million from a life insurance company. It was in order to save its investment that the oil firm brought in Michael Wilder to replace Finch.

Opinions and Complaints

Some members of Sharon's management left over from Finch's days blamed the project's failure on the architects and designers. They claimed that the community reflected Finch's personal tastes and not those of the general public. Other employees believed that the concept and design were sound but, because they were new, traditional sources of financing were unwilling to take a chance on Sharon. The tight financial situation prevented the project from gaining the momentum it needed to succeed, according to this view.

In talking to residents of the community, Wilder discovered that most were very happy in Sharon. One tangible piece of evidence supporting this feeling was the scarcity of "For Sale" signs or vacancies. According to one resident, the best thing about Sharon was the people.

On the other hand, there was some disenchantment expressed by other residents. A local psychiatrist, Dr. Paul Bavagnoli, served as an advisor to Sharon's planning officials. He believed that some unhappiness was inevitable whenever people moved to a planned community expecting perfection.

An opposite viewpoint was expressed by a woman who was planning to leave Sharon. She complained that the community was *too* planned for anyone with nonconformist tendencies. She also believed that the cluster environment was too confining; she preferred to be separated from her neighbors.

Dr. Bavagnoli warned Wilder of other problems faced by residents of Sharon. Vandalism had become a serious problem during the previous summer. It was never proven whether youth from Sharon were involved or whether the damage had been caused by young people from Hughville, a less affluent neighboring city. However, Bavagnoli believed that Sharon children were at least partly responsible, and he blamed the parents for relying too much on community facilities to rear their children.

Parents in turn blamed the planners for leaving a gap in community facilities. There were child-care centers for children under nine and recreation centers for teenagers. There was nothing for children aged nine to thirteen.

In an open meeting with residents, several other complaints were aired. Oil company officials felt an obligation to make Sharon a racially and economically integrated community and had submitted an application for aid to the Department of Housing and Urban Development. Many residents were critical of these efforts to bring government-aided housing for low-income families to Sharon. Others, however, defended the concept of mixed housing.

Another complaint mentioned at this meeting concerned the high level of fees assessed against homeowners. In addition to mortgage payments, residents had to pay several hundred dollars a year for yard care, maintenance of common grounds, air conditioning, and recreational facilities.

The president of the Sharon Business and Professional Association added a final grievance. According to this man, local residents did not support the Sharon business community. He believed that this was true for two reasons: first, because the small number of stores offered an incomplete selection of merchandise, and second, because the specialty shops charged high prices.

After this series of meetings with residents and employees, Wilder saw that he had a challenging job ahead of him. He wondered how he could make Sharon a financial success as well as a pleasant place for homeowners to live.

Questions
1. Why has Sharon failed up to now under Charles Finch's management?
2. What could be done by Michael Wilder to modify the product?
3. Describe any social responsibility issues that Wilder and the oil corporation would have to handle.

Price

PRICING IN A MARKETING PERSPECTIVE

After completing this chapter, the reader should be able to:

1. State how consumers, marketers, and society view pricing.
2. Evaluate the contribution of the economic view of pricing.
3. Explain the nature of the pricing objectives—profit-oriented, volume-oriented, and status quo-oriented.
4. Describe the various internal and external forces that shape pricing strategy.
5. Identify the steps in the strategic pricing process.

The task of determining the **price** for a market offering is most complex. The organization faces many problems in making its decisions on pricing. This work can become less troublesome if executives are guided by a solid conceptual framework. The purpose of this chapter is to offer such a framework, in order to help evaluate pricing within a marketing perspective.

THE GREAT FLYING PRICE WAR

In the spring of 1975, another air-fare war broke out among the major domestic airlines.[1] Companies like Eastern Airlines, United Airlines, American Airlines, and Trans World Airlines all lost millions of dollars in the first quarter of 1975. The result was a general panic in the industry.

The main response from the airlines was a number of new discount fare plans. Traditionally, such plans have given no benefits to steady business travelers, but were intended to attract new travelers because of the cut rates. But these discount attempts have rarely produced enough new business to offset the various costs involved.

Only two years earlier, the Civil Aeronautics Board had conducted an extensive survey of airline pricing. It determined that all air fares should be based strictly on costs. The board recommended that discounts which discriminated in favor of or against certain kinds of travelers should be eliminated. However, jet fuel costs skyrocketed shortly after the survey became public, and the single fare of the airlines was raised rather than lowered. Traffic fell off as a result of the price boost.

Despite the CAB findings, airline marketers once again returned to discount pricing in an attempt to interest more passengers. They gave discounts for flying during the week or at night, for flying during off-peak months or booking 60 days in advance, for staying not less than 7 and not more than 30 days. Many of these discounts ran as high as 20 to 30 percent off normal rates. The airlines hoped that these discount passengers would fill up planes that were operating well below capacity. The most striking discount plan was National Airlines' no-frills coach fare. Under this plan, regular coach fare on a trip such as New York to Miami was reduced by 35 percent on certain midweek, off-peak flights.

PRICE, VALUE, AND MARKETING

The aviation industry's price war is a good example of the relationship between pricing and marketing considerations. Environmental pressures such as recession, slump in demand, and higher fuel costs had an important impact on the

327

industry. In a time of diminishing profits, price was used as a fast and aggressive marketing strategy element. National Airlines hoped that reducing certain fares by 35 percent would help its overall image and boost its passenger rolls. The assumption was that consumers would be responsive to such price changes. But demand was not very elastic, meaning that not enough added tickets were sold to offset the lower revenue each ticket brought in.

Pricing has been defined as "the art of translating into quantitative terms (dollars and cents) the value of the product to customers at a point in time."[2] The notion of **value** here is flexible and subjective and is basically determined by the customer. Value may be concrete, such as the cost savings of replacing worn-out sneakers with a new pair. It may be intangible, such as the owner's pride in having a new car. The same product may have a different value for two different customers, or it may have a different value for the same customer over time. Having a sports car may seem important to a 19-year-old, but by the time the person reaches 25 he or she may be more concerned with economy or safety.

Pricing parallels the "total product offering" concept that we explored in Chapters 12 and 13. The buyer, for the stated price, receives not only the

Figure 14-1   PRICING IN THE MARKETING MODEL

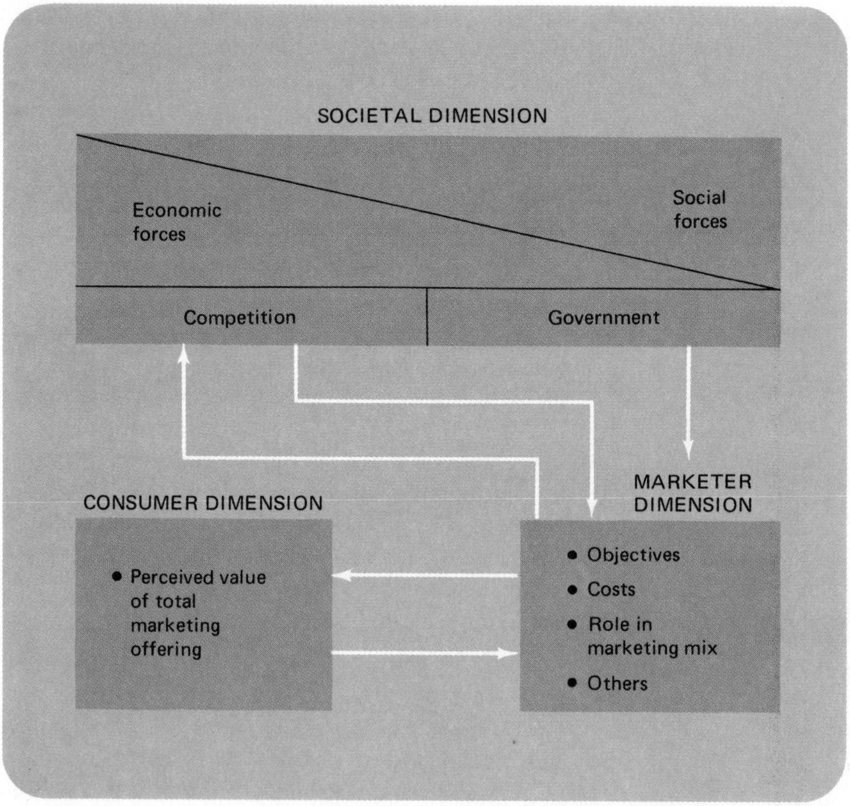

Historically, many public museums charged no regular admission fee, partly because they were seen as centers of public enlightenment. Museum directors often believed that the less affluent would be unable to afford admission and would thus miss out on museum benefits. But in the 1970s most museums faced severe financial problems, despite fund-raising campaigns and private and governmental donations. The policy of free admission no longer seemed possible. Instead, museums began to consider three alternative approaches:

1. A regular admission charge, but with one free day each week. This would allow the poor, young, and old people to come without charge.

2. A "pay as you wish" admission policy. This would encourage donations from more affluent citizens, but would allow others to enter for lesser contributions or at no cost.

3. Special membership plans. Members would receive benefits such as monthly magazines, invitations to preview openings, discounts at gift shops, and free admission. Membership rates might vary from a basic rate for regular members (perhaps $15 to $20) to much higher rates for sustaining or lifetime memberships ($100 or more).

Based on Philip Kotler, *Marketing for Nonprofit Organizations* (Englewood Cliffs, N.J.: Prentice-Hall, 1975), pp. 177–78.

product, but the total product offering. This offering may include repair and maintenance services, a brand name (which may be helpful in future promotion), a relationship with the seller (which is valuable if there are shortages of goods), and credit terms.

The price also covers the "total marketing offering." This means that the consumer also buys the information received through advertising or personal selling and the distribution method that has been chosen. The consumer obtains these "values" and also covers their costs (including profit to the business participants).

In general, we only think of consumer and industrial goods as having a "price." But there are many different way to express a price, especially for services. Who do you think the buyers and sellers are for the prices listed in the margin?

Price is an important concern of nonprofit as well as profit-making organizations. The nonprofit group may wish to set a "fair" price for its service (such as tuition in a university), or it may wish to become self-sufficient through normal client fees rather than large gifts from donors. This question is examined in the accompanying box (shown above).

Tuition
Rent
Fare
Fee
Salary
Toll
Interest
Honorarium

THREE DIMENSIONS OF PRICE

For the pricing element of the marketing mix to work, it must both be accepted as a concept and agreed upon by consumers, marketers, and society. Figure 14-1 presents an overview of the forces affecting pricing that will be examined in this section.

THE CONSUMER DIMENSION

Consumers view price in various ways according to their buying behavior. Their perceptions of price and the benefits they obtain from it are described below:

1. *Value of total marketing offering.* Marketers want to know what value particular segments of the market will place on the firm's product offering. In other words, they need to know what volume of goods can be sold at a given price. Marketers must also know the relationship between price changes and consumer demand.

2. *Effect of affluence.* Because of rising income and a high level of discretionary spending over the last few decades, consumers are enjoying a wider range of products and services than ever before. This includes both an increase in durable goods, such as air conditioners and color televisions, and an increase in convenience products. The general effect has been to desensitize consumers to specific prices and to make price comparisons less important.

3. *Price consciousness.* Surveys suggest that over 80 percent of consumers remember a price that they paid for groceries, and nearly 60 percent recall the correct price.[3] Price consciousness appears to be inversely correlated with social class. The more affluent they are, the less likely consumers are to be conscious of prices. Price consciousness varies greatly from item to item, but generally is lower for brand name items.

4. *Price importance.* Market research indicates that the brand name may be more important than price in consumer purchases of most grocery products and beverages.[4] In clothing purchases, consumers are influenced by price, but the fit, style, and quality of the clothing appear to be even more important.

5. *Price standards and ranges.* Buyers often have ranges of acceptable prices for a particular purchase and will reject any price that is outside that range. In many cases, buyers will become accustomed to a standard price that functions as a yardstick for evaluating new products.

6. *Price as a quality indicator.* The relationship between price and quality is of great interest to marketers. Consumers may purchase more of a firm's product if the price is high rather than low, possibly because of increased prestige (snob appeal) of the product or because consumers genuinely believe that higher prices mean higher quality. In the tire-replacement market, for example, product quality is directly related to price. It is also true, however, that prices are often a monetary expression of the opinions and buying patterns of uninformed consumers.[5]

THE MARKETER DIMENSION

The pricing element occupies a special place in the marketing mix and is intimately related to other elements of the mix. Manipulation of these other elements (such as through differentiation) affects price, while price changes can generate income to cover the cost of all the other elements. Price is crucial in marketplace competition; it is the part of the marketing mix that competitors watch most closely so that they can respond to it quickly. It is the factor most sensitive to changing economic conditions. Although the relationship between marketers and the pricing process may vary, the following considerations must generally be taken into account:

1. *Pricing is important.* Pricing is one marketing task that can *never* be bypassed. A product cannot enter the marketplace without a price tag or at least some guidelines for bargaining. Actually, pricing decisions are a critical part of corporate affairs, and are generally made by top management officials. The price of a product will have a noticeable (and sometimes dramatic) effect on its sales, on the firm's total revenues, and on ultimate profits.

2. *Pricing is discretionary.* Pricing is greatly influenced by who controls the market. There are three principal possibilities: the market can be market-controlled, business-controlled, or government-controlled.

In a **market-controlled** situation, the seller has no control over market prices; the forces of supply and demand dictate pricing. Certain commodity exchanges and agricultural markets are examples of this kind of structure. In a **business-controlled** situation, business firms set prices and buyers must either agree to these terms or not make a purchase. The forces of supply and demand can affect pricing decisions, but the marketer retains a significant amount of control. Most prices in our economy are business-controlled, whether at the local drug store or at Holiday Inns. **Government-controlled** market situations will be discussed in later sections of this chapter. Obviously, in a government-controlled market, the firm is not free to set whatever price it pleases.

3. *Pricing is difficult to determine.* Ideally, a price might be established simply by feeding all of the essential marketing data into a computer and awaiting the results. But in most pricing situations, marketers do not have all of the essential information. Critical factors such as elasticity of demand for a product or the reactions of competitors to price changes are often unknown and unpredictable. Generally, the best a firm can do is to gather all of the available information and come to an informed judgment.

4. *Nonprice competition may be preferred.* **Nonprice competition** in business revolves around such factors as personal selling, advertising, product development, delivery service, and credit terms. Executives often prefer nonprice competition to price competition because there is no risk of pricing errors or price wars. Also, competitors cannot copy nonprice improvements as easily as they can duplicate a price change. In fact, one survey of marketing management indicated that product research and development was far and away the most important element of current competitive strategy.[6] In line with this thinking, companies like Hewlett-Packard have begun to focus on the development of sophisticated and expensive products. In 1974 Hewlett-Packard raised its prices by over 10 percent and at the same time increased its spending on research and development by 20 percent.

THE SOCIETAL DIMENSION

Pricing plays a role in and is influenced by a variety of social issues. How the price mechanism fits into the values of our society has itself become an issue.

1. *Pricing and competition.* Philip Kotler has observed, ". . . the price mechanism affords an elegant rationale for the efficiency of a competitive free-enterprise system."[7] When there is an oversupply of goods, sellers cut prices. When there is a shortage, prices rise and production is encouraged. In prin-

ciple, flexible prices thus lead to optimal economic performance. (The context of competition in which price occurs was discussed in Chapter 6.)

2. *Pricing and ecology.* Because of ecological problems associated with industrialization, the market pricing mechanism may need to be restructured to include social and environmental costs along with marketer's product costs. We have routinely used our environment (air, water, and other resources) as if it were free. But the costs of our consumption are now being paid in taxation, social ills, and biological problems.

3. *Pricing and consumerism.* **Unit pricing** has become a well-publicized issue in which the price mechanism and social responsibility come together. Consumer advocates pushed for unit pricing in supermarkets and groceries in order to allow the consumer to quickly determine the best buy through informing him or her of the price of the product on a unit (such as an ounce or a quart) basis. Thus, many supermarkets now display both actual prices and unit prices on the goods themselves or on shelf signs. But some researchers insist that consumers do not care about unit pricing, do not use the system, or are confused by it.[8] This may be due to the lack of consumer education.

4. *Pricing and the ghetto.* A 1969 staff report of the Federal Trade Commission pointed to higher food costs in inner-city supermarkets than in suburban stores.[9] The study determined that inner-city stores had less competition than most supermarkets, and as a result were under less pressure to maintain high-quality service or offer low prices. Food bargains advertised by chains were often unavailable in inner-city locations. Furthermore, inner-city residents seemed to have considerably less chance of winning promotional games, such as sweepstakes contests, than suburban residents. Some studies made since the FTC's report have found that pricing in a variety of store types is similar in both ghetto and non-ghetto areas. Others, however, confirm that differences do exist.

5. *Pricing and ethics.* Some observers have predicted that, if economic conditions continue to be gloomy, unethical business practices will inevitably result. These include the use of shoddy ingredients and hidden reductions in quantity. The ethics of pricing is a touchy subject for business under any circumstances—because pricing decision makers are not expected to relate price to cost. If you can add $10 worth of frills to your product and sell it for an extra $30, you are expected to go right ahead and do so. Yet, after a decade of consumerism and post-Watergate feelings, the American public has forced some reexamination of business ethics.

ECONOMIC VIEW OF PRICING

Price theory is an essential ingredient in marketing activity. It provides a framework for understanding price decisions and helps to pinpoint and examine the critical economic forces involved. Although economists have not always been successful in making predictions for business, their method of analysis is valuable for our purposes.

A THEORY OF PRICING The way in which prices are determined has much to do with the market structure of a particular industry (or society). The market structure is shaped by three principal factors—the number of firms in an industry, the size of those firms, and the degree of product differentiation of goods or services.

Pure competition (introduced in Chapter 6) exists under the following conditions:

1. there is a large number of sellers and buyers;
2. no individual or firm can dictate the market price;
3. it is easy to enter or leave the industry;
4. the offerings of various competitors are relatively the same.

In this kind of situation, which is virtually unknown today, the economic model of traditional price theory applies. As illustrated in Figure 14-2, an upward-sloping "supply curve" shows that as the price of a product rises, more firms will enter the field and the supply will rise. A downward-sloping "demand curve" suggests that as prices fall, the sales in the industry will increase. Under this theory, market conditions become stable at the point where these two curves cross. At this price, there is no incentive to produce more goods or to buy more goods.

In the theoretical model, the critical functions are *demand* (the quantity of goods demanded per time period at various possible prices) and *cost* (the total costs for various quantities of goods per time period that might be pro-

Figure 14-2 HOW SUPPLY AND DEMAND CURVES SHAPE PRICE

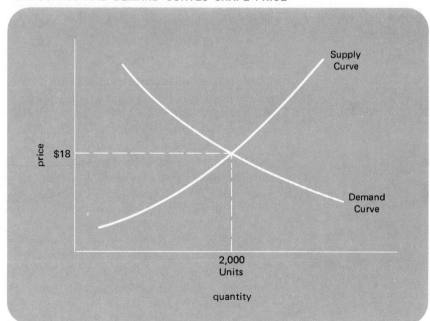

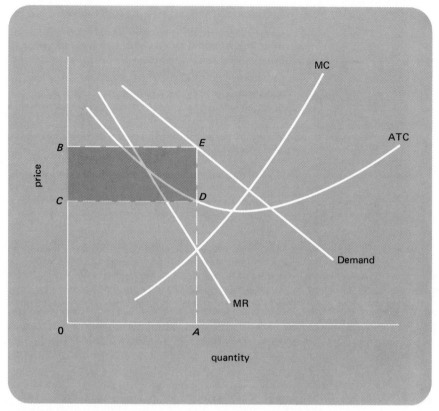

Figure 14-3 SHORT-RUN PRICING UNDER MONOPOLISTIC COMPETITION

duced). Total revenue equals the price times the quantity of goods sold; total profits equal total revenue minus total costs.

This theory may be modified to apply to conditions of **imperfect competition.** For example, Figure 14-3 represents a model of short-run pricing in monopolistic competition. This condition includes a large number of sellers and buyers and a relatively high level of product differentiation. As a result, the demand curve is somewhat inelastic and slopes downward. In the short run, the firm will produce a quantity of units of goods (0A), which it will sell at price (0B). The rectangle *CDEB* shows the firm's total excess profit. Since *marginal cost* (MC) is equal to *marginal revenue* (MR) at this point, the firm is making maximum profits. As in pure competition, excess profits will attract new competitors. Supply will increase, and the level of profits will often be reduced.

The use of price theory can help marketers. It is useful in isolating and examining the most important economic forces affecting pricing. The theory provides standards against which actual situations can be compared. Finally, it underscores some of the social and economic implications of pricing strategies.

EVALUATION OF PRICE THEORY As we have described, conventional price theory, while useful, nevertheless rests on a variety of unrealistic assumptions about the business world. As we examine the criticisms of the economic model, we can understand the greater complexity of the marketing perspective on pricing.

1. *Pricing is not so rational.* Price theory assumes that the person setting the price is a rational individual who carefully weighs all available information on demand and costs. In fact, human beings are not always rational, and the information is often unavailable or incomplete.

2. *Pricing is affected by changes over time.* The model applies to the short run and does not take into account the way that demand changes over time (due to changes in tastes, population, and income), or the way costs change over time (due to technological innovations and changes in input prices).

3. *Pricing may have several objectives.* The model assumes that firms are concerned only with maximizing profits. Yet, once a firm has a secure short-run profit, it may turn its attention to goals of financial liquidity, economic stability, or socially beneficial actions.

4. *Pricing is affected by other forces.* Pricing is affected by many forces not represented in the model, including labor costs, antitrust regulation, and foreign competition. This subject will be examined in more detail later in this chapter.

5. *Pricing interacts with the marketing mix.* The model assumes that other marketing elements (product, promotion, and distribution) can be regarded as neutral while the relationship between sales and price is pinpointed. In actuality, the optimal price can be calculated only by considering all of the marketing elements as part of a total marketing offering.

6. *Pricing is affected by limits in estimating.* There are severe problems in developing estimates of actual demand and costs. The knowledge that most firms possess is rather inexact. Decisions are often made on the basis of projections and even outright guesses.

7. *Pricing is affected by multiple products.* Price theory assumes that a firm produces only a single product or service. In today's business world, a firm is often involved in many lines of goods and services at the same time.

8. *Pricing is affected by marketing objectives.* Two firms may enter the same market with very different objectives. American Balloons may wish to make a quick profit and then leave the competition, while Continental Balloons may want to slowly build a secure base and corner a stable segment of the market. Since each has a distinct objective, each may determine a price that suits its own objective. Price theory is unsatisfactory because it assumes that each firm has the same objectives and is simply looking for a price that maximizes profits.

PRICING OBJECTIVES

Generally, a firm will pursue more than one objective at the same time. While it pursues maximum profits in the short and long run, it may also wish to maintain good relations with labor, the government, and consumers. It may wish to build a prestigious company name and to increase its rate of growth (even if this means reducing immediate profits). The firm's pricing decisions will reflect all of these objectives. One goal may be dominant at a particular time, but often pricing decisions will represent a balancing of different concerns.

PROFIT-ORIENTED OBJECTIVES

The goal of making a profit is usually the major influence in pricing decisions. In the past, many firms concentrated on building greater volume, even when this meant decreases in profit margins. More recently, the main focus of companies is on maintaining profit margins, keeping costs down, and attempting to price for profit as well as for sales.

Profit Maximization

We might assume that most business firms are constantly working to maximize profits above all else. Yet few firms seem to operate entirely in this way. More common is the use of sales quotas of target profit levels. But the concept of maximum profits is either unfamiliar to most marketers or difficult for them to plan for.

Long-run profit maximizing is actually a dubious goal for an organization. Not only are the available data on costs and demand limited, making projections impossible, but there are many other problems as well. If a firm opts for the price that maximizes profits in the short run, it may lose the opportunity to establish a broad market clientele, thus leaving the field open for competitors. To gain long-range profits, the firm must take actions that are not profit oriented, such as expanding the firm's market share and promoting a favorable public image.

Target Rate of Return on Investment

Many firms strive for a specific level of profit, generally known as the **target rate of return on investment.** This can serve as a kind of guideline for judging improvement, especially in a new product line. The actual market conditions in each industry dictate the target rate—anywhere from 8 to 20 percent after taxes.

Robert F. Lanzillotti has studied large companies engaged in target-return pricing.[10] He found that they set a rate of return that they consider satisfactory and then calculate a price level that will guarantee that rate if their plants are operating at perhaps 80 percent of capacity. More recent research by J. Fred Weston has cast doubts on the findings of Lanzillotti.[11] Weston insists that top executives use the target rate of return on investment as a helpful reference point, but little more. He found that pricing decisions cannot be separated from other types of business decisions.

Satisfactory Profits

Some firms are not interested in maximum profits or in a target rate. Instead, they seek a "satisfactory" level of profit. Prices are determined from costs so that a satisfactory return on investments is forthcoming. What is defined as satisfactory may change over time, due to need for increased production, stockholder pressure, or other causes.

VOLUME-ORIENTED OBJECTIVES

Firms pursue a variety of volume-oriented objectives. In many cases, an impressive volume of sales can help promote widespread consumer acceptance of the firm's products. Organizations assume that a satisfactory level of profits will result, but that may not be what actually happens.

Maximization of Sales Revenue

Many businesses have traditionally pursued maximum sales revenue through high volume of sales. Conventional wisdom has dictated that sales growth was a positive business indicator, that high sales led inevitably to high profits, and that high production levels built a sizable work force. However, recession and economic shortages have resulted in a reexamination of this volume-oriented thinking. Firms have realized that sales growth does not necessarily lead to higher profits. Certain product lines with high marginal costs may be popular with consumers, but may yield only limited profits for the firm.

Maximization of Market Share

The pricing policy of some firms is geared toward maximizing the firm's market share. When volume is increasing but the firm's competitors are multiplying at an ever faster rate, a false sense of security may develop. To offset this danger, firms keep a close watch on their percentage of the market share. In the field of calculators, firms such as Texas Instruments, Bowmar, Casio, Keystone, Sinclair, Hewlett-Packard, and Novus all reduced their prices in order to increase their share of the market.[12]

Maximization of Customer Volume

A business firm may elect to offer an unusually low price in order to increase dramatically the number of customers using its product. This is known as a **rapid-penetration objective.** The firm hopes to increase its share of the market through this strategy.

Nonprofit organizations in particular often set low prices in order to increase awareness and acceptance of their products and services. An environmental protection group may distribute its literature at a low cost or even free. The aim is to circulate the material and to build knowledge of the issues and of the organization's program.

Minimization of Customer Volume

There are sometimes unusual circumstances in which a firm wants to *discourage* the public, or certain segments of the public, from using its product or service. This dilemma has become more common in recent years because of the energy crisis and growing pollution problems. Many cities want to limit the number of automobiles using highways and bridges and entering the central business areas from the suburbs. Therefore, bridge and tunnel tolls are raised and parking lots are heavily taxed (causing higher rates for parking).

STATUS QUO-ORIENTED OBJECTIVES

As we have already seen, pricing strategy can be used to bring about changes in the marketplace. But when a favorable situation exists, any change represents a threat, whether from customers, competitors, or government. To protect its position, a firm may pursue status quo-oriented objectives.

Maintenance of Market Share

Often a firm will be content to maintain its share of the market. This is especially true for a corporate giant like General Motors, which may fear government antitrust action if its market share rises too far above 50 percent. Even smaller firms may find it to their advantage to live with a constant market share. In some industries, the fight for an increased share is so expensive that profits decline in the process.

Meeting Competition

A firm may adopt a policy of meeting competitors' prices as a rather passive pricing strategy. The firm may feel that it can better improve its sales, market share, and profits through nonprice mechanisms, such as promotional efforts and product development. The firm may be satisfied with its current level of profits and may fear a damaging price war (price cuts create losses) more than it hopes for a better competitive position.

Maintenance of an Image

A company needs a solid and dependable image in the marketplace in order to survive and prosper. If its basic strategy is to produce high-quality, high-prestige goods, then putting out a low-budget line could damage the company in the long run—even if the economy line made initial profits. The reverse is also true. A company respected for putting out inexpensive but reliable goods could tarnish its image and reputation by promoting a different line that long-time customers see as "showy" or "snobbish."

Maintenance of Stable Prices

Some firms prefer to keep prices stable because they wish to avoid unpredictable consequences of changes (such as price wars). Security-minded executives may be satisfied that stable prices will result in stable profits (and stable job tenure). A firm may also view price stability as vital to the overall health of an industry. An industry leader often fights for stable industry-wide price policies.

Achievement of Certain Markups

Wholesalers and retailers are especially likely to rely on markups (which will be discussed more fully in Chapter 15). It may be difficult for them to calculate demand or operating costs for their many products. Thus, markups become a convenient means of making pricing decisions. It is more or less assumed that markup policies will, if properly arrived at, lead to favorable market share and profits.

Recovery of Costs

Nonprofit organizations must rely on various types of fees in order to help offset their costs. A city's transit authority charges a fare for buses and subways, while a college charges tuition for enrolling in classes. These "prices" do not fully meet the financial needs of nonprofit institutions, but they may be essential in providing funds for day-to-day operating expenses.

FORCES SHAPING PRICING

Within what limits can the marketing executive set a price for a product? In most cases, the marketer faces traditionally structured upper and lower limits. The upper limit is the value of the product to the buyer; the lower limit is the cost of producing, promoting, and distributing the product or service. Within these boundaries, the actual price of a product or service is affected by

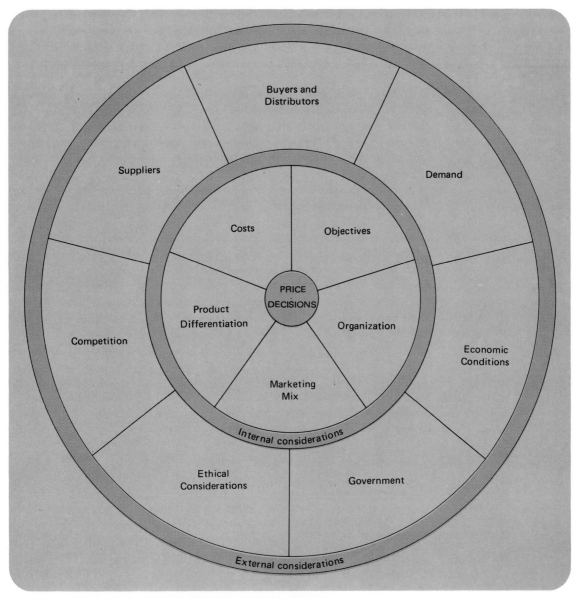

Figure 14-4   MODEL OF THE PRICING FORCES

Adapted from Donald V. Harper, *Price Policy and Procedure* (New York: Harcourt Brace Jovanovich, 1966), p. 293.

many economic factors. But these elements do not apply in any set way to particular products. Pricing decisions are shaped by many internal and external considerations.[13] These forces are illustrated in Figure 14-4.

INTERNAL FORCES   Internal pricing considerations—such as pricing objectives, product characteristics, and costs—can be controlled by the firm itself. By contrast, the external forces—such as suppliers, competitors, and legal and ethical constraints—cannot be controlled in any meaningful way. These internal and external pressures narrow the latitude that a firm has in making its final pricing decision. In some cases, the firm may have virtually no choice at all (especially when it must attempt to meet or undercut competition).

Objectives   The variety of possible pricing objectives was discussed in the previous section of this chapter. The influence of these objectives depends upon how well-defined they are, especially in quantitative terms (for example, a 15 percent increase in sales). Setting specific objectives for each product permits the multiproduct marketer to compare performance among products.

Organization   There are two basic levels of pricing decisions. A firm will decide on its overall price strategies, and these will be used to determine particular product price strategies. The latter function, known as the "mechanics of pricing," may be handled at lower levels of a firm's organizational hierarchy. But the firm's overall pricing strategies are discussed and decided at a high level, perhaps by the board of directors or a committee of senior executives.

Pricing organization varies widely. In some firms, production and marketing specialists have an important say in the pricing process. In others, computer printouts have become a vital instrument. Some firms with nation-wide enterprises conduct pricing on a centralized basis, while others rely on lower- and middle-management personnel as part of a more decentralized price-setting system.

Marketing Mix   Marketing experts see price as only one of many important elements in a marketing mix. A pricing decision must be understood as one integrated ele-

"I know Azzinns Auto Repair used to do it cheaper — that's Mister Azzinns over there."

Automotive News, December 13, 1965, p. 10. Reprinted from Automotive News.

ment of a total marketing strategy and must be coordinated within the framework of this overall strategy.

In some industries, a firm may use price cutting as a marketing technique. Other firms may raise prices as a deliberate strategy to build a high-prestige product line. In either case, the effort will not succeed unless the price manipulation is combined with a total marketing strategy that supports the price change. Thus, a firm that raises its prices may add a more impressive-looking package and may begin a new advertising campaign. If it increases its prices without this kind of total marketing effort, the results may be disastrous.

Product Differentiation Generally, the more a firm's product is differentiated from competitive offerings, the more leeway it has in setting prices. If the public sees all fast-food restaurants as identical, it will be difficult for any company to deviate sharply from the common price level. When a firm cannot differentiate its product easily from competitors, it may choose to differentiate the image of the entire organization by building a solid reputation among customers.

Costs Costs are an often misunderstood factor in pricing. There are two common misconceptions. Because people know that prices should generally cover costs, conventional wisdom holds that costs are the chief factor in pricing. Yet, while prices must absorb costs in the long run, factors other than costs may be the prime influence on pricing in the short run.

It is generally assumed that costs are a price-determining factor. Actually, the reverse may be true; prices may be a cost-determining factor. A firm may decide to market a new product and may examine what prices it can project for the product given the demand and competition in the marketplace. Afterward, the firm will determine an acceptable level of costs for producing the product, given its projections on prices, sales, and profits. We will explore this topic further in Chapter 16.

EXTERNAL FORCES Marketing managers face two difficult tasks which are related to the external forces that determine pricing. Managers must measure and analyze these forces; in some cases they can try to change the marketing environment and create an atmosphere that is more conducive to the firm's pricing strategy.

Demand The market demand for a product or service has an important impact on pricing. Many factors shape demand, including the price of the product and other firms' offerings, the income and preference of buyers, and the number and size of competitors. In deciding upon a price, marketers must study the character of demand in the industry and must gauge the effects of price changes on demand.

Competitors The dynamics of competition are a key factor in pricing strategy. Before a firm makes a pricing decision, it must observe the prices and develop predictions on the behavior of present competitors in the industry. The firm must also analyze the likelihood of other companies entering the industry and joining the competition. Here the critical consideration is how difficult and expensive it is for a new firm to enter the field.

Suppliers   Suppliers can have a significant effect on the price of a product. Manufacturing firms that buy raw materials from suppliers may increase their prices if the suppliers increase theirs. Wholesalers and retailers may work on direct mark-ups; thus, their prices may be a direct reflection of suppliers' charges. Also, if suppliers determine that manufacturers are making large profits from sales of the product, they may attempt to increase their prices in order to get their share of the profits.

Distribution   When a producer makes a pricing decision, it must take into account the needs and expectations of all of the various intermediary firms in its distribution system. In general, the more intermediaries there are in an industry, the less influence any one of them may have on the price policies of the producer. When the potential intermediaries are very few, they may have a significant impact on pricing.

Economic Conditions   When the business cycle is in a favorable stage, the demand for a product or service may increase. This may allow a firm greater independence in its pricing strategy. However, if sales are rising, competition may grow—which may restrict pricing independence. New firms may enter the industry once they sense that there are substantial profits to be made.

Price strategy is also affected by less favorable economic conditions. Among these are:

1. *Inflation.* When prices are rising, marketers must make renewed efforts to reposition products and to make appeals stressing both price and performance. Thus, if the prices of meat and fish are skyrocketing, marketers can develop a new marketing strategy promoting soybeans or peanut butter as a cheaper but still efficient source of protein.

2. *Recession.* When a national recession continues over a prolonged period of time, companies find it necessary to begin cutting prices in order to reduce large inventories or to keep production at an acceptable level. This can increase price competition at a time when it is least desirable.

3. *Inflation–recession.* When inflation and recession occur simultaneously, firms may face shortages, rising prices, and diminishing demand all at the same time. A number of new pricing strategies may be attempted. Among these are boosting prices to protect profits against rising costs, developing price protection systems to link the price on delivery to current costs, and shifting emphasis from volume to margin and cost reduction.

4. *Shortages.* When shortages of a raw material occur, the price of obtaining it rises. Therefore, a firm may choose to suspend production of its weakest product lines, where the profit pinch is greatest. It will probably become necessary for the firm to raise the prices of its most successful products. These price increases will be limited by various pressures, including the government, competitors in the industry, and customer reactions.

The Christmas season of 1974 was a time of confrontation and, eventually, negotiation between the federal government and the leading steelmakers. The industry's giants had raised prices in a number of areas, and the President's Council on Wage and Price Stability (COWPS), headed by Albert Rees, opposed the raises. (COWPS was the government agency that replaced the powerful price control board.)

On Friday, December 20, Rees met with the Chairman of the Board of U.S. Steel, Edgar Speer, and William Whyte, the firm's chief Washington lobbyist. Rees examined the steelmaker's justification data for its raises, and accepted some of the decisions. But he opposed others, and pushed for price rollbacks using the technique of jawboning (bringing government pressure to bear on a private industry). After a second meeting, U.S. Steel agreed to follow some of Rees' recommendations. The end result was that roughly 40 percent of the industry's products received price hikes of at least 6 percent.

Rees later called the negotiations "a reasonably successful use of the 'jawbone.'" Nevertheless, the steelmakers did win a sizable price increase.

Based on "Where the Jawbone Left Steel Prices," *Business Week*, January 13, 1975, pp. 31–32.

Government

Pricing in the private sector of the economy is subject to government antitrust regulation. Pressures may come through high government officials, congressional committees, or legislation such as the Sherman Antitrust Act and the Federal Trade Commission Act (see Chapter 3). The government closely watches prices and market shares of firms in major industries.

One example of government regulation is the outlawing of price fixing among firms at the same level of competition.

The government also influences pricing in other ways. It is, of course, the largest buyer in the domestic market, and in some industries (such as defense) it is the only buyer of certain goods. In addition, the government sets prices on the products or services that it controls, such as postal rates, electrical power rates for the Tennessee Valley Authority, and charges for local government street improvements. The federal government also tries to inhibit large firms from making price increases that will contribute to inflation (see the accompanying box).

Ethical Considerations

Although a pricing practice may not be considered illegal by the government, it could still run afoul of commonly accepted ethical standards. Ethics usually involve how high prices can go. Charging what the traffic will bear may be criticized when a market segment has a valid need for the product but limited resources to spend on it. Such products include groceries for the poor and medicine for the elderly.

PLANNING STRATEGIC PRICING

Deciding on a strategy for pricing—given all of the internal and external factors mentioned above—is no easy matter. The larger an organization is, the more it goes through the agonizing process of weighing many variables in order to come to a pricing decision. When we examined the major forces that shape prices in the previous section, the decision as to how to set prices may have looked mechanistic—a simple matter of weighing all of the variables listed. While this might be ideally accomplished through a computer simulation, no such model is available. In this section, we will focus on a discussion of the decision-process approach.

Figure 14-5 offers a concise, six-step model of the **strategic pricing process**. This kind of model can be quite useful to decision makers, especially since it is designed to simplify each step so that the subsequent tasks of the next stage will appear more clearcut. The six steps in the process are:

1. *Select target markets.* This is perhaps the most fundamental marketing decision—what kinds of consumers will the firm pursue with its product? The firm should decide on one or several important market segments with a promising sales potential.

2. *Study consumer behavior.* Market research should be designed to present a picture of the target markets—their buying motives, location, sensitivity to price, prior attitudes about the marketer and the industry, and so forth.

3. *Identify competition.* The firm should conduct an extensive investigation into its competitors in the industry (and also into other firms that may enter the industry in the future). What kinds of price, promotion, and other marketing strategies do these firms employ?

4. *Assign price a role in marketing mix.* At this stage, the firm desires esti-

Figure 14-5   MODEL OF THE STRATEGIC PRICING PROCESS

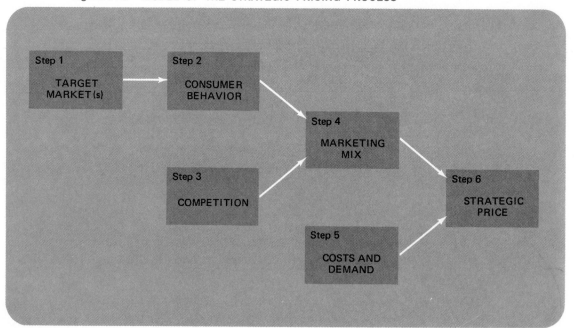

mates of the number of units that could be sold at various price levels. These estimates will be developed only after some thinking about nonprice marketing strategies, for the firm may want price estimates that conform to these nonprice elements. Another task at this stage is to project the competitive reactions of other firms to each of the proposed pricing strategies.

5. *Relate costs and demand.* Costs will be estimated for producing the product at a number of possible levels of output. These levels will reflect projections of the demand for the product (which will be influenced by the price options in stage four).

6. *Determine strategic price.* The previous five stages set limits for the possible price range of the product. At this point, marketing management will reflect on its overall objectives (satisfactory profits, share of the market, higher volume, ethical standards, and so forth). It will then choose the price that best coincides with those objectives and the economic realities developed in stages one through five.

For this process to function effectively, the firm has a critical need for accurate and complete information. Without this, an involved planning process will produce only an incorrect (and possibly disastrous) pricing strategy. Management must strive to develop the most efficient research and statistical techniques. Obviously, a key mistake at any one stage will throw the entire process off.

Pricing strategy is a most difficult challenge for marketers. Even so, marketers have little choice but to struggle to do their best. For there is no retreat from the uncertainties of the strategic pricing process.

CONCLUSION

Price is a monetary expression of value. Pricing is the art of translating the value of a product into dollars and cents—the amount that it is worth to consumers at a particular point in time. Marketers are interested in price because it has traditionally been a dominant variable in studying consumer demand and because it retains an important impact on marketing strategy today.

Price theory is a useful model for evaluating the workings of the market place. Yet its limitations must be understood—for the theory rests on some fundamental assumptions about the economy that are incorrect or oversimplified.

A firm may pursue one or many pricing objectives at the same time. These may be profit-oriented, volume-oriented, or status quo-oriented.

Various internal and external forces shape pricing decisions. The internal forces include objectives, organization, marketing mix, product differentiation, and costs. The external forces include demand, suppliers, competitors, buyers, the government, and economic conditions.

Chapters 15 and 16 which follow will provide details on methods and procedures of price determination. This will help us to better understand the full dimensions of pricing strategy.

DISCUSSION QUESTIONS

1. Are there any built-in conflicts between the way price is viewed by consumers and the way it is viewed by marketers? between the way it is viewed by marketers and the way it is viewed by society?
2. Of what use is the economic theory of price in determining the price of each of the following: aluminum garden furniture, scientific instruments, photocopying services?
3. Describe the pricing strategy that results from the specific pricing objectives for each of the following:
   a. profit-oriented for a dance studio;
   b. volume-oriented for Citizens Band radio;
   c. status quo-oriented for textile machinery.
4. Which of the various internal and external forces that help to determine an organization's pricing strategy have the most impact on the following (more than one force may operate for each): international airline travel, laser beam medical equipment, French cookware, and nuclear power plant contracting?
5. Trace the strategic pricing process for each of the following:
   a. advertising rates for an FM country and western music station;
   b. tuition for a private New England college with an experimental education program;
   c. a doll with a high-fashion wardrobe.

NOTES

1. *Business Week*, April 21, 1975, pp. 126–28, 132.
2. E. Raymond Corey, *Industrial Marketing* (Englewood Cliffs, N.J.: Prentice-Hall, 1962), pp. 125–26.
3. Kent B. Monroe, "Buyers' Subjective Perceptions of Price," *Journal of Marketing Research* 10 (February 1973): 71.
4. Ibid., p. 73; "They 'Switch' and Trade-off More Today Too," *Chain Store Age*, General Merchandise Edition, June 1975, pp. 32–33.
5. A. G. Bedean, "Consumer Perception of Price as an Indicator of Product Quality," *MSU Business Topics* 13 (Summer 1971): 59–60.
6. Jon G. Udell, "How Important Is Pricing in Competitive Strategy?" *Journal of Marketing* 28 (January 1964): 44.
7. Philip Kotler, *Marketing Management: Analysis, Planning, and Control*, 2d ed. (Engle-wood Cliffs, N.J.: Prentice-Hall, 1972), p. 515.
8. Donald O. Schnuck, "Unit Pricing—Current Public Policy Issue," *1973 Combined Proceedings* (Chicago: American Marketing Association, 1974), p. 461.
9. "Inner-City Food Costs at Supermarkets Top Those in Suburbs, FTC Study Shows," *Wall Street Journal*, July 28, 1969, p. 3.
10. Cited in Gilbert Burck, "The Myths and Realities of Corporate Pricing," *Fortune* 85 (April 1972): 88.
11. Ibid.
12. James Schneider, "Calculator Prices Slide to Separate Men from Boys," *Merchandising Week*, October 14, 1974, p. 10.
13. This section is based largely on Donald V. Harper, *Price Policy and Procedure* (New York: Harcourt Brace Jovanovich, 1966), p. 292.

15

PRICE DETERMINATION APPROACHES

After completing this chapter, the reader should be able to:

1. Identify the cost-oriented, demand-oriented, and competition-oriented methods for determining prices.

2. Provide the rationale and state the limitations of these price determination approaches.

3. Apply price determination methods to the calculation of basic prices.

4. Explain the major new product pricing approaches—skimming and penetration.

5. Describe the special situation of setting prices for items in a product line.

In Chapter 14, we examined pricing from a marketing perspective, focusing on pricing objectives and the factors involved in price setting. In this chapter, we will consider the major approaches that are most often used to determine prices.

A PROFILE OF DETROIT'S PRICING

No other country in the world has such close psychological ties to the automobile, nor such close economic ties to the automobile industry as the United States.[1] It is hardly surprising, therefore, that when General Motors raises its prices, more than one Washington committee raises its collective eyebrow.

During the early 1970s, automobile prices became part of a high-inflation trend affecting many products. In one fifteen-month period, the cost of cars rose an average of $1,000; at the same time, the recession caused sales to decrease by 25 percent. Since traditional economic theory would call for sales to be stimulated by a price reduction, the automobile manufacturers found themselves facing unwelcome pressures to cut prices at a time of rising costs. Pressure was applied not only by the government, but also by the growing voice of consumers as well.

Much of the pressure was understandably directed at General Motors. GM is the Big Brother of the automobile industry (with an approximate 50 percent share of the market); when GM sets the price, everyone falls into line simply as a matter of survival. Neither Ford, Chrysler, nor American Motors can hope to overprice GM and stay in the game. Undercutting is just as dangerous, since GM's per unit costs at the start are almost invariably lower.

GM prices its cars on the basis of cost plus profit and dealer margin. Everyone else bases their prices on GM's. And all the industry runs scared when the question of price cuts comes up. The feeling is that substantial price cuts, even if they do result in volume increases, will create trouble for the industry as it tries to cope with rising costs of material, labor, and new model developments designed to meet energy conservation demands. A cut of $200 or $300, on the other hand, would be too small to increase volume enough to offset higher per unit costs.

PRICING IN PRACTICE   The GM pricing system relies on selling a standard volume of cars that is large enough to cover all fixed and variable costs. Cars are then priced at what the market is willing to pay to yield a target profit or return on investment. Once the standard volume is reached, fixed costs have been charged off and per unit profits jump dramatically. But with sales volume reduced by the recession and costs pushed up by inflation, a failure to reach the standard volume results in a drastic cut in profits.

The pricing strategy of any product starts with the establishment of a **basic**

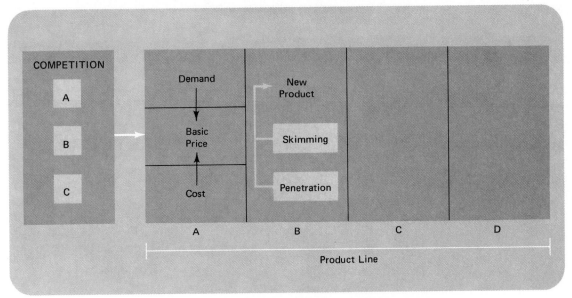

Figure 15-1   MAJOR APPROACHES TO SETTING THE BASIC PRICE

price. As illustrated in Figure 15-1, this amount is set by considering the major constraints on the product's price, including production cost, market demand, and competition. The basic price may then be modified by distribution arrangements and legal or social considerations.

Most of our attention will be devoted to a single product, shown as A in Figure 15-1, where cost, demand, and/or competition are major influences. We will also look at basic price setting for a new product, B, where skimming and penetration pricing strategies become considerations. Finally, we will consider the factors involved when products are part of an organization's product line, A to D in Figure 15-1. This model presents a simplified view from which to explore more intricately the characteristics of cost-oriented, demand-oriented, and competition-oriented pricing. While we will be examining each of these areas separately, they are, in actual practice, interrelated.

Becoming more accurate and effective in the pricing process is largely a matter of employing sound techniques instead of guesswork and hunches. Techniques may include simplified approaches such as straight cost-plus or the establishment of specific goals such as with the target rate-of-return technique. Pricing methods must be properly and expertly applied with provision for review and flexibility. Sound control by the executives involved is essential. Approaches that are too rigid can not only spell disaster in a changing marketplace but can often give the competition the advantage of being able to anticipate pricing moves before they happen.

COST-ORIENTED PRICING

Setting prices on the basis of **costs** is one of the most common pricing procedures, particularly in highly competitive markets. Total costs are calculated and a margin of profit is tacked on. The simplicity and ease of application of this method is one of the main reasons for its popularity. Sales volume forecasts are sometimes taken into consideration in order to figure costs per unit more accurately.

Often the process works in reverse: costs are adjusted to the most desirable selling price. For example, in the mid-1970s, appliance manufacturers tried to hold selling prices of their products against inflation by eliminating many extra features, thereby keeping production costs down.

COST-PLUS APPROACH   There are many industries in which cost is the major determinant of price. Among these are manufacturers of special products made to customer specifications, most service companies, utilities, and contractors. Wholesalers and small retailers also usually follow a cost-plus approach.

The basic method is to add a percentage of cost on top for profit, using this simple formula:

Price = Direct costs + overhead costs + profit margin

Direct costs include materials and labor; overhead costs include a share of fixed indirect costs; and profit margin includes a fair amount of return.

A distinction is made between the cost-plus and markup methods, based on the calculations illustrated in Figure 15-2. **Cost-plus** is the profit margin as a percent of full costs (direct costs and overhead):

$$\frac{C}{A + B} \times 100 = \frac{\$10}{\$60} \times 100 = 16.7 \text{ percent}$$

Figure 15-2   FIGURING COST-PLUS AND MARKUPS

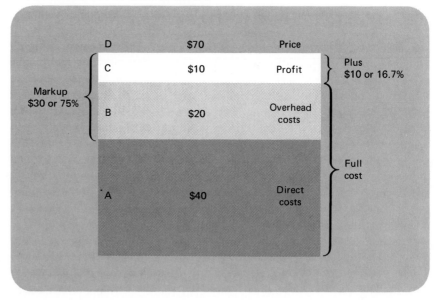

Markup may be figured "on cost," in which case the same cost-plus formula is used. However, business custom may state markup in another way. Markup may cover overhead costs and profit as a percent of the price, as follows:

$$\frac{B + C}{D} \times 100 = \frac{\$30}{\$40} \times 100 = 75 \text{ percent}$$

Besides being simple to calculate, cost-plus has a potential public-relations value. A prudent executive does not publicly boast that his firm is charging all that the traffic will bear. Recoiling "from branding himself a 'profiteer,' he admits only to wanting a 'fair' return."[2]

Cost-plus pricing is also used to gain security in an uncertain market. By taking what is considered a fair profit, a marketer may feel relatively safe from price cutting by competitors, assuming costs are about the same. The approach also assumes, however, that the competitors will not attempt to increase their market share by taking a below-normal profit.

Another common use of cost-plus pricing is for pricing jobs that are difficult to estimate in advance, as with government contracts for military weapons development. Retailers using cost-plus do not necessarily apply the same percentage markup to every item. Competition may be an influence. On a highly competitive product, the retailer may settle for a lower profit in order to get a decent share of the market. A slow economy, too, may cause a general drop in profit margins so that sales are kept moving. On the other hand, it is difficult for retailers to pass up an opportunity to take an extra layer of profit on scarce items with high demand.

Most services are charged on some form of cost-plus pricing. The major component of the cost is invariably labor. As labor costs go up, the costs of services go up. This has been noticeably true in the health field with the rising costs of hospital care and treatment. This ratio also leads to a pertinent consumer question: In a market with a low competitive factor or a highly limited choice, are there adequate safeguards to prevent overcharging? Parents who have paid questionably high prices for having their children's teeth straightened will understand why the question needs to be asked.

Rigid vs. Flexible Markups

The use of a customary **rigid markup** over cost generally works only in special circumstances where the unit cost and price elasticity are fairly constant over a long period of time. These conditions occasionally prevail in retailing, but almost never in manufacturing.

For maximum profits, pricing must allow for changes in market situation, seasonal demand, product life cycle, and other factors affecting potential sales. The popularity of rigid cost-plus pricing results mainly from the fact that it is easy to use; there has been, however, a trend away from it in both large and small businesses.

An effective **flexible markup** system requires that demand, competition, and markets be observed and analyzed. Some highly competitive markets, for example, may necessitate low markups, while the reverse situation permits a higher markup for the same product in other areas.

Full vs. Direct Costs

Direct costs are the costs of labor and materials that actually go into the making of the product. **Full costs** include the direct costs plus a portion of overhead costs such as rent, insurance, and selling and administration costs.

Normally, since overhead costs have to be paid, a product's price should always be higher than its full cost plus a profit margin. The full cost does not, however, represent an absolute floor for price. If market pressure forces the price down below full cost and the firm is not working at full capacity, the product is at least paying for all of its fixed costs plus a part of the overhead. In such circumstances, the fixed cost makes a more economically realistic floor. As long as the price is above that, the company is making more profit than if the products were not being sold at all.

When it sells below the fixed cost, of course, the company is losing more with every unit it produces and only exceptional circumstances would make that feasible. Examples might be a short-term loss sustained to keep an uninterrupted supply available for customers or to maintain the labor force and keep the plant machinery in operation.

Future Cost Issues

Since yesterday's or today's costs may not be the same as tomorrow's, pricing policies should be based on a reliable estimate of **future costs**. The accuracy of this estimate will be influenced by the length of time being estimated for, the complexity of the product, and the experience of the company in producing it. A company starting to make a new, fairly sophisticated product can expect unit costs to go down as volume expands and as the company gains more experience. See the example in the accompanying box.

Inflation can further complicate future cost estimates. Many producers, faced with cost rises even higher than expected, find themselves with the un-

---

The electronics industry provides a typical example of the economic forces affecting pricing policies. At one end of the spectrum are the mature, established products such as standard transistors. Their development costs have been amortized and their prices show stability and, usually, a steady drop in spite of increasing material costs. This is the result of their position on the learning curve, which correlates a steady increase in production and manufacturing experience with a steady decrease in unit costs.

At the opposite end of the spectrum are the new products, which are priced to pay their way out of the learning curve, often sacrificing profit margin for market share. One semiconductor memory device, for example, started out at a price of $28. Its popularity became quickly established and three years later it was available for $4.

In the long run, other economic forces and pressures should keep the electronics industry pricing in continual change as long as new developments in product design can be expected.

Based on "The Complexities of Electronics Pricing," *Business Week*, April 6, 1974, p. 44.

PRICING RIDES THE LEARNING CURVE

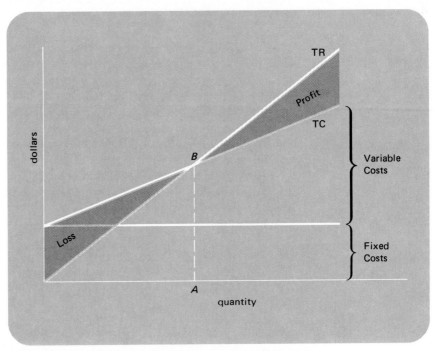

Figure 15-3   THE BREAK-EVEN POINT SEPARATES PROFIT AND LOSS

From Donald V. Harper, *Price Policy and Procedure* (New York: Harcourt Brace Jovanovich, p. 57.

welcome task of choosing between accepting lower profits or raising prices higher than they hoped, just to stay within their profit target area.

Evaluation   The first problem in a cost-plus system is finding an accurate means of figuring realistic cost. The amount of overhead to be charged to each unit, for example, will vary with the number of units sold. Another problem is in accurately allocating costs among different company product lines.

The major drawback to cost-plus, however, is its lack of consideration of demand and of competitive activity. This can seriously alter the estimated sales and production; since cost-plus prices are based on the assumption that sales will be as estimated, a wrong estimation can mean trouble.

The popularity of cost-plus pricing rests primarily with its simplicity. Costs are easier to estimate than demand and are more likely to remain constant. If competition also uses cost-plus pricing, costs and markups are likely to be similar and thus price competition will be minimized. Many companies also feel that cost-plus is fairer to both buyer (when the product is scarce) and seller (when the product is overly plentiful), reducing the chance of one taking unfair advantage of the other.

For a firm with a great number of items to be priced, cost-plus offers the quickest method—even if it is, by necessity, also the most simplistic.

BREAK-EVEN   A **break-even analysis** (as shown in Figure 15-3) relates total cost (TC) to total
ANALYSIS   revenue (TR). The point where TC and TR intersect shows the volume of the

product that must be sold in order to break even (no loss and no profit). These lines may also be used to set prices calculated for maximum profits.

As a cost-oriented approach to pricing, break-even analysis puts more emphasis on sales volume than the cost-plus approach. The standard break-even model shown in Figure 15-3 indicates two kinds of cost: **fixed cost**, which includes executive salaries, depreciation, and all other overhead charges; and **variable cost**, such as labor and materials that are proportional to the number of units produced.

The difference between fixed and variable costs depends theoretically on the passage of time. In the extreme short run, all costs are fixed: products sitting in inventory are gaining no return, regardless of how much has been invested in manufacturing them. If they are about to become obsolete, they should be sold for whatever price can be obtained. In the extreme long run, all costs are variable because money invested in new plant should result in increased production and more executives should be able to sell more goods. Thus, there is a long-term relationship between overhead costs and the number of units produced.

The chart in Figure 15-3 is designed to show relative profit at each level of quantity sold. A loss may be expected up until point A has been reached on the output line; this is the break-even point, represented by B, where total revenue intersects with total cost. After that, a profit may be anticipated. Note that the amount of profit theoretically increases from the break-even point on as the quantity produced increases. This provides a basis for pricing, with price reductions possible in the later stages while the company still maintains the same profit margin.

The break-even point can be calculated with the following formula:

$$\text{Break-even point} = \frac{\text{Fixed cost}}{\text{Price} - \text{variable cost per unit}}$$

For example, consider a stuffed toy animal produced by a company in southeast Kentucky. The product has a fixed cost of $50,000 a year, a variable cost of $6 per unit, and sells at a price of $10. The number of units necessary to break even for the year would be:

$$\text{Break-even point} = \frac{\$50,000}{\$10 - \$6} = 12{,}500 \text{ units}$$

A method related to the break-even approach is **contribution analysis**. Rather than showing the difference between total revenue and total costs so as to measure profits at different levels of output, contribution analysis shows the difference between total revenue and variable cost in order to measure the contribution to fixed costs and profits made at different levels of output. The product's contribution, then, is total revenue minus variable cost. This method has the advantage of focusing attention on the critical fact that any revenue over and above variable costs makes a contribution to overhead and profits. Different contributions can then be calculated at different prices and outputs.

Evaluation Because the TC and TR lines are straight, break-even analysis assumes that the product can be sold throughout the time period shown at the assumed price. In other words, break-even analysis assumes a steady demand that has no influence on price. The longer the period of product life, the more risky that assumption. Also, the break-even chart does not provide any information on whether or not the quantity required to break even can actually be sold at the required price. Break-even analysis, then, is only partially helpful in price determination; it shows, rather, the comparative effect of alternative prices, costs, and quantities on the break-even point.

TARGET RATE-OF-RETURN APPROACH A company may express **target rate-of-return** as a desired percentage return on investment (ROI) or as a specific dollar amount. Either way, it may be used as a pricing policy. The main difference between this approach and cost-plus is that the markup added to costs, in this case, is determined by the rate-of-return objective.

The target amount for the rate-of-return may be set through a variety of criteria, ranging from what the company feels is fair and just, through the amount traditionally earned in the industry, to the "grab all you can get" school.

Prices of services are typically set to achieve a desired rate-of-return. In the case of utilities and public transportation, the rate is regulated by government supervision in order to achieve a fair balance between profit and public interest.

Any target rate-of-return system, to be effective, needs an element of flexibility. Profit goals may have to be adjusted in the face of a blitz from competition or, alternatively, unexpected sales volume may call for price reductions. The desired return is usually averaged over a number of years with expectations of exceeding the target in some years, and not making it in others.

To adapt the break-even point model to target rate-of-return pricing, all that is necessary is to add the required profit figure to the fixed cost. This gives a new break-even point that indicates the quantity of sales necessary to achieve the target return at each price alternative.

The procedure for target rate-of-return pricing can be understood through the example in Figure 15-4. The total cost line is nearly horizontal until it rises sharply as capacity is approached. Suppose a producer of blenders estimates that it will operate at 80 percent of capacity, which means selling 400,000 units. The estimated cost of producing this volume is shown as $8 million. Assuming a target of 15 percent over costs, which equals $1.2 million, target revenue at that point is $9.2 million. Total revenue divided by estimated number of units gives a unit price of $23. Thus, if the company sells 400,000 units at $23, it will reach its target return of 15 percent (and make a $1.2 million profit).

Evaluation Although target rate-of-return is frequently used as a pricing method, particularly by large manufacturers, it has serious drawbacks. Principally, it does

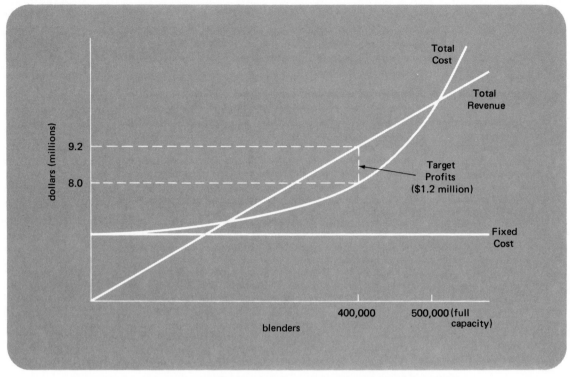

Figure 15-4   GETTING TARGET PRICING FROM BREAK-EVEN ANALYSIS

not allow satisfactorily for the relationship between price and demand. An estimate of sales volume is used to determine price; price, however, is a major influence on sales volume. The price may have to be adjusted to achieve the sales target as well.

Another problem with target pricing is the difficulty in accurately estimating costs and overhead. This can be a major complication for companies with many different product lines and markets. It is often unrealistic to set the same target for widely differing markets where competition may be a strong influence on sales volume and price.

DEMAND-ORIENTED PRICING

Demand-oriented pricing is based on an estimate of how much sales volume may be expected at various prices. Usually these figures are then related to cost estimates at various levels to arrive at a price most likely to meet the sales and profit objectives.

DEMAND ANALYSIS   The basic principle of demand-oriented approaches is to charge high prices when demand is high and low prices when demand is low, even though unit costs are the same in both cases. Essentially, this means basing the price not on cost but on the consumer's perceived value of the product. Cost becomes a factor only if consumers place too low a value on the product to allow for an adequate profit.

The task of the organization, then, is to accurately predict a demand curve for the product. This usually means preparing a stratified projection showing the number of customers who will be willing to buy at each price level. Once the actual price is established, all those willing to buy at that price level will consider the product good value for the money; all those above that price level will consider it a bargain since they were willing to pay more. That, at any rate, is the theory.

Some products and services are sold at **customary prices:** consumers expect to pay just so much for them. Candy bars, chewing gum, and soft drinks are good examples. Charging more than the customary price reduces demand drastically; charging less has little effect and therefore little purpose. Customary pricing simplifies the problem but puts emphasis on cost control in order to be able to sell at a particular price. During times of rising prices, the problem becomes more serious. Often, the only solution is to cut quality or quantity. (Remember how big a candy bar used to be?)

The discussion of profit maximization on p. 336 is relevant here. A number of demand-oriented pricing formulas have been used to determine the best prices for maximum profit. These formulas are usually built on the inverse relationship between price per unit and quantity demanded. For example, the lower a Polaroid camera's price, the higher the demand will be.

DEMAND ESTIMATION APPROACHES Estimating future demand for a product, particularly for an item new to the market, is one of the most difficult, frustrating, and least-developed steps in pricing. Nine factors need to be considered in this process: availability of substitutes, ease of want satisfaction, durability, urgency of need, impact of total price, income, promotion, population, and competitive pressures.[3]

Generally, an important change in any one of these factors will result in a change in demand.

Even with existing products, a company is usually sure of only one point on the demand curve: the number of units being sold for the existing price. The effects of raising or lowering the price by any given percentage are seldom easy to estimate. Certainly, an effective use of demand curve estimation takes vast amounts of time and energy to transpose theoretical treatment to the realities of a dynamic marketing environment. Strangely enough, the more complex that environment is, the more tempting it is for the price setters to stick with simpler systems, such as cost-plus or break-even pricing, in an effort to retain their sanity and get on with the job.

Still, over half of the companies in today's market are believed to be participating in demand studies of some sort. More sophisticated techniques are being developed and are beginning to prove their usefulness, with the result that more and more price-setting executives are gaining confidence in them.

Marketers with more than one product need information not only about the demand for each product but also about what effect a demand change for one product will have on the sales of their other products. Once again, this may become doubly important if a company has little or no experience with a particular product or market.

Basically, there are five demand estimation approaches in common use, depending on the company and the situation: experience, substitute products, survey of buyers, statistical analysis, and experimentation.

1. *Experience.* Experience is an executive commodity that can command high prices in the marketplace. Although such estimates made from experience take demand and price characteristics into account, they are, by nature, subjective and could probably be improved with the help of more sophisticated information gathering.

2. *Substitute products.* Perhaps the simplest, and often most feasible, method of pricing a new product is to compare it with the closest competitive substitute available. This may be a direct comparison—say, a new type of razor blade with the old type it is designed to replace. Or it might be a related comparison, such as a new labor-saving device related to the old method in terms of efficiency and hours saved. The substitute approach works in a surprising number of cases, but rarely in areas of true innovation.

3. *Survey of buyers.* Another approach to demand estimation is to survey prospective buyers, gauge their interest in the product, and estimate what price they might be willing to pay for it. This method is approximate at best and misleading at worst, especially for consumer products. Many consumers find it extremely difficult to predict their reactions to an actual buying situation. The survey method may have a better chance in industries where buyers have a better idea of what prices they are willing to pay for what products.

4. *Statistical analysis.* Demand estimation by statistical analysis is the process of looking over past company and industry records of sales and price changes and using them as a basis for future predictions. To work efficiently, there must be ample figures available and a market situation that has not changed significantly since the figures were gathered. This is not always the case. The past does not necessarily repeat itself like night and day; competitive situations change, as do conditions of supply and demand. Price changes in the past may be too infrequent to demonstrate much range of relationship with demand. There is also the considerable problem of establishing that past correlations between price fluctuation and demand did indeed have a cause-and-effect relationship and were not influenced by some third factor, such as advertising.

5. *Experimentation.* Experimentation is an attempt to set up controlled conditions so that only one variable is present. Any changes that occur can then be attributed to that variable. The usual method is to select two comparable markets and charge a different price for the same product during a test period. This method has the big advantage of a close simulation of real market conditions, with real consumers buying the product for real money.

Dynamic Dimensions of Demand   In evaluating demand-oriented pricing, it is important to be aware of the possible dynamics that may take place when a price change is actually made in a market. For example, the psychological effect of a price cut may be to lead consumers to the suspicion that the item is about to go out of production or be replaced by a newer model. Secondary consumer reactions must also be anticipated. Consumers may stock up on the product, thinking the low price is temporary. This is then followed by a drop in sales as consumers draw on their supplies.

How consumers perceive a new price can dramatically change their concept of the value of the total market offering. Southwest Airlines, for example, cut the fare in half on their Dallas to San Antonio run. At first, when sales volume stayed the same, the airline took a loss. Business people, however, soon took advantage of the lower fare, and Southwest's passenger increase over the long run gave them a profit. Their pricing strategy, in effect, changed the travel patterns of many consumers.

MARKET SEGMENTATION PRICING

Market segmentation pricing, also known as **price discrimination**, is a form of demand-oriented pricing in which one product is given different prices, depending on the segment of the market it is sold in. For example, vending machines normally command higher prices than chain stores for candy bars, presumably because consumers are willing to pay a premium for the convenience or for the availability when other stores are closed.

The bases for market segmentation pricing are the customer, the product version, the place, or the time.

Customer segmentation is classically illustrated by the new car market. Two customers may buy identical cars from the same showroom, from the same salesperson, on the same day, for different prices. The difference is a result of the customers' bargaining power; or, from the dealer's viewpoint, that he or she has managed to sell at a premium to one of the buyers.

Product-version price differences occur when two slightly different products are sold for prices that differ by more than the cost of the product differences. Usually, the difference is largely psychological. The price difference between first class and coach on airlines is a good example.

Place as a basis for price segmentation is illustrated by the sometimes startling difference in cost between similar rooms of a resort hotel, depending on whether the view is of the lake or the parking lot.

Time segmentation may take many forms, from seasonal price swings to cheap parking rates in the evenings. On weekends, it costs more to fly, less to phone. Theater tickets are often priced lower for the matinee than for evening performances of the same play.

BREAK-EVEN PLUS DEMAND

Figure 15-5 illustrates the **break-even plus demand** method—"a modified form of break-even analysis, in which demand curves may be used to remedy the cost-only weakness of the basic BEP [break-even point] approach, while retaining its concreteness and focus upon a relatively few key price alternatives."[4]

The upper part of the figure shows four TR (total revenue) curves that result in four break-even points where each intersects with the TC (total cost)

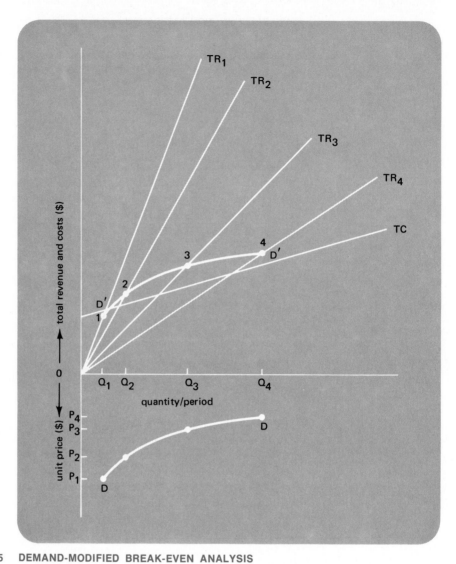

Figure 15-5   DEMAND-MODIFIED BREAK-EVEN ANALYSIS

From Mark I. Alpert, "Pricing: Decision Areas and Models," in Frederick D. Sturdivant et al., *Managerial Analysis in Marketing* (Glenview, Ill.: Scott, Foresman, 1970), p. 468. Copyright © 1970 by Scott, Foresman and Company. Reprinted by permission of the publisher.

line. Without demand considerations, it would be necessary to select whichever of these four prices was felt to have the best chance of exceeding its break-even point.

The figure is, in effect, two graphs in one. The lower half shows a typical demand curve (line DD) with the quantities estimated to be sold at different prices. When this graph is superimposed on the upper graph (line D'D'), we can locate points 1, 2, 3, and 4, the expected revenue points for each pricing alternative. We then note that price P_3 produces the greatest difference between expected total revenue and expected total costs. Thus, profits should be maximized by choosing P_3 as the unit price.

In situations where pricing alternatives are limited, this type of analysis may be more practical than marginal analysis. Although both systems share the difficulty of obtaining a reliable demand curve, the break-even plus demand technique provides somewhat of a hedge against error by including the more easily obtained estimates of total cost, revenues, and profits.

LEGAL CONSIDERATIONS AND DEMAND
Any efforts at price setting, and particularly market segmentation pricing, must take into account federal pricing regulations. Special attention should be given to the Robinson-Patman Act, which regulates against certain forms of price discrimination, including advertising allowances, brokerage fees, and special services. Different discounts for different classes of customers need careful justification. The size of a single order is usually the most acceptable rationalization. Wholesalers typically receive larger discounts than retailers, although this practice may run into trouble if the wholesaler also sells to the public—hence the government may claim "unfair competition."

To prove price discrimination, the plaintiff must first establish that the goods sold were of "like grade and quality" and that the prices in question "may substantially lessen competition" or result in an injury to competitors or consumers. If the defendant can show that the price differences do not exceed the cost differences, his prices are legal regardless of the effect on competition. A seller may also grant a discriminatory price if he acts in "good faith" solely to meet a competitor's equally low price.

Deceptive pricing also comes under federal scrutiny. New cars must now have full prices, including extras and delivery charges, listed on the window. Sellers of other goods who claim that their prices are "wholesale" may be open to complaint unless the claim is true. Inflating "original" prices in order to make discounts seem larger is no longer done without either a lot of nerve or a lot of nervousness.

COMPETITION-ORIENTED PRICING

One of the easiest methods of pricing is to base your price on what the competition is charging. This does not necessarily mean to charge the same as the competition—many companies will try to keep their prices a set percentage above or below competition. The distinguishing characteristic of competition-oriented pricing, however, is that the prime relationship is not between price and cost or demand. Costs may vary, but the company tries to keep its price in line with competitors. The firm assumes, usually quite logically, that the average price level represents a reasonable one.

Competition is the major consideration in setting prices in many markets. Standardized commodities, such as steel and wheat, are usually priced this way. In highly competitive consumer markets, a company often has little choice but to keep prices at the same level as other suppliers. Charging more than the market-determined price might drastically reduce sales. Pricing below this has little value when a company is assured of selling all its output at the going rate; at worst it could start a damaging price war that could quickly hurt all but the strongest of companies in the field (see the accompanying box). Price cuts generally should be made only if competition prices must be met to maintain market share or if the price cut is based on a cut in product cost.

In the late 1960s, hundreds of independent companies were in the business of making computer accessories that IBM customers could use with their IBM systems. Prices and profits were protected by the high leasing prices maintained by IBM for the same equipment. Early in the game, IBM paid little attention to what was, to them, a relatively insignificant part of their total business.

THE EXCESSES OF A COMPUTER ACCESSORIES PRICE WAR

As more and more companies moved in to grab a handful of the action, IBM decided it was time to go after this market. They lowered prices of their most important accessories by 15 percent and more. The independents had no choice but to follow; profits, in the words of one competitor, fell from "unbelievable to merely excellent."

Other companies were not so fortunate. With all their resources concentrated in the one field, they were forced to diversify quickly or, in many cases, disappear. Even those who remained in business were forced to live with the uncomfortable feeling that, if IBM decided to lower prices even further, they could be hurt or go under.

Based on "IBM's Price War Hurts the Independents," *Business Week*, December 18, 1971, pp. 53–56.

One reason for the popularity of competition-based pricing is that it is the easiest method. Costs are often hard to compute; measuring demand is usually even more devilish; competitive prices can be accurately obtained in minutes.

The most notable exception is the service field. Services are harder to compare both for cost and for quality. Thus, only limited flexibility for price competition is possible.

PRICING IN AN OLIGOPOLY

An oligopoly exists when the market for a particular product or service contains so few sellers that the marketing action, including pricing, of any one has a direct effect on all the others. Although the products within an oligopoly tend toward similarity, there are many different kinds of oligopoly with varying characteristics that make generalization difficult. There are, however, two basic kinds of oligopoly: a pure or homogeneous oligopoly (aluminum), and a differentiated oligopoly (trucks).

A **homogeneous oligopoly** is made up of a small number of firms selling a homogeneous product or service. All normally sell at the same price. Prices can be cut by any one of the firms where a gain is to be made—though competitors will probably match the lower price. Price rises, on the other hand, are almost always made first by a recognized industry leader with the others following suit.

In a **differentiated oligopoly**, consumers are aware of real or imagined product differences so prices may vary in direct proportion to the degree of these differences.

Figure 15-6 shows a **kinked demand curve** that demonstrates the short-run effect of a price change in an oligopoly. The normal, established price is represented as *OB*. If a firm drops its price to *OD*, competing firms will probably follow. The result is that the initiating firm has the same, or possibly less, market share with less revenue. If a firm raises its price from *OB* to *OE*, competitors will probably not follow the change. In this case, the firm will lose a substantial amount, or possibly all, of its market share. Given this situation, it is easy to see how prices tend to be stable in an oligopoly unless industry-wide cost changes occur, making a price change logical for all firms.

Price Leadership   **Price leadership** implies that a price change instituted by a leading member of an oligopoly will be automatically adhered to by all the other members. In this way, individual firms give up the privilege of following their own market analysis in return for a much greater certainty as to what action their competitors will take.

    Although actual collusion and price-fixing are clearly illegal, the companies within an oligopoly usually reach agreements and understandings through "signal actions" that, for all intents and purposes, are as explicit as if they had sat down and discussed the matter in detail. For example, the announcement of a price change by Reynolds Metals may lead within hours to a

Figure 15-6   OLIGOPOLY AND THE KINKED DEMAND CURVE

From Donald V. Harper, *Price Policy and Procedure* (New York: Harcourt Brace Jovanovich, 1966), p. 10.

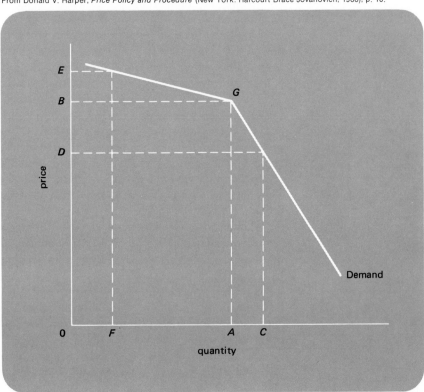

similar change by Alcoa or Kaiser. A price change by an aggressive stereo dealer may be imitated by competing dealers days or weeks later.

The role of the price leader, still, is one of responsibility. Theoretically, at least, the company must make decisions that consider the industry as a whole, the possibility of foreign competition, and the ever-present threat of government inquiry or intervention.

One oligopolistic pricing practice is the concept of **umbrella pricing**, which takes place when one or more giants in a particular field hold a protective economic umbrella over smaller competitors. They do this by maintaining prices high enough for the smaller companies to make a profit even though their per unit costs are higher than that of their high volume, efficient protector. U.S. Steel and General Motors have both been said to assume this role at one time or another.

The opposite philosophy applies to **keep-out pricing**, in which companies will sometimes even take a temporary loss in order to discourage competition and gain a larger market share in the long run.

DYNAMICS OF COMPETITIVE BIDDING

Competitive bidding may be requested by customers ranging from the Defense Department (for new ships) to consumers (for house painting). For the competing sellers, the goal is to submit the lowest bid, all other things (reputation, quality, services) being equal. To do so, each firm must estimate two variables: the profit at each level of bid price and the probability of getting the business.

Estimating competitors' probable bids is the tricky part. Each firm's past experience, current commitments, and degree of hunger for new business must be considered along with profit and probability estimates. At the same time, a firm's own needs will change from time to time and it is desirable to maintain flexibility in bidding. If nothing else, this makes it harder for competitors to forecast the firm's actions, since that is all part of the bidding game.

For companies producing standard products for sale, bidding procedures can be divided into pre-bid analysis and bid determination. **Pre-bid analysis** calls for a clear definition of company objectives. These may range from normal profit goals to minimum company survival, which is achieved by keeping machines and labor force working until a more profitable opportunity comes along. Competition for the bid must also be taken into account. For example, a known competitor who is just trying to survive can be expected to submit a minimum bid.

Manufacturers must take into account their plant capacity, the quantity of items requested, and delivery dates. If quantities and delivery deadlines will tie up production for a length of time, relationships with other customers may be damaged.

The final consideration is, of course, profit. Unless the company is fighting for survival, the bid figure will include a reasonable profit margin. This is so even though the object of bidding is to set the price low enough to beat out competitors for the contract.

Bid determination involves balancing the probability of getting the contract (which diminishes as the amount of the bid goes up) with the potential

Table 15-1

FIGURING THE BEST BID BASED ON EXPECTED PROFIT

COMPANY'S BID (A)	COMPANY'S PROFIT (B)	PROBABILITY OF THIS BID WINNING* (C)	EXPECTED PROFIT (B × C)
$100,000	$5,000	.70	$3,500
125,000	12,000	.40	4,800
150,000	25,000	.10	2,500

*A probability of 1.0 means an assumed certainty that the bid would be accepted.

profit (which diminishes as the amount of the bid goes down). In skillful bidding, the producer bids as high a figure as possible and still winds up winning the contract.

Let us suppose that a supplier of building maintenance services wants to bid on a contract with a large hospital complex. One approach to bid determination, shown in Table 15-1, is to estimate the probability of getting the contract with different bid amounts. At a bid of $100,000, the company expects only a $5,000 profit, with the chances of getting the bid estimated at 70 percent. The expected profit, then, becomes $3,500 (or $5,000 × .70). The expected profit figure ($3,500) is not "real" in the sense that the company actually anticipates receiving that much. Rather, it reflects the "attractiveness" of the bid's actual profit ($5,000) in light of the good chance (70 percent) that it would be accepted. At the other extreme, a bid of $150,000 yields a higher profit, but there is less of a chance (10 percent) that it will be accepted. Here, the expected profit is only $2,500 ($25,000 × .10). The logic behind these calculations is that the higher the bid, the greater the risk that a competing company will bid lower. From this simplified table, it would appear that the company's best alternative would be to bid $125,000, a figure that yields the highest expected profit ($4,800).

Of course, whether the company gets the job or not depends upon the nature of the competing bids. Other criteria may also enter into the picture. These include the buyer's estimate of seller reliability, the probable speed of job completion, and the nature of any special requirements or services the buyer may have.

LEGAL CONSIDERATIONS AND COMPETITION

Price fixing among competitors is not only unethical but decidedly illegal. Other forms of collusive behavior, such as allocating sales territories or production restraints, are equally open to legal attack by government agencies when two or more competitors are involved.

The art of price fixing can take several forms. These involve agreements on selling bids or prices, enforcing resale price, purchase price to be paid, price differentials on discounts, and the addition of arbitrary charges to or deductions from sales prices.[5]

Collusion does not necessarily have to involve price fixing: agreement to undertake discriminatory price cutting to destroy competition is an example. Predatory, or keep-out prices (low prices intended to drive a weaker competitor out of business) are an illegal ploy of powerful firms striving for a monopoly.

NEW PRODUCT PRICING

The problems in pricing new products are related to how different the product is from existing products already on the market. A new breakfast cereal or bath soap, for example, will be priced in line with competitive products. A new product without close substitutes (as DuPont's Teflon once was) presents a different problem. In the past, such products were typically priced at cost plus a predetermined markup and then adjusted to anticipate competition. Now, many companies are taking advantage of the temporary monopoly the product enjoys to set market-oriented prices as high as a reasonable demand-curve would seem to allow.

To set prices accurately for maximum profit, the company has to project potential demand and the relation of price to sales. Consumer preferences must be established and a range of prices set out that will make the product economically attractive to buyers. High initial prices may help to recoup development costs; low initial prices may help to keep competition at bay for a longer period. Both approaches are plausible depending on individual circumstances.

The basic decision, then, in pricing a new product is whether to (1) go in with a high initial price, thus **skimming** the top off the market, or (2) start low with the goal of market **penetration**.

SKIMMING APPROACH   With the introduction of every new and innovative product, there is a group of consumers who are willing to pay premium prices in order to be the first to own or try it. This provides a unique opportunity to launch the product at a high price and skim this lucrative top off the market before competition inevitably forces prices down.

This is, of course, not a high-volume segment of the market; production, however, may not be at a high volume at this stage anyway. Skimming can help cover research and development costs, hold sales figures down while design and production problems are solved, and create prestige for the product.

The objectives of skimming should be clearly laid out by the company. The lower the skimming price, the more visibility can be expected for the product among those who won't buy initially but who will be prospects once the price comes down. In other cases, the company may wish at first to limit production of a semi-experimental model by setting a high initial price.

Skimming works best when there is little chance of competitors entering the market quickly, especially when the product is protected by a patent. This advantage must be balanced against the extra incentive a high skimming price may give to competitors to speed up their entry plans.

Skimming also succeeds among certain products with high visibility and prestige. Wristwatch calculators, electric cars, and home video recorders are some examples.

PENETRATION APPROACH   The penetration approach calls for a price low enough to get the product as deeply into the market as possible, establish brand loyalty, and keep two steps ahead of the competition. Penetration may be instituted as a strategy at the time of the product launch or it may follow a skimming period.

Penetration pricing requires a carefully constructed program, especially if it is part of a plan to reduce prices gradually. As initial costs begin to be paid off either by skimming or initial sales volume, the unit cost goes down and many companies are tempted to base their selling price reductions on a cost-plus basis. For full effectiveness, however, penetration strategy should take market demand into consideration. It is also wise to anticipate competitive pressure and stay ahead of it, rather than reduce prices in response to it.

A penetration approach in some ways requires more courage and commitment than skimming, in that the break-even point is farther down the line and therefore there is no promise of early profits. One danger of a penetration strategy is in setting the price so low that demand exceeds supply, thus hindering market penetration and allowing competitors time to catch up.

PRODUCT-LINE PRICING

Most firms sell not just one product but complete lines of products. The pricing strategy applied to each product, therefore, must work in relation to the other products in the line. Products must be positioned in the market so as to maximize profits for the entire line. Pricing is one factor in achieving that goal.

An efficient product-line pricing policy should consider cost figures for differing levels of output for each product in the line. Next, competitive products and their prices have to be considered, along with the price elasticity of demand of each product group.

In extreme cases, such analysis may lead to the dropping of some products in order to maximize market coverage and profits with the rest of the line.

COST CONSIDERATIONS   The effect of any product on the costs of others in the line depends to a great extent on what costing method the company uses. In full costing, with each product assigned a proportion of the overhead, a decline in sales will mean an increase in costs. This is so because the overhead share per unit will go up. A direct costing system might show only minor cost variations in the same circumstances because overhead costs are not charged on a per unit basis.

If excess capacity exists, this can have a bearing on cost considerations. It may be economically feasible to sell some products below full cost, if the market demands such a price, in order to pay for at least a portion of the overhead. Anything above variable costs will actually decrease the total costs of the other products. This philosophy works effectively only if the products appeal to separate markets. Otherwise, the low price of the one product may force prices down on the others as well.

Many formulas for product-line pricing add an extra margin for those items that require a scarce resource. In the past, this resource was usually skilled labor; now it is just as likely to be a scarce material.

In practice, costs are usually the basis for balancing prices of interrelated products in a line. Since different results may be obtained depending on which costs are used, the company requires careful analysis to be certain that it is proceeding in the most effective manner possible.

PRICE-CROSS ELASTICITIES

Price-cross elasticity refers to the actual effect a price change for one product in the line has on sales of the others. A positive elasticity means that a rise in price of one product causes increased sales of another: a manufacturer charging more for his deluxe washing machine may increase sales of his economy model. Such products are called **substitutes**. The opposite of substitutes are **complements**: increasing the cost of washing machines might lower the demand for dryers. If no correlation exists, the two products are said to be unrelated: raising the price on washing machines would have little effect on demand for dishwashers.

The seller needs to consider these possibilities before changing the price on any item in his product line. The psychological impact of a price change must be considered. The washing machine manufacturer, for example, could conceivably shift sales from the economy model to the deluxe model by lowering the latter's price. On the other hand, this may merely arouse suspicions about the quality of the product and cause a shift to a competitor's similarly priced model.

DEMAND CONSIDERATIONS

While there is a normal price–demand relationship for individual products, additional considerations apply for product-line pricing. The $500-a-day VIP suite at a resort hotel, for example, may have a low demand response, yet it lends prestige to the hotel, possibly increasing overall demand. Some products may be sold at prices showing little or no profit in order to stimulate sales of more profitable items. (Sell the razor at cost and make the profit on the blades.)

A company needs to keep a sharp eye on the market, looking for areas of demand that are presently unfulfilled and that may be profitably explored with a new product that fits into the company's product line. Detroit's discovery of the market for economy-sized cars is an example.

One common method of taking advantage of demand at different levels of the market is in positioning different models in the line to appeal to separate segments of the market—the premium/regular, deluxe/standard, first class/economy approach.

For some types of product, accessories are an important part of the pricing process. It can be argued that, if there is demand for the product, it makes sense to price the accessories high since the consumer will make the decision to buy on the basic product. A price of $120 for a car radio seems unimportant when it is part of a $5,000 buying decision.

CONCLUSION

In order to develop a pricing strategy for any product an organization must start with the establishment of a basic price. The determination of accurate and effective prices is largely a matter of employing better techniques instead of guesswork.

Prices should be set on the basis of costs, demand, competition, and other factors (recall Chapter 14). In practice, however, marketers frequently rely on a single technique or approach to determine basic prices. Focusing mainly on cost, demand, or competition seems to work in many industries for many products. The astute marketing analyst should always examine the assumptions of the price-setting method being used, its track record in terms of pricing objectives, and current or possible future changes in the marketing environment.

Basic decisions in new product pricing involve whether to aim first for skimming of the market with a high initial price or to keep prices down and opt for market penetration.

In product-line pricing, the relative effects of price changes on sales of the entire line must be considered. Individual product goals must be coordinated with the overall company profits and growth goals.

DISCUSSION QUESTIONS

1. Which of the major price determination approaches—cost-oriented, demand-oriented, or competition-oriented—would be most appropriate for pricing these products or services: instant coffee, aluminum ingots, funeral services, private university tuition, pianos? Explain your choice in each case.

2. Hobby City, a large hobby, toy, and gift retailer in Spokane, Washington, wants to use the cost-plus method to price its ten-week ceramics course. The course will take two hours per week. The direct cost (mainly clay and other supplies) will be $80 per student, with overhead cost figured at $30 per student. Assuming the company seeks a 20 percent profit margin, what fee should it charge each student for the course? Would you recommend the same markup on a photography course?

3. A plastic furniture manufacturer, Polliplastics in Los Angeles, California, is adding a new plexiglass bookcase to its product mix. It feels it can use break-even analysis to determine the price of this new product. The new equipment needed to produce the bookcase creates a fixed cost of $14,000. The variable cost per unit will be $80. A price of $150 per bookcase will be competitive. What is the break-even point?

4. The Lapidus Luggage Company of Little Rock, Arkansas, is introducing a canvas tote bag line. The line will be operated as a profit center, with a target rate-of-return of 20 percent over costs. Lapidus plans to run the plant at 90 percent of capacity, for an output of 150,000 tote bags. The total cost of production will be $3 million. What price should it charge to realize its target rate-of-return?

5. What type of market segmentation pricing would be appropriate for these products or services: umbrellas, freight elevators, sailboats, computer time-sharing services, college football games?

6. What are the limitations of being the price leader in an oligopoly? (In your answer, refer to the concept of the kinked demand curve.)

7. Mardini and Goodman Office Furniture is about to make a bid on furnishing the waiting room of a large law firm. Mardini and Goodman want the business, but they know the competition will be rough. Based on the expected profit and the probability of the bid winning, which of the bids given below should they make?

BID	PROFIT	PROBABILITY BID WILL BE ACCEPTED
$14,000	$ 800	.80
18,000	1,500	.50
21,000	2,200	.30
23,000	3,000	.20

8. Make a case in support of the market skimming or the market penetration approach to the pricing of these new products: a digital weight scale, a high-yield grass seed, a downtown museum parking lot, a low-calorie peanut butter.

9. What type of price-cross elasticity relationship describes these product-line items: venetian blinds and draperies, cameras and film, figure skates and ski boots?

NOTES

1. "Detroit's Dilemma on Prices," *Business Week,* January 20, 1975, pp. 82–83.
2. G. Burck, "The Myths and Realities of Corporate Pricing," *Fortune* 85 (April 1972): 85–89.
3. Eugene J. Kelley, *Marketing Planning and Competitive Strategy* (Englewood Cliffs, N.J.: Prentice-Hall, 1972), p. 94.
4. Mark I. Alpert, "Pricing: Decision Areas and Models," in Frederick D. Sturdivant et al., *Managerial Analysis in Marketing* (Glenview, Ill.: Scott, Foresman, 1970), pp. 468–70.
5. Louis W. Stern and John R. Grabner, Jr., *Competition in the Marketplace* (Glenview, Ill.: Scott, Foresman, 1970), p. 111.

16

FINALIZING PRICE STRATEGY

After completing this chapter, the reader should be able to:

1. Describe the rationale for different degrees of price flexibility.

2. Explain the different types of consumer-related adjustments to the price of a product.

3. Describe the major types of discounts—trade, quantity, and cash.

4. Distinguish among the different types of geographical pricing systems.

5. Define the several approaches to promotional pricing.

6. Identify the key consumer and competitor considerations involved in a price-change strategy.

7. Evaluate pricing from the managerial and social viewpoints.

In Chapter 14, we discussed the background of price setting in terms of objectives and price-shaping forces. In Chapter 15, we examined the major methods for determining "basic" prices. In this chapter, we will analyze the reasons for adjustments in the price structure and price changes.

DO-IT-YOURSELF PRICING

Discount structures are an important element in the pricing strategies of many organizations. But to determine discounts, marketers have to come to grips with difficult issues. Distributors are often forced to calculate discounts based on information in suppliers' literature coming from a home office. This central office, however, may be unaware of local costs or of special burdens that the distributor faces in cutting and fitting the price.

One supplier of industrial belting, L. H. Shingle Company, helped ease this problem by refusing to publish its discounts.[1] Jack Keating, a vice-president of the firm, explained that this policy allows distributors to pass along the rising costs of belting. "We understood that the distributors had different pricing requirements from region to region. Their cost increases could vary erratically."

Charles Reeves, a vice-president of Southern Belting and Transmission in Atlanta, notes that L. H. Shingle's action has helped his firm offset the inflated cost of equipment and goods. "It's hard to say if the unpublished discounts policy has added sales or just helped to prevent losses. But it has given us an opportunity to fine-tune our marketing."

FINAL TOUCHES ON PRICING STRATEGY
In the situation just described, the important question is: What is the price a company pays the SB&T distributor for L. H. Shingle belting, and how is it arrived at? Shingle publishes a list price, which is used by SB&T salespeople as a guide. Other factors that go into price determination include:

1. the amount of product preparation that must be done by the distributor;
2. the rising costs to the distributor for equipment and materials;
3. regional differences in distributors' requirements;
4. variations in customer demand level caused by changes in the economy.

Figure 16-1 presents a cumulative model of price strategy. This figure summarizes Chapters 14 and 15 and brings us to the determination of "basic" prices (also called base prices or list prices). In this chapter, we will add two more dimensions to marketing strategy. The first dimension is **price administration**, which involves the degree of **price structure** (discounts, freight charges, promotional considerations, and so forth). The second is **price-change**

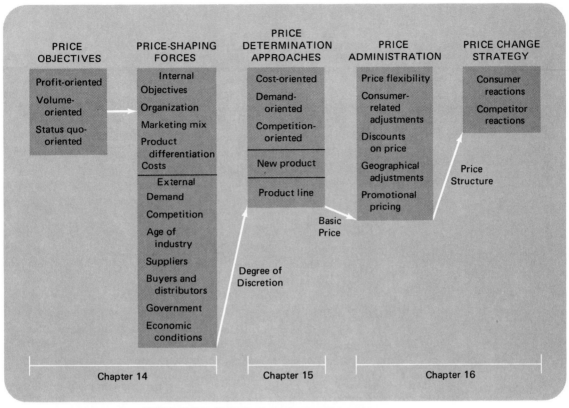

Figure 16-1 CUMULATIVE MODEL OF PRICE STRATEGY

strategy—initiating or responding to price changes that occur on account of consumer and competitor reactions. Both of these dimensions also contribute to harmonizing and integrating pricing strategy with other elements of the marketing mix—product, promotion, and distribution.

PRICE ADMINISTRATION

Not all customers, especially organizations, actually pay the announced basic prices. Usually marketers use some strategy modifications or related terms of sale so that prices differ for different customers under different circumstances. Together, all these possible price modifications make up a price structure. Implementing the price structure is called price administration.

PRICE FLEXIBILITY POLICY

Price flexibility is determined by the options in the price structure that raise or lower the price. It is also influenced by variations that occur through negotiation between buyer and seller. For example, widespread shortages of materials might force many marketers into more flexible sales contracts.

Most retailers today use what is known as a **single-price policy**.[2] This means that all buyers must pay the same price for the product, regardless of the quantity being purchased or any other market factors. For example, a student at a private university must pay a fixed fee for tuition each semester, regardless of sex, racial, or ethnic background, income level, age, class standing, grade point average, or similar factors.

A **one-price policy** offers the same price to all customers who purchase the same quantity of goods under similar circumstances. But, unlike a single-price policy, it allows for price to vary according to the *quantity* of the purchase. Many retailers favor a one-price policy because it is easy to administer. Also, it is equally fair to all buyers because it eliminates bargaining.

Under a policy of **varying prices**, different buyers purchasing the same quantity of a product under identical conditions may pay different prices. Competitive market factors (including a desire to make the sale) may lead to price reductions or increases. This type of policy is advantageous to sellers, since it allows for adjustments to meet prevailing market conditions. But varying prices often means that pricing authority must be delegated to sales personnel in the field. This can be counterproductive, especially if a sales manager continually lowers prices in order to complete difficult transactions.

Price shading has become a dominant practice in some industries. Under this policy, list prices become little more than a starting point for negotiations with a salesperson in the field. For example, an item may be purchased for 30 percent or more below the list price. Some companies have found these practices intolerable and have begun procedures to encourage or require the restriction of price shading.

Escalation clauses have become common in business deals. The buyer pays the going prices at the time of shipment (rather than at the time of the order) for labor, materials, and production costs. On the surface, this may seem a fair way for sellers to cover their costs in a time of inflation. But, as one manufacturer has noted, "The price quoted to you when you place the order no longer means a thing."[3] As a result, some firms have discarded such clauses and now add surcharges to a fixed base price. This is designed to give the buyer a better idea of the likely increases.

Limits on Price Flexibility

A seller usually has full latitude to determine the price at which he chooses to sell a particular product. But what power does a manufacturer have in setting a resale price for wholesalers and retailers?

Distributors may choose to accept the recommended prices of the supplier. Many wholesalers and retailers make no independent pricing judgment, but simply mark up their purchase price by a given percent. Distributors are especially likely to follow the suppliers' preferences if they have been granted limited or exclusive distribution rights on a product.

Price flexibility can also be limited by government action. In 1975, the Council on Wage and Price Stability blasted Union Carbide for raising its wholesale antifreeze price by 21 percent. It threatened that if the rest of the industry went along with this hike, it would demand cost data from all firms and would release data to the public about industry sales and market share.

CONSUMER-RELATED ADJUSTMENTS

As we have seen, an accurate reading of consumer perceptions is an essential marketing task. Setting prices based upon such a reading may be a form of demand-oriented pricing. In other cases, after the basic price has been determined, the presence of strong consumer reactions may lead to certain pricing adjustments.

Psychological Pricing

The technique of **psychological pricing** has been touched on in Chapter 14. This type of pricing is an attempt to choose prices that have some kind of psychological payoff. Usually, this means choosing a price that appears to be lower than it actually is. Thus, the consumer who feels that $3 is too much to pay for a paperback novel may select the same book for a cover price of $2.97, which seems like a lot less money.

In some cases, the application of psychological pricing techniques may actually lead to higher prices. If a price looks too low, the consumer will wonder, "If it's so cheap, how good can it be?" Consumers often link high prices to high product quality. Thus, some goods (perfume) and services (hairstyling) may sell more easily if their prices are raised.

Some firms have attempted to build a permanent premium image through product quality, pricing, and other marketing techniques. One example is the Green Giant Company, which has successfully promoted its food items as top-quality choices through the famous "Jolly Green Giant" advertising campaign. When an image is promoted effectively, a firm can capture a solid market share and make a very satisfactory level of profit.

Odd Pricing

Odd pricing is a particular form of psychological pricing that involves the use of unusual, odd-numbered prices, such as 69 cents or $2.97. As noted before, odd prices can be used to give the impression of lower prices, especially when the price is slightly below a dollar figure. Interestingly, odd prices can result in benefits for the seller even when the odd price is higher than the "normal" price. One Midwestern department store chain was able to move certain clothing items much more easily at a price of $1.77 than at the lower price of $1.69.[5]

One study of the last digit of the retail prices for processed meats indicates the striking popularity of odd pricing among retail grocery chains.[5] Fifty-seven percent of all prices surveyed ended in the digit "9" while another 15 percent ended in the digit "5."

Behind the use of odd pricing is the belief that consumers will respond positively to items marked with such unusual figures. Yet scientific data backing up this conventional wisdom seems to be lacking. A number of studies have turned up no conclusive evidence of the supposed high sensitivity of consumers to odd prices.[6]

Price Lining

Price lining occurs when a manufacturer offers products or services at a limited number of prices (known as **price lines**). Thus, instead of selling men's hats at many different prices, the manufacturer may decide to sell hats at only three prices: $10, $20, and $35. Price lining is effective because the price lines (and the associated levels of quality) become clearly fixed in the minds of consumers. One price may stand for the economy choice, another for the medium-quality product, and the third for the most prestigious and luxurious model.

This device also helps reduce pricing decisions and makes retailers' inventory control a much less difficult problem.

DISCOUNTS ON PRICES

Most manufacturers and wholesalers offer some form of discount on the list price of their products. The formulation of **discount structures** has become a critical task of pricing strategy.

The three main types of discounts are trade, quantity, and cash. Discounts are also given with trade-ins, as well as for providing installation and repair service, financing, prepayment, warehousing, and stocking a complete line. Some firms give seasonal discounts to buyers who accept delivery during certain desired periods.

Trade Discounts

Trade or **functional discounts** are compensation to a distribution intermediary who performs essential services for a manufacturer. A wholesaler may assume the responsibility (and the cost) of storing goods that will later be resold to retailers. The manufacturer repays the wholesaler through a trade discount, for without the wholesaler the manufacturer's storage costs would probably rise. The structure of these discounts is often set by industry-wide custom.

The service sector of the economy does not use trade discounts, since services are not resold to clients. Agents' commissions are paid by the seller or by the buyer, depending on the particular industry practice, such as real estate or travel service.

Quantity Discounts

Sometimes a seller will reduce the unit price of an item if the buyer is willing to buy in bulk or agrees to make many orders over a long period of time. This is known as a **quantity discount**. Such arrangements are common in industrial sales (a hospital's order for 200 beds), but also in certain service industries (a commuter railroad's 30-ride ticket).

There are two types of quantity discounts. A **noncumulative quantity discount** is based only on the size of a particular order. A baseball team might be willing to sell tickets to a game at a cut rate to a block of 25 fans. The purpose of this kind of discount in most industries is to stimulate the buyer to make a large purchase. In manufacturing, this reduces the seller's costs for sales, storage, processing, and delivery.

The **cumulative quantity discount** extends over a given period of time, generally a year. A buyer who makes enough purchases over the year—even if each individual purchase is small—can qualify for the discount. This builds a long-term relationship between that buyer and the seller, and it allows the buyer to more easily plan a production schedule.

Quantity discounts allow larger marketers to make the process of production and distribution more efficient and predictable. However, small marketers are penalized by this process because they are generally unable to buy enough goods to qualify for the discounts.

Cash Discounts

Although rarely used in consumer transactions or service industries, **cash discounts** are offered by many firms to business clients. If the buyer pays the bill within a limited period of time (often ten days), he or she receives a discount. Industry practice tends to determine the amount and terms of the cash discount.

2/10 net 30 is a typical form for a cash discount. This symbolic equation means that the buyer is expected to pay the bill within 30 days. If he does, there is no penalty; if he pays after the 30-day period, he may be subject to an interest charge. But, if the buyer pays within ten days of the invoice date, he will receive a 2 percent cash discount. For example, abrasive steel conditioning wheels list at $124.51. If the terms include a 2/10 net 30 cash discount, the wheels will sell at 2 percent off—or $122.02—if the buyer pays the bill within ten days.

We can expect to see new kinds of consumer cash discounts in the future. In one New Jersey experiment, holders of a savings "cashcard" received 10 to 20 percent discounts at 1,200 stores.[7] The use of credit cards may have spread around the world, but many organizations will still offer a discount in order to see folding currency.

Legal Considerations

As we mentioned in Chapters 3 and 15, the 1936 Robinson-Patman Act governs all business pricing policies. The law was created to eliminate unfair competitive practices and to prevent discrimination in prices or terms of sale among buyers of the same product.

Trade discounts seem to be permissible under the Robinson-Patman Act as long as they are offered on the same terms to all buyers in a particular class. While some legal questions of this law remain unsettled, it appears that a seller may offer different trade discounts to various trade groups as long as all buyers in each group have the same privileges. Thus, wholesalers can be subject to separate types of discount arrangements from retailers.

Quantity discounts are a risky venture under the Robinson-Patman Act. When the same price is charged to all buyers regardless of quantity, there is no problem. But noncumulative quantity discounts are lawful only if they are extended equally to all buyers and if they can be justified on a cost basis. The discounts cannot be greater than the cost savings of the seller. Cumulative discounts are particularly questionable, because they may generate unfair competitive practices. For example, the Federal Trade Commission ruled in the Universal-Rundle case that the firm's trucking discounts unlawfully discriminated against small buyers, who could not hope to benefit from the lower rates.[8]

Cash discounts are clearly acceptable within the terms of the Robinson-Patman Act as long as they are offered to all buyers on the same terms. This is common business practice with cash discounts such as 2/10 net 30. Thus, in this area there have been no legal problems between business firms and government regulatory agencies.

GEOGRAPHICAL ADJUSTMENT

Geographical factors are a serious concern of marketers in determining pricing policies. This is especially true in industries where transportation costs are high, such as steel and heavy machinery. Regardless of how a manufacturer plans to ship his goods to buyers, he must decide how these costs will figure in the overall price structure. Buyers may not be willing to absorb the full responsibility for transportation expenses.

There are two principal approaches to geographical adjustment of prices. One is based on the supplier, the other on the destination of the goods.

Supplier-Based Systems

When a manufacturer quotes prices **f.o.b.—free on board**—it means that the buyer must select the mode of transportation and pay all freight charges. The buyer may wish to hire a shipping firm or may pick up goods with his or her own trucks. Under this policy, the geographical distance between seller and buyer becomes a critical factor in the actual transportation costs. If a manufacturer has no competitor in the immediate geographical area, he will enjoy a clear advantage in dealing with buyers in that region.

Product differentiation is one way of offsetting this situation. If a manufacturer has a distinctive and attractive product, buyers from distant geographical areas may prefer (or be compelled) to deal with that manufacturer rather than competitors in the buyer's territory. Thus, f.o.b. pricing does not always lead to restrictions on the seller's ability to interest buyers over a wide geographical area.

Freight equalization is one method used by manufacturers to compete more effectively for business. A manufacturer who is anxious to undercut f.o.b. competitors may choose to "foot the bill" for some or all of the freight costs involved in the transaction. One technique is to offer buyers the following deal: goods can be purchased and delivered for the seller's normal factory price f.o.b., plus the freight costs that the buyer would incur if he or she purchased the goods from the nearest available competitor in his region.

Uniform delivered prices mean that all buyers pay the same charge for the same quantity of delivered goods, regardless of their location. The seller quotes a purchase and delivery price that actually includes an average freight cost. This system of pricing is realistic only when the product has relatively low transportation costs. It does have the advantage of allowing for nationwide advertising of prices.

Destination-Based Systems

In f.o.b.-delivered pricing, the manufacturer's price includes both the normal purchase price and shipping costs. In effect, the buyer is contracting for transportation services from the manufacturer, who determines the best mode of delivery and pays all freight bills.

With the **zone system**, there is a uniform delivered price for all buyers within a geographical zone. In a single-zone system, any buyer within the seller's entire market area is charged the same uniform delivered price. Many wholesalers adopt this method of pricing since their buyers (retailers) may all be in the same metropolitan area as the wholesaler. In a multiple-zone system, the delivered prices are the same within each particular zone. Price differences between zones are usually based on the distance from the factory where goods are stored. The farther the zone from the factory, the higher the price within the zone. Under these zoning systems, buyers usually pay less for transportation than the actual costs incurred by the manufacturer.

Under a **freight-absorption pricing system**, buyers arrange and pay for transportation, but can deduct their costs from the seller's bill. Thus, if buyers go to great expense to transport the products—which will happen if they are particularly far away from the seller—the seller will settle for a smaller payment. This is quite similar to a delivered-pricing system, but in this case the buyer controls the method of transportation and the choice of carrier.

Basing-point pricing begins with the designation of one or more cities as "basing points" for pricing of transportation costs. The delivered price for a shipment reflects the cost of transporting goods to the buyer from the nearest basing point (regardless of where the actual point of shipment is). Industries with a few dominant firms and price leaders often employ this form of pricing to restrict price warfare.

In a single basing-point system, all firms at the basing point receive the same net return from sales regardless of the buyer's location. But firms that are located away from the basing point receive differing net returns, since their compensation for actual transportation costs comes from a formula of basing point to buyer, rather than plant location to buyer.

Figure 16-2 illustrates the complex workings of a single basing-point system. In this case, the basing point is Chicago. Producer A, located in Chicago, ships goods to Buyer B in Little Rock. He charges Buyer B a price of $50 per unit, plus a freight charge of $10 per unit, for a total delivered price of $60 per unit. But what if Producer B, in Little Rock, is shipping the same goods to the same Buyer B in Little Rock? He must calculate the price as if the goods were actually travelling from Chicago to Little Rock. Producer B also charges Buyer B $60 per unit—the base price of $50 plus a "phantom freight" charge of $10.

If Producer A in Chicago is selling goods to Buyer A in Chicago, there is no freight charge. The goods are not travelling away from the basing point, so the delivered price is the same as the base price—$50 per unit. But if Producer B in Little Rock is selling to the same Buyer A in Chicago, he must act as if the goods were not being transported, since Chicago is his basing point. Therefore he cannot charge Buyer A for shipping. He must absorb the freight charge of $10 per unit himself, and can charge Buyer A only the delivered price of $50 per unit.

In a multiple basing-point system, all firms receive varying net returns from different sales. The basing point used for a particular buyer will be the one that offers him the most reasonable transportation costs.

Legal Considerations No one has ever really challenged the legality of f.o.b. pricing. But some forms of delivered pricing have fallen under close government scrutiny.

Organizations having zone pricing systems have been charged with price discrimination, since some buyers in a zone may be paying more for transportation than it costs the manufacturer, while others are paying less. Nevertheless, the Federal Trade Commission and the federal courts have been reluctant to attack zone pricing. Single-zone pricing has been approved, since there is no price discrimination at the point of destination of goods, but only at the point of origin of the product. Multiple-zone systems have been subject

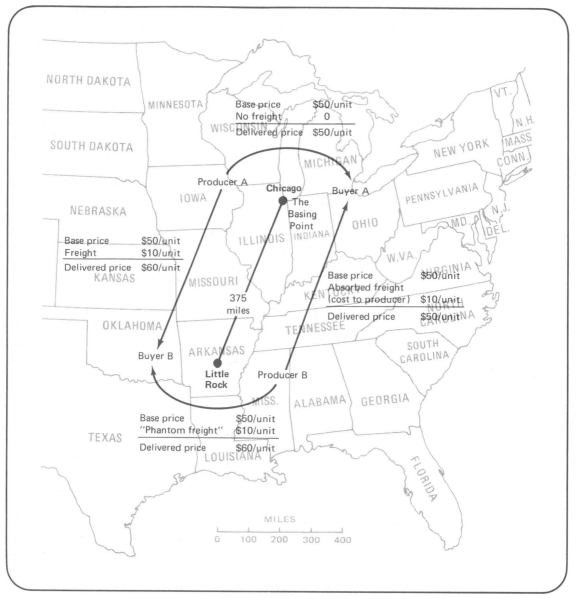

Figure 16-2   BASING-POINT PRICING ILLUSTRATED—CHICAGO AND LITTLE ROCK

to legal action only when price fixing involves many leading firms in an industry.

Basing-point pricing systems have been much more controversial under the Robinson-Patman Act and the Federal Trade Commission Act. As we saw in Figure 16-2, some firms are paying extra transportation costs for phantom freight, while others are benefiting from freight absorption. This raises questions about price discrimination. The legal status of basing-point pricing systems remains somewhat unclear. In general, the FTC has been most concerned with avoiding industry-wide systems of identical delivered prices that result from price fixing.

PROMOTIONAL PRICING

Price is often used as one part of a total marketing campaign to promote a good or service. The term **promotional pricing** is generally applied when low prices are offered as the major advantage of a particular product or service. Other examples include special low-price sales events, offers of premiums or trading stamps, and combination offers. In each, there is some sort of direct or indirect price cut, or at least the appearance of such a cut. Some firms do promotional pricing regularly; others do so only when sales are slow.

Promotional Allowances

A manufacturer may wish to supplement his or her own promotional efforts by encouraging wholesalers and retailers to take on special promotional work for his products. If this occurs, the manufacturer will probably grant the distributors **promotional allowances** in the form of discounts in return for local advertising or special displays.

Another form of promotional allowance is **push money.** A retail salesperson will be given extra money for vigorously promoting the products of a particular manufacturer. Promotional allowances may also be granted for accepting trade-ins, providing installation and repair service, or handling financing, prepayment, or storage.

Leader Pricing

Roasting chickens usually sell for anywhere from 55 cents to 75 cents a pound in Julio Valdez's neighborhood. But one day he notices that the local Daitch-Shopwell supermarket is selling the highly advertised Perdue chickens for only 49 cents a pound.

This is more than a typical supermarket sale. Daitch is using the Perdue chicken as a **price leader** (or loss leader). It is hoping that customers will come into the store to get a bargain on Perdue chickens, and while there will decide to do all the rest of their normal grocery shopping at Daitch's regular store prices. In order to make this strategy work, Daitch must have a price leader with a real drawing power and value for the consumer. It must also have sufficient stock to handle a high volume of business.

Daitch's primary concern is not the sales of the price leader itself. The store may assume that if sales of Perdue chickens are high, many customers are coming in to benefit from the sale and are purchasing other food products. The danger, of course, is that Julio Valdez and others will come into the store, buy only the special, and leave. If this happens, the supermarket's reduced profits on the chickens will not be made up in higher overall business.

Manufacturers are wary of having their products used as price leaders. It may not be in Perdue's interest to see its chickens selling too often at 49 cents per pound. People may link that price to the product and then resist buying it at the usual retail price.

Price leading is also risky for distributors, since it can lead to retaliation and ultimately to price wars. If Daitch is too successful using Perdue as a leader at 49 cents, A&P may have to sell Perdue or another brand of chicken at 45 cents, and Safeway may be forced down to 42 cents.

Some firms use price leaders in the opposite way. They develop a line of premium products and offer them at high prices to build their overall image. For example, a Safeway store in Washington, D.C., introduced a profitable line of exotic foods such as kangaroo steaks. What was most important was not that the exotic foods sold themselves, but that they helped improve the overall image of the store. This helped sales of several product lines.

Customer Category Discounts

When a business firm or industry attempts to give particular discounts to certain categories of customers, it advances into questionable legal ground and raises the danger of outraging other customers. For some years, it was common practice among the Big Three automobile manufacturers to sell new cars at a discount to car-leasing companies like Hertz and Avis. Some wholesale car dealers were angered by this practice and threatened legal action to prevent such discounts. Eventually, General Motors and Ford agreed to end all such discounts.

Price-Reducing Specials

A wide variety of techniques are used to provide consumers with **indirect price reductions**, including the offer of premiums, coupons, trading stamps, and combinations of these. Such promotions offer unlimited possibilities for creative marketing. A company can provide a larger package of the normal product for the regular price. It can promote cans of shaving foam with coupons for discounts on razor blades.

Coupons have become an increasingly popular marketing technique. From 1970 to 1975, their use rose by over 80 percent. In 1974, manufacturers' coupons reached a peak of 29.8 billion, a more than two billion increase over 1973. In 1975, supermarkets' redemption rates for in-ad coupons averaged 30 percent.[9]

Trading stamps may have passed their prime in the 1960s. When the energy crisis began in the winter of 1973, many gas station owners, who had been major distributors, found it unnecessary to promote stamps in order to attract business. As the economic recession of the 1970s deepened, many supermarkets began cutting back on the use of trading stamps. It was claimed that if trading stamps were reduced, prices would be lowered correspondingly. This does not appear to have been the case, however, as so many other costs were affected by inflation as well.

Rebates, in the opinion of one advertising firm, were "pounced on" by marketers as the "magic elixir which would not only soothe the pains of sales stagnation, but revive our ailing economy."[10] The best-known move was the automobile industry's use of $200 to $600 cash rebates for certain purchases of new cars in 1974–1975. But the rebate idea quickly caught on at General Electric and with home furnishings makers, homebuilders, retailers, and packaged goods dealers. In many of these industries, there was a noticeable jump in sales. Stocks in auto dealer lots and salesrooms were quickly reduced by billions of dollars.

There seem to be a number of important advantages in the use of rebates. First of all, they can reshape consumer attitudes toward buying, at least in the short run. Rebates also leave the normal price structure of an industry untouched, which may be important in heading off government price freezes.

Retail Markdowns   **Markdowns** are a frequent occurrence in retail pricing. A distributor reduces the original prices by some figure or percentage for a variety of reasons:

1. because of mistakes in buying merchandise, such as poor choices of goods or overbuying of an item;

2. as a periodic clearance and sale device;

3. because particular items simply are not selling;

4. as a consistent marketing strategy. A retailer may price goods at a fairly high level and plan to make reductions and advertising campaigns at the right time.

Markdowns vary greatly in size; one rule of thumb is to have a markdown that is no less than 15 percent—sizeable enough to be interesting to customers. For some retailers this means marking down at least one full price range; for others, it means whatever reduction will initially move at least 25 percent of the stock on hand. The only limit on a markdown is the retailer's need to protect the overall revenue of the firm.

Legal Considerations A promotional allowance is, as we have seen, a form of price reduction. As such, it is subject to the provisions of the Robinson-Patman Act. The allowances are unlawful "unless such payment or consideration is *available on proportionately equal terms* to all customers competing in the distribution of such products or commodities."

This places a number of limits on the promotional allowances:[11]

1. To be considered "available," promotional allowances must be made known to all distributors.

2. The manufacturer must be getting a service of some real marketing value.

3. The size of the allowance must be reasonably linked to the value of the service.

4. The service rendered by the distributor or dealer must be a function that any competitor in the group can perform (such as window display).

5. The manufacturer must determine that the service being compensated is actually performed.

Bait pricing is an unlawful marketing practice that can resemble leader pricing. A supermarket may advertise an unprecedented special on lamb chops. Consumers enter the store to take advantage of this sale, but—guess what!—the store can't seem to find any more lamb chops. "Maybe tomorrow," they say. The "special" was a form of bait, designed to get you into the store to buy other products. But, unlike price leading, bait pricing is a situation in which the retailer is hoping (and sometimes making sure) that you won't be able to buy the product that was advertised. Bait pricing is considered to be a deceptive and unlawful technique by the FTC. Some states have passed legislation to prevent such advertising frauds.

Fictitious pricing occurs when a firm announces the price of a product as a reduction from some "normal" price, when in fact there is no real reduction at all. The firm may say that the price was "formerly $25" or "reduced from $130." This technique is practiced by unethical dealers who wish to benefit from the consumer's legitimate desire for sales and discounts. It has been attacked by the FTC and by state legislation. But fictitious pricing is difficult to fight through legal efforts, because of the enormous volume of prices and advertisements.

PRICE-CHANGE STRATEGY

Making a price change is an important decision for a firm. A price reduction may stimulate demand or outflank weak competitors; a price increase may be necessary in order to pass on higher costs. Either way, the action is going to affect not only the firm itself, but also buyers, competitors, distributors, suppliers, and perhaps the government.

Planning can be a critical element in price changes. No firm wants to be in the position of always following competitors in making price changes. It is risky to be the innovator, but such action can lead to an enhanced reputation and to higher profits. Planning allows a firm to make price changes at the most desirable time, and good timing has many advantages. If there is an increase, the firm should schedule it at a time when it will not be readily apparent.

A firm has a number of options if it finds it must raise its prices. It can eliminate costs, such as volume discounts or freight absorption, rather than boost list prices. It can shift production toward a new emphasis on higher priced models. Or it can preserve the familiar price but advertise a lesser weight content. These alternatives may be essential if the firm feels it cannot sustain a straight price increase.

CONSUMER REACTIONS The reactions of consumers to price changes are measured through the concept of **price elasticity of demand** (see also our discussion in Chapter 6).[12] The degree of elasticity depends on a number of factors. If the price change is small, many consumers may accept it; if it is large, there may be a widespread shift to a competitor's product. Price elasticity may also depend on the original price level. A 10 percent hike on a product that costs $1 may be received very differently from a 10 percent hike on a $50 product.

Price elasticity also varies over time. In some cases, demand may be stable in the short run but elastic in the long run. Buyers may have no alternative but to accept the price increase at first, but by the next buying season they may be ready to switch brands. The reverse situation is also possible. Buyers may immediately switch out of anger about a price increase, but may return to the original product later if they realize it is still the best buy.

When a price is increased, a seller is wise to introduce some form of improvement—even if this means higher costs and an even greater increase than originally planned. Consumers are not happy when the only reason for a price hike seems to be the producer's costs; they believe that business profits are high enough already. They may respond more favorably if they can see that they are at least getting a better product for their money.

Price cutting is based on the assumption that it will lead to a higher volume of sales and, therefore, a higher profit. It has proven to be most effective when the brand is well known and has an established quality reputation. High-volume retailers try to pass on a saving to consumers through low prices and build up sales figures as a result.

COMPETITOR REACTIONS To understand competitive reactions to price changes, we must distinguish price reductions from price cutting. Price reductions are instituted to gain benefits from a projected consumer response. Price cutting is a direct move to draw consumers away from rivals (rather than into the industry as a whole). Once price cutting begins, it can be difficult to stop. There are usually few winners in this kind of competitive warfare. Many industries have long-time traditions that discourage price wars, for it is believed that they can only damage all firms in the long run.

Initiating a Price Change Whether in terms of the initial pricing decision or the analysis of a price change, pricing has an element of strategy similar to a poker game. In pricing as in poker, it is necessary to analyze the possible reactions of all the players in the game.

Similarly, the firm planning a price change must make extensive efforts to estimate the possible reactions of its competitors. In doing so, the firm must decide whether any important competitor has a set price-reaction policy, or whether the competitor reacts differently to each unique situation. If a competitor has a set policy, it can be pinpointed through statistical analysis or through inside information (one firm may hire a key executive from its competitor). If a competitor has no set policy, it becomes important to analyze the competitor's financial situation and determine which objectives seem most important.

When a price reduction is initiated, a competitor's reactions are affected by a number of principal factors:[13]

1. *Costs.* If costs are high, a competitor may not want to cut prices and reduce profits.

2. *Speed.* If a change in production method is necessary to reduce costs and prices, it will probably take time.

3. *Conflict of interest.* If prices are cut, the competitor's "quality line" and "standard line" may be selling too close to each other in a way that harms both.

4. *Relative sales volume.* It is particularly costly for a large supplier to reduce prices to protect a certain segment of the market.

Figure 16-3 presents a logical flow model of competitors' reactions to a price cut. The model goes beyond the elementary question—will he or won't he match my price cut—to an examination of the more complex possibilities involved.

A price increase raises different sorts of problems in terms of evaluating competitors' reactions. In most situations, the competitors will be asking three crucial questions.[14]

1. Will an industry-wide price hike reduce the total size of the market?

2. How many other marketers are interested in following the initial rise?

3. Has the initiator acted in the best interests of the industry as a whole?

Responding to a Price Change How does a firm respond when a competitor makes a price change? In a homogeneous product market, the firm may have no choice when a competitor cuts prices. If the firm "holds the line," customers will probably switch to the product with the lowest prices. If one firm in a homogeneous product market raises prices, the situation is less clear. All firms may follow suit if an overall increase will help the industry. But one firm may choose to maintain its prices—an action that, if successful, can lead to a general rollback by other firms.

In a nonhomogeneous product market, buyers have many criteria for choosing among the products of competing firms. They consider pricing, of course, but service, quality, and reliability are also important. Thus, when one

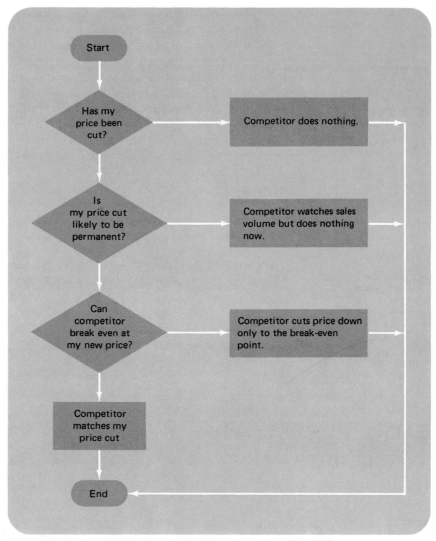

Figure 16-3 CONSIDERING COMPETITOR'S REACTIONS TO A PRICE CUT

From William F. Massy and Jim D. Savvas, "Logical Flow Models for Marketing Analysis," *Journal of Marketing* 28 (January 1964): 32. Reprinted from *Journal of Marketing*, published by the American Marketing Association.

firm makes a price change, the others will not necessarily be forced to follow suit. If a firm with a reputation for mediocre products raises or lowers its prices, a firm with an established name may feel no need to respond to the change.

EVALUATION OF PRICING STRATEGY

We have now completed three chapters on pricing. It therefore seems appropriate to evaluate this element of the marketing mix in terms of management performance and society.

**MANAGEMENT
PERFORMANCE**

Of all the elements in the marketing mix, price is the one most closely related to the economic health of the organization. For this reason, it has always been closely watched by the financial managers of an organization. In terms of its marketing impact, it serves another role in matching consumers to the total market offering. The ideal state combines both these viewpoints.

While pricing is of critical importance to marketing, it is also an area of continued uncertainty and confusion. The economic theory and operating precision of pricing both leave much to be desired. Some observers have referred to business thinking about pricing as "superstitious" and "fuzzy."[15]

In the inflationary economy of the mid-1970s, pricing became even more unpredictable than ever. In the oil and food industries, some prices rose 10 to 50 percent in a year. In the calculator business, electric hand-held models fell in prices from $240 to $19.95 over a three-year period. These examples suggest what all too many marketers have come to realize: pricing in a complex economy is a totally perplexing process. What seems most certain is that the past assumptions about pricing strategy and tactics must be re-evaluated.

The key challenge is how to create value in a total marketing offering through the use of price and other marketing mix variables. The automobile rebates discussed earlier were highly successful in boosting short-run sales in the industry. But some advertising specialists have warned that the industry still has failed to create a product that has solid value for car buyers.[16]

**SOCIAL
VIEWPOINT**

Traditional economic theories of market behavior place price at the heart of the economy. According to these theories, price functions as a means of resource allocation in the private sector. (Decisions in the public sector are generally made through the political process.) In addition, the price mechanism influences the welfare of consumers.

Jennifer Cross, author of *The Supermarket Trap*, argues that consumers should have an opportunity to save on prices.[17] She claims that a careful and selective consumer can reduce food bills by 10 to 20 percent. But, as Cross observes, the food industry has many built-in obstacles for the consumer, including dubious benefits such as trading stamps, premiums, and promotional games. Cross urges consumers to make active efforts to defend their rights, but points out that the overwhelming number of competitive choices tends to paralyze many consumers.

The social issue of administered pricing is especially complex. Some economists believe that price leadership in a highly concentrated industry tends to produce unusually high prices. Other economists argue that there is little difference between price changes in concentrated and unconcentrated industries. The question of whether concentration has inflationary effects—and helps promote unemployment and recession—remains a subject of intense debate and controversy.

Some theorists feel that higher costs and prices can actually benefit the consumer. In their view, "higher costs may produce a better product or add valuable services."[18] While this may be true in many cases, the possible side effects of inflation can be negative. It has also been argued that efficiency, rather than high prices, is actually the key variable in building corporate profits.

CONCLUSION

To administer prices, an organization must have a certain degree of flexibility and well-defined techniques for structuring prices. Price-change strategy means that the organization must weigh consumer and competitor reactions when making changes. These are two essential tasks of pricing strategy.

Price flexibility is an important part of price administration. Marketers want to know what options in the price structure would raise or lower the price of a product. Price flexibility is affected not only by market conditions but also by legal constraints.

There are many types of adjustments to prices. Among these are consumer-related adjustments (psychological pricing, odd pricing, price lining, leasing); discounts on prices (trade, quantity, and cash discounts); and geographical adjustments (supplier- and destination-based systems).

Price-change strategy is a complex process that works best when a firm is committed to careful planning and research. The reactions of consumers and competitors must be weighed before any price change is initiated, or before a firm responds to the price change of a competitor.

With this chapter, we conclude our discussion of pricing and its function within the marketing mix. We have seen that pricing is the translation of a product's value into dollars and cents. This dollar value may be arrived at by various methods, including cost-oriented pricing, demand-oriented pricing, and competition-oriented pricing.

Whatever method is chosen, the price arrived at will have an impact on the other elements in the marketing mix, and on consumers and society as well.

DISCUSSION QUESTIONS

1. What degree of price flexibility would you expect to find among polyvinyl chloride makers, surfboard renters, photography studios, and men's clothing stores?
2. How would these consumer-related price adjustments apply to these products:
   a. psychological pricing—sun glasses;
   b. odd pricing—small, used computers;
   c. price lining—motel rooms.
3. Which of these products' pricing strategy would be subject to trade, quantity, and/or cash discounts: X-ray supplies, life insurance, mobile homes, and Florida oranges?
4. Explain how freight terms affect pricing in these long-distance selling situations:
   a. Hallmark Cards, St. Louis, Missouri, bills a card shop in Waco, Texas, for greeting cards.
   b. A shipment of fried noodles from a San Francisco, California, manufacturer goes through three price zones to a restaurant in Boise, Idaho.
   c. A furniture manufacturer in Shreveport, Louisiana, uses High Point,

North Carolina, as the basing point for an order going to Chattanooga, Tennessee.

5. How would these promotional-pricing techniques be applied to these products:
   a. leader pricing—a travel agent;
   b. customer-category discounts—a campus theater;
   c. promotional allowances—a dairy products company;
   d. price-reducing specials—Gronkowski Opticians, Langhorn, Pennsylvania.
   e. retail markdowns—a florist in downtown San Antonio, Texas, late Friday afternoon.

6. What consumer and competitor reactions to a price change would be relevant under these circumstances:
   a. Sears, Roebuck lowers the price of its central air conditioning units.
   b. AT&T raises the price for its business telephone equipment rentals.
   c. Seven-Up bottlers lower the price of their beverage.

NOTES

1. "Supplier Encourages Do-It-Yourself Pricing," *Industrial Distributor*, April 1975, p. 64.
2. This section is based largely on Donald V. Harper, *Price Policy and Procedure* (New York: Harcourt Brace Jovanovich, 1966), pp. 173–75, 235–40.
3. "Pricing Strategy in an Inflation Economy," *Business Week*, April 6, 1974, pp. 45–46.
4. Benson P. Shapiro, "The Psychology of Pricing," *Harvard Business Review* 46 (July–August 1968): 18.
5. Dik Warren Twedt, "Does the '9 Fixation' in Retail Pricing Really Promote Sales?" *Journal of Marketing* 29 (October 1965): 54–55.
6. Kent B. Monroe, "Buyers' Subjective Perceptions of Price," *Journal of Marketing Research* 10 (February 1973): 70.
7. *Business Week*, July 14, 1975, p. 100.
8. Harper, p. 287; Louis W. Stern and John R. Grabner, Jr., *Competition in the Marketplace* (Glenview, Ill.: Scott, Foresman, 1970), p. 121.

9. "The New Price-Cut Phase," *Chain Store Age*, May 1975, pp. 40–41.
10. Grey Advertising, Inc., *Grey Matter* 46 (1975): 1.
11. Albert Wesley Frey, ed., *Marketing Handbook* (New York: Ronald Press, 1965), p. 8;33; Harper, p. 291.
12. Philip Kotler, *Marketing Management: Analysis, Planning, and Control*, 3d ed. (Englewood Cliffs, N.J.: Prentice-Hall, 1976), pp. 261–62.
13. E. Raymond Corey, *Industrial Marketing* (Englewood Cliffs, N.J.: Prentice-Hall, 1962), pp. 222–23.
14. Ibid., p. 224.
15. Shapiro, p. 14.
16. Grey Advertising, Inc., *Grey Matter* 46 (1975): 3–4.
17. Jennifer Cross, *The Supermarket Trap* (Bloomington, Ind.: Indiana University Press, 1970).
18. F. E. Brown and A. R. Oxenfeldt, "Should Prices Depend on Costs?" *MSU Business Topics* 16 (Autumn 1968): 77.

CASE STUDIES

THE CENTER FOR NEW BEHAVIOR

A New Way to Kick the Habit

The Center for New Behavior (CNB) packages "Sease-Smoking Cruises" to Caribbean islands such as Martinique and the Bahamas. The Miami-based firm was conceived by Willie T. Kleinrock, 39, who left East Germany in 1955 and became a successful insurance broker in Venezuela. Kleinrock defines himself as an "inventor and idea man."

In 1971, Kleinrock determined that many chain-smokers might want to come together to "kick the habit" in a pleasant, luxurious atmosphere. He established the CNB, hired ten consulting psychiatrists and psychologists to devise an antismoking program, and chartered a boat. Chet Ragus, a Miami management consultant, became the chairman of CNB. Seven business associates of Kleinrock contributed an initial capital outlay of more than $250,000. Of this sum, $65,000 went for initial advertising budget, $10,000 for other administrative expenses, and $220,000 for the ship rental and the crew.

Laura English, a Baltimore schoolteacher who smokes three packs of cigarettes daily, has signed up to sail on the CNB two-week cruise to Nassau, departing November 20. She and her shipmates will be paying an average of $1,500 for the voyage, with the most desirable staterooms running as high as $2,200.

Laura learned of the cruise by reading the travel section of the Sunday *New York Times* of September 19. On that date, Rockwell Advertising Agency placed promotional notices for the CNB cruise in leading newspapers in New York, Boston, Philadelphia, Washington, and Chicago. Laura English was fascinated by the idea of combining seminars and self-hypnosis sessions with swimming, movies, and elegant dining.

Rockwell account executive Aida Turell originally estimated that 300 people would sign up for the cruise after reading the September 19 ads. But, as of October 18, only 200 had done so, and Kleinrock and CNB faced an important decision.

Not Enough Passengers

"Here's the situation as I see it," explained a disturbed Willie Kleinrock at the CNB board meeting. "We've already laid out more than a quarter of a million to get this cruise rolling. It's going to cost us roughly $200 per passenger for the two weeks, mostly for food. Rockwell predicted that 300 people would respond to the advertising campaign, but the fact is that we're just under 200.

"I see three basic options: (1) we cancel the cruise and take our losses; (2) we run the cruise with the 200 and a few more that will trickle in over the next month; or (3) we shell out some more money and hope that we can pull in many more people.

"My recommendation to this board is that we try to recruit more passengers. There are simply too many empty rooms on that boat. Each one costs us a bundle."

At this point, Aida Turell addressed the board: "I've worked out two possible advertising campaigns for the October 24 papers. The first, the limited campaign, will cost $6,000. I estimate it will bring in 20 more passengers. The more ambitious campaign, which I personally recommend, would cost CNB another $15,000. I believe this campaign will bring in a *minimum* of 40 more passengers.

"I realize that our first attempt was somewhat disappointing. But we're dealing here with a new concept, and a follow-up ad might work with many newspaper readers who were curious and interested when they read our first notice.

"One thing is absolutely certain," Turell emphasized. "We must act *immediately* if there's any hope of getting more people on board. The deadline for the Sunday papers is in less than 48 hours. And if our ads don't appear by this weekend, you can forget it. No one signs up in early November for a November 20 sailing date."

Kleinrock interrupted, shaking his head. "I just don't know what to say. I've looked over Aida's proposals, and they're excellent. Absolutely first-rate. But our problem, to be blunt, is money. Our funds are tight, and our investors are already nervous. I get more calls each day, asking me where the 300 passengers are. It won't be easy to squeeze another $6,000 out of these people. And $15,000—well, I just don't know how we can justify it."

Questions

1. What is the minimum number of passengers that CNB must plan to sign up by October 18 in order to break even with the Sease-Smoking Cruise?
2. Because CNB has actually signed up 200 passengers by October 18, should it go ahead with the cruise?
3. Would it be worthwhile for CNB to spend either $6,000 or $15,000 for advertising on October 24?

NORTHERN UTILITY COMPANY

The Time-of-Day Rates Concept

The Northern Utility Company is the largest utility in New Hampshire. It provides electricity for some 100,000 customers. But Northern Utility is currently in difficult financial shape, due in part to the public's spiralling demand for electrical power during peak periods of the day.

In September, 1975, the Northern Utility Board approved the concept of time-of-day rates for billing. Under the board's ruling, Northern Utility was allowed to experiment with such billing by charging selected customers more than six times as much to use electricity from 8 A.M. to 11 A.M. and 5 P.M. to 9 P.M. as it charged at other times.

Erik S. Briggs, the president of Northern Utility, was relatively neutral on the idea of time-of-day pricing. In an effort to better evaluate this alternative, he asked two marketing trainees, Julia Wong and Carl Whitehall, to study and report on the advantages and disadvantages of time-of-day metering.

**Evaluating
Time-of-Day Rates**

The meeting was held in Briggs' office. Present were Briggs, various senior staff personnel of Northern Utility, and marketing trainees Julia Wong and Carl Whitehall. Briggs opened the meeting: "As all of you know, Julia and Carl have been hard at work during the past four months studying time-of-day metering. Today, we will hear their conclusions. Carl, why don't you begin?"

Carl Whitehall approached a blackboard filled with statistics. "The main reason we should pursue the idea of time-of-day pricing is that both the consumer and the company will benefit. Look at these figures I have here.

"Under this plan, an expensive kilowatt hour would cost 9.86 cents, while an off-peak kilowatt hour would cost 1.52 cents. Let's translate that into a common electricity need. Once a week, I do one load of laundry. An hour of drying would cost me 60 cents during peak hours. During off-peak hours, it would cost me only 9 cents!

"Extend this over a year, for a typical family, and the data is even more striking. I calculate that the average middle-income household could cut $520 off its electric bill through intelligent use of off-peak electric power. In a decade of inflation and unemployment, that's no small saving."

At this point, Julia Wong interrupted. "I agree with everything you've said so far, Carl. But you're overlooking an important point. Very few customers will be eligible for this saving. We've got permission to institute this pricing for only 30,000 people in one section of the state.

"Furthermore, this system of metering is terribly expensive. It costs $25 to wire an appliance into the 'ripple control' mechanism, and that's only experimental. Full conversion to the new rates would cost an average of $375 per household for new equipment.

"Who's going to pay for all this? Sure, the National Science Foundation has been giving grants for testing time-of-day metering, but they're not going to pay for rewiring the whole state. The consumers aren't going to pay $375 for new meters, most of them don't have that kind of extra money lying around.

"I just think this plan has too many pitfalls. The money, the installation work, the resistance from the public to *any* new billing system; there are so many ways we could run into trouble. And it will take 15 years or more to find out if the experiment can really reduce Northern Utility's costs. We could go broke long before then."

Carl returned to the conference table. "I know there's cause for concern; I know that Julia's presentation has a lot of merit. But, remember, this type of pricing alternative has broad national support. The Environmental Defense Fund, Federal Energy Administration chief, the staff of two other state regulatory commissions—all have voiced the need for time-of-day metering.

"I believe this metering *can* save the consumer enough money to change electricity demand patterns. And *if* it works, *if* we can spread energy usage around the clock more evenly, Northern Utility can reap enormous benefits. We won't have to keep building inefficient, high-cost peaking units. Instead, we can concentrate on efficient, baseload generating plants.

"Both the consumer and the company can benefit from this plan. And, in the long run, so will the nation. We can get along with less power plants, and there will be many fewer brownouts and blackouts at peak electricity periods."

Julia Wong looked at President Erik Briggs. "It's a beautiful vision, but I just don't buy it. There are too many financial risks, too many uncertainties, too much speculation. This isn't a roulette game!"

Questions
1. What are the major forces affecting Northern Utility's pricing strategy?
2. What would be your evaluation of time-of-day metering?
3. What other types of marketing strategy could Northern Utility use to make time-of-day metering succeed?

AMERICAN STEEL COMPANY

American Steel Company holds more than $2.6 billion in worldwide assets. The firm owns steel plants, shipyards, and manufacturing facilities in many parts of the United States, and mining properties all over the world. In 1970, American Steel registered sales of $2.7 billion—thus accounting for 14.9 percent of all domestic steel shipments.

In the past decade, under the leadership of chairman Bernard M. O'Brien, American Steel has earned an impressive reputation as the price leader and policeman of the steel industry. As a leading business magazine notes, "Whether American Steel is raising, lowering, or freezing prices, its goal is to set the pace for the industry."

Price Setting Meets with Government Opposition

The scene was an elegant mansion in a suburb of Pittsburgh—the home of American Steel chairman O'Brien. Meeting with O'Brien was Wayne L. Levchuk, the firm's president. This was no ordinary business meeting or social chat. In January, 1976, American Steel had issued a brief statement announcing an 8.7 percent net increase on plates and structural steel products. The statement anticipated the end of a one-year voluntary price freeze on these items. Company officials expected that American Steel's solid reputation would promote wide acceptance of this hefty price hike.

But their expectations proved to be incorrect. The White House reacted angrily to the firm's statement, and made clear its intention to force a reduction in the desired price increase. As American Steel leaders O'Brien and Levchuk met at O'Brien's house, each knew that the prospect of a difficult battle with the federal government was just around the corner.

Two Views on Pricing

Levchuk spoke first. "Look, Bernie, we need this increase! It's as simple as that! Our profits were down by 39 percent last year. The industry as a whole was down 36 percent. These products account for more than a third of all industry shipments. It's the only way we can make up for the losses we've been taking. And, with a strike threat over our heads for August, we can't afford to pass up this opportunity."

O'Brien peered glumly at the figures in front of him. "Yes, Wayne, I know what you're getting at. I know we need that margin. But we can't get caught up in the short-run outlook.

"I became president of American in 1969. Ever since then, my stand on pricing has been clear and well known. Price selling doesn't have any place in an industrial market. If this is the only way we can survive, we're really in trouble.

"Our firm has made a dedicated commitment to maintaining price stability. The industry won't survive otherwise. Sure, the difference between a 5.7 percent increase and an 8.7 percent increase would mean badly needed revenue for us. But what about the long-range picture? What about the steel industry in 1990? We need to make sure that there *will be* a steel industry in 1990."

Wayne Levchuk got up from his chair and began nervously pacing the room. "Bernie, I've always supported you on these policies. I want to support you this time, too. But how can we talk about 1990 when our profits dropped 39 percent last year? When industry profits have been dangerously static for a decade before that? When steel consumption may not even grow by 3 percent in the next decade?

"Bernie, if we don't get a decent price hike now, American Steel may not be around in 1980 to worry about 1990."

"I understand, Wayne, I really do. But you're forgetting a critical factor. Even if I supported price selling—which I don't—we can't forget the White House. They're really mad at us, and we can't buck them. There's no way to win. If they want us to get no more than 6 percent, that's all we'll get. We can fight a bloody battle and lose, or we can concede gracefully. But, either way, we *will* lose in the end.

"I see no alternative other than recommending to the board that we scale down our increase."

Questions
1. How should American Steel respond to the government's opposition to the 8.7 percent price hike?
2. What pricing objectives would be appropriate for American Steel?
3. What price strategy would help American Steel face the future marketing environment?

Promotion

CHAPTER

17

MARKETING COMMUNICATION AND PROMOTION STRATEGY

After completing this chapter, the reader should be able to:

1. Explain the benefits of promotion for the consumer, management, and society.

2. Diagram the communication process that takes place between marketers and consumers.

3. Explain how the promotion mix is determined.

4. Define the decisions that must be made concerning the promotion budget.

5. Distinguish between the promotion strategies of sales promotion and publicity.

The third major marketing strategy element is **promotion**. It is based on the need of the marketer to communicate with consumers. This chapter gives an overview of integrated marketing communication and the promotion strategy decisions. Two individual elements of the promotion mix—advertising and personal selling—will be featured in the following two chapters.

THE DOWN-UNDER DISCO

Sylvia Plachy/Magnum

Brian Zyk, a 29-year-old architect and real estate magnate in Melbourne, Australia, plans to open a new discotheque. Zyk has consulted marketing experts in planning his new venture and has developed a sophisticated strategy for building a successful enterprise.

Zyk is working from a particular type of enterprise concept that he hopes will give him a distinct advantage over local competitors. One element is the American idea of the discotheque. Admissions policy is another critical element in Zyk's strategy. He plans to maintain a high cover charge to attract a young, affluent, "swinging" clientele—while keeping beverage and food prices low. A final important element in Zyk's enterprise concept is layout and decor. He has hired a young highly professional, Australian architectural firm to design "Cape Kennedy." The firm intends to integrate the American theme through various visual techniques.

Zyk's overall promotional plans include advertising, publicity, sales promotion, and personal selling. The opening of the new discotheque will be a highly publicized event, complete with a "name" rock band, various American and Australian music and entertainment celebrities, and one free drink per customer during the first weekend. There will be an exhaustive advertising barrage, with special emphasis on radio commercials. Zyk has instituted a number of sales promotion devices, including American gourmet dishes and discount prices on Tuesday and Wednesday nights. In addition, he has invested in a personal selling campaign by hiring the popular Melbourne disc jockey Tom Smythe as a weekend host and assistant manager.

PROMOTING THE MARKETING OFFERING

Promotion has been defined as "the coordination of all seller-initiated efforts to set up channels of information and persuasion to facilitate the sale of a good or service, or the acceptance of an idea."[1] In formulating his promotional strategy, Brian Zyk was guided by two major concerns: (1) projecting an image that would appeal to his target market of young Australian swingers, and (2) integrating his promotional efforts into a carefully designed enterprise concept geared to consumer preferences.

The role of promotion in marketing strategy is illustrated in Figure 17-1. As we have seen in previous chapters, marketing strategy is determined by the

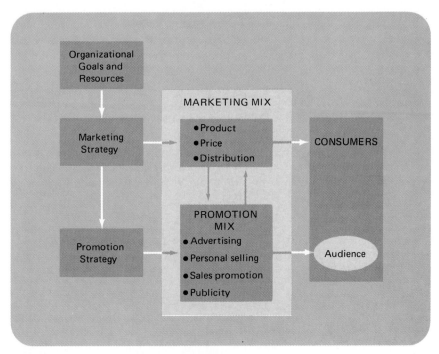

Figure 17-1   PROMOTION IN A MARKETING CONTEXT

overall goals and resources of the organization. In turn, the marketing strategy determines the **promotion strategy**. As a part of the marketing mix, promotion strategy is affected by decisions concerning product, price, and distribution. For example, some prices, such as those labeled "prestige" or "discount," are more easily promoted than others. There is also a **promotion mix**, consisting of a combination of strategy elements (advertising, personal selling, sales promotion, and publicity).

Promotion overcomes consumer ignorance concerning a situation by providing **information** about the organization, product and brand attributes, prices, availability, and uses of the product. Promotion also overcomes consumer inertia by using **persuasion** to create a favorable psychological association. This may induce a consumer to act as the promoter wishes.

The general business rule is that promotion truly makes a difference, assuming that the product has some real merit and the other marketing mix elements are compatible. A dramatic example is given in the accompanying box on p. 400.

In the 1970s, **marketing communication** became a key ingredient in marketing strategy. As we saw in Chapters 11–13, the product communicates a distinct image—such as respectability, conservation, or youthfulness. The brand name suggests various physical and psychological attributes of the product. The package can carry a message that the manufacturer of the product really cares about the consumer—or that he or she is saying "take it or leave it." The price (Chapters 14–16) is taken by consumers as a significant index of quality. Even retail stores can be said to communicate noticeable "brand" images and personalities. Thus, all of the vital elements of the marketing mix

**IT PAYS TO
PROMOTE PEOPLE**

can help or hinder communication (and eventually sales) efforts.

We generally think of communication strategy in terms of marketing
within the business world. Yet advertising, personal selling, and other promotional techniques have gained greater acceptance in other areas of American life, including the work of nonprofit organizations. Marketing consultants
are busy promoting political candidates, aid to higher education, family planning, highway safety, and physical fitness.

THREE DIMENSIONS OF PROMOTION

It is helpful to think of marketing communication as a transaction. Both the communicator (the marketer) and the receiver (the buyer) contribute something,
and each wants to gain some advantage from the communication. Society also
has an interest in how promotion functions.

**THE CONSUMER
DIMENSION**

The consumer derives both direct and indirect benefits from promotion. Direct
and immediate benefits to the consumer include the following:[2]

1. *Promotion arouses desire.* Promotional activities are aimed at the individual identity and feelings of the consumer. The marketer is always there,
reminding consumers of what they want, what they need, what they do not
have, what they fantasize, what their neighbors have, and so forth.

2. *Promotion informs.* Promotional messages actually bring concrete information to the consumer—here is our new product, it can perform the following tasks, it costs so much (and less than the product you are now using),
it comes in the following sizes, it carries the following guarantees.

3. *Promotion entertains.* We all know that television and radio commercials and even magazine advertisements can be entertaining. They can make
us laugh, identify with a character, even sing along with a McDonald's jingle.

4. *Promotion influences.* Promotion builds on our hopes and fantasies to

400

provide images of what life might be like. In a sense, people buy these expectations when they buy the product. When a consumer buys a Honda motorcycle, he or she is buying more than transportation. This purchase expresses a desire for control, freedom, speed, and/or sex.

The consumer also derives various indirect benefits from promotion. These include subsidizing mass media and generally supporting an economy that expands through new products.

THE MANAGEMENT DIMENSION

The viewpoint of the promoter is that of any communicator. He or she intends to share an idea with a receiver (consumer), and encourage the receiver to act in a certain way.

Figure 17-2 illustrates the effects of promotion on the demand curve. The main goal of promotion activities is to shift the demand curve to the right (from D_1 to D_2). In other words, promotion is used to maintain the price while increasing sales, or to raise the price while maintaining the sales level.[3] Each effort, if successful, will result in higher sales income.

In Chapter 6, we described marketing as a form of demand management. We can now see that promotion may be used to influence demand in the following ways:[4]

1. *To increase or maintain high sales.* A firm has three general approaches

Figure 17-2   EFFECTS OF PROMOTION ON THE DEMAND CURVE

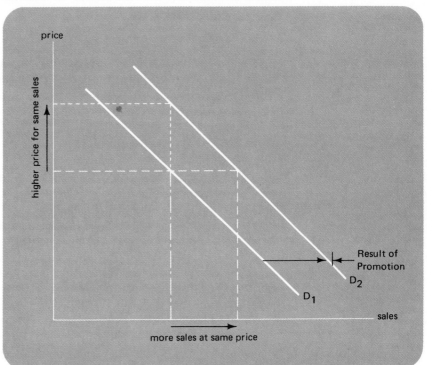

for using promotion to achieve or maintain a high sales level. It can place intensified pressure on salespersons, distributors, and consumers through incentive programs, special sales, coupons, and other unusual favors. (One California appliance retailer offered 100 free McDonald's hamburgers with the purchase of a television or stereo.) The firm can redirect its advertising strategies to improve the image of the company or brand. Finally, it can aim promotion at special market segments.

2. *To reverse declining sales.* Promotional work often is at the center of a firm's efforts to revive a sinking product. Lysol, a 100-year-old product, is a good example.[5] In the 1960s it seemed that Lysol disinfectant was a dying brand. But strategic marketing reversed this. Lysol was positioned as a laundry aid; advertisements convinced consumers that it fought germs in the wash. It was promoted for cleaning bathrooms, toilet bowls, basins, and tile. During garbage strikes, it was advertised as a killer of odor and germs; during rainy spells, it was advertised as a killer of mold and mildew. As a result, in the mid-1970s Lysol captured more than half of the disinfectant market.

3. *To demarket.* Because of the energy crisis and increased ecological and consumer awareness, marketers are now more than ever using promotional techniques for demarketing. Some utilities, instead of encouraging energy consumption, are promoting conservation of energy.

4. *To launch new products.* Here the promotional goal is to teach the consumer about the attributes and advantages of an unfamiliar product. There is no prior experience with the product and the potential buyer has few preconceived notions. Thus, marketers have a real opportunity to promote a new and different image.

THE SOCIETAL
DIMENSION

Promotional practices are an important societal concern. Promotional strategies affect many contemporary political and social issues, including waste disposal, media control, private consumption vs. general welfare, deceptive advertising practices, and differing judgments about good taste.

Criticism of promotion is greatest when the product is one that some people disapprove of, such as cigarettes or liquor. Even when the product is socially acceptable, however, promotion may still be objectionable. Many consumers see the promotional message as separate from the product. They believe that the promotional message is used to pressure them to evaluate the product on some basis other than its merits.

A key question for promotion is "when does *informing* become *persuading* and when does *persuading* become *deceiving*?"[6] The answer to this question is complicated by the fact that the same communication may mislead some persons and not others. Recent regulatory efforts have focused on the *capacity* of an advertising message to mislead, rather than on the intent of its marketers or the fact of deception. Meanwhile, the consumer movement has pressed for more informative and less "persuasive" marketing communications.

A common form of potentially misleading advertising is **puffery**. It occurs when a marketer describes his or her product in superlatives and uses exaggeration—the best, finest, most efficient. The Federal Trade Commission has attacked claims that seem to imply specific facts that are not true. In some cases, it has asked firms to document their claims with product tests and opinion polls.

In 1974, the National Organization for Women (NOW) attacked the puffery of National Airlines' "fly me" advertisements.[7] Previously, NOW had persistently criticized these ads for being sexist and demeaning to stewardesses and all women. In early 1975, it changed its strategy and charged that the ads were deceptive. It asked the FTC to require National to substantiate such claims as "I'm going to fly you like you've never been flown before."

To avoid this type of conflict in the future, Stanley Tannenbaum, chairman of Kenyon and Eckhardt advertising agency, has developed a set of guidelines for proper and ethical advertising.[8] His main recommendations are:

1. Don't mislead the average consumer.

2. Don't abuse research findings.

3. Be accurate and fair in making comparisons with the products of competitors.

4. Any endorsements should tell of personal use.

PROMOTION IN A MARKETING COMMUNICATION PERSPECTIVE

As we noted earlier in this chapter, promotion is a form of marketing communication. In order to understand how promotion works, we must first develop an understanding of the **communication process** itself.

THE COMMUNICATION PROCESS

The communication process consists of six basic elements:

communicator—the sender or the source of the message;

message—the set of meanings being sent and/or received by the audience;

channels—the ways in which messages can be carried or delivered to the audience;

audience—the receiver or the destination of the message;

results—feedback to the communicator concerning what the audience learned or how they behaved;

noise—conditions that distort the communication process.

The communication process begins when the sender decides what idea he or she wants to get across. Since the sender wants the receiver to understand the message, he or she learns as much as possible about the receiver before deciding on the form and content of the message that contains the idea. The receiver getting the message will attempt to understand it and may (or may not) choose to send a return message (feedback). At any point in the process noise can inhibit the effectiveness of communication. Noise includes poor message planning, inappropriate media selection, the competition's messages, busy audience members, and careless measurement of results.

**PROMOTION AS
COMMUNICATION**
With the communication process outlined above in mind, let's examine how promotion functions as a communication tool within the marketing strategy context.

Figure 17–3 presents a marketing communication model. As the model indicates, there are various ways in which marketers communicate with consumers. The controllable communications channels include the promotion mix and other marketing elements. Although word-of-mouth communication occurs mainly among consumers. it can be indirectly influenced by marketers (as we saw in Chapter 8). The reverse communication (feedback) involves results (attitudes and sales). Promotion mix elements—which are primarily communication approaches—are preceded by decisions concerning budgets, objectives, and messages.

Figure 17-3   A MARKETING COMMUNICATION MODEL

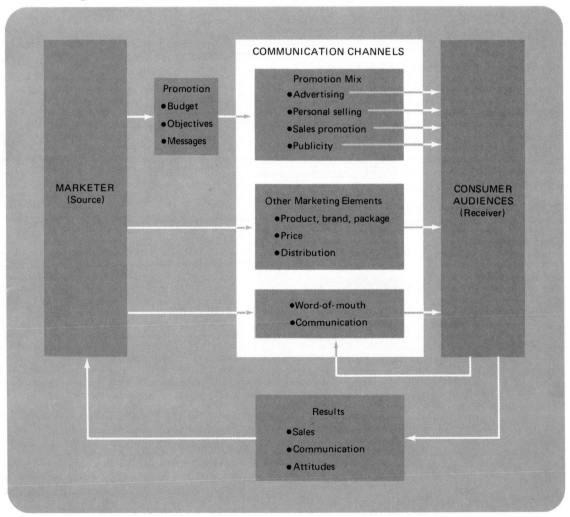

Let's take a closer look at the key variables in the model in Figure 17–3:

1. *Audience.* An audience may be defined as "any group of people who can be thought of as having some more or less common characteristics of interest to the marketer, and to whom he wishes to address himself to achieve some marketing purpose."[9]

The first rule of mass communications is to "know your audience." This means refining the specific groups that you will address, and determining the relevant needs and goals of the target market. As Philip Kotler has explained, "The communicator must start with the audience because the audience determines *what* is to be said, *how* it is to be said, *when* it is to be said, *where* it is to be said, and *who* is to say it."[10]

Audiences must fulfill two important marketing criteria. First, there must be enough of a target population to justify the costs of the communication. Second, the audience must include a sufficient number of persons who want the sender's product or brand, and who are able to pay for it. If the audience does not meet these criteria, the sender is probably wasting time and money in pursuing this target market.

2. *Objectives.* Promotion is most likely to be successful when a firm begins with clear, realistic, and carefully researched objectives. A good example is the decision to strive for primary or selective demand. If the makers of Maxwell House coffee feel that their sales will benefit most from a promotion of the product class as a whole, they will undertake **primary promotion**. Their advertising will focus on the benefits of coffee (perhaps as opposed to tea or other beverages) for consumers. If the firm believes that its sales will benefit most from promoting its own individual brand, it will engage in **selective promotion**. In this case, advertising will focus on why Maxwell House is a better brand than others on the market.

3. *Messages.* There are two fundamental decisions in message strategy: what is to be said and how it is to be said. The most recent development in message strategy within marketing has been the concept of market positioning (introduced in Chapter 7). The product can be positioned by promotional appeals (Seven-Up is the Uncola), as well as by product characteristics, so that it becomes the choice of a target market. All messages must be formulated with the product's market position in mind.

4. *Communications channels.* There are four principal communications channels available to the marketing manager: media (television, radio, newspapers, direct mail), face-to-face (salespeople), publicity (news releases), and word-of-mouth (among consumers). Of course, as we noted earlier, *all* marketing elements (product design, packaging, pricing, and so forth) communicate with buyers in one way or another.

A marketer often uses more than one channel of communication at the same time, since the two channels may reinforce each other's influence. Prudential Insurance uses television advertising so that its sales representatives may make more appointments with potential customers.

The task of selecting the most effective communications channels for the firm's promotional work is made simpler when an organization has defined its market segments clearly. The manager can then consult market research to determine which channels are most appropriate for reaching the target audience.

5. *Source.* A marketing message can come from the company manufacturing the product, the retailer who sells the product, the salespeople or announcers in commercials, and/or the media as a whole. The reaction of an audience to a promotional message is greatly influenced by the audience's feelings about the source of the message. Receivers may not be willing even to "receive" a message if it comes from a disliked source.

6. *Results.* Marketers face a number of critical problems in evaluating the results of various promotional efforts. Feedback can arrive in somewhat hazy ways, such as consumer sales or mass audience norms (10 percent of the readers of the magazine read 50 percent of our copy). Such data are not easy to analyze, for there are many factors involved in the decision to buy or not buy, and in responses to advertising campaigns. Also, most feedback on mass media promotion comes weeks or even months afterwards. This makes marketing analysis even more difficult.

PROMOTION STRATEGY

Promotion influences demand by communicating pro-product and pro-company messages to the marketplace. Promotion strategy involves the coordination of all communication efforts aimed at specific audiences: consumers, stockholders, dealers, government, and so forth.

THE PROMOTION MIX

The promotion mix is usually coordinated on a **campaign** basis, making the campaign the relevant unit of promotion strategy. The campaign may last for a few weeks, months, or the year; or, if successful, it may run over several years (for example, Avis' "We Try Harder" theme). The most desirable marketing effort includes a total campaign with one unified theme. All promotional messages tie into this theme in one way or another, rather than conflicting with it.

As we have seen, the promotion mix consists of four basic elements: advertising, personal selling, publicity, and sales promotion. We will define these elements as follows:[11]

1. *Advertising:* any paid form of nonpersonal presentation and promotion of ideas, goods, or services by an identified sponsor.

2. *Personal selling:* oral presentation in a conversation with one or more prospective purchasers for the purpose of making sales.

3. *Sales promotion:* those marketing activities, other than personal selling, advertising, and publicity, that stimulate consumer purchasing and dealer effectiveness, such as displays, shows and exhibitions, demonstrations, and various nonrecurrent efforts not in the ordinary routine.

4. *Publicity:* nonpersonal stimulation of demand for a product, service, or business unit by planting commercially significant news about it in a published medium or obtaining favorable presentation of it upon radio, television, or stage that is not paid for by the sponsor.

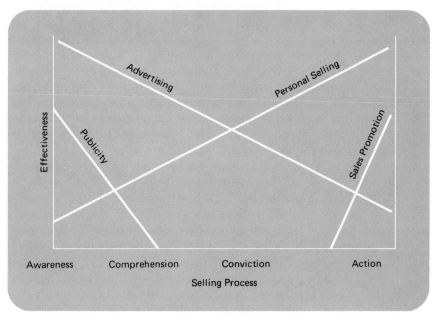

Figure 17-4   PROMOTION MIX DURING THE SELLING PROCESS

Figure 17–4 represents the role of the four promotion mix elements in the selling process (based on the stages an individual buyer and market segment go through). *Publicity* is generally effective in the awareness stage. *Advertising* becomes less and less effective over a period of time. *Personal selling* becomes more effective as consumer needs dictate a more personal relationship. (Products can succeed on advertising alone although a combination of advertising and personal selling techniques is usually desirable.) *Sales promotion* can be effective in providing added incentives for buyer action.

As we discussed earlier, it is difficult to arrive at the best kind of promotion mix. The results of promotional efforts are hard to measure, and we do not fully understand what a particular medium can do for one product as opposed to another. Most marketing managers will select more than one channel to promote a product. Their choices will be affected by the nature of the intended audience, the kind of message they wish to send, and the kind of action they want to get. The advantages and disadvantages of the four promotion elements may be balanced off against each other. These advantages and disadvantages are summarized in Figure 17–5.

Effectiveness indicates how much impact the element has on communicating and persuading to action. **Efficiency** indicates how much you get for the cost involved. The cost dimension of personal selling, however, may be a major liability for marketers. In a two-year period, 1971 to 1973, the cost of an average industrial sales call jumped from $57.71 to $66.68, a rise of 16 percent.[12] By comparison, a television commercial "message" to a prospective buyer may cost the sender only a few cents (or less) per person. The figures point out a real paradox in mass market promotional techniques. Advertising, which is probably the most efficient channel in terms of costs vs. results, is also the least effective as a communication tool.

Bob Haley, the controversial coach of Metuchin College's varsity basketball team (commonly known as "Haley's Comets") could be considered a marketing expert. He approaches player recruitment with all of the intensity, intelligence, and calculation of a top-level planner for General Motors.

Haley, his assistant coaches, and friendly alumni identify the target market (top high school basketball players) by studying statistics and visiting high schools around the country. Then Haley outlines his sales approach (the unique benefits of studying and playing ball at Metuchin) for his recruiters. Each recruiter is given a territory (a part of the country), a travel schedule, and various sales aids (films of Metuchin, newspaper clippings on "Haley's Comets," and so forth).

Once prospects are contacted by Haley and his recruiters, they are offered the option of a trial period (an all-expenses-paid visit to the campus, along with a chance to meet the coach and practice with the team). The recruiting pitch is coordinated with other college departments, including Admissions and Financial Aid.

"Bob Haley" is a fictional character based on Frederick E. Webster, Jr., *Social Aspects of Marketing* (Englewood Cliffs, N.J.: Prentice-Hall, 1974), p. 89.

**DETERMINING THE
PROMOTION MIX**

Aside from the effectiveness/efficiency differences of the promotion mix elements, the following factors should be considered in arriving at the promotion mix:

1. *Life-cycle stage.* The concept of the product life cycle was introduced in Chapter 11. According to this concept, a product moves through five stages—introduction, growth, maturity, saturation, and decline. The promotional emphasis changes with each stage.

During the introductory period, buyers must be informed about the new product. Personal selling may be useful, especially with industrial goods. The promotion task may center on generating primary demand rather than selective demand for the individual brand.

During the growth phase, the marketer aims at higher volume and a sizable

Figure 17-5   RELATIVE ADVANTAGES OF PROMOTION MIX ELEMENTS

	Efficient	Effective
PERSONAL SELLING	High	Low
NONPERSONAL SELLING (Advertising, Sales promotion, Publicity)	Low	High

share of the market. Promotional work has as its main goal selective demand—establishing the desirability of the marketer's brand. Profits are high during this stage, and the firm may allocate high budgets to corner a substantial brand share.

In the maturity and saturation phases, a balanced promotion mix is used to maintain the sales level. In the decline phase, manufacturing and marketing costs (including promotion) are reduced. The firm may turn increasingly to personal selling rather than advertising. It may also invest in new market research to locate areas of weakness or possible improvement.

2. *Type of product.* The characteristics of a product may dictate its "natural" audience. A nondifferentiated product (detergents) may be promoted with psychological advertising. A product with hidden emotional qualities (cosmetics) will be given a careful and subtle mass media promotion. A convenience good (cold remedies in winter) depends on mass advertising techniques. An industrial good (office copiers) is generally promoted through personal sales efforts.

Personal selling is given special emphasis when the buyer requires service and specialized knowledge (insurance or investments), when large sums of money are involved (real estate or automobile sales), and when products need a favorable shelf position (certain consumer goods). It is also used when the buyer seems to want advice, understanding, or personal support of one form or another (fine furniture or quality cameras).

3. *Size of budget.* The amount of money available is an obvious limitation on the choice of promotional channels. If the budget that an organization allocates for promotion is small, it may be impossible to buy enough mass media advertising for it to count. The organization may then rely on personal selling and publicity. A nonprofit organization may use volunteer "salespeople" and special fund-raising events.

4. *Push and pull strategies.* The key variable is the direction of influence in the distribution marketing channel. In a **push strategy**—generally used in industrial marketing—products have high unit value and need adjustment for consumer needs. Personal selling is the favored promotional channel. Dealers must promote the product line aggressively; thus, they are granted high margins and an exclusive distribution territory.

In a **pull strategy**, mass communications are emphasized. The marketer wants to create end-user demand. He or she hopes that customers will ask retail dealers for the product, retailers will demand it from wholesalers, and wholesalers will order it from the manufacturer. Advertising and sales promotion are stressed in beginning this cycle. Pull strategies are most effective with a product that has low unit value and is suitable for broad, public distribution. In most cases, marketers will use both push and pull strategies, but one is usually emphasized.

5. *Organization philosophy.* Paul Chammings has built a highly successful electrical contracting enterprise through the use of a "people-oriented" sales approach.[13] All shop mechanics are given special training to underscore their role as sales representatives of the firm. Special programs exist to preserve good customer relations, including a monthly publication *(Bits and Pieces)* and

even humorous business cards thanking customers for an order or noting a special occasion. As Chammings explains, "I'm convinced that you really can't survive on price alone. . . . I really believe that the key to success . . . is to know your customer, know his needs, and make the concept of selling a 24-hour, 100 percent effort involving everybody in the organization. If you look at it that way, how can you fail?"

BUDGETING THE PROMOTION MIX

How much should a firm spend on promotion? In order to determine this, a marketing manager must have estimates of the effects of communications allocations. He or she will often rely on computer planning models to project sales response estimates.

Ideally, a firm might choose to spend promotion funds up to the point where marginal cost equals marginal revenue. This formulation recalls our discussion of marginal analysis in a price-setting context in Chapter 14. Such analysis can also be used for promotion budget decisions. The problem lies in the difficulty of calculating the effect of promotion costs on sales. Also, the "payoff" from promotion may be realized only over a long period of time, further complicating economic projections.

The most common methods of setting a total promotion budget are the following:

1. *Percent of sales.* This is a simple, workable, and relatively safe way of handling the problem. A predetermined percentage of the firm's past sales revenue (or projected sales revenue) is allocated for promotion. However, this method avoids the important question: What is the relationship between advertising expenditures and sales revenue?

2. *Competitive parity.* There are various ways of applying the competitive parity method, but all are based on spending approximately the same amount or percentage of sales as one's competitors. This approach may be better than the methods previously described in that it recognizes competition as a key element in marketing and promotes stable relationships rather than market warfare. But competitive parity totally loses sight of the buyer.

3. *All-you-can-afford.* Some firms may spend whatever dollars are available for promotion, with the only limit being the firm's need for liquidity. This strategy can backfire very easily. The firm may actually end up spending more than it needs to, simply because the money is available. Or it may lose a golden opportunity simply because of the upper limits on its advertising.

4. *Objective and task.* The most desirable method of setting a promotion budget seems to be the objective and task approach. This method is goal oriented. The firm agrees on a set of marketing objectives after intensive market research. The costs of relevant promotional tasks are then calculated. Assuming that the resulting figure is within the firm's financial means, it becomes the promotional budget for the project.

The main problem with this approach is that it is not easy to determine the costs of fulfilling an objective or to decide whether an objective is worth fulfilling. Many firms eventually choose a realistic approach that seems valid in terms of marketing research for products, territories, or market segments. They estimate costs for each category and then total up the budget.

Promotion can be viewed as a long-run process. Product image and company reputation are built over time by continuous and related promotion elements. Thus, Joel Dean has argued that advertising should be seen as a business investment, in much the same sense as opening a new plant or spending additional funds on improved package design.[14] Treating advertising in this manner would require projections of the dollar return on advertising—or at least some sophisticated estimates.

SECONDARY PROMOTION ELEMENTS

Separate chapters will be devoted to advertising (Chapter 18) and personal selling (Chapter 19), the primary elements of the promotion mix. They are most frequently part of any promotion mix, and most often receive the largest share of the promotion budget. The so-called secondary elements—sales promotion and publicity—are covered more briefly in this chapter. These elements are secondary only in relation to the primary elements. They are still vital parts of the mix and in some cases may account for a larger part of the budget than either (or both) of the primary elements.

SALES PROMOTION

Sales promotion is a selling activity that coordinates advertising and personal selling into an effective persuasive force. It is claimed that sales promotion moves buyers toward the product. Well-known media of sales promotion include packages, samples, premiums, coupons, contests, and trading stamps. In some circles, sales promotion techniques are grouped together under the label "marketing services." The full range of responsibilities of sales promotion managers is described in Table 17–1.

Many sales promotion campaigns involve the use of incentives. **Incentives** are "something of financial value added to an offer to encourage some overt behavioral response."[15] They increase the presumed value of a product in the hope it will gain wider acceptance from consumers. Some of these sales promotion elements were discussed in Chapter 16 because of their close relationship to pricing (for example, leader pricing, trading stamps, and price-reducing specials).

It is important to add that sales promotion incentives are used by nonprofit organizations as well as profit-making ones. For example, charitable organizations typically have particular strategies aimed at offering "free" merchandise in order to increase contributions.

The following sales promotion methods are commonly used:

1. *Sampling.* One way of promoting a product is to give out free samples. When Procter & Gamble started manufacturing the detergent Top Job, it distributed millions of free samples. Marketers hope that sampling will encourage consumers to try out, and then purchase, the product. A free trial of a health club's facilities is a sampling of a service.

One problem of sampling is the cost. It is expensive not only to manufacture the product but also to distribute it across the country to consumers. Also, 20 percent of all samples are wasted. They either go to consumers who are not interested or to people who already use the product.

Table 17-1
PROMOTION RESPONSIBILITY OF THE SALES PROMOTION MANAGER

ACTIVITY	PRIMARY AND PART-TIME DUTIES (%)
Design and production of sales presentation kits, manuals, and other sales tools	98
Point-of-purchase displays and other materials	77
Direct mail to consumers, jobbers, distributors, and dealers	55
Incentive programs for sales organizations	88
Sales incentive programs (contests, premium plans, prize drawings, games, grand openings) for dealers and consumers	62
Shows and exhibits	66
Demonstrations	66
Sampling and couponing	54
Sales meetings	85
Sales training (company's own people, jobbers, distributors, and dealers)	43
Production and editing of house publications for company people, distributors, dealers, and consumers	41
Sales bulletins	62
Slides and films	86
Improved communication (correspondence, conferences, channels, use of audio-visual devices)	94

Adapted from William R. Kelly, "Sales Promotion: Super Success Is Still to Come," *Sales Management,* June 1, 1970, p. 27.

2. *Point-of-purchase displays.* The point-of-purchase display industry (for example, items for sale at the check-out counter) has been booming in the last decade. In the years 1967 to 1972, sales practically doubled (from $1 billion to $1.8 billion).[16] Marketers are investing in such displays in order to "grab" the shopper while in a store. Some studies suggest that this approach has a real payoff. In one survey, sales jumped 15 percent in areas where displays were used and in some cases rose by more than 100 percent.

3. *Contests and games.* As one advertising agency executive has observed, "The desire to win easy money via *games of chance* is spreading like wildfire. As it penetrates more deeply into American life, it is inevitable that its impact on the marketing world will be significant.[17] Supermarkets have been fond of using promotional games to boost business.

Some stores favor games of chance, while others prefer contests with some element of skill involved. Experts on games have specified seven criteria that contribute to the success of a promotional game: simplicity, fun, suspense, minimum frustration, continuity, low cost, and appeal to both sexes.[18]

4. *Demonstrations.* Some products seem to require demonstrations in order to sell successfully. Microwave ovens are a good example. Manufacturers have invested in frequent demonstrations in stores, community centers, and even churches. One sales manager claims that "The secret of selling micro-

waves is demonstrations. If you get customers to see the oven in use and the advantages of cooking with it—the faster time and convenience—it plants a seed in their mind, which becomes an eventual sale."[19]

5. *Trade shows and exhibits.* The same principle is at work here as in the case of demonstrations. The difference is that trade shows are more elaborate and reach retailers as well as individual consumers. Most marketers find demonstrations at these events particularly useful in promoting new products or product innovations.

PUBLICITY   **Publicity** is also known as "marketing public relations." It is distinguished from advertising in that publicity is not paid for by the organization. Instead, the firm actively seeks to gain favorable notice in communications media for its overall image or for particular products or programs. The publicity comes from newscasters, columnists, and the like; it comes to the receiver as "the truth" rather than as a "commercial."

Nevertheless, publicity has significant disadvantages. The marketer cannot control publicity as easily as he or she conducts advertising or personal selling. A newspaper columnist may print part of a firm's publicity release and then criticize it line by line. Also, public relations personnel may find it difficult to promote products aggressively, since they often need to placate threatening or hostile audiences (including consumers, stockholders, and government).

Kotler has outlined three principal tasks that an organization must undertake if it wishes to use publicity for promotional purposes:[20]

1. *Define the objectives of the publicity effort.* This includes the target market, the target variable in the market, and the time frame for the publicity campaign.

MARKETING TO THE RESCUE

In 1974, Owens-Corning Fiberglas was attacked by some women's columnists for deceptive washing instructions on its Fiberglas draperies. The instructions —in large type—said "completely washable." Yet, at the bottom of the package, in small type, was the following message: "Hand wash in tub only. Do not machine wash."

As a result of this bad publicity, the Federal Trade Commission ruled that the product must carry a health hazard statement. It found that when the draperies were machine-washed, fibers remained in the washing machine. The ruling did not satisfy the columnists, who insisted that the FTC had ducked the problem.

Owens-Corning's public relations specialist, James H. Dowling, investigated the matter and found that the columnists' criticisms were justified. He rewrote the copy on the washing instructions and then took it to one of the columnists for her opinion. She approved the new copy, and even wrote a later column praising the company for its response to the problem.

Based on "Marketing PR Can Ring Cash Registers, Change Items, Get Inquiries," *Marketing News,* April 1, 1974, p. 5.

2. *Search for publicity ideas to achieve these objectives.*

3. *Plan for specific media involvement.* Set up face-to-face events and coordinate coverage in newspapers, magazines, radio, and television.

Publicity, like sales promotion, is also important for nonprofit organizations. Since many of these organizations have limited advertising budgets they often depend on mass media publicity to spread their message and boost membership and contributions.

CONCLUSION

Promotion has been defined as "the coordination of all seller-initiated efforts to set up channels of information and persuasion to facilitate the sale of a good or service, or the acceptance of an idea." There are four important types of promotional activities—advertising, personal selling, sales promotion, and publicity.

Promotion must be understood as a form of communication occurring in a marketing context. The seller hopes to establish a meaningful dialogue with the buyer and must develop a message that speaks to the particular needs and language of the target audience for the product.

The main focus of promotion strategy is the planning and implementation of persuasive communication with potential buyers. The marketer hopes to establish an optimal mix of the four channels of promotion: media, face-to-face, publicity, and word-of-mouth. To do so, he or she must study many factors, including the nature of the product, the nature of the target audience, and the characteristics of the four elements in the promotional mix.

Many factors contribute to the eventual decision about the promotion mix, including long-time firm traditions that may or may not make sense. Other noteworthy influences are the life-cycle stage, the type of product, the size of the budget, push and pull strategies, and organizational philosophy.

Sales promotion and publicity are often defined as secondary promotion mix channels when compared with advertising and personal selling. Yet each offers its own distinct advantages for the firm, and in some cases may be the prime means of promoting a commercial product or a nonprofit service.

DISCUSSION QUESTIONS

1. "Promotion is more beneficial for marketers than for either consumers or society." Explain your agreement or disagreement with this statement.
2. Using the marketing communication model, diagram the communication process that takes place between these groups:
   a. American Express and credit-card holders;
   b. candidate for governor and the voters;
   c. Pfizer Drugs and doctors;
   d. IBM and retail chains.

3. What would be appropriate promotion mixes for these marketing situations and marketers:
   a. Clothes-pressing machines for drycleaning plants;
   b. Mexican frozen foods producer in the Southwest with limited funds;
   c. An apple growers' association believing the apple to be in the maturity stage of its life cycle;
   d. The American Dental Association's tooth decay reduction campaign using a pull strategy;
   e. A small church-affiliated college that believes in a humanistic way of communicating with prospective students.
4. How would the U.S. Postal Service use the objective and task method for arriving at its total promotion budget?
5. The blue jeans manufacturer Levi Strauss has always sought ways to use publicity to stretch its promotion strategy. After years of sponsoring soap box derbies (by providing jeans to contestants), it is reconsidering its alternatives. What types of sales promotion and publicity programs would you recommend for Levi Strauss?

NOTES

1. Edward L. Brink and William T. Kelley, *The Management of Promotion* (Englewood Cliffs, N.J.: Prentice-Hall, 1963), p. 6.
2. This section is based largely on Sidney J. Levy, "Promotional Behavior," in Frederick D. Sturdivant et al., *Managerial Analysis in Marketing* (Glenview, Ill.: Scott, Foresman, 1970), pp. 409–11.
3. Harper W. Boyd, Jr., and Sidney J. Levy, *Promotion: A Behavioral View* (Englewood Cliffs, N.J.: Prentice-Hall, 1967), p. 3.
4. This section is based largely on Boyd and Levy, pp. 385–88.
5. "Lysol Wrinkle-Free at 100," *Advertising Age*, August 18, 1975, p. 16.
6. Frederick W. Webster, Jr., *Social Aspects of Marketing* (Englewood Cliffs, N.J.: Prentice-Hall, 1974), p. 33.
7. "Aviation: Feminists Fly to the FTC," *Business Week*, February 24, 1975, p. 26.
8. "Guides Given to Cut Complaints," *New York Times*, January 22, 1975, p. 63.
9. Boyd and Levy, pp. 20–21.
10. Philip Kotler, *Marketing Management: Analysis, Planning, and Control*, 3d ed. (Englewood Cliffs, N.J.: Prentice-Hall, 1976), p. 325.
11. Committee on Definitions of the American Marketing Association, *Marketing Definitions: A Glossary of Marketing Terms* (Chicago: American Marketing Association, 1960).
12. "Cost of an Industrial Sales Call Continues to Rise," Laboratory of Advertising Performance, McGraw-Hill research report no. 801312 (1974), p. 1.
13. "Profiles in Management," *Electrical Contractor*, January 1975, pp. 31–33.
14. Joel Dean, *Managerial Economics* (Englewood Cliffs, N.J.: Prentice-Hall, 1972), p. 102
15. Philip Kotler, *Marketing for Nonprofit Organizations* (Englewood Cliffs, N.J.: Prentice-Hall, 1975), p. 217.
16. "A P.O.P. Art Form That Turns Shoppers On," *Business Week*, January 8, 1972, pp. 36–38.
17. Grey Advertising, Inc., *Grey Matter* 45 (May 1974): 1.
18. Watson Dunn and Arnold M. Barban, *Advertising: Its Role in Modern Marketing* (Hinsdale, Ill.: Dryden, 1974), p. 460
*19. Mary Ellen Figueroa, "Demos Still Hot Hand for Microwaves," *Merchandising Week*, October 7, 1974, pp. 1, 18.
20. Kotler, *Marketing for Nonprofit Organizations*, pp. 212–13.

18

MANAGING ADVERTISING STRATEGY

After completing this chapter, the reader should be able to:

1. Describe the importance of advertising in the organization's marketing strategy.

2. Assess social and economic criticisms of advertising.

3. Describe the processes used to determine advertising opportunites and to set advertising objectives.

4. Explain how advertising messages are created.

5. Identify the criteria for selecting advertising media.

6. Contrast communication and sales results as approaches to measuring the effectiveness of advertising.

Although **advertising** is only one element of the promotion mix, it often takes special prominence on the overall marketing mix design. Because of its high visibility and pervasiveness, within our society, it is an important social and economic topic.

OTB HITS TV

O.T.B.

In April 1975, New York City's Off-Track Betting Corporation (OTB) initiated its first television advertising campaign.[1] Six television commercials, featuring such celebrities as Imogene Coca, Professor Irwin Corey, and former jockey Eddie Arcaro, became the center of a six-week blitz on OTB. The $350,000 promotional effort was aimed at bringing in new bettors for the "Triple Crown" of horseracing—the Kentucky Derby, the Preakness, and the Belmont Stakes—which takes place in May and June.

At the time that the television push began, OTB was reaching about 200,000 customers per day. The advertising agency expected this effort to increase that figure substantially. A central part of the agency's strategy was a concentrated promotional pitch. Of OTB's $1.4 million advertising budget, one-fourth was poured into this critical six-week period.

Before 1975, the Code Board of the National Association of Broadcasters had prohibited OTB from advertising on television. The Code Board changed its position and allowed OTB to use the air waves—but only with supervision. The agency could inform the public of its workings, but was not allowed to engage in high-pressure selling.

MASS MAGIC

OTB undertook its television campaign because, as a public benefit corporation, it wished to increase public demand for its services. To do so, it planned and implemented an advertising campaign. Advertising may be defined as "the use of paid-for, sponsor-identified material in mass media (including direct mail)."[2] In its campaign, OTB took the following steps, which sum up the work of advertising management.

1. It set **objectives** (public awareness, winning new bettors, increasing the number of bets placed).
2. It created **messages** (betting is pleasurable, interesting people [as symbolized by the endorsing celebrities] do it).
3. It selected **media** (TV rather than print).
4. It measured **results** (in terms of communications and sales [bets]).

As was the case for OTB, most advertising is an attempt to stimulate sales to present, future, and even former customers. But, as we can see in Figure 18-1, advertising has other purposes as well. It is used to reassure buyers that they have made the best purchase, thus building loyalty to the brand name or

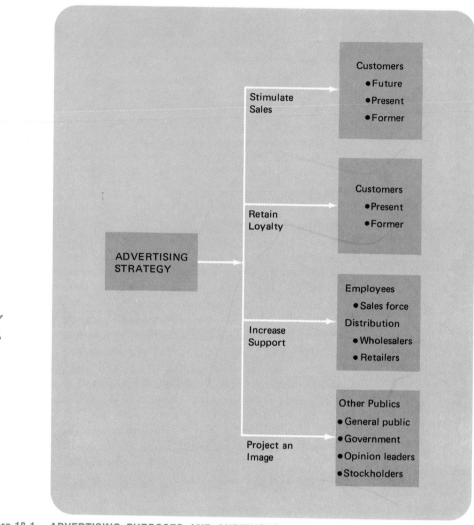

Figure 18-1   ADVERTISING PURPOSES AND AUDIENCES

Based on S. R. Bernstein, "What Is Advertising? What Does It Do?" *Advertising Age,* November 21, 1973, pp. 14, 16.

the firm. It bolsters the morale of the sales force and distributors, thus contributing to an enthusiastic and confident spirit within the organization. Finally, advertising is used to promote an overall image of respect and trust for an organization. This message is aimed not only at consumers, but also at government, stockholders, important opinion leaders, the general public, and so forth.

Does advertising actually accomplish these goals? Most corporate executives believe that advertising is essential to business success, that it is a definite asset in winning public confidence for a product. As a representative of the Whirlpool Corporation has stated, "Our automatic ice maker . . . has become a profitable product over its 13 years of existence. We certainly would not have invested nearly two million dollars in improvements . . . had we not had advertising to help us tell its story to the public."[3]

On the other hand, some research has indicated that advertising is less influential in determining demand than are environmental variables (population, income) or other marketing elements (product quality, price). One study found that a 1 percent increase in advertising costs leads to an average sales increase of only 0.1 percent in the short run and 1.25 percent in the long run.[4] These statistics back up the view of an advertising executive at Quaker Oats: "Very few companies continue to advertise products that don't sell. Very few companies stop advertising products that do. And that's the relationship between advertising and sales."[5]

A SOCIAL PERSPECTIVE ON ADVERTISING

Critics attribute to advertising an awesome ability to persuade millions of Americans to do almost anything. Serious observers of advertising would disagree, contending that it is not that powerful or influential. Nonetheless, in 1974 over $26 billion was spent on advertising, or 2 percent of the gross national product. Over the last 30 years, advertising volume has increased 1,000 percent.

THE ADVERTISING INSTITUTION

Historically, the main task of advertising has been to promote mass consumption of goods and services. It gets the message to the consumer quickly, and thus cuts the time span between production and consumption. Advertising also accelerates the change from older, low-quality products to improved models. It reshapes consumer attitudes and speeds up the introduction of new products into the economy.[6] It is worth noting that even in the planned and production-oriented economies of the Soviet Union and other developed communist states, advertising is now being used to coordinate production with consumer demand.

Unlike the 1950s and the 1960s, however, the 1970s have been a time of recession, inflation, unemployment, energy shortages, and worsening pollution crises. In this climate of "unabundance" and ecological danger, advertising has taken on new functions. It must promote conservation of resources rather than unchecked consumption, control of waste rather than industrial pollution, recycling of materials rather than thoughtless depletion.

If we think of advertising as a social institution, we can define it as "the set of all the people and activities concerned with the sending and seeking or receiving of information for economic purposes."[7] Figure 18–2 provides an overview of the major components of the **advertising institution**. A discussion of two of the key components of this model—advertising agencies and advertising regulators—follows as an introduction to the rest of the chapter.

Advertising Agencies

The **advertising agency** normally has two critical functions. It creates an advertising message for an organization and it decides on the proper media for that message. The key consideration is the target audience: the message must be tailored to the kind of clientele the advertiser hopes to attract. Thus, the adver-

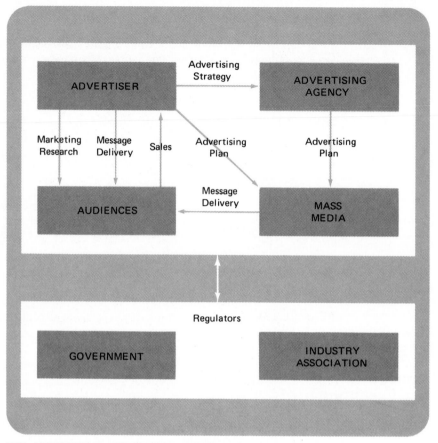

Figure 18-2   THE ADVERTISING INSTITUTION MODEL

Based on Francesco M. Nicosia, *Advertising, Management, and Society: A Business Point of View* (New York: McGraw-Hill, 1974), pp. 3–16. Copyright © 1974 by McGraw-Hill Book Company.

tising agency acts as an intermediary whose goal is to effectively bring together the senders and receivers of messages (who are often the sellers and buyers of products or services).

The major contact between advertiser and agency is made through the agency's account staff, which transmits the advertiser's strategy to various agency personnel (artists, media planners, researchers). Later it brings the finished advertising back to the client for approval. The account staff thus has a sensitive role. It must help the advertiser send effective messages to the general public and at the same time encourage the advertiser to keep the feelings of consumers (and the public interest) in mind. If public interest is not served, both advertiser and agency may have to deal with the unpleasant possibility of strict government regulation.

The main compensation for agencies comes from media commissions. Generally, the agency receives a fee equivalent to 15 percent of the advertiser's cost for gross time or space used when it places the advertising with a television station, newspaper, or magazine. In more and more cases, however, advertising agencies receive set fees for doing a particular job.

Advertising Regulators Government agencies and/or industry associations may assume the role of **advertising regulators**.

Government Regulation. All advertising, especially through the mass media, is subject to government regulation. In recent years, the FCC, the FDA, and other government agencies have significantly narrowed the range of acceptable advertising messages. In part, this is a result of increasing pressure from the consumer lobby. The FTC has adopted a new concept of **corrective advertising**. If a firm's advertising is found to be deceptive, it must devote a certain percentage of new advertising to remedial, confessional messages acknowledging the unfair practices of the past.

Research studies indicate that many American legislators have a consistently negative image of advertising practices. Many legislators support stiffened government regulation of the industry. One observer has warned that, unless advertising becomes more socially responsible, "we may see a U.S. Bureau of Advertising that has the power to approve or reject all advertising," and "a congressionally chartered Food and Drug Testing Laboratory that . . . might take product research out of the marketer's hands altogether."[8]

Industry-Wide Regulation. Some structures have already been established for the self-regulation of advertising. The Council of Better Business Bureaus maintains a National Advertising Division (NAD), which studies complaints and acts as a sort of fact-finder and trial court.[9] Appeals of NAD decisions can be made to the National Advertising Review Board (NARB). For each review, NARB sets up a panel of five members—three advertiser representatives, one agency expert, and one public member.

NARB has no legal power to compel obedience to its decisions. The review board, however, can easily gain publicity—and can point out to the public an advertiser that will not even follow the dictates of an industry-wide self-regulating body. This accounts for the noticeable influence of the NARB over advertisers.

CRITICISM OF ADVERTISING It is easy to see why critics of marketing practices focus much of their energy on advertising. Advertising is something we see all around us—whether we want to or not.

The Critics' Viewpoint There is little doubt that criticism of advertising has become widespread. Typical of this trend was a comment from an ad agency president: "A look through almost any newspaper or a few hours in front of a TV set will make it clear that much advertising continues to be false, boring, and irritating."[10]

Even many businessmen are coming to this conclusion. One survey found that less than a third of the business leaders questioned believed that ads present a true picture of a product.[11] Many of these leaders conceded that advertising has unhealthy effects on children and persuades consumers to buy products that they do not really need.

There are several lines of social attack on contemporary advertising practices.[12] The critics claim that advertising encourages senseless materialism, which in turn wastes national resources. They also charge that advertising minimizes price competition, that it emphasizes immoral (or at least amoral) behavior, and that it lowers the general level of taste. Finally, they maintain that it is too shrill, too insistent, and too pervasive.

In this kind of climate, it is hardly surprising that the public has developed a rather cynical view of advertising. A survey conducted by a major advertising agency found that more than 60 percent of the respondents believed criticism of advertising to be fully justified.[13] Less than half of all advertising was seen as honest and informative.

Closely related to social criticism is the economic controversy over advertising in the context of competition (see Chapter 6). But one large-scale European study has concluded that the economic influence of advertising has actually been overestimated (see Table 18-1).[14]

The Defenders' Viewpoint

The viewpoint of many of advertising's defenders is summarized in the following statement:

> *Advertising, as we have seen it, is merely a tool and a technique, and attacks on advertising per se are therefore meaningless. It can equally well be used to promote materialism or asceticism, the purchase of cosmetics or U.S. bonds, the sale of smut or scriptures. . . . Opposition to specific advertising forms or uses of advertising may be meaningful and sensible; opposition to "advertising" is not.*[15]

Many defenders of advertising believe that opponents are actually indicting the entire social and economic system. They see the criticism of advertising as a stab at our entire way of life in an industrial society. "There is no evidence . . . to support a claim that advertising and other forms of promotion have caused the materialism and affluence of the United States in any direct sense. The desire to consume is much more basic than that."[16]

Defenders also scoff at the much-heralded power of advertising. They point out that many manufacturers have gone out of business despite lavish advertising campaigns for their products. Many "packaged" political candidates have not been able to translate media dollars into votes on election day. To these defenders, the notion that advertisers can magically hypnotize the American public is simply a myth.

The Middle Ground

The defenders of advertising have spoken forcefully, but the critics have made their point with the American public. There is growing public skepticism of advertising, even within the business community. As one business executive has charged, "The quality of life in a society is determined by the quality of its culture. . . . The advertising industry helped create it and is continuing to make it worse."[17]

The psychological manipulation involved in advertising has left many Americans feeling cheated. Television commercials promise sex appeal from using the right toothpaste, or a vacation feeling from drinking a sponsor's beer. Can such messages be justified? The toothpaste and the beer may both be of

Table 18-1
THE ECONOMIC IMPACT OF ADVERTISING

STEPS IN THE ADVERTISING CONTROVERSY	ASSUMED ROLES OR EFFECTS OF ADVERTISING	OBSERVED ROLES OR EFFECTS OF ADVERTISING
1. Advertising	Large companies advertise in order to create a preference for their brands	**Yes, but . . .** they also use advertising to perform communication tasks required by the market situation; large-scale advertising has no built-in advantage for the large companies, although a threshold level exists that may benefit the big spenders
2. Consumer buying behavior	Consumers perceive real or apparent differences among brands and develop preferences	**Yes, but . . .** the advertising effect is modest in both absolute and relative value; consumers are less responsive to noninformational advertising
3. Barriers to entry	Preferences lead to brand loyalty, or consumer inertia, that constitutes a barrier to entry of new brands into the market	**Yes, but . . .** many other factors explain consumer inertia or loyalty; where consumer inertia is high, advertising intensity is not necessarily also high
4. Market power	Protected brand positions reduce active rivalry and give the company more discretionary power	**No . . .** we observed no basic incompatibility beween the presence of intensive advertising in a market and the degree to which that market exhibits active rivalry, **but . . .** advertising escalation does not benefit the consumer as does a price war or a technological race
5. Market conduct	Discretionary power allows the company to ignore more tangible forms of competition (price and product quality) and lets it charge higher prices	**No . . .** consumer responsiveness to price and product quality remains high in advertising-intensive markets; a company may react to rival advertising by advertising, price, or even quality adjustments
6. Market performance	Higher prices result in high profits that furnish incentive to continue advertising	**Yes . . .** advertising increases the capacity of the company to charge higher prices to the consumer, **but . . .** no continuous association is observed between market concentration and advertising intensity; sales maximization under profit constraints seems to be the company's objective, although long-term profitability is likely for several brands

From Jean-Jacques Lambin, "What Is the Real Impact of Advertising?" *Harvard Business Review* 53 (May–June 1975): 145.

high quality, but they cannot give viewers what the ads imply. The result may contribute to an aroused, stimulated, frustrated, and outraged consuming public.

There is also a hidden cumulative effect of advertising on social values and roles. One particular advertiser can develop a television commercial with a humorous appeal picturing a helpless, confused housewife. But when our television screens are filled day after day with this image, then the overall impact is degrading to women. For this reason, advertising portrayals of women, blacks, Chicanos, senior citizens, and other groups have come under increasing scrutiny in the last decade. A corporate advertisement with a negative image of women or blacks may truly reflect the majority opinion of a society. Yet the advertisement has its own effect; at a minimum, it contributes to perpetuating the discriminatory conventional image.

CLASSIFYING ADVERTISING

Figure 18-3 presents an overview of the subject matter in this section. It provides a perspective on various kinds of advertising and the appropriate senders and receivers.

TYPE OF CONSUMER

In this section, we will look at the nature of advertising when the marketer's product is aimed at consumers, industrial customers, and clients of nonprofit organizations.

The major national marketers engage in **consumer-product advertising.** Marketers of food, drugs, cosmetics, automobiles, detergents, tobacco, and

Figure 18-3   TYPES OF ADVERTISING IN PERSPECTIVE

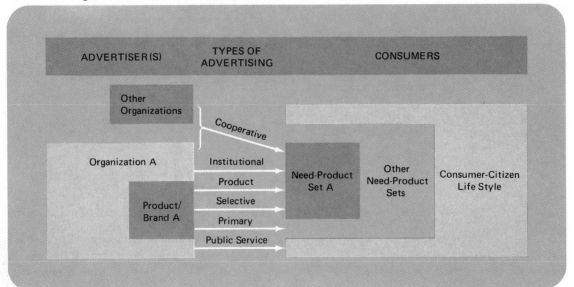

We don't
like being No.1

The Arthritis Foundation

Reprinted with permission from
the October 21, 1974 issue of Advertising Age. Copyright 1974 by
Crain Communications Inc.

alcoholic beverages are included here. Aside from automobiles, these products
are all **package goods** that the individual consumer will buy many times
during a year. Advertisers in this area compete to establish an advantage for
their particular brand.

Industrial-product advertising is another important type of advertising.
Interestingly, a study by a market research firm found that industrial executives have little confidence in advertising.[18] They seem to rely on this form of
promotion mainly out of fear that competitors will benefit if they stop their
advertising efforts.

Nonprofit advertising is a growing part of the total advertising picture.
Nonprofit organizations currently account for more than 20 percent of the
American economy, spending between $2 billion and $3 billion annually on
advertising.[19] They generally rely on advertising to achieve the goals of fund
raising ("send us a check"), persuasion to action ("get a check-up"), and attracting clients ("hear your city's symphony orchestra").

**FOCUS
OF CONTENT**

We can also examine advertising in relation to what is being advertised—
products, institutions, or public services. Because product advertising is the
focus of most of this chapter, we will concentrate here on institutional and
public service ads.

**Institutional
Advertising**

Institutional advertising attempts to build for a firm a positive public image in
the eyes of stockholders, employees, suppliers, legislators, opinion leaders,
or the general public. In some cases, a company will use a public affairs program as part of an effort to improve its image. In the mid-1970s, Mobil Oil
spent $10 million per year on a multimedia campaign that included ads on
company policy on energy and ecology, and on its sponsorship of a public
broadcasting television series and varied community projects.[20]

**Public Service
Advertising**

Public service advertising is directed at the social welfare of a community
or a nation. While the effectiveness of product ads may be measured by a rise
in sales, the effectiveness of public service ads must be measured in terms of
goodwill toward the sponsoring organization. Some examples of public service
advertising include General Motors on safe driving, Metropolitan Life Insurance on the signs of drug addiction, and Abbott Laboratories on health problems.

**DEMAND
INFLUENCE
LEVEL**

Another way of classifying advertising is based on demand influence level.
This includes primary and selective demand concepts, which were introduced
in Chapter 17. Since most of this chapter is concerned with stimulating **selective demand,** we will now touch briefly on **primary demand** stimulation.

Advertising that focuses on primary demand represents a form of inter-
industry competition. Ads that promote margarine may cut into the sales of
butter. Ads that glorify "Ski New England" may lure vacationers away from
the slopes of Colorado or other western areas.

Most primary demand campaigns come from leaders within an industry. They generally have the most resources to invest, and they assume that they will reap most of the benefits from an increase in primary demand. On the other hand, the smaller the firm, the more likely it will be to aim its advertising at selective rather than primary demand. Industry trade associations by their very nature engage in primary demand advertising.

SPONSORSHIP ARRANGEMENT

Sponsorship of advertising may be undertaken by an individual organization or as a cooperative activity. Because most of this chapter is concerned with individual advertising, we will discuss the cooperative arrangement here. The cooperation may be horizontal (firms on the same level of production or distribution) or vertical (firms in a distribution channel).

Horizontal cooperative advertising usually occurs through trade associations. The Douglas Fir Plywood Association, the United States Savings and Loan League, and the Mobile Homes Manufacturers Association all promote primary demand for a specific type of product.

Vertical cooperation can take place at various points in the distribution channel. It is in the interests of a product's manufacturer and its wholesalers to promote the product to retailers. To do so, they may decide to join forces in advertising the product. Or there may be cooperation between a manufacturer and retailers.

GEOGRAPHICAL SCOPE

Advertising may be national, regional, or local in its scope. In 1974, $14.8 billion was spent on national ads and $12 billion on local ads.

National advertising is practiced by more than 17,000 firms. They encourage the consumer to buy their product wherever it is sold. Most national ads concentrate on the overall image and desirability of the product. The top five national advertisers in 1975 were:[21]

Procter & Gamble	$274 million
General Foods	150
Bristol-Myers	134
American Home Products	121
General Motors	104

Local advertising is generally done by retailers and service firms rather than manufacturers. Retail ads usually provide specific information for the consumer (ice cream sundaes are only 50 cents on Thursday nights at all Baskin-Robbins locations in Savannah, Georgia). These ads should save the customer time and money by passing along specific information about products, prices, store hours, locations, credit terms, and so forth.

Regional advertising is another geographical alternative for organizations. Vlasic Foods, Inc., which claims to be the leading pickle producer in the United States, is based near Detroit. But, until recently, it confined its distribution to the area east of Texas.

THE ADVERTISING MANAGEMENT PROCESS

Advertising will not be successful if it is a haphazard process. Like other marketing activities, it requires efficient planning. Market research and strategic thinking are needed to answer two fundamental questions: What is the task of the advertising in question? How can this advertising best fulfill its role in the overall marketing effort?

Figure 18-4 presents the advertising management model we will use as a basis of this section.

ADVERTISING OBJECTIVES

First, we must look at the role of advertising in marketing and promotion strategies. (Does a sufficient opportunity exist to make advertising worthwhile?) Second, we will focus on the advertising objectives for a given advertising program. (How is a given campaign projected to result in a specific program?)

Advertising Opportunity

A successful advertising plan must be part of a total marketing strategy that coordinates all important marketing elements, including personal selling, pricing, and distribution. Clear marketing goals must be established before the specifics of an advertising campaign can be formulated. Of course, the more the firm can pinpoint its exact objectives (and its target audiences), the better it will be for advertising purposes.

It is important to consider the **advertising opportunity**—the likelihood that the proposed campaign can generate sales increases substantial enough to pay its own costs and boost the firm's profits. An intelligent marketer will ask, "Should we advertise?" before committing the firm to an expensive campaign. Advertising opportunity varies among different industries, different products, and even different brands.

Primary advertising is often necessary when a firm is the first to introduce a new product category (as Xerox did with dry copying and as 3M did with cellophane tape) or is opening up a new market for an established product

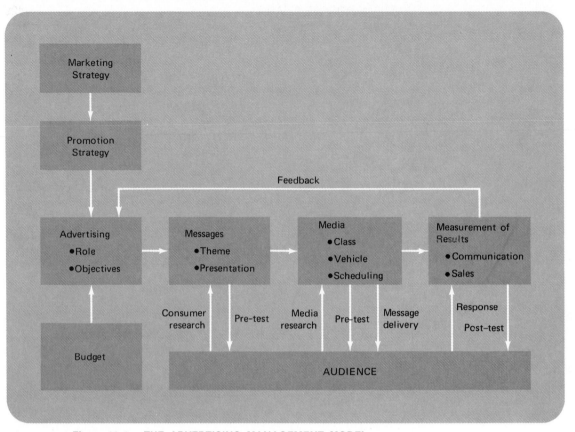

Figure 18-4   THE ADVERTISING MANAGEMENT MODEL

(frozen foods overseas). It may also be used if a firm has a leading market share of an established product and wants to expand sales.

Selective advertising is aimed at promoting awareness and sales of the brand or service. Six factors shape the opportunity for selective advertising:

1. The product offering meets some important consumer need.
2. The product is unique or highly differentiated.
3. The product has hidden attributes that the consumer cannot evaluate simply by inspecting it.
4. Primary demand is already expanding because of favorable market acceptance.
5. Adequate quantities of the product are available at the end of the distribution channel.
6. There are sufficient funds to cover the cost of the advertising campaign.

Advertising Campaign Objectives   One market research study has indicated that only one-fourth of all industrial advertisers set any basic objectives for their promotional work.[22] And even when objectives were set, they were usually vague and somewhat superficial. Nevertheless, it is considered essential for the success of an advertising campaign that clear goals be mapped out.

428

For an advertising objective to be meaningful, it should demonstrate the following qualities:

1. *It must be precise.* As some promotion experts have observed, "A vague objective is really no objective at all. A benchmark should be stated at the beginning of the campaign so that results can be assessed."[23]

2. *It must be communication-oriented.* Advertising objectives should emphasize communication tasks. These include developing brand awareness, changing consumer attitudes, associating desirable themes with products, and informing consumers about product attributes.

3. *It must be related to sales and profit goals.* Advertising objectives must be linked to overall marketing tasks and to short-term and long-term goals. The message must always have some impact on consumer buying action. If an ad stresses a unique product feature that has no relevance to buying behavior, the resulting product awareness will be useless.

The general philosophy that advertising should focus on clear and measurable communication objectives has become known as **DAGMAR** (*D*efining *A*dvertising *G*oals, *M*easuring *A*dvertising *R*esults). It was pioneered by Russell Colley in a 1961 position paper. At that time, he wrote: "Advertising succeeds or fails depending on how well it communicates the desired information and attitudes to the right people at the right time and at the right cost."[24]

MESSAGE CREATION
The creative part of advertising involves selecting appeals and presenting them. This is sometimes called the "art" of advertising. **Message development** may be defined as "what is said, how it is said, where it is said, and how often it is said."[25] There seems little doubt that the creative element in advertising can make or break a promotional campaign. One study even found that the quality of advertising was far more important in determining success than the amount of dollars spent.[26]

The conventional wisdom of advertising theory includes the concept of **AIDA**—*A*ttention, *I*nterest, *D*esire, and *A*ction. Many advertisers believe that their messages must attract the attention and interest of receivers if action (buying) is to result. Consumers may not know that a product exists or may not feel they have any need for it. Advertising tries to persuade these consumers that they need the product.

But how exactly does advertising capture the attention, interest, and desire of target audiences? One study suggests that national advertising communicates one or more product attributes to consumers.[27] If the communication is effective in building a favorable image, and if the product attributes have a strong impact on consumer buying, then the advertising will probably lead to more purchases. This is why advertisers take great interest in which product attributes have the most significance in consumer buying patterns.

Theme Development
The **theme** of a message strategy should be the logical outcome of decisions on market positioning, product concept, and other marketing objectives. Most creative people work inductively by building advertising ideas on the input from consumers and dealers. When a clear differential advantage exists for the

product over competitors (especially when it is new), a good advertising theme stands out.

The Coca-Cola Company has relied on a number of key advertising themes over the last few decades. These themes have changed as marketplace conditions changed. "Things Go Better with Coke" was a people-and-good-times theme initiated to counter Pepsi's successful "Pepsi Generation" pitch. The message "It's the Real Thing" emphasized Coke's classic formula and taste as distinct from the flood of new soft drinks that were entering the market.

As one of the most powerful influences on the success or failure of advertising (and marketing in general), decisions on positioning must be made before advertising is created. Will Bufferin be promoted as a cold remedy or a headache cure? These decisions imply marketing priorities—and thus advertising priorities.

A successful advertising theme cannot always rely solely on positioning. It must promise some tangible and valuable benefit. Because advertising must capture the attention of an audience and arouse its interest and desire, it must speak to a real and unfulfilled need. A newer view is that the message must tell consumers how they can solve a problem by using the product.

Advertising can also be related to the overall brand image of a product. Some 95 percent of all advertising has no connection to any consistent brand image. This leaves the way open for those firms who do not promote an attractive and distinctive brand image. If their advertising is well designed and positioned, they can gain a much larger share of the market.

Message Presentation

The presentation of a message involves careful evaluation of the **message structure** (the arrangement of major arguments for maximum impact) and the **format development** (the choice of words, pictures, symbols, colors, and action to conceptualize the advertising theme).

There are many distinctive forms of advertising messages. Among the most common are:

1. *The "sales pitch" presentation.* The audience is informed about a product with a sense of urgency ("You can't afford to miss this opportunity").

2. *The demonstration presentation.* The main goal is to show the viewer how to use an unfamiliar product while at the same time stressing its value.

3. *The mood presentation.* This focuses on creating an emotional climate in which to mention the product, rather than on the attributes of the product itself. We see a young couple out in the woods, obviously in love, quiet and contented—any one of many products come to mind.

A **testimonial** can be presented as any one or a combination of these three message forms. In Mr. Coffee's highly successful series of commercials, Joe DiMaggio comes across as honest, believeable, and sincere. He doesn't seem like a hustling salesman. The mood created is pleasant—a familiar, trusted celebrity presents a product in a low-key manner.

Humorous messages have become an increasingly popular way of creating a mood. Another common mood-setter is the sex-oriented message (from cosmetic to conveyer belt advertising).

MEDIA SELECTION Henry Schachte, an expert in the field of advertising, has pointed to a critical and yet somewhat obscured element of promotional success. He notes that advertising agency personnel "spend 90 percent of their time sweating over copy." Yet, in Schachte's view, "The quantum leaps in advertising effectiveness . . . have come much more from smart media moves than from brilliant advertising copy."[28]

The harsh reality is that two-thirds of every organization's advertising budget goes into the purchase of time and space in the various media, rather than copy design or any other activity. This makes it even more evident why a "smart move" by an organization in **media selection** can be essential for advertising success.

Advertisers ideally match consumer preferences with media attributes. Each of the mass media has specific characteristics, potentials, and liabilities that must be taken into consideration when selecting media for advertising efforts.

Media selection involves a basic understanding of the capabilities and costs of the major advertising media. The media profiles shown in Table 18-2 enable us to make a comparison among the different categories.

Media Selection Criteria In media selection, a target audience is pinpointed and media are chosen to reach that segment of the population. There are six elements of a successful media proposal:

1. *The communication requirement.* If a visual demonstration of a product seems necessary, the advertiser may turn to television. If a musical mood is desired, radio may be favored. If detailed discussion of sales points is required, print media may be most useful.

Cass Student Advertising of Chicago commissioned a survey of 506 college students on twenty-four major campuses. The study indicated that the most trusted media for students were their college newspapers.

In terms of usage, 87.6 percent of the students had read their college papers in the last week. This compared with figures of 58.1 percent for local city papers, 36 percent for *Time*, 33.6 percent for *Playboy*, and 28.5 percent for *Reader's Digest*.

In addition, 66.7 percent of the students had read their college papers "yesterday." This figure contrasts with 61.5 percent for television, but 83.6 percent for radio.

The critical question in the survey asked which media seem most honest and credible. Here 29.6 percent of the students chose their college papers. This exceeded the scores for magazines (21.3 percent), city papers (14.2 percent), radio (7.3 percent), and television (5.9 percent).

Based on Philip H. Dougherty, "Reaching On-Campus Spenders," *New York Times*, July 17, 1975, p. 45.

MEDIA PROFILE OF COLLEGE STUDENTS

Table 18-2
PROFILES OF MAJOR ADVERTISING MEDIA

MEDIUM	VOLUME (IN BILLIONS)*	EXAMPLE OF COST	NATURE OF THE MEDIUM	ADVANTAGES	LIMITATIONS
Newspapers	$8.0	$12,000, one page, weekday, *New York Times*	Immediacy, emphasis on facts, changes with times	Territorial flexibility, wide coverage of target communities	Quickly out of date, short attention span
Magazines	1.8	$40,000, one page in *Time*	Serious, sustained leisurely investigation of problems	Reaches specialized target audience	Limited flexibility
Direct mail	4.5	$40 for names & addresses of chief executives of 500 largest manufacturers	Quick dissemination of information	Quick handling takes advantage of timing	Skyrocketing postal costs
Television	4.9	$70,000 for one minute of NBC network time	Entertainment	Wide dissemination, flexibility	Cost, high mortality rate of programs and ads, short attention span
Radio	1.5	$121 for one minute of prime time in Baltimore	Entertainment	Mobility, flexibility, specialization	Intense competition, short attention span
Outdoor	.4	$1,200 prime set of billboards, monthly, Los Angeles	Immediate	Repetition creates needs	Visual pollution annoys consumers

*Data in column 2 from *Advertising Age,* December 17, 1975.

2. *Emphasis on the prime prospect.* The media expert must have a precise picture of the target audience for the product. Daytime television serials tend to reach younger housewives while quiz shows reach older women.

3. *Geographic sales analysis.* Will the campaign be national or regional? Will it aim at 150 television stations or at ten choice urban targets?

4. *Efficiency/effectiveness balance.* Media vary in their efficiency as measured in cost per reaching a thousand viewers. They also vary in their effectiveness in communicating the message. Advertising choices often represent a balance of these factors.

5. *The pressure of competition.* Advertising decisions are often made with an eye on the opposition. An organization may not want to abandon a key market to competitors.

6. *The budget.* Most budgets for advertising do not come up to the most desirable level of expenditures. Thus, priorities must be determined for allocating the money that is available.

Advertising Scheduling

An advertiser wants to schedule advertising so that it reaches a good proportion of the target audience at the most favorable time. This raises problems of macroscheduling.[29] **Macroscheduling** problems center on how to respond to seasonal patterns of sales. Should the firm pursue constant, seasonal, or even counter-seasonal advertising? **Microscheduling** problems center on how to gain the most advantageous timing and impact for an advertisement. Should a thirty-second television commercial run five times a day for two weeks, or once a day for a month, or an increasing or decreasing amount of time as the month goes on?

Budweiser beer is advertised with a **pulsing** approach. A study done for its brewer, Anheuser-Busch, found that, even if there were no advertising in a particular market over a long period of time, it would take a year and a half before sales would be adversely affected.[30] And a six-month spurt at this point could restore the previous growth rate. As a result, Anheuser-Busch adopted a concentrated pulsing policy.

MEASURING ADVERTISING RESULTS

Advertisers are interested in knowing what they are getting for their advertising dollars. Thus, they test the proposed ads with a **pre-test** and measure actual results with a **post-test**.

In the past, pre-testing of advertising messages was handled mainly by advertising agencies. But increasingly, advertisers are taking a more active role in the pre-testing process. There may be pre-testing either before an advertisement has been designed and executed, after it is ready for public distribution, or at both points.

During pre-testing, there is often research on three vital questions.[31]

1. Do consumers feel that the ad communicates something desirable about the product?

2. Does the message have an exclusive appeal that differentiates the product from competitors?

3. Is the advertisement believable?

Although advertisers spend money primarily on pre-testing, they also post-test their promotional campaigns. There are at least three distinct reasons for measuring advertising results:

1. to produce more effective advertising;

2. to prove to management that a higher ad budget will benefit the firm;

3. to determine what level of ad expenditures is most promising.

It is a striking fact that business firms spend millions of dollars on advertising without any clear sense of the "payoff" from this investment. Often there is no measurement or detailed evaluation. Even when a ratio between advertising and sales can be established, it is still of dubious value—since the relationship between advertising and sales is so unclear.

Most research focuses on communication effect rather than on sales effect. As John Treasure explains, "the short-term effect of advertising on sales is, no doubt, tiny and unimportant, whereas, in the long run, its effect on brands and companies may be of great importance."[32] For this reason, advertisers are particularly concerned with their impact on consumer awareness and attitudes.

Communications and Sales Results

The main goals of most advertising are to capture the attention of a potential buyer and promote brand awareness. Figure 18-5 presents a model of how an advertising campaign can lead to purchase and repurchase. Awareness builds a favorable or at least curious attitude toward the product, which leads to experimentation ("I'll try it once and see how it is"). If the trial is satisfactory, the consumer may stick with the product.

There are many critical and unresolved issues in determining how to test the communication effects of advertising. Among these are:

1. *Exposure conditions.* Should advertising be tested under realistic conditions (an actual, on-the-air commercial) or under more controlled laboratory conditions?

2. *Execution.* It is often expensive and time-consuming to pre-test a finished advertisement. Does pre-testing a preliminary execution produce accurate and useful data?

3. *Quality vs. quantity data.* Quantitative data are easiest and most precise for measurement purposes (42 percent of *Newsweek* readers recognized New England Life's cartoon ad series). But qualitative data from in-depth interviews can provide information that short-answer questions never can (a strong negative attitude exists regarding the use of humor in life insurance ads).

There are many types of advertising tests used. In theater testing, a sample of people are invited to a studio to view a television program with commercials included. The audience is then surveyed about the commercials. Print ads are tested through "dummy" magazine tests and portfolio tests. In the former, a magazine with test advertising in it is sent to a sample of readers, who are later surveyed. In the latter, about 10 to 12 ads are placed in a booklet that is shown to respondents; one of these is the test ad. The readers are asked to examine and comment on all of the advertising in the booklet.

As noted earlier, it is much more difficult to assess the sales effect of advertising than the communications effect. Advertising des not occur in a vacuum. Hertz may introduce a brilliant new advertising campaign in 1980. But if Avis slashes its prices and undercuts Hertz, what will the resulting sales figures prove? If Avis takes away 5 percent of Hertz's market share, will this mean that the Hertz advertising was a flop? Or that pricing was the key variable? And how can Hertz test this to learn the truth?

Figure 18-6 offers a model that may help define the advertising–sales relationship. In the lowest range of advertising expenditure (Y_1), sales increases do not parallel advertising increases. In the intermediate range between Y_1 and Y_2 sales are highly responsive to advertising. A 10 percent rise in advertising may produce an even greater boost in sales. In the range beyond Y_2, however, the sales response to advertising falls off again. The dilemma for the organization is how to calculate the optimum advertising expenditure. A firm may project its figures on the high side, risking the wasted expenditures of the Y_3 range to be sure that it at least meets the desired Y_2 level.

There are two noteworthy approaches to measuring the sales effect of advertising. With the historical approach, a researcher uses a statistical technique to link past sales and advertising data for the firm. With the experimental design approach, there is actual field testing. A firm may spend 50 percent more

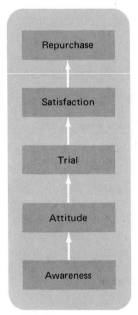

Figure 18-5
THE STAGES OF CONSUMER DECISION PROCESSES

From Francesco M. Nicosia, *Advertising, Management, and Society: A Business Point of View* (New York: McGraw-Hill, 1974), p. 98. Copyright © 1974 by McGraw-Hill Book Company.

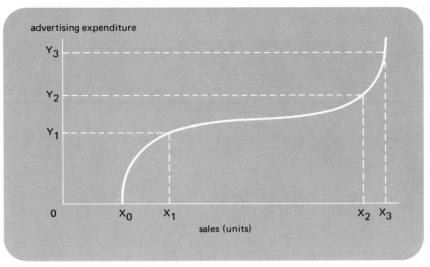

advertising expenditure

Figure 18-6   THE ADVERTISING-SALES RELATIONSHIP

From Jerome B. Kernan and James U. McNeal, "The Closest Thing to Measuring Advertising Effectiveness," *Business Horizons 7* (Winter 1964): 77.

than its typical advertising budget in one area, 50 percent less in a second, and the previous normal amount in a third. It will then calculate the effects of these advertising changes on sales figures in each region.

THE FUTURE OF ADVERTISING

It is no easy matter to speculate on the future of advertising. But we can briefly survey interesting projections that may be borne out in the years ahead.

Volume Growth. One group of 158 experts predicts that advertising volume will grow at an average rate of 7 percent from 1975 to 1980 and 8 percent from 1980 to 1985.[33] If this is true, total advertising volume ($26 billion in 1974) will reach the $60 billion figure by 1985.

Social Constraints. It is open to debate whether society can afford to have certain consumer wants (big automobiles, high-power-consumption appliances, cigarettes) reinforced by advertising. If society cannot afford health hazards, unlimited growth, energy use, and economic waste, it may not be able to afford the kind of advertising that promotes these very goals.

Consumer Expectations. Consumers will be increasingly skeptical of advertising practices in the future. They will demand accurate and useful product information, and will retaliate against advertisers who engage in deceptive or untrustworthy advertising practices.

Education-Oriented Messages. More and more, firms will be educating the consumer. An example is Whirlpool's Care-a-Van program—a 90-minute stage show on the construction, care, and proper use of appliances.

"I just realized—I've been leaving the room during the movie and coming back for the commercials."
Wall Street Journal

435

Advertising Agencies. A survey of business executives found mixed opinions about the future role of advertising agencies.[34] Half saw agencies becoming even more powerful in the coming years, while the other half expected that more firms will turn to providers of specialized services or the in-house advertising department.

CONCLUSION

Advertising can be defined as the process of buying sponsor-identified media space or time in order to promote a product, a service, or an idea. Advertising is perhaps the most visible of all the elements in the promotion mix. As such, it is the subject of much criticism from consumer groups. It is also subject to government and industry-wide regulation.

Advertisers fall into four main groups: individuals, nonprofit organizations, government agencies, and business firms. Based on their organizational goals and material resources, these groups must choose among many alternative media for advertising. These include print media, broadcast media, outdoor media, and direct mail. The selection of the proper medium or media is a critical marketing activity. The advertiser wants the best medium at the ideal cost at the right time in order to reach a target audience.

Advertising may serve many different purposes. Primary demand advertising promotes an industry or a product; selective demand advertising promotes an individual brand. Advertising may be conducted in national, local, or regional campaigns. Its goal may be increased profits (in the case of a business firm) or public service (in the case of a nonprofit organization).

DISCUSSION QUESTIONS

1. Does advertising expenditure determine an organization's sales level, or does the sales level determine its advertising expenditure? Discuss.
2. Is there now too much government regulation and self-regulation for advertising to work effectively, or too little to protect consumers? Explain.
3. In 1975, the U.S. Postal Service asked Congress for $30 million for advertising purposes. Can you justify this request? Explain.
4. What factors would account for the effectiveness of selective advertising for these products: microwave ovens, an urban monorail system, a vacation in Spain, and Sears brand power tools.
5. Create an advertising theme based on market positioning for these products: a diet foods restaurant, French cookware, an indoor tennis club, and a low-energy light bulb.
6. Which advertising media lend themselves to effectively reaching potential customers for these products: an investment advisory service, ping pong tables, a rock album, and sound-proofing wallcovers.
7. Would communications results or sales results be more appropriate for measuring the advertising effectiveness of these products: mail-order micro-

scopes, a "Keep America Beautiful" campaign, industrial natural gas power, and heavy duty trucks.

NOTES

1. Philp H. Dougherty, "OTB Plans Television Campaign," *New York Times*, April 21, 1975, p. 44.
2. Seymour Banks, "Trends Affecting the Implementation of Advertising and Promotion," *Journal of Marketing* 37 (January 1973): 22.
3. Stephen A. Greyser and Bonnie B. Reece, "Businessmen Look Hard at Advertising," *Harvard Business Review* 49 (May–June 1971): 20.
4. Jean-Jacques Lambin, "What Is the Real Impact of Advertising?" *Harvard Business Review* 53 (May–June 1975): 142.
5. Kenneth Mason, "How Much Do You Spend on Advertising? Product Is Key," *Advertising Age,* June 12, 1972, p. 41.
6. Floyd L. Vaughan, *Marketing* (New York: Farrar and Rhinehart, 1942), p. 569.
7. Francisco M. Nicosia, *Advertising, Management, and Society: A Business Point of View* (New York: McGraw-Hill, 1974), pp. 2–4.
8. Leo F. Greenland, "Advertisers Must Stop Conning Customers," *Harvard Business Review* 52 (July–August 1974): 28, 156.
9. Edwin D. Etherington, "Originality and Aptness of Thought" (Speech, May 17, 1974), p. 2.
10. Greenland, p. 18.
11. Greyser and Reece, p. 22.
12. S. R. Bernstein, "What Is Advertising? What Does It Do?" *Advertising Age*, November 21, 1973, pp. 8–9.
13. "The Public Is Wary of Ads, Too," *Business Week*, January 29, 1972, p. 69.
14. Lambin, pp. 145–47.
15. Bernstein, p. 18.
16. Frederick E. Webster, Jr., *Social Aspects of Marketing* (Englewood Cliffs, N.J.: Prentice-Hall, 1974), p. 46.
17. Alan L. Otten, "The Good Guys Come Through," *Wall Street Journal*, November 11, 1970, p. 8.
18. "Big Steel Gets Back into Advertising," *Business Week*, May 30, 1970, p. 92.
19. Bernice Finkelman, "Growing Nonprofit Sector, Now 20% of Economy, Becoming Marketing-Conscious," *Marketing News*, January 15, 1974, p. 1.
20. "Mobil's Advocacy Ads Lead a Growing Trend, Draw Praise, Criticism," *Wall Street Journal*, May 14, 1975, p. 1.
21. "Top 100 National Advertisers in 1975," *Advertising Age*, May 24, 1976, p. 32.
22. "Industrial Ads: The View from the Top," *Business Week*, May 30, 1970, p. 92.
23. James F. Engel, Hugh G. Wales, and Martin Warshaw, *Promotional Strategy* (Homewood, Ill.: Irwin, 1967), p. 103.
24. Russell H. Colley, *Defining Advertising Goals* (New York: Association of National Advertisers, Inc., 1961), p. 21.
25. Philip Kotler, *Marketing Management: Analysis, Planning, and Control*, 3d ed. (Englewood Cliffs, N.J.: Prentice-Hall, 1976), pp. 356–57.
26. Ibid., p. 357.
27. Alvin A. Achenbaum, "Advertising Doesn't Manipulate Consumers," *Journal of Advertising Research* 12 (April 1972): 12.
28. Henry Schachte, "They Did It with Media Magic—Can Today's Ways Match Them?" *Advertising Age*, November 24, 1975, p. 35.
29. Kotler, *Marketing Management*, 3d ed., pp. 364–66.
30. Philip H. Dougherty, "Bud 'Pulses' the Market," *New York Times*, February 18, 1975, p. 40.
31. Kotler, *Marketing Management*, 3d ed., p. 358.
32. John A. P. Treasure, "How Advertising Works," in Yale Bronzen, ed., *Advertising and Society* (New York: New York University Press, 1974), p. 153.
33. "Marketing Observer," *Business Week*, March 31, 1975.
34. Banks, p. 28.

19

MANAGING PERSONAL SELLING STRATEGY

After completing this chapter, the reader should be able to:

1. Explain the nature of professional personal selling today.

2. Identify the elements that account for effective personal selling.

3. Describe the major steps in the personal selling process.

4. Explain the importance of setting a series of objectives for the selling effort.

5. Point out the considerations for structuring the sales force.

6. Describe the major processes in developing the sales force.

7. Explain the activities that direct sales force performance.

8. Describe how sales force performance is evaluated for the salesperson and the sales staff.

Personal selling is an extremely effective but expensive form of promotion. Because it involves people and professional relationships, management of personal selling is a challenge. All too often, personal selling is confused with marketing itself. It is important to distinguish between the two: personal selling is only one part of the promotion mix, which in turn is part of the marketing mix.

SELL NOW, PLANT LATER

William E. Frost

Bill Keller of Collinsville, Illinois, farms about 500 acres of mixed grains.[1] On 60 acres he grows sweet corn of the Sundance, Northern Belle, and Gold Cup varieties.

Bill lives by the philosophy that a crop must be sold before it is grown. If you grow first, then sell, you just depress the market for everybody, he maintains. Each winter, Bill meets with purchasing agents and merchandisers of his two major buyers, Kroger Company and United Fruit and Produce, who operate in the St. Louis wholesale market. He asks for a rundown on their future plans and solicits their opinion on his past year's performance, including any suggestions for change.

"At this point, we usually complain that they don't take good enough care of the sweet corn," he relates. Both Bill and the stores are concerned with quality, and the stores' management usually try hard to keep the crop cool and in good condition. "But it seems the closer the corn gets to the consumer, the less care it is likely to get. What sometimes happens is that in transfer from warehouse to retail store, the produce is put on a truck with a load of paper goods, soap products, and so on—there's so much paper on the truck that they may not bother to turn on the refrigerator units."

Generally, Bill's relationship with his buyers is a good one. Back in the 1930s, Bill's father started dealing with Kroger. Now, supplying Kroger is a family project that involves Bill's brother, two cousins, and brother-in-law.

THE PERSONAL SELLING CONNECTION

Bill Keller's story is not unique, even though many farmers still operate on the "plant now, sell later" philosophy. But for Bill, personal selling is the heart of his business. It is the step that pulls together his other marketing variables: type of corn, quality, physical distribution, and price. He has built a long-term sales relationship with his two major customers, which he personally cultivates with as much effort as his crop.

Selling is a universal human occupation. Almost everyone lives by selling something. Personal selling refers to the use of speech and personal conviction to bring about some action on the part of another. Some actions that might result from personal selling are buying an insurance policy, leasing a car, con-

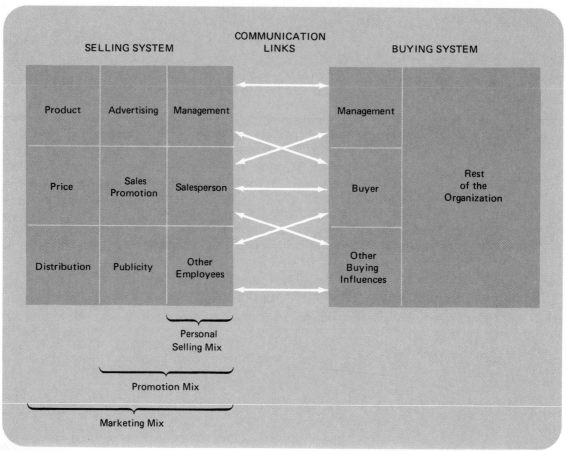

Figure 19-1

PERSONAL SELLING
IN THE MARKETING
RELATIONSHIP

tributing to a charity, voting for a certain candidate, or making a job offer. Figure 19-1 illustrates personal selling within the promotion mix. Besides those people in the selling system who have the title "salesperson," personal selling may be done by anyone in the organization who personally communicates with members of the buying system.

The sales force consists of those people who actually do the personal selling. With organizational customers such as steel manufacturers, printers, or hospitals, sales force performance has always been the key to marketing success. As one analyst points out,

> Other elements of the marketing mix—i.e., advertising, promotion, and merchandising—simply cannot have the same pull through impact in industry as they do in the consumer goods world. . . . There are very few situations in industry where the buying decision is either made impulsively or triggered by some especially creative advertising or promotion appeal.[2]

An estimated 8 million Americans are designated "salesperson," but many millions more in the marketing organization have an impact on the selling process. In 1974, some $26 billion was spent on advertising, compared with the roughly $80 billion spent each year on selling. In the past, companies tried to keep their sales expense ratio at about 10 percent of sales volume. But today, with rising costs, personal selling is becoming even more expensive.

In reading this chapter, it is important to bear in mind that selling and marketing are not the same thing, even though firms that are still in the "selling era" (see Chapter 1) may use the terms almost interchangeably. In a marketing approach, sales do not result simply from personal selling efforts. Rather, they are the result of the combination of all the elements in the marketing mix. In some cases, the personal selling element has even been eliminated entirely, with other factors in the marketing mix performing the "selling" function. Such is the case with some advertising and promotion campaigns and with distribution methods such as self-service retailing or vending machines.

THE PERSONAL SELLING ROLE

Buying system changes, the salesperson's role, and the sales manager's role in personal selling are all related. In the promotion mix of an organization, personal selling often becomes the dominant note.

TYPES OF SELLING

All personal sales jobs are not created equal. For this reason, several ways of classifying them have been devised. The one we will use identifies four basic types of selling: trade, missionary, technical, and new business.[3]

1. *Trade.* Trade selling is done in many industries, particularly food, textiles, apparel, and wholesaling. These are areas where products are well established, so that high-powered selling is not necessary.

The trade salesperson's job is to build up volume by providing customers with promotional assistance. This type of salesperson sells *through*, rather than *to*, customers. As a result, the trade salesperson must understand how the customer runs his or her business. Being helpful and persuasive are more important than being aggressive, since the trade salesperson must wear well with customers.

2. *Missionary.* Personal selling assistance is the key to stimulating more or seeking new sales. The medical detail person is a good example. He or she calls on physicians as the representative of a drug company, attempting to persuade them to prescribe the company's products for their patients' problems.

Missionary salespeople, like trade salespeople, use a low-key approach. They are, however, selling *for* direct customers rather than *through* them. A successful missionary salesperson is thoroughly familiar with the market and can make an effective presentation of product benefits.

3. *Technical.* The technical salesperson is like a professional consultant: he or she must be able to tell the customer what his buying needs are. The company views such a salesperson as a means of increasing sales volume to existing customers through additional product uses—especially in chemicals, machinery, and heavy equipment categories. Since the technical salesperson

sells directly to the user or buyer, technical competence is as important as being personable.

    4. New business. The new-business salesperson, as the name indicates, is concerned with obtaining new accounts. This process is also referred to as "canvassing," "bird-dogging," and "cold-calling." A new-business salesperson has to be tough and able to withstand rejection. Because the demands are so great, the turnover rate in new-business selling is high.

THE BUYER–SELLER RELATIONSHIP

In recent decades, changes in the buying system of consumers and organizations have had a great impact on what type of personal selling arrangements and behavior are appropriate. First we will identify the new buying situations that have resulted from these changes and then we will see how the role of the salesperson has changed to fit them. In terms of distribution, preselling permits many products to be sold without personal contact (as in supermarkets, catalogs, and direct mail). Complex goods and services, however, often require professional selling assistance (as with mutual funds, stereo systems, and health maintenance organizations).

    Changes in organizational buying patterns have had a very heavy impact on the sellers of industrial goods and services. There are fewer and larger organizations doing business today. In the mid-1970s, only 14 percent of all business firms accounted for 84 percent of total receipts. Of course, many small, independent firms must still be reckoned with in designing a selling program. But the relatively few corporate giants will determine survival of many sales organizations.

    As we saw in Chapter 10, the role of the organization's purchasing agent has been very much modified by the centralization of purchasing decisions. The responsibility for long-term supply programs is rarely left in a single buyer's hands, but is entrusted to upper level executives. This centralization is an inevitable outgrowth of customers' growing needs for information and technical expertise.

    Diffused buying responsibility has also affected buying system changes. Organizations now commit themselves to long-term relationships with sellers, not to specific purchases. This means that purchasing decisions are influenced by personnel from various departments and sometimes outside experts as well.

    The introduction of systems buying is another element in the picture. Today, as firms grow larger, they are less likely to buy merchandise on an individual basis. More often, they think in terms of a product package, such as computer hardware, software, and support services.

    Change has also been brought about by the increase in negotiated transactions. Such transactions have followed the reorganization of sales forces into large, disciplined complexes. At one time, business was conducted on a local basis. Now, giant retailers usually prefer to deal directly with their suppliers' executives without the aid of salespeople.

    Lastly, the emergence of supplier development is coloring the buying picture. Supplier development refers to the creation of a new source of supply by the purchaser. The purchaser himself, in other words, takes the initiative in developing new sources of supply.

THE CHANGING ROLE OF SALESPEOPLE

In response to these important changes in buying systems, the role of salespeople has often changed beyond recognition. The essence of the salesperson's new role is to serve as the link between the selling and buying systems, not just as someone who makes a sale. Most salespeople today have more education and technical training than their predecessors. Probably, they are backed by a team of specialists, such as financial experts, engineers, and marketing researchers. They are more interested in establishing long-term relationships than in making quick sales. Even the salesperson's title has changed—to "field manager," "account manager," "sales engineer," and so forth. No longer is the salesperson merely the pitchman for a product. Instead, he or she must be the diagnostician of a customer's needs and problems as well as the consultant who makes recommendations.

As one top executive explains, "more and more companies are selling on many different levels, interlocking their research, engineering, marketing, and upper management with those of their customers. This way, today's salesman becomes a kind of committee chairman within his company.... His job is to exploit the resources of his company in serving the customer."[4] At Del Monte, the giant food producer, the actual selling is handled by an account representative who makes the direct calls and writes up the orders. Below the representative is the sales representative, who works with the store managers on shelf management, restocking, and display.

Another new role the salesperson must play is financial adviser. As new product lines appear constantly, the modern salesperson must deal with a customer as an investor as well as a purchaser. If a salesperson is trying to sell a product that will outdate a product the customer already has, he or she may have to help the customer figure out how to unload the current equipment economically.

Like other professionals, salespeople are at the mercy of the economy and can feel unneeded if shortages develop in product lines. But while they may relinquish one type of selling temporarily, they still maintain relationships with clients and with management. And they can sell other company products that are not in short supply. For example, when the oil crisis struck, salespeople for Sun Oil began promoting a new product called "hydrocarbon management."[5] This industrial lubrication package included field test kits for checking lube quality, a computerized system for preparing correct lube schedules and matching the right lube with the right machine, and oil reclaiming units.

ROLE OF THE SALES MANAGER

What does the **sales manager** do in the context of the buyer-seller relationship? Answers to that question will vary widely from one firm to another. In some places, the sales manager is the marketing manager in everything but title. In others, the sales manager functions only to make forecasts and budgets or to supervise salespeople. Still, there are certain basic functions that most sales managers share:[6]

1. development and planning of specific personal selling goals;
2. accomplishment of these goals through the sales organization;
3. evaluation of goals and accomplishments and revision of these goals.

As a result of organizational pressures to increase selling productivity, the sales manager's job emphasizes two major areas. First, the new sales manager does much more development of strategy at a higher marketing level. The manager is a planner, not just an operator. Second, he or she is increasingly involved in new profit responsibilities. Use of computers allows for faster accumulation of large amounts of data (which salespeople are most productive, which products sell best, and so forth). The successful sales manager must be able to interpret that information for profit.

HOW PERSONAL SELLING WORKS

The systems approach is useful for understanding the dynamics of personal selling and the elements of a successful personal selling strategy.

THE PERSONAL SELLING SYSTEM

A model of a personal selling system should be general enough to include any possible sales situation.[7] And it should allow for insight into a particular sales situation: What's good about it? What's wrong? Has one approach been overstressed at the expense of the system as a whole? Figure 19-2 shows such a model of the selling process.

It is the seller's job to select the most desirable combination of human, technological, and organizational **input** from the environment to make the sale.

Human input comes from salespeople, managers, and other personnel, as well as the customer. Technological input refers to a whole complex of factors relevant to the sales process: physical equipment such as order forms and showroom, as well as advertising and organization of the sales department. Organizational input refers to the hierarchy of goals, policies, and procedures specific to a situation, including the system of reward and the division of labor.

How these input elements are combined affects the **transformation** process. As the customer and salesperson interact, the attitudes and behavior of each are modified.

A successful sales encounter is more likely to occur when:

1. the characteristics of consumer and salesperson are closely matched;
2. the consumer perceives the salesperson as credible and trustworthy;
3. the consumer is susceptible to persuasion;
4. the salesperson impresses the buyer favorably.

Feedback refers to the rebounding of information from the sales encounter. Information can be used to modify any of the sales inputs (closed system), or to seek new input from the environment (open system).

SUCCESSFUL PERSONAL SELLING

Clearly, one of the most important elements in the personal selling system is the individual salesperson. Bethlehem Steel, for example, provides this information to would-be salespeople: "We're seeking college graduates who are personable and intelligent, who have good appearance, and who enjoy dealing with other people. You have to be able to think, to absorb training, to master product knowledge, and finally, to put that knowledge together with your personal sales acumen. The sales experience and maturity will follow."[8]

Certain elements are critical in developing effective personal selling strategies. First, the salesperson must analyze the market situation and the buyer's needs. He or she must be aware of what is happening within the industry, what the competition is doing, how market patterns are changing, what related lines of merchandise are moving onto the market.

The salesperson must also be thoroughly grounded in all aspects of the product. Product knowledge often compensates for many shortcomings. If a salesperson's employer does not provide him with enough product information, he or she should seek it independently.

In addition to product knowledge, the salesperson must have solid organizational orientation. This means knowing precise terms of pricing, credit, order handling, delivery. It also means having information on the company's reputation, organization, and management. He or she should be able to name executive personnel, as well as anyone with whom the buyer might have contact.

Figure 19-2   A SYSTEMS MODEL OF THE SELLING PROCESS

From Thomas S. Robertson and Richard B. Chase, "The Sales Process: An Open Systems Approach," *MSU Business Topics* 16 (Autumn 1968): 48. Reprinted by permission of the publisher, Division of Research, Graduate School of Business Administration, Michigan State University.

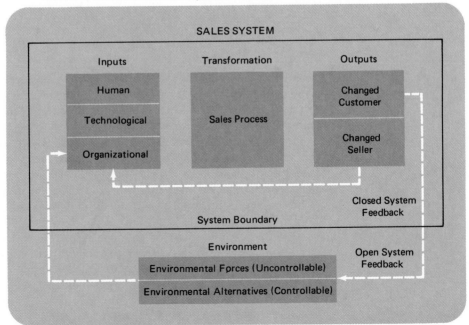

One survey of 1,000 male college students unearthed the following stereo-types about selling:

> Selling is a job—not a profession or a career.
>
> Salespeople must lie and be deceitful in order to succeed.
>
> To be a good salesperson, you have to be psychologically maladjusted.
>
> One must be arrogant and overbearing to succeed in selling.
>
> Selling benefits only the seller.
>
> Selling is no job for a person with talent and brains.

Obviously, salespeople do not share these attitudes, although they have learned to live with those who do. The rewards of selling have been spelled out many times. Selling experience is a reliable avenue for promotion to executive positions. Selling offers excellent opportunities to make top money. And a personal selling background is often a valuable prelude to establishing one's own business.

Perhaps the most important reward for the good salesperson is a personal one—the sense of achievement. C. N. Painter of Armstrong Cork Company raises these questions: "What equipment salesman first persuaded a dentist to try those nearly painless high-speed drills? What salesman first persuaded an office manager to try a photocopying machine, or an electric typewriter?" What salesman first induced a supermarket manager to stock and display frozen foods?"

Based on Donald L. Thompson, "Stereotype of the Salesman," *Harvard Business Review* 50 (January–February 1972): 21; and C. N. Painter, *Selling as a Career* (Lancaster, Pa.: Armstrong Cork, 1972), pp. 11–12.

The Salesperson Profile

There is no one set of personality traits required for success in sales. A salesperson cannot walk into a job interview confident of having all the "right equipment." However, the presence of motivation and general competence in a salesperson are encouraging.

The process of becoming a good salesperson is a dynamic one. Almost every bookstore contains a shelf of volumes that offer to teach sales success. These books have titles like *How I Sold a Billion* or *Learning to Sell to Tough Clients*. Many of these books are interesting to read, as they usually relate the tale of a self-made success. But as manuals of salesmanship, they have limited value. First, the reader is far removed from the writer's experience in time, space, and perception. Second, such books focus almost exclusively on the salesperson, consigning the customer to a minor, passive role.

Although there may not be an ideal salesperson profile, salesperson stereotypes are traditional. It has been remarked that "Perhaps no other occupation has been subjected to quite so much amateur analysis and pseudo-psychology as personal selling, without moving one step closer to an understanding of the problems and influences involved."[9]

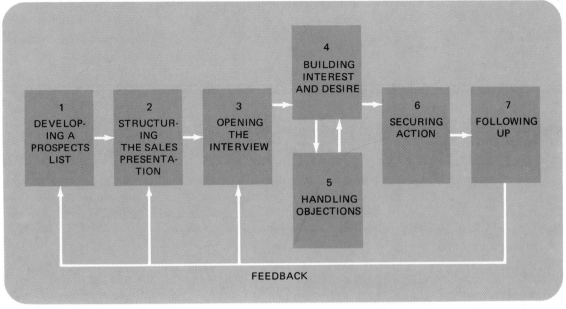

Figure 19-3   STAGES OF THE PERSONAL SELLING PROCESS

Good salespeople are both born and made. Most often success comes from a combination of innate talent and acquired skills.

THE PERSONAL SELLING PROCESS

The basic steps in the personal selling process must be mastered by every salesperson. In professional selling, the process may be carried out by a team of specialists (as with electrical equipment) and may take months or even years (as with aircraft).

The personal selling process is shown in Figure 19-3. The first step is to develop a list of prospects. Prospects include existing and potential customers who have a likely need for the product and the ability to purchase it. In some companies this list is provided; in others, the individual salesperson must develop contacts by scouting out leads.

The next step is to create a presentation. It can be completely unstructured—that is, the salesperson describes the product any way he or she sees fit—or fully automated, accompanied by sound movies, slides, or film strips. Or it can fall anywhere in between. Generally, firms use several types of presentation simultaneously. The unstructured approach is particularly popular, especially once a salesperson has gained experience and confidence.

The third step is to conduct an interview. The interview should generally go according to the **AIDA** theory. This theory (which was introduced in Chapter 18) divides the buying process into four stages through which the buyer passes mentally: attention, interest, desire, action. Unless favorable attention is secured, the interview won't go much further. Next, the salesperson tries to arouse the buyer's interest and desire, often by exploring his or her needs and problems and how the product relates to them.

Handling objections is part of the salesperson's job during the interest and desire stage. It can rarely be assumed that the interview will go exactly

Attention

Interest

Desire

Action

447

as the salesperson wishes. In reality, the customer often raises objections. He or she may want more time to think, may question the product's value, dislike the terms of sale, or indicate a lack of confidence in the salesperson. The ability to face objections is acquired with time and experience.

The climax of the sales presentation is the securing action. The sale may be closed with the customer's decision to buy or not to buy, or a meeting may be scheduled with other personnel who influence the buying decision. The customer may be ready to say yes early in the interview, or not until much time and talk have passed.

The successful salesperson does not let the matter end even with the closing of a sale. Following up is an important part of the selling process. It includes checking on how well the product is selling for a retail customer or how satisfied the organizational customer is.

SALES FORCE MANAGEMENT

The heart of the managerial task has been defined as "coordinating and combining individual efforts into a total organizational effort to achieve some overall goal or a set of goals."[10] The range of activities in managing the sales force is illustrated in Figure 19-4, which will serve as the basis for our discussion of sales management.

The managerial task is a difficult one. Sales managers have been accused of many mistakes, including hiring by instinct, pushing trainees too quickly,

Figure 19-4   THE SALES MANAGEMENT PROCESS

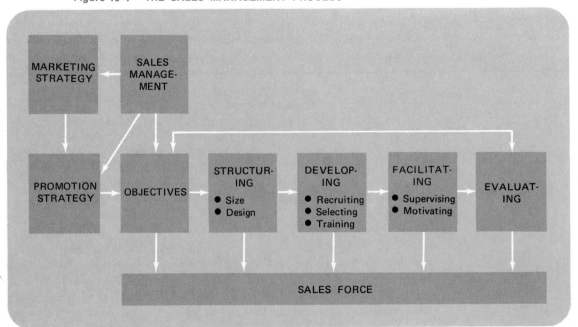

ignoring the importance of motivation, not communicating properly, and failing to show sales leadership. They have been criticized for not being properly "scientific" in their decision making, for pursuing sales volume instead of profit, for neglecting comprehensive planning and preferring to think on their feet.

On behalf of the sales manager, it should be said that his or her stock in trade is salespeople and customers, not machinery and parts. Many variables in the human equation are difficult to predict or allow for. Even known quantities can interact in unpredictable ways.

OBJECTIVES FOR THE SALES FORCE

In working out **sales force objectives**, many factors deserve consideration: What selling strategy should be used with a particular customer? With a particular product? Should the emphasis be on cost, performance, reliability, or something else? Whatever conclusions the sales manager reaches, the selling job must be defined closely enough so that employees have guidelines to follow in any situation.

Figure 19-5 illustrates a hierarchy of selling objectives.[11] Calculating the sales potential is the first step. The sales potential for any product is a measurement of the maximum sales revenues or units of sale of that product available to the firm in a given time period. In other words, it indicates the upper limit of sales. The forecast provides anticipated sales levels—usually a smaller figure than the potential. From the forecast, a determination of anticipated sales revenue can be made and a sales budget drawn up. A budget is a plan for selling, including all expenses and the amounts needed to hit a certain forecast level. It must be lower than anticipated revenues in order to make a profit.

The next step in the hierarchy is setting goals for market area divisions or sales territories (that is, groups of customers). The last step is the development of sales quotas against which sales results will be checked. Quotas can be set for more than sales volume alone. Often they are determined for individual product lines or specific types of customer.

STRUCTURING THE SALES FORCE

In planning an organizational **structure** for the sales force, management should take many things into consideration. These include size of the firm, nature of the market and of product lines, types of personnel in the organization. No single organization system is suited to all sales forces. In one firm, management may decide that all sales people should sell all products. In another, it may be more practical to have individuals assigned to single products.

Size

What is the right **size** for the sales force? One analyst has worked out a system based on equalizing workload.[12] The method assumes that management has determined the economical number of calls to make on accounts of different sizes. Using this formula, a company might estimate that there are 1,000 A-accounts and 2,000 B-accounts in the entire country. A-accounts require 36 calls a year and B-accounts 12 calls. The company then needs a sales force that can make 60,000 sales calls per year. If the average salesperson can make 1,000 calls per year, the company needs 60 full-time salespeople.

Some managers have the mistaken impression that the number of salespeople should be determined by the number of sales, rather than the other way around. These managers are likely to add to the sales force when dollar sales are up and to fire when they are down. But this represents a distorted view of the salesperson's role. The salesperson is the one who brings about new sales, and adding to the force is a capital investment. The manager should compare the expected rate of return with the expected rate for other corporate investments before deciding to hire or fire.

Design   The effectiveness of a sales force depends primarily on how it is organized. Various types of **design structure** are possible, and we will briefly examine a few of the more common ones.

Territories. Under the simplest sales structure, each salesperson represents the firm's full product line in a specific territory. Such a setup defines the salesperson's responsibilities clearly, as failure in sales in the area must be laid directly on the individual's shoulders. This structure encourages the salesperson to develop personal and business ties in the area. Such a structure also reduces travel expenses.

Products. Many companies find that assigning the sales force according to product line has advantages, especially when the products are technically complex, highly unrelated, or very numerous. But just because a company offers different products does not mean that a product-structured sales force is necessary. If one customer buys many separate product lines, for example, the setup can be a disadvantage. Company salespeople may be treading on each other's toes, lining up to see the same customers.

Customers. A customer-structured sales force has a major advantage in that it allows sales personnel to be more thoroughly aware of the customer's needs. There are several ways of structuring a sales force by customer. These include breakdowns by size, nature of business, and method of distribution. But like the product-oriented structure, a customer-oriented setup has disadvantages of overlapping coverage of territories.

National Cash Register is an example of a major firm that sells by industry rather than by product line.[13] The 3,000-person domestic sales force is assigned to specific markets such as retailing, financial, commercial/industrial, and medical/educational/governmental. A salesperson who sells a cash register to a department store, for example, would also sell a computer to the same store.

Key Accounts. With increasing frequency, sales efforts are being organized on the basis of major accounts. Usually, a major buyer has a number of units whose purchases are directed by a central corporate group, although individual branches may make the actual purchases. For example, J. P. Stevens & Company sells towels to executives at the Holiday Inn headquarters in Memphis,

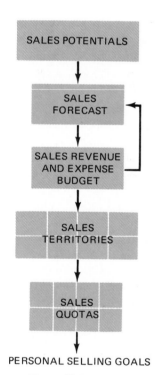

SALES POTENTIALS

SALES FORECAST

SALES REVENUE AND EXPENSE BUDGET

SALES TERRITORIES

SALES QUOTAS

PERSONAL SELLING GOALS

Figure 19-5
HIERARCHY OF SELLING OBJECTIVES

From Thomas R. Wotruba, *Sales Management: Planning, Accomplishment, and Evaluation* (New York: Holt, Rinehart and Winston, 1971), p. 13.

Tennessee, which buys for all its franchised motels across the nation. At Koppers Company, a national account executive looks after the broad buying needs of a given metals customer.

Other Variations. Some firms have developed still other variations on sales organization. At IBM, salespersons specialize by function, including maintenance and upgrading of systems, equipment protection, and installation. Other firms organize on a sequential basis: executives isolate the separate markets for each product line and focus on a single market before moving on to the next.

DEVELOPING THE SALES FORCE

The success of a sales program depends on developing a high-caliber sales staff. If salespeople are not properly developed for the job, no amount of supervision or compensation will make them effective.

Proper staffing (recruiting and selecting) is crucial. Yet some have charged that, today, selection of salespeople is a hit-or-miss proposition. One critic maintains that:

> *few managers recognize that there are significant variations among sales jobs; know precisely what qualities they need in a man for their own sales activities; understand how to locate and attract suitable candidates in sufficient numbers; have a plan to screen out the unqualified quickly and courteously; and are proficient in evaluating the qualifications and potential of the more promising applicants they see.*[14]

Management's aim is to find people with potential that can be developed through training and motivation. The selection process begins with careful job analysis and job description. It proceeds to recruiting potential salespeople, and to choosing from among available candidates. Finally, the new salespeople receive some type of training.

Recruiting

The selection of potential salespeople usually begins with **recruiting** efforts. Typically, the personnel department recruits by placing want ads, contacting employment agencies, and asking salespeople already on staff to suggest possibilities. Some recruiting is also done on college campuses.

A national products manager at Powers Regulator Company reports that "we contact employment agencies, professional societies, and use referrals within the industry. We just can't afford to take the guy, make the major investment in him for two or three years, and then have him sell the training that we gave him to someone else."[15] Powers Regulator is looking for salespeople (both men and women) who can become productive immediately. Sales quotas are so large and selling costs are so high that the company cannot afford nonproductive employees.

Selecting

Many criteria dictate the selection of a sales force. Does the organization want experienced professionals or qualified trainees? Training is expensive, and it may be more economical to select people who already know the job. If very specialized experience is being sought, however, the search may prove difficult and costly.

In general, companies are concerned with the individual's health, physical appearance, verbal fluency, and adaptability. Many companies routinely give psychological screening tests. These tests are useful in identifying traits of character and personality, but they cannot be used as the sole criterion. Other companies have developed lists of qualities deemed important to the good salesperson. But such lists are static: they cannot be used to predict how the salesperson will interact with customers in a dynamic situation.

Training   The training process is most effective when there is real interaction between salesperson and trainer. It is influenced by individual attitudes, the goal of training, and methods of teaching and evaluation.

Training can range from on-the-job training, to formal classroom sessions. **On-the-job training** means that the salesperson actually learns by doing the new job under the supervision of a seasoned salesperson or sales manager. This approach is attractive because it is cheaper and faster. But it runs the risk of producing graduates who are little more than imitators of people with relatively narrow experience.

There are several methods for **off-the-job training**. Choice will depend on specific objectives as well as on content of the training.[16]

1. *The case method.* Trainees are asked to discuss problem situations in a classroom setting. (These might resemble the cases in this book.) The situations are usually selling encounters with difficult customers.

2. *Role playing.* The trainee acts out a problem in order to experience it emotionally. This experience is used to test insights into the problem.

3. *The T-group method.* Trainees interact with each other while discussing specific topics. The aim is to increase understanding of how people interact with each other.

4. *Operational gaming.* A computerized or manually operated model of a hypothetical organization allows the trainee to use decision-making capabilities. Certain questions are answered about selling strategies and tactics. Rapid feedback reports the results of decisions.

Deciding which training approach is best means analyzing objectives. If memorization of technical information is the goal, written tests will probably serve the purpose. Whatever method is used, the test of value is subsequent performance. A student may do well in training, but the real test is his or her ability to interact and communicate in the actual selling encounter.

DIRECTING THE SALES FORCE   Even the most capable and motivated salesperson needs **direction** to bring out his or her top potential, as well as an incentive to keep performing at a top level.

Effective direction of the sales force means keeping open the lines of communication between management and sales. A two-way system keeps each side sensitive to the other's problems. If salespeople feel that management is accessible and sympathetic, they will be more productive. Coordination pays off.

A breakdown in the two-way system may have unhappy consequences.

Insecurity on the part of sales managers about their own ability to communicate leads to increasing emphasis on management and control which in turn leads to a decrease in the salesmen's competence requirements. As salesmen perceive the apparent unimportance of their jobs, performance falls off, leading to more management and control. This circular trend cannot be broken without substantial changes in the concept of the role of personal selling.[17]

Supervising

Sales **supervision** integrates the interests of the individual salesperson with those of the organization as a whole. In larger companies, the first-line manager is the district, divisional, or branch manager. In a smaller company, the sales manager or even the owner may serve as first-line manager. The first-line manager's job is to follow through on any actions regarding call quantity, quality, or time allocation. By training and motivating the first-line manager, the sales manager can bring about improved performance by the staff.

A sales force is usually made up of people with a wide variety of backgrounds and experience. Often staff members are hundreds of miles from headquarters. The first-line supervisor is physically close enough to direct, advise, and help them solve daily problems.

Companies have different philosophies about how much direction salespeople need. When salespeople work on commission, they are generally left

"If we have to fire someone, let's make it Preston—his pin is bent, anyway."

From the *Wall Street Journal*

to fend for themselves. When they are salaried, they will undoubtedly receive some supervision.

By the nature of the profession, the salesperson spends a lot of time waiting, for a phone call or an appointment—and traveling. With the sales manager's help, wasted time can be kept to a minimum. The salesperson can learn to fill out sales charts during odd moments. He or she can learn how to use the phone more effectively—particularly, to determine which prospects aren't worth seeing.

The sales manager may select potential accounts carefully, rather than having the staff cold-call. It is his or her job to allocate sales efforts and to make such decisions as whether to increase sales specialization, sell directly or through agents, grant price concessions. He or she analyzes which **sales calls** are productive and which special customer demands should be met.

Providing the sales staff with planning aids is part of sales supervision. Many companies issue monthly printouts that show how much business a salesperson is doing and how he or she stacks up against competitors or other salespeople in the company. Supervisors may also provide selling aids such as audio/visual cassettes, films, and soundstrips.

The effectiveness of sales performance can be tied directly to the effectiveness of the reporting system used to control the sales force. When management insists on frequent and regular reports, performance is better.

Motivating

Motivating salespeople is not an easy task, yet it is a vital one. If performance and morale are to remain high, the sales manager must be capable of building and sustaining motivation. Because people are individuals, a system of rewards and incentives should be individualized. It should be structured to encourage participation rather than simply to influence behavior.

People take jobs or go into business because they need money to survive. But money is not the only motivation. Psychological needs for security, approval, and self-esteem must also be satisfied.

Compensation

In most organizations, **compensation** programs are set up to attract qualified salespeople, keep them, and motivate them to maintain high performance levels. Some companies work on an all-commission or all-salary basis, but a combination of the two is frequent. In 1967, a survey of 444 manufacturers (employing 16,263 salespeople) found that 65 percent paid their sales force on a salary-plus-incentive basis.[18] The survey showed that salespeople tend to be more highly paid in large companies that use heavy advertising and sales promotion to sell nontechnical products. Pay is lower in businesses that work through personal contact and whose products are custom-made—shoes, for example.

Paradoxically, smaller companies tend to pay better than larger firms in the same industry. First, a smaller company relies more heavily on personalized selling, and must seek top sales personnel. Second, the smaller company usually has no training program, and must hire experienced salespeople away from competitors or other industries.

A company often works out an incentive plan by determining the gross amount of compensation it can afford to pay the average salesperson. Next, it decides how much should be in the form of base salary and how much bonus and/or commission. In the survey mentioned, the average salesperson received incentive pay amounting to more than a quarter of his regular salary.

A problem that may arise in compensating salespeople is identifying who is responsible for a sale. When the customer is a large organization, it may not be easy to pinpoint where the sale was made.

Should a $13,500 sale of Bausch & Lomb lenses be credited to the salesperson in Omaha who convinced the Techinstruments branch executive, or to the salesperson in Milwaukee who processed the order at the Techinstruments headquarters? Many companies feel that it is only fair to credit sales to the office where the sale originates (Omaha), rather than where it takes place (Milwaukee).

Other Incentives   The self-starter who is able to perform well without encouragement or inducement is rare. Most salespeople need **incentives** that reinforce morale and provide a psychological reward that is even greater than the financial one. Field selling is often frustrating. First, a salesperson is likely to follow a schedule that interrupts being with family and friends. Loneliness and a sense of disorientation may result. Second, it is human nature to resist going all out for a goal in the absence of reward. Third, salespeople can be preoccupied with personal problems, like anyone else, and they need incentives to make the job effort seem worthwhile.

Attempts to create sales incentives have taken many forms. Some companies offer frequent sales contests. Others set yearly sales quotas, granting a bonus to those who exceed their quota. Sales meetings are often scheduled with the idea of providing incentive. Relaxing in a partly social situation, salespeople have a sense of belonging to a larger effort. And they feel more free to express their feelings about the job. Favored locations for meetings include Miami, New Orleans, and Honolulu.

One analyst has singled out three nonfinancial incentives to sales efforts: status pay, privilege pay, and power pay.[19] Status pay refers to public recognition of a salesperson's success and of his or her good standing with management. Privilege pay refers to the freedom granted to an employee to approach and discuss special problems and ideas with the manager. Power pay rewards an individual by making his job more important, for instance, by giving him added responsibility.

EVALUATING THE SALES FORCE   The process of **evaluation** extends to the individual salesperson as well as to the sales force as a whole.

Salesperson Performance   A salesperson's value cannot stand on whether or not he or she makes a specific number of sales. Good salespeople have bad years, and mediocre salespeople can do well when the market is good. The following criteria have been proposed for analyzing sales performance:[20]

1. *Physical activity or efficiency.* How many calls did the salesperson make? How much time was spent with clients? How much of the company's money was spent?

2. *Adaptive behavior.* Can the salesperson understand different buying situations well enough to be persuasive in each?

3. *Instrumental performance.* Can the salesperson work without constant direction? Has he or she worked out an individual selling style and thinking process?

4. *System integration.* Can the salesperson integrate different performances and behaviors and bring them to bear on a situation?

5. *Value integration.* Is the salesperson competent to perform the total selling job? Is he or she committed to his employer's goals?

Evaluation of a salesperson is inevitably colored by qualities of the evaluator. A salesperson may be held in high esteem by the supervisor, while a member of the engineering department wonders why he doesn't know more about the intricacies of the product.

The salesperson's periodic work plan report provides management with one of the best barometers of performance. Work plans describe the calls the salesperson anticipates. From these, management can judge how well activities were projected and how closely the plan was followed. A supervisor will also evaluate on the basis of other salespeople's and customers' reports, and on personal observation.

The salesperson's career follows a natural life-cycle pattern, as Figure 19-6 indicates. The cycle of preparation, development, maturity, and decline can be repeated over and over, with each stage occupying different periods of time.

Figure 19-6

THE SALESPERSON'S CAREER CYCLE

From Marvin A. Jolson, "The Salesman's Career Cycle," *Journal of Marketing* 38 (July 1974): 39. Reprinted from *Journal of Marketing* published by the American Marketing Association.

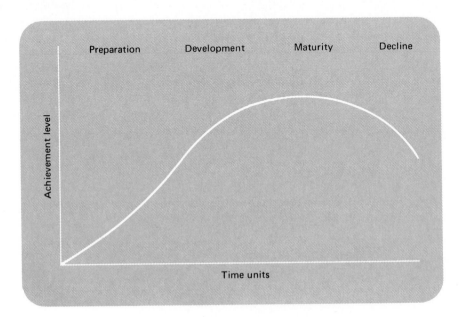

To maintain interest and motivation among sales personnel, many organizations have adopted a career path concept. Under this philosophy, salespeople undergo frequent evaluation and counseling from management. They are encouraged to set specific performance objectives, which become the basis for the next evaluation session.

The career path concept allows for a clear distinction between selling and management potential. It also recognizes the value and importance of the professional salesperson. And it defines an "up or out" policy at lower levels so that qualified juniors can get ahead.

The diagram shown here illustrates the steps in the sales career path. You can see that within each job designation, there are at least two levels of performance and competition.

After some experience, a sales trainee with the consent of the firm may decide to take on major selling responsibilities rather than supervise. This person would then become an account manager. At the first level, the account manager can still switch into sales supervision (and vice versa). But switching would not be possible at higher levels.

Perhaps the most important advantage to the career path approach is that it allows an individual to develop his or her managerial skills within the organization. It also guarantees that the salesperson's personal development will be carefully planned and evaluated. And it gives a young salesperson a clear path of opportunity ahead.

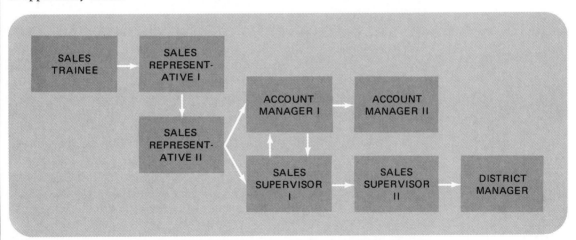

Based on Frederick E. Webster, Jr., *Marketing for Managers* (New York: Harper & Row, 1974), p. 271.

Ideally, the curve between preparation and development is steep, flattening out in the maturity stage. If employers can assess where each salesperson stands on the curve, they can better assess needs and deficiencies in his or her selling effort.

The Selling Function Five yardsticks have been suggested for evaluating the total selling function of the sales force:[21]

1. *Contribution to profit.* This figure can be determined by taking the cost plus markup figure for a product and subtracting all costs of the selling operation.

2. *Return on assets managed.* Current sales expenses such as salaries, travel, and entertainment are subtracted from gross profit on sales volume.

3. *Sales–cost ratio.* This index is the ratio of sales expenses divided by dollar sales volume. However, it shall not be used as the sole yardstick.

4. *Market share.* If product quality, pricing, advertising effectiveness, and competitors' activity do not change, an increased market share could be attributed to a more productive sales effort.

5. *Achievement of company marketing goals.* Sales performance can be judged on whether certain sales and profit targets have been realized.

Judgment of the sales force is also based on turnover rate—the hiring, firing, and quitting of salespeople. Although there is no direct relationship between turnover rate and quality of the staff, a turnover rate higher than 10 percent is costly. Customers' ordering routines are interrupted when a salesperson leaves, and customer-salesperson rapport must be re-established.

CONCLUSION

Selling is a much more complex business today than ever before. Millions of people are involved in the selling process, not all of them with the title "salesperson." Today, sales takes many forms—trade, technical, missionary, new business. Many kinds of selling are removed from face-to-face confrontation. The modern salesperson is often backed by a strong force of marketing, financial, and technical experts.

But while selling reaches ever wider horizons, the nature of the selling process remains essentially unchanged. Successful selling means developing personal qualities and technical expertise. There is no one ideal salesperson profile, but top salespeople are highly motivated, energetic, and knowledgeable about their product. And they know how to win others to their side. Effective selling is based on a knowledge of techniques to draw the potential customer's interest and bring about an action goal.

The good salesperson must understand the needs of the customer. And the good sales manager must understand the needs of the staff. He or she must be able to choose among various means of structuring the sales force for maximum productivity. In addition, the manager must know how to recruit, select, train, motivate, and evaluate.

Personal selling has come in for its share of social criticism. This includes complaints about high pressure, unethical selling techniques on the part of door-to-door salespeople (especially in ghetto areas) and incompetent or discourteous salespeople in retail and service firms. The vast majority of professional salespeople, however, perform this important marketing task in a responsible, professional manner.

Some analysts predict that in the future, selling will rest on a par with marketing. Others foresee the day when the salesperson will become the most important employee in an organization, with management playing a supportive role.

DISCUSSION QUESTIONS

1. In the context of professional personal selling today, why is a sales order an inadequate measure of a saleperson's success? Would your opinion differ for a computer salesperson and an encyclopedia salesperson?
2. Design a comprehensive list of criteria for reviewing the elements of a successful personal selling effort for sailboats, industrial furnaces, and museum fund-raising.
3. Describe how you would plan the personal selling process in the following situations:
    a. Espresso coffee machines to the owners of small restaurants.
    b. An improved version of Astroturf to a planned sports stadium in Portland, Oregon.
    c. A radio communications (one-way paging) system to Detroit area firms.
    d. A new low-calorie cake line to a supermarket chain buying committee.
4. What would be an appropriate series of objectives for the selling effort of: a new suburban department store branch, a university's centennial anniversary alumni-giving campaign, a window-cleaning service for private houses, and a surgical instruments manufacturer?
5. SealAmerica Corporation markets foam sealants to the automobile, construction, mobile home, and appliance industries. Explain how you might structure its sales force.
6. Which is more important: finding the right person for the selling job or designing the right selling job for competent people? Explain.
7. What type of assistance could a sales supervisor give to salespeople who are new on the job, who are coping with product shortages, or who are spending too much time in prospects' waiting rooms?

NOTES

1. "First You Sell It—Then You Plant It," *American Vegetable Grower*, May 1975, p. 19.
2. B. Charles Ames, "Build Marketing Strength into Industrial Selling," *Harvard Business Review* 50 (January–February 1972): 48.
3. Gary M. Grikscheit and W. J. E. Crissy, "Personal Selling: A Position Paper," in Ross Lawrence Goble and Roy T. Shaw, eds., *Controversy and Dialogue in Marketing* (Englewood Cliffs, N.J.: Prentice-Hall, 1975), p. 270.
4. "The New Supersalesman: Wired for Success," *Business Week*, January 6, 1973, p. 45.
5. "The Salesman's New Job: Drumming Up Supplies," *Business Week*, October 26, 1974, p. 58.
6. Thomas R. Wotruba, *Sales Management: Planning, Accomplishment, and Evaluation* (New York: Holt, Rinehart and Winston, 1971), p. 9.
7. This section is based largely on Thomas S. Robertson and Richard B. Chase, "The Sales Process: An Open Systems Approach," *MSU Business Topics* 16 (Autumn 1968): 45–52.
8. Bethlehem Steel, "Careers in Sales," p. 6.
9. Patrick J. Robinson and Bent Stidsen, *Per-*

sonal Selling in a Modern Perspective (Boston: Allyn and Bacon, 1967), p. 227.

10. Albert Wesley Frey, ed., *Marketing Handbook*, 2d ed. (New York: Ronald Press, 1965), pp. 9:8–9.

11. This section is based on Wotruba, p. 12.

12. Walter J. Talley, "How to Design Sales Territories," *Journal of Marketing* 25 (January 1961): 7–13.

13. "NCR's Radical Shift in Marketing Tactics," *Business Week*, December 8, 1973, p. 102.

14. Robert N. McMurry and James S. Arnold, *How To Build a Dynamic Sales Organization* (New York: McGraw-Hill, 1968), p. 9.

15. "The New Supersalesman," p. 49.

16. This section is based on Robinson and Stidsen, pp. 238–39.

17. Ibid., p. 227.

18. Richard C. Smyth, "Financial Incentives for Salesmen," *Harvard Business Review* 46 (January–February 1968): 109.

19. Robert Dubin, *Human Relations in Administration* (Englewood Cliffs, N.J.: Prentice-Hall, 1968), pp. 297–99, 317–20.

20. Robinson and Stidsen, p. 245.

21. Porter Henry, "Manage Your Sales Force as a System," *Harvard Business Review* 53 (March–April 1975): 75.

CASE STUDIES

SAINT VINCENT'S COLLEGE

College Statistics

Saint Vincent's College is located on an 1100-acre campus in Cordova, Alaska, roughly a one-hour drive from Anchorage. It was established in 1922 by the Society of the Precious Blood, a Roman Catholic religious order. Many brothers of the Society continue to teach and work at the college, though the board of trustees is now composed of local business leaders.

Saint Vincent's was originally a junior college for male students. In 1937 the first four-year class was graduated, and in 1966 the first women students were admitted. Currently, the college has approximately 1300 fulltime students.

The Present Situation

In February, 1976, Saint Vincent's College suffered a devastating fire. The oldest building on campus—which housed important administrative offices, classrooms, and laboratories—was burnt to the ground. Only courageous action by students saved the entire college from destruction.

Soon after the fire, Dan Reiner and Paul Soccoli met to devise advertising strategy for a large capital campaign to replace the central building. Dan Reiner, the college's vice-president for public relations and development, formerly handled similar duties for a Canadian public utility. Paul Soccoli, a talented young art director and writer for an Anchorage advertising agency, is a Saint Vincent's alumnus.

Suggestions for the Advertising Campaign

"Dan, we're at a crisis point. If we don't raise a bundle of money quickly, morale on this campus will sink to zero. Students will transfer, faculty and administrators will leave, alumni will lose interest in the college. We need a bold, new strategy to raise money.

"I suggest we start with an ad in the *Wall Street Journal*. This is perhaps the most important newspaper in the nation, certainly one of the finest and most impartial. If we can reach this kind of readership with our story, we'll get all sorts of dividends. I know we're short on advertising budgets, but at least we can put something in the western regional edition."

"I don't know, Paul," Dan Reiner responded. "Don't you think we should stick with the 'old reliables' (direct mail and phone campaigns to alumni)? We tried an ad in *Newsweek* three years ago with a message about fund raising and student recruitment. We got our money back, but the ad didn't really work."

"Oh, come on, Dan. You know as well as I do that the *Newsweek* ad had no real focus. We've got a unique story here. Our students risked their lives to save their college. People will be interested in that. These students aren't burning down their campus, they're preventing it from burning down!

"We can try an ad in *Time*. A photograph of a priest who teaches for $60 a month. Plus statistics showing that the cost of educating college students has jumped 30 percent in two years. We can place this in the western and midwestern editions, and, with luck, we'll raise maybe $50,000 and get national exposure.

461

"At the same time, we put an ad in *Seventeen*. We tell readers that Saint Vincent's is anxious to recruit more women students. We stress the advantages of a Christian humanist education. And we include a coupon on the bottom so readers can write to us for information. I'll bet we can pull 1000 responses."

"Look, Paul, these ideas are exciting, they're creative—but are they practical? My advertising budget doesn't begin to cover this kind of stuff. And our board of trustees wasn't tossing money around even before the fire. Now they're watching every penny like hawks. To put these ideas into action, we'd have to squeeze them hard with a proposal for a long-term promotional program."

"Dan, this is our only chance! And there are so many potential payoffs. A good advertising campaign can be a springboard for free nation-wide publicity, for foundation grants, for emergency appeals to alumni. We've got a dramatic story, we've got a serious need, all we need is a good push. Let's give it a try."

Questions
1. Should Saint Vincent's College go ahead with the "fire" advertisement in the *Wall Street Journal*?
2. What other promotional efforts, if any, would you propose for a long-term promotional strategy?

SOUTHEAST MICHIGAN TRANSIT AUTHORITY

The Present Situation

The Southeast Michigan Transit Authority (SEMTA) was created in the mid-1970s to administer the Michigan Central Railroad's commuter lines in the Detroit metropolitan area. The Michigan state legislature delegated broad powers to SEMTA, including the power to establish fares and schedules without external regulation from the Public Service Commission.

SEMTA is basically a way for the state to absorb out-of-pocket expenses for labor and equipment for the commuter lines. Personnel from Michigan Central still run the railroad. But there have been several noticeable changes since SEMTA took over. Within two years, a deteriorating commuter line has been transformed into a modern and efficient mass transit system. Nearly three-fourths of the railroad's oldest cars (35 years and more) have been replaced. At the same time, the on-time performance of all trains rose from 55 percent to 90 percent.

Unfortunately, SEMTA has not proven that it can pay its own way. As of November, 1975, revenues were not substantially greater than they were at the time of the takeover—despite all of the improvements in service. A series of marketing innovations aimed at rush-hour commuters and potential off-peak riders has achieved disappointing results. To put it bluntly, SEMTA is in trouble.

Memorandum

FROM: Diane Gottlieb, Marketing Researcher
TO: De Witt S. Bradshaw, President, SEMTA

DATE: December 15, 1975

SUBJECT: Analysis of SEMTA marketing innovations

As you asked, I have surveyed the recent marketing innovations instituted by SEMTA. These fall into two broad categories: (1) attempts to reach rush-hour commuters; (2) attempts to increase the number of off-peak riders.

1. *Rush-hour commuters.* Eighty percent of all SEMTA revenues come from weekday rush-hour riders. In an attempt to improve services for these riders, we have instituted two principal reforms. We cut a few minutes off normal commuting time by adding extra trains in rush hours. Also, we devised Check-it, a ticket mail service. This allows rush-hour commuters to purchase monthly commutation tickets through the mails. The tickets are sent out during the third week of each month, and commuters can pay by check or money order.

Results: We have improved morale among regular rush-hour commuters by reducing travel time. But Check-it has been a failure. Only 20 percent of regular commutation ticket buyers have taken advantage of this service. The principal reasons for hesitation seem to be the commuters' fear that their tickets will be lost in the mail, and the ticket agents' fear that Check-it threatens their jobs. The latter fouls up the entire strategy, since ticket agents are not informing regular commuters about Check-it.

2. *Off-peak commuters.* Our marketing research suggested that the general public was largely unaware of special excursion rates in off-peak riding hours. As a result, we developed four new rate schemes for non-rush-hour commuters: the student plan, the shoppers' plan, the excursion rate, and the family rate. Schedule changes were announced in all stations. Information on fares was listed in new timetables. Notices were placed in local newspapers throughout the Detroit metropolitan area. And leaflets were left in evening rush-hour trains.

Results: Again, our innovations brought about only minor changes in riders and revenues. Here the main mistake begins with marketing strategy. We failed to do a proper analysis of desirable market segments. Not knowing *who* we really wanted to reach, it's not surprising that we didn't figure out *how* to reach them. Furthermore, our main promotional campaigns were geared to people who were already riding SEMTA trains (particularly during rush hours.) This was an extremely inefficient method for attracting the interest of off-peak shoppers, bus riders, students, etc.

Memorandum

FROM: De Witt S. Bradshaw, President, SEMTA

TO: Diane Gottlieb, Marketing Researcher

DATE: December 21, 1975

SUBJECT: Analysis of SEMTA marketing innovations

Your memorandum of December 15 was concise, informative, and disturbing. It certainly seems that we've been misguided in our marketing approach.

I'd like you to do further research on potential conflicts between SEMTA and the auto industry. We've got to gain riders by convincing them not to ride their cars to work, school, and shopping centers. But, if we're effective, the General Motors and Ford lobbyists may be after us at the state capital. Please look into this for me.

Questions

1. Design the coming year's promotion mix for SEMTA to include strategies for: (a) advertising; (b) sales promotion; (c) publicity; and (d) sales force.
2. What, if any, other marketing strategies would you recommend?

MARSHALL, VEGA, AND HOE

Marketing Background

Thomas I. Neumann is the senior vice-president and executive creative director for Marshall, Vega, and Hoe, a New York City advertising agency. One evening, after the phones had finally quieted down, Neumann sat at his cluttered desk munching a sandwich. In three days, he faced a meeting with Holden marketing executives about their newest product—Holden Hardy II razor blades. Neumann's task was to create an advertising campaign and positional strategy for the Holden innovation.

In January, 1974, Finedge had introduced a new razor blade: the Finedge Two-Trak. This move was a dramatic development in the industry, because it featured two razor edges on the same side of the blade. Finedge promoted the product heavily, promising buyers "closeness" and a "revolutionary new shave." It aimed its advertising campaign at the single-edge shaver, including long-time Holden users. Ironically, Holden had already developed working models of a similar product, but failed to bring out its Hardy II in time. Finedge had beaten Holden to the punch.

The Proposed Advertising Campaign

Neumann carefully considered this background data, then began speaking into his dictaphone:

"Advertising campaign for the Holden Hardy II shaver.

"OK, let's take a quick look at the market. Finedge has historically been the double-edge-man's company. Holden, on the other hand, has concentrated on the single-edge injector shaver. Yet Finedge comes out with its Two-Trak and goes after the single-edge market. It assumes that it can hold its double-edge users without any special marketing effort.

"My general theory in these situations is to combine a two-pronged approach. First, we develop a better product than our competitors. Second, we determine and attack their marketing weakness.

"I believe we have the better product. We've done thousands of shaving tests with a reputable testing firm. And the clear result is that the Holden Hardy II delivers *more better* shaves.

"*More better* shaves. Now what does that mean to the engineer in Edwardsville? Here's where we have to be extremely careful in our advertising and positioning. If we put an ad on television stating that the Hardy II gives more better shaves, we'll do nothing more than offend every high school English teacher in the country. We won't communicate anything to our market.

"Our research shows clearly that Holden and Finedge users don't care about getting more shaves per blade. They believe that if you get many more shaves per blade, it can only be because the blade isn't as sharp after a while. So, emphasizing this point—even if we convince them we're right—won't help any.

"But our research shows something else that's a lot more helpful. The key words and concepts in defining a *better shave* are closer, safer, comfortable, and smoother.

"Finedge's magic word has always been *closeness*. The words Finedge and closeness are practically synonymous in the minds of shavers. So we can't attack them on that battlefield; we'll only lose.

"Holden's traditional image, on the other hand, is one of safety and comfort. This is our strength, and I believe it's also Finedge's soft underbelly.

"I think we have a chance of denting their market with a campaign based on Holden's superior *safety*. We run a series of ads with the Two-Trak and Holden Hardy II next to each other. We read our test results—impartial surveys by respected authorities suggest that the Holden Hardy II gives better shaves. Then we focus on the safe and comfortable shave you get with Holden.

"I think we can do two things with this campaign. We can retrieve some of the single-edge users we've lost to Finedge. And, interestingly, I believe we can make a successful pitch to the Finedge double-edge users. They've been neglected recently and they just might be ripe for a marketing raid."

Neumann sat back in his chair with a contented look on his face. "I think it can work because I honestly believe we have the better product. I've been saying this all along. Advertising can only become credible when it has something real to promote. Give me a good product, and I'll give you a great marketing prospect."

Questions
1. What factors account for Tom Neumann's dilemma with Holden Hardy II marketing?
2. What advertising position should Neumann propose to the client?

XABS/AM RADIO STATION

XABS/AM Radio Station of Tucson, Arizona, is affiliated with the National Broadcasting Company's News and Information Service (NIS). NIS is a $10 million NBC investment that allows local stations to play only news and features all day long. The 250-member NIS staff develops programming for affiliates in Dallas, Cleveland, Minneapolis, Miami, Honolulu, Las Vegas, and many other cities and towns across the country.

Evaluating XABS's Problems

One evening toward the end of November, 1976, Roy Cedergreen sat yawning on the half-empty plane heading from Tucson to New York City. Cedergreen, a key representative for the NBC/NIS Station Relations Staff, had just finished a week in Tucson examining the problems of XABS. NIS had hoped that a good sales showing from XABS could convince Ustinova Broadcasting, the owners of nine radio stations throughout the Southwest, to affiliate *all* of its stations with the national news service. But UB was disappointed with the performance of XABS, its only link to NIS. Cedergreen's task was to find the problems and recommend solutions to UB and NIS.

The Problem Is at the Top

Cedergreen switched on his dictaphone. "November 19, 1976. This is a report on station XABS/AM, Tucson, Arizona. Mark it confidential."

"I have just completed a week in Tucson at the XABS offices. My basic finding is that the station's sales situation is distressing.

"Incredibly enough, until two months ago, XABS had only one salesperson. Now there are three: Carl Moncure, Eva Battle, and K. C. Kane. All are qualified and eager. When I spoke with them about the "how to" and "where to" of selling all-news, they became fascinated. It was as if they hadn't heard anything on the subject before. And perhaps they hadn't.

"The three of them are constantly developing new ideas for advertising time. Battle and Kane are working on a plan to encourage retailers to place more public service ads on XABS. Their argument is that an all-news station is a logical vehicle for commercials about special sales and events. Thus far, a number of retailers have shown real interest.

"Unfortunately, enthusiasm and creativity aren't enough. Moncure, Battle, and Kane all need training and direction. They're getting *nothing*. Neil Seidman, the new sales manager of XABS, is the cause. He has a poor attitude and he constantly bad-mouths Tucson—the local agencies, the local business people, the XABS staff, everything. He puts little time and effort into supervising the salespeople. And he's very distant when they come to him with new ideas. When Battle and Kane told me about the public service advertising campaign, I was impressed and told them so. Kane mentioned that this was the first time a station "higher up" had given them any encouragement.

"The station's general manager, Ralph Lindsay, is not much better than Seidman. Lindsay is a genuinely decent person, but he's not very competent. Whereas Seidman is talented but lacks motivation, Lindsay can't even read his own budget or locate critical financial figures. He told me that the FM station was making a profit of $15,000 per month. I checked this out for October, and my investigation showed a *loss* of $5,000.

"It's really unfortunate. Here we've got three young, energetic salespeople who could be the best in the market if they had proper leadership from above. The news director, Karen Clements, has the whole staff jumping— I never saw one of them sit down except to write news or read stories on the air. There's a wealth of talent at XABS, especially for a city the size of Tucson.

"This could be one of the most profitable stations in the NIS chain. I'm convinced of that. But there have to be changes at the top.

Questions

1. What would you recommend that XABS do to improve the productivity of its salespeople?
2. What role would you have sales promotion play in the XABS sales effort?
3. Assuming that Sales Manager Neil Seidman can get it together, what should his job description be?

Distribution

CHAPTER

20

DISTRIBUTION CHANNEL SYSTEMS

After completing this chapter, the reader should be able to:

1. Diagram the distribution structure, the distribution channel, and vertical marketing systems.

2. Describe the points of view of the major participants of the distribution structure—consumers, management (producers and intermediaries), and society.

3. Provide the rationale for conventional distribution channels and for vertical marketing systems.

4. Contrast the leadership characteristics of producers and intermediaries for control of the distribution channel.

5. Identify the major reasons for distribution conflict and the approaches to conflict management.

6. Explain the important considerations for determining distribution strategy and channel formation.

7. Describe the steps in managing distribution relations.

As part of the marketing mix, **distribution** adds the elements of channel relations and physical distribution to strategy planning. This chapter gives an overview of distribution systems, their strategy, and management. The distribution picture is expanded in the discussions of wholesaling and retailing intermediaries (Chapter 21) and physical distribution (Chapter 22).

products

Formica Corporation

FOLLOW THE FORMICA ROAD

Dawn Holeywell is a business student who has spent the past four summers working in the marketing department of the Formica Corporation.[1] In that time, she has witnessed dramatic changes in the firm's distribution channels.

"When I first began working at Formica, the firm had one door manufacturing plant. I spent most of my time helping our sales force promote these doors. We handled all distribution within the company.

"By the next summer, sales were way up. The firm couldn't handle all of the sales and distribution work anymore. We began dealing with selling agents who also represented other construction materials manufacturers.

"But this was no real solution. The firm's major goal wasn't really selling doors; it was developing and selling laminated plastic that could be used in the door field. So Formica located and developed 25 independent door manufacturers, who were then advertised as "approved sources" for our goods. These independents began buying laminated plastic from our sheet factory.

"With this step, Formica had realized its ultimate goal—selling sheets for a new market application. We could then convert the original door manufacturing plant into an operation focused on specialty doors for our independent dealers. The firm's door market had been established; we had 25 manufacturers using our laminated plastic sheets."

ALLIANCE FOR AVAILABILITY

Formica used three simple criteria in evaluating a particular means of distribution.[2] Will the distributor (person or company) help to provide service, financial credit, or sales power? By applying these criteria, it saw that the selling agents were giving inadequate distribution support. The door manufacturers changed the physical form of Formica's product and then used their own distributors.

All goods must move through some sort of **distribution channel**. This may be a direct sale from the producer to the consumer (when you buy corn on the cob at a farmer's roadside stand), or it may include an extensive series of intermediaries between producer and consumer. We can define the distribution channel as "the set of institutions which participate in the marketing activities undertaken in the movement of goods or services from the point of production to the point of consumption."[3]

The term distribution channel generally refers to one type of distribution

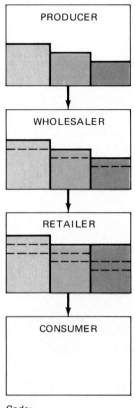

Code:

▨ Product

▨ Promotion

▨ Price

Figure 20-1

THE DISTRIBUTION SYSTEM BUILDS THE TOTAL MARKETING OFFERING

alliance (for example, toy maker to department store). The term **distribution structure** is used to describe all available arrangements in a particular industry (toy maker to wholesaler to specialty store, toy maker to discount house, toy maker to mail order catalog company, and so forth).

Customers, whether of consumer or industrial products, should be viewed as important participants in the distribution process. It is their continued patronage of distribution intermediaries that determines which channel members (retailers, wholesalers, producers) prosper or disappear.

For the distribution process to be successful, a marketer must understand distribution channels from a total-channel point of view. "It is entirely *wrong* to view a channel from the standpoint of the manufacturer only, or to think that what is good for the manufacturer is good for the channel."[4] There must be cooperation, compromise, and a sense of interdependence among producers, wholesalers, retailers, and facilitators (such as truckers and finance companies). This is why we will refer to the distribution channel system.

In terms of the conventional approach to distribution, the channel is made up of three levels of independent firms: producers, wholesalers, and retailers. Of course, there may be several levels of wholesalers. And in an increasing number of cases, two or more of these functions may be performed by a single organization.

Three principal types of activities are essential to the **distribution mix:**

1. *Distribution relations.* At one (or many) points in the distribution system, the ownership of the product will change. This must be carefully arranged.

2. *Physical distribution.* The product must be moved to a specific place at a specific time in order to be delivered most efficiently to the consumer. Important physical distribution functions include transportation, warehousing, and inventory management.

3. *Facilitating activities.* The collection of marketing information, the financing of marketing activities, and standardization and grading all assist the distribution process.

Figure 20-1 shows how the distribution system helps build a total marketing offering. Let's use a Sony Trinitron color television as an example. The producer (Sony) initially develops the marketing offering by manufacturing the product, and adding the brand, the package, and the warranty. In addition, the producer runs national advertisements for Sony televisions and sends sales representatives to call on authorized wholesalers and retailers. Finally, setting the wholesale price is Sony's responsibility.

The wholesaler adds to the marketing offering by storing and transporting the Sony televisions. Other tasks include contributing funds for retail advertising, sending salespeople to give merchandising advice to retailers, and adding a markup to the price he paid.

Finally, the retailer completes the marketing offering by actually selling the product to the customer. The retailer is responsible for store location, store atmosphere, hours open, product assortment, delivery, credit, return goods privileges, local advertising, and sales assistance. The final purchase price for the general public includes the retailer's additional markup.

Distribution is unquestionably vital to the overall marketing process. It has been described as "the managerial battlefield in which marketing strategy

One way of characterizing marketing channels is to analyze the number of channel levels. Each institution (including the producer) that takes ownership of a product or selling responsibility for it constitutes a level. The number
of channel levels determines the length of a channel. Channels are also characterized by the dimensions of width—intensity and directness. Intensity
refers to the number of separate arrangements at each distribution level, especially the number of final sales outlets. Directness refers to the number of
separate distribution units in a vertical channel.

The figure shown here presents various distribution channels for phonograph records. As new market segments (classical music collectors, teen-age
rock fans, and so forth) have been targeted, the distribution of records has become more complex. The length of channels in the distribution system varies
from two-level (record manufacturer to clubs) to six-level (record manufacturer,
to record distributor, to one-stop distributor, to jobber, to retail outlet, to customer). The width of the distribution system spans the possible channels or
channel segments. In this industry, also, certain intermediary roles have been
eliminated. Record manufacturers may own distributorships, record distributors may own rack jobbers, and retail stores may service jukeboxes.

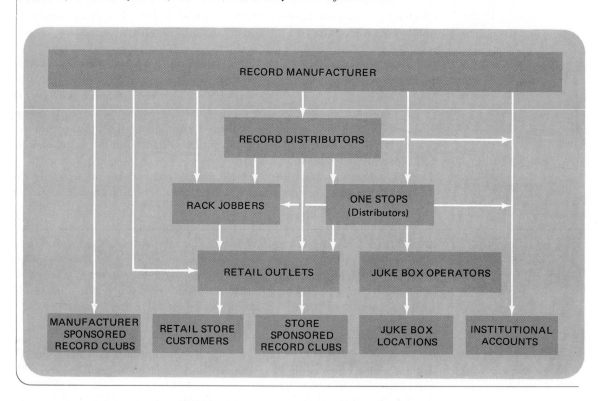

and marketing tactic activities of each business unit either succeed or fail."[5]
Distribution decisions exert a strong influence on the rest of the marketing mix,
including pricing, advertising, and sales force priorities. And the dollar costs of
distribution are one of the greatest expenses in marketing. For example, distribution costs account for one-fourth of the sales dollar in metals, chemicals,

and petroleum, and over 30 percent in the food industries. Also, a channel decision often involves a relatively long-term commitment to other firms. The selection of an inefficient or unethical set of wholesalers could be disastrous for a manufacturer.

Most often, we think of channels in terms of distributing physical goods. However, services are also involved with distribution decisions, as in the case of bank branches, travel agencies, health care facilities, and college extension divisions.

Distribution decisions must be made by organizations at all levels in the channel. Most of the examples in this chapter, however, will be concerned with the producer's distribution decisions.

DIMENSIONS OF DISTRIBUTION

The major participants in distribution channels include consumers, management (producers and intermediaries), and society. Each has a stake in the distribution channel and contributes to its functioning.

CONSUMERS   Consumers derive the following benefits, among others, from the distribution structure, especially at the retail level:

1. *Availability.* Washington's National Gallery of Art produces slide shows that reach some 3.5 million Americans—or five times as many people in the 1970s as in the 1960s.

2. *Convenience.* Shopping-center chapels have been opened across the country as a way of providing religious services "where the people are."

3. *Service.* Consumers can choose the degree of service they want (and want to pay for), from a self-service supermarket to a full-service department store (offering sales assistance, credit, free delivery, return privileges, and so forth).

4. *Savings.* In 1975 some meat producers began experimenting with direct sales to consumers. By eliminating the profits of intermediaries, these producers arranged a 10 to 30 percent saving for consumers.

5. *Enjoyment.* Studies suggest that many consumers derive a variety of sensory, interpersonal, and recreational pleasures through shopping.

PRODUCERS   Channel management is generally the responsibility of the producer, although, in some cases, retailers and wholesalers may exert middle-level channel leadership. It is common to think of producers as designing their own distribution systems. For example, in 1975 Homelite, a light construction division of Textron, Inc., began restructuring its marketing and distribution systems. In order to accomplish this, it enlisted the services of distributors in selling Homelite construction and farm equipment. Direct-sales efforts were gradually phased out.

Confusion can develop regarding the concepts of distribution and sales force management. When Homelite was selling direct to customers, the two concepts were almost the same (except for physical distribution). After the change, the distributors functioned as an extension of the sales force.

INTERMEDIARIES An **intermediary** in the distribution process is traditionally defined as "a business concern that specializes in performing operations or rendering services directly involved in the purchase and/or sale of goods in the process of their flow from producer to consumer."[6] Intermediaries are wholesalers, retailers, or facilitators.

Wholesalers A **wholesaler** (or "jobber") buys goods from manufacturers and sells them to retailers and industrial users. A merchant wholesaler takes title to goods before reselling them, while an agent wholesaler negotiates sales without owning the product. Merchant wholesalers accounted for $448 billion in business in the mid-1970s. This figure would be much larger if it also included agent wholesalers and internal transfers (the value of products moving from one level of distribution to another within the same corporation).

In certain service industries, there has been a recent trend toward a "wholesaler" role. For example, one agent may represent the composers, the orchestra director, and the individual musicians of a symphony orchestra. The agent will speak for all parties in dealing with a local civic association.

Retailers A **retailer** is "a merchant, or occasionally an agent, whose main business is selling directly to the ultimate consumer."[7] Retailers were responsible for a total volume of business of $538 billion in the mid-1970s.

In the service marketing channel, brokers and agents are the main intermediaries who deal with the consumer. They often represent the owner of services, but may also represent the buyer. Rental agents, travel agents, and insurance agents are familiar examples of intermediaries in service industries.

Facilitators A **facilitator** is a person or organization that neither takes title to goods, nor negotiates purchases or sales. They do play an important marketing role by assisting in the performance of various marketing tasks. Banks, railroads, stock yards, insurance companies, advertising agencies, market research firms, and shippers are all facilitators.

SOCIETY The impact of distribution on society can be considered in two ways. First, distribution, as a part of marketing, takes on a societal dimension when marketing is defined as everything that happens after production; this view is discussed in Chapter 27. Second, the performance record of the distribution channel itself, especially the interaction of its intermediaries with the public, can be viewed in a social context. Three aspects of this latter dimension of distribution are:

1. *Consumerism.* Since retailers are located at the "bottom" of the distribution chain, they come into direct contact with consumers. This places them in an ideal position to respond to consumer demands and serve as con-

sumer advocates with suppliers. For example, the retailer could pressure a supplier by threatening to take business elsewhere unless the supplier met responsible consumer standards. Unfortunately, few retailers have thus far chosen to play this kind of role.

2. *Ghetto distribution.* As we saw in Chapter 4, the most disadvantaged American citizens are generally serviced by the least efficient units of our economic system. Ghetto shopping areas are mainly filled with small, "mom and pop" type stores that offer high prices, poor quality merchandise, and shabby physical settings. In addition, ghetto residents must contend with many unscrupulous merchants who use the lure of "easy credit" to disguise their deceptive advertising and huge retail mark-ups.

3. *Protecting intermediaries.* The interests of giant marketers are not always in harmony with the intermediaries. Class action suits have been filed against large franchisers like Kentucky Fried Chicken Corporation by groups of franchisees. Federal and state legislators have become increasingly interested in the contractual relationships between various members of the distribution system.

THE MAKING OF DISTRIBUTION SYSTEMS

Both suppliers and consumers are served by efficient distribution. Each will benefit if a product reaches the market in the shortest possible time. The best market route is not, however, simply the shortest distance between producer and consumer. Rather, cost, time, and risk affect distribution decisions the most.

Eight basic marketing functions must be handled within the distribution channel: buying, selling, transportation, storage, standardization and grading, financing, risk bearing, and marketing information. These functions are essential and some member of the channel must take responsibility for each of them. If the producer cannot handle one (or more) of these tasks, an intermediary will have to take over.

Ideally, the channel members divide the various functions in a way that promotes overall efficiency. But, if one member sees an innovation that may improve his own interests, he may attempt to change the workings of the channel. This is why the position of an intermediary can be most insecure. The intermediary's value is that he offers the producer specialized knowledge, contacts, and experience—all of which are vital in performing distribution functions. But if the producer finds a more convenient or less costly way of getting the work done, the intermediary may be out of work.

How does the intermediary make distribution more efficient? At first glance, adding another distribution member might be seen as placing one more level of red tape and costs between the producer and the consumer. But the value of the intermediary must be understood through the logic of sorting, as illustrated in Figures 20-2a and b.

In Figure 20-2a, there is no intermediary. But there are four producers of the same product who must deal separately with each of four potential consumers. Thus, there are sixteen trade relationships. In Figure 20-2b, the intermediary brings producers and consumers together. Now there are only eight trade relationships. If we apply this logic on a much larger scale, we can see how intermediaries greatly narrow and simplify the infinite number of trade relationships possible in our complex economic system.

Intermediaries also figure significantly in the **assortment** of goods. Now let's assume that the four producers in Figure 20-2b make different products. The intermediary will then put together different combinations of quantities and qualities of product lines to satisfy the needs of different customers. His or her role is to handle sorting in a way that leads to savings in physical distribution and exchange costs.

Figure 20-2
**MARKETING
ORGANIZATION—THE
ROLE OF THE
INTERMEDIARY**

Adapted from Albert Wesley Frey,
ed., *Marketing Handbook,* 2d ed.
Copyright © 1965 The Ronald
Press Company, New York.

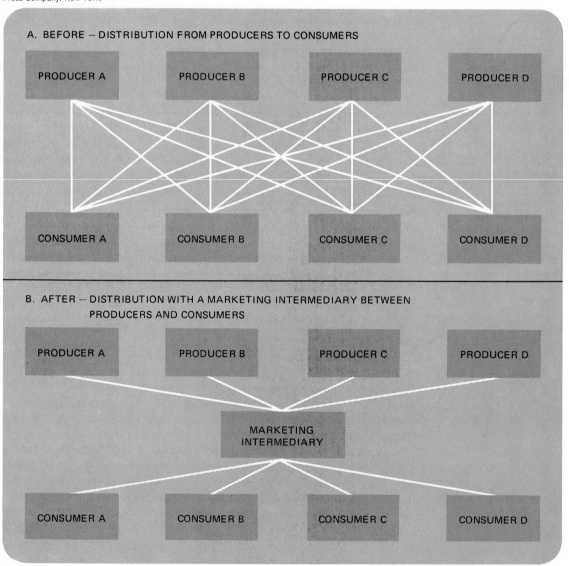

A. BEFORE -- DISTRIBUTION FROM PRODUCERS TO CONSUMERS

PRODUCER A   PRODUCER B   PRODUCER C   PRODUCER D

CONSUMER A   CONSUMER B   CONSUMER C   CONSUMER D

B. AFTER -- DISTRIBUTION WITH A MARKETING INTERMEDIARY BETWEEN
     PRODUCERS AND CONSUMERS

PRODUCER A   PRODUCER B   PRODUCER C   PRODUCER D

MARKETING
INTERMEDIARY

CONSUMER A   CONSUMER B   CONSUMER C   CONSUMER D

CONVENTIONAL
DISTRIBUTION
CHANNELS

Conventional distribution channels have been defined as "those fragmented networks in which loosely aligned and relatively autonomous manufacturers, wholesalers, and retailers have customarily bargained aggressively with each other, established trade relationships on an individual transaction basis, severed business relationships arbitrarily with impunity, and otherwise behaved independently."[8] The most common image we have of these channels is that of a pipeline, with products moving from market (producer), to market (wholesaler), to market (retailer), to market (consumer).

In a conventional channel, members see only their self-interest. They have no total-channel concept, being only concerned with the people from whom they buy and to whom they sell. A producer in such a channel may not even picture himself as being at the head of a distribution chain. He may simply sell his goods to wholesalers and then take no interest in what happens after that.

MARKETING
(DISTRIBUTION)
SYSTEMS

In marketing (distribution) systems, more complex products and services are "produced" by several participants in a system. Each participant realizes that his or her individual success will be significantly affected by the success of the entire system. These types of systems may be either vertical or horizontal in nature.

Vertical
Marketing Systems

In the past, conventional distribution channels were the dominant model for our economy. Today, however, **vertical marketing systems** are emerging as a growing form of organization. Vertical marketing systems are "networks of horizontally coordinated and vertically aligned establishments which are managed as a system."[9] These arrangements save money for marketers by their large size, bargaining power, and elimination of duplicated services. More than 60 percent of consumer goods are currently distributed through a vertical marketing system.

The travel industry is one area in which vertical marketing arrangements have become quite popular. For example, there are many alliances between hotels and airlines: Hilton International and TWA, Americana hotels and American Airlines, Western International and United Airlines. The hotel and airline may also develop vertical ancillary services such as auto rentals, credit cards, and travel insurance.

Figure 20-3 illustrates the three principal types of vertical marketing systems: the corporate system, the contractual system, and the administered system.

The Corporate System. In the corporate system, a member of the distribution channel expands through ownership into another area in order to promote vertical integration. Thus, a producer may open wholesale or retail outlets for the product; a retailer may integrate backward by beginning production of certain goods for his or her stores; or a wholesaler may move in either direction.

The rationale for **forward integration** (a manufacturer entering wholesaling, for example) is often to secure a desirable market share. The manufacturer may also wish to exert more direct control over the marketing operations of

Figure 20-3 TYPES OF VERTICAL MARKETING SYSTEMS

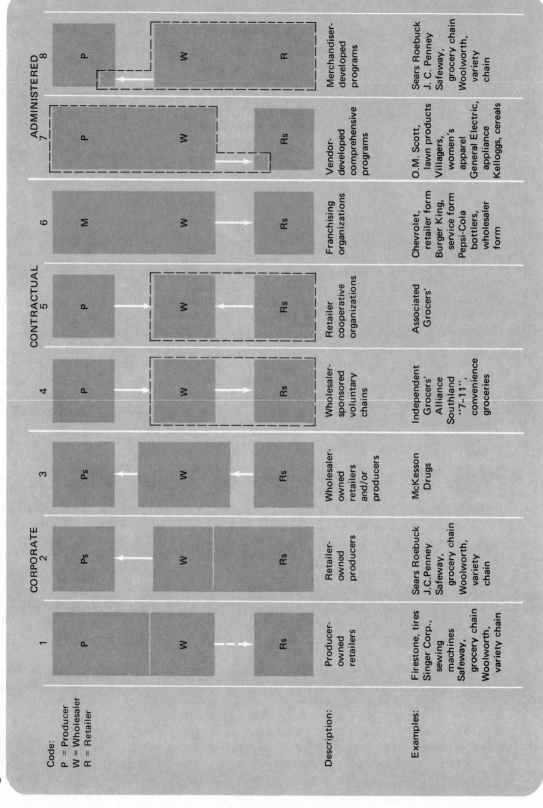

Code:
P = Producer
W = Wholesaler
R = Retailer

	CORPORATE			CONTRACTUAL			ADMINISTERED	
	1	2	3	4	5	6	7	8
Description:	Producer-owned retailers	Retailer-owned producers	Wholesaler-owned retailers and/or producers	Wholesaler-sponsored voluntary chains	Retailer cooperative organizations	Franchising organizations	Vendor-developed comprehensive programs	Merchandiser-developed programs
Examples:	Firestone, tires Singer Corp., sewing machines Safeway, grocery chain Woolworth, variety chain	Sears Roebuck J.C.Penney Safeway, grocery chain Woolworth, variety chain	McKesson Drugs	Independent Grocers' Alliance Southland "7-11", convenience groceries	Associated Grocers'	Chevrolet, retailer form Burger King, service form Pepsi-Cola bottlers, wholesaler form	O.M. Scott, lawn products Villagers, women's apparel General Electric, appliance Kelloggs, cereals	Sears Roebuck J. C. Penney Safeway, grocery chain Woolworth, variety chain

intermediaries in the distribution chain. **Backward integration**, of course, has a different rationale. A retailer (such as Sears, Roebuck) may wish to reduce the costs of goods purchased for later sale. Through backward integration, it may be able to avoid inflated wholesale or manufacturer's prices.

There is little doubt that corporate systems are becoming an increasingly popular business form. Chains with 11 or more store units now account for more than 30 percent of all retail business.

The Contractual System. There are three types of contractual systems: wholesaler-sponsored voluntary, retailer-cooperative, and franchising. In each, independent firms integrate their work on a voluntary and contractual basis to develop a more efficient distribution system. Typically, one member of the system develops a total marketing approach to be used by all members of another level of distribution and assists them with support services (central buying, advertising, financing, and so forth).

In the wholesaler-sponsored voluntary arrangement, a wholesaler seeks out retailers who will go along with the marketing formula suggested by the wholesaler. In the retailer-cooperative arrangement several retailers start or acquire their own wholesaler in order to develop a common marketing program and perform central and coordinate services.

The franchising organization links by contract a franchiser with a comprehensive marketing program to a group of franchisees. Franchising has long been popular for automobiles and gasoline, but in the last 20 years it has grown dramatically for a wide range of service industries (from fast-food restaurants to temporary help). In 1973, 380,000 franchising firms totalled $151 billion in retail sales—or almost one-third of all retail sales revenue for the year.

The Administered System. In an administered system, one firm develops a coordinated marketing strategy for one line of merchandise for firms at another level of distribution. This arrangement contrasts with the other two vertical marketing systems in which organizations at one level agree to operate their entire business according to another's program. Firms may submit to an administered strategy when the sponsoring firm has valuable expertise, substantial consumer loyalty, or provides financial incentives. One goal of these administered strategies is to reduce friction within the distribution network.

Competition among the three types of vertical marketing systems has become an important phenomenon of business life. The success of McDonald's restaurants is the success of one franchising system operating against other franchising systems (Burger King), corporate systems (Howard Johnson), and administered systems (catering services operating college cafeterias.) More and more, marketing strategy will not be developed in terms of manufacturer versus manufacturer or retailer versus retailer, but channel system versus channel system.

Horizontal Marketing Systems

In **horizontal marketing systems** there is some sort of cooperative arrangement between two or more companies at the same level of distribution. The firms may simply exchange information (data on sales, expenses, or profits), or they may engage in a joint venture to increase their power (as when a merchant association fights for urban renewal in a downtown center).

The basic principle behind horizontal marketing is "give a little to get a little." Business firms have traditionally developed within a competitive system that places a high value on independence. Yet, in a horizontal marketing arrangement, a firm will yield some part of its autonomous decision-making power in order to create a new (and more powerful) institutional force.

There are six important variables that define horizontal marketing systems:

1. *Number of participants*—anywhere from two to thousands.

2. *Time period involved*—short-term, long-term, or undefined.

3. *Level of operations involved.* There may be joint efforts at management level, in technical departments, or on the selling floor.

4. *Competitiveness of cooperators.* The retailers may closely cooperate with competitors or only with firms in unrelated fields.

5. *Legality.* Courts are examining a wide variety of horizontal marketing arrangements for possible violations of antitrust and other legislation.

6. *Formality.* There may be binding contracts, or nothing more than handshake agreements.[10]

There are numerous examples of horizontal marketing arrangements. Retailers located on the same block may purchase a parking lot together for customers in any of the stores. A tax specialist, such as H & R Block, may arrange with a bank to take office space in all branches during the months of income tax preparation. Many firms in the same industry may establish a trade association to promote a cooperative campaign to educate the public about the industry's products and job opportunities. In many communities, different charities and hospitals join forces to collect for a united fund.

DISTRIBUTION SYSTEM DYNAMICS

It is relevant to examine the dynamics of power, leadership, and conflict situations within distribution systems. These behavioral dynamics influence distribution strategy and channel management decisions.

POWER AND LEADERSHIP

For a distribution channel to function efficiently, there must be coordination of operations among the various members. But this does not always happen spontaneously. Someone must take charge and make sure that all units work together effectively. Under the channel systems concept, it is generally agreed that this responsibility should fall on the **channel captain** (the most powerful firm in the distribution channel). The captain usually has the greatest economic power and stands to lose the most if the channel does not perform adequately.

Financial strength is not the only measure of the power of a channel member. Other important criteria include:

1. brand ownership;
2. a channel member's role within its channel;
3. ownership control over other channel members;
4. contractual agreements among members of the channel.

These other criteria result in a more diverse set of possibilities for defining channel dominance than the economically based channel captain approach. For example, if a small manufacturer has established an impressive brand name, he or she can dominate the channel and force giant retailers to meet his terms.

A key question that is often asked is: "Which level of the channel is best suited for leadership?" Often the answer depends on the nature of the product. Upper levels of the channel generally exert leadership when a product requires heavy developmental costs or extensive advertising. When demand is difficult to estimate and influence, the lower level units become particularly powerful. As a general rule, the channel level that can most effectively absorb the relevant risks will probably be in control.

Producer Power

Automobiles, soft drinks, patent medicines, toothpaste, television sets, and cameras are all examples of manufacturer-controlled products. Why is it that these types of products result in channel dominance for the producers? Money is perhaps the decisive factor. In order to market any of these products successfully, a firm must invest heavily in new product development and national advertising. The ads alone may run into millions of dollars for a national campaign. Few intermediaries are in a position to invest so much capital, and most lack the skill to focus so much attention on a single product.

In most marketing situations, the power of the producer is reduced as the distribution channel becomes longer and more complex. If wholesalers are involved, the producer loses direct contact with retailers and may find that communications are becoming distorted along the way. Also, the more intricate the distribution channel, the more the participating firms are likely to focus on their individual priorities. A total-channel strategy becomes difficult to implement.

In some cases, however, the producer can hold a degree of power that threatens other channel members. Service station operators can easily attest to this truth. One operator has claimed that: "The oil companies have made the gas station operator the last of the sharecroppers, the serfs of the industrial world."[11] In part, this is because the company serves as both landlord and product supplier for the station owner or lessee. Legally, oil companies cannot dictate pricing policy to their dealers. Since the dealers have often invested their life savings in the stations, it becomes difficult to buck the company.

Intermediary Power

In recent years, large retailers have taken a more aggressive marketing approach. As one executive of a retail chain has explained, "Sure, it's the manufacturer who actually develops the product; but more and more, it's the chain merchandise managers and buyers who draw up the programs and marketing concepts."[12]

Certain products, such as household goods and fashion items, seem particularly suited to channel control by intermediaries. These products face rapidly shifting demand in local markets. The manufacturer cannot easily predict or shape local demand conditions. As a result, leadership falls into the hands of merchants. They will pick out the items they want for their customers and may decide on the promotion and even the price.

Another basis for the intermediary's power is the distributor's controlled brand (or private label), which was introduced in Chapter 12. When products enter the maturity stage of their life cycle (as have appliances, frozen foods, and tires), there is little risk for a retailer in marketing its own brand in place of or along side of the usually higher priced manufacturers' brands.

DISTRIBUTION CONFLICT

Although distribution systems are held together by cooperation, some degree of **conflict** is likely to occur (as in any marriage). If the conflict is excessive, it may be harmful to channel members' performance or even fatal to the channel arrangement. Some conflict, however, keeps the participants on their toes. If managed properly, it may actually lead to an improved channel system.

Conflict Dynamics

Generally, the members of a marketing channel work cooperatively for their collective gain. But conflict between members of a channel is not unusual. In the service sector, for example, diversification has led to new types of channel conflicts. Commercial banks handle insurance, credit cards, and computer services. All of these expanded functions can cause conflicts between firms that have a joint interest in a particular distribution process.

One continual source of conflict between large corporate enterprises and retail stores arises from their differing psychologies. Business leaders operate under a type of growth psychology: they are constantly striving for more and more, both in their own lives and for the firms that they direct. But the typical retail dealer has more limited aspirations for money, status, and power. He is not as anxious to advance higher each year, or to build profits upon profits. If he reaches a satisfactory level of performance, he may be content to stay there. The conflict between the dynamic goals of the corporate manager and the more static goals of the retail manager often spills over into business decision-making.

Frequent and important conflict issues within distribution channels include: delivery of product, product shortages and inventory problems, procedures for handling complaints, errors in billing, disagreements over pricing, resistance to changing policies and programs, containers and packaging, perceptions of efforts and fairness.

The dynamics of the conflict process can be illustrated by examining a grocery distribution channel. The setting for the conflict is external circumstances: a preholiday week, a snowstorm, and a resource shortage. The morale of the manufacturer is low, while the retailer is under a great deal of pressure. When an incorrect order arrives from the manufacturer, the retailer complains and a flare-up occurs. Eventually, the conflict is resolved. The manufacturer sends an emergency delivery of goods to the retailer and later reassesses truck scheduling procedures. The retailer feels more powerful, knowing that he was able to insist upon swift action to make up for the original error.

Most firms react to conflict rather than plan for it or attempt to anticipate it. Generally, they see conflict as a destructive process that can only hurt the marketing operation. But this view needs to be modified, for conflict has both negative and positive aspects. The negatives include economic inefficiency, emotional disruption, and resistance to resolving future conflict issues. The benefits of conflict have been summarized as follows:

> It [conflict] represents a strong motivating force for management to remain active in reviewing and upgrading its activities. Conflict may provide a reliable and dramatic, although not painless or inexpensive, means of indicating the need for change and evaluating management performance.[13]

Conflict Management A spontaneous, haphazard, and ill-considered response to conflict can be immediately or ultimately disastrous for a distribution channel. It seems logical that the channel captain must take responsibility for promoting effective **conflict resolution**. The captain must not only encourage among all channel members a sense that conflict resolution is essential, but must also devise workable ways of converting this spirit into positive actions.

A number of specific guidelines can be suggested for resolving channel conflicts:[14]

1. Establishing personal relationships between representatives of channel members—and holding regular joint meetings—can help to build an atmosphere of trust and interdependence.

2. When an error is made, it must be quickly admitted. Immediate action must be taken to redress the harm done.

3. Distribution executives must be given an important role in the decision-making processes of manufacturers. They must also be given adequate resources to perform their work.

Exxon has taken action to improve conflict resolution within its marketing channels. Since the late 1960s, the company has maintained Region and Headquarters Dealer Relations Committees to review serious complaints from local Exxon dealers.

These committees are actually intended as a kind of "court of last resort." Exxon prefers that any conflicts be brought to its Sales Representatives or to the Sales Supervisor or District Manager. Most dealer complaints are still received and settled at this level. The firm believes that such personnel are in the best position to understand the local problems of Exxon dealers. However, when satisfaction is not obtained at this level, a dealer has the option of approaching a Dealer Relations Committee to pursue the matter further.

Based on *The Exxon Extra*, January 1975, p. 14.

In recent years, **arbitration** has become a more accepted technique for resolving disputes among channel members. This avoids slow and costly litigation that only increases the problems of each party. In the textile industry, arbitrators commonly rule on whether the goods that a manufacturer shipped match the promised quality and on whether the merchandise was shipped too late in the season to be sold at a full markup. These conflicts often develop among members of a textile channel, and they are frequently settled by an impartial arbitrator who enjoys the confidence of both parties.

DEVELOPING DISTRIBUTION STRATEGY

The necessity of developing distribution strategy is lost on many business and nonprofit organizations. Operating executives often "stand pat" with traditional distribution processes, regardless of changes in market conditions. And, in many cases, no one in the firm has any real interest in or responsibility for distribution development.

A more constructive approach is to view the marketing channel as a system, and to develop strategy for the most efficient functioning of the channel system. This is a complex process, with different channels for different purposes at different times. Whatever the product or market conditions, a firm will wish to select a channel that best complements its overall marketing strategy.

Certain specific situations often lead to changes in channel strategy:[15]

1. When a new company or subsidiary is formed.
2. When a new product or product line is created.
3. When the firm shifts its marketing strategy, or decides to target its product for a new market.
4. When a product reaches a new stage in its life cycle.
5. When the available structure of channels for the product changes (a new channel opens up, or a wholesaler or retailer changes its policies).

How many channel systems can a marketer serve? Generally, even the most well-financed firms must concentrate their efforts on one principal channel system. The firm may establish secondary channels, but cannot afford to risk overlooking its primary market.

Figure 20-4 presents an overview model for planning distribution strategy and managing the distribution system.

STRATEGIC MARKETING ROLE In earlier chapters, we described how the firm's relative stress on price, product, and promotion formed a marketing mix. In the same sense, we will define the **channel mix** as the way in which the firm allocates funds to influence other institutions within the vertical marketing system.

In Chapter 17, we discussed "push" and "pull" promotion strategies.

Figure 20-4 DISTRIBUTION SYSTEM STRATEGY AND MANAGEMENT

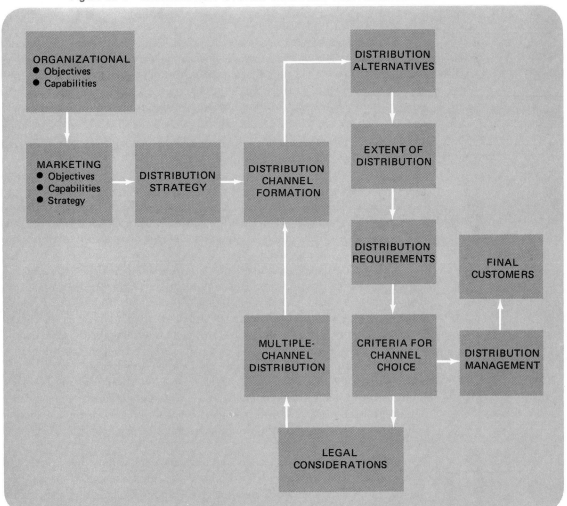

Actually, these promotion strategies function simultaneously as distribution strategies. In a "push" (or frontal attack) strategy, the primary emphasis is on internal promotion within the channel. In a "pull" (or flanking attack) strategy, the producer bypasses the intermediaries and concentrates his promotional efforts on the consumer.

One of the key questions in channel strategy is: Who makes up the market that we wish to reach? There is often a strong relationship between the selection of markets and the selection of channels. If the existing channels of distribution cannot effectively reach the target markets, the firm may have to revise its marketing strategy.

One critic has pointed to "a tendency for distribution channel planning to be neglected in favor of plans concerned with product development, promotion, and pricing."[16] This makes little sense, since efficient performance on all of the "three Ps" will be pointless if the distribution system is in trouble.

FORMATION OF THE DISTRIBUTION SYSTEM

The channel captain usually assumes the dominant role in channel formation. This is true whether the channel is manufacturer-dominated or retailer-dominated. The channel captain wants to have enough leverage to implement a successful marketing strategy. Interference from other channel members may prevent the channel captain from putting distribution priorities into practice.

Channel Determinants

Figure 20-5 shows the relationship among major factors that determine what channel an organization will become part of:

1. *Market.* The nature of the market determines distribution strategy. Direct marketing is most successful when there is a large number of potential customers, a likelihood of a high sales volume, and a high geographic concentration of customers. When a market is widely scattered and when the purchasing pattern of customers is irregular, intermediaries will play a more important role in distribution.

2. *Product.* Product characteristics can dictate channel decisions in certain instances. Perishable products require direct marketing because of the dangers of delay and handling problems. Specialized products, particularly when they need special servicing, may also need direct marketing. A seasonal product is generally sold by the sales force of an intermediary (who can handle many different seasonal products) rather than the producer. Intermediaries may also be employed when a product has a low unit value.

3. *Organization.* If a firm is large, financially strong, and has a wide product mix, it will be able to engage in extensive direct marketing activities. The weaker the firm, the fewer resources it has to concentrate on distribution activities. The result is that intermediaries must be employed to handle the essential tasks.

4. *Intermediaries.* Wholesalers and retailers reach widely differing groups of consumers and vary greatly in their advertising, storage, credit requirements, return privileges, and frequency of shipment. Marketers want an intermediary who can best reach and meet the needs of their target segments.

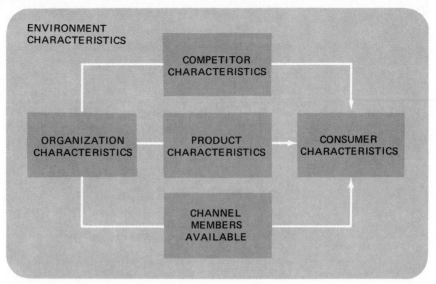

Figure 20-5   FACTORS AFFECTING DISTRIBUTION CHANNEL CHOICE

In addition, the intermediary's financial strength is also significant in channel consideration.

5. *Competitors.* In some industries, marketers may find it essential to match competitors' channel selections closely. A dog food manufacturer may want his brand in all of the same supermarkets as other industry leaders. As Philip Kotler has cautioned, however, "The marketing channels used by competitors sometimes define what the producer wants to avoid rather than imitate."[17] Using this type of strategy, for example, Avon bypassed retail store distribution and built its operations on door-to-door sales (where it had no competition).

6. *Environment.* Changes in the marketing environment will reshape channel strategies. When economic conditions are depressed, producers turn to the shortest and cheapest channels. Technological innovations can also have dramatic impact. The development of refrigeration totally revamped the distribution of perishable goods. The resulting storage capabilities led to an expanded role for intermediaries between the producer and the consumer.

A firm must carefully weigh all distribution alternatives before making its channel decisions. It must balance the advantages and disadvantages of conventional channels and vertical marketing systems. The key questions that must be considered are:[18]

1. What are the purchasing needs of the target market?
2. How can each channel alternative meet those needs?
3. Which channels are most efficient in distribution?

Extent of Distribution   The extent of distribution is measured in two ways. The first is the geographical coverage of the channel. The second is the intensity of distribution within a given geographical area—in other words, how many intermediaries give how much support to a product or services?

A firm may opt for general or limited distribution, depending on how it

485

uses intermediaries to handle its products. Convenience goods tend to receive wide distribution, while specialty goods may be distributed only by a small number of dealers with exclusive rights from a manufacturer.

We can break down distribution further into three types of distribution intensity: intensive distribution, selective distribution, and exclusive distribution. The key variable here is the degree of market exposure sought by the business firm.

Intensive Distribution. Producers of convenience goods and common raw materials tend to pursue a strategy of intensive distribution. They want as many sales outlets as possible for their retail products. The more supermarkets, drug stores, and grocery stores that stock Bufferin, the better for its manufacturer (Bristol-Myers).

Firms find intensive distribution essential when the price of their product is low, buying is frequent, and brand-switching is fairly common. Many consumers looking for soft drinks will buy Pepsi-Cola if Coca-Cola is not stocked, or vice versa. Thus, each firm wants to saturate the market in order to maximize its sales.

Selective Distribution. This strategy can be defined as "the use of more than one but less than all of the intermediaries who are willing to carry a particular product."[19] Often, the marketer chooses as wholesalers and retailers only those firms that will be most likely to contribute to high sales volume and profits.

Selective distribution is employed in the sale of many convenience, specialty, and shopping goods. It allows the marketer to focus attention on a relatively limited number of intermediary relationships, while maintaining adequate market coverage. The costs of this strategy are typically less than the costs of intensive distribution.

Exclusive Distribution. In some cases, a manufacturer will grant exclusive distribution rights within a territory or market to a particular wholesaler or retailer. Thus, Panasonic may agree that it will sell stereos in the town of Butte, Montana, only through one retailer. It will not distribute its goods to any other stores in Butte.

Such exclusive arrangements are common at the retail level for musical instruments, furniture, radios, watches, sporting goods, and other specialty items. They are not practical for convenience goods (where the buyer will usually not go out of his or her way to find one specific store that sells the item).

There are obvious benefits for a wholesaler or retailer in gaining exclusive rights to a specialty product within the intermediary's territory. The manufacturer can also benefit from such a relationship. He or she may receive a more enthusiastic selling effort from the dealer and may be able to exert more influence over intermediaries' marketing policies (including price, promotion, and credit terms). In addition, the prestige of the brand may be strengthened because it will seem more "exclusive."

Distribution Requirements

One way of understanding distribution decisions is to look at a channel as a series of tasks that must be completed as efficiently and inexpensively as possible.[20] The producer turns to an intermediary who can perform one of these tasks more effectively than the producer or other intermediaries. Each task in the distribution chain thus may be included among one firm's distribution requirements.

In pinpointing the essential tasks of distribution, the producer must keep in mind the basic **trade-relations mix**, which is made up of four elements:

1. *Price policy.* The manufacturer generally sets a list price for an item. Discounts may be allowed for favored intermediaries or for a designated quantity purchase.

2. *Conditions of sale.* The most important of these are payment terms and producer guarantees. The "2/10 net 30" (2 percent discount for the distributor if payment is made in ten days; or full cash price payable within 30 days) is a familiar example that we examined in Chapter 15.

3. *Territorial rights.* The distributor may want guarantees that the producer will not set up another franchise too close to his or her own operations. Or he or she may want full credit for all sales in the territory, whether he or she was directly responsible for them or not.

4. *Mutual services and responsibilities.* These are extensive and precisely defined in most franchise and exclusive distribution arrangements. However, in intensive distribution, the producer may give only minimal assistance to the distributors.

CRITERIA FOR CHANNEL CHOICE

After analyzing the major distribution tasks, the producer will have identified the most attractive channel options for the product. The question then is: Which alternative best coincides with and promises to fulfill the long-run marketing objectives of the firm? To answer this question, each alternative is weighed against economic, control, and adaptive criteria.[21]

Economic Criteria

Economic criteria are most important in making channel decisions, since profits are such an essential marketing goal. In order to evaluate the economic potential of various distribution alternatives, a firm may employ a total cost approach. It will map out the distribution impact on each marketing cost that seems relevant (such as warehousing, inventory, transportation). The firm will then attempt to assess the profit impact on each distribution strategy, and select the most desirable alternative.

Unfortunately, this is easier said than done. It is no simple matter for a firm to project the profits of a distribution system, even when it has all the available data from intermediaries. Furthermore, in evaluating a number of channel alternatives, it is difficult to obtain all of the vital information necessary for the projection.

Control Criteria

Among the many difficult control questions that a marketer must face in weighing channel alternatives are: Will the self-interests of two or more levels be so opposed as to produce dangerous conflicts? Will the self-interests of two or more levels be so harmonious as to create an alliance against the producer?

Will the channel contain any features that may present legal problems? (An example might be a fight over exclusive distribution rights.)

In 1972 only four out of ten buyers expected in-store service from suppliers.[22] By 1975 eight out of ten buyers expected such service. This has become a major area of control conflict within the distribution system. One Woolworth buyer notes that free shelf-maintenance can save the firm six cents on every sales dollar. Thus, chain stores are pressuring suppliers to provide more and more services (especially as expenses force them to cut down their sales forces).

Adaptive Criteria A channel alternative sometimes seems ideal but carries a hidden danger. If it severely restricts the flexibility of the producer, it may cause many problems later on as market conditions change. The producer who makes a ten-year contract with a sales agent may be "stuck" if better alternatives appear three years later. Thus, many producers are wary of channel alternatives that require long-range commitments—unless the future of the industry is clear and marketing conditions are likely to remain stable.

LEGAL CONTROL OF DISTRIBUTION

Exclusive agency or franchise agreements may be subject to the restrictions of antitrust legislation. The key considerations are: (1) does the manufacturer control a significant share of the market? and (2) does the agreement seem to exclude competitors from a substantial share of the market? If either of these conditions exist, the government will often take action against an exclusive agreement or franchise.

Territorial restriction is another critical legal issue in distribution. It has always been considered legal and proper for a manufacturer to establish dealer sales territories. But exclusive territorial arrangements may act as a means of restricting competition (in violation of the Sherman Antitrust Act). Certain court decisions suggest that such practices are acceptable only when the manufacturer maintains title, dominion, and risk over the product until it is transferred to the consumer.

Manufacturers have a legal right not to sell to a particular distributor. The only limitation is that they may not refuse in order to pursue illegal ends (such as monopolistic control). As long as this is not the case, a manufacturer retains the legal right to decide which firms it will do business with.

Full-line forcing is a requirement by a manufacturer that a dealer carry all of his goods if he wishes to carry any. This practice seems within the law as long as there is no exclusive dealing arrangement between the parties.

MULTIPLE-CHANNEL DISTRIBUTION

In many cases, a firm may use more than one distribution channel. Most retail and wholesale organizations rely on a number of channels because they carry such diversified types of products. The **multiple-channel approach** is advantageous for a producer since he or she can potentially reach a greater number of markets. But the approach is also risky. Many intermediaries resent being "one of the crowd," and may not promote the products of such a manufacturer with any great enthusiasm. For the producer, the decentralization of the multiple-channel strategy can lead to confusion and a lack of focus.

There are a number of specific forms of multiple-channel distribution. A firm may sell only certain parts of a given line to each channel. It may sell its least expensive hardware to certain discount dealers, while reserving the quality merchandise for dealers who specialize in costly, high-status models. Another possibility is to design special lines with separate brand names for each channel. Revlon sells its basic mass consumption items to smaller drug and department stores. Its limited lines—Moon Drops, Ultima II, and Braggi—are distributed only through larger selected outlets.

A third alternative is to use distributor-controlled brands in order to attract specific market segments. This may be necessary for the producer in dealing with large retailers (such as J. C. Penney and Sears, Roebuck) who usually insist on using their own brand names.

If a producer wishes to pursue different market segments, he may find it helpful to establish separate divisions within the firm. Each would carry its own name and marketing strategy and would operate independently (though, of course, each would be under the control of the firm's central executives).

MANAGING DISTRIBUTION RELATIONS

Once distribution strategy has led to a given channel or set of channels, the firm takes the next series of steps in managing its relations with other channel members as part of a total channel system.

Traditionally, manufacturers and retailers have competed against one another for a larger share of business profits. But in recent years, these long-time adversaries have joined forces more and more against some common difficulties. These include competition from rival systems, material shortages, energy crises, government intervention, consumer pressure, and continuing inflation. The producers and intermediaries have realized that they may "sink or swim" together, and they cannot afford to continue the old antagonisms.

SELECTING SPECIFIC CHANNEL MEMBERS

After an organization has developed a firm understanding of the kinds of channels it needs, it must then choose specific individuals and firms as its "partners" in distribution. The accompanying box suggests some of the basic criteria for selection for producers.

Some producers—either because of their prestige or the appeal of a specific product—find it easy to interest intermediaries in joining a channel. Others must do extensive recruiting. In either case, the producer wants an intermediary with a solid reputation, a good economic base and growth potential, and a cooperative and trustworthy organization.

In 1959, Dr. Pepper tried to crack the lucrative New York market and failed.[23] The firm's intermediaries—a number of small bottlers—could not market the product with any skill. But, in 1970, Dr. Pepper appeared on the New York scene again. This time it was promoted by the well-financed Coca-

Cola Bottling Company of New York, which launched the most costly campaign in the history of the soft drink industry. As a result, Dr. Pepper became firmly established as part of the New York soft drink market.

The retailer or wholesaler faces enormous problems in selecting vendors. A drug store may carry some 12,000 different items during a single year. How can the manager of the store decide which vendors are reliable? Generally, the key considerations are:[24]

1. Is the manufacturer financially stable?

2. Does the product seem likely to sell at this store?

3. Are the manufacturer's policies on discounts, inventory, and investment favorable?

4. Will the supplier provide training and technical assistance where it is needed?

MOTIVATING CHANNEL MEMBERS

The producer must steer a delicate course in motivating the intermediary. Sometimes, he may use the carrot (encouragement), sometimes the stick (threats that he will find another intermediary). Sometimes he will offer generous financial arrangements for the intermediary; yet, he cannot afford to make the terms so generous as to dilute profits. Finding the right balance—and the terms that will motivate the intermediary to an enthusiastic sales effort—is a difficult task.

There are a number of techniques used by producers to gain trade cooperation and support from retailers. The producer may grant price concessions to the retailer—either discounts or discount substitutes. He may offer financial assistance through lending arrangements or extended dating. Finally, the producer may give the retailer preferential treatment on certain lines to protect him against certain business risks.

Training has become an important concern of manufacturers in improving the distribution channel. Producers are working harder than ever to insure that distributors have advance training in the installation, servicing, sales appeals, and promotional aids of specialized products. For example, in the carpet industry, the American Carpet Institute developed a simple sales-training package that could be used by retail salespeople. It emphasized "selling from the customer's point of view," and included slides, phonograph records, and complete training manuals.

EVALUATING CHANNEL MEMBERS   A supplier uses many standards in evaluating the performance of an intermediary. Among the most important indicators of effectiveness are:[25]

1. comparisons of actual sales with sales objectives or quotas;
2. trends in sales;
3. trends in proportionate share of the market;
4. reports of contacts with distributors by distributors' customers;
5. customer visitations for evaluation purposes.

If the performance of the distributor seems to be unsatisfactory, the supplier must decide whether or not to find a replacement. Of course, making a change does not always bring improvement. The supplier may feel that it is better to stay with the known quantity, even if the distributor is not doing the best possible job.

Some suppliers attempt to meet the problem in advance by defining specific standards of performance and sanctions. There may be understandings between supplier and distributor involving sales intensity and coverage, average inventory levels, treatment of damaged and lost goods, and training programs. The producer may also set target sales quotas for each distributor and territory. This gives the distributor a clear picture of his or her responsibilities.

WILL THIS MEETING OF THE DISTRIBUTOR COUNCIL PLEASE COME TO ORDER?

In the past, most firms had meetings with distributors on a yearly basis. These meetings were either cheering sessions ("Aren't we all terrific?") or pep rallies ("Let's all work a little harder for the team next year so we can be Number One!").

A more serious approach has finally emerged. Some producers have helped to create permanent distributors' councils with regular meetings. These conferences feature serious evaluation of policies, products, and manufacturer–distributor relationships. The meetings also include training sessions for the distributors in sales approaches and in general business practices.

These meetings do more than simply pass along valuable information. They also build a more cooperative business relationship based on mutual understanding and an airing of opinions, problems, and innovations.

Based on Peter Hilton, *Handbook of New Product Development* (Englewood Cliffs, N.J.: Prentice-Hall, 1961), pp. 131–32.

MODIFYING THE DISTRIBUTION SYSTEM

A given channel or set of channels should be evaluated from time to time, since the marketing environment does not remain static. Such evaluation means starting the strategy process (Figure 20-4) over again. Channel member modifications may result.

Kotler has identified three different levels of channel change: adding or dropping individual channel members, adding or dropping particular market channels, or devising a totally new strategy for selling goods in all markets.[26] The most difficult, of course, is a revision of the entire marketing system. A firm will not undertake such drastic action without extensive study and authorization from the highest executive officers.

CONCLUSION

Distribution means moving a product from the point of production to the point of consumption. The institutions that perform this task constitute the distribution channel. Each product type has its own distribution structure, which includes all networks connecting producers of the product with buyers.

When we think of distribution, we immediately think of producers and consumers. But intermediaries between these groups are a vital element in the distribution process. Wholesalers and retailers handle important tasks, such as sorting, that producers often cannot do as efficiently.

Power conflicts are a particularly troublesome distribution issue. The interests of manufacturers, wholesalers, and retailers do not always coincide, even when all stand to gain if a product sells well. There may be competition for channel dominance, or disagreement over fundamental marketing goals. As a result, some firms are making more sophisticated efforts to insure intelligent conflict resolution.

Strategic thinking has become an increasing part of all distribution decision making. Marketers view the distribution channel as a total system, and attempt to determine how the system as a whole can best complete its functions. Often, definitions of the target market segments will significantly shape the selection of distribution channels.

The next chapter (Chapter 21) goes into further detail on the wholesaling and retailing processes and the intermediaries that perform them. Chapter 22 provides another layer of understanding of the channel system by looking at the dynamics of physical distribution in the organization and throughout the system.

DISCUSSION QUESTIONS

1. Diagram the distribution channel for travel services consisting of American Airlines and 87 outside travel agencies and corporate travel departments tied in by wire to AA's national reservation computer center. What are the advantages of this system for each channel member?

2. Create the appropriate goals and operating strategy for a type of vertical marketing system in these marketing situations:

   a. a corporate system for Max Factor's beauty and health spas;

   b. a contractual system for "Let's Face It," a line of cosmetics that can be sampled in the store before buying;

   c. an administered system for Kline's Kushion Korner line of pillows of all shapes and sizes.

3. The distribution channel for Carrier brand commercial and residential central air conditioning units includes Carrier Air Conditioning Co. (the industry leader and growth-oriented manufacturer), a nation-wide network of distributors (independent, volume-oriented firms with exclusive contracts to handle the full Carrier line and other noncompeting merchandise lines and serve area dealers), and dealers (owner-operated, gross margin-oriented, heating and air conditioning equipment, sales, installation, and service firms that handle some to all of the Carrier line along with competing air conditioning lines). What segment of this channel is a contractual system? What segment is an administered system? What distribution conflicts could emerge during a period of product shortages? What could the channel members do to resolve these conflicts?

4. What would be suitable distribution channel arrangements for these marketing situations:

   a. a line of home knitting machines manufactured by a small Japanese producer (initially rejected by major department stores as "too complicated");

   b. United Church Publishing's new Walt Disney characters version of the Bible;

   c. First National of Louisville's automated banking center;

   d. Parker Pen realizing that its direct distribution approach for its $1.95 to $150 product line is resulting in too many low-volume retail accounts;

   e. an American Indian crafts cooperative in South Dakota seeking new sales in large cities.

5. What marketing strategies would give maximum control of the distribution channel system of these organizations:

   a. Texas Instruments, with fine jewelers handling its digital watches;

   b. Milton Bradley games, with discount houses;

   c. Snap-on Tools, with industrial distributors serving metal contractors;

   d. Balanced Books, Inc., with its network of franchised accounting services for minority-owned small businesses.

6. How could these distribution problems be managed in these channel system situations:

   a. selection criteria for franchises being considered by rapidly expanding Wiener King;

   b. motivating optometrists to feature the lesser-known Optico brand of soft contact lenses;

   c. evaluating the year-end performance of Quality Court motel franchisees;

   d. the decision to modify the one-location-only policy of a city's art museum.

NOTES

1. A. L. Munsell, "Evaluating Channels of Distribution," in *Allocating Field Sales Resources* (New York: The Conference Board, 1970), pp. 45–47.
2. Ibid., p. 50.
3. Louis P. Bucklin, "The Marketing System and Channel Management," in Frederick D. Sturdivant et al., *Managerial Analysis in Marketing* (Glenview, Ill.: Scott, Foresman, 1970), p. 550.
4. Reavis Cox and Thomas C. Schutte, "A Look at Channel Management," *1969 Fall Conference Proceedings* (Chicago: American Marketing Association, 1970), p. 102.
5. David A. Revzan, "The Evaluation of Channel Effectiveness," in William G. Moeller, Jr., and David L. Wilemon, eds., *Marketing Channels: A Systems Viewpoint* (Homewood, Ill.: Irwin, 1971), p. 359.
6. Philip Kotler, *Marketing Management: Analysis, Planning, and Control,* 2d ed. (Englewood Cliffs, N.J.: Prentice-Hall, 1972), p. 551.
7. Ibid.
8. William H. Kaven, "Channels of Distribution in the Hotel Industry," in John M. Rathmell, *Marketing in the Service Sector* (Cambridge, Mass.: Winthrop, 1974), pp. 115–16.
9. William R. Davidson, "Changes in Distribution Institutions," *Journal of Marketing* 34 (January 1970): 7.
10. C. Merle Crawford, "Needed: A New Look at Retailer Horizontal Cooperation," *Journal of Retailing* 46 (Summer 1970): 67.
11. William D. Smith, "Angry Gasoline Retailers Boil Over," *New York Times*, December 13, 1970, sec. 4, p. 3.
12. "Sharing the Burden with Supply Sources," *Chain Store Age*, Supermarket Edition, September 1975, p. 135.
13. Larry J. Rosenberg, "A New Approach to Distribution Conflict Management," *Business Horizons* 18 (October 1974): 67, 73.
14. Ibid., p. 72.
15. Maureen Guirdham, *Marketing: The Management of Distribution Channels* (Oxford: Pergamon, 1972), pp. 129–30.
16. Ibid., pp. 118–19.
17. Philip Kotler, *Marketing Management: Analysis, Planning, and Control*, 3d ed. (Englewood Cliffs, N.J.: Prentice-Hall, 1976), p. 288.
18. Guirdham, p. 136.
19. Kotler, 3d ed., p. 290.
20. This section is based largely on Kotler, 3d ed., pp. 290–92.
21. Ibid., p. 292.
22. "Sharing the Burden with Supply Sources," p. 135.
23. Arthur M. Louis, "What Happened When Dr. Pepper Began Thinking Big?" *Fortune* 88 (December 1973): 123.
24. Ronald D. Michman, *Marketing Channels* (Columbus, Ohio: Grid, Inc., 1974), p. 133.
25. J. L. Heskett, "Distribution Channels," in Albert Wesley Frey, ed., *Marketing Handbook*, 2d ed. (New York: Ronald Press, 1965), p. 20:33.
26. Kotler, 3d ed., pp. 299–300.

21

RETAILING AND WHOLESALING INTERMEDIARIES

After completing this chapter, the reader should be able to:

1. Distinguish between retailing and wholesaling intermediaries.

2. Identify the distinctive characteristics of the major types of retailing and wholesaling intermediaries.

3. Explain the relationship between retailing and wholesaling and the retailer and wholesaler intermediaries.

4. Describe the classification schemes for major types of retailing and wholesaling.

5. Relate past and future changes in the environment to innovations in distribution intermediaries.

In the previous chapter, we discussed the dynamics of distribution channel systems and described channel membership as well as the roles of the various retailers (from discount stores to vending machines) and wholesalers (from rack jobbers to manufacturers' agents). This chapter takes a deeper look at who these different retailers and wholesalers are and what they do for each other, for producers, and for customers (organizations and individual consumers).

THE ULTIMATE CONVENIENCE RETAILER

Westinghouse Electric Corporation.

The time is the mid-1980s. Jane and Ralph O'Neil are sitting at home in their downtown apartment on a quiet Thursday evening.[1] Each is reading, when suddenly Ralph remembers that it is his turn to do the grocery shopping for the week.

"Jane, I'm going to do the shopping now. Is there anything you particularly want?"

"Be sure to get a big order of brown rice and lentils. We're almost out of grains."

Ralph walks into the kitchen and sits down in front of a color television screen. He picks up a portable Direct-Shop console with a set of buttons on it. This console connects him directly with the customer communications department of City-Wide Distribution Center.

For several minutes, images of various grocery products appear on the screen, and Ralph presses buttons to indicate his preferences. Finally, he pushes the "tally" button on his console. A full accounting of the order appears on the screen, including itemized purchases and total cost. Ralph examines the tally and pushes a red button to confirm and clear the order. This completes his shopping for the evening—all done in under ten minutes! City-Wide will begin processing the order immediately and the costs will be deducted from the O'Neils' bank account.

**ORGANIZATIONS
IN THE MIDDLE**

The system of consumer buying described above will probably be in use within the next decade. Originally, it was forecast for the 1970s, but bugs in the system have caused delay.

The development of central distribution facilities—linked to homes through electronic devices—is certain to revolutionize mass merchandising. Companies such as City-Wide will become the major suppliers of common foods, household supplies, and convenience items. The new system will threaten the operations of conventional stores and place even greater pressure on producers to create media advertising and brand images that will stimulate sales.

This threat underscores an important point: distribution is a central marketing element. There are two critical reasons why marketers must understand the role of intermediaries:

1. Distribution changes affect all other participants in the marketing process.

2. How distributors function is important in selecting retailers and/or wholesalers for membership in distribution channel systems.

In this chapter, we will look first at the retailers who serve final customers. Then we will examine the wholesalers who serve retailers and organizational users (industry, government, education, health care, and so forth). The relationships among wholesalers, retailers, and then customers are illustrated in Figure 21-1.

In the field of consumer marketing, **retailing** is the front line, the final step, and also the early warning system for producers. It is the producer and retailer who "take the temperature" of the consumer and gather information for future marketing strategies. In retailing the consumer generally purchases only a small quantity of goods, with the retailer expecting an ultimate profit. Thus, retailing has been defined as "all activities involved in the sale of small quantities of goods and services, at a profit, to ultimate consumers for personal use."[2] A retail sale is one in which the buyer is the final consumer and the purchase is for a nonbusiness use.

Wholesaling, in a broad sense, includes all business that is not transacted on a retail level, or between business suppliers and organizational customers. For purposes of classification, however, the Bureau of the Census categorizes

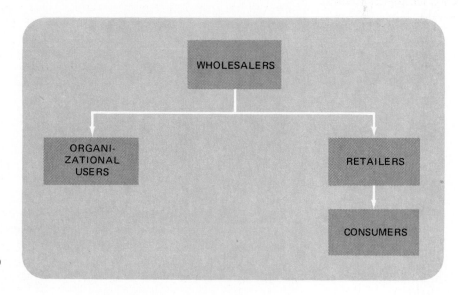

Figure 21-1
THE DISTRIBUTION INTERMEDIARIES AND THEIR CUSTOMERS

a firm as a retailer if more than 50 percent of its sales are to consumers. A firm is considered a wholesaler if more than 50 percent of its sales are to other business firms.

    Distribution intermediaries can be understood by looking at the functions they perform. One of the major themes of this chapter is the interrelationship between functions (wholesaling and retailing as subsets of marketing functions) and intermediaries (wholesalers and retailers as business units in the distribution process). It is the dividing and shifting of functions that creates different types of intermediaries.

RETAILING INTERMEDIARIES

Figure 21-2 illustrates the position of retailers in the distribution process. What retailers are and can become is limited by their location in the channel between producers/wholesalers and consumers. Retailers are, at the same time, the outlet of their suppliers and the purchasing agent of their customers.

DYNAMICS OF RETAILING

The following are important characteristics of retailing:[3]

    1. *The customer generally initiates the transaction.* This differs from marketing on the producer/wholesaler level, where a salesperson will actively pursue customers.

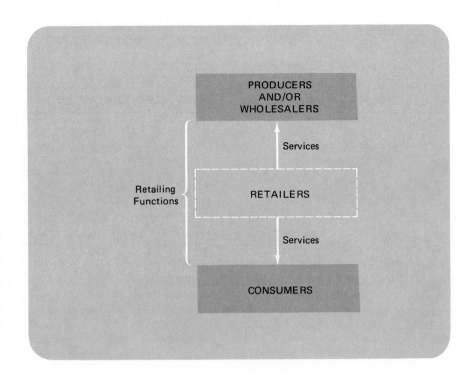

Figure 21-2

THE POSITION OF RETAILERS IN THE DISTRIBUTION CHANNEL

2. *Retailing has a sense of urgency.* People want to buy (and use) many retail goods immediately.

3. *The typical sale involves a small quantity of goods.* In 1974 the average supermarket transaction was $8.64.

4. *Retailing is usually localized.* Food stores, service stations, restaurants, and variety stores are often located near potential customers. This contrasts with the situation of the industrial buyer, who may have to cross a continent to find the right materials for the firm.

A retail firm has four major alternatives for conducting business. It may perform the retailing itself, give specialized companies contracts to do the work, share the work with other retailers, or shift the work to suppliers or consumers. The last three alternatives may reduce the firm's total costs of operation. On the other hand, if the firm does not handle the work itself, there is a loss of individuality and differentiation.

The retail sector of the economy is also influenced by shifting environmental and financial conditions. When the energy crisis was at its worst in the mid-1970s, fast-food outlets and motels along major highways were desperate for customers. Regional shopping centers that could be reached only by car were also hurt by the gasoline shortages.

RETAILING INNOVATIONS Figure 21-3 illustrates the life-cycle curve in retailing. Retail institutions pass through four stages of development: early growth, accelerated development, maturity, and decline. In the initial stages of development, new retail institutions grow rapidly and generate high profits (as was the case with super-

Figure 21-3   THE LIFE-CYCLE CURVE IN RETAILING
From Bert C. McCammon, Jr., "The Future of Catalog Showrooms: Growth and Its Challenges to Management," Marketing Science Institute working paper (1973), p. 2.

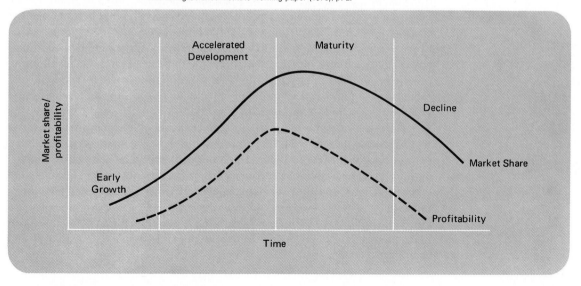

Table 21-1
LIFE CYCLES OF RETAIL INSTITUTIONS

RETAIL INSTITUTIONS	EARLY GROWTH	MATURITY	APPROXIMATE TIME REQUIRED TO REACH MATURITY
Department stores	Mid-1860s	Mid-1960s	100 years
Variety stores	Early 1900s	Early 1960s	60 years
Supermarkets	Mid-1930s	Mid-1960s	30 years
Discount department stores	Mid-1950s	Mid-1970s	20 years
Fast-food service outlets	Early 1960s	Mid-1970s	15 years
Home improvement centers	Mid-1960s	Late 1970s	15 years
Furniture warehouse showrooms	Late 1960s	Late 1970s	10 years
Catalog showrooms	Late 1960s	Late 1970s	10 years

From Bert C. McCammon, Jr., "The Future of Catalog Showrooms: Growth and Its Challenges to Management," Marketing Science Institute working paper (1973), p. 3.

markets in the 1930s and discount department stores in the 1960s). As these institutions mature, both market share and profit share performance drop. Competition is more intense, and the markets for products become oversaturated. Eventually, the mature retailing institution enters into the decline stage.

Research has suggested that institutional life cycles are accelerating (see Table 21-1).[4] It took variety stores roughly 60 years to go from the "early growth" stage to maturity. More recent retail innovations (such as furniture warehouse showrooms and catalog showrooms) are making this transition in only 10 years. If this trend persists, contemporary forms of retail selling will quickly be faced with the spiraling competition, intense price wars, and diminishing profit margins that characterize the declining phases of the cycle.

We can better understand retailing if we examine two important descriptive theories. In the **wheel of retailing** concept, new forms of retail selling begin their operations with low prices and costs. As competitors notice the success of the innovators, more and more of them pursue the same customers. Costs of business then begin to rise as each firm looks for methods of differentiating itself from competitors. In time, the most successful retailers become caught in an increasing cost-and-price spiral. They come to resemble the established firms that they originally challenged. And, ironically, the former innovators may find themselves open to attack by small, low-priced firms.

The concept of the **retail accordion** focuses on product assortment among retailers. Research findings and practical business experience suggest that a retailer cannot carry an unlimited number of items.[5] The competitive appeal of the specialty store has forced many large department store chains to cut out entire divisions. In other words, if you stretch the accordion too far, it may break.

As we look at traditional and emerging types of retailing, we will see that innovation and change result from a mixture of social, technological, and competitive factors.

TYPES OF RETAILERS

Figure 21-4 presents and summarizes our classification scheme of major retailing types. It follows traditional patterns of classifying retail institutions along five basic criteria:[6]

1. the nature of product lines sold;
2. the number of outlets owned and/or controlled;
3. the relative emphasis on prices;
4. the nature of the business premises;
5. the number and nature of neighboring stores.

Of course, we must exercise caution in applying this classification system —an individual retailer may meet more than one of the above descriptions. Furthermore, even the categories themselves raise serious questions. Retail institutions are changing continually. Today food stores sell drugs, gas stations sell toys, and drugstores handle photodeveloping. In this kind of business climate, any retail classification system cannot be exact.

Product Lines Sold

One of the most conventional ways to classify retailing types is to group them according to the product lines they sell, either single (food, drug, auto supply) or multiple product lines (food–drug, clothing–housewares). Table 21-2 presents the share of the consumer dollar held by different types of retailers in 1974.

Figure 21-4   CLASSIFICATION OF MAJOR RETAILING TYPES

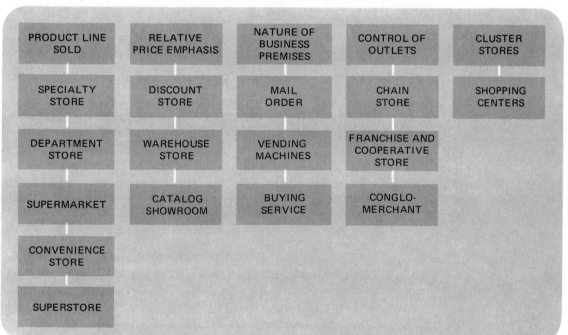

Table 21-2
HOW RETAILERS SHARED THE CONSUMER'S DOLLAR IN 1974

RETAILER	SHARE OF CONSUMER'S DOLLAR
Food stores	22.3%
Automotive dealers	17.3
Other retail stores	12.4
Department stores	10.4
Eating, drinking places	7.8
Gasoline service stations	7.4
Furniture, home furnishings, equipment stores	4.8
Apparel, accessory stores	4.6
Lumber, building materials, hardware dealers	4.0
Drug stores, proprietary stores	3.1
Nonstore retailers and mail order firms	2.3
Liquor stores	2.0
Variety stores	1.6
TOTAL	100.0%

From *Progressive Grocer*, April 1975, p. 62.

It is important to distinguish between the variety and the assortment that can be found in a retail store. **Variety** refers to the different kinds of products in the store—shoes, candy, clothing, furniture, leather goods, comic books, and so forth. **Assortment** refers to the range of choice within a product category. Thus, a store may display a dazzling assortment of women's and men's shoes, but may have no variety (that is, the store sells only shoes).

The rural general store was once the dominant retail institution in the nation. Many towns also had small specialty shops that sold baked goods, candles, and other products. Today, we call a store "general" when it has great variety. But such an establishment may be found in an urban area and it may carry hundreds or even thousands of products.

Specialty Stores. A store with a large assortment is often a specialty store that concentrates on the sale of a limited number of goods. Examples of specialty stores are jewelry, hardware, and plant stores. In most cases, the specialty store is identified by the principal product sold.

Specialty stores have been sprouting up in increasing numbers in large shopping centers and downtown malls. The gourmet food store, the early American furniture store, and the women's sportswear store all offer a distinctive and extensive assortment of goods that no general retailer can match. As one chain-store executive has observed, "As income and taste levels are upgraded, customers are becoming more fastidious in their wants. . . . The real 'pros' in retailing will pick out certain specific areas of the market and concentrate on fulfilling consumer wants."[7]

An example of this new type of specialty store is the six-store chain of Calculator Shops in the Boston area.[8] The first store opened in 1972 and was an instant success with students, business people, and housewives. One reason was the emphasis given to providing each customer with the calculator that best suited his or her needs. The firm carries more than 60 models of calculators from roughly 20 manufacturers, thus offering a wide range of choices.

Department Stores. The department store offers at least three important types of merchandise: home furnishings and appliances; apparel for men, women, and children; and housewares. The main clientele are women, but different divisions of the store amy appeal to different market segments. The record department may be geared toward teenagers and young adults, while the sporting goods department may emphasize merchandise for skiers, tennis players, and golfers.

Department stores offer a high level of service; there are many employees on the floor to assist customers. As a result, there is a high margin—about 42 percent.[9] Some department stores run extensive sales and concentrate on selling a large quantity of lower-priced goods. Others pursue a more affluent clientele and stock only the most respected brand names.

Supermarkets. In 1974 there were more than 31,000 supermarkets in the United States that handled at least $1 million in business.[10] These stores accounted for a total of almost $94 billion in sales, or more than 70 percent of all grocery store business.

Although the first supermarket probably appeared around 1930, there is still no firm agreement on what exactly a supermarket is. The Supermarket Institute offers one definition: "A complete, departmentalized food store with a minimum sales volume of one million dollars a year and at least the grocery department fully self-service." Other trade sources, however, prefer a $150,000 yardstick.[11]

One recent trend has been a proliferation of nonfood items in supermarkets.[12] In part, this resulted from the economic squeeze of the 1970s. Although supermarket sales have risen since 1970, margins have slipped. In 1972, the margin figure was only 0.6 percent of sales. As a result, many supermarkets stocked high-margin nonfood items (antifreeze, toys, picture frames).

Convenience Stores. In 1960 there were 2,500 convenience stores in the United States, with annual sales of $375 million. In a little more than a decade, these figures showed a staggering rise. By the early 1970s, there were 18,000 convenience stores, with a sales volume of $3.75 billion.[13]

The convenience store provides consumers with place convenience (stores are small and can be located near residential areas) and time convenience (more flexible hours than supermarkets). Even the names suggest convenience: Minit Market, Jiffy, Stop-n-Go. The stores are typically open 16 hours a day, 7 days a week. They focus sales efforts on national brands of tobacco, soft drinks, beer, bread, milk, and other favorites of the shopper with a short shopping list. Most offer fast checkout service and parking for a small number of customers.

Superstores. The average supermarket has an area of 17,000 square feet and handles roughly 8,000 items, mostly food, laundry, and household products. By contrast, the "average" superstore, as we noted in Chapter 13, has an area of 60,000 square feet. It handles over 17,000 items. The basic principle behind the superstore is to provide the consumer with any or all items that are routine purchases. These include all items offered by supermarkets, as well as fast foods, personal care products. alcohol, standard apparel, housewares, leisure goods, lawn and garden materials, gasoline, stationery, and household services.

In the late 1970s, superstores brought in more than 20 percent of all sales in food retailing, and may register half of all grocery sales by 1980. The average superstore brings in $100,000 a week in sales, as compared with $20,000 for the standard supermarket. One reason is the high margin on certain specialty and nonfood items. A normal supermarket takes a 16 percent margin on grocery items. A superstore runs margins of 70 percent on bakery products, 50 percent on snack bar and delicatessen products, 29 percent on household supplies, 45 percent on pet supplies, and 30 percent on health and beauty aids.[14]

Relative Price Emphasis

Another method of classifying retail stores is to examine the relative emphasis that they place on price in competing with other retailers. Within any field, there are usually some retailers who stress low prices as the most significant part of their marketing appeal. Yet having a discount image is no guarantee of success in retail competition. Some retailers are often quite effective in convincing consumers that their products are worth the additional cost.

Discount Stores. Discount stores have boomed since the end of World War II. While they accounted for only $2 billion in sales in 1960, this figure had risen to over $30 billion by the mid-1970s. The pure discount retail outlet has the following characteristics:[15]

1. It has comparatively low margins (between 20 and 25 percent of net sales).

2. It stresses nationally advertised brands.

3. There are few sales clerks (to encourage self-service buying).

4. Store decoration is limited and inexpensive.

5. It is usually located in isolated areas where rents are cheap and free parking is feasible.

Some observers believe that the discount industry has reached maturity. They point out that discount stores are suffering from excessive competition within the industry itself and further competition from mass merchandisers such as Sears and J. C. Penney's. One retailer has insisted that, "Discounters no longer take customers from others—they take from each other. With lots of discounters in the field, the strong will get stronger—the weak, weaker."[16]

Warehouse Stores. In the early 1970s, there were more than 30,000 furniture dealers across the country. The industry was totally fragmented. But a new marketing concept has come along to reshape furniture retailing. It is known as the warehouse store, and represents an application of the supermarket concept to the furniture business. It is now being used to retail appliances, building supplies, sporting goods, and the like.

Levitz Furniture Corporation pioneered this marketing revolution, and the San Diego-based Wickes Corporation followed the Levitz pattern.[17] A typical Wickes furniture outlet has an area of about 150,000 square feet. Two-thirds of this space is run as a conventional warehouse, while the rest is a showroom with more than 200 room settings. Wickes gears its sales efforts toward middle- and upper-income consumers, while Levitz concentrates on those in the middle- and lower-income brackets.

Catalog Showroom. The discount-catalog showroom is a unique operation. The customer walks in, armed with a detailed catalog of the available goods and prices (which are attractive because of the discount savings). Sales personel provide service and information. The customer makes a purchase and almost always takes the product home immediately.

Most discount-catalog showrooms feature high markup items, such as jewelry, luggage, and small appliances. In 1973 these showrooms sold $1.5 billion worth of goods, a huge jump from the 1972 figure of $1 billion. It has been suggested, however, that the boom period for catalog showrooms will be short-lived, in keeping with the general acceleration of retailing life cycles that we examined earlier in this chapter.[18]

Nature of Business Premises   Our discussion of retailing up to this point has centered only on retail stores. Now it is time to take a look at **nonstore retailing**.

More than 95 percent of all retailing is done by stores. Many firms, however, also engage in nonstore retailing. They sell through mail and phone solicitations, run vending machines, and employ in-home salespeople. All of this nonstore retailing adds up to roughly 10 percent of retail sales, or about $45 billion.[19]

Mail Order. Mail-order business is an important part of retailing. In the period 1970–1975, the number of catalog companies jumped 20 percent, to 6,500. In 1974 alone some 2.26 billion catalogs went out through the mails.[20]

Mail-order retailing is most effective in reaching markets that are not concentrated. The total nation can be seen as a potential market. Of course, a good mailing list is critical, for a retailer handling specialized goods will not want to send out a brochure to 200 million Americans.

There are three important types of retail mail-order operations:

1. *The general merchandise mail-order house.* Firms like Sears, Roebuck

and Montgomery Ward distribute catalogs that include a wide variety of merchandise.

2. *The "novelty" operation.* The retailer carries a small line of products that have a particular appeal for a limited audience.

3. *The department store or specialty shop that accepts mail orders.* Generally, this is handled through newspaper coupon advertising.

Mail-order buying rarely saves the consumer money, since freight and postal charges are skyrocketing. But it does save time for the consumer, and it is often more convenient and pleasant than running from one crowded store to another.

Vending Machines. Products such as candy bars, soft drinks, and cigarettes are commonly sold through vending machines. This type of retailing has grown steadily in volume since the late 1920s. In 1965 vending machine sales reached $3.8 billion; by 1972, the total volume was almost $7 billion. Part of this increase reflected the rising cost of cigarettes (which accounted for some $2.3 billion in vending machine sales in 1972). Yet the 1972 figures also included sales of $533 million for hot drinks, $18.2 million for cold drinks, and $707 million for confections and snacks.[21]

Buying Services. Figure 21-5 illustrates the role of the buying service. This storeless retailer serves a specific clientele—generally the employees of large organizations with whom it contracts. These may include government agencies, schools, hospitals, and unions. The members of the organization become members of the buying service.

The service also signs up a selective list of retailers, who allow special discounts to service members. Thus, a member of the buying service who wants a new automobile or refrigerator would first get a special form from the service. He or she would then take this form to retailers on the approved list and make the purchase (with discount) from one of these dealers. The buying service receives its fees in the form of a small charge on the customer's bill. The retailer then gives the fee to the buying service.

Control of Outlets   Retail stores can also be classified by their ownership characteristics and their relationship to suppliers. A retail store may be an **independent**, in other words, not part of a chain or a group of cooperating stores. Independents include 90 percent of all retail stores and account for two-thirds of all retail sales. Other types of owner relationships include franchised retailers (already covered in the previous chapter), cooperative retailers, and the merchandising conglomerate.

Chain Stores. A chain is made up of "more than one store selling similar lines of merchandise, having similar architectural motifs, and featuring centralized buying. . . ."[22] In a chain store operation, the buying of stock for all units is centralized. Thus, if a firm has 20 outlets in cities across the country, it can purchase a mass order of tennis sneakers from a manufacturer and then distribute them among its 20 stores. This centralization allows for economies of scale in buying—which results in lower prices for the retail customer.

Because of this characteristic, the chain store is most effective in handling staple merchandise. If people in all cities are anxious to buy Converse sneakers, then the chain can make a bulk order and feel comfortable about achieving the necessary sales. But the chain faces greater difficulty in selling products with great variation in local appeal. Such goods do not fit well into the centralized economic approach of chain store purchasing and distribution.

In 1964, chains of eleven or more units handled 26 percent of retail business. This figure rose to almost 31 percent in 1972, and has remained relatively constant since then. The importance of chains varies significantly according to the product area. In 1971, chain sales accounted for 77.4 percent of variety retailing, 51.5 percent in foods, and 42.4 percent of shoe retailing. Yet chains represented only 8.7 percent of eating and drinking sales and 8.6 percent of furniture and appliance retailing.[23]

LONG LIVE SMALL RETAILERS

Of 1,913,000 retail establishments in the United States in 1972, some 58 percent had fewer than four employees, and 53 percent did less than $100,000 in annual sales. This is the scope of what we generally call small business. While definitions of small business vary, one popular approach sets an upper limit for a small business at $1 million in sales per year.

Small business makes many distinctive contributions to the American economic and social system:

1. *Small business is a prime agent of social change.* The small firm can often institute new policies much more easily than the giant corporation.

2. *Small business offers leeway for the individuals who want to control their own destiny.* This is vital to people who feel trapped in bureaucracies.

3. *Small business is a critical supplier for large business.* The specialized firm may provide materials or services essential for the success of more diversified organizations.

4. *Small business offers convenience for the consumer.* A small retailer generally can adapt to the needs of a particular community and can offer more personal services.

5. *Small business can make possible new life styles.* Working at such an enterprise can be a way for a senior citizen to hold a part-time job, or for a small group of people to run a business together.

Of course, small business is a risky venture. Many such retailers barely exist from year to year. The rate of failure is high—perhaps as much as 75 percent fail after five years or less. Because of this rate of failure, there has been a growing need to combine the advantages of small business with the financial stability of larger enterprises. Franchising has emerged to fill this void.

Based on Roger A. Dickinson, *Retail Management: A Channels Approach* (Belmont, Cal.: Wadsworth, 1974), pp. 75–79.

Franchised and Cooperative Retailers. When a retail or wholesale firm is a cooperative, it is actually owned by its customers. Such arrangements usually develop when the citizens of a community feel that the local retailers are not serving them adequately. They may wish better quality products, or they may feel that the retailers are making excessive profits from some or all product lines. This discontent can lead consumers to create their own store.

Cooperative retail stores have varying means of dividing their profits among members. Some include a patronage dividend—a special form of discount for members based on the volume of purchases. Other cooperatives concentrate on establishing a fair market price in order to boost their image (and, ultimately, their sales revenue).

Cooperatives are more popular in the North Central part of the United States. They have also emerged as one outgrowth of the counterculture of the late 1960s in cities and university towns. But on the whole, this form of retail enterprise is still quite rare.

Conglomerchants. The newest entry into the retail field is the "conglomerchant" or the free-form corporation. A conglomerchant is "a multi-line merchandising empire under central ownership, usually combining several styles of retailing with behind-the-scenes integration of some distribution and management functions."[24]

A conglomerchant's empire could include department stores, discount houses, food stores, restaurants, catering facilities, specialty chains, regional distribution centers, wholesale divisions, service specialty outlets, and even foreign stores. All would be managed through centralized corporate services, including market information systems, computerized inventory control, credit processing, and central buying staff assistance.

The immense marketing power of large retailers has given rise to the conglomerchant. J. C. Penney moved into the discount field with its Treasure Island stores and has begun an income tax preparation service. Montgomery Ward began adult education schools for computer programmers as well as grooming and etiquette classes for teenagers. These developments suggest that the immense marketing power of large retailers will be tested in new fields throughout the late 1970s.

Clustered Stores   Ever since retailing began, there has been a tendency for stores to cluster together into selling districts. In contemporary society, there are four principal types of **retail clusters**: the central business district, the regional shopping center, the community shopping center, and the neighborhood shopping center.

Each of these clusters operates under the principles of "aggregate convenience." Consumers who shop in a cluster area can reduce the aggregate effort necessary to collect the goods they need. The consumer does not need to buy shoes in one part of town, pants in another part of town, and shirts in the next city. "One-stop shopping" is possible in a cluster district. In the process, the consumer saves time, energy, and travel costs and is more likely to be satisfied with the shopping venture.

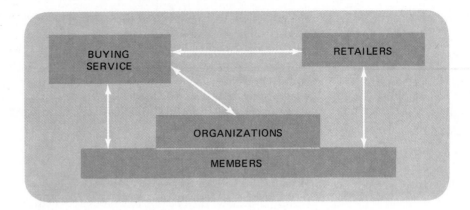

Figure 21-5
ROLE OF THE
BUYING SERVICE

Shopping Centers. The shopping center has become the dominant cluster institution in modern retailing. The Urban Land Institute defines a shopping center as "a group of commercial establishments planned, developed, owned, and managed as a unit related in location, size, and type of shop to the trade area that it services, and providing on-site parking in definite relationship to the types and sizes of stores it contains."[25]

By the end of 1964 there were some 4,500 shopping centers across the United States. This figure rose to over 12,000 by 1971. In 1972, roughly 44 percent of all sales of the types of products found at shopping centers were actually sold at shopping centers, as opposed to other retail outlets. The total of these sales was $123.5 billion.[26]

In the 1950s, a shopping center was generally constructed around one major department store. But it is not unusual for the giant shopping centers of the 1970s to include five or more department stores. The center may consist of 100 to 200 stores—including 15 to 20 dress shops, 20 to 30 shoe stores, and so forth. The consumer faces a mind-boggling array of choices; as a result, the concept of store loyalty can become a bit obsolete. Retailers in a shopping center sometimes work out joint promotion campaigns stressing the advantages of the shopping center over competing clustered stores.

Central business districts, found in most cities and larger towns, normally are areas for comparison shopping. Department stores and specialty stores are the most common retail institutions. Many central business districts have suffered in recent years from urban decline and deterioration; they need rehabilitation and improvements in parking and traffic conditions.

The **regional shopping center** generally consists of 40 to 100 stores serving from 100,000 to 1 million people. The center is often laid out as a mall, allowing for pedestrian traffic in the middle of the shopping area and parking on the outskirts. Most regional centers have an assortment of store types, which are often balanced as part of the planning for the center.

The **community shopping center** contains 15 to 50 retail stores that serve from 20,000 to 100,000 people. Normally, there is one primary store—either a department store branch or a large variety store. The community center often includes a supermarket, convenience goods stores, professional offices, and a bank. It generally sells an equal amount of convenience goods and comparison goods.

The **neighborhood shopping center** usually has five to fifteen stores for a neighborhood of less than 20,000 people. There is substantial walk-in trade, and driving time to reach the center is minimal. Tenants might include a supermarket, a drug store, a laundry, a dry cleaning firm, a beauty shop, a shoe repair store, and so forth. Virtually all retail business involves convenience goods or personal services.

WHOLESALING INTERMEDIARIES

Figure 21-6 shows the position of wholesalers within the distribution channel. Wholesalers are the customers of producers; they also supply retailers and organizational customers.

DYNAMICS OF WHOLESALING

As we noted earlier in the chapter, there is no firm agreement on the definition of wholesaling. In most cases, however, the wholesaler is an intermediary who takes title to goods from a producer and/or passes them along to users or retailers. For producers, the wholesaler supplies market information, promotional and selling assistance, and financial support. Wholesalers' knowledge of

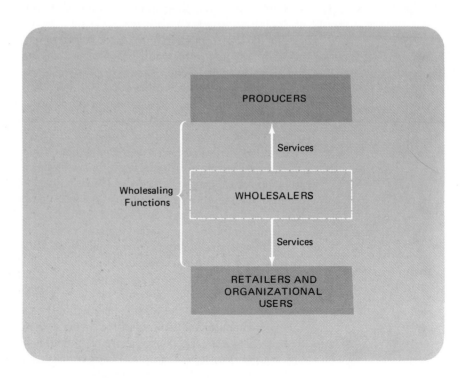

Figure 21-6
THE POSITION OF WHOLESALERS IN THE DISTRIBUTION CHANNEL

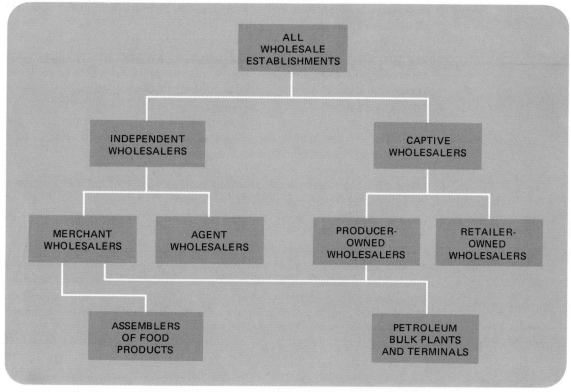

Figure 21-7 CLASSIFICATION OF MAJOR WHOLESALING TYPES

Based on Louis P. Bucklin, *Competition and Evolution in the Distributive Trades* (Englewood Cliffs, N.J.: Prentice-Hall, 1972), p. 205.

particular markets makes them a prime source of data on consumer preferences and buying patterns. These same services are of value to retailers as well. In addition, wholesalers may provide retailers with advice concerning store engineering and management, accounting systems, and adjustments. All of these services are of particular value for the small retailer, who may lack essential resources or experience. Finally, the wholesaler serves the organizational user by providing technical assistance and reliable delivery service at favorable rates.

Some manufacturers have attempted to eliminate this intermediary role in the distribution system, in the hope of cutting costs and improving efficiency. But they have often come to realize that the wholesaler performs essential services for producers, retailers, and organizational users.

TYPES OF WHOLESALERS

Figure 21-7 classifies the major types of wholesalers. These types are based on terms of ownership, functions performed, and products handled.

Independent wholesalers include agents (or brokers) and merchants who are engaged in wholesale business. Agents do not take title to goods; merchant wholesalers do.

Captive wholesalers may be owned either by producers or retailers.

Assemblers of food products are merchants or agents who are engaged in gathering food crops. They are separated from other wholesalers in the figure because the functions they perform occur at the initial stages of the distribution process.

Petroleum bulk plants and terminals have a unique product line and method of storage. Within this grouping, some wholesalers function as merchants, some as agents, and some as producer-owned branches.

Merchant Wholesalers

Merchant wholesalers are the most important group of intermediaries between producers and retailers or users. They have a vital role in the distribution of grocery products, tobacco, alcoholic beverages, hardware, and plumbing equipment.

The merchant wholesaler is an independent firm that takes title to the goods that it handles. In addition to buying and selling products, the merchant wholesaler may take charge of a number of marketing functions, including installation, servicing and repairs, sorting, and storage.

Merchant wholesalers are commonly divided into two main categories: service wholesalers and limited-function wholesalers.

Service Wholesalers. The service wholesaler performs many diverse marketing tasks. Most of these firms carry complete stocks, handle delivery of goods, and offer credit. Some service wholesalers engage in personal selling and assist their clients in merchandising functions. There are three broad types of service wholesalers: wholesale merchants, industrial distributors, and rack jobbers.

The **wholesale merchant** buys within the domestic market and sells to retailers or organizational users. The wholesale merchant handles more marketing functions than most wholesalers. An example is Drug Guild, a New York City firm that runs weekly advertisements in the local newspapers promoting the cut-rate prices of its retail customers.

The **industrial distributor** buys industrial products and sells them to factories, mining companies, and other business customers. It performs the same marketing functions in the distribution of industrial goods that wholesale merchants perform in the distribution of consumer goods.

The **rack jobber** is a new breed of wholesaler whose main retail customers are supermarkets. This distributor provides supermarkets with nonfood items such as housewares, health and beauty aids, magazines, toys, and children's books. He or she takes over most marketing functions for these items within retail outlets. A 1974 survey of supermarket buyers found that 62 percent of their stores used rack jobbers to supply some or all of the soft goods sold.[27]

Limited-Function Wholesalers. Limited-function wholesalers take on fewer marketing functions than service wholesalers. Some may carry only limited stocks; others may refuse to extend credit to retailers. There are four principal types of limited-function wholesalers: cash-and-carry wholesalers, drop shippers, truck wholesalers, and mail-order wholesalers.

Cash-and-carry wholesalers provide no credit or delivery services. Retail customers visit the wholesaler's warehouse, pick out the goods that they want, pay immediately in cash, and carry the goods back to their stores. This operation is common in the grocery trade. The cash-and-carry wholesaler services small retailers who are looking for staples and fast-moving items.

Drop shippers do not physically acquire or store goods. They take legal title to merchandise, ship it directly from the producer to the buyer, and serve as intermediaries for purchase and payment. This arrangement is common in the distribution of lumber products, building materials, and coal. Such items are bulky and transportation is costly; the drop shipper usually arranges it efficiently.

Truck wholesalers are small wholesalers who operate warehouses and trucking operations. Salespeople stock the trucks, drive through a region, and sell and deliver goods at the same time. Truck wholesalers stock a limited number of items, including nationally advertised specialties, fast-moving products, and goods that need special handling such as produce, cheese, and bakery items. Most of their business is done with cash.

Mail-order wholesalers are quite similar to wholesale merchants, except that they do not engage in personal selling efforts. The major share of business is conducted through the mails. Such operations are found in a wide range of wholesale fields.

Agent Wholesalers   **Agent wholesalers** sell and buy goods primarily for others. They rarely take title to the merchandise being sold. Instead, they help distribute goods from

---

PROFILE OF A FOOD BROKER

A food broker is a business firm that serves as a sales agent for major manufacturers of food (and nonfood) products. The average food broker represents twenty-three clients; thus, when a chain store buyer speaks with a food broker, he or she can save the time that might be spent dealing with twenty-three different salespeople. The most important services that food brokers provide include discussing manufacturer advertising with chains and wholesalers, recommending orders, offering merchandising ideas, supplying advertising allowances, and building displays.

Many manufacturers have turned to food brokers to perform retail sales functions. Examples are Sara Lee, Stokely-Van Camp, and Miracle White. Such firms turn to food brokers because the brokers make more sales calls than the manufacturer's own sales staff and are able to more effectively service retail clients at a lower cost.

Based on National Food Brokers Association, "Everything We Always Wanted to Know about Food Brokers," n.d.; and *Grocers' Spotlight* 39 (December 1972): 1.

a producer to a buyer in return for some form of fee or commission. There are five types of agent wholesalers: brokers, commission merchants, purchase agents, selling agents, and manufacturers' agents.

Brokers. These wholesalers do not take title or possession of goods in a transaction. Their job is simply to help bring together a buyer and a seller to complete a sale. Generally, brokers represent the seller, who pays some type of fee or commission.

Their main asset is knowledge about market conditions within one or more industries. Because of a detailed knowledge of supply and demand, brokers can give clients up-to-date information about the value of the product, likely buyers, and the best selling approach.

Commission Merchants. Unlike brokers, commission merchants take physical possession of the goods they sell. Sellers are always represented by commission merchants and pay them a commission based on sales or the number of units handled. Commission merchants play an important role in the distribution of farm products such as cotton, grain, livestock, and produce. They are also instrumental in many textile and lumber transactions.

Purchase Agents. The purchase agent is a particular type of buying broker. Agents only represent buyers, and generally have a long-term relationship with their clients. Not only do agents purchase merchandise, they may also receive, inspect, warehouse, and ship goods to the ultimate buyers. In some cases, a purchase agent will combine the orders of a number of clients as a means of gaining quantity discounts and preferential sales terms.

Purchase agents are influential in the hardware, grocery, and building materials industries. In the dry goods and apparel markets, a purchase agent is known as a **resident buyer** and maintains an office in central market cities. This helps the agent to provide market information for clients.

Selling Agents. A selling agent has contractual authority to sell the entire output of a client on a commission basis. The agent has no territorial limitations and has significant influence over prices, terms, and conditions of sale. In effect, the agent becomes the sales department for the manufacturer, who prefers to concentrate on production tasks.

Selling agents have played an important role in the textile industry. They also market industrial machinery and equipment, coal and coke, metals, home furnishings, chemicals, and canned foods.

Manufacturers' Agents. Manufacturers' agents have much less power than selling agents—they do not sell the entire output of a producer. These agents have exclusive rights over a limited territory only and can exercise little influence over pricing and terms of sales.

Manufacturers' agents are more numerous than any other type of agent wholesaler. Some of the kinds of products they distribute include textile mill products, furniture, apparel, electrical goods, metals and machinery, and equipment.

Retailer-Owned Wholesalers

Many producers establish their own sales offices and branches rather than relying totally on independent wholesalers. These offices perform wholesale functions and help distribute goods directly to retailers and other customers. Producers' outlets do more business in the sale of drugs, chemicals, and metals than do any type of independent wholesaler.

Sales Offices. Producers' sales offices are maintained in cities where the producer does not have a central office or plant. These offices rarely stock the firm's products, but serve as a base for the producer's sales force in the region. When sales are made, the goods are shipped from the nearest production plant or from the warehouse of a merchant wholesaler.

Sales Branches. The sales branch, like the sales office, serves as a base of operations for a producer's selling and promotional efforts. But the sales branch also carries a limited inventory of the firm's products. It fills some local orders from its own stock, and may also handle installation, maintenance, and repair work.

Sales branches are commonly maintained by firms that produce chemicals, special electrical goods, and industrial machinery. In these industries, a few large firms sell their products over a wide geographical area.

Producer-Owned Wholesalers

As we have seen, some producers find it desirable to set up their own units to carry out the duties of the wholesaler. Interestingly enough, certain large retailers also find it profitable to eliminate the independent wholesaler and create their own wholesaling units. Such chain-store warehousing operations have become a particularly popular innovation among major grocery retailers. Also, retail cooperative systems (as was discussed in the previous chapter) control their own wholesaling operations.

Administrative and Purchasing Offices. More than 200 retailers have established purchasing offices in urban market centers such as New York, Chicago, Cincinnati, and St. Louis.[28] These retailers—who are not located in central market regions—make a significant number of purchases in nearby cities each year. They have learned that their operations are more efficient when a permanent purchasing office exists in the market center.

Warehouses and Auxiliary Offices. Many chain-store organizations establish one or more warehouse operations to stock a satisfactory level of inventory and distribute the necessary goods to various retail units. There is no typical pattern for the operation of these warehouses, since the chains vary in the number of retail stores, the volume of business, and the variety of products offered.

Chain stores also rely on auxiliary offices, which do not perform retailing or warehousing functions. These offices may handle research, development, testing, and receiving and shipping.

Other Wholesalers   Two groups of wholesalers are generally catergorized separately from all others because of the unique nature of their operations and physical facilities. These are assemblers of farm products and petroleum bulk plants and terminals.

Assemblers of Farm Products. Assemblers collect farm products from farmers and commodity dealers and ship them in larger lots to food retailers. Whereas most wholesalers buy goods in large lots and break them into smaller ones, assemblers buy in small lots and concentrate the merchandise. This provides sufficient bulk to transport the products at a reasonable cost. The assembler must be able to buy goods at a price below the going rate in central markets. The difference between the two price levels represents the assembler's profit margin.

Petroleum Bulk Plants and Terminals. Petroleum products need highly specialized distribution facilities because of their bulk and their highly flammable nature. As a result, intermediaries in this field form a distinct category of wholesaler. These firms sell petroleum products to filling stations and other retailers and to organizational users. Some bulk plants and terminals are owned and operated independently; some are owned by major petroleum producers.

FUTURE OF DISTRIBUTION INTERMEDIARIES

Because retailing tends to be more dynamic than wholesaling, most of our glimpses into the future of distribution will involve retailers. Of course, retailing is particularly difficult to predict or forecast. The retailer is caught between the needs and demands of the producer and the needs and demands of the community. The retailer's future cannot be understood without first assessing the future of the forces that shape the retailing environment.

A number of interesting modifications of current practices are likely in retailing. Among these are:

1. Computer technology will improve the buying process. Merchandising errors will be reduced, and unnecessary costs will be cut back significantly.

2. The conglomerate retailer may represent the wave of the future. If this is the case, concentration within retailing will have to be assessed across product lines, rather than within each distinct retailing line.

3. The new high-yield specialty stores will force changes in retailing practice. As one analyst has pointed out, "They're already changing the rules and success requirements of general merchandising in dramatic and recognizable ways."[29] Franchise-operated and chain-run specialty networks represent a clear challenge to general merchandise retailers.

4. One business executive predicts that: "We may see, within the next decade, many shopping areas located in high density urban areas which will be integrated with other uses, such as offices, hotels, and apartments."[30]

5. We can expect increasing conversion of buildings from one retail pur-

pose to another. Old gas stations may become fast-food stores, satellite bank branches, or small supermarket outlets. Abandoned movie theaters may be used as community centers. Some one-room school buildings have already been converted into gift shops.

There will also be more dramatic changes in retailing in the coming decades. Some of these innovations will totally alter the face of retailing as we know it today:

1. We are already witnessing the beginnings of cross-country credit systems wired into computerized data banks. By the year 2000, cashless retailing may be a common experience for most Americans.

2. Many more stores may be eliminated. By 1985, nearly half of all American homes will have some form of cable TV system. This opens the way for nonstore selling on a massive scale.

In Chapter 5, we discussed the Delphi technique of forecasting. A 1973 research study of the future of retailing using this technique came up with these predictions:[31]

1. By 1985 sales per net square foot will be 20 percent higher.

2. By 1990 self-service racks will handle double their present sales.

3. More and more branches will become specialty stores rather than general merchandise outlets.

4. Furniture warehouse selling will increase its share of the market by as much as 400 percent.

In 1972 the Sun Oil Company issued a report by its Marketplace of the Future Task Force, entitled "U.S. Retail Gasoline Marketplace." The report examined the future of the retail gasoline business in terms of five important marketplace factors: product differentiation, convenience, business mix, service, and product variety.   **GASOLINE RETAILING, 1990-STYLE**

1. *Product differentiation.* There will be a significant attitudinal shift; consumers will show decreased interest in differentiated gasoline brands.

2. *Convenience.* Gasoline retailing will increasingly focus on convenience factors such as proximity, time, and cost. Marketers will link the need for gasoline to other, more satisfying needs (as in a car wash that sells gasoline).

3. *Business mix.* Many new retailers will add gasoline marketing to other operations. The combined fast-food outlet and gas station is one example.

4. *Service.* The gasoline station will become more of a refueling stop than a service station. Full-scale car-repair centers will handle most servicing work while large roadside facilities will aid transient drivers.

5. *Product variety.* While there will be a growing demand for product variety in most consumer areas, gasoline will probably be an exception. Consumers may not exhibit any serious demand for more grades of gasoline.

Based on Sun Oil Company, Marketplace of the Future Task Force, "U.S. Retail Gasoline Marketplace," April 1972, pp. 20, 30, 32–36.

5. Discounters will raise their share of general merchandise business from 15 percent in 1972 to 25 percent in 1986.

One final forecast is worthy of special emphasis.[32] Some experts predict that services, which currently represent less than 25 percent of total general merchandise sales, will account for 50 percent of sales by the year 1990. This would be a dramatic development in retail business practices.

CONCLUSION

Retailing has been defined as all activities involved in the sale of small quantities of goods and services, at a profit, to ultimate consumers for personal use. Wholesaling is more difficult to define. A firm is classified by the Bureau of the Census as a wholesaler if more than 50 percent of its sales are to other business firms.

There are many types of retail enterprises and new types continue to appear. It is difficult to classify retail intermediaries, but it can be done according to several important characteristics, including product lines, number of outlets, price emphasis, business premises, and store clustering.

In the last decade, the retail industry has been dominated by fewer and fewer firms. At first, there were mergers within product lines—department stores merged with other department stores, food chains with other food chains. This served to increase concentration within each field. The second stage of centralization saw a blurring of product specialization lines. Large retailers have moved into new enterprises, as we saw earlier in the discussion of J. C. Penney and Montgomery Ward. Countering this trend is the entry and growth of retail innovations, which are generally introduced by newer, smaller firms.

It is the great diversity and continuous change in retailing that offers consumers a wide range of choice in the goods they buy. For all firms engaged in distribution management, the existence of so many retail options requires the on-going review and modification of existing channel systems.

Wholesalers fall into a number of major classifications. Some are independent, such as merchant wholesalers and agent wholesalers. Others are said to be "captive"; they are wholesale enterprises owned and operated by producers or retailers.

Some wholesalers continue to resist the application of new business techniques and marketing concepts into their work. But a growing number of wholesale firms are relying on the most recent innovations. A few companies are going so far as to open their own manufacturing and retailing outlets. This type of action inaugurates a new type of marketing relationship in which the wholesaler is the leader of the distribution channel, rather than just another intermediary.

The future of distribution intermediaries—and in particular, of retailing intermediaries—is likely to be quite dynamic over the next 25 years. Technological innovations, especially cable TV and computers, may be instrumental in reshaping the retailing process.

DISCUSSION QUESTIONS

1. The 500-store Tiltco hardware chain orders all merchandise directly from manufacturers. Tiltco distributes surplus merchandise to about 100 small independent hardware retailers. It has a catalog that brings in over 200,000 orders per year. Six manufacturers are contracted to provide Tiltco with 65 to 100 percent of their output. What distribution classifications does Tiltco fit into?

2. Complete the following dialogue:

    MS. DIAZ: Current trends all point to the demise of wholesalers. Their margin adds to costs, which in turn means higher prices for consumers. Moreover, they just aren't as important to distribution as they used to be.

    MR. ZAJKOWSKI: Wholesaling is one of the most vital and dynamic areas of distribution. Innovations made by wholesalers benefit all members of the distribution community.

    YOU: I think that . . .

3. In the following marketing situations, which of the given pair of distribution intermediaries is more appropriate:

    a. custom-made kitchen cabinet—department store or catalog showroom;
    b. art supplies—supermarket or specialty store;
    c. lawn seed—discount store or convenience store;
    d. plumbing equipment—truck wholesaler or merchant wholesaler;
    e. natural, vitamin-based cosmetics—cash-and-carry wholesaler or manufacturers' agent.

4. Which types of retailers would be suitable for the marketing of services? Which types of wholesalers? Explain.

5. Which types of wholesale intermediaries are most responsive to distribution trends today? Which types are least responsive? Explain.

6. Concerning the nature of the distribution environment in 1985, what recommendations would you make to these organizations: Woolco discount house chain, Burger King fast-food franchise, and G. E. appliance manufacturer?

NOTES

1. Alton F. Doody and William R. Davidson, "Next Revolution in Retailing," *Harvard Business Review* 45 (May–June 1967): 4–5.

2. Carl M. Larson, Robert E. Weigand, and John S. Wright, *Basic Retailing* (Englewood Cliffs, N.J.: Prentice-Hall, 1976), p. 6.

3. Larson et al., pp. 6–7.

4. Bert C. McCammon, Jr., "The Future of Catalog Showrooms: Growth and Its Challenges to Management," Marketing Science Institute working paper (1973), pp. 1–4.

5. Roger A. Dickinson, *Retail Management: A Channels Approach* (Belmont, Cal.: Wadsworth, 1974), pp. 22–25.

6. This section is based largely on Ronald R. Gist, *Retailing: Concepts and Decisions* (New York: Wiley, 1968), p. 40.

7. Alton F. Doody and William R. Davidson, "Growing Strength in Small Retailing," *Harvard Business Review* 42 (July–August, 1964): 77.

8. Marilyn Nason, "Calculators—Only Store Chain Scores Instant Hit in Boston," *Merchandising Week*, March 11, 1974, p. 20.

9. Dickinson, pp. 11–12.

10. *Progressive Grocer*, April 1975, p. 59.

11. Dickinson, pp. 10–11.

12. "The Spectacular Rise of the Consumer Company," *Business Week*, July 21, 1973, p. 51.
13. Philip D. Cooper, "Will Success Produce Problems for the Convenience Store?" *MSU Business Topics* 20 (Winter 1972): 40.
14. "Can Jonathan Scott Save A&P?" *Business Week*, May 19, 1975, p. 134.
15. Gist, pp. 45–46.
16. "Hard Times Hit the Discount Stores," *Business Week*, February 10, 1973, p. 87.
17. "Wickes Seeks Profits to Match Its Growth," *Business Week*, June 2, 1973, p. 70.
18. McCammon, p. 4.
19. Dickinson, p. 5.
20. Stanley H. Slom, "While Retail Stores Have Ups & Downs, Catalog Shopping Gains in Popularity," *Wall Street Journal*, June 6, 1975, p. 30.
21. Dickinson, p. 7.
22. Gist, pp. 76–77.
23. Dickinson, p. 10.
24. Rollie Tillman, "Rise of the Conglomerchant," *Harvard Business Review* 49 (November–December 1971): 44–51.
25. Dickinson, p. 9.
26. Ibid.
27. *Chain Store Age*, Supermarket Edition, August 1974, p. 59.
28. Richard M. Hill, *Wholesaling Management* (Homewood, Ill.: Irwin, 1963), p. 47.
29. *Chain Store Age*, General Merchandise Edition, September 1975, p. 48.
30. Grey Advertising, *Grey Matter* 46 (1975): 5.
31. Dickinson, pp. 333, 335.
32. *Chain Store Age*, General Merchandise Edition, September 1975, p. 124.

22

MANAGING PHYSICAL DISTRIBUTION

After completing this chapter, the reader should be able to:

1. Explain the relationship of physical distribution strategy to distribution channel management.

2. Define the customer service concept and total cost approach within the physical distribution system.

3. Describe the managerial considerations of the major elements of physical distribution—order processing, inventory, transportation, storage, and information systems.

4. Provide the rationale for the systems approach to physical distribution organization.

Chapter 20 provided an introduction to distribution channel systems. In Chapter 21, we examined retailing and wholesaling intermediaries. In this chapter, we will complete our study of distribution with an analysis of how physical distribution strategy is managed.

THE TEN-MILE PEPSI PIPELINE

There's something running at Yonkers raceway besides horses.[1] If you could see through the walls, you would discover ten miles of insulated tubing carrying the syrup to make Pepsi, Teem, Patio Orange, and ginger ale for thirsty fans. Beginning at seven supplying tanks, the tube snakes up the walls of the stadium, along ceilings, through walls, and eventually to the 56 racetrack stations that serve these drinks.

This unique distribution system was the brainchild of Ogden Foods, food concessionaire at Yonkers raceway in Westchester County, New York. After winning the Yonkers contract, Ogden's physical distribution specialists had to figure out an efficient way of getting huge quantities of the syrup to the raceway's restaurants, refreshment stands, and cocktail lounges. They decided to divide the initial delivery of 520 tanks among seven "factories," or centralized locations. The longest run of tubing from one location is 450 feet. The factory with the heaviest demands needs refilling every two weeks. It contains some 150 tanks pumping 50 to 60 gallons per hour to one stand. The Ogden people are hopeful that the Pepsi lines will keep running as long as the horses.

KEEP THE PRODUCT MOVING

Although the Ogden system is unique, it was nonetheless designed in response to a universal marketing problem—how to keep the product moving efficiently. To solve this problem, Ogden's distribution manager had to identify points of supply, arrange for truck transportation and product storage, and devise a method of getting the product to its ultimate destination. Like all distribution managers, Ogden's was concerned with production scheduling, packaging, warehouse location and operation, shipping methods, schedules, costs, and order processing.

As is illustrated in Figure 22-1, the two types of distribution functions are demand oriented and supply oriented. **Demand-oriented** operations are concerned with creating a market for the products handled by the distribution channel system. **Supply-oriented** operations are concerned with getting those products to the consumer after the demand has been created. Although the functions are separate, they are nevertheless interdependent. If you know that delivery of a new sofa bed will take eight weeks (supply), you may decide not to buy at that particular store (demand).

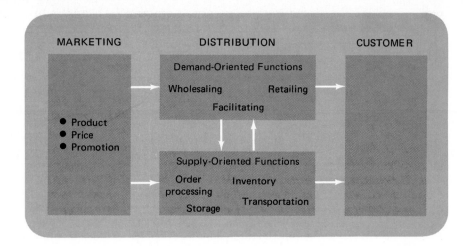

Physical distribution can be defined broadly or narrowly, depending on the marketing context within which it functions.[2] In the broad view, physical distribution is virtually identical with the marketing system itself. That is, distribution is concerned with all steps from raw materials to the delivery of finished product. This definition is most suitable in a new product development situation where there are no previously existing distribution systems. Working backward from its target markets, the firm develops a network of intermediaries that will most effectively meet its distribution needs.

The narrow perspective, which we will be concerned with in this chapter, is used by an established company with commitments to certain factories, suppliers, intermediaries, and final markets. In this case, distribution management means locating, stocking, and shipping goods to serve particular markets.

Physical distribution has been called "the other half of marketing."[3] Although it often accounts for about half of the total costs of marketing, physical distribution has often been given little attention by marketing analysts. Because firms are under increasing pressure to cut costs while at the same time increasing consumer satisfaction, more and more attention is now being paid to the management of distribution functions.

As a part of the marketing mix, distribution influences and is influenced by the other key factors we have examined so far—product, price, and promotion. Distribution management must take into account the physical form of the product and the style of its packaging. The price includes not only the cost of production but also of delivery to the ultimate consumer. Promotional programs must be coordinated so that sufficient stock is available to meet the anticipated demand. Ineffective distribution management will result in increased costs and may even decrease consumer satisfaction.

Physical distribution is mainly of interest to producers, retail and wholesale intermediaries, and facilitating organizations such as railroads, freight forwarders, and public warehousers. It is also a consideration for nonprofit organizations, such as fire and ambulance services, which must allocate emergency equipment.

THE PHYSICAL DISTRIBUTION SYSTEM

Our discussion of the physical distribution system is based on the systems approach we first defined in Chapter 2. The object of a **physical distribution system** is to get the right goods to the right places at the right time for the least cost. A system that satisfies both customer and supplier is achieved through coordination of material allocation, scheduling, and control. Many industries have cut physical distribution costs and improved service by carefully analyzing the system, making changes in it, and controlling results. The experience of Branch Industries, a trucking company, illustrates the savings that can be achieved.[4] Two major auto companies served by Branch were shipping items such as exhaust pipes and transmissions to their own warehouses throughout the country. Dealers would then draw on the warehouses for supplies. Branch decided it could help the companies operate more profitably by making fewer but bigger shipments. The trucking firm took the items to their own bulk terminals and filled dealer requests from there. This saved the auto manufacturers 10 to 15 percent in paperwork and transportation costs.

Whatever approach a company takes, it can expect increasing pressures for better product quality and service. Customers will take delivery and reliability for granted, and in addition will expect service at every point of contact with the marketer—salespeople's calls, maintenance and repair service, engineering advice, claims processing, and so forth.

CUSTOMER SERVICE OBJECTIVES

Customers are highly attracted by the level of service a physical distribution system can provide. A slight improvement in **customer service** can often produce an encouraging upsurge in sales.

Selecting the right service level is important for two reasons. First, when a company sets a service level, it is in effect placing a value on the role of service in creating demand. Second, the operating objective of physical distribution managers is to keep down the cost of supply activities while achieving the service level set by the company. Thus **cost minimization** is relative to service level, not a goal in itself.

A few years ago, evaluation of a supplier's service performance was considered too cumbersome a process to be undertaken very often. Today, manufacturers, wholesalers, and many retailers routinely use sophisticated inventory control systems to determine service requirements. Thanks to computer technology, customer service has become a measurable factor in the total marketing program.

Several elements are involved in customer service.[5] One is **order cycle time**—the period between placement of an order and receipt of goods. Another is **inventory reliability**—how much the customer can depend on the item's being in stock and available for shipment. A third is **order privileges and restraints**—the organization of customer ordering practices.

TOTAL COST APPROACH

Inventory, freight, and warehousing costs are the main expenses that a company must sustain in order to maintain customer service. Because companies often lack centralized accounting for physical distribution, the total of these costs is frequently unknown. As a result the efficiency of the distribution system cannot be controlled.

Some distribution costs are visible, others hidden. Operating costs, typically reported on expense statements as "distribution expense," are one type of **visible cost**. These include transportation, warehousing, handling, and order processing. Indirect costs associated with data processing, inventory, property taxes, and insurance are other visible costs. **Hidden costs** of distribution are those resulting from lost profit opportunities (cancelled orders, failure to ship products on time). These costs never appear on a profit-and-loss statement, but they can bite heavily into profits.

Del Monte Foods has sharply reduced inventories by examining intended levels of service from the end of the fiscal year until the new products are available.[6] Del Monte used to aim at 100 percent availability so that a customer would never be out of stock. But they found that by rearranging the physical distribution system to achieve 98 percent availability, they could save tremendously.

Figure 22-2 illustrates a simplified version of the **total cost concept**. The alternatives listed at the right of the cost graph include high inventory costs,

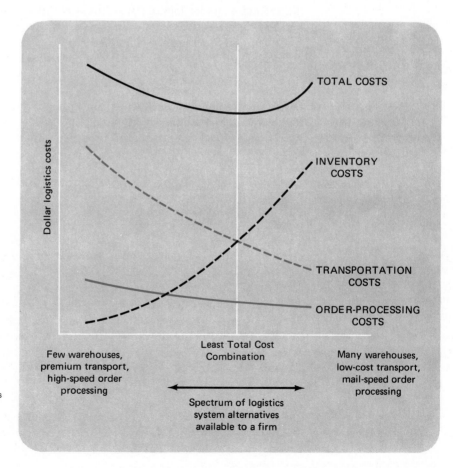

Figure 22-2
HYPOTHETICAL TRADE-OFFS AMONG TRANSPORTATION, INVENTORY, AND ORDER-PROCESSING COSTS

From James L. Heskett, Nicholas A. Glaskowsky, Jr., and Robert M. Ivie, *Business Logistics: Physical Distribution and Materials Management*, 2d ed. Copyright © 1973 The Ronald Press Company, New York.

low transportation costs, and cheap but slower order processing. Those at the left feature relatively low inventory expenses, high transportation charges, and high-speed order processing. The lowest total cost system is achieved by the use of an intermediate number of inventory locations and a combination of low- and high-priced transportation services. As Figure 22-2 illustrates, the total cost concept can be viewed as the management of trade-offs. Cost increases in some supply activities are exchanged for greater cost cuts in others; centralized cost control may result in increases in some areas that are offset by reductions in others.

A total cost approach allows the physical distribution manager to spot ways of reducing operational expenses, simplifying the system, reducing inventories, improving packaging, and using more efficient methods and procedures. It allows the manager to use technological innovations, revise distribution channels, and study the system with an eye toward improving profit opportunities.

COMPONENTS OF THE PHYSICAL DISTRIBUTION SYSTEM

A basic grasp of physical distribution activities and their interrelationships is essential to understanding how levels of service are maintained and how trade-off costs are calculated.

Figure 22-3 presents a simplified model of the key components of the physical distribution system. Those components will be discussed here.

ORDER PROCESSING— KEY TO SERVICE

Order processing includes receiving, recording, filling, and assembling orders for shipment. Management's interest in this process extends to the amount of time required and quality control procedures that ensure proper shipment.

Figure 22-3　OVERVIEW OF THE MAJOR PHYSICAL DISTRIBUTION SYSTEM COMPONENTS

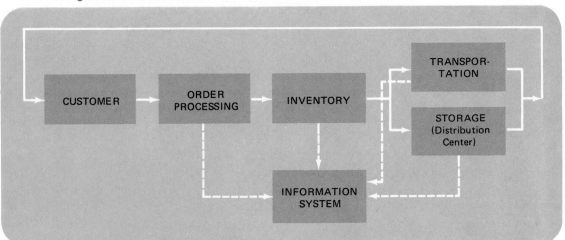

If Howard Johnson's orders orange tablecloths from the producer, a shipment of red cloths would be a disaster.

High-speed data processing techniques allow for rapid order processing. Sometimes speed is so essential that customers have a direct computer tie-in with suppliers. They can find out at a moment's notice how many units of a product are on hand, how many on order, how many have been shipped, and when they are expected to arrive.

When customers place an order, they set in motion a flow of products and information through the distribution network. The crucial events in this transaction between buyer and seller are the receipt of the order by the seller, the initiation of the actions leading to assembly of ordered goods, and the shipment of the goods themselves. If responsibility for these events is centralized, processing can be accomplished quickly and more efficiently. For this reason, many firms have assigned the responsibility for processing to the physical distribution department. Figure 22-4 illustrates this **order cycle**.

INVENTORY— AVAILABILITY OF SUPPLY

Although marketing managers usually have little control over **inventory policy**, they want to have a say in its formulation, since inventory policy is an instrument in the demand-creation and demand-satisfaction process. Ideally, the manager would like to be able to tell customers that all orders will be filled and shipped immediately. But economic reality does not allow a company to carry enough stock to guarantee that shortages will not occur. Some compromise must therefore be reached in which inventory costs and the desired customer service level are reconciled. In general, the desired level of inventory is computed by balancing the added cost of maintaining inventory against the expected profit from the additional sales that may result from increased product availability.

Inventory management has always been a major headache. On the average, nearly 30 percent of a firm's total assets are tied up in inventory. One of the key factors in inventory management is accurately predicting demand levels (remember Chapter 5 on sales forecasting). If manufacturers could determine when demand would occur and how heavy that demand would be, they could hold inventory and costs down to the minimum needed to guard against production failure.

Several other elements besides demand go into the inventory decision-making process. One is critical value analysis, or the decision as to which items need most attention in the inventory control system. Many inventories are managed on a multi-system basis, whereby a firm concentrates on popular items, paying less attention to less popular items and to orders to replace them. A larger stock of the slow-moving items is maintained to reduce costs of managing them. This system would not work for products that spoil easily (dairy products) or become obsolete (fashions).

Distribution management must also take into account sales rate, or average demand over lead time (the time between placement of order and receipt of goods), and sales variability. Since demand is seldom constant, a firm must figure out how much safety stock is needed to account for fluctuations. Mana-

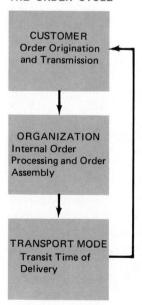

Figure 22-4
THE ORDER CYCLE

CUSTOMER
Order Origination
and Transmission

ORGANIZATION
Internal Order
Processing and Order
Assembly

TRANSPORT MODE
Transit Time of
Delivery

Economic Order Quantity, or EOQ, is a mathematical formula used to deter- **INVENTORY AND** mine base stock requirements. It provides a guide to efficient inventory man- **THE EOQ METHOD** agement. The formula is:

$$EOQ = \sqrt{\frac{2as}{i}}$$

where a = order cost (per order)
   s = annual sales rate (in units)
   i = interest costs per unit per year

Let's assume that a = $20, s = 5,200 units, and i = 25¢ per unit. Then:

$$EOQ = \sqrt{\frac{2 \times 20 \times 5,200}{.25}} = 912 \text{ units}$$

Base stock refers to the amount of stock required to meet the average level of demand. A firm that provided only base stock inventory would probably be out of inventory half of the time. To guard against shortages in times of high demand, firms carry safety stocks.

Based on Richard J. Lewis, "Physical Distribution: Managing the Firm's Service Level," in E. Jerome McCarthy, John F. Grashof, and Andrew A. Brogowicz, eds., *Readings in Basic Marketing* (Homewood, Ill.: Irwin, 1975), pp. 225–26.

gers making inventory decisions must also take into account such factors as the cost of carrying inventory, the end use of products, and geographical variations in demand.

TRANSPORTATION— PRODUCTS IN MOTION

A firm that ships its products generally has five **transportation** alternatives: railroad, highway (motor carrier and private truck), water, air, and pipeline. After an analysis of the capabilities of each of these modes of transportation, physical distribution managers are then able to select the best mode (or modes) for the job.

Legal Regulation of Transportation

Two forms of transportation—common and contract—are subject to federal economic and safety regulations if their operations cross state lines. Two other forms—exempt and private—are subject to regulations only within the states that they serve.

Common carriers, the most frequently used form of transportation, can carry goods any time and to any place, as the local operating authority allows. Their rates for service must be published openly, and must be the same for all customers for a given service. When shippers or carriers dispute those rates, they apply to government agencies for rulings.

Contract carriers, which do business on a selective basis, may ask a different price of two customers for the same service. But they must make public the actual rates charged to shippers. Regulatory agencies issue permits to contract carriers on a less restrictive basis than to common carriers. Such permits specify commodity to be carried, routes to be used, and other aspects of the transporting operation.

The term **exempt carriage** applies to a whole range of activities. Transport of unprocessed products of agriculture and fishing, for example, is by and large exempt from economic regulation. Companies that use their own **private carriers** can transport their own goods without regard to state or federal economic regulations. Private transportation is particularly desirable for manufacturers with a constant volume of need, multidirectional material flows, and a desire for greater control over carriage of goods, more flexibility, and specialized equipment.

Modes of Transportation

As was mentioned above, there are five basic modes of transportation for physical distribution: railroad, highway, water, air, and pipeline. Table 22-1 shows that rail, air, and water carriers are generally used for long-distance shipping, while highway carriers are used for shorter shipments. We can also see that highway carriers account for the largest percentage of tons shipped (a combined total of 57 percent).

Special Transport Agencies. Within each of the major transportation modes there are a number of special transport agencies. While some of these maintain their own equipment, there are others that depend on outside carriers. These auxiliary users generally limit themselves to shipments from 20 pounds to less-than-carload, less-than-truckload, or container quantities. These special agencies include air express, United Parcel Service, freight forwarders, and shippers' cooperatives.

Table 22-1
SHIPMENTS BY MODES OF TRANSPORTATION

MODES OF TRANSPORTATION	AVERAGE LENGTH OF HAUL (STRAIGHT-LINE MILES)	TONS (AS A PERCENTAGE OF THE TOTAL)	TON-MILES (WEIGHT × DISTANCE, AS A PERCENTAGE OF THE TOTAL)
Rail	577	37.8	55.9%
Motor carrier	306	35.7	28.2
Private truck	166	21.3	9.0
Air	850	.1	.2
Water	507	4.6	6.1

NOTE: Data excludes shipments moving by pipeline, parcel post, by own power or towed; shipment transported less than 25 miles from the plant, and within the same city.
source: U.S. Bureau of the Census, *Census of Transportation, 1972* (Washington, D.C.: U. S. Government Printing Office, 1975), p. 8–1.

Air express, which is very expensive, is useful when a shipment must be made quickly. The agencies pick up goods at the point of origin and deliver them to the customer's door. Goods are loaded on planes after the mails, but before air freight.

United Parcel (UPS) operates in the East, Midwest, and Far West, but does not deliver to all states or all towns. UPS prices compare favorably with parcel post for select shipment sizes. They provide regular pickup and delivery at a small weekly charge.

Freight forwarders pick up small shipments, consolidate them, and distribute to markets. The operating margin of this intermediary comes from the low-volume rates paid to rail or truck companies and the higher, less-than-volume prices charged to the shipper. The advantage to the shipper is that he or she buys single carrier responsibility and the services of a carrier who will then be responsible for arranging the best possible combination of pick-up, line-haul, and delivery.

Shippers' cooperatives are usually set up by a related group of shippers who are interested in cutting volume rates by increasing the quantity of freight offered to the carrier. The cooperative office collects orders from members, designates a local pickup carrier, arranges for transport from origin to destination, and pays all bills to carriers involved.

Coordinated Transport. The concept of coordinated transport has recently received renewed attention. Coordinated services usually represent a compromise among the services (and costs) offered by the individual cooperating carriers. Figure 22-5 gives a simplified scheme of the forms of coordinated transport and shows how each is the result of combining the services of two basic modes.

Of the many coordinated transport possibilities, the most popular is **piggyback**, or the trailer-on-flatcar (TOFC). This method is cheaper than trucking alone, but provides the same convenience and flexibility. Piggyback shippers

Figure 22-5

MAJOR COORDINATED TRANSPORT TYPES

Based on James L. Heskett, Nicholas A. Glaskowsky, Jr., and Robert M. Ivie, *Business Logistics: Physical Distribution and Materials Management*, 2d ed. Copyright © 1973 The Ronald Press Company, New York.

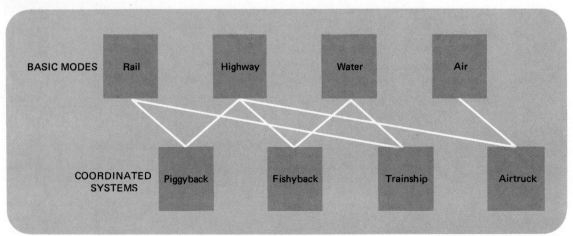

BASIC MODES — Rail, Highway, Water, Air

COORDINATED SYSTEMS — Piggyback, Fishyback, Trainship, Airtruck

pay reasonable rates for the convenience of door-to-door service over long distances.

Containerized freight refers to the shipment of an entire trailer on a railroad flatcar. In a truck-rail combination service called container-on-flatcar (COFC), only the container or box in which the freight is packaged is hauled, not the chassis. The shipper who uses containerized freight avoids the expense of rehandling small shipment units at point of transfer.

Fishyback (combined water-truck services) is a new but expanding industry. The **airtruck** combination has also been successful. The container is important to air transportation, since the high costs prohibit transport of the chassis of a highway trailer. The **trainship** system is used only moderately

Transportation Selection Criteria

Generally, firms use a variety of transportation modes. Raw materials are often moved by a combination of rail, water, or pipeline; finished goods by truck; small shipments by truck, air, UPS, bus, or the post office. The method chosen depends upon distribution patterns, some of which are illustrated in Table 22-2. There are, of course, exceptions to these general rules. For example, a magazine publisher will usually use the post office, while a petroleum firm will move its product from field to refinery in pipelines.

Decisions about transportation require trade-offs. For example, as we can see from Figure 22-6, air freight is fast but expensive. However, as Kent Instruments Ltd. (England) has found, it may be less costly in the long run, since it leads to lower insurance, packaging, and storage costs.[7] In addition, air freight has enabled the company to reduce its inventory holdings and thereby improve its cash flow and profitability. Trade-offs must be made in areas other than transportation in order to minimize transportation costs. For example, decentralization of warehousing and inventory lowers total transportation costs. But it also raises warehousing and inventory expenses.

STORAGE—FIXED DISTRIBUTION FACILITIES

Storage management must take into account the size, number, and location of facilities needed to provide service. Basic inventory stocks are supplied by storage, and it also serves as a buffer between differences in supply and demand.[8]

Table 22-2
TRANSPORT NEEDS SUGGEST TRANSPORTATION MODES

PATTERN	NEED	PROBABLE MODE
Plant to plant	Production scheduling	Rail or Truck
Plant to warehouse	Replenishing stock	Rail or Truck
Warehouse to warehouse	Balancing stock	Truck
Warehouse to customer	Service	Truck
Plant to customer	Emergency	Air

From Edward W. Smykay, *Physical Distribution Management,* 3d ed. (New York: Macmillan, 1973), p. 196. © 1973 by Macmillan Publishing Co., Inc.

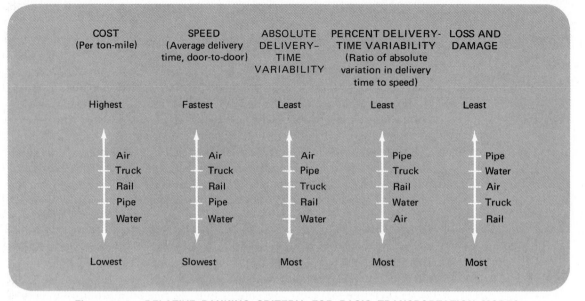

COST (Per ton-mile)	SPEED (Average delivery time, door-to-door)	ABSOLUTE DELIVERY- TIME VARIABILITY	PERCENT DELIVERY- TIME VARIABILITY (Ratio of absolute variation in delivery time to speed)	LOSS AND DAMAGE
Highest	Fastest	Least	Least	Least
Air	Air	Air	Pipe	Pipe
Truck	Truck	Pipe	Truck	Water
Rail	Rail	Truck	Rail	Air
Pipe	Pipe	Rail	Water	Truck
Water	Water	Water	Air	Rail
Lowest	Slowest	Most	Most	Most

Figure 22-6 RELATIVE RANKING CRITERIA FOR BASIC TRANSPORTATION MODES
Based on Ronald H. Ballou, *Business Logistics Management* (Englewood Cliffs, N.J.: Prentice-Hall, 1973), p. 147.

Inventory is stored in relation to the market, in order that the time lapse between order and delivery be as short as possible. Also, storage makes up for differences in supply and demand in the case of goods produced seasonally and consumed constantly, produced constantly and consumed seasonally, or produced in one season and consumed in another. Such storage is appropriate to fruit and vegetable growers, who face difficulty in transporting goods during periods of peak transportation demand.

Today, national producers can usually obtain overnight trucking service for nearly all of their customers by maintaining only 12 to 18 distribution centers. In the early part of this century, the same manufacturers usually had 150 warehouses, each one serving an area with a radius of 100 miles or so. Territories have widened as a result of improved order communications, the interstate highway system, air cargo, and better rail and water transportation.

Conventional Warehousing

A **warehouse** differs from a **distribution center** in that the products remain in one place for some time, and cost minimization is given priority over throughput (moving goods in, through, and out). As noted, many products require long-term storage—seasonal agricultural products, items in limited demand. If space is available, economy dictates that such products be stored near the production site. If the producer ships too far ahead of demand, extra transportation charges and regional variation in demand may increase costs.

Warehouse facilities are of three types: private and owned, private and leased, and public. A warehouse user usually decides to go public or private depending on capital commitment and degree of control. For the user, public warehousing entails variable costs and few fixed asset commitments. However, the user has less direct control over operations in the warehouse, since the owner is an independent operator.

But **public warehousing** offers many advantages. A long-term lease or real estate investment is not necessary, and the user has more flexibility in adjusting to variables in transportation and distribution relationships. The company that uses public warehousing can obtain readily negotiable receipts from the warehouse which allow it to finance or borrow against stocks. If it stores only a small number of goods, it does not worry about keeping a warehouse busy all year.

Private warehousing also has advantages. A company may find it profitable to run its own warehouse when its product is sufficiently stable or diversified to keep the warehouse filled. Private warehousing is preferable when a company has a large concentration of customers within a small area and required storage space is about 100,000 square feet. It is also preferable when a product demands special safety or quality control, or when unusual skill on the part of warehouse operators is needed. Special handling facilities (for broadloom carpets, for example) may call for private warehousing.

Distribution Centers

Careful location of distribution centers is important if a company is to reach markets quickly. By shipping large amounts of a small number of products from several centers, the company can also economize on inbound movements. After World War II, expanding business activities stimulated the growth of distribution centers to serve new markets, and to cut down inventory, storage, handling, and transportation costs.

Unlike a warehouse, a distribution center provides services for shippers and/or consignees of goods, often using a computer and sophisticated materials-handling equipment. Distribution centers serve a regional market, and the staff is primarily interested in moving rather than storing goods. The center consolidates large shipments from production points, processes and regroups products according to the customer's orders, and maintains a full product line.

Many companies are shifting from warehouses to distribution centers in their distribution planning. Ten years ago, Federal-Mogul Corporation had 120 warehouses.[9] Today they have 47. A new distribution center in Jacksonville, Alabama, handles more than 90 percent of the production of manufacturing facilities in 16 states. Products are repackaged there and batched for shipment to company warehouses. By shipping all production to the Jacksonville center rather than from factory to warehouse, Federal-Mogul more than offsets the costs of extra travel time to Jacksonville.

INFORMATION— MONITORING DISTRIBUTION FLOWS

The people who handle physical distribution need information about inventory, transportation, and warehousing and unit loading. Most important is knowing about inventory—present stock positions at each location, future commitments for shipment, and replenishment capabilities.

Planning the best transportation means day-to-day selection of transport modes and carriers. Before a mode is chosen, relative charges and service preferences are weighed. Performance reports by carrier form the basis for daily decision on specific carriers. The top performer, whether private or common carrier, will probably earn the business.

Warehousing reports usually cover:

1. space utilization, or the placement of products in storage and picking lines;

2. labor utilization, or scheduling of the work force;

3. unit-load performance reports, reflecting whether shipments result in full loading of vehicles and unit loading to reduce handling costs.[10]

A well-conceived distribution management information system is vital to controlling cost and service. The system should be tailored to provide management with information for planning and controlling all distribution operations. It should include data from areas that determine the effectiveness of distribution and should measure costs against effectiveness rather than against sales. Finally, the system should provide facts for assessment of ways to improve cost and service performance of the entire network.

Marketers are often unaware of the true cost of physical distribution operations.[11] Either the computer is not fed the information it needs, or the right questions (about inventory costs and level) are not asked.

ORGANIZING PHYSICAL DISTRIBUTION

Top management is becoming increasingly aware of the importance of clearly defining responsibility for controlling results of physical distribution. As the role of distribution management is increasingly appreciated, companies are placing it at a higher level in the organizational structure.

FRAGMENTED APPROACH

Coordination is essential to making valid decisions on inventory levels, transportation, and warehousing. Unfortunately, many companies divide physical distribution functions arbitrarily among several departments. When this happens, each department tends to view physical distribution objectives from its own perspective.

While the traffic manager tries to minimize freight bills by shipping large quantities infrequently and with cheap modes of transportation, the sales manager wants large inventories and faster, more expensive transportation in order to satisfy customers. The inventory control manager wants small inventories in order to keep costs down. This fragmentation often creates stress and tension within a firm. It also makes the task of pinning down responsibility for specific costs such as inventory or transportation extremely difficult.

INTEGRATED APPROACH

Some companies that have recognized the importance of integrating physical distribution functions have established a permanent committee that meets regularly to determine policy. Others have increased the efficiency of the distribution system by putting authority into the hands of one person.

A company that sets up a special department to handle distribution

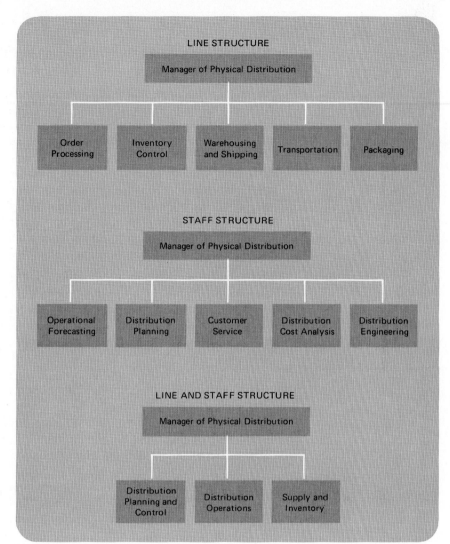

LINE STRUCTURE

Manager of Physical Distribution

- Order Processing
- Inventory Control
- Warehousing and Shipping
- Transportation
- Packaging

STAFF STRUCTURE

Manager of Physical Distribution

- Operational Forecasting
- Distribution Planning
- Customer Service
- Distribution Cost Analysis
- Distribution Engineering

LINE AND STAFF STRUCTURE

Manager of Physical Distribution

- Distribution Planning and Control
- Distribution Operations
- Supply and Inventory

**Figure 22-7
ALTERNATIVE PHYSICAL DISTRIBUTION ORGANIZATIONS**

From William M. Stewart, "Physical Distribution— Coordinating Inventory, Warehousing, and Transportation for Optimum Service at Lowest Cost," in Victor P. Buell, ed., *Handbook of Modern Marketing* (New York: McGraw-Hill, 1970), pp. 4:66–67.

must decide whether that department should have separate status or be integrated with an existing unit. Usually, physical distribution departments are a part of the marketing unit, especially in competitive packaged goods industries. In those industries, marketing and physical distribution functions must be coordinated with those of advertising and promotion staff.

Regrouping of activities is only one element in creating an effective physical distribution system. The company must also decide whether responsibility should be advisory or control in character. A physical distribution manager can be a line administrator, a manager with responsibility for staff activities only, or the overseer of both staff and line functions. An informed decision rests on thorough analysis of the nature of a company's business and the administrative talents of its personnel. Various possible distribution structures are illustrated in Figure 22-7.

One marketing analyst has noted that in the 1970s, distribution finally entered a period of maturity as a corporate organizational entity:

> *The major roles of the distribution organization today encompass not only daily administration of order processing, inventory control, distribution center management, and traffic, but a new emphasis on coordinative and analytical input at the top management level.*
>
> *Many distribution organizations in major corporations are increasingly taking on the mission of acting as a partner to the finance function in the process of analyzing, diagnosing, and suggesting changes in methods of operation in order to increase the effectiveness of the whole corporate organization. Changes in accounting practices and managerial accounting techniques have made it possible to evaluate the distribution function in terms of its contribution to the overall business.*[12]

While far-sighted executives have recognized the changes that must be made in concepts of physical distribution, their ideas have not been universally realized. Some companies have established solid lines of communication between marketing and manufacturing, yet have stopped short of making the distribution function a concern of top management.

FUTURE OF PHYSICAL DISTRIBUTION

Several trends in today's economic environment will have an impact on physical distribution. One such trend is the growth of consumerism—the customer is demanding better service and quality. Competition is increasing. New products and processes are being created. Labor, transportation, and investment costs are rising. Telecommunications are improving, and computerization, mechanization, and automation are increasing. These changes will force the redesign of physical distribution systems for greater effectiveness (customer service) and efficiency (costs).

Change in physical distribution will also result from institutional developments, including reordering of functions and facilities.[13] One new development is the creation of distribution utilities—companies that provide a complete range of warehousing, transportation, order processing, and inventory control services. A distribution utility contracts with a manufacturer to remove finished stock from the manufacturer's production line and make it available for sale. This arrangement permits the manufacturer to concentrate on the other marketing mix elements.

The concept of shared services has been created by inflated distribution costs and heavy capital expenditures required for physical facilities. Instead of relying on private distribution systems, companies turn to comprehensive systems of shared facilities and services. As a result, they are able to take a new view of some old distribution problems.

The operation of distribution centers is beginning to form new patterns. For example, storage space is being used more intensively. Fewer and larger distribution centers are being operated in order to cut inventory carrying costs.

Some firms have opened specialized supplementary centers. Analysts predict that firms will turn more often to sharing of storage space and equipment in order to deal with rising costs, shortages, and government pressure.

Changes in physical distribution will have an international impact—for example, on food shortages in underdeveloped countries. In those countries, good management is essential to the distribution of what is available. In that sense, physical distribution can serve as an instrument of social change.

CONCLUSION

The physical distribution process has been defined as getting the right goods to the right place at the right time for the least cost. The system which aims at that goal is a complex and changing one. One of the first objectives of distribution planners is to determine a level of customer service that will be satisfactory to the customer and profitable to the seller.

The physical distribution manager determines inventory policy—how much of a product must be made available to satisfy fluctuations in demand. The manager must choose among many forms of transportation—common, contract, exempt, and private. Transport agencies use five basic modes: rail, highway, water, air, and pipeline. Often, one shipper will use a combination of services, depending on the amount being shipped and the marketing distribution patterns.

The physical distribution manager also makes decisions about how products will be stored and distributed. Today, many companies are using distribution centers rather than warehouses. A distribution center provides services for shippers and serves a regional market. The emphasis is on moving rather than storing goods.

The flow of distribution is monitored by an information system that contains data about inventory, transportation, and warehousing. Such an information system is an important element in controlling costs and service.

Companies today recognize the fact that physical distribution functions must be integrated and not fragmented. Often, recognition of this fact has led to restructuring within an organization. Trends in modern business only make more apparent the fact that physical distribution will continue to be a vital marketing element.

DISCUSSION QUESTIONS

1. What characteristics of a physical distribution system indicate how close an organization is to the marketing concept?
2. What would be some management guidelines regarding physical distribution for: (a) a bank with several branches, (b) U.S. Steel and its distributors, (c) and Montgomery Ward and its many suppliers?
3. What implications does the order cycle have for the management of inventory control, transportation, warehousing, and information systems?

4. The industrial customers for a specific high-pressure pump require fast delivery in the event that their present equipment breaks down. Paladin Pumps, a major manufacturer of this type of pump, maintains a distribution center in Atlanta to serve the Southeast, a market which amounted to sales of 20,000 units last year. The cost per order to Paladin is $50.00 and the annual interest cost per unit is $.50. What base stock of this pump should the company carry?

5. Sun Giant brand fresh produce is primarily transported nationally by rail. Truck transport is the next most frequently used method, with air shipments used only rarely. Does this setup make sense? Explain.

6. Why is the "fast in and fast out" principle so important to distribution center management for a discount store chain?

7. Cheery Greeting Cards wants to restructure its physical distribution organization under a single manager, Pamela Sklar. Among the fragmented activities she is considering assuming are inventory control, packaging, order processing, manufacturing, sales forecasting, materials handling, complaint handling, and transportation. Which of these activities do you feel should be Ms. Sklar's direct responsibility? Which should be her indirect responsibility? Which should not be her responsibility?

NOTES

1. "Win, Place, and Flow," *Pepsi-Cola World* 33 (Summer 1972): 32–34.

2. Philip Kotler, *Marketing Management: Analysis, Planning, and Control*, 3d ed. (Englewood Cliffs, N.J.: Prentice-Hall, 1976), p. 304.

3. Paul D. Converse, "The Other Half of Marketing," in Alfred L. Seelye, ed., *Marketing in Transition* (New York: Harper, 1958).

4. "Cheaper Ways to Reach the Customer," *Business Week*, September 9, 1972, p. 120.

5. Wendell M. Stewart, "Physical Distribution," in Victor P. Buell, ed., *Handbook of Modern Marketing* (New York: McGraw-Hill, 1970), p. 4:54.

6. "Del Monte Living with New Labeling Rules," *Business Week*, February 3, 1973, p. 45.

7. Gerard Tavernier, "Controlling the Soaring Cost of Distribution," *International Management* 30 (August 1974): 14–15.

8. James L. Heskett, "Physical Distribution," in Albert Wesley Frey, ed., *Marketing Handbook*, 2d ed. (New York: Ronald Press, 1965), p. 21:15.

9. "The Changing Channels of Distribution," *Industrial Distribution* 66 (February 1976): 38.

10. Edward W. Smykay, *Physical Distribution Management*, 3d ed. (New York: Macmillan, 1973), p. 37.

11. "The Changing Channels of Distribution," p. 28.

12. Ward A. Fredericks, "Emerging Patterns of Physical Distribution—Domestic," in Smykay, p. 376.

13. James L. Heskett, "Sweeping Changes in Distribution," *Harvard Business Review* 51 (March–April 1973): 123–32.

CASE STUDIES

GRANADA BAKERIES, INC.

Granada Bakeries, a firm operating in the Dallas-Fort Worth metropolitan area, began in 1962 as a small family business run by Mr. and Mrs. Tony Mendoza and their older children. Initially, they operated a small store in a Mexican-American neighborhood of Fort Worth, and sold meat patties, bread, spice buns, and small rolls. But Granada's meat patties showed an astounding popularity. As a result, the Mendozas obtained an SBA loan to assist them in opening separate manufacturing facilities for Mexican meat patties.

Granada currently generates almost $1 million in annual sales. Roughly $200,000 represents retail sales from the original bakery shop. The remaining sum reflects wholesale trade to the fast food market and small retail stores.

Distribution Is the Problem

There are three principal means of distribution for Granada's meat patties: (1) direct sales—the firm has two company trucks; (2) local wholesaler jobbers, who service bodegas; and (3) fast food wholesale supply companies, which service fast food outlets such as taco stands and pizza parlors.

The patties are distributed in two assortments. At present, roughly 65 to 75 percent of Granada's wholesale business involves distribution of 60- and 100-pack cartons to fast food outlets. The other 25 to 35 percent of wholesale trade represents sales of three-packs to retailers.

Pricing is entirely cost-based. Granada has not studied any pricing alternatives for its patties. The firm allows no discounts for quick payment, and refuses to sell any patties on a consignment basis. The Mendozas believe that flexible credit terms will not boost product sales.

Granada has only one person working on direct sales. Frank Santos, the sales manager, has two primary responsibilities: (1) he looks for new accounts through contacts with wholesale distributors and jobbers who service retail food stores and fast food markets; (2) he speaks with representatives of supermarket chains in the hope that Granada can distribute there.

Because of its limited budget, Granada cannot engage in any advertising. The small printed signs that the firm provides for fast food outlets are Granada's only sales promotion effort.

In most instances, Granada handles servicing in Fort Worth directly with its own delivery trucks. Outside distributors handle most of Granada's wholesale trade in the Dallas area. This distinction seems to be quite important in evaluating Granada's marketing success. Most retailers in Fort Worth are satisfied with Granada's distribution, but this is not true in Dallas.

Fifteen of Granada's 25 largest outlets in Dallas complained about poor servicing from independent distributors. The complaints centered around three areas: (1) delivery schedules are erratic and unpredictable; (2) when a retail outlet needs more patties, the manager finds it almost impossible to contact the distributor to place an order; and (3) even when an order is placed, the distributor does not always appear on time, and sometimes not at all.

Almost half of the Dallas outlets reported that they lost significant sales of Granada meat patties because they were often out of stock. Many of these outlets are considering dropping business with Granada, even though they like the product, and switching to a competitor (probably Mexi-man). It should be noted that Mexi-man owns four delivery trucks and regularly makes stops at retail outlets at least two or three times a week.

Most dealers are satisfied with the quality of the Granada meat patties. However, six outlets suggested that the present patty should be enlarged with more dough (while retaining the same amount of meat as before). In the opinion of these dealers, this change would give people "more for their money." The dealers believe that, by adding more dough, Granada patties could more effectively compete against other fast food products such as tacos, tortillas, and pizza.

Granada owner Tony Mendoza feels that the firm's best opportunities for growth lie in the supermarket field. He hopes to interest Fort Worth and Dallas supermarket chains in carrying the Granada meat patties. Ultimately, Mendoza hopes that entrance into these chains will foster acceptance in other large markets—particularly Houston, Oklahoma City, Denver, Albuquerque, and New Orleans.

Granada is considering these ways of getting into supermarkets:

1. Giving one free case of patties to each store in a chain. This has already been done for Safeway, at the chain's request.

2. Offering product samples (in the form of hors d'oeuvres) in individual stores. The samples would be precooked and reheated in microwave ovens in the supermarkets.

3. Using local radio advertising to back up and support supermarket sales.

Questions 1. What are Granada's distribution channel problems? What other marketing strategy problems are related to distribution?
2. How can Granada solve its distribution channel problems? What other marketing strategy recommendations would you make?
3. Should Granada enter supermarket distribution channels at this time? If so, what should Granada's strategy be?

PEMBROOK PETROLEUM COMPANY

Background The Pembrook Petroleum Company (PPC) of Denver, Colorado, is one of the nation's fourteen largest oil companies. Gerald S. Dunphy has been a marketing vice-president of PPC for the past eight years.

Since 1973, his work had focused on responding to the energy crisis and the effects of oil shortages on the marketing of gasoline products. But, in 1976, the crisis seemed to be over—at least temporarily. Oil producers, dealers, and consumers had become accustomed to a world of expensive gasoline. In this marketing climate, Dunphy felt a new freedom to consider possible major revisions in PPC's distribution channel mix.

Dunphy decided to make a determined attempt to institute changes in PPC marketing strategy: he set to work on an original and daring position paper.

Notes for a Position Paper

Market Share. The "independents" in the retail gasoline business are on the rise. They concentrate mainly on pumping as much gasoline as cheaply as possible. In the last decade they have expanded retail business by 50 percent. They now control one-third of the retail market. In the last two years, nine of the top ten oil companies have lost some of their market share to these independents.

Dealer and Jobber Revolt. Dealers are pressing damage suits against major oil companies in six states. They claim that the majors are stifling competition and are selling gasoline to independents at a lower cost than to their own branded jobbers.

Environmentalists. There is growing pressure on oil companies because of the blight of abandoned gas stations. In Detroit, 8 percent of the stations are now boarded up. It costs $4,000 to tear down a station, and if we're pressured by environmental groups to spend that for each station that closes across the country, it will cost PPC a pretty penny.

Capital Squeeze. A decade ago, we only had to borrow 15 percent of our capital funds. Now the figure is 30 percent. Price wars are forcing us into a cash-flow squeeze.

Self-service. Five years ago, self-service stations were almost nonexistent. Today, they control 10 percent of national gasoline sales. The projection for 1980 is 25 percent.

Gas Station Food Stores. Tenneco, a Texas-based firm, has set up 100 combination gas station/convenience goods stores across the country. This started a trend that has been followed by many convenience and grocery store chains and even by mass merchandisers such as Sears, Roebuck and Montgomery Ward.

Diagnostic Car-Care Centers. Exxon now has 100 huge car-care stations in operation. These stations have complex electronic gear and can diagnose all sorts of car "illnesses."

Questions

1. How should PPC go about revising its distribution channel mix?
2. Assuming some changes are made in PPC's distribution channels, what should be the strategy toward its conventional service station dealers?

NEWMET CORPORATION

Background

Newmet Corporation is a Wilmington, Delaware firm specializing in national metals distribution. It was founded in 1970 by Marc Trippe, a young graduate of Stanford Business School. In its first four years of operation, Newmet's sales soared to over $22 million.

The rise of Newmet reflects recent marketing developments in the metals service industry. Increasingly, steel mills are filling customer orders (especially for small buyers) at separate service centers rather than at the mill. These independent centers were supplying some $15 billion worth of metals annually as of 1976.

Two Views of Newmet

In New Orleans, Louisiana, Philip Mackey, a regional sales manager with Davis Steel, and Guy Skeeter, the president of a garden furniture manufacturing firm, were discussing the Newmet Corporation. Skeeter had been considering the Newmet Corporation as a supplier. He was especially impressed by a presentation he received from Marc Trippe, the president of Newmet. Mackey has also been hearing a lot about Newmet over the last few years, but he is a conservative executive noted for his reluctance to experiment with anything new and different.

Guy Skeeter began their conversation. "I'm impressed with Newmet. I think these people are the up-and-coming force in metals' distribution.

"Their approach is a new one for the field. They focus on *buying* the right products as much as on selling them. He plans ahead—he's always one step ahead of the market.

"Trippe saw the shortage of stainless steel in 1972 coming months before anyone else. Newmet stocked up on stainless steel metal sheets, and waited patiently. When the crunch came, their orders went up 60 percent.

"Newmet has maintained a high profitability over its four years of operation. And that allows a flexibility that most of its competitors don't have. They can get products from the outside for a regular customer and take a slightly lower profit. Most firms can't afford to do that."

"Sure, Guy, they can stretch the dollar like that," answered Philip Mackey. "But that's just the kind of wheeling and dealing I don't trust, especially with these new whiz-kid operators. If Newmet has to go to a competitor for a product in order to service Guy Skeeter, the competitor may not be in any rush to help them out. And you sit there waiting while Newmet sits there waiting.

"I'd much rather trust my business with a solid, reputable firm that handles a full range of product lines and preprocessing services. With *that* kind of distributor, you know they're right there to take care of *all* of your needs."

Mackey got up and started pacing. "There's another danger area, too. What about shortages? What happened with these whiz kids in 1973 and 1974 when metal shortages tore the industry apart? Did these guys take care of their long-time customers?"

"I don't know the answer to that," replied Guy Skeeter. "Frankly, I should have asked Trippe that question, and I didn't. But I'm certainly going to check into it. Even a whiz kid can guess wrong, and *his* wrong guesses could put *me* out of business.

"But even so," continued Skeeter, "I still think Trippe is on to something. This man doesn't wait for customers to come to him. My current supplier, Standard Brass, sends out a mailing once a year. Newmet sends out mailings every three weeks. They're constantly buying new products, updating their stock lists, and filling us in on what they've got. I think it's good business.

Questions

1. Does Newmet have what it takes to succeed as a metals distributor? Why?
2. Should Skeeter's company agree to use Newmet as a supplier?

Carrying Out Marketing Strategy

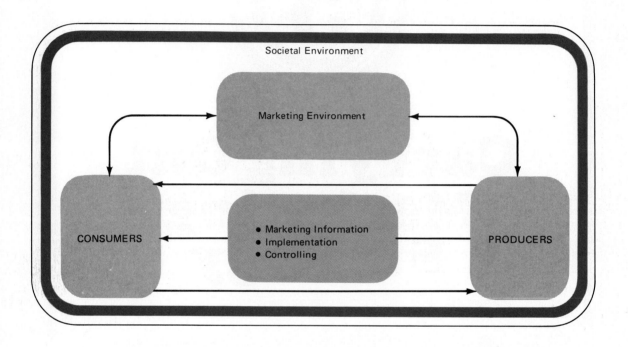

23

MARKETING INFORMATION SYSTEMS AND RESEARCH

After completing this chapter, the reader should be able to:

1. Explain the role of information in the marketing decision-making process.

2. Describe the major components of the marketing information system.

3. Contrast the dynamics of the marketing information system with the marketing research process.

4. Point out the necessary steps in marketing research.

5. Describe conditions under which a research design and marketing data sources are selected.

6. Show how marketing research data are analyzed, reported, and followed up.

7. Evaluate the management performance and social issues linked to marketing research.

Marketing strategy doesn't just happen. Several managerial processes are needed to carry it out. One of these is the marketing information system; another is marketing research. In this chapter we will discuss ways of gathering information and how it is used in marketing decision making.

THE SPEED-CAR ANTIFREEZE

A few years ago, the Dow Chemical Company consulted a market research firm in connection with its antifreeze products.[1] Dow wanted a forecast of the demand for a new type of antifreeze aimed at owners of speed cars (souped-up models of standard cars).

The research firm determined that two basic questions had to be answered: (1) Were speed-car drivers similar to or different from other motorists in their purchasing habits? (2) What kind of positioning would be best for such a product?

After further study, it was learned that antifreeze not only prevents damage to cars in the winter, but also protects against boil-overs in the summer. A sample survey found that it would be more effective to position the new Dow product as a "summer coolant and antifreeze," than as an "antifreeze and summer coolant."

The consultants eventually recommended targeting the product at the preventive-care motorist rather than the speed-car owner. The preventive-care group was found to be most willing to experiment with a new brand. Furthermore, since such motorists tended to buy automotive supplies in discount stores, it was decided that the Dow marketing campaign should emphasize mass merchandise outlets.

INFORMATION IS THE LIFEBLOOD OF MARKETING   As this example illustrates, the market researcher must always search for the essential questions and problems for study. If the consultants for Dow Chemical had simply assumed that the product should be geared toward winter sales, they would have ignored vital marketing alternatives. But this research firm asked the right question (Should we stress the summer or winter advantages of the product?) and also found a good answer.

Information has been defined as "those cues which have the potential to affect managerial decisions."[2] Since marketing decision makers cannot control all the factors in a given situation, there is always the risk that they will make a wrong choice. Such wrong choices cost money, so it is the task of market researchers to provide the information that will enable the decision makers to make fewer wrong decisions (risk reduction). The role of marketing information in the decision-making process is illustrated in Figure 23-1.

The marketing manager must make frequent decisions about price, adver-

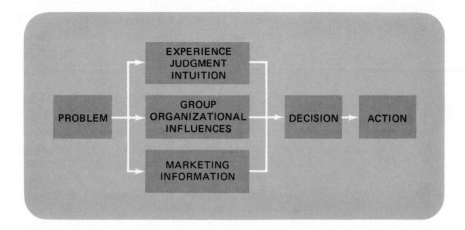

Figure 23-1
THE ROLE OF
INFORMATION IN
DECISION MAKING

tising, promotion, distribution, sales efforts, and branding. Marketing information is used to predict the probable results of decisions, evaluate those results, and anticipate new profit opportunities. This information is vital for decision making in the goal setting, planning, implementation, and control stages of the managerial marketing process.

Marketing information comes from two sources: marketing research and marketing information systems. **Marketing research** is conducted when specific information is needed to solve a particular problem (which market segment prefers motels, which advertising theme for a new plant store will attract more customers). Despite its importance, much of what has passed for "marketing research" has actually been unsystematic data collection on isolated problems. Irrelevant facts have been obtained while truly valuable information has been lost in the shuffle. As a result, some firms have attempted to develop marketing information systems. These regularly pull together various scattered sources of information from inside and outside the organization. The purpose of these systems is to provide information and analytic capabilities (thanks to the computer) that are needed by executives who must make decisions on a broad range of marketing topics. These include sales results, competitive activities, inventory movement, sales force performance, forecasts of economic conditions, changing consumer attitudes, and the like. The possible sources of information for the marketing information system include accounting records, salesperson reports, and contracted data-gathering services, as well as marketing research studies.

MARKETING INFORMATION SYSTEMS

Increasingly, firms are integrating various information-gathering mechanisms into more general **marketing information systems (MIS)**. There are a number of reasons why this has happened:

1. Economic managers are becoming overwhelmed by the flood of data around them. We live in the midst of a true "information explosion."

2. The pace of consumer change and competition in the business world

has increased the need for faster decision making. Managers must make important decisions often and with little time to think them through.

3. The marketing process has become much more complex. The information needs of a firm keep escalating, thus requiring a more systematic approach to information management.

4. Consumers have repeatedly challenged the isolation of marketing managers from day-to-day marketing realities. Marketing information systems have been developed to help reduce this isolation.

It has been mainly larger business firms that have developed MIS, often as part of a comprehensive management information system. With the availability of smaller-scale computers, even small businesses can set up an MIS. Nonprofit organizations, from hospitals to charities, are beginning to recognize the benefits of an MIS.

WHAT IS AN MIS?   The information needs of marketing managers depend on the particular problems that they must solve. As a result, marketing information systems differ widely in their complexity, flexibility, data sources, and information yields. Basically, a marketing information system is:

> *A structured, interacting complex of persons, machines, and procedures designed to generate an orderly flow of pertinent information collected from both intra- and extra-firm sources, for use as the bases for decision making in specified responsibility areas of marketing management.*[3]

A number of important assumptions underlie this definition:

1. The MIS is a carefully developed master plan for information flow.

2. There must be coordination among many departments and individuals, including top management, sales management, marketing research personnel, finance, systems analysts, programmers, and computer experts.

3. Advances in computer technology, data copying, storage, and retrieval have been instrumental in the growth of sophisticated MIS.

4. Such technological advances are meaningless unless a firm can precisely define the target data and the most desirable research sources.[4]

All successful MIS's share a few common characteristics. First, the system must selectively generate information in a form that can be easily applied to decision making. Second, management must fully understand what sources are included in the MIS boundaries. And finally, the system must allow for expansion and change with the filing of new inputs, which should be designed so as to make the most of the flexibility of the system.

Since each MIS is constructed to serve the needs of an individual business firm, there is no "general" marketing information system model. Thus, in our discussion of MIS in this section, we will refer to the ideal type of system on which each of the individual systems should be based.

OVERVIEW OF MIS   Figure 23-2 presents an overview of the marketing information system and how it functions within the marketing environment. Let's take a look at the five major components of the MIS.

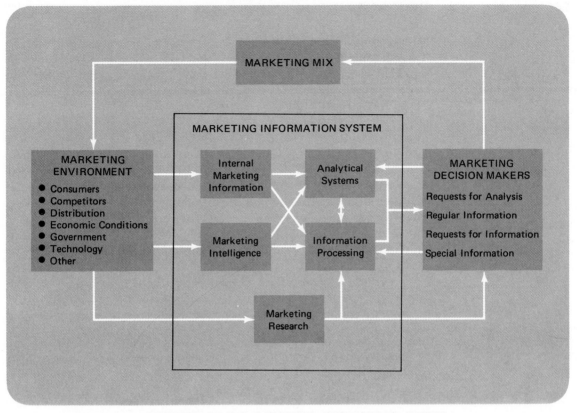

Figure 23-2   OVERVIEW OF THE MARKETING INFORMATION SYSTEM

1. *Internal marketing information.* A firm's internal accounting system supplies data on the firm's sales, costs, inventories, cash flows, accounts receivable and payable, and so forth. This information will help marketers to assess the firm's current activity and performance.

2. *Marketing intelligence.* The firm needs census data, trade association statistics, market studies, and the like to maintain an up-to-date picture of the marketing environment.

These two components, which we will discuss in more detail later, help the firm to monitor the marketing environment through both internal and external information. They provide an accurate and continual report on "how things are going."

3. *Information processing.* The MIS requires information processing systems that efficiently store and retrieve data. Multisubject coding and indexing structures help marketers to locate the information they need.

4. *Analytical systems.* Several large companies, including Pillsbury and Monsanto, have developed complex analytical MIS's. These systems allow a firm to ask, "*Why* did that happen?" and "What will happen *if . . . ?*" Mathematical models are used to solve media selection problems, to evaluate new product acceptance, and to weigh sales and pricing alternatives.

All of the above components are concerned with the ongoing MIS activities that provide information for regular marketing decisions.

5. *Marketing research.* Marketing research obtains unique information

for special decision-making needs. It is considered part of the MIS because it can develop large amounts of marketing information. Many marketing research efforts are project-oriented. Management points to a problem that must be researched and the research personnel carry out the necessary data collection and analysis and prepare some type of report.

INTERNAL MARKETING INFORMATION

First, let's look at the marketing information in the MIS that is found right under the organizational nose. We begin with the **internal accounting system**, which reports orders, sales, inventory levels, receivables, payables, and other important data. Central to this system is the order–shipping–billing cycle, which begins when orders are received from sales personnel, dealers, and customers. The order department transmits invoices to various departments within the firm. The goods are shipped to the buyer, and billing documents are prepared and sent.

Every firm wants its order–shipping–billing cycle to function with maximum speed and accuracy. One firm had its order routine studied with an eye toward greater efficiency. The average elapsed time between the receipt and issuance of an order was cut from 62 hours to 30 hours while the costs of the cycle did not rise.[5]

Other internal data that should be available to marketing executives on a regular basis include:[6]

1. *Customer billing*. This helps management in sales evaluations and customer relations.

2. *Sales activity*. There should be summaries by product line, geographic or sales area, and customer. Comparisons to quotas and past history should be provided.

3. *Information by selling activity*. Profits and losses should be summarized by product line, by geographic or sales area, and by customer. Sales discounts and selling expenses should be analyzed.

4. *Stock availability*. Accurate product-inventory data is essential in setting production goals.

5. *Product costs*. Accounting costs must be clearly examined in establishing pricing strategies.

MARKETING INTELLIGENCE

The **marketing intelligence system** has been defined as "the way in which company executives are kept current and informed about changing conditions in the [marketing] environment."[7] The intelligence gathering is often a decentralized and rather haphazard process. In general, firms rely on salespeople, special agents, and suppliers for marketing intelligence.

Salespeople are the company personnel best placed for intelligence work. They are out in the field, constantly meeting with the general public and with dealers. However, typical salespeople have been trained for *selling*, not for intelligence gathering. They may not be looking for information, and may not report findings to company executives. If firms hope to gain maximum advantage from salespeople's strategic location in the marketplace, they must revise their training programs and redesign internal lines of communication.

There are many other options for the firm that desires an active intelligence effort. It may use other personnel, including sales managers or dealers, or it may hire full-time specialists. The firm may stress interviewing or comparison shopping. It may purchase data from marketing intelligence services such as the A. C. Nielsen Company. A firm may turn to industrial espionage. This alternative is not unknown in the world of business competition.

In mid-1975, *Business Week* observed that ". . . with business more complex and the economic climate so uncertain, corporations are becoming far more sophisticated at scrutinizing the competition. Direct mailers, cataloguers, printers, and lithographers were cited as popular "leaks" of information about competitors' products. One marketing manager claimed that, in the electronics industry, "tactics for keeping track of the competition are at times sneaky, maybe even immoral or unethical."[8] As a result, strict security precautions have become the rule in many industries, for example, fashion and high technology.

MIS IN PRACTICE The list of firms that have made serious efforts to develop MIS includes such notables as American Airlines, AT&T, Coca-Cola, General Electric, Johnson & Johnson, Pillsbury, and RCA. A study of 193 of the nation's top 1,000 business firms found that 77 percent either had an MIS or were installing one.[9]

Clearly, MIS is being used by a wide variety of industrial firms, consumer packaging companies, and service institutions. It does appear, though, that large firms are the principal developers of the MIS concept. Smaller business outlets may follow suit when operating costs are less severe, and when the experiences of large firms provide more evidence that the MIS is desirable.

One analyst has written that, "Anyone who has worked with marketing information systems frankly must admit that progress to date has indeed been modest."[10] Among the most difficult and continuing problems with MIS are:

1. Marketing research efforts have not been effectively integrated into MIS. Accounting departments generally have a large role in marketing information systems; they are not always skilled at marketing research and may prefer to avoid such analytical work.

2. Some firms have not conducted the necessary monitoring of consumer attitudes and opinions. Marketing research has been done sporadically and without a systematic approach.

3. Different executive officers supervise marketing research activities and MIS. This can lead to a lack of coordination or cooperation.

MARKETING RESEARCH

Marketing research is "the systematic and objective search for and analysis of information relevant to the identification and solution of any problem in the field of marketing."[11] The key words in this definition are "systematic" and "objective." All methods and analytical techniques must be precisely planned in accordance with the highest social science standards. Any slanting of the facts to arrive at a desired result will be not only unethical, but also damaging to the interests of the decision maker.

Table 23-1 makes a few general comparisons between MIS and marketing research. As we can see, marketing research generally operates within a more restricted sphere, focusing on a specific problem within a business project or program. This differs from the system-wide scope of MIS.

OVERVIEW OF THE MARKETING RESEARCH PROCESS

Marketing research cannot begin until the investigators have established their objectives. They must be clear on what information they need and how it is to be used. We can look at the marketing research process as a seven-step sequence, as illustrated in Figure 23-3.

1. *Situation analysis.* The first step in the research process is to survey all available information about the firm, its products, the industry, the market, advertising, and so forth. Sources include personal interviews, internal company records, library materials, and trade papers.

2. *Preliminary investigation.* Researchers make some initial efforts to get a "feel" of the problem. Interviews with consumers, dealers, and industry executives help the investigators focus on the most critical issues for study.

3. *Research design selection.* Here the researcher develops a formal plan that anticipates the character of the study and specifies the general procedures and methods to be used.

4. *Marketing data sources.* Once the general goals and direction of the study are determined, the researchers will pinpoint the data sources they wish to consult. A written set of research guidelines is developed, and experiments with data collection are conducted and analyzed. After necessary modifications are made, the main research efforts are completed.

5. *Information analysis.* Data from the research must be tabulated and analyzed. The marketing research team makes interpretations of the data, which generally lead to recommendations for action.

6. *Reporting the findings.* The researchers must prepare all findings and recommendations for submission to company executives. The report must be written in a way that clearly and effectively demonstrates the relationship among the data, the interpretations, and the recommendations.

7. *Recommendations follow-up.* An excellent research report is wasted when its recommendations are not adopted by the firm. Thus, a marketing re-

Table 23-1
MIS AND MARKETING RESEARCH AT A GLANCE

CHARACTERISTIC	MARKETING INFORMATION APPROACHES	
	MIS	MR
Scope	System based	Project based
Time frame	Continuous	Intermittent
In response to	Recurring problems	Specific problem
Data source	External and internal	External

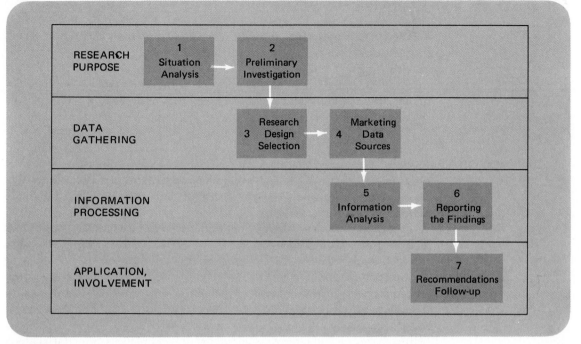

Figure 23-3
THE MARKETING
RESEARCH PROCESS

searcher often continues to work with decision makers after the report is submitted. The researcher helps the firm convert the findings of the report into new strategies and procedures.

SITUATION ANALYSIS

The first step in conducting market research is to identify and state the problem. The analyst begins by examining all available sources of information in order to get a general understanding of the situation. Sources include company records and personnel, library and trade association materials, and past research efforts.

Often the researcher will notice *symptoms* of the central problem that point to the deeper issues. There are three types of common symptoms:

1. *Overt difficulties*. A major competitor launches a huge advertising campaign. It is clear that there must be some marketing response.

2. *Latent difficulties*. An important dealer for the firm is dissatisfied with a recent price increase. Such difficulties are not always apparent, yet they can ultimately lead to more serious problems if not corrected.

3. *Unnoticed opportunities*. A firm producing water analysis equipment achieves a reasonable sales level by the early 1970s. Then a new law is passed requiring manufacturers to monitor their pollution of the waters. The firm realizes that it could serve as a consulting service to help these manufacturers comply with the law. For example, DuPont may consider new uses for the special coating on Teflon cookware that prevents sticking.

Marketing researchers must analyze four principal types of problems:[12]

1. *Market targets*. The *who* and *why* of the potential customer.

2. *Product positioning*. What critical benefits of the product can be promoted competitively?

3. *Consumer decision making.* How does the consumer decide which products and brands to purchase? How can a marketer influence the consumer's choices?

4. *Media selection.* Which media should the firm employ—and when—in order to reach consumers most effectively?

PRELIMINARY INVESTIGATION

Situation analysis initiates personal interviews with the staff of the firm and extensive study of written research materials. By contrast, the second stage of the marketing research process, **preliminary investigation**, includes extensive interviewing in the field. Consumers, dealers, and executives from other firms may be visited by the analyst.

There are two main goals of preliminary investigation. One is obtaining a better "feel" of the market. The researcher who sticks too closely to books and records may not understand important dynamics of the industry.

Second, preliminary investigation is vital in the development of testable hypotheses for the study. A **hypothesis** is a statement of an expected relationship between variables (consumer resistance to buying insurance is caused in part by the complicated language of policies). These hypotheses narrow the scope of the research and define its central focus. Situation analysis produces many tentative hypotheses; preliminary investigation suggests which ones are most valuable and realistic. In addition, the interviews with consumers and dealers may generate new hypotheses that did not emerge from previous data.

RESEARCH DESIGN SELECTION

A **research design** is "the specification of methods and procedures for acquiring the information needed."[13] The planning of the research design is perhaps the most important step in the entire marketing research process. If the methods and procedures for the research are shoddy or insufficient, the resulting data and findings will be inadequate or even misleading.

Figure 23-4 shows alternatives in selecting a research design. In many cases just one research design (A_1, A_2, or A_3) is appropriate. In other situations, an exploratory design may lead to a descriptive design (B_1) or a conclusive design (B_2). In some cases, the study will go through all three designs (B_3).

Exploratory Research

Exploratory studies are designed to help identify problems, locate relevant variables, and produce new hypotheses. Such studies must be quite flexible, since the researcher is still somewhat uncertain about the exact nature of the problem. Hopefully, the exploratory study will generate data that suggests meaningful research questions.

There are three principal stages in exploratory research. The first is a search of secondary information sources. Next come interviews with knowledgeable persons. After these interviews are completed, the research team will analyze them in two ways. They will study both the unique suggestions of each interview subject, and the aggregate conclusions that can be drawn from the majority of the sample.

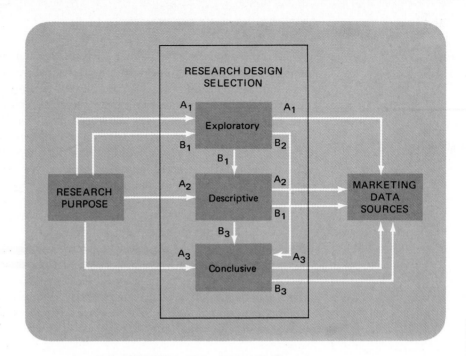

Figure 23-4
SELECTING A
RESEARCH DESIGN—
ONE OR MORE

The last stage is examination of analogous situations, including case histories and simulations. Case histories help the researcher to focus on past marketing approaches to similar problems. Simulations, which are often computer based, involve experiments with a research model of the actual marketing situation (reactions of competitors in the snowmobile industry).

Descriptive Research

Some market research studies attempt to describe market characteristics or functions. For example, a market-share study of the shoe industry may describe the share of the market held by leading competitors in men's, women's, and children's shoes. A sales analysis for a shoe manufacturer may show the firm's sales by territory, type of account, model of product, and other variables.

There are three common characteristics of descriptive research studies:

1. *Association of two or more key variables.* A sales analysis may break down the frequency distribution along various income levels. This can help the firm develop predictions and marketing strategies.

2. *Specific research questions.* In this type of study, the researcher begins with a solid knowledge of the problem and clear ideas about hypotheses and testing methods.

3. *Preplanned and structured design.* Whereas the exploratory study is broad and somewhat unfocused, the descriptive study must be precise and systematic. The research design strictly controls sources of information and procedures for information gathering.

Conclusive Research

One of the important limitations of **descriptive research** is that it cannot establish causation—why something happened. A descriptive study may show a strong connection between two or more key variables (for example, Sears cuts prices on stereo systems in its Minneapolis stores, and sales rise steadily over the next three months). But a descriptive study cannot provide solid scientific evidence that the Sears price cut caused the rise in stereo sales. Sales may have jumped because economic conditions were improving in the area, and people felt more able to invest in entertainment goods.

In some research situations, a marketer feels a need for research to determine causal connections. The marketer may not wish to change marketing strategy because a descriptive study has resulted in suggestive data that may be misleading. Thus, marketing researchers may review the descriptive data and then attempt to develop the causal relationship between the market factors with a conclusive study.

MARKETING DATA SOURCES

After marketing researchers have defined the problems for study, they will begin the important and time-consuming process of **data collection**. The researcher must be careful in selecting data. For any marketing hypothesis, there may be many types and sources of data. If the researcher is not discriminating, a great deal of effort may be wasted in collecting interesting but useless data. At the same time, a key piece of data may be overlooked in the confusion.

A research study may require both primary and secondary data. Primary data must be assembled by the researchers for the first time. Secondary data has already been collected by another source.

Table 23-2 illustrates the major uses of marketing data sources in the three research designs discussed above. Exploratory studies rely on secondary and observation data; descriptive studies employ secondary, observation, and survey data; explanatory studies use survey and experiment data.

Secondary Data

Almost every research project includes a review of **secondary data** sources. Yet, many marketing executives have a very limited view of secondary research.[14] They see such data merely as a narrow extension of "library" type research, rather than as a dynamic inquiry into past market performance, current conditions and realities, and future prospects. Secondary data may be collected from such sources as government statistics, trade publications, newspapers, surveys, and interviews with experts.

Such research must be systematic and analytical if it is to accomplish its

Table 23-2
MAJOR USE OF MARKETING DATA SOURCES IN RESEARCH DESIGN

MARKETING DATA SOURCE	RESEARCH DESIGN		
	EXPLORATORY	DESCRIPTIVE	EXPLANATORY
Secondary	X	X	
Observation	X	X	
Survey		X	X
Experiment			X

The experiences of one marketing research firm suggest the value of secondary research. An overseas trade association wanted information on the market for printed textiles in the United States. At first, the researchers studied U.S. Government statistics and reports by trade associations within the textile industry. Much information was collected, but the researchers were skeptical about its usefulness for future projections.

To test out these fears, the research team initiated telephone conversations and personal interviews with industry personnel. The first set of calls yielded little in the way of feedback on the data. But the researchers learned which industry experts would be most able to answer their questions.

Finally, after consultations with certain knowledgeable textile executives, the researchers prepared a report for their client. Based on selective application of secondary data, they were able to project the market in printed cloth with impressive accuracy. In addition, the report provided a timely prediction about the impact of knits and double knits on the apparel market.

This secondary research was highly successful in forecasting conditions in the textile industry. It was also noteworthy in another respect. By avoiding the necessity of a field survey, the researchers kept the costs of their work comparatively low.

Based on Walter K. Storm, "Secondary Research—The Overlooked Opportunity," *Marketing Review*, pp. 12–13.

---

goals. The data cannot be collected in a scattered or imprecise manner. Investigation must proceed carefully from one source to additional and more detailed references. Furthermore, the data collected must be quantifiable and projectable if analytical projections are an important goal.

In addition to being systematic and analytical, the data must also meet the following criteria:[15]

1. *Impartiality.* Are the data deliberately or unintentionally slanted in order to encourage certain conclusions or attitudes?

2. *Validity.* Are the data likely to provide a relevant research tool, or are they out of date, misleading, or otherwise unrepresentative of "typical" or "average" industry conditions?

3. *Reliability.* How large or small is the sample being used? How accurately does it reflect the target group under study?[16]

Primary Data—Observation

The major methods of gathering primary data include observation, surveys, and experiments. The following is an example of direct observation:

> *Investigators observing a special display of foam rubber pillows in a department store checked the number of persons passing by, the number who stopped to look at the display, the number who handled the product, and the number who purchased it. The objective was to evaluate the effectiveness of the display.*[16]

Some observation studies are even more imaginative. A "garbage can audit" may indicate that people drink more than twice as much beer and liquor as they would admit to in an interview. A "bumper sticker check" has suggested that drivers with "law and order" stickers are less likely to have paid an automobile tax than those who have no such stickers.[17]

The observation method is generally contrasted with the survey method. Instead of asking people what brands of breakfast cereal they use, researchers may wish to make an inventory of pantry supplies in the home or station observers at supermarket aisles in a neighborhood. In theory, this method is more accurate and objective than the survey method. The researcher does not have to wonder if the respondent's answer is honest and complete. Either the family has Wheaties or Special K in its pantry, or it doesn't.

Unfortunately, the observation method itself is not necessarily objective. The potential problems in this area include:

1. The investigators are not always precise and diligent. For this reason, many observation studies rely on tape recorders and television cameras rather than human researchers. (Though, again, a human will ultimately have to scrutinize the tape or film.)

2. The very presence of the observer may affect the behavior of the people being studied. A shopper may notice a researcher making notes on a pad, become nervous, and decide not to buy anything in that part of the store. Because of this, some research studies attempt to conceal the observer.

3. Observation studies provide little information on the feelings, desires, attitudes, and buying prejudices of buyers. Important data on buyers' incomes and education may also be lost. An interviewer can explore *why* a buyer prefers Tide detergent to Cold Power; a television camera can only record the purchase.

4. The observation method is extremely costly. It is expensive to station a researcher in the right place at the right time for a period long enough to make the survey valid.[18]

Primary Data— Surveys

Surveys are the most common means of gathering primary marketing data. They usually lead to a broader range of data than the observation or experimentation methods. Surveys are used to plan product designs, advertising copy, sales promotions, and other marketing elements.

The **questionnaire** is the most important element in many survey efforts. In this method, an investigator asks direct questions of interview subjects. In many people's minds, the questionnaire is synonymous with market research.

Figure 23-5 presents alternative ways of gathering survey data. These include various sampling plans (unrestricted random, restricted random, judgment, quota, convenience); survey methods (telephone, mail, personal); and types of research questions (short, objective; long, objective; long, subjective). The many possible combinations of these methods yield a wide variety of research designs. For example, AT&T used a complex sampling plan in testing Dataspeed 40, a data communications terminal.[19] Using quota and business probability samples, the firm located 711 private and governmental units that might be potential buyers of the terminal. To locate the target organizations and the key decision-makers within them, investigators had to make a total of 3,690 preliminary telephone calls.

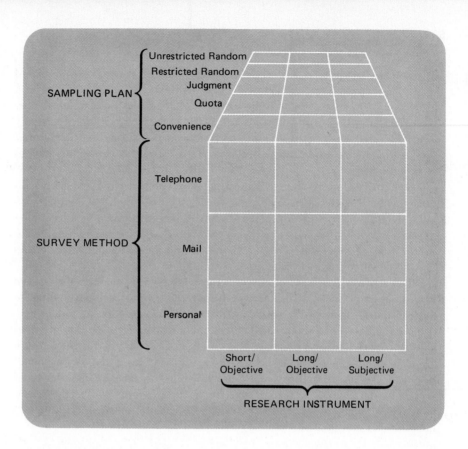

Figure 23-5
ALTERNATIVE WAYS
OF GATHERING
SURVEY DATA

Survey Methods. The three principal survey methods are the telephone interview, the mail questionnaire, and the personal interview.

Telephone interviews have certain distinct advantages. A large number of interviews can be handled quickly at a comparatively low cost. The interviewer can talk with a number of family members during the same call, and can clarify or elaborate on questions whenever necessary. The response rate for telephone interviews appears to be more favorable than for mail questionnaires.

On the other hand, telephone interviews do not always provide an ideal sample. Some people do not have telephones, some have unlisted numbers, others may be difficult to reach. Many resent being bothered at home with a telephone survey. Finally, the interview must be short and cannot be as relaxed or as revealing as a personal discussion.

Mail questionnaires have a number of noteworthy advantages. Whereas telephone and personal interviews necessarily contain an element of bias—because of the critical role of the interviewer—mail questionnaires represent a more objective and controlled presentation. In addition, the mail questionnaire allows respondents to answer questions at their own pace. The haste and distractions of many personal and telephone interviews can be avoided.

The most serious problem with mail questionnaires is the difficulty of obtaining returns. Most people do not answer such queries; even when they do, the returns may trickle in over a long period of time. The low return rate

Two somewhat controversial approaches to qualitative data have appeared on the horizon over the past 30 years. These are motivation research and the focus group concept. In the early 1950s, marketing was bombarded by the lively fad known as motivation research. MR practitioners, using unusually long and free-flowing interviews and a vast array of psychoanalytic techniques, produced dramatic explanations of the "real" reasons why consumers bought certain products.

TWO APPROACHES TO QUALITATIVE DATA

One motivation researcher, Ernest Dichter, conducts studies which typically involve 100 initial in-depth interviews, each of which lasts between 30 minutes and an hour. Dichter then tests 100 or more consumers to substantiate the initial findings. The major criticism of Dichter's method is that the qualitative findings of such small samples do not permit generalizations to be made about how all consumers would behave.

The second approach, focus group interviewing, has been the subject of even more controversy than motivation research. In this technique, eight to ten consumers meet to discuss a product, a product category, a product concept, an activity, or a company. The researcher involved with this group is able to collect firsthand evidence of consumer satisfactions and frustrations. Critics of this method charge that the group situation itself and the personalities of the researcher and consumers are variables that have an important, and unmeasured, influence on the opinions expressed by group members. Furthermore, they point out, there are often discrepancies between what the group members say and how they actually behave in the marketplace.

Based on William D. Wells and Douglas J. Tigert, "Activities, Interests and Opinions," *Journal of Advertising Research* 11 (August 1971): 27–35; Roger Ricklefs, "Ernest Dichter Thrives Selling Firms Research on 'Hidden Emotions,'" *Wall Street Journal*, November 20, 1972, pp. 1, 23; and William A. Yoell, "How Useful Is Focus Group Interviewing? Not Very . . . Post-Interviews Reveal," *Marketing Review*, pp. 15–20.

leads to a distorted sample, no matter how precisely the target population for the mailing was determined. Finally, mail questionnaires can be deceptively costly. They are often considered the least expensive of the survey methods, but the low rate of return actually makes the per-response cost very high.

Personal interviewing is the most versatile and informative type of survey method. The interviewer can observe subjects, ask follow-up questions, and draw out the respondents in a way that is impossible over the telephone or through the mails.

The main disadvantage of personal interviewing is the cost. Companies must invest heavily if they wish to maintain or hire a staff of professional interviewers. The expenses for training, supervision, travel, and salaries run high. The danger of bias is also quite significant in a personal interview situation. A good rapport between interviewer and subject may lead the subject to try to provide anwers the interviewer seems to want. On the other hand, if the two are not comfortable with each other, the subject may become abrupt or misleading. The interviewer might ask questions in a way that leads to a certain type of response. Or, when noting the answers to open-ended questions, he or she might distort what the respondent actually said.

Research Instruments. Constructing a good questionnaire is a difficult task. Imprecise or leading questions can lead to useless data. The following general rules should be followed in making up a useful questionnaire.[20]

1. *Ask only for data that is remembered, or accessible from records.* Many respondents will guess when they cannot recall the answer to a factual question. This brings in a mass of unreliable data.

2. *Ask for reports of specific events rather than generalizations.* It is better to ask a consumer, "Where did you buy your groceries last week?" than to ask, "What percentage of the time do you buy groceries at each of the local supermarkets?"

3. *The meaning of all questions must be obvious to all respondents.* The language must be simple, direct, and clear. Technical words and terms with ambiguous meanings should be avoided.

4. *Eliminate all leading questions.* Do not suggest answers to the respondents. The question, "Don't you think that Disneyland is a good value?" almost compels the respondent to agree with the interviewer.

5. *Avoid questions on intimate subjects unless they are vital to the study.* It is not wise to touch on deep personal opinions or biases of a respondent unless they are relevant to the issues under study.

6. *Concentrate on obtaining facts and attitudes.* There is a danger in concentrating too much time and effort on motivation questions like, "Why do you use your college library? It is often more useful to collect objective data on the respondent (school, year, residence, age, sex, study patterns) and specific attitudes (toward library hours, availability of books, reference assistance).

7. *Make questions as easy to answer as possible.* A written questionnaire should be attractively laid out and readable. There must be clear instructions for all short-answer questions, and ample space to respond to open-ended essay questions.

8. *Do not include questions with more than one element.* For example, a researcher might be tempted to ask, "Why did you stop buying *Time* and switch to *Newsweek*?" Actually, these are two distinct activities: (1) the respondent stopped buying *Time*; (2) the respondent began purchasing *Newsweek*. If the question jumbles both activities together, the interviewer may not get all of the necessary information. (The respondent may only discuss his or her disenchantment with *Time*, and may not mention *Newsweek*.)

9. *Allow for conditional answers on all questions.* Give the respondent a chance to choose "Don't know" or "No choice" or "Unsure" rather than a simple "Yes" or "No." Learning the percentage of respondents who are doubtful or confused often provides valuable information.

10. *Arrange all questions in a proper sequence.* Keep a logical flow from beginning to end. Create interest with the opening questions. Place difficult and personal questions toward the end of the questionnaire.

Sampling Plans. A sample is "a part of the whole population that is used to make inferences about the characteristics of the population."[21] If a marketing executive needs information on the public's attitudes toward different ice cream brands and flavors, it is not necessary to interview everyone. Instead, the researcher will hope to find a representative sample of the total population (or universe). The views of this sample should correspond to the views of the general public.

The first critical task in sampling is to decide who is to be surveyed. The population from which the sample will be drawn must be defined with absolute precision. Improper designation of the universe or sample can lead to critical errors. One manufacturer of surgical sutures asked a market research firm to study the reading habits of surgeons.[22] The manufacturer was interested in influencing the persons who direct the purchase of sutures in hospital operations, and assumed that surgeons had that power. But the market research firm learned that operating room supervisors—rather than surgeons—made the decision about what brand of sutures to use.

The actual selection of the sample from the universe is a complicated matter. First, the researcher must make a decision about size. A large sample is generally more trustworthy than a small sample, but it is also more expensive. In some cases, careful selection of a representative sample of fewer than 100 persons will suffice.

A key question is whether to use nonprobability sampling procedure or probability (random sampling) design. In a random sample, everyone in the universe theoretically has an equal chance of being chosen. People with special characteristics (dog owners, the unemployed, Irish-Americans) should all be represented in rough proportion to their percentage of the total population.

Unfortunately for marketers, random sampling is a costly procedure that can pose vexing problems for marketing researchers. On the other hand, it limits the likelihood of sampling errors and produces a sample that the marketer can study with real confidence.

Because of the difficulties and expense of random sampling, market researchers often turn to a number of restricted probability sampling methods. These include:

1. *Stratified sampling.* The population is split up into strata (smaller populations). Divisions are made on the basis of some factor important to the study. A simple random sample is drawn from within each stratum.

2. *Judgment sampling.* This is a subjective and nonrandom method. A sampling expert uses his or her judgment to define a sample that is believed to be representative.

3. *Quota sampling.* Here the interviewer simply fills a quota. The requirement may be, "Interview 450 owners of private houses, or 30 women who teach college-level biology courses."

4. *Convenience sampling.* Under this method, a sample is determined simply by the relative ease of reaching people. The sample may be the shoppers in a particular department store, the subscribers to *Mad Magazine*, or the audience at the premiere of a new movie.

Primary Data—
Experiment

An **experiment** is "a research design in which the selected hypothetical solution or solutions are put into effect and the results measured. In other words, a hypothesis is actually applied or put into action to see what its results are and whether it solves the problem."[23]

Two groups of subjects generally take part in the experiment. One (the experimental group) is introduced to the new stimuli, while the other (the control group) is not. Researchers measure the reactions of each group. The difference suggests the impact of the selected stimuli.

Figure 23-6 presents the marketing research experiment visualized as a system. Various inputs affect the subjects and lead to particular outputs. The subjects of the experiment are those who receive the experimental inputs and whose responses are being measured. Subjects may include consumers, sales representatives, stores, sales territories, dealers, and so forth. The experimental input is the marketing variable under study. It could be product, price, ad, display, or distribution. Environmental inputs are other factors that may influence the experiment, such as shortages, inflation, or increases in shipping costs. Experimental outputs are the results of the experiment. These may include changes in sales, attitudes, or behavior.

The experimental method is not easily applied to marketing research. One major reason is the expense of developing experiments; another is the presence of so many marketing variables. A store may raise prices on costume jewelry over a six-month period and be interested in the effect on sales. Yet the target variable (price change) interacts with many other marketing factors (competitors' activities, effectiveness of advertising, changes in local citizens' buying power, nationwide fashion trends, general image of the store). It is difficult to construct an experiment that sorts out the importance of one of these variables when all are interacting at once.

Nevertheless, it is only through the experimental method that we can determine cause-and-effect relationships. Although the method has never been used extensively by marketers, there is some evidence that this may be changing. Firms such as DuPont and Scott Paper have relied on large-scale experiments to evaluate the effectiveness of their advertising programs. The most widely used form of experiment is the test market, which was described in Chapter 11.

Figure 23-6
THE EXPERIMENT
VIEWED AS A
SYSTEM

From Philip Kotler, *Marketing Management: Analysis, Planning, and Control*, 2d ed. © 1972, p. 318. Reprinted by permission of Prentice-Hall, Inc., Englewood Cliffs, N.J.

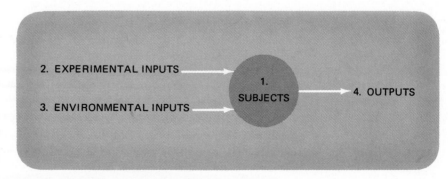

Primary Data—
Other Methods

There are a number of other methods of obtaining marketing information. These include expert opinion, consumer panels, and store or warehouse audits.

Expert Opinions. If an organization cannot invest the time and money to gather objective data, it may decide to sound out experts (consultants, salespeople, dealers, and so forth). Expert opinion provides a subjective yet important source of data and interpretation.

The most serious pitfall in this method is the possibility of bias. All questions must be carefully worded, and all answers must be evaluated with some caution and skepticism. If the "expert" is within the firm itself, he or she may have a personal stake in stressing a certain answer to a problem. (The advertising manager believes that sales will skyrocket if the advertising budget is increased; the product manager wants more money invested in research and development.) Some firms handle this problem by rewarding employees for correct projections. They may also maintain written records that will eventually suggest the biases of personnel.

Consumer Panels. Panels are ongoing groups of consumers who report from time to time on their buying behavior, attitudes, preferences, frustrations, and so forth. The main advantages of the consumer panel relate to its stability. Once the panel has been selected, there is no need for new sample designs for each study. Observing a group of people over a significant period of time gives marketers a deeper understanding of their buying behavior.

Unfortunately, there are also certain problems of bias associated with panels. When panel members drop out (and as many as 50 percent may within a short time), the resulting sample may be unrepresentative. Panel members also age over time, which distorts the applicability of the data. Finally, panel members often fail to keep accurate records about their purchases.

Store and Warehouse Audits. Store audits provide information about the sales of specific products and brands at certain outlets during limited time periods. The effects of deals, coupons, discounts, and special promotions are also supplied by this type of audit. The main difficulty with this method is getting a sample of retail stores to cooperate in the study. The labor involved in counting stock and checking invoices can be exhausting and expensive.

INFORMATION
ANALYSIS

Once all information has been collected, the analyst faces a huge array of data. Rarely will this data fit neatly a preconceived explanation. Instead, the investigators will have to make sense of the data. Through the use of **analytical tools**—cross-tabulation, frequency distributions, averages, and so forth—the investigator will attempt to establish meaningful patterns in the data.

The analytical ability of the researcher is crucial to the success of the research project. Even the most brilliant command of mathematical tools is not sufficient. The investigator must be able to take a huge "jigsaw puzzle" of data and see the relationships between various pieces of information.

Information analysis is thus a delicate and vital stage in the market research process, as is illustrated in the following example. The ABC Television Network pre-tested viewer response to the TV movie, *Satan's Triangle*. Analysts suggested that the public was more intrigued by the mystery elements of the Bermuda Triangle disappearances than by the supernatural aspects of the story. As a result, ABC promoted the mystery theme in the advertising for the movie, and it received a high audience rating when it appeared on television.

REPORTING THE FINDINGS

Making a good presentation of the results of research studies is as important as collecting and analyzing the data itself. Reports may be too long or too short, too technical or casual in language—or simply boring. A poor presentation may be discarded even when the analysis is first rate.

As a result, the marketing analyst must clear two important hurdles in reporting findings:

1. The report must hold the interest of readers or listeners—it must be well written, easily understandable, and convincing.

2. The report must include solid scientific evidence that the data, interpretations, and conclusions are sound.

In some instances, the marketing researcher will prepare two versions of the report. One, the technical report, provides a detailed explanation of the research design. The other, the popular report, is written in less technical language and focuses on the research findings.

FOLLOWING UP

Many organizations commission market research studies, read findings and and recommendations with interest—and then do nothing. The entire value of these studies is thereby lost.

If the firm makes a serious effort to implement the recommendations of the study, researchers can be most helpful. They already have become quite familiar with marketing personnel, conditions, and operations. This knowledge and experience should not be wasted.

There are a number of guidelines that the researcher can use to ensure a successful follow-up process:[24]

1. Become thoroughly acquainted with the business.

2. Cultivate the personal friendship of all employees—from high-level executives to lower-level sales personnel.

3. Try to reassure people that you have the best interests of the company at heart—rather than your own advancement.

4. Explain to personnel how your research can make their jobs easier and more rewarding.

5. Be ready to admit errors and shortcomings. Don't promise more than you can actually deliver.

6. When discussing your report, focus on the main issues and recommendations. Don't get bogged down on minor technical points.

7. Keep a careful eye on all applications of your recommendations. Find improvements and point them out to the company personnel.

MARKETING RESEARCH IN PRACTICE

A 1973 study of marketing research activities within the business world provided the following picture of actual conditions:[25]

> Since 1922, the number of marketing research departments has grown steadily.
>
> More than half of all firms responding to the survey have some form of marketing research department. This includes 70 percent of consumer companies, 66 percent of publishers and broadcasters, and 59 percent of industrial companies.
>
> The bigger the firm is, the more likely it is to have a marketing research department.
>
> Marketing research directors are reporting more often to top corporate management . . . and less often to sales and marketing management.

These figures do not suggest the full extent of marketing research. Many firms categorized as having no formal market research department may be performing the same work in a different way. Some employ private firms to do their research; others rely on product managers or marketing executives to handle research tasks.

Table 23-3 presents the percentage of companies using each of the most common marketing research activities. These include determination of market characteristics (conducted by 68 percent of firms in the study), measurement of market potentials (68 percent), market-share analysis (67 percent), and sales analysis (65 percent).

EVALUATION OF MARKETING INFORMATION

The two most relevant viewpoints for evaluating the quality of marketing information and the impact of its usage are those of management and society.

MANAGEMENT VIEWPOINT

Marketing research is not always viewed with enthusiasm by top corporate management. Many executives see research as a costly and time-consuming process that yields few definitive conclusions. They doubt whether the benefits of research (in terms of sales and profits) justify the expenses involved.

An additional strain can be found in the relationship between marketing managers and research professionals. As one analyst has pointed out, many brand managers "view researchers as rigid academicians who have their heads in the clouds and very little understanding of what business is like."[26] At the same time, researchers resent it when marketing managers exclude them from the decision-making process. Obviously, this situation does no one any good. A harmonious and mutually respectful relationship between managers and researchers can benefit both sides and promote the long-range interests of the

Table 23-3
MOST COMMON MARKETING RESEARCH ACTIVITIES

RESEARCH ACTIVITY	PERCENTAGE OF COMPANIES ENGAGED IN THE ACTIVITY
Advertising research	
Motivation research	33
Copy research	37
Media research	44
Studies of ad effectiveness	49
Business economics and corporate research	
Short-range forecasting (up to 1 year)	63
Long-range forecasting (over 1 year)	61
Studies of business trends	61
Pricing studies	56
Plant- and warehouse-location studies	47
Product-mix studies	51
Acquisition studies	53
Export and international studies	41
Company-employees studies	45
Corporate research responsibility	
Consumers' "Right to Know" studies	18
Ecological-impact studies	27
Studies of legal constraints on advertising and promotion	38
Social values and policies studies	25
Product research	
New-product acceptance and potential	63
Competitive-product studies	64
Testing of existing products	57
Packaging research: design or physical characteristics	44
Sales and market research	
Measurement of market potentials	68
Market-share analysis	67
Determination of market characteristics	68
Sales analysis	65
Establishment of sales quotas, territories	57
Distribution-channels studies	48
Test markets, store audits	38
Consumer panel operations	33
Sales compensation studies	45

From Dik Warren Twedt, ed., *1973 Survey of Marketing Research* (Chicago: American Marketing Association, 1973), p. 41. With permission of American Marketing Association.

firm. To remedy these problems, it has been suggested that top management do the following:

1. *Define research responsibilities.* Provide written guidelines for the functions and limitations of the research department.

2. *Budget realistically.* Researchers must be paid adequately and given reasonable budgets.

3. *Be objective.* Managers must be open-minded in evaluating research efforts. Solicit suggestions and consider them seriously.

4. *Emphasize high-yield projects.* Keep the work of the department centered on studies that may boost profits for the firm.

5. *Minimize management filters.* Do not obstruct the easy flow of research findings between researchers and top management.

At the same time, marketing researchers should:

1. *Reflect management viewpoint.* Keep research efforts in line with overall profit goals.

2. *Be decision oriented.* Avoid dull, windy reports that seem to bypass key decision areas.

3. *Be imaginative.* Don't rely forever on old, tired approaches. Look for something that will represent a real advance.

4. *Seek opportunities*. Make active efforts to develop projects that have profit potential.

5. *Communicate persuasively.* Speak to management in language that they can understand.[27]

SOCIAL VIEWPOINT

Most marketing researchers like to think of their work in terms of its benefits for the consumer. They may argue that their studies give consumers a chance to "vote in advance" on marketing innovations. This is a valid viewpoint for those organizations that have adopted the marketing concept. However, there is growing evidence that consumers do not accept this rosy picture of market research activity.

Many citizens are becoming more hostile to research inquiries. Interviewers find resistance because people see them as salespeople posing as researchers in order to disguise a "sales pitch." Specific complaints have been lodged about hidden tape recorders, one-way mirrors, and other research techniques.

A 1974 survey of interview respondents illustrates the discontent people feel.[28] Of those surveyed, 19 percent found some questions to be overly personal. Seventeen percent judged the interview to be too long (this figure jumped to 45 percent for respondents who were interviewed for more than 20 minutes).

A related social and ethical issue is the rights of respondents and subjects in research experiments. The research code outlines three general rights:[29]

1. A research interview must not become a disguised sales call.

2. If the researcher promises the respondent anonymity, the commitment must be maintained.

3. All information given must be confidential and used only for research purposes.

In theory, these guidelines seem entirely appropriate, but they have no force in law. The absence of legal protection is even more significant in view of the development of computer technology. Many citizens fear the possible abuses of information storage by the federal government and private business. They see the potential for private information being passed around casually

New York Times, November 16, 1975, Section 4, p. 9.

Mort Gerberg

among banks, insurance firms, department stores, law enforcement agencies, the IRS, and other institutions that they must contend with daily.

One marketing researcher has commented, "Perhaps we are not treating the respondent with respect as a human being. There is a tendency among statisticians to regard the person as only incidental to the information about the person."[30] If such trends continue, we can expect increasing public pressure on legislators to restrict invasions of privacy. Marketing researchers must curb such abuses before an outraged public shuts them out entirely.

MARKETING INFORMATION IN THE FUTURE

The future of marketing information will inevitably involve greater use of computer-based systems. There are two principal reasons for this trend. The costs of computer data storage and use will continue to decline—in marked contrast to the costs of conventional systems. Also, more and more firms will be led by executives who have had long exposure to sophisticated mathematical and data-processing concepts.

In addition, the following trends in research methodology have been projected.

1. *Greater use of experimental design.* Many valuable research techniques have been discarded in the last decade, but are gradually being reintroduced.

2. *Greater use of trend- or longitudinal-type studies.* Researchers will repeat the same study over time in order to determine relationships among variables.

3. *Greater use of sequential research.* Researchers will work in a series approach, with each study helping to shape the next.

4. *Growing concern over the quality of field work, coding, editing, and tabulation.* Researchers will be giving more careful scrutiny to the quality of data collection and processing.[31]

CONCLUSION

Information is a primary tool of marketing managers. They must make constant decisions about price, advertising, promotion, distribution, and so forth and require up-to-date, accurate information to make effective decisions.

Sophisticated marketing information systems (MIS) have emerged to meet the information needs of business firms. MIS has five basic components: internal marketing information, marketing intelligence, information processing, analytical systems, and marketing research.

Marketing research is the systematic and objective search for and analysis of information relevant to the identification and solution of any problem in the field of marketing. It must be efficiently organized and free from bias.

There are seven steps in the marketing research process: situation analysis, preliminary investigation, research design selection, marketing data sources, information analysis, reporting of findings, and recommendations follow-up.

Marketing research raises a number of difficult social issues. The general public is increasingly hostile to interviewers and other researchers. People are fearful that computer technology may lead to further invasions of privacy. Unless marketers and marketing research firms respond to the public's grievances, there will be mounting pressure for legislation to limit the pervasiveness of marketing research studies.

DISCUSSION QUESTIONS

1. About $7 out of every $10 spent on marketing research is by consumer nondurable producers (food, household items, drugs). How would you convince the following organizations that they should use more information in these marketing situations:
   a. the Denver public library as it experiences sharp budget cuts;
   b. a specialty steel producer wanting to expand beyond its Midwestern market;
   c. a Tallahassee, Florida shoe repair shop considering a new location in the same city.
2. What would be some of the major elements of a marketing information system for these organizations: life insurance company, college alumni offices, and supermarket chain.
3. Should the following marketing information activities of *Newsweek* magazine be classified as "marketing information system" or as "marketing research":
   a. learning that *U.S. News and World Report* is testing new advertising rates on the West Coast;
   b. hiring a key marketing research executive away from *Time*;

   c. telephoning magazine distributors to find out their reactions to a new billing procedure;

   d. reviewing quarterly consumer attitudes toward editorial content?

4. Deep Sea Ventures, producer of deep-sea mining vehicles, wants to perform a comprehensive marketing research of market opportunities in South America. Describe how it might apply the steps in the marketing research process.

5. The U.S. Department of Agriculture reports that milk consumption per capita has declined for the last 20 years. A dairy category that has grown, however, is cheese. To find out what's behind this trend, describe three research designs: exploratory, descriptive, and conclusive.

6. Octagon Oil conducted a study of consumer predispositions to oil advertising. To plan a new advertising strategy, three different campaign themes were developed: **Search** (S) expresses the company's effort to locate and recover more oil; **Concern** (C) expresses its innovation and social responsibility regarding the ecology and safety issues; and **Public Confidence** (P) expresses its product mix being offered with a sense of trust and honest helpfulness. The results of a national sample of consumers include these data:

CONSUMER GROUP	WITH RESPONSE PATTERN	PERCENTAGE OF CONSUMERS IN THE GROUP
1	Favorable to S, C, P	42
2	Favorable to S, C; negative to P	20
3	Favorable to S; negative to C, P	18
4	Negative to S, C, P	13
5	Other combinations	7
		100

How would you analyze these data? What would be your recommendations regarding Octagon Oil's next advertising theme?

7. John Molloy, special markets director for the Photographic Products Division of Honeywell, Inc., was upset about the conflicting findings of two marketing research studies of the Division's new Strobolite, a flashing warning light for motorists and sportspeople, selling for $19.50. The first study, done with a selected group *without* a sample of the product, showed the light would not sell. In a subsequent study, the light was shown to another sample group and the results were favorable. Molloy's reaction (heard down the hall): "This doesn't say much about the capability of research to cut the risk in marketing decisions!" What is your evaluation?

NOTES

1. Emanual H. Demby, "Psychographics: Problems and Solutions, or, 'How Do You Know a Problem?'" *Marketing Review* 30 (February 1975): 19.

2. Gerald Zaltman and Philip C. Burger, *Marketing Research: Fundamentals and Dynamics* (Hinsdale, Ill.: Dryden, 1975), p. 529.

3. Richard H. Brien and James E. Stafford, "Mar-

keting Information Systems: A New Dimension for Marketing Research," *Journal of Marketing* 32 (July 1968): 21.

4. Ibid., pp. 21–22.

5. Philip Kotler, *Marketing Management: Analysis, Planning, and Control*, 2d ed. (Englewood Cliffs, N.J.: Prentice-Hall, 1972), pp. 297–98.

6. Thomas C. Kelley, Jr., "The Marketing–Accounting Partnership in Business," *Journal of Marketing* 3 (July 1966): 9–11.

7. Kotler, 2d ed., p. 302.

8. "Business Sharpens Its Spying Techniques," *Business Week*, August 4, 1975, p. 60.

9. Richard H. Brien, "Marketing Information Systems: The State of the Art," *Combined 1972 Conference Proceedings* (Chicago: American Marketing Association, 1973), p. 20.

10. David B. Montgomery, "The Outlook for MIS" *Journal of Advertising Research* 13 (June 1973): 5.

11. Paul E. Green and Donald S. Tull, *Research for Marketing Decisions*, 2d ed. (Englewood Cliffs, N.J.: Prentice-Hall, 1970), p. 3.

12. Demby, p. 20.

13. Green and Tull, p. 73.

14. Walter K. Storm, "Secondary Research—The Overlooked Opportunity," *Marketing Review*, p. 11.

15. Kotler, 2d ed., pp. 315–16.

16. Ibid., p. 316.

17. Philip H. Dougherty, "Market Research Is Now a National Pastime," *New York Times*, November 16, 1975, sec. 4, p. 9.

18. Kotler, 2d ed., pp. 316–17.

19. "Three AT&T Research Projects Show Variety of Methods Used," *Marketing News*, January 31, 1975, p. 8.

20. Charles S. Mayer, "Marketing Research," in Albert Wesley Frey, ed., *Marketing Handbook*, 2d ed. (New York: The Ronald Press Company, 1965), pp. 24:27–32.

21. Demby, p. 18.

22. Ibid.

23. David J. Luck, Hugh G. Wales, and Donald A. Taylor, *Marketing Research* (Englewood Cliffs, N.J.: Prentice-Hall, 1970), p. 91.

24. Frey, pp. 24:56–58.

25. Dik Warren Twedt, ed., *1973 Survey of Marketing Research* (Chicago: American Marketing Association, 1973), p. 8.

26. William P. Hall, "Industrial Marketing Research Future Lies in Continuous Tracking, More Like a Motion Picture Than the Current 'Snapshot' Approach," *Marketing News*, January 16, 1976, p. 16.

27. John G. Keane, "Some Observations on Marketing Research in Top Management Decision Making," *Journal of Marketing* 33 (October 1969): 13–15.

28. George S. Day, "The Threats to Marketing Research," *Journal of Marketing Research* 12 (November 1975): 463.

29. Zaltman and Burger, p. 626.

30. Robert Reinhold, "Polling Encounters Public Resistance; Decision-Making Process Is Threatened," *New York Times*, October 26, 1975, p. 58.

31. Phil Levine, "Trends in Research," *Marketing Review*, p. 13.

24

IMPLEMENTING MARKETING STRATEGY

After completing this chapter, the reader should be able to:

1. Apply decision-making tools to a marketing decision.

2. Describe how an integrated marketing program is constructed.

3. Explain how marketing plans are prepared for implementation.

4. Identify those organizational factors that aid the implementation of marketing strategy.

Most of this book has been about marketing strategy. In Chapter 23, we discussed marketing information gathering and usage, an important aid in determining strategy. This chapter will focus on the implementation of strategy—those managerial activities that convert marketing plans into action.

SCORE WITH EVERY DETAIL

The marketing history of Wheaties illustrates the relationship between strategy and tactics.[1] For years, the firm relied on a central marketing theme: associating the product with sports. The bulk of Wheaties advertising was placed in publications such as *Sports Illustrated* and *Sport*, while commercials were presented during televised football games and the World Series. The slogan "Breakfast of Champions" summed up this approach.

Initially, these tactics were quite successful. But declining sales in later years led to a marketing re-evaluation. Analysts concluded that the firm's promotional efforts were reaching a narrow and overwhelmingly male audience. If Wheaties were to reverse its downward spiral, the firm would have to pursue a more diverse cross-section of Americans.

Wheaties did not change its essential marketing strategy; it continued to stress the association between the cereal and athletics. But the firm adopted a new tactical approach. Popular Olympic hero Bob Richards was hired as the principal, on-the-air representative of Wheaties. Commercial spots featuring Richards were placed on prime-time evening television shows. His "family" appeal went far beyond hard-core sports fans. As a result, Wheaties brought its sports-associated message into many more homes, and sales figures started looking healthier.

PUTTING MARKETING INTO ACTION

Marketing strategy is a design for an organization's commitment of resources to achieve its marketing objectives. The strategy must emerge from the basic nature and appeal of the product in the marketplace. **Marketing tactics** are steps taken to carry out marketing strategy. Tactics must correspond to the central strategic plan, yet they may be revised or even scrapped as market conditions change. In the example given above, Wheaties retained its principal marketing strategy but developed a new tactical campaign.

Figure 24-1 gives a streamlined version of the managerial marketing process that was discussed in Chapter 2. The purpose of this figure is to highlight what is needed to get the marketing plan ready and then to put it into action. The elements of the marketing mix—product, price, promotion, and distribution—which make up the major elements of strategy were discussed in Chapters 11 to 22. Along with marketing information, the elements in Figure

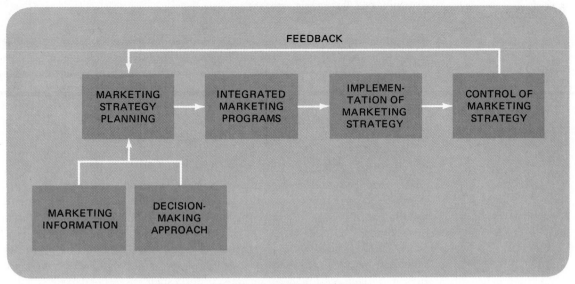

Figure 24-1 **WRAPPING UP THE PLANNING PROCESS**

24-1 must be taken into account by the management of an organization in the planning process.

This chapter takes planning several steps further. We will analyze the decision-making process that separates those plans that will be put into action from the many others that are proposed. We will see how the plans for several elements of the marketing mix are integrated into one master strategy. Finally, we will discuss implementation—those activities that convert strategic planning goals into action. Control of marketing performance will be analyzed in the next chapter.

Planning may be considered as constituting one half of the success (or failure) of an organization's marketing efforts. The other half is made up of implementation. While effective implementation cannot save a bad plan, poor implementation can wipe out good planning. Marketing managers must both plan and implement. Except for marketing planning and research specialists, however, most marketing personnel are engaged mainly or totally in implementation. This is equally true for large and small business firms and for non-profit organizations.

Integration and coordination are essential elements in the marketing planning and implementation processes. Integration refers to marketing functions and activities, while coordination involves actual performance of people on the job. As one executive has noted, "You can often integrate by organization, by chart, and by directive; but you coordinate only through patience, perspiration, and practice."[2]

DECISION MAKING IN MARKETING

It has been observed that, "All too often, the end product of present-day strategic planning is a strategic plan—period. Nothing really new happens as a result of the plan, except that everyone gets a warm glow of security and satisfaction now that the uncertainty of the future has been contained."[3]

Many marketing organizations seem to be unable to translate planning into day-to-day decision making. There are a number of reasons why even the best plans are sometimes ignored:

1. *To do so is risky.* The corporate executive may be putting his or her career on the line in endorsing the recommendations of a plan.

2. *To do so is difficult.* Strategic planning tackles the most complex problems faced by business firms. Assembling the data properly is no easy task; effective analysis and interpretations are even more demanding.

3. *To do so requires leadership.* Often the need for change is apparent, but top executives do not have the courage to abandon old, familiar methods of operation.

4. *To do so is counter to traditional value systems.* Executives are not promoted because they have excelled in strategic decision making. Instead, they are judged on short-term business criteria such as sales or earnings. Thus, many managers who rise to the top of the hierarchy are not comfortable with long-range planning techniques.

FROM PLANS TO DECISIONS

The number of decision makers within an organization varies greatly, depending on its size, its philosophy, and its style. Some have four or five levels of marketing management, while others concentrate decision-making power in a few highly influential executives. Ultimately, however, the marketing manager is responsible for all key decisions. There are a number of basic **decision-making concepts** that managers must deal with. First, he or she must take account of the organization's marketing objectives, which represent its desired goals. These may be measured in return-on-investment, cash flow, or sales figures. With these goals in mind, the decision maker examines alternatives ("What are my choices?") and implications ("What are the possible results of each choice?"). Finally, the manager must assess the possible risks and gains that accompany each course of action.

We can break the decision-making process down into a series of four basic steps.[4] First, all available data must be brought together. Second, all reasonable alternatives must be evaluated. Third, all controlling limiting factors that may restrict the range of possible decisions must be identified. Fourth, and perhaps most important, the moment of truth must be faced—the decision must be made.

While following through on this four-step procedure, the marketing manager will find that the task is made easier by:[5]

1. Maintaining clear-cut lines of authority.

2. Applying new decision-making techniques, but using them with caution.

3. Not ignoring the judgment factor. Employees can provide vision, intuition, wisdom, and foresight.

4. Being sure to act and then standing firm with the decision that is made.

5. Constantly preparing and retraining so that decision making does not become a casual routine.

INTEGRATED MARKETING PROGRAMS

The purpose of integration is to mold all of the marketing programs of an organization into one total marketing system. This system can be effective only if it takes into account the characteristics of each program. The system must also be flexible enough to adapt to changes in any one of its components.

MARKETING MIX INTERACTION

The marketing manager is shortsighted if he or she considers only the individual elements of a program without looking at its total picture. The way in which marketing elements interact has a great effect on the success of the effort. For example, if an advertising campaign can be coordinated with a strong sales effort in the field, the results can be most impressive. Skilled marketing strategists will not be content to assess the work of the sales force or the advertising department separately. Instead, they will be alert to the opportunity for an overall, system-oriented marketing approach.

The best marketing plan does not result simply from lumping together all the plans for the individual elements in the marketing mix. Instead, "the optimum marketing mix is that combination of marketing's product, price, channel and promotion inputs that produces the closest conformity to the firm's overall profit objective."[6] But determining the optimum marketing mix is no easy matter, since there are an infinite number of ways to combine marketing elements. Moreover, different elements may even conflict with each other. The marketing manager has no simple measuring device that can aid in testing all the variables and coming out with the best package.

The only real response to this dilemma is to ask the right questions. In building an integrated marketing approach, the manager must pinpoint the critical issues and potential conflicts. The central question is, What is the relationship between marketing elements (inputs) and market response (output)? Market response includes sales, market share, consumer attitudes, buying intentions, and so forth. The following specific questions can be asked:[7]

1. *What is the productivity level of a marketing input?* Here the manager looks at the relationship between dollar input and dollar output. Here, a dollar spent on training the sales force is compared to a dollar spent on a dealer contest, to see which dollar increased sales or profit more.

2. *What is the elasticity or rate of market response to changes in a marketing input?* This involves the rate of market response to a change in a marketing input level in the total marketing program. If expenditures for advertising or packaging are increased by 20 percent, how will this affect sales of the product? Will sales rise by 20 percent, by 30 percent, or not at all? Price and promotional elasticity are important in marketing calculations.

3. *At what level of input for a marketing variable is a "threshold of effectiveness" reached?* In other words, how much of an increase (or eventual decrease) in market response is caused by an additional dollar of marketing input. In product modifications a marketer may need to spend a certain minimum amount to make any impact at all on market response. But, beyond that point, will additional expenditures be as productive as the initial spending, or will the market response tend to level off regardless of spending?

4. *How do economies and diseconomies of scale affect the total marketing program?* Here is an area where conflicts often develop. For example, a marketer may choose to close six warehouses and operate only four warehouses across the country to handle its distribution. This economy move may result in the lowest possible average unit cost for shipping. But if this leads to slow delivery of goods—and consumers are dissatisfied as a result—the long-range damage may outweigh the immediate savings.

5. *What is the decay rate of market response to an input in the total marketing offering?* When the March of Dimes introduced its Walkathon, the effect was dramatic and a large increase in contributions resulted. But when this campaign is repeated for several years in a row, the market response will drop off over time.

6. *What inputs in the marketing program can be effectively substituted for one another?* Can a new nonprice element be effective enough to offset a competitor's price cut? Can more effective promotion be substituted for product quality, or product quality for promotion? Recognizing these kinds of trade-offs can keep the marketing program flexible and well integrated.

7. *What inputs in the total marketing program seem to reinforce each other and produce the best impact?* Will the firm be most likely to succeed if it combines product quality with channel efficiency, or price cuts with mass promotion? Also, certain inputs can destroy each other's effectiveness.

8. *What inputs in the marketing program are most difficult for competitors to copy or resist?* Marketers want, as much as possible, to design a program that competitors cannot easily counteract. If a firm cuts prices by 5 percent, a competitor may follow suit, or may cut prices even further. But if a firm makes an important new innovation in product quality, packaging, or distribution procedures, competitors may find it impossible to do the same.

Figure 24-2 illustrates the effect of the interaction of different elements in the marketing mix. The two elements of advertising and distribution are shown in terms of their relationship to time and market response. The ultimate question is: How much will sales increase if a firm increases expenditures (for advertising or distribution) or if the firm alters the expenditures over time?

PROGRAMS OVER TIME   Time is an important variable in the marketing process. Many marketing variables, such as promotion, advertising, and distribution, are time-dependent. It may take six months for a salesperson to learn the territory; it may take years to establish a new physical distribution system. Thus, marketing managers must always give careful consideration to the time dimension of strategy and tactics.

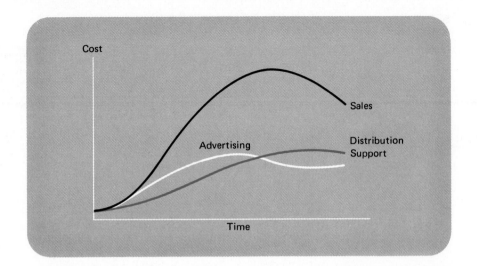

Figure 24-2
MARKETING MIX INTERACTION EFFECTS

Time lags are a particular concern when a promotional campaign is being planned. In a given industry, a television advertising blitz may induce a quicker market response than newspaper advertising. Of course, television advertising may also be much more expensive. The firm will have to determine whether the extra expenditures are worth it. If the product does not need to be sold immediately, the firm may select the cheapest advertising method. But if the product is likely to spoil or become outdated, there may be good cause to choose the marketing approach with the smallest time lag.

The conventional wisdom of marketing suggests that **sequential marketing activities** produce a favorable market response. This knowledge is often applied to problems of introducing or scheduling the distribution of new products. Promotional functions are best known for their sequential character; we all can recall television advertising campaigns in which one commercial is actually an offshoot of the firm's previous effort.

Table 24-1 presents the stages of the **product life cycle**—introduction, growth, maturity-saturation (combined here), and decline—and relates them to various types of marketing action. For example, in the introductory phase, retail prices tend to be high. The costs of initiating a new project can be steep, and marketers want an immediate return on their investments. Then, during the growth phase, prices remain high, since heavy consumer demand for the the product exists. When maturity is reached, prices usually level off and the firm attempts to avoid price wars. Finally, in the decline stage, retail prices are lowered so that high inventory levels can be reduced.

PREPARATION FOR IMPLEMENTATION

Once an integrated marketing plan has been developed, it must be implemented effectively by all levels of the marketing organization. Effective implementation depends to a large extent on the groundwork that is laid for the plan. The first prerequisite is that the plan must be fully understood and accepted by all key personnel in the marketing organization.

Table 24-1
IMPLICATIONS OF THE PRODUCT LIFE CYCLE FOR MARKETING ACTION

EFFECTS AND RESPONSES	STAGES OF THE PRODUCT LIFE CYCLE			
	INTRODUCTION	GROWTH	MATURITY–SATURATION	DECLINE
Competition	None of importance	Some emulators	Many rivals competing for a small piece of the pie	Few in number with a rapid shakeout of weak members
Overall strategy	Market establishment; persuade early adopters to try the product	Market penetration; persuade mass market to prefer the brand	Defense of brand position; check the inroads of competition	Preparations for removal; milk the brand dry of all possible benefits.
Profits	Negligible because of high production and marketing costs	Reach peak levels as a result of high prices and growing demand	Increasing competition cuts into profit margins and ultimately into total profits	Declining volume pushes costs up to levels that eliminate profits entirely
Retail prices	High, to recover some of the excessive costs of launching	High, to take advantage of heavy consumer demand	What the traffic will bear; need to avoid price wars	Low enough to permit quick liquidation of inventory
Distribution	Selective, as distribution is slowly built up	Intensive; employ small trade discounts since dealers are eager to store	Intensive; heavy trade allowances to retain shelf space	Selective; unprofitable outlets slowly phased out
Advertising strategy	Aim at the needs of early adopters	Make the mass market aware of brand benefits	Use advertising as a vehicle for differentiation among otherwise similar brands	Emphasize low price to reduce stock
Advertising emphasis	High, to generate awareness and interest among early adopters and persuade dealers to stock the brand	Moderate, to let sales rise on the sheer momentum of word-of-mouth recommendations	Moderate, since most buyers are aware of brand characteristics	Minimum expenditures required to phase out the product
Consumer sales promotion	Heavy, to entice target groups with samples, coupons, and other inducements to try the brand	Moderate, to create brand preference (advertising is better suited to do this job)	Heavy, to encourage brand switching, hoping to convert some buyers into loyal users	Minimal, to let the brand coast by itself

From Nariman K. Dhalla and Sonia Yuspeh, "Forget the Product Life Cycle Concept!" *Harvard Business Review* 54 (January–February 1976): 104.

The second step is to establish who is responsible for carrying out the plan. Many individuals and departments become involved in this process, and often the responsibility for execution becomes too diverse. Where everyone has responsibilty, no one is ultimately responsible. Thus, many firms have found that they must take great care to build accountability into marketing strategy plans.

MARKETING PLAN FORMAT

As we have seen, a formal, written marketing plan is essential if the firm hopes to implement its marketing objectives successfully. To illustrate such a plan, let's examine the sample outline of a two-year operating strategy for a marketer of data processing machines which are leased or sold outright.[8]

The following elements of the plan may be expressed in narrative form:

1. *General economic outlook.* A two-year projection of the firm's activities should be prepared.

2. *Assumptions and constraints.* The firm should make assumptions about corporate income tax rates, pricing formulas, product quality, and available capital.

3. *Statement of the competitive situation.* There must be clear and honest analysis of the strengths and weaknesses of major competitors, and the relative position of the firm within the industry.

4. *Statement of marketing objectives and strategies.* Both qualitative and quantitative objectives must be outlined, as well as strategies designed to help the firm attain these goals.

The other parts of the written plan are entirely quantitative:

1. *Sales and sales backlog summary.* The data processing manufacturer in this case produces goods at many different sizes and prices. Thus, for statistical purposes, some unifying type of measurement must be found. Sales units are defined in terms of "points"; one point reflects a monthly rental revenue of one dollar. Table 24-2 shows the kind of charting used to outline sales and sales backlog data. Cancellations and replacements are subtracted from gross sales figures in order to calculate a net sales statistic.

2. *Income summary.* Table 24-3 illustrates the kind of analysis-of-income summary that is included in the marketing plan. Income is classified in a number of distinct categories, including regular rental, extra-shift, and purchased equipment.

3. *Program data sheets.* Each program will have its own individual sheets, which reflect sales, sales development, and sales support activities.

4. *Personnel and expense summaries.* Here the plan projects the resources (in terms of employees and money) necessary for each program. A personnel flow summary, including forecasts of attrition and hiring difficulties, will be included.

Even the best written plan is no guarantee of successful marketing. Supervision and auditing are critical tasks if the firm's marketing objectives are to be realized. Marketing managers must be constantly aware of how well the plan is being carried out. If there are not adequate checks in the system, a deviation from the plan may not be discovered until after the damage has already been done.

Table 24-2
CURRENT OPERATING PLAN—SALES AND SALES BACKLOG SUMMARY

SALES AND SALES BACKLOG SUMMARY	LAST YEAR	THIS YEAR (PROJECTED)	FIRST YEAR OF PLAN		SECOND YEAR OF PLAN	
			AMOUNT	% CHANGE	AMOUNT	% CHANGE
Sales (points):						
Gross sales						
Cancellations						
Replacements						
Net sales						
Backlog (points):						
Opening balance						
Net sales						
Deliveries						
Closing sales						

From Mark E. Stern, *Marketing Planning: A Systems Approach* (New York: McGraw-Hill, 1966), p. 125.

Table 24-3
CURRENT OPERATING PLAN—INCOME SUMMARY

INCOME SUMMARY	LAST YEAR	THIS YEAR (PROJECTED)	FIRST YEAR OF PLAN		SECOND YEAR OF PLAN	
			AMOUNT	% CHANGE	AMOUNT	% CHANGE
Installed equipment (points):						
Rental equipment:						
Opening balance						
Gross delivered						
Cancellations						
Closing balance						
Purchased equipment:						
Opening balance						
Deliveries						
Closing balance						
Income from sales:						
Rentals—regular						
Rentals—extra-shift						
Equipment sales						
Other revenue						
Total:						

From Mark E. Stern, *Marketing Planning: A Systems Approach* (New York: McGraw-Hill, 1966), p. 126.

SCHEDULING APPROACH In order to make effective monitoring possible, the marketing plan must set precise, month-by-month tasks and goals for each department involved in the program. It must assist and direct interdepartmental coordination. There can be no doubt left as to the responsibilities of any operating division, or the procedures for joint efforts of two or more departments.

One well-known way of dealing with the intricacies of scheduling is **PERT** (Program Evaluation and Review Technique). Its central theme is the **critical path method**. This approach was used successfully in the construction of the Polaris Missile in 1958, and has been adapted for other situations since. The method is illustrated in Figure 24-3, where it is applied to one part of the marketing planning process (from screening to first review of a new product).

Under the critical path method, all project activities are arranged in paths based on their performance sequence (the PERT chart). Since various sequences will occur at the same time, there may be a number of paths leading to each key review point in the project implementation. Time estimates are calculated for each path; the one with the longest total time is designated as the critical path. Only by reducing the time length of that path can the duration of the project be shortened. Any delays on the critical path will increase the time needed to complete the project.

It is no simple matter to perform these calculations. In most cases, computers will be necessary for handling this work. Furthermore, each delay or speedup in a part of the project will require new calculations. Nevertheless, there are significant benefits to be gained from the critical path method. It is quite valuable to marketers in projecting income cash flow, scheduling, time control, cost overruns, and personnel requirements. All elements of the marketing program can be viewed more effectively with a time–cost perspective in mind.

MAKING IMPLEMENTATION POSSIBLE

One important (and often hidden) limit on implementation of the marketing plan is **organizational capacity**. To put the question simply, can the organization handle the changes suggested by the plan? Can the personnel of the organization adapt in the necessary ways? If a plan calls for expenditures on distribution to be reduced by 5 percent while transferring additional revenues into product quality research, this is restructuring of financial priorities. But people cannot be restructured or shifted as easily as dollars. If the advertising department and the sales force cannot work together—because of personal tensions or professional rivalries—a brilliant plan can go down the drain.

Failure to match the marketing program to organizational capacity can be very costly. It is also more likely to occur than other types of errors, since organizational capacity cannot be easily predicted by quantitative data. Therefore, marketing planners must carefully evaluate the human resources in their organization before committing themselves to dramatic reforms and changes that are unrealistic and doomed.

Figure 24-3   DEVELOPMENT CRITICAL PATH—SCREENING TO FIRST REVIEW
From John M. Brion, *Corporate Marketing Planning* (New York: Wiley, 1967), p. 258.

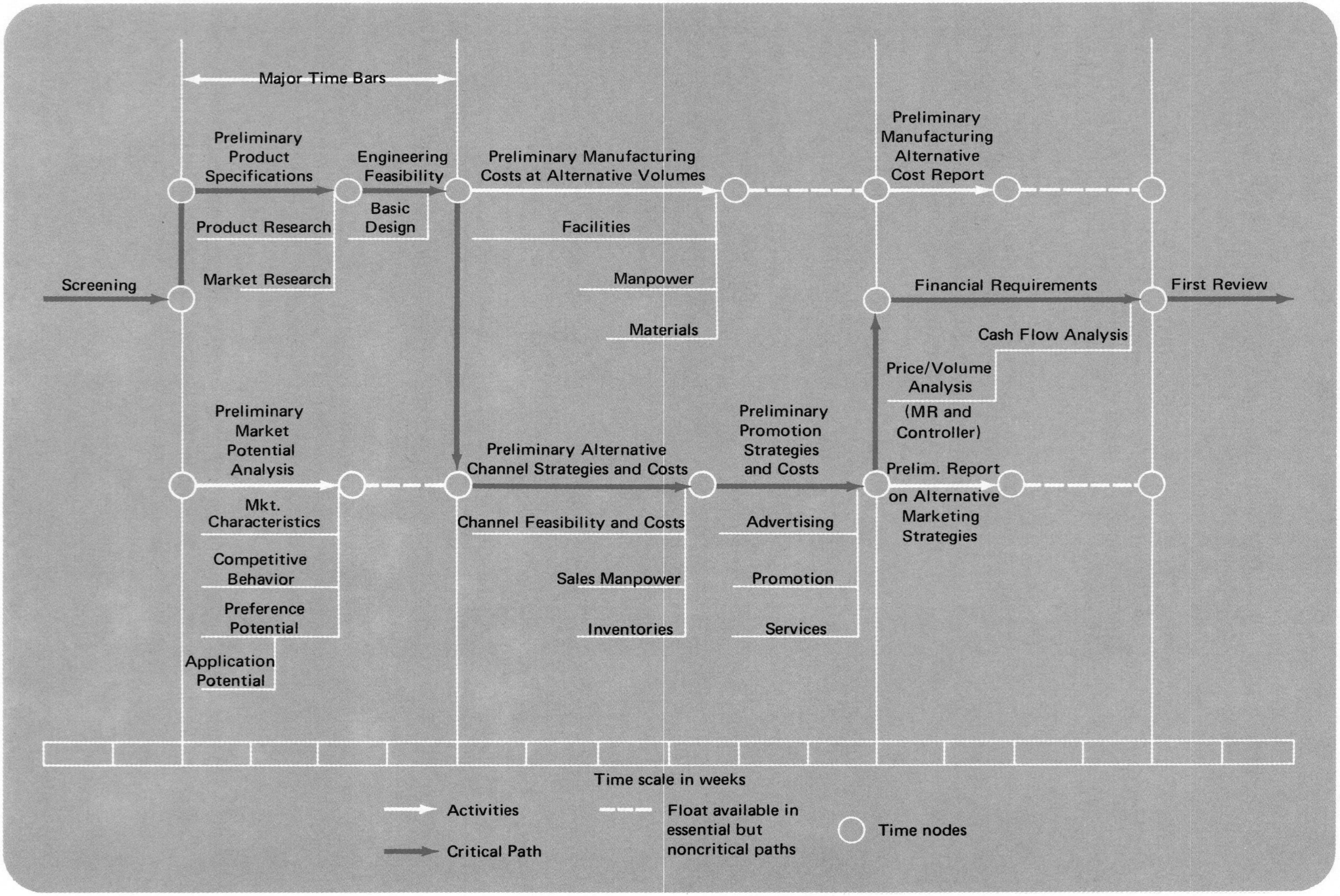

First Review

Preliminary Manufacturing Alternative Cost Report

Financial Requirements

Cash Flow Analysis

Price/Volume Analysis (MR and Controller)

Prelim. Report on Alternative Marketing Strategies

Preliminary Promotion Strategies and Costs

Advertising

Promotion

Services

Preliminary Manufacturing Costs at Alternative Volumes

Facilities

Manpower

Materials

Preliminary Alternative Channel Strategies and Costs

Channel Feasibility and Costs

Sales Manpower

Inventories

Major Time Bars

Engineering Feasibility

Basic Design

Preliminary Product Specifications

Product Research

Market Research

Preliminary Market Potential Analysis

Mkt. Characteristics

Competitive Behavior

Preference Potential

Application Potential

Screening

Time scale in weeks

Float available in essential but noncritical paths

Time nodes

Activities

Critical Path

ORGANIZING FOR
IMPLEMENTATION

Three different types of functions are especially important in the implementation of marketing strategies: product management, interface management, and resource scheduling.

Product
Management

As discussed in Chapter 11, the **product manager** has primary responsibility for coordinating marketing and production tasks for a specific product or product line. Manufacturing schedules must be adjusted to market demands, and the product mix must be geared to current sales requirements. To perform these tasks, the product manager focuses on four key factors: plant capacity and flexibility, production expertise, standardization, and quality standards.

The product manager also has a major role in integrating general marketing objectives into the product development process. New products and applications must be created as a reflection of the overall marketing strategy for the firm, not simply because they are interesting or original.

The product manager balances efficient production goals with consumer needs and demands. He or she tries to keep plant costs down while maintaining a cost-competitive product that will satisfy consumers. In the DuPont Textile Fibers Department,

> *each Sales Program Manager was charged with looking after the "health" of his particular fiber and for serving as a clearing house for all information on it. Specifically, he worked with groups in the sales, research, and manufacturing organizations on scheduling production, allocating available supplies, planning new plant capacity, developing new products and new applications, and promoting the use of his fiber in the market.*[9]

Interface
Management

The **interface manager** in a resource department (sales advertising, physical distribution) is responsible for the allocation of resources to particular programs. He or she performs two important functions: (1) evaluating cost, profit, and consumer considerations to determine whether a change in the program would benefit the organization; and (2) setting priorities for the personnel, money, and so forth, that the organization will invest in the program.

The personnel manager for the organization has an indirect but important role in resource allocation. Each new employee is actually a potential resource for the firm—if allocated properly. The personnel manager has overall responsibility for recruiting, selecting, training, and assigning marketing personnel. The manager must have a firm grasp of the nature of all work performed within the company in order to place employees in the right slot.

Resource
Scheduling

Resource scheduling is another essential element in the implementation process. In some firms, an independent department for scheduling the use of resources is created outside of the program structure and the resource structure. The task of this scheduling function is "to satisfy given levels of demand in the several markets the business served at the maximum profit without sacrificing long-run market position."[10] Usually, such independent units are only established when a firm's scheduling problems are complex.

Other Approaches

Marketing organizations employ many methods to promote an overall, integrated marketing approach. Among the most common are the committee approach, departmental meetings, and mixed training programs.

In the committee approach, a general marketing committee is formed, which may replace various sales committees, advertising committees, and the like. Members of the committee include specialists in production, engineering, purchase, finance, and other important activities related to marketing. Such committees rarely do any policy making; their main work consists of discussion and recommendation.

Some organizations prefer departmental meetings to permanent committees. These meetings may be attended by members of two departments whose work is closely interrelated (such as production and marketing), or they may include many internal departments. Often leadership is alternated. For example, at one monthly meeting, the production department may present its problems on a specific project. This will be followed by an open discussion among all the departments represented. The next month the advertising department may present its viewpoint and outlook.

The basic theory behind mixed training programs is that they will promote a sense of interdependence among personnel in the firm. Marketing training sessions are conducted for a variety of employees, including engineers, buyers, technicians, and advertising copywriters. Each comes to a better understanding of the work of other individuals and departments within the firm. One result is a deeper realization that marketing is a total, integrated process in which the whole is truly greater than the sum of its parts.

SUSTAINING COMMUNICATION

Clear, decisive communication is vital to marketing success. But this goal is not easy to achieve. In one large pharmaceutical house, various divisions of the company kept secrets from each other. At one point, two divisions were secretly allocating large sums of money for new projects. After more than two years of research, one division finally announced its findings. Then the truth came out. Each division had been working on virtually the same problems.

Such secrecy and in-fighting is not the rule among major marketing firms. Yet poor communication can take many other, if less dramatic, forms. An ambiguous policy statement from a top executive can create confusion up and down the line. What if the heads of the production, advertising, and marketing research departments each interpret the policy statement differently? The likelihood of developing an integrated marketing approach is certainly lessened. In fact, low-level executives may get wrapped up in arguments about whose interpretation is correct.

Effective communication must begin at the highest levels of the organization, and it must flow freely in all directions and at all levels. It has been noted that the chief "must be both willing *and able* to communicate. It must be the policy of the organization to communicate. And executives must be trained in the art of effective communication; otherwise, they will hesitate to communicate for fear of being misunderstood."[11]

Lafayette Keeney, the president of the Sage-Allen department store chain in Connecticut, is a good example of the "communicating" executive. Keeney walks through the chain's flagship store in Hartford three times daily, exchanging thoughts and jokes with managers, salespeople, and customers. "I like to keep my relations with our people friendly and informal. That way they can level with me if something goes wrong."[12]

Under the marketing concept, communication is more essential than ever. If marketing is most successful as an integrated process, then one communications breakdown may echo all through the organization. Thus, many firms are studying and experimenting with new methods of improving internal communications. In order to develop the right kind of atmosphere, the firm must make it clear that it wants to hear the views of personnel. Employees must feel that their opinions are considered important, and that their colleagues and superiors truly want an exchange of information and experiences.

CONCLUSION

Having a first-rate marketing strategy is a good beginning for an organization, but by itself strategy means nothing. The firm must be able to implement that strategy; it must be able to convert its marketing objectives into action, into a total marketing offering.

Integration is a central theme of marketing implementation. The marketing manager wants to bring every element of the marketing program together into a total marketing system. The firm does not need a good advertising campaign as an end in itself, or a high standard of product quality isolated from other marketing elements. Instead, the firm needs a solid and effective marketing mix, an overall package of marketing elements that will seem attractive to potential buyers.

Implementation requires that an integrated marketing plan be developed, and that the plan be accepted on all levels of the organization. Generally, the plan must be written. It must clearly spell out such factors as the firm's economic outlook, the competitive situation, and summaries of sales, income, and manpower data. The plan must also take into account the organizational capacity of the firm to absorb the changes suggested.

Communication is a key stumbling block in the implementation of marketing strategy. Some firms have used special coordinated approaches in order to build understanding among the individuals and departments involved in the marketing program. There must be strong executive leadership in establishing an atmosphere of open, relaxed, and clear communication.

DISCUSSION QUESTIONS

1. What would be examples of strategy and tactics in these marketing planning situations:
   a. advertising a new condominium in Tampa, Florida;
   b. selecting distributors for a new line of high-pressure pumps;

    c. researching the small town market for band concert bookings.

2. In what ways can decision-making concepts help improve the solving process in these problem areas: selecting a new package for frozen pizza; pricing an annual membership fee for a tennis club; motivating the sales force for an industrial park.

3. Solar Products Company, Long Beach, California, is considering the introduction of a modernistic, solar-powered, outdoor clock. It operates by direct sunlight during sunny days and by stored solar energy on cloudy days and at night. To test market the product in California, marketing director Nancy Pollack will have to make several decisions. What decision-making guidelines can you give her?

4. Contrast the marketing mix elements in the introduction stage and in the maturity stage of the product life cycle of Electric Stars, Inc., the first computerized astrology service, based in Dayton, Ohio.

5. Construct a PERT chart for launching a new men's cologne, given this information:
    a. product concept testing, 3 weeks;
    b. develop formula, 7 weeks;
    c. develop prototype bottle, 6 weeks;
    d. decide brand name, 6 weeks;
    e. make up product samples, 4 weeks;
    f. plan advertising campaign, 6 weeks;
    g. develop and produce display materials, 5 weeks;
    h. run consumer preference tests, 4 weeks;
    i. produce for inventory, 3 weeks;
    j. distribute to dealers, 2 weeks.
    How many weeks long is the critical path?

6. Scandinavian Catering Service in Milwaukee, Wisconsin, has developed a formal marketing plan in its effort to expand its sales in the suburbs. The president complains, "I'm never sure who is supposed to do what we've agreed on." His wife, the executive vice-president, admits, "The direct mail campaign went out too long before our follow-up phone calls to potential customers." Their daughter, the vice-president, says, "No one told me that anything was wrong!" Diagnose their implementation problems and recommend some solutions.

NOTES

1. C. W. Plattes, "Strategic and Tactical Decision-Making in Marketing," in *Decision-Making in Marketing: A Colloquium* (New York: The Conference Board, 1971), pp. 15–16.

2. Hector Lazo and Arnold Corbin, *Management in Marketing: Text and Cases* (New York: McGraw-Hill, 1961), p. 563.

3. Louis V. Gerstner, Jr., "The Practice of Business: Can Strategic Planning Pay Off?" *Business Horizons* 16 (December 1972): 5–9.

4. W. Gifford Myers, "The Decision-Making Process," in *Decision-Making in Marketing: A Colloquium* (New York: The Conference Board, 1971), p. 21.

5. Ibid., pp. 24–25.

6. R. P. Willett, "A Model for Marketing Programming," *Journal of Marketing* 27 (January 1963): 40–41.

7. Ibid., pp. 41–44.

8. This discussion is based largely on Mark E. Stern, *Marketing Planning: A Systems Approach* (New York: McGraw-Hill, 1966), pp. 123–27.

9. E. Raymond Corey and Steven H. Star, *Organization Strategy: A Marketing Approach* (Boston: Harvard University Graduate School of Business Administration, 1971), p. 41.

10. Ibid., pp. 41, 47.

11. Lazo and Corbin, pp. 503–505.

12. "Taking on the Giants," *Chain Store Age*, General Merchandise Edition, April 1975, p. 40.

25

CONTROLLING MARKETING PERFORMANCE

After completing this chapter, the reader should be able to:

1. Identify the key dynamics of the marketing control model.
2. Explain the control considerations that are related to sales.
3. Allocate marketing costs to marketing segments.
4. Apply the different methods for calculating profit.
5. Describe budgeting as a control technique.
6. Explain how a marketing audit is conducted.

In the two preceding chapters we described how marketing information is used to plan marketing strategy, and then how this strategy is put into action by the organization. As a result, developments in the marketing environment take place (consumers buy, competitors react, government watches, and so forth). In this chapter we will discuss the final phase of the managerial marketing process—control of marketing performance.

HOOKED ON CONTROL

When the chairman of the board of a very successful drug store chain was asked how he turned his conventional chain operating in a restricted trading area into a major competitor, his answer came quickly: control.[1] Hook Drugs in Indianapolis, Indiana, began as a small chain at the turn of the century. Now, there are 200 stores statewide—only fifteen other drug chains in the country have more units.

In a highly competitive industry, Hook has become a major, publicly held chain by "sticking to drug store basics," as Bud Hook explained. The chain's annual volume hovers around the $120 million mark, making it the twentieth largest in the business. It is also one of the most profitable chains on a dollar and percentage basis. And an 18 percent return on investment puts Hook at the top of the list for a drug chain.

Centralized control of operations is a major reason for Hook's success. This control is exercised largely through the Indianapolis warehouse, which supplies up to 90 percent of each store's merchandise. No store is more than two hours away by truck, according to Bud Hook. Direct shipments are restricted, and no jobbers are used. Deliveries are made weekly, with a three-day turnaround for orders. With one large facility handling almost all merchandise, the company can keep tight reins on inventory levels and transportation costs.

KEEPING MARKETING UNDER CONTROL

The story of Hook Drugs illustrates the importance of **control**. Hook gained when the head office took strong centralized direction, thereby reducing costs and maximizing profits. Without this tight marketing control, the most elaborate marketing plans may be wasted. Control is necessary to ensure that all the company's resources—human, physical, and financial—are used effectively and efficiently. Through the use of control systems, managers can evaluate the ways in which plans and performance are fulfilling organizational objectives, and make adjustments where necessary.

Figure 25-1 provides a view of control from a managerial marketing perspective. The two major influences on control are planning and information. Planning ensures that performance is always geared to meet the overall objectives of the company. Information provides the data on which evaluations are

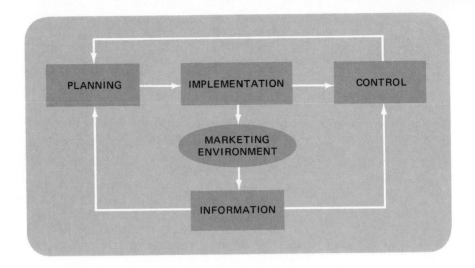

Figure 25-1
CONTROL IN A MANAGERIAL MARKETING PERSPECTIVE

based (see Chapter 23). In a company where there are good controls, the planning includes suggestions of needed changes to increase the effectiveness of the company's marketing program.

One reason for a renewed emphasis on marketing control is the quickening pace of economic change. As we saw in Chapter 3, the U.S. economy in the 1970s moved from surpluses into shortages, then into substantial inflation, then into recession. Because even the wisest planners could not have foreseen all of these developments, the burden of coping with them has fallen more heavily on management control. Better ways of evaluating marketing effectiveness are constantly being sought. Also, nonprofit organizations have become more aware of the need for greater control over their resources and marketing strategies.

THE MARKETING CONTROL MODEL

Control is a major part of marketing that influences all other phases of the management process. To make marketing control more understandable, let us look at the model of the control system illustrated in Figure 25-2.

The central job of the control system is to evaluate and compare results from the marketing environment with performance standards that are consistent with company objectives. This comparison and evaluation leads to formulation of plans for corrective action. Once the corrective actions have been taken, the control cycle begins again.

What kind of corrective action is put into effect will depend on the source of the company's problem. It may be necessary to make changes in the way the marketing plan is implemented, in the plan itself, or in the objectives upon which the plan is based. Changes in any one of these will, of course, result in changes throughout the entire marketing system.

WHAT SHOULD BE CONTROLLED? The first step in establishing a control procedure is to identify the boundaries of the control system. It has been suggested, for example, that 20 percent of an organization's customers are generally responsible for 80 percent of sales.[2] Control over the transactions with this small segment of the marketplace would therefore be more effective than control over all the other segments combined.

The marketing manager not only controls events in the marketing department but also controls the relationship that department has with other organizational units and with outside suppliers.[3] Within the organization, the marketing department is heavily dependent on activities of other units, such as production and finance. The reverse relationship is also true, with other units depending on the performance of the marketing department. In most cases, control is the result of compromise, rather than the total domination of one unit over another.

Effective control also demands flexibility. Since events in the marketplace are often uncontrollable (material shortages, strikes, recession, surprise moves by competitors, and so forth), management must be prepared with alternative plans of action. Moreover, the introduction of a new product or advertising campaign will require changes in schedules and budgets, as well as the reallocation of personnel. Coping with these "unusual" demands, while maintaining performance standards, is an important aspect of the control system.

Figure 25-2 MARKETING CONTROL MODEL

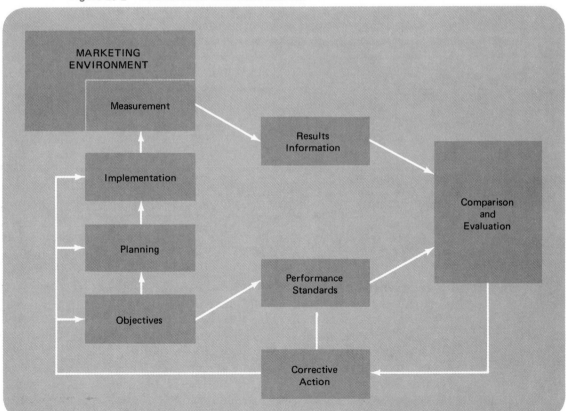

PERFORMANCE STANDARDS

Close monitoring of progress means breaking down broad **standards of performance** to specifics such as monthly sales goals. Defining goals is a vital task, but not always an easy one. It means developing standard figures that answer questions such as whether new accounts should be added or whether more of a certain product should be stocked. Standards are based on industry norms, past performance, and the expectations of management.

Fernando Gumucio of Del Monte has described how the company judges the performance of its research department. Analysts question "how much in our research activities is in the 'nice to know' category and how much is 'actionable and conclusive.'" The theory, he explains, is that "having high performance and measurable standards where the payoff will be the greatest is the basis for sound and productive marketing management."[4]

Measures of efficiency can be used to develop standards of performance. In an efficient system, production is achieved at the lowest possible cost. The sales force is one key area that should be continually checked for efficiency. As we said in Chapter 19, personal selling is the most expensive form of promotion. Managers must question the size of the sales force and whether certain of its tasks could be transferred or eliminated. They need to know if individual salespeople are using their time productively. Efficiency is also a primary concern in advertising, physical distribution, and packaging.

MEASUREMENT APPROACHES

Once the areas of control have been defined, the next step is to determine what performance measurements should be used. An important question here is what kind of data the measurement is based on. As is the case with all marketing information, the data used for measurement must be in a form that is relevant to the task at hand. In many cases, companies restrict measurement to material factors such as time, quantity, and quality, which are usually expressed in units of production or cost. But human factors are often important as well, especially those that serve as a barometer of personnel performance (sales force) or consumer attitudes (satisfaction).

Today, many marketing information reports are designed to point specifically to differences between standards and actual results. Management can then zero in on problem areas. For example, executives may be cheered to read that overall sales are up 10 percent from the previous year. But when they discover that the product group that has always generated the biggest profit is down 10 percent, their cheer usually fades.

EVALUATION PROCESS

Procedures for **evaluation** should be set up before they are actually needed. "Management by crisis" doesn't work very often. Of course, it is impossible to make every decision in advance, because the unexpected is always happening. But a good marketing manager will schedule points of decision at the beginning of an operating period.

History will provide a guideline to many decisions made in the normal cycle of activities. Looking at the past record, the marketing strategist can often plan times when new strategies should be launched. And even if there

"How do we know it's the recession? Maybe we've got a lousy product."

are no new plans on the drawing board, past experience can identify times of the year likely to be the best testing points for current strategy.

Since control usually involves the investigation of differences between standards and actual performance, it is important to determine what types of deviations will be considered. Often, it is only when results fall below expectations that a re-evaluation of strategy is called for. However, significant achievements above the norm should also be investigated. These may be evidence of a change in the marketplace that will have serious consequences for the marketing effort.

CORRECTIVE ACTION

Assuming that the workings of the control process have signaled a need for change, the next step is to determine what that **corrective action** should be. The strategists should determine what the current situation is, evaluate possible modifications of existing strategy, and, if necessary, come up with a whole new strategy.[5]

At Reliance Electric & Engineering, for example, sales analysis and profitability studies go hand in hand. Management determines profit objectives for the major product groups by examining divisional costs plus overhead. A running summary of division costs according to product groups supplements the bookings fed constantly into the computer. Each month the current profit figure is compared with objectives.

"If a product's profit is down," the marketing vice president has explained, "we must analyze whether costs are rising or income is falling. If the price of copper is rising, say, we can't do anything about it. So we ask for an engineering redesign which would cut down on the amount of that metal. If less income is the culprit, we have to analyze why and explore for positive steps."[6]

Marketing decision makers face three procedural problems in taking corrective action: identifying the causes of a problem; adjusting for time lags between the point of decision and the point of action; and budgeting elaborate and costly control procedures. Costs may be so heavy that they outweigh benefits.

Personnel problems also become obstacles to corrective action. An employee may be too strongly committed to one way of doing something to adapt to change. A corrective decision may affect organizational morale, to the point where it is not worth taking. And traditions of the organization may also run against proposed changes.

MARKETING CONTROL APPROACHES

There are many marketing control approaches, but they can all be translated into the common denominators of revenue, expense, and profit dollars. As the last decade has shown, many marketing control elements are interdependent. Computer technology has allowed for the recognition of those complex relationships.

Although the computer is an extremely useful tool, it cannot solve all marketing control problems. An integrated, systems-oriented approach is vital. And while productivity is crucial, a marketing organization cannot run efficiently if sales and profits are the only end. The system should also produce information that will make better planning possible.

SALES-RELATED ANALYSIS

Traditionally, current sales are regarded as the best barometer of marketing performance. Marketing managers are elated when sales are high and despondent when they plunge. There is a danger that interest in sales may outweigh interest in virtually every other aspect of performance.

While sales information is fundamental, it can be used improperly, or its value can be overstressed. Data on competitors' sales, marketing costs, and sales standards must also be weighed. Each marketing manager must define the most useful level and type of sales analysis.

The basic piece of sales information is the **sales transaction**. It has been defined as "the order of (1) a particular customer for (2) a particular quantity of (3) a particular company product from (4) a particular sales representative on (5) a particular date (6) under particular terms."[7]

With the complete record of a sales transaction, marketing managers can break down sales according to:

1. *Customer.* A company with only a few large customers will want to keep a close check on their purchases. Another with many customers may also need sales summaries by type of customer and/or geographic location.

2. *Salesperson.* A record of sales according to personnel shows who is performing satisfactorily and who is not.

3. *Product.* Information gathered according to product or product version can be very useful.

Sales volume figures are valuable in measuring a company's growth and indicating its standing among competitors. To create good staff morale, a company might choose to set sales volume as a goal: employees of a firm that has a healthy sales level often feel better about their jobs.

Today, sales analysis is speeded and simplified by electronic data processing (EDP) equipment. A U.S. Rubber Company executive reports that before EDP, the company usually furnished sales figures to the marketing people in the chemical division no earlier than the twentieth of the following month. With EDP those figures are now available in the first week.[8]

Market Share   A common alternative to measuring sales performance in absolute terms is to use the relative measure of **market share,** or sales performance as measured against competition. This type of analysis enables management to decide whether changing sales patterns are due to outside forces or to weaknesses within the marketing program.

If sales drop but market share remains constant, forces within the marketing environment are probably affecting all companies within an industry. But if its share of the market starts to slip, a company may conclude that something is wrong with the marketing mix or with its implementation.

Like sales analysis, market share analysis is most precise when data are broken down according to customer, product, region, or other area. With these subdivisions, market share becomes a very effective tool for evaluating marketing objectives.

Share figures eliminate the influence of uncontrollable forces such as amount of disposable income and cost structure. They are simple and easy to understand. And they provide a measure of a company's image in the marketplace. A high share offers a positive image to the customer and retailer, and is one of the best ways to attract and keep customers (the bandwagon effect).

COST ANALYSIS   No two marketing operations are alike, and consequently no two marketing managers will evaluate sales dollars the same way. Nor are they likely to hit the same levels of marketing costs. Company philosophy, quality of product, market coverage, and other factors vary widely.

Marketing costs include the outlays required for all activities that determine the needs of the market, make products available, price, promote, and distribute them. Some marketing costs are incurred after sale, such as administrative expenses. Marketing cost analysis, then, is the organizing of marketing cost data to show profit and loss, and thus to indicate ways of making better marketing decisions.

Several uses for marketing cost analysis have been suggested:[9]

1. To determine the kinds and amounts of expense incurred in individual marketing activities such as outside selling, billing, warehousing, and delivery;

2. To evaluate marketing methods, policies, and operating procedures;

3. To determine the marketing cost and profitability of the company's various products or customers;

4. To determine the relationship between cost and order size.[10]

Allocating   As shown in Figure 25-3, there are four steps in allocating marketing costs. The
Marketing Costs   process begins with a list of **natural business costs,** such as salaries and wages, office supplies, insurance, rent, and so forth. These natural costs are then apportioned into **functional costs,** which represent all the costs associated with

Figure 25-3 MARKETING COST ALLOCATION FOR A WATER COOLER MANUFACTURER

NATURAL BUSINESS COSTS

Simplified Profit-and-Loss Statement ($ Million)

Sales	100,000
Cost of goods sold	60,000
Gross margin	40,000

Expenses

Salaries	15,000	
Supplies	4,000	
Advertising	4,500	
Depreciation	3,500	
Rent	2,500	
Insurance	4,000	
Bad Debts	2,000	
		32,500
Net profit		7,500

FUNCTIONAL COSTS

Partial List ($ Million)

	Personal selling	Advertising	Storage	Order filling	Delivery	Market research	Nonmarketing
Salaries	4,000	100	500	300	200	150	9,750
Supplies	300			200			3,500
Advertising		4,500					
Depreciation					1,000		2,500
Rent			1,000				1,500
Insurance			100		200		700
Bad Debts							2,000

MARKETING SEGMENTS

Products
- Bottle cooler
- Pressure cooler
- Hot-and-cold unit
- Compact refrigerator

Customers
- Factories
- Waiting rooms
- Schools
- Hospitals
- Homes

Territories
- East
- Midwest
- South
- West

Sales representatives
- Carr
- D'Amico
- Espinosa
- Finkel
- Hartmann
- Others

Order size
- $0 – $999
- $1,000– $1,999
- $2,000– $4,999
- $5,000 and over

Distribution channels
- Refrigeration
- Office suppliers
- Spring water suppliers
- Department stores

each marketing activity. In Figure 25-3, where a water cooler manufacturer is used as an example, the storage function includes the percentages of the natural costs of salaries, rent, and insurance that are spent on storage.

These functional costs are then assigned to **marketing segments**. In Figure 25-3, bottle coolers and hot-and-cold units are included under the product breakdown. Distribution channels are subdivided into refrigeration, office suppliers, spring water suppliers, and department stores. Finally, after sales and costs have been allocated to each of these segments, profit can be determined. (For the specifics of this step, see pp. 601–602.)

Natural Business Costs

Most businesses classify accounts according to object of expenditure, such as office supplies, salaries, and insurance. This natural cost method simplifies recording since each check or voucher can be charged to a specific account. However, information provided by this type of accounting is limited. "Natural costs, by definition, are not viewed in light of their purposes or the outcomes they have produced. If travel costs are 15 percent higher than in the corresponding period last year, does this mean that they are now too high?"[10] Possibly, he suggests, travel costs were too high for some purposes and not for others. The natural cost method does not provide any answer to this type of question.

Functional Costs

Functional costs are classified according to purpose or activity. In the case of travel expense given above, these figures would be broken down according to the purpose for which the travel was undertaken. For example, travel expenses incurred by salespeople would be grouped together. To this would be added the salaries of the salespeople, the rent for office space occupied by them, and other sales force-related costs. In this way, the cost of the entire sales function can be determined.

Sometimes, the major elements of total marketing costs are separate (direct) marketing expenses associated with a particular subdivision of sales. An organization with broad-scale marketing activities is especially likely to devote a large portion of the total budget to direct marketing costs. Often the organization sets up individual departments for marketing particular product groups and searching out particular types of customers.

Marketing Segments

After functional costs have been determined, they are allocated according to the marketing segment to which they apply. Each segment is charged with the cost of its share of the activity of each functional cost group. A marketing segment is the "application or end toward which functional activity is directed."[11] In most cases, the marketing segments considered are products, customers, and sales territories. (Marketing segments should not be confused with market segments. Market segments, which were discussed in Chapter 7, are groups of consumers with similar characteristics and, therefore, similar buying habits.) A typical allocation of some functional costs to marketing segments is illustrated in Table 25-1.

Product Segments. Product analysis allows for evaluating product profitability, making price decisions, and providing legally necessary information.

Table 25-1
FROM FUNCTIONAL COSTS TO MARKETING SEGMENTS

FUNCTIONAL COSTS	BASES OF ALLOCATION		
	TO PRODUCT GROUPS	TO CUSTOMER GROUPS	TO SALES TERRITORIES
1. *Direct Selling Expenses* Personal calls by salespeople on existing accounts and prospective accounts. Sales force salaries, commissions, traveling, etc.	Selling time devoted to each product as shown by special sales call reports or other special studies.	Number of calls times average call time as shown by special sales call reports or special studies.	Direct.
2. *Indirect Selling Expenses* Field supervision. Sales administration—clerical and office costs. Sales training. Sales management expenses. Marketing research costs. Sales statistics and accounting.	In proportion to direct selling time.	In proportion to direct selling time.	Equal charge for each salesperson.
3. *Advertising* Media costs. Production costs. Fees. Salaries.	Direct, or on basis of space and time by media. Other costs in proportion to media costs.	Cost of space for each customer group, or equal charge to each customer.	Direct, or on basis of analysis of media circulation records.
4. *Transportation* Payment to carriers. Transport department costs, etc.	Applicable rate times weight.	Analysis of sample of bills of lading.	Applicable rate times weight.
5. *Storage and Shipping* Storage, packing, handling, loading, assembling shipments, preparation of documents, rent and warehouse charges. Labor costs, etc.	Space occupied times average inventory; number of shipping units; the invoice line.	Number of shipping units; the invoice line; average order size.	Number of shipping units.

Adapted from R. M. S. Wilson, *Management Controls in Marketing* (London: Heinemann, 1973), p. 97.

As Table 25-1 shows, analysis is usually directed at groups of products, not specific items.

Customer Segments. Figures for customer cost are arrived at by combining the total of the shares of the allocated functional cost groups with any direct expenses. To arrive at a figure for relative profitability for a customer class, management deducts this cost from the total dollar gross margin (see p. 601) received from that customer class during the same period. In Table 25-1, indirect selling expenses are allocated to customer groups in proportion to direct selling time.

Territory Segments. Analysis of distribution cost by territory is intended to control expenditures and direct sales efforts.

Table 25-2
DIFFERENT WAYS TO MEASURE PROFIT ($ MILLION)

	GROSS MARGIN	PROFIT CONTRIBUTION	NET PROFIT	
Sales	24,000	24,000		24,000
Cost of goods sold	16,000	16,000		16,000
Gross margin	8,000	8,000		8,000
Escapable marketing costs		5,500	5,500	
Profit contribution		2,500		
Inescapable costs			1,400	
				6,900
Net profit				1,100

Based on Thomas R. Wotruba, *Sales Management: Planning, Accomplishment, and Evaluation* (New York: Holt, Rinehart and Winston, 1971), pp. 505–507.

Other Segments. There are still other types of segments that may be analyzed, including channels of distribution or size of order. With the former, the usual procedure is to take the same expenses used for analysis by territories and allocate them to channels of distribution and methods of sale.

PROFIT ANALYSIS   As illustrated in Table 25-2, profits can be analyzed according to gross margin, profit contribution, or net profit. **Gross margin is the measure of net sales minus cost of goods sold.** It does not reflect marketing costs, and for this reason gross margin figures are not of great interest to marketing managers from the standpoint of control. But they are a function of net sales, which are very much in the interest of marketing and sales planners.

Profit contribution is defined as "gross margin for that subdivision minus the marketing costs which would not be incurred if the subdivision were not present."[12] These marketing costs are sometimes termed "escapable." They include direct costs that stem from a particular marketing entity, as well as variable indirect costs that are fixed in relation to the time period and the segment under study (inescapable costs).

Analysis by profit contribution indicates what profit would be lost if a product were discontinued or a territory abandoned. Rather than eliminate a major product, most managers look first for alternative strategies to change the relative sales volume within the segments. Profit contribution information then shows where marketing efforts must be refocused. It is most useful in short-term analysis, where fixed costs remain the same.

Net profit measures are calculated by subtracting all costs from net sales revenues. Results will vary according to the basis of allocation used. In net profit analysis, costs are attached to segments in three ways:

1. direct costs are assigned directly to segment subdivisions;

2. costs that are both indirect and variable are allocated to segment subdivisions;

3. costs that are both indirect and fixed (inescapable) are distributed proportionately to segment subdivisions.

One disadvantage to the net profit approach is that gross profit per unit can vary greatly between periods of fluctuation in production. Measures of effectiveness may become distorted when marketing costs are analyzed as a percentage of gross margins.

Although no one disputes the necessity of including direct costs in cost analysis, there is some disagreement on whether traceable common (indirect) costs should be included. And there is major disagreement over whether non-traceable common (indirect) costs should be allocated to the marketing entities. Advocates of the **full-cost approach** say that all costs ultimately must be taken into consideration in order to determine true profitability. Those in favor of **partial-cost allocation** think it is wiser to determine margin by measuring merely the contribution made by a particular segment to unallocated cost and net profit. In reality, both approaches can be useful.

BUDGET CONTROL **Budget control** is necessary if actual performance is to be kept in line with plans. Usually good control means having enough past experience to know what standards are workable. To the marketing expert, budget control is essentially a process of estimating future sales, then allocating costs.

Table 25-3
FIXED VS. FLEXIBLE BUDGET ANALYSIS

FIXED BUDGET			
	BUDGET	ACTUAL	VARIANCE
Sales (Units)	10,000	11,000	+1,000
Sales Revenue	$15,000	$16,500	+$1,500
Expenditure:			
Direct	10,000	11,000	+1,000
Indirect	4,000	4,200	+200
Profit	$1,000	$1,300	+$300

FLEXIBLE BUDGET				
	FIXED BUDGET	FLEXIBLE BUDGET	ACTUAL	VARIANCE
Sales (Units)	10,000	11,000	11,000	—
Sales Revenue	$15,000	$16,500	$16,500	—
Expenditure:				
Direct	10,000	11,000	11,000	—
Fixed Indirect	1,500	1,500	1,450	−50
Variable Indirect	2,000	2,200	2,240	+40
Mixed Indirect	500	520	510	−10
Profit	$1,000	$1,280	$1,300	+$20

Adapted from R. M. S. Wilson, *Management Controls in Marketing* (London: Heinemann, 1973), pp. 82–83.

Good budget control means setting up not only sales budgets, but budgets for expenses in advertising, sales promotion, branch operations, and other areas. A budget can be drawn up monthly, quarterly, semiannually, or annually.

A realistic budget is a valuable tool. By keeping close watch on actual performance and comparing this with budgeted performance, management can quickly spot deviations and bring them into line. A good budget keeps the marketing machine on track, and it also provides for better analysis, planning, and coordination.

With a **flexible budget,** the marketing manager can vary projections according to differences in operations. A simple way of building a flexible budget is to start with one for the most likely level of activity, then to derive budgets for 5 percent, 10 percent, and 15 percent above and below this level.[13] A flexible budget does not have to be revised when sales and production programs are altered.

The differences between fixed and flexible budget analysis are shown in Table 25-3. Both the fixed and the flexible budgets here are designed for a situation in which 10,000 units were expected to be sold but actual sales amounted to 11,000. The fixed budget method, shown at the top of Table 25-3, gives the impression that an increased profit of $300 was realized, due to the increase in sales. But this is misleading. The actual sales figure becomes the flexible budget (bottom of Table 25-3). The total actual profit ($1,300) is the same in both the fixed and flexible budgets. But when the flexible method is used, which takes into account variations in costs, the actual profit *increase* is only $20.

THE MARKETING AUDIT

Periodic reviews of operations are essential to any well-run organization. This is particularly true in marketing, where objectives and strategies can quickly become out of date as a result of changes in the environment and within the marketing organization itself. One way to keep up with these changes is to conduct a **marketing audit.**

WHAT IS THE MARKETING AUDIT?

The marketing audit is "a periodic, comprehensive, systematic, and independent examination of the organization's marketing environment, internal marketing system, and specific marketing activities with a view of determining problem areas and recommending a corrective action plan to improve the organization's overall marketing effectiveness."[14] The marketing audit makes sense for such diverse organizations as General Motors, Barney's Clothes, Inc., and the Kansas City Public Library.

The marketing audit has several specific objectives. One of these is to determine how the organization uses the marketing concept. Is it able to develop and market products that customers want to buy? What is the profit picture? A second objective is to determine how well the organization understands its market environment.

One specialized type of marketing audit is the **consumer affairs audit,**

In 1972 a group of independent investors made news when they purchased Roman Products from H. P. Hood Company. Hood had dropped plans for national expansion of marketing for Roman Products, and many people predicted a tough uphill route for the new owners. Small manufacturers were not having an easy time, and Roman Products faced stiff competition.

The new owners of Roman were able to turn a losing operation into a profitable one. It wasn't easy. A marketing audit was the key to success.

"Our initial strategy called for a retrenchment to those markets and products where we could support our franchise with reasonable promotional activity," top executives explained. "We moved away from dependence upon home office executives to maintain contact with the trade and brokers, reorganized our sales management structure, and increased the decision-making responsibility of our field managers."

Roman has now begun to expand its product lines in response to consumer demands: for example, a greater variety of pizza items, such as pepperoni pizza. "We believe these products will secure our position as the leader in this category—and initial trade and consumer response supports this belief," the executives noted.

Based on "The Fall and Rise of Roman," *Quick Frozen Foods*, February 1975, pp. 37–72.

which was discussed in Chapter 4. Fernando R. Gumucio of Del Monte has explained the importance of this type of audit:

> *Perhaps it is time that we take a more objective view of the new consumer and environmental issues. [May I suggest that pre-emptive self-audit of polities and correction may be needed now more than ever and building consumer issues into contingency productive plans may not be a bad idea to be thinking about.] How will they affect our future marketing plans? In some instances our objective analysis may indicate that, at the very least, we must build these issues into our alternative business plans or that we must open up an earnest dialogue with consumers and responsible media people to establish the facts.*[15]

CONDUCTING THE MARKETING AUDIT

There are four basic steps in conducting a marketing audit:[16]

1. Obtain a clear statement of objectives and evaluate them in terms of adequacy, attainability, and marketing orientation.

2. Look at the plans developed to attain the objectives, and examine how the available resources are allocated to segments to ensure that these reflect the company's philosophy and priorities.

3. Study the means by which the plan is put into effect to ensure that objectives are attained.

4. Review the organizational structure, including such matters as delegation, human relations, the means used to allocate duties, the competence of the marketing team, and the adequacy of particular individuals.

Who should conduct the marketing audit? There are various possibilities, beginning with a self-audit. Since the marketing executive knows most about marketing operations, he or she may be in the best position to audit them. A disadvantage of the self-audit is that it will lack the objectivity of an outside audit. The marketing executive may consciously or unconsciously overlook information that reflects poorly on the marketing operation.

A second possibility is audit by a task force of personnel from other company units. Again, objectivity may be lacking. A third possibility is an internal staff audit by company specialists in auditing procedures. This would be more expensive. Fourth, a marketing audit could be conducted by an outside consultant. Again, this would be a costly approach, although an objective one.

The question of timing is important. Frustrated executives may be tempted to call for an audit in times of trouble, when they are pressed to find out what is going wrong. But a time of crisis is probably the worst time for a systematic analysis. An audit conducted under normal circumstances is more useful.

CONCLUSION

Control of marketing performance is the final phase of the managerial marketing process. Without adequate control, the most elaborate, best thought-out marketing programs may be wasted.

Effective control depends on planning and information. Planning formulates the organizational goals against which performance is measured. Information from the marketplace provides the data on which evaluations are based. The result of the control process may be a change in the marketing strategy itself or in the way it is carried out.

The control process must be both continuous and systematic. Since dealing with crisis situations only is largely ineffective, regular evaluation of performance is essential. Deviations from objectives can be spotted before a crisis develops and corrective action taken.

There are varying approaches to control, all of which can be related to revenue, expenses, and profit. Popular methods are sales-related analysis (including market share), cost analysis, and profit analysis. A key factor in any of these methods is the presence of good budget control.

One way of conducting the periodic reviews that are essential to control is to undertake a marketing audit. The audit is an examination of the organization's marketing environment and the way it practices marketing in that environment.

DISCUSSION QUESTIONS

1. What aspects of these marketing situations should be subject to close control: new product planning with a brief lead-time; pricing in times of inflation; distribution channels management during a period of intense vertical conflict?
2. What would be appropriate descriptions of these control process steps in these marketing situations:
   a. performance standards for a museum's membership drive;
   b. measurement approaches for retail furniture sales force quotas;

    c. evaluation process for account loss by a Spanish language-oriented advertising agency;

    d. corrective action for customer complaints regarding a new minicomputer's operating complexity.

3. On what basis could these functional costs be allocated to these marketing segments:

    a. sales force cost to customer segments;

    b. warehouse cost to product segments;

    c. bad debts cost to territory segments.

4. The Do-It-Yourselfer Book Company is evaluating profit on each of its three books. According to the following figures, are any of the books candidates for being dropped? Describe the basis for your decision.

	($ THOUSANDS)		
	A	B	C
Gross sales	$400	$350	$500
Cost of goods sold	300	210	370
Gross profit	100	140	130
Direct marketing expenses	70	90	90
Contribution profit	30	50	40
Indirect marketing expenses and administrative overhead	20	60	35
Net profit (or loss)	$10	($10)	$5

5. What would be some of the major areas to be examined in a marketing audit for a state tourist board? A church organ manufacturer?

NOTES

1. "Hook at 75: A Study in Traditionalism," *Chain Store Age*, Drug Edition, December 1974, pp. 26–29.
2. R. M. S. Wilson, *Management Controls in Marketing* (London: Heinemann, 1973), p. 44.
3. This section is based on Philip Kotler, *Marketing Management: Analysis, Planning, and Control*, 2d ed. (Englewood Cliffs, N.J.: Prentice-Hall, 1972), pp. 755–57.
4. Fernando R. Gumucio, "Productivity in Grocery Marketing," Speech to the Grocery Products Manufacturers of Canada (April 7–9, 1975), p. 12.
5. David J. Luck and Arthur E. Prell, *Market Strategy* (New York: Appleton-Century-Crofts, 1968), p. 119.
6. Thayer C. Taylor, "Sales Cost and Profit Analysis," *Sales Management*, March 4, 1966, p. 55.
7. Kotler, 2d ed., p. 782.
8. Taylor, p. 53.
9. Robert B. Miner, "Distribution Costs," in Albert Wesley Frey, ed., *Marketing Handbook*, 2d ed., (New York: Ronald Press, 1965), pp. 23:2–3.
10. Thomas R. Wotruba, *Sales Management* (New York: Holt, Rinehart and Winston, 1971), p. 495.
11. Ibid., p. 500.
12. Ibid., p. 505.
13. Wilson, p. 82.
14. Kotler, 2d ed., p. 448.
15. Gumucio, p. 14.
16. Wilson, p. 104.

JOE SHORT PRODUCTIONS, INC.

Company Background

Joe Short Productions, Inc., is located in San Francisco. The firm began operations in 1968 under the leadership of film producer Joe Short. It has been basically a family enterprise. Ruth Short, Joe's wife, serves as bookkeeper and controller. Ike, their son, often acts as production manager.

Joe Short Productions has become well known for its award-winning documentary films on contemporary social problems. These films are mainly sold to government agencies, industry associations, and trade unions. Originally, the films were distributed by a publisher. But Short became dissatisfied with this and set up his own independent distributorship.

Joe Short Re-evaluates His Company

It was late Thursday evening, and Joe Short was tired after a draining business day. He decided to walk home, for the San Francisco hills were always a pleasurable experience for him. Short had just completed the final editing of a feature film on marijuana. With that project ready to sell, he knew it was time for a major re-evaluation of his company. Joe Short Productions seemed in need of a total marketing overhaul, and Short was honest enough to admit that he didn't have the skills necessary to conduct that evaluation.

But thinking things over was at least a first step. As he walked, he began formulating a mental balance sheet about the strengths and weaknesses of his company.

"Our financial situation is excellent. We have ample working capital. Our 1975 sales were $2.5 million—we returned 40 percent of the dollar on investments. That's a fine record. Yet I know that neither Ruth nor I has the best possible grasp of the firm's financial prospects. We've grown faster than we expected, and it's getting past the point where we know where we stand.

"All of our documentaries are sponsored on a contract basis before production begins. Government agencies account for about two-thirds of the films' sponsors; major corporations such as Time-Life and Gulf Oil take on the others. But we always retain the rights to our films so that we can rent or sell them to as many customers as possible.

"Our promotional work is limited. We do almost no advertising. Public relations is usually the result of the awards we've won in film festivals. Without these awards, we couldn't attract new sponsors. This is the cheapest possible way of promoting the firm, but it's also risky. If we go two years without winning any new awards, people might start to think that we're slipping.

"At present, we have three films in distribution, one film (on marijuana) all set to go, plus rights to twenty to thirty additional films. And we're close to final terms with Corporate Public Broadcasting (CPB) for an advance to produce five thirty-minute documentaries for their stations.

"I think it's fair to say that we're in a solid position as a producer of documentary films. But feature films is where I really want to go. The marijuana film is a real test case. It's 90 minutes long, our longest in a few years. If it sells, maybe we can really start branching out into features. If we focused too

607

much on features, our documentary production might suffer.

Joe Short was nearing his home. He stopped for a minute and finished his speech to himself "I know we have to stick with the documentaries. Our first priority has to be improving the distribution of our current documentaries, and producing new ones that are as good if not better.

"And I know that our distribution system is not all it could be. We need some real professionals to handle it. No one in the family knows *anything* about promotion. It's such a waste to produce a great documentary and then have it sit in the office because we can't promote it properly."

Questions
1. Design a complete marketing information system for Joe Short Productions, based on the on-going marketing decisions you feel should be made in the years ahead.
2. Describe those marketing research studies that will be needed to provide information for the strategic decisions you feel should be made in the next few months.

HOLLIS STORES

Hollis Stores is a chain of eight medium-sized discount department stores located throughout Vancouver, Canada. In mid-November, 1975, Hollis president C. H. Brodersen, Jr., assigned merchandising vice-president Gregory Geyer the responsibility for studying consumer attitudes toward Hollis stores.

Brodersen believed that Hollis' success resulted from its discount price policy and its good quality merchandise. But the concept of consumerism had grown in Canada over the past few years, and he decided to investigate consumer satisfactions and dissatisfactions.

Geyer, involved in planning for the Christmas shopping rush, passed the matter along to his chief assistant, Arne de Navacelle. Geyer relieved de Navacelle of all other duties for a three-month period, and told him his only job was to devise, supervise, and report on the Hollis attitude survey.

A Contest To "Serve You Better"

De Navacelle went right to work. Within one day, he had developed the idea for a "Serve You Better" contest during December. The attitude survey would take the form of a contest with prizes! To enter, the customer had to fill out a "Serve You Better" entry blank that included eight different areas of questions based on why he thought customers pick a store. Completed entry blanks would be placed in a bin, and drawings would be held on December 22nd.

De Navacelle presented Geyer with the questionnaire to be used on entry blanks. Geyer gave the plan a quick look and approved it. He noted de Navacelle's estimate that 200 customers per store—or a total sample of 1600 persons —would enter the contest. With Geyer's approval in hand, de Navacelle sent out a memorandum to the eight Hollis store managers, explaining that the contest would begin on December 1 and run until December 15.

ENTRY BLANK

HOLLIS "SERVE YOU BETTER" CONTEST

Our goal is to get your opinion on how to make Hollis a better place to shop. After all, who would know better than you—our customer?

Rules
1. Please fill in the form below completely. Be sure to include your name and address. **2.** Contest ends at store closing on December 15th. **3.** Winners will be picked at random at 8:30 PM on December 22nd at the Hollis Courtesy Desk. **4.** Winners will *not* have to be present at drawing in order to win. **5.** Not more than one prize will be awarded to a family. **6.** Employees and their families will not be eligible.

Name _____

Age: Circle one: 14 and under   15 and over

Address _____ **Phone No.** _____

Directions: Circle the description that best reflects your opinion.
1. How do our everyday prices compare overall?
usually lower/often lower/at times higher/often higher than competitors.
2. How often is Hollis out of advertised specials?
never/not usually/often/almost always
3. How are the values in Hollis circulars and newspaper ads?
always great/usually good/often not so good/rarely good
4. How knowledgeable is Hollis sales help?
know a lot about the merchandise/can answer most questions/adequate/know very little
5. How is the Hollis checkout procedure?
never a long wait/rarely a long wait/sometimes have to wait/usually a long wait
6. How is the Hollis merchandise selection?
always have/usually have/sometimes do not have/rarely have what I want
7. How courteous is Hollis sales help?
always very courteous/usually courteous/sometimes courteous/rarely courteous
8. How easy is it to find sales help when you need it?
always very easy/usually pretty easy/often not too easy/usually very difficult

Some Results of the Survey

On January 12, 1976, Gregory Geyer received a report from Arne de Navacelle describing the progress of the attitude study. While the results were not completed, the report did spell out some disappointing facts.

The total number of respondents for the study (in other words, contestants) was 1007. This was far below the 1600 projected by de Navacelle. Interestingly, the number of respondents varied greatly from store to store, from 41 at Store A to 233 at Store E.

Another disappointing result involved questionnaire completion. A total of 85 entries failed to answer *any* of the eight attitude questions, despite elaborate instructions that doing so could lead to disqualification in the contest. Another 173 entries answered fewer than eight questions.

Geyer was most disturbed at the figures in de Navacelle's report. Originally, they had hoped that 1600 Hollis consumers would answer all eight attitude questions on the survey. Instead, only 1007 people had entered the contest, and, of these, 258 had failed to answer all of the questions. As a result, *only* 749 Hollis customers completed the entire survey.

Questions

1. Describe the problems you see with the research design of the "Serve You Better" contest.
2. What specific criticisms do you have of the questionnaire?
3. Give your suggestions as to how this marketing research might be done again next time.

NATIONAL WIRE CORPORATION

In late 1975, the National Wire Corporation launched its Send-a-Gift subsidiary, boosting this new service as "the most successful innovation in retail merchandising since the introduction of the supermarket 40 years ago."

The basic appeal of Send-a-Gift was that a consumer could choose among eighteen gift item lines illustrated in National Wire ads. He or she could call a central toll-free number and have the gift wrapped and delivered almost immediately by one of 4,000 retailers across the country. The selection of gifts included blankets, golf balls, steak knives, electric fondue pots, sterling silver bowls and candlesticks, clock radios, and blenders.

One year later, however, Send-a-Gift had not fulfilled the lavish predictions of National Wire. The firm had projected sales of 1,000,000 units in the first year, but the actual figure was a paltry 92,000. This represented less than 10 percent of the sales estimate.

In September, 1976, *Advertising Age* reporter Della Pruitt interviewed J. Andrew Connolly, the president of Send-a-Gift. Pruitt hoped to find out why Send-a-Gift had had such a disappointing year.

One View of Send-a-Gift's Problems

"Mr. Connolly, a year ago some of your executives were boasting that Send-a-Gift might sell as many as 2,500,000 gift units in the first year. Your official projection was for 1,000,000 units. But you sold only 92,000. What happened?"

"Well, obviously we made some drastic mistakes. When you hit less than 10 percent of your projection, something is very, very wrong."

"I think a lot of the problem was with our ad agency, Ritter and Yano. Philosophically, they were not set up to handle the entire marketing structure."

"But, Mr. Connolly, talk around the industry suggests a very different story. The word is that you repeatedly overruled the advice of marketing professionals from R&Y; that the agency was dead set agaonst your airing national television commercials without pre-testing, but you went ahead anyway; that you were slow to follow R&Y's suggestion about direct mailing of brochures to credit card holders. . . ."

"I object to those statements, Ms. Pruitt. I'm not here to defend myself or Send-a-Gift or National Wire. It happens that we followed most of the advice that we received from Ritter and Yano, and that's *exactly* how we got into this mess. I'm happier with our new firm, Hartz Advertising.

"We thought there was a tremendous demand for this service. All of our work was tied to that basic assumption. Perhaps we were wrong, but I'm not convinced. One bad year doesn't prove that the whole idea was a mistake. It only proves that our execution was lousy.

"For example, we chose our product lines by surveying consumers. We asked them what gifts they had given to friends and relatives in the past year. From these responses, we selected the "average popular gift" of retail customers across the country. Now some merchandising experts who evaluated our first year sales say that the product line was too narrow and dull.

"We also got hung up with credit card problems. Our customers couldn't charge purchases on their phone bills, as they could with Mailgrams and

Candygrams. And we were only able to work out approval for one oil company card and some bank and entertainment/travel cards. As a result, our service was only convenient for roughly 30 million of the 50 million unduplicated credit card holders in the United States."

"I understand what you're getting at, Mr. Connolly," replied Della Pruitt. "But how do you plan to turn this situation around? Your firm has already taken some heavy losses on Send-a-Gift. What about the future?"

"I'm not at liberty to answer that question with specifics."

Questions
1. Identify any oversights in the planning and decision-making process regarding Send-a-Gift.
2. How was the Send-a-Gift marketing mix inadequately integrated?
3. If the planning lead-time and the first year of Send-a-Gift were to be done over, how would a PERT chart have helped?
4. What should Send-a-Gift's marketing strategy be next year?

FRAMEWOOD COMPANY

Steven Berman and Roger McMurray are the owners of the Los Angeles-based Framewood Company. The two men originally learned the skill of framemaking during their service as Peace Corps volunteers in a small Bolivian town in the early 1970s. Upon returning to the United States, they decided to continue working together as framemakers.

In February, 1976, Berman and McMurray decided that they needed some objective advice on their marketing operations. Each of the two men was a skilled craftsman, but neither had much of a head for business. As a result, they hired Kathy Zane of the management consulting firm of Roberts, Thayer, and Zane. Zane's job was to do a marketing audit for Framewood.

Two weeks later, Kathy Zane submitted her report (excerpts follow).

Basic Company Operations and Directions

Framewood concentrates its wholesale activities on high-quality "custom framework." New frames are constructed and fabricated, and existing frames are restored and repaired. Within these fields, the firm specializes on frames requiring gilding in gold or silver leaf, antique finishes, and specialized corner work. This is the kind of quality work in which the proprietors are most experienced. In addition, the firm accepts some retail business of routine framing in order to help its cash flow. . . .

The company is small and new; it has only been in business for three years, and registered sales of $146,000 in 1975; its cash flow is always low.

Primary Market Areas to Be Entered

These areas have been suggested to Framewood as marketing possibilities:

1. High quality retail frame shops in upper-income areas, particularly those engaged both in the sale of new frames *and* the repair and/or restoration of existing frames.

2. Museums, particularly small and medium-sized museums with no frame shops.

3. Art galleries, particularly those that deal with pretwentieth-century art employing ornate, traditional-style frames.

4. Those antique dealers actively engaged in the sale of traditional art work (framed).

5. Interior designers and decorators. The main concentration here should be on the residential and contract markets. However, few contacts have been made to those designer/decorators active in both fields.

One problem here has been the low prices of Framewood. Some customers have assumed that the quality must be inferior. The owners of Framewood have resisted raising prices because they want to charge "fair" prices for ethical reasons.

I believe that the primary focus of the firm should be on restoration and repair work rather than on the sale of newly constructed frames. The owners of Framewood do not agree with this suggestion, in part because they have hired some part-time workers to turn out ordinary frames.

Nevertheless, I feel that this concentration could initially help to differentiate Framewood from larger frame manufacturers in the eyes of customers. By proving their superior capabilities at restoration and repair work, the firm can build a solid base of support that will assist the sale of customized frames in succeeding years.

Summary of Information Gathered and Conclusions

A summary of the information contained in this report follows:

1. On Framewood as a supplier, the consensus of opinion among customers is:

workmanship is excellent;
frames are top quality;
owners are cooperative but unreliable in meeting delivery schedules;
prices are very competitive but strangely below the average.

One fairly typical remark was that "all Framewood has to do now is to let more people know about them."

2. Recommendations regarding sales materials and sales servicing for established accounts:

a. *Frame manufacturers*—a good set of molding samples with gold and silver leafing is required. . . .

b. *Retail frame shops*—Nothing else is needed or warranted other than a good set of actual molding samples in corner sections, in the different paint finishes available. . . .

c. *Art galleries*—a really good set of sample moldings in the different finishes available is mandatory. . . .

Questions

1. How close does Kathy Zane's report come to being a "marketing audit"?
2. What recommendations do you have concerning Framewood's marketing?

Broadened Marketing Perspectives

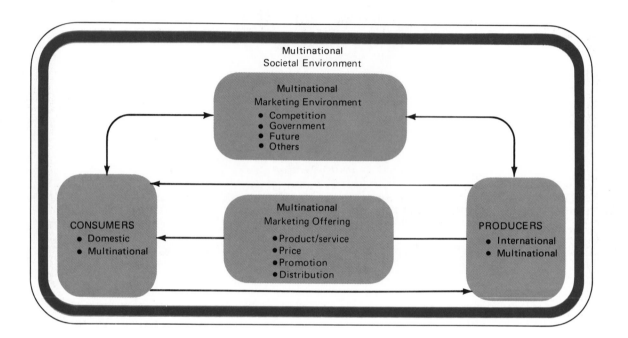

26

THE MULTINATIONAL MARKETPLACE

After completing this chapter, the reader should be able to:

1. Distinguish between the perspectives of domestic marketing and multinational marketing.

2. Explain why companies enter the multinational marketplace.

3. Compare the alternative company commitments available for multinational marketing.

4. Identify the decision-process stages and key environmental elements in evaluating multinational marketing opportunities.

5. Describe the alternative managerial arrangements available to organizations for multinational marketing.

6. Explain what considerations affect the planning of marketing strategies in multinational markets.

So far, our marketing story has been largely confined to the American scene. But there are many markets around the world in which foreign and American firms are operating. Let us now take a look at the multinational marketplace and how marketing is carried out in it.

IT'S THE REAL STRAWBERRY SOY MILK, ECUADOR

The Meals for Millions Foundation of Santa Monica, California, believes that poor people in the developing countries of the world need high-nutrition food products.[1] The Foundation has conducted a marketing research study to determine what types of soybean-based foods can be successfully marketed for young children in Ecuador.

As the Foundation soon discovered, it is not easy to conduct marketing research in a developing nation such as Ecuador. Phone and mail communications are poor, retailers uncooperative, and politicians suspicious. Moreover, census information is limited. But despite these difficulties, the Foundation was able to complete a number of surveys. The most important finding was that a strawberry-flavored soy milk product seemed most acceptable to local residents. The study also indicated that low-income consumers in Ecuador tend to buy food for young children on the basis of brand names and taste rather than quality and nutrition. They usually buy food at corner stores and open markets, rather than supermarkets.

The next step for the Foundation will be to convert these survey results into action. An enterprise will be formed to produce a strawberry-flavored soy milk product. Local citizens in Ecuador will be trained to operate production plants. A broad marketing campaign will be created to help promote the new product among the target population.

THE WONDERFUL WORLD OF MARKETING

The work of the Meals for Millions Foundation in Ecuador suggests the importance of marketing. Without sophisticated marketing research techniques, it would be impossible to develop a nutritional food product that could be successfully marketed to low-income consumers in Ecuador. A producer might introduce a food item that was inexpensive, highly nutritional, and yet totally unacceptable to the target market. If it were orange-flavored instead of strawberry, a soy flakes product instead of a soy milk product, or sold in supermarkets but not in corner stores, it might never reach poor families in Ecuador.

International or multinational marketing follows the same basic principles as domestic marketing. The problems faced by an American textile manufacturer who sells products throughout Europe are not so different from those of a textile manufacturer who operates in all 50 states of the Union. Each must tailor his or her marketing strategy to the particular environmental conditions

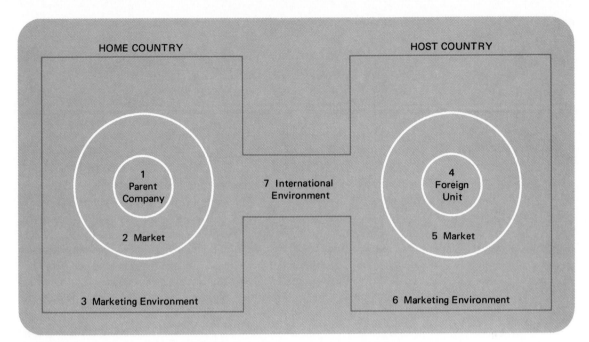

Figure 26-1
THE INTERNATIONAL
MARKETING MODEL

Adapted from H. B. Thorelli,
*International Marketing
Strategy* (Hammondsworth,
England: Penguin, 1973), p. 330.

of many diverse markets. The only fundamental difference is that the marketing environment varies more widely from nation to nation than from state to state.

In this chapter, when we speak of **multinational marketing**, we include both the activities of U.S.-based firms and foreign-based firms (British, Dutch, Japanese, Canadian, and so forth) in many parts of the world, including the United States. In most cases however, we will concentrate on the foreign activities of U.S.-based firms.

Figure 26-1 illustrates the complex environment in which multinational marketing takes place. The international marketer must take into account the local marketing environment at home, the marketing environment in each host country, and the overall international environment.

Let's take a look at the key elements in the international marketing model illustrated in Figure 26-1:

The parent company. International marketing management must not limit its activities to selling a product in different parts of the world. It must also coordinate international marketing activities and provide local personnel in the host country with a marketing orientation. On a broader level, it must integrate the organization's marketing strategy into the international environment.

Home country marketing environment. This is another factor that constantly changes. For example, the United States Congress voted in 1975 to tighten tax regulations on foreign income. One result may be to restrict the activities of foreign multinational firms within the United States.

Foreign unit. As noted above, a significant degree of local autonomy is desirable in multinational marketing. This may create certain problems, however, since management in foreign countries may be unfamiliar with American budget and control systems. Also, marketing information for successful planning is usually harder to obtain in foreign markets than in the United States.

Host country marketing environment. The important factors in the marketing environment of the host countries are climate, distance and communications, and differences in business and social customs. Language barriers and variations in market structure must also be taken into account, along with the stage of economic growth that has been reached.

International environment. There are many basic factors in the overall multinational marketing environment. Among these are political arrangements, relations between home and host countries, tariff policies and nontariff barriers, and national monetary systems and currency controls. Transportation costs of international commerce and differing business standards around the world (such as systems of measurement) are also important.

In view of all these factors, we might well ask why an organization makes the decision to go multinational. Philip Kotler has noted two common patterns.[2] In the first, a company is pushed into multinational operations by difficulties in the home market. These difficulties might include a domestic profit squeeze, declining returns on investment, stiff competition, or unused production capacity. In the second pattern the company is pulled into multinational operations by desirable conditions in other countries. A rising gross national product (GNP) and the absence of competition are common lures.

The "pulling" power of international marketing can be seen in the growth of Levi Strauss International.[3] In 1962, just before the boom in bluejeans around the world, sales of Levi's outside the United States accounted for about $2 million. By 1973, this figure had made an astronomical rise to $228 million. Such prospects lure other American firms into multinational operations.

MARKETING COMMITMENTS ABROAD

More and more, business firms are operating on a global scale rather than confining their activities to one nation. This change has forced a rethinking of marketing goals, strategy, and organization.

MARKETING ORIENTATION

Figure 26-2 illustrates five common approaches to international marketing. Many firms have changed from one orientation to another over time. Some, however, operate under two or more of these orientations at any one time. Each orientation suggests particular organizational goals and leads to related marketing strategies.

1. *Domestic-only orientation.* Some firms have no interest in foreign sales. The domestic market satisfies their needs and foreign operations are seen as complicated and risky.

2. *Home-country orientation.* Some firms view foreign operations as clearly secondary to business activity in the home country—overseas sales are an aid in distributing surplus goods. An organization with this orientation generally exports its products to foreign nations that are most like the home country. It will not conduct extensive marketing research or promotional ac-

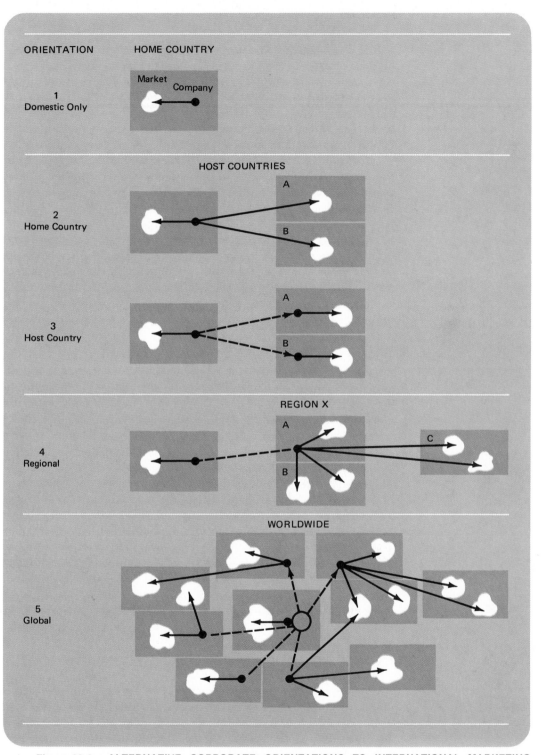

ORIENTATION   HOME COUNTRY

1
Domestic Only

Market
Company

HOST COUNTRIES

2
Home Country

A

B

3
Host Country

A

B

REGION X

4
Regional

A

B

C

WORLDWIDE

5
Global

Figure 26-2   ALTERNATIVE CORPORATE ORIENTATIONS TO INTERNATIONAL MARKETING

Based on Yoram Wind Susan P. Douglas, and Howard V. Perlmutter, "Guidelines for Developing International Marketing Strategies," *Journal of Marketing* 37 (April 1973): 14–23. Published by American Marketing Association.

tivities in its international markets. Nor will it invest in costly product modifications in order to meet the specific needs of foreign consumers.

3. *Host-country orientation.* Some firms establish subsidiaries in each overseas market; these subsidiaries are generally managed by local nationals. Marketing activities are planned and administered on a country-by-country basis. The crucial considerations in planning strategy are the legal and environmental conditions in each nation.

4. *Regional orientation.* Certain firms find that the host-country orientation leads to many problems with coordination and control. As a result, they gear operations to a regional orientation. This allows for more economical and systematic planning and administration. It also offers the opportunity to pursue market segments that cross national boundaries.

5. *Global orientation.* A firm may choose to see the entire world as its "marketing region" and to pursue global market segments. There are severe problems, however, associated with this approach. National differences in laws and currencies make global marketing strategy a difficult undertaking. The worldwide orientation appears more useful for production and research development than it is for marketing activity.

MULTINATIONAL MARKETING MANAGEMENT

A **multinational corporation** has been defined as "an enterprise which allocates company resources without regard to national frontiers, but is nationally based in terms of ownership and top management."[4] This definition distinguishes the multinational corporation from the **transnational** corporation (which is owned and managed by persons of more than one nationality) and the **supernational** corporation (a transnational corporation that has been legally denationalized by incorporating through an international agency).

American-based multinational corporations tend to dominate in Latin American countries. In other parts of the world, multinational corporations from Great Britain, France, and the Netherlands have established themselves, often continuing in patterns that date back to earlier periods of colonialism. The most recent entries into the multinational field are Japanese firms, which have expanded into many lesser developed countries such as Brazil and Indonesia. Table 26-1 lists the world's ten largest multinational corporations. (As you can see, six of the ten are based in the United States.) The foreign sales of these corporations range from 19 percent (General Motors) to 88 percent (British Petroleum) of total sales. The number of subsidiaries each has in foreign countries ranges from 21 (General Motors) to 62 (Mobil Oil).[5]

Social responsibility has become a controversial issue in multinational marketing in recent years. Many nations have few effective legal restraints on advertising, packaging, product quality, credit terms, and after-sale service. Critics of multinational corporations charge that many firms take advantage of this opening to manipulate uneducated consumers in developing nations.

In the mid-1970s, several American multinational firms admitted paying large bribes to foreign officials in connection with their marketing activities. These bribes are a common feature of the business practices of a good many

Table 26-1 THE TOP TEN MULTINATIONAL COMPANIES		($ BILLIONS)	
COMPANY	HEADQUARTERS	TOTAL SALES	TOTAL NET INCOME
Exxon	New York	$44.9	$ 2.50
General Motors	Detroit	35.7	1.25
Royal Dutch/Shell Group	London/The Hague	32.1	2.11
Texaco	New York	24.5	.83
Ford Motor	Dearborn, Mich.	24.0	.32
Mobil Oil	New York	20.6	.81
National Iranian Oil	Teheran	18.9	16.95
British Petroleum	London	17.3	.37
Standard Oil of California	San Francisco	16.8	.77
Unilever	London	15.0	.32

nations. But they violate the American sense of ethics, not to mention a few federal laws. The concern here seems to center on the immense power (and money) these firms possess as well as the question of to whom they are accountable. As one observer has maintained, "Our tax laws, labor laws, disclosure requirements, and antitrust laws are hopelessly obsolete in dealing with a corporate entity which makes its home everywhere and nowhere."[6]

WORLDWIDE MARKETING OPPORTUNITIES

In evaluating worldwide marketing opportunities, a firm must be flexible and open to new strategies and innovations. Any proposal to begin operations in other countries must be evaluated on the basis of potential returns on investment and risks.

SELECTING THE MARKETS The first crucial question that a firm faces in entering the international market is: "Where can we sell our products?" Local governments and international associations publish valuable population statistics, which assist firms in pinpointing market segments. Unfortunately for most multinational marketers, market share information is relatively difficult to find.

In general, the marketing manager starts off with little firsthand knowledge of the marketing opportunities in a foreign country. But the basic tools of marketing analysis are the same for foreign markets as for the domestic market. Figure 26-3 summarizes the five-step process by which managers evaluate multinational marketing opportunities.

1. *Environmental analysis.* This includes studying economic, political, and social conditions in the target country. It is most important that marketers understand the rate of cultural change of the host country.

2. *Market potential.* Here the marketer begins by evaluating the current

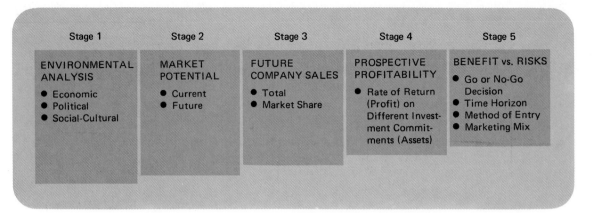

Stage 1	Stage 2	Stage 3	Stage 4	Stage 5
ENVIRONMENTAL ANALYSIS	MARKET POTENTIAL	FUTURE COMPANY SALES	PROSPECTIVE PROFITABILITY	BENEFIT vs. RISKS
● Economic ● Political ● Social-Cultural	● Current ● Future	● Total ● Market Share	● Rate of Return (Profit) on Different Investment Commitments (Assets)	● Go or No-Go Decision ● Time Horizon ● Method of Entry ● Marketing Mix

Figure 26-3   STAGES FOR EVALUATING MULTINATIONAL MARKETING OPPORTUNITIES

Based on David S. R. Leighton, *International Marketing: Test and Cases* (New York: McGraw-Hill, 1966), pp. 22–27.

size and nature of the market. If accurate production and sales figures are not available, the firm will turn to its own marketing research to develop the necessary data. Once marketers understand the dimensions of the current market, they can forecast future market trends (such as industrywide sales) over a five- or ten-year period.

3. *Future sales.* What percentage of all industrywide sales can the individual organization expect to capture? To answer this question, the firm must conduct some kind of market analysis of its industrywide projections. The crucial factors here are competition (the size, market share, facilities, and financial resources of major rivals) and the strengths and weaknesses of the firm (how it measures up to the competition). Careful evaluation should produce a reasonably accurate estimate of the anticipated market share and sales volume.

4. *Prospective profitability.* When this estimate is completed, the firm must weigh the possible profits of entering the multinational market. Involved in this evaluation is a forecast of the necessary capital, facilities, and personnel. The firm must also analyze the desirability of entering foreign markets through an export approach, a joint venture, or direct operation.

5. *Benefits vs. risks.* The last stage in the evaluation process is often the most difficult, for there are no simple mathematical tools to guide marketers in weighing the risks of international business. Predicting economic trends is no simple matter, but the political risks of multinational investment can be even more serious than the economic uncertainties. Decisions are also made in this stage as to the time period covered by the entry plan, the organizational method of entry, and the initial marketing mix.

ENVIRONMENTAL ANALYSIS

Environmental information is often understood intuitively by managers and planners in domestic markets. But in multinational marketing, environmental information must be carefully defined, gathered, and absorbed. There may actually be a hidden benefit to unfamiliarity with the local conditions—the outsider may spot a marketing opportunity that the familiar insider overlooked.

ECONOMIC DIMENSIONS

A firm must gauge the size of potential markets in order to develop needed business projections. Population is therefore a crucial factor. But raw population data are not the only concern of marketers. Population shifts, changes in size of age groups or families, and changes in the structure of the work force are also crucial.

Gross national product is also an important consideration. Figure 26-4 illustrates the estimated growth in per capita gross national product of various nations from 1965 to 1985. The slope of the line between the three yearly points plotted for each nation suggests the percentage growth in GNP per year.

Another key economic dimension is the degree of development and competition in a country. In industrialized nations (such as the United States, Canada, West Germany, Japan), a multinational marketer faces competition from local producers and also from other multinationals. These nations are typically contrasted with other countries labeled "underdeveloped," "less developed," "developing," or "Third World."

In general, the marketplaces of developing countries are less competitive than those of industrialized nations. Local manufacturers are generally not well established, thus allowing an opportunity for extensive penetration by multinational companies.

Income is also an important economic dimension in multinational marketing. When people have little to spend, marketers must compete feverishly for sales. This problem is most significant for multinational marketing, since in many parts of the world only upper-class citizens can afford to buy more than the bare necessities in goods and services.

POLITICAL DIMENSIONS

The attitudes of host countries toward foreign companies varies from place to place. The Belgians have been accepting of multinational investors, the Japanese suspicious, and the French hostile. In any multinational marketing opportunity, the marketer must examine the likely reactions of the citizens and government of each host country. Of particular concern is government policy on the substitution of goods produced by local industries for import goods, incentives for new business development, and taxation.

The flow of business across national boundaries is affected by a number of common control mechanisms. The character and use of each depends on the particular nation and government involved. These controls include tariffs, quotas, licenses, and import taxes.

Tariffs may be levied either on the physical quantity of goods being transported or on the total value of the shipment. Many nations maintain tariffs on both imports and exports.

Quotas are imposed when a government wishes to set absolute limits on imports and exports of a product. They are especially popular in regulating the import or export of agricultural goods.

Licenses are still another means of regulating international trade. In some

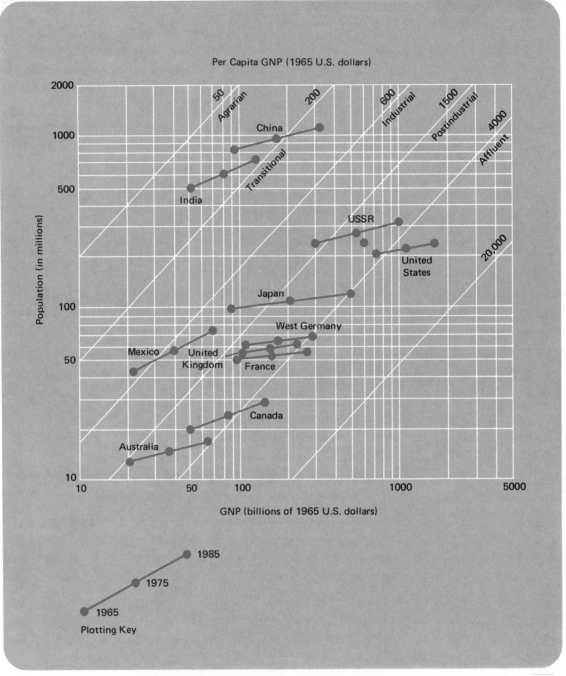

Per Capita GNP (1965 U.S. dollars)

Figure 26-4   PER CAPITA GNP GROWTH, 1965–1975–1985

From J. E. Steiner, "Commercial Air Transport Development Considerations," Boeing Company Report, January 1973, p. 2.

cases, an exporter may want proof that an importer has the required licenses before making a final commitment on a deal.

Legal problems often develop in conducting international business. As one American marketing executive has explained:

Our law is based on the Anglo-Saxon. U.S. contracts tie everything down. Some countries have purposely ambiguous laws, meant to be interpreted by government officials. In a lot of those places they're offended by U.S. business methods. They think we just don't trust them.... They can't understand why we want everything spelled out.[7]

It is interesting to contrast American marketing patterns with those of socialist nations. In the People's Republic of China, foreign trade is a state monopoly under the direction of the Ministry of Foreign Trade. A number of government-run foreign trade corporations conduct business in accordance with overall economic planning.

SOCIAL AND CULTURAL DIMENSIONS

Religions, family systems, educational systems, and social systems are all part of the social and cultural dimension of multinational marketing. The influence of these factors is as diverse as the many peoples and nationalities of the world.

National character is a general term used to describe the style of life and thought of a group of people. While the concept is somewhat vague and ab-

---

THE SUPRANATIONAL GOVERNMENTS

The European Economic Community (EEC, or "Common Market") is the best known supranational economic organization. The EEC nations have adopted common standards on food additives, labeling requirements, and packaging sizes. Tariffs have been lowered and it has become less difficult to transport goods across national boundaries.

Latin America has three important supranational organizations. The Central American Common Market (CACM) was created in 1961 by Costa Rica, El Salvador, Guatemala, Honduras, and Nicaragua to promote economic integration and attract foreign investment.

The Latin American Free Trade Association (LAFTA) was established in 1961 by eleven Latin American nations. Its primary objective has been to formulate a treaty to reduce tariffs between member nations. However, the deadline for the treaty has been delayed from 1973 to 1980.

In 1967 six members of LAFTA (Bolivia, Chile, Colombia, Ecuador, Peru, and Venezuela) united to form the Andean Common Market (AnCom). The main goals of AnCom include joint planning of industrial development and the creation of multinational enterprises.

The socialist nations of Bulgaria, Czechoslovakia, the German Democratic Republic, Hungary, Poland, and Romania belong to the Council for Mutual Economic Assistance (CMEA). Roughly 60 percent of the total international trade of socialist countries takes place within the CMEA framework. American multinational corporations have entered socialist markets by participating in long-term agreements with CMEA.

Based on Arthur F. Woelfle, "Marketing in Western Europe" (Chicago: International Trade Club of Chicago, 1975), p. 55; O. B. Parrish, "Marketing in Latin America" (Chicago: International Trade Club of Chicago, 1975), p. 61; and G. Peter Lauter and Paul M. Dickie, "Multinational Corporations in Eastern European Socialist Economies," *Journal of Marketing* 39 (October 1975): 42.

stract, it can nevertheless be useful to marketers in understanding the feelings and attitudes of a market segment. Generalizations about national character can be especially helpful in preparing advertising campaigns.

The status of women is an important cultural dimension in multinational marketing. Women still face legal discrimination and subordination to men in most societies in the world. Many cultures maintain a rigid division of labor between women and men. Marketers need to understand the social roles for each sex in a potential host country in order to develop marketing strategy.

Differences in social and cultural traditions lead to significant variations in market behavior. For example, 93 percent of Swedes eat crackers, while only 3 percent of French people do so. Yogurt can be found in 50 percent of Dutch homes, but in less than 5 percent of Portuguese homes.

In studying such national patterns, marketers place particular emphasis on how purchases are made by a family, in order to focus their promotion on the person or persons most likely to influence purchase decisions. Does the family shop together and come to a joint decision? Is mass-media influence a critical factor in the decision-making process? Are the views of local opinion leaders (clergy, politicians, influential citizens) important? (These same considerations were considered in Chapters 8 and 9).

MARKETING RESEARCH "OVER THERE"

As we saw at the beginning of the chapter, market research is a difficult undertaking in many foreign nations. For example, only 3 percent of the people of Ceylon have telephones. At least fourteen different languages are spoken in India. Census data and area maps are not available in many countries. And many citizens in other parts of the world will not cooperate with a strange interviewer who comes to the door.

We often think of the problems of conducting marketing research in the developing agricultural nations of the world. But even in the industrial countries of Western Europe the job is not easy. For example, telephone sampling, which is popular in the United States, may not be reliable in Great Britain, West Germany, France, or Italy, since so few residents have telephones.

As a result of these limitations, there are three principal methods of obtaining information on overseas markets:[8]

1. collecting and analyzing published data;

2. interviewing knowledgeable individuals within the home country;

3. sending representatives to the overseas nations for personal inspection and research.

The importance of reliable marketing research has been underscored in the last decade by the worldwide phenomenon of inflation. This inflation has led to an increase in the risks of international forecasting. In Great Britain, the price of bacon jumped by 80 percent in less than three years; it is now a luxury item for most English people. The demand for automobiles and air conditioners in India has fallen sharply due to inflation. When prices rise so rapidly, it is more difficult than ever to develop accurate projections about international business prospects.

MULTINATIONAL MARKETING OPERATIONS

When an organization expands from purely domestic to multinational operations, it must decide on the type of organizational arrangements that will link headquarters to foreign markets. The major alternatives include exporting, joint ventures, and direct investment. These alternatives parallel the marketing orientations of companies that were described on pp. 618–20.

One of the most critical problem areas in the expansion into multinational marketing is ownership-control. Figure 26-5 shows various alternatives in the degree of control of international marketing maintained by the home country corporation. Most American firms prefer the first two forms of organization shown, which allow for the strongest central control. In some cases, however, a firm will sacrifice the goal of management control when it conflicts with the opportunity for maximum profit. For example, an American company with limited sales volume or capital may choose to develop cooperative marketing arrangements with local African companies, rather than building its own marketing divisions all over Africa.

EXPORTING

A company may become involved in international business simply by agreeing to sell some of its products to foreign markets. This is known as **exporting**. The company does not invest in overseas production plants and generally makes few changes in its product.

There are two principal types of exporting arrangements. A company may hire an independent intermediary to take responsibility for foreign sales. This reduces the company's investments and risks. Or the company may eliminate the intermediary and negotiate directly with foreign buyers. This leads to greater investments and risks, but also greater potential returns.

JOINT VENTURES

One alternative to exporting is to establish some form of **joint venture** with companies in a foreign nation. There may be production and marketing facilities in both the host country and the home country. The joint venture may take the form of licensing, contracting, or joint ownership.

Licensing

In a **licensing** arrangement, the company offers the licensee the right to use a manufacturing process, trademark, patent, or trade secret in exchange for a fee or royalty. For example, Continental Can Company has licensees in 133 nations of the world, including West Germany, the Netherlands, and Poland.

Some companies, such as Westinghouse, have relied on licensing because they feel it reduces the risks and investments of multinational marketing. However, this view is becoming less popular among major marketers.[9] Many firms believe that they stand to lose substantial income if their licensees are incompetent. As a result, they have turned to other marketing arrangements that allow for more direct central control.

Contracting

A firm may not wish to license other companies to produce and market its products. Instead, it may **contract** with local manufacturers for production,

Figure 26-5 ORGANIZATION FOR INTERNATIONAL MARKETING

Adapted from John Fayerweather, *International Marketing*, 2d ed. (Englewood Cliffs, N.J.: Prentice-Hall, 1970), p. 105.

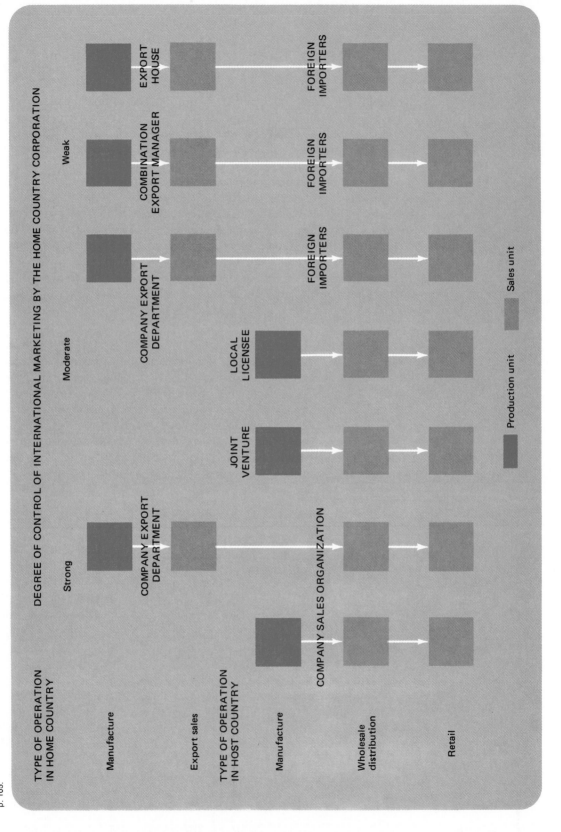

while retaining the responsibility for marketing. Or it may supply marketing and management services to a foreign firm. In other words, it sells its management know-how rather than an actual product.

Joint Ownership

Joint ownership resembles licensing in that both involve foreign production. But, in a joint ownership arrangement, local and foreign investors share ownership and control of the marketing firm. For example, Mitsubishi, the largest foreign trader in Japan, has entered into joint ownership arrangements with Kentucky Fried Chicken and Shakey's Pizza.

American multinational corporations are often forced into joint ownership arrangements because of political pressures from foreign businesses or governments.[10] Local capitalists want to profit from American technological expertise rather than compete against powerful multinationals. In addition, there is a strong nationalistic sentiment in many foreign nations against American dominance of local economies. Most American companies prefer to avoid joint ownership relationships, especially when they can hold only a minority interest (less than 50 percent) in the firm. But, in order to reach certain international markets, there may be no other choice.

DIRECT INVESTMENTS

In the past decade, American business has turned to **direct investment**—rather than exporting and licensing—as the most desirable means of entering foreign markets. One 1975 estimate pinpointed American investment abroad at $110 billion (compared with $22 billion of foreign investment within the United States).[11]

By making a company the sole owner of facilities in a foreign country, direct investment allows for complete control of all production and marketing decisions. Some decentralized decision making is commonly allowed, but international marketing executives in the central office retain final responsibility for planning strategy.

MULTINATIONAL MARKETING STRATEGY

The development of a strategic marketing view for multinational operations is a critical business goal. As one analyst has observed, "The overriding talent which I would wish on all is the managerial ability to visualize our products overseas in marketing terms. But this quality of marketing-mindedness is all too rare around the world."[12]

ADAPTING THE MARKETING MIX

When a corporation expands into overseas operations, it must determine if its domestic marketing mix can be adapted to foreign markets. Of course, as John Fayerweather has pointed out, "There is nothing absolute or sacred about a particular marketing mix. . . . Goods may well be sold by one combination of efforts in one market area and a second combination in another."[13]

Standardization is a key issue in adapting a marketing mix to foreign operations. Some marketing specialists have stressed the differences between foreign markets and have argued for differentiation in multinational marketing efforts. An international manager for Levi Strauss has explained, "Today, there are great differences between what sells in Sweden and what sells in Italy and sometimes there are real differences even within national borders."[14]

On the other hand, standardization has at least three distinct advantages:

1. the costs of product design, packaging, advertising, and other marketing elements can be reduced;

2. a solid international image can be promoted through worldwide advertising media;

3. the firm can gear some of its efforts toward the growing number of international travellers and tourists.

The growth of standardized marketing practices in the multinational arena has been documented in a study made in 1975.[15] The researchers surveyed roughly 100 executives from 27 multinational firms engaged in packaged goods marketing. The European and American operations of these firms formed the sample. Among the high standardization areas reflected in the study were brand names, physical characteristics of products, packaging, basic advertising message, and distribution channels. An overall 63 percent of the rating fell into the "high standardization" category. The study also singled out planning systems as a key area for standardization.

PRODUCT STRATEGY When a firm shifts from domestic to multinational marketing, it may need to alter basic product characteristics. These changes may be minor in nature (adding a protective coating for equipment needed in the tropics), or more fundamental (removing extra features from a tractor so that more farmers in Turkey can afford it).

Figure 26-6 identifies five product strategy alternatives that are available to international marketing planners:

1. *Standard strategy,* or *product extension.* This is the easiest and often the most profitable option. When customer need and use conditions are the same around the world for the product, the marketer can sell a standardized product with standardized promotional messages.

2. *Communication redesign.* This strategy is appropriate when use conditions are identical to those in the domestic market, but the product serves a different function overseas. An example is the bicycle, which is mainly used for recreation in the United States, but provides basic transportation in many nations of the world. The marketer will maintain a standardized product, but will adjust all marketing communications to local needs and customs.

3. *Product redesign.* This strategy is used by marketers when a product fills the same need around the world but use conditions vary. The marketer will maintain the standard promotional appeal, but will vary the product to local use conditions. For example, Exxon made certain alterations in its gasoline to suit weather conditions in foreign markets, but relied in all cases on its standard message, "Put a Tiger in Your Tank" (translated into the appropriate language).

4. *Dual adaptation.* Dual adaptation strategy represents both communi-

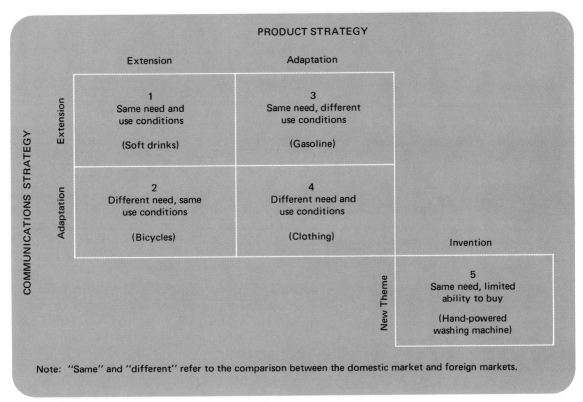

PRODUCT STRATEGY

	Extension	Adaptation
Extension	1 Same need and use conditions (Soft drinks)	3 Same need, different use conditions (Gasoline)
Adaptation	2 Different need, same use conditions (Bicycles)	4 Different need and use conditions (Clothing)

COMMUNICATIONS STRATEGY

Invention

New Theme

5
Same need, limited
ability to buy

(Hand-powered
washing machine)

Note: "Same" and "different" refer to the comparison between the domestic market and foreign markets.

Figure 26-6
**MULTINATIONAL
PRODUCT
COMMUNICATION MIX**

Based on Warren J. Keegan,
"Multinational Product Planning:
Strategic Alternatives," *Journal
of Marketing* 33 (January 1969):
59.

cations and product redesign. It is applied when a marketer wants to reach overseas markets in which both environmental use conditions and basic product functions differ from the home country. An example is clothing. The marketer must alter both the product characteristics and the standard marketing appeal.

5. *Product invention.* The first four strategies depend on the ability of the overseas consumer to buy the firm's product. But if target market segments cannot afford the price, the company must invent a new, cheaper product to fill the need. The marketing theme must also be changed to fit the new product. The hand-powered washing machine is an example of a product that was "invented" for this reason.

PRICE STRATEGY What price should be charged for a product when it is sold in international markets? Three guidelines have been suggested:

1. periodic review of prices;
2. setting of prices on a one-country basis;
3. consideration of price discounts.[16]

One study of multinational marketing executives found that 45 percent considered pricing to be a most important marketing strategy factor.[17] Among price-setting considerations, production costs and the prices set by multina-

631

tional competitors were ranked as most influential. The prices of local firms in the host country scored third among price considerations, and consumer demand was ranked fourth.

Marketers may not have absolute (or even *any*) freedom to set prices abroad. Some governments in developing countries legislate low retail prices in order to promote a higher standard of living, especially on necessities such as food.

Dumping of products is a common practice in international marketing. A manufacturer of television sets may have an oversupply of last year's models in its warehouses. It dumps these goods by selling them at a lower price than consumers in its domestic market are being charged. This practice has become unpopular in many nations, and import duties may be raised when there is a suspicion of dumping.

PROMOTION STRATEGY

The ideal promotion mix for a foreign nation depends on the characteristics of the society. For example, Nigeria has a low literacy level and there are few important print media. Only 14,000 Nigerian homes own television sets. But there are 1.5 million radios in use in the country, and motion picture advertising reaches 5 million Nigerians each year.

As we can see from the Nigerian example, the use of advertising abroad is determined mainly by the importance of various communications media. French people listen to the radio three times as much as West Germans. Twice as many Germans read daily newspapers as Italians.

Occasionally, an advertising theme or slogan can be "translated" for foreign appeal. In 1974 Chevrolet initiated a successful new campaign in the United States around the theme, "Baseball, hotdogs, apple pie, and Chevrolet." This led General Motors Holden of Australia to introduce the theme, "We love football, meat pies, kangaroos, and Holden cars." But some slogans can lose a lot in the translation process. In Japan, the General Motors slogan "Body by Fisher" becomes "Corpse by Fisher."

In order to be effective, international advertisers should follow three important guidelines:[18]

1. Make the message meaningful to people in terms of their day-to-day lives. Don't center a theme around automobiles if they are virtually unknown to most citizens in a rural country.

2. Strike a responsive chord. Use images or comparisons that reflect the feelings of the target audience.

3. Do not offend. Understand the sensitive points and biases of the people of the country, and stay away from dangerous themes.

Marketing management faces several key issues in designing strategy for personal selling in foreign markets. These include design of sales territories, control systems for field salespeople, and type of compensation to be paid.

Displays are a popular means of sales promotion in multinational operations. Wording and layout arrangements are selected with local conditions and cultural norms in mind.

DISTRIBUTION STRATEGY

Before making decisions about distribution strategy, a multinational marketer must first gather as much information as possible about the available alternatives. Ultimately, the complexity of the selling job is a key factor in all distribution decisions. If servicing the product is likely to be frequent and difficult, the marketer may find it necessary to perform the distribution task directly rather than relying on a local intermediary.

There are three main channels of distribution for international marketing:[19]

1. representatives of foreign firms;

2. resident buyers within the United States who work for foreign firms or governments;

3. intermediaries, such as export commission houses, export merchants, export agents, export brokers, and export managers.

A company may choose different distribution channels for each nation it views as a market. For example, Del Monte relies on distributors to handle its operations in Holland, West Germany, Austria, Sweden, Spain, and France. Food brokers are responsible for the sale of Del Monte products in Norway and a number of Mideast states. In Switzerland, Del Monte products are sold exclusively through a powerful supermarket chain known as the Federation of Migros Cooperatives.

Physical distribution systems vary greatly in different nations. Centralized warehousing has become the dominant approach to food distribution in the United States, the Netherlands, Switzerland, West Germany, and the Scandinavian nations. Large central warehouses are run by retail food chains. But, in France, small wholesalers are more important, and in Italy food retailers are licensed by location.

THE MULTINATIONAL FUTURE FOR MARKETING

Although rapid change and shifting conditions in the multinational marketplace make prediction a risky undertaking, the following trends seem likely:

1. *Economic environment.* Shortages will persist through the end of the 1970s. Export managers will be competing with domestic divisions for output.

2. *Government influence.* Multinational marketers will be under increasing political pressures. Decisions about production, expansion, and allocation of profits will be deeply affected by political and social forces. The days of the "free hand" for American multinational corporations in many part of the world are coming to an end.

3. *Third World development.* The trend toward economic nationalism among Third World nations will continue to grow. This will conflict with the desire of multinational corporations to expand operations in Third World nations in order to obtain raw materials and reach new markets.

4. *Growth of multinational corporations.* Multinational corporations have become a fixture in the business world. Despite political opposition and legislative restrictions, it seems inevitable that they will continue to grow and multiply.

CONCLUSION

Multinational marketing works on the same basic principles as domestic marketing, except that the environment itself is different. Overseas marketing involves interaction among the parent company, home country marketing environment, foreign unit, host country market and marketing environment, and international environment.

There are five basic marketing orientations among international marketers. A company may have a domestic orientation, home-country orientation, host-country orientation, regional orientation, or global orientation. The multinational corporation can be defined as an enterprise that operates internationally yet is nationally based in terms of ownership and executive management.

When a firm decides to "go international," several decisions must be made. It must choose the specific nations that provide solid marketing opportunities. Then it must arrange its entry method. The major entry forms include exporting, licensing, joint ownership, and direct investment. Finally, a marketing mix must be tailored to each foreign market. In many cases, standardized elements of the marketing mix may be used in different countries.

DISCUSSION QUESTIONS

1. NCR Corporation is seeking to market its Century 300 computers to Spain's nationwide system of 87 thrift institutions with 6,000 branch offices. What should NCR be aware of concerning this marketing operation in contrast to its U.S. operation?

2. One study found that small American manufacturers believe they can perform successfully either in the domestic or foreign market, but not both. Therefore, they feel that greater involvement in marketing abroad would mean a loss of marketing activity at home. How would you convince these producers to market internationally?

3. Euromedico, Paris has signed up 60 French hospital-equipment companies for exclusive sales rights in developing countries. In these countries "turnkey" hospitals order a package deal on all equipment. Also competing in this potentially vast market is the leading supplier, Hospitalia of Frankfurt. A major U.S. hospital equipment firm withdrew from this market, stating, "Constant delays from bureaucracies and contractors in developing countries left our equipment rotting in overseas warehouses and our technical personnel running in circles." If the European-based firms are prospering in this lucrative market, why aren't the American? What would you recommend?

4. What is your estimate on how well these products would do in these countries:
   a. blue jeans in Vietnam;
   b. cosmetics in Libya;
   c. instant coffee in Japan;
   d. private aircraft in Saudi Arabia.

5. Two Mexican executives from different American-owned multinational

corporations were overheard in a Monterrey hotel lobby discussing Mexican subsidiary and U.S. headquarters relationships. One executive commented on the procedures used by the many experts at the Chicago-based headquarters to approve nearly all marketing decisions made in the subsidiary. The other executive replied that the Houston-based headquarters lets the subsidiary run practically every aspect of marketing as long as profit objectives are reached. Which managerial strategy makes more sense for the multinational corporation as a whole?

6. A British marketing executive once said, "Ninety percent of the commercially successful new products in Europe were first developed in the U.S. So were 90 percent of the failures." What guidelines would you recommend to a multinational corporation considering marketing its products abroad?

7. It has been claimed that because multinational corporations are bound everywhere by national restraints, they fall short of their full productive potential. Is this situation more positive or more negative for consumers in these nations?

NOTES

1. Robert V. Caruso, "Marketing Research Aids Development of Strawberry Soy Milk to Help Feed Ecuador's Poor . . . at a Profit," *Marketing News*, December 5, 1975, p. 8.

2. Philip Kotler, *Marketing Management: Analysis, Planning, and Control*, 3d ed. (Englewood Cliffs, N.J.: Prentice-Hall, 1976), pp. 467–68.

3. "Levi Strauss International," *Saddleman's Review* 19 (Spring 1975): 3.

4. Donald S. Henley, "Multinational Marketing: Present Position and Future Challenges," *1972 Combined Proceedings* (Chicago: American Marketing Association, 1973), p. 42.

5. "The U.N. Sizes Up the Global Giants," *Business Week*, August 18, 1973, p. 26.

6. Richard J. Barnet, "Not Just Your Corner Drugstore," *New York Times*, June 19, 1975, p. 35.

7. "Levi Strauss International," p. 5.

8. Edward M. Mazze, *International Marketing Administration* (San Francisco: Chandler, 1967), pp. 59–60.

9. John Fayerweather, *International Marketing*, 2d ed. (Englewood Cliffs, N.J.: Prentice-Hall, 1970), p. 104.

10. Ibid., pp. 106–07.

11. Lindley H. Clark, Jr., "Multinational Firms, Under Fire All Over, Face a Changed Future," *Wall Street Journal*, December 3, 1975, p. 24.

12. E. J. Enright, "Modern Concepts of Marketing for International Success," *1969 June Conference Proceedings* (Chicago: American Marketing Association, 1970), p. 68.

13. Fayerweather, p. 99.

14. "Levi Strauss & Co.: Jeanmakers to the World," *Newsweek*, August 27, 1973, p. 39.

15. Ralph S. Sorenson and Ulrich E. Wiechmann, "How Multinationals View Marketing Standardization," *Harvard Business Review* 53 (May–June 1975): 38, 50.

16. Mazze, p. 103.

17. James C. Baker and John K. Ryans, Jr., "Some Aspects of International Pricing: A Neglected Area of Management Policy," *Management Decisions* (Summer 1973): 177–82.

18. Mazze, p. 80.

19. Ibid., p. 68.

27

YOUR PRACTICAL PHILOSOPHY OF MARKETING

After completing this chapter, the reader should be able to:

1. Explain the current major criticisms of the marketing system.

2. Identify the trends in the marketing environment that will shape future marketing practice.

3. Explain the need to integrate productivity goals and responsibility goals in marketing performance.

4. Describe ways to increase productivity in marketing.

5. Define the nature of the evolving marketing concept.

6. Evaluate career opportunities in the marketing profession.

So far we have touched on many aspects of the marketing concepts, tools, and issues relevant to today's marketing manager. In this chapter we look backward to evaluate marketing performance, then forward to the future marketing world, including possible career opportunities. These perspectives should give you a framework for forming your own practical philosophy of marketing.

CB—THE INNOVATIVE EARS

In the mid-1970s, some 6 million Americans owned a Citizens Band radio.[1] Each could get in touch with another operator via the two-way radio system. All a person needed to join the CB ranks were $100 or so for the basic equipment, a Federal Communications Commission license (available to anyone over 18), official call letters, and the nickname ("handle") of his or her choice.

The CB phenomenon mushroomed rapidly in a short time. Chrysler has predicted that by 1979, nearly 80 percent of its cars will be equipped with CB. In 1975, retail sales for the equipment plus accessories hit the $1 billion mark. On the negative side, owners of radio stations have watched glumly while the CB craze has taken off, fearful that CB will win a large share of their audience. Telephone companies are also unhappy about the new source of competition.

How did this form of anonymous, personal broadcasting come into existence? Truck drivers are given the credit. When 55 mph speed limits were imposed—originally to conserve gas and later to save lives—drivers began using the two-way radio system to warn each other of speed traps and the location of highway patrolmen.

The CB craze may one day go the way of the hula hoop, but at least one commentator doesn't think so. "The reason Citizens Band radio will not fade is that it answers the need to answer," William Safire has written in the *New York Times*. "Newspapers, recognizing this pent-up desire to talk back, have expanded their letters-to-the-editor column; radio stations have featured listener call-ins on discussion shows."

The lonely crowd wants company, he pointed out. "A human being is not merely a receiver. Behind locked doors in cities, behind locked cliques in suburbs, behind the lock of isolation in rural areas, individuals want to say—with no loss of safety or privacy—'Hello, I'm me; let's talk about something.'"

GETTING READY FOR MARKETING'S FUTURE The story of CB illustrates how society affects marketing by providing opportunities, in this case for a more personal mode of communication. Marketing also influences society by supplying innovations, such as the CB radio. Marketing organizations have both economic and social power, then, and a corresponding amount of responsibility.

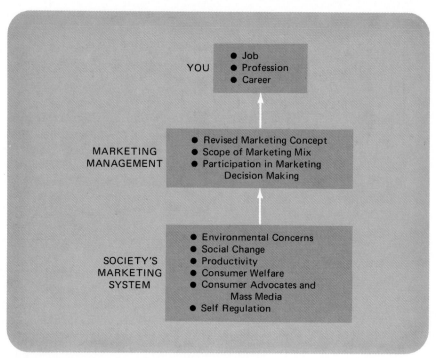

Figure 27-1   THREE PERSPECTIVES ON MARKETING ISSUES

Ultimately, it is society, not marketing managers, that evaluates marketing performance. Thus the marketing manager can take his or her cues from society's evaluation, translating it into a practical philosophy of planning and action.

Figure 27-1 provides an outline for this chapter. We will begin with an examination of the marketing system in society (**macromarketing**) and progress to a discussion of marketing management issues (**micromarketing**). In this context we will discuss career opportunities in marketing.

Many people feel that organizations should concern themselves more with the "net benefits" of marketing to society and less with gross economic benefits. As William Lazer has pointed out, "marketing must become more socially concerned and involved not for altruistic reasons, but for reasons of long-term, enlightened self-interest and system survival."[2]

The future of marketing is naturally of direct concern to the marketing professional. Developments in the marketing field will coincide with the growth and productivity of the marketing person's professional career.

In your future development as a marketing specialist, or as an individual who deals with marketing people, you will be concerned first with learning concepts and techniques. In fact, that is why you have been reading this book. Next, you will apply this knowledge either in school exercises (problems, cases, papers, and so forth) or in on-the-job experience.

A third step is a value orientation toward what you are doing: What do you believe about the social, ethical, and human issues that touch on marketing? Beliefs affect decisions and actions, and you should be able to formulate your own practical philosophy of marketing. If you aren't yet sure what that is, examining the points of view presented here may help you come to some conclusions.

MARKETING IN SOCIETY

In this book we have approached marketing through the eyes of management—the decision makers. It has also been necessary, of course, to examine trends and interactions within the broader marketing environment to understand what influences marketing strategy.

This chapter focuses on marketing within the context of society—the "macromarketing perspective." What happens at this level is what ultimately determines how the marketing system and the people in it (marketers, consumers, government advocates, and so forth) function and, therefore, how effective marketing managers are in performing their role.

What exactly is macromarketing? One analyst has explained that macromarketing "analyzes marketing in a larger framework than the firm; it studies marketing within the context of the entire economic system, with special emphasis on its aggregate performance."[3] It has also been defined as the study of the cumulative results of individual decisions influencing the demand for products.

Macromarketing encompasses the systematic broadening of the analysis of market exchange issues and relationships. It emphasizes aggregate performance with respect to such units as industries, sectors, regions, and the marketing system as a whole.

Macromarketing is chiefly concerned with the analysis of marketing exchange theory. Improvements in the welfare of the consumer and of society are also primary concerns. With improvements in both areas, more people will be better off, since their needs and expectations will be met through market transactions.

CONTROVERSIAL ISSUES IN MARKETING

Today, marketing is under heavier fire than ever. Often it is seen as opposed to the new social and political norms determined by young people, environmentalists, and consumerists. Business people may be tempted to brush aside their critics, noting that America has grown rich by virtue of its philosophy of mass production and mass consumption. They may argue that a little bit of waste and excess is a small price to pay for material well-being.

This type of thinking is dangerous, however. Already, new attitudes are giving a different shape to the future. For reasons of conscience and self-interest, business people should listen closely to their critics. The following dialogues examine some key issues in today's marketing environment.[4] Where do you stand on these issues?

Encouraging a Materialistic Culture

Ms. A: The American business system has created an unhealthy interest in possessions. As a result, people often judge each other according to what they have, not what they are.

"I didn't get shot in the foot on Pork Chop Hill for frozen pizzas, super highways, and canned martinis."

The Wall Street Journal, September 23, 1975.

Mr. B: That's true to some extent. But more and more Americans are losing interest in material goods, particularly people with a lot of money. Even wealth can get boring after a while. American materialism may finally be turning on itself.

Ms. A: I think you're wrong. Materialism is here to stay, because it is intrinsic to the workings of our production and consumption systems. Materialism is part and parcel of business. Advertisers present us with a materialistic model of the good life. We see some people living well and we wonder why we shouldn't have what they have.

Mr. B: But is business really all that powerful? Hasn't the ability of business to stimulate wants been exaggerated quite a bit? Statements about American consumers and how easily they can be manipulated are often based on a simplistic and outmoded stimulus-response psychology applied under laboratory conditions. Pavlov's dog was a dog, after all. The high failure rate of new products is evidence that consumers can't be manipulated all the time. And also think about the influence of family, peer groups, religion, education, and so on. The mass media are not dictators.

Ms. A: Maybe not. But they do push us to want things we don't need—often at public expense. An increase in private goods usually requires a proportionate increase in public service. But often such services are not forthcoming. Do car manufacturers really think about the need for more parking spaces and highways when they push new car sales?

Mr. B: In principle you're right—marketers should bear the full private and public costs of their operations. But this would mean building public costs into the price of an item. Prices would go up, up, up.

Ms. A: Isn't this already happening because of higher taxes? Besides, business is also polluting our cultural atmosphere. Our senses and intelligence are constantly assaulted and our privacy invaded by lifeless music, silly commercials, and scenery-defacing billboards.

Mr. B: That's often a matter of taste. Muzak, for example, is a nuisance to some people and relaxing to others. And cultural pollution may be less evident as advertisers are able to narrow their markets.

Ms. A: Business is much too powerful in areas outside its own concerns—politics and the press, for example.

Mr. B: Business has a right to claim its own interests through lobbying, for example, just like any individual or group. And don't forget that the power of many businesses has been weakened through government regulations and the efforts of consumer and other groups.

Generating Anticompetitive Effects

Mr. C: One of my objections to the business system is that firms so often expand by acquiring other firms rather than by developing within themselves.

Mr. B: That's because it is usually cheaper and less risky to enter a new field by acquisition. Of course, some people fear that the acquisition and merger movement may reach the point where only a few giant firms are doing business. To prevent this, the courts have recently prevented or dissolved a number of mergers.

Mr. C: Another way that businesses try to stay powerful is by putting up barriers to entry into a field. By keeping out others, they protect themselves against competition. The higher the barriers, the greater the potential profits.

Mr. B: Yes, but some barriers to entry are associated with the real economies of large-scale enterprise. Others could be challenged both by existing law and by new legislation.

Mr. C: Even so, many businesses are predatory in their assault on other firms. They intend to hurt and destroy, by means of price slashing, threats to cut off business with suppliers, and downgrading of competing products.

Mr. B: Of course, the business world is not like a children's nursery. On the other hand, there are government regulations to prevent different forms of predatory competition. But often it's difficult to prove that an intent was really predatory.

Inhibiting Full Consumer Welfare

Mr. C: As an American citizen, I see a lot of room for improvement in the marketing system that would directly affect me as a consumer.

Ms. D: There is always room for improvement in any system, but don't forget that the American marketing system has given you the highest standard of living in the world.

Mr. C: I'm paying for it. Our marketing system keeps prices higher than they would be under other systems. The middleman adds his markups to the cost of a product far above the value his service adds. In 1939, the Twentieth Century Fund published the most thorough analysis ever conducted of distribution costs in *Does Distribution Cost Too Much?* The answer to the question in the title is yes. Duplication of sales efforts, multiplicity of sales outlets, excessive services, proliferation of brands, unnecessary advertising, and misinformed buying all add to costs. As do ignorance, greed, poor management, and unwise pricing on the part of marketers.

Another point: charges and markup are often way out of proportion to their true cost. A good example is the prescription drug industry. The manufacturers say that they have to charge those high prices—something like 40¢ for one pill—in order to recover their research investments.

Ms. D: Okay, undoubtedly prices are higher in some areas than is necessary. But there are many reasons for this. Sometimes, price-inflating forces are actually in the consumer's long-range interest. You may see red when you pay $7.00 to have a pair of shoes repaired. But that high price may protect you.

"As we move toward a more structured society, I suppose we'll see fewer and fewer days when clouds are scattered lazily across the afternoon sky."

You are less likely to be dealing with an unscrupulous repairman who charges for work not done or parts not added.

Another important point: often prices are driven up purely by consumer demand. Gas stations proliferate because drivers want a lot of them available. Food prices are high partly because consumers demand more convenience: frozen foods, convenient packaging.

Mr. C: Now I have a criticism not of the marketing system as such but of some of its practitioners. A number are willing to engage in deceptive practices that mislead consumers into believing that they will get more value than they actually do.

Ms. D: Businesses who use such tactics should be controlled through self-regulation and legal means.

Mr. C: But even though they aren't using deliberately deceptive practices, certain organizations pressure people into making purchases they are later sorry for.

Ms. D: People who feel they are victims of a hard sell should apply to better business bureaus, government consumer affairs departments, or the courts.

Mr. C: A lot of people are bothered by the fact that products are often so poorly made. They don't deliver what they promise, and many are unsafe.

Ms. D: For many reasons, certain companies have had trouble producing high-quality products. Poorly trained labor and increased product complexity are two of the reasons. But the long-range picture looks good. As marketers grow, they become more concerned with their reputations. Also, consumer groups are putting heavier pressure on marketers.

THE FUTURE OF THE MARKETING ENVIRONMENT

The outcome of many of the issues we have been discussing will be determined by environmental forces beyond our control. The American economy has been shaped by the rapid socioeconomic changes of recent years, and the pace of those changes promises to increase.

As was noted in a business publication:

[T]racking change—with a view to managing it—increasingly holds the key to successful marketing. Thus, astute companies have made and are making major investments of time and money, forecasting technological and economic developments likely to affect the future course of their business. To chart their course through the rocks and shoals ahead, companies need profound insights into the social changes under way.[5]

Many marketing situations have been and will be changed dramatically by events. For example, the oil policies of the Middle Eastern countries have forced major changes in the operations of the Detroit auto manufacturers. Many other dramatic changes in the marketplace have been brought about by explosive gains in knowledge, communications techniques, and applications of operations research.

Changes determined by biological or physical factors are fairly easy to predict. The direction of economic forces, however, is being predicted with less and less confidence. As one analyst has put it, "this seems to be because a number of the forces effecting change are sociological or psychological. They relate to man as a human being, to his inner life and his life in relation to others. The changes occasioned by these forces are often imperceptible and consequently extremely difficult to predict."[6]

Social Trends   The marketing manager's future will be shaped basically by influences that are changing the environment in which he or she operates, particularly by relationships among people and between people and products.

Some analysts feel that individual needs and values will form the primary forces for change in the marketplace of the future (see Table 27-1). In this context it might be interesting to point out once again the universal hierarchy of five need levels postulated by Abraham Maslow. As we noted in Chapter 8, Maslow saw human development as a progression upward from the level of physiological needs to the level of psychological needs. In many respects this needs hierarchy is compatible with the concept of market segmentation that we examined in Chapter 7.

Louis Harris, the pollster, made the following remarks on the values of American consumers as he had surveyed them:

If given a choice between seriously trimming their material life styles or enduring more cycles of double-digit inflation and high levels of unemployment, they find that decision relatively easy. By 77 percent to 8 percent, they would opt for cutting back in their material life styles. . . . [The] three bathtub and three car syndrome would disappear from American life. People are no longer content to watch their possessions pile up. Instead they yearn for a more satisfying kind of existence.[7]

A few years ago Americans were fairly well sold on the myth of progress: they felt that standards of living would improve as a matter of course. But in the rapid economic changes of the past decade, they have begun to take a second look at their beliefs. They have come to distrust the operations of government and business. They have become concerned with corruption and unfair

Table 27-1
DOMINANT NEEDS AND EVOLUTIONARY TRENDS

NEED LEVEL	DOMINANT NEED	EVOLUTIONARY TREND
Survival	Need for that which sustains life.	Broadening view of what is essential to stay alive.
Security	Need to feel unthreatened, safe, protected.	Security demands lengthen in time span, increase in amounts, and cover wider variety of situations.
Belonging	Need to be a part of something bigger than oneself.	Object of belongingness is extended to broader groups.
Esteem	Need for achievement, success, recognition.	Focus shifts from need for esteem for others to need for self-esteem, and from achieving esteem through conspicuous consumption and ostentatiousness to achieving it through meaningful actions.
Growth	Need to achieve full inner potential.	Areas of interest broaden from specific to general, from local to universal, from concrete to abstract, from mundane to transcendental.

SOURCE: Stanford Research Institute. From "U.S. Gasoline Marketplace," Report of the Marketplace of the Future Task Force, Sun Oil Company, April 1972, p. 13.

practices, and are not convinced that they are buying top-quality products or living the best quality life.

Economic Trends   The economy of the future will be much influenced by the fact that some natural resources are becoming ever more scarce and commanding an ever higher price. This situation means that the rate of economic growth will be held in check.

Inflation will also be with us for some time. As governmental spending increases, so do the tremendous budget deficits. This spending is just one of the many factors keeping inflation at such strength.

The growth of producer-cartels, which try to corner the market for their products, will also have an effect on prices. Capital shortages will increase as companies find it harder and harder to obtain external financing at affordable interest rates. One result will be a deceleration of the rate of investment, especially in capital-intensive industries.

The soaring cost of energy has been pointed to as the biggest growth inhibitor of all. The days of cheap energy are gone, and the major growth economies can no longer build on cheap and abundant sources of power. Until long-range solutions can be found, energy conservation is crucial.

Political Trends More and more often, people are looking to government for economic solutions. And government is increasing its control over the economy. Both trends are expected to continue. Business will also be subjected to a growing list of rules and regulations, which will further limit the free market system.

When a group of executives from major U.S. corporations were asked to predict how business would look in 1985, only 5 percent saw a rosy picture.[8] Less than 25 percent foresaw increased recognition of the overall cost-benefit ratio by consumer and environmental legislation. And only 16 percent thought that industry would become less regulated as a result of increased competition to protect the public interest.

Technological Trends Of that same group of executives surveyed above, 63 percent predicted:

This will truly be "an age of change" as the knowledge explosion of the seventies and early eighties bears a major crop of new technology. Cable TV communications systems, rapid mass transit, cashless computerized financial transactions and medical equipment breakthroughs will be representative of the harvest of new technological products and processes that will be operative in the society.[9]

Although pollution and ecological damage have been called the tragic consequences of technological advance, some feel that abuse of technology is the essence of the problem. They maintain that if America abandons technology, it will be throwing out the baby with the bath water.

MEET THE FEDERAL PRODUCT COMMISSION— FICTION OR FUTURE FACT?

The Federal Product Commission decides whether new products will be beneficial to the people who will buy them. Manufacturers are required to submit every new product to the FPC. Because the agency is understaffed and has a backlog, approval may take months. Some critics charge that the FPC gives early approvals to certain companies while others wait in line.

The FPC considers several questions when judging a new product:

1. Is it sufficiently different from existing products?

2. Are the product differences, if they exist, of sufficient benefit to buyers and society?

3. Is the product relatively safe and healthy for the user? (Marketers may build a minimum of safety features into their products for reasons of cost and also because they don't think the consumer will value the safety aspects.)

4. Is it designed for minimum ecological harm? (The FPC urges designers to minimize the use of nonbiodegradable materials in their products.)

Many people fear that the FPC will someday regulate the entire economy. They urge manufacturers to take "anticipatory responsibility," asking of themselves the questions they would expect from the FPC.

Based on Philip Kotler, "Future Shock for Marketing," in Conference on *Social Responsibility Is Good Business* (Tokyo: Japanese Advertising Industry, 1973).

In many areas, new combinations of previously unrelated materials and processes will be developed. The traditional boundaries between areas of technology will become less sharp. And while governmental control will continue, there will still be plenty of room on the marketplace for innovation.

In communications we will see greater use of video tape cassettes and laser beams. By the year 2000, one analyst predicts, most homes will have complex communication systems.[10] Examples of other technological innovations are given in Table 27-2.

DOES THE MARKET SOCIETY HAVE A FUTURE?

Traditionally, America has respected the concepts of individual enterprise, private property, free competition, and limited government. That philosophy of individualism has become a national ideology.

In a Harvard Business School survey of nearly 2,000 business people here and abroad, more than two-thirds said they preferred individualism.[11] But an even larger majority predicted that communitarianism will be dominant in this country by 1985. And even while holding to their belief in individualism, some respondents admitted that a communitarian approach would be better for the solution of future problems.

Proponents of individualism were more often Americans, while supporters of communitarianism were usually foreigners. According to the authors, American business people are refusing to confront reality by clinging to their outmoded ideology. As a result they are trying to impose solutions that fail and that prevent more effective means of dealing with the nation's problems.

There are arguments to be made for both sides, as the following dialogue illustrates. How do you feel about it?

Mr. E: The free enterprise system has worked in this country for 200 years. Individuals make decisions and are accountable for their actions. When a group or government makes decisions, you don't always know who is in charge. Historically, government is ineffective, slow, and clumsy. With free-market mechanisms, we can solve even the most complex problems, such as energy shortages and environmental pollution.

Ms. D: The common welfare is more important than individual freedom. Let's face it, the individualist ideology has never worked very well. Look what we've done to our environment in the name of individualism.

Mr. E: I still think you can't beat a system that rewards individual competence and productivity. If this kind of system is allowed to function, it will produce a society that will compete with other countries for the resources needed to maintain our high standard of living. Man is a selfish animal, and a philosophy of individualism uses this trait for the common good.

Ms. D: As moral creatures, we have an obligation to support and help each other. We need some new form of competition. I cannot accept the simplistic "jungle" view of humans that you propose. Anyway, while your philosophy may have been suited to the American frontier days, it doesn't make sense in today's world.

Mr. E: The communitarian ideology is accepted in many countries of Western Europe where the Social Democratic parties are in power. But a lot

Table 27-2 SOME LIKELY TECHNOLOGICAL INNOVATIONS BY THE YEAR 2000

General and substantial increase in life expectancy, postponement of aging, limited rejuvenation

Generally acceptable synthetic foods and beverages

Physically nonharmful methods of overindulging

Use of robots as "slaves" for humans

Chemical methods for improving memory and learning

Greater use of underground buildings

Adapted from Herman Kahn, "The Next Thirty-Three Years," *13th Annual Conference Proceedings* (Advertising Research Foundation, 1968), pp. 36–41. Copyright 1968. Advertising Research Council, Inc.

of people say that the system is not the Utopia it was meant to be. Even citizens of those countries will admit that they live in a docile, drab society where initiative is stifled.

Ms. D: You must have spoken to very few people. The successes of the system are obvious: an absence of destructive social tensions, a much lower crime rate, a dedication to community goals, a gradual removal of class barriers, and participation of workers in management. The sustained GNP has made possible a vast array of services, including good public transportation, subsidized performing arts, and prompt street cleaning. And the general level of employment, income, health and social services is high.

THE SOCIETAL MARKETING CHALLENGE

In the future, the marketing system will be called upon to perform a balancing act between productivity and responsibility. **Productivity** is a familiar but difficult goal, especially in this decade of turbulent economic conditions. **Responsibility** imposed on marketing by social and political forces is the newer goal.

Marketing Productivity

Despite economic ups and downs, the highest levels of productivity in the world are in the United States. Some industries have been able to maintain high levels throughout the economic crises.

Productivity has been defined as "the output-input ratio of an economic process. The productivity measure is obtained by dividing the quantity of goods or services produced during some period of time by the quantity of resources used to accomplish those ends. Productivity is simply the terminology economists use to express the concept of efficiency."[12]

Productivity and profitability are not the same. Profitability refers to dollar earnings on a product, productivity to the amount of labor or other resource required to make the product.

"Those pills have made us a profit of five million dollars and you people call them worthless?"

Len Herman in *The Wall Street Journal*, October 7, 1975.

But for many reasons, marketing is not trusted as a productive business effort. This mistrust is compounded by poor decision making and missed opportunities for growth and development, resulting in substantial—but in many cases unspecified—costs.

Industry, government, and education do not agree on what constitutes marketing production as opposed to other types of production. No body of data has been systematically gathered and organized to provide for a measurable basis of marketing production. Of course, some efforts have been made by private industries and trade associations. But often their data are safely guarded from public scrutiny. Table 27-3 shows that one study has found marketing productivity to be rising.

According to some recent studies, various marketing costs are consuming a steadily increasing share of consumers' expenditures. Why is this so, and what can be done about it?

Marketing Responsibility

In some prosperous times the attitude of "business-as-usual" and "the market will right itself" was often expressed. But with today's growing consumerism and economic surprises, such attitudes are being put forth with a lot less conviction. And business people who think that way may not continue to make

1. Health and safety
   Personal and environmental health
   Public and environmental safety
2. Education, skills, and income
   Basic schooling and higher education
   Skills and jobs
   Amount, adequacy, and continuity of incomes
3. Human habitat
   Housing
   Quality of neighborhood
   Access to the area
   Recreational opportunities
   Quality of larger environments
4. Finer things
   Arts and sciences
   Nature and beauty
5. Leisure and production
   Interrelationships between economic growth and availability of discretionary time
6. Freedom, justice, and harmony
   Concerns with liberty
   Concerns with democratic values
   Quality of social environment

From Harry A. Lipson, Eugene J. Kelley, and Seymour Marshak, "Integrating Social Feedback and Social Audits into Corporate Planning," in William Lazer and Eugene J. Kelley, eds., *Social Marketing: Perspectives and Viewpoints* (Homewood, Ill.: Irwin, 1973), p. 177. Reproduced with permission.

profits. The system of free markets and open competition was fine at one time, but today an increasing concern for "quality of life" has forced new obligations on the business world.

The box on this page lists the national social goals that should be of concern to the marketing manager. Today the accumulation of material wealth is no longer equated automatically with social progress. Often a sharp distinction is made between economic and social interests. National goals and government programs are of interest to business because they are indicators of what directions business should move in for its own interest as well as that of society as a whole.

An Integrated Approach to Marketing All measures of marketing productivity are the expression of a ratio of output to input. But developments in today's marketplace have resulted in three different ways of measuring productivity: efficiency, consumer satisfaction, and social satisfaction.[13] The meanings of output and input differ with each measure (see Figure 27-2).

Efficiency is usually measured in numbers such as profit per dollar of capital invested, sales per square foot of space, units produced per man hour.

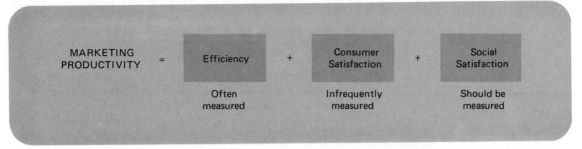

Figure 27-2   THE ULTIMATE EQUATION OF MARKETING PRODUCTIVITY

**Table 27-3
AN INDEX OF
MARKETING
PRODUCTIVITY***

YEAR	INDEX
1948	78.7
1949	80.1
1950	86.8
1951	85.7
1952	86.4
1953	88.7
1954	91.5
1955	96.6
1956	97.7
1957	98.9
1958	100.0
1959	105.1
1960	105.5
1961	108.3
1962	114.2
1963	118.6
1964	123.1
1965	127.3
1966	132.7

*Calculations expressed in terms of output per unweighted labor hours.
Reprinted from Louis P. Bucklin, "A Synthetic Index of Marketing Productivity," *1975 Combined Proceedings* (Chicago: American Marketing Association, 1975), p. 559. Published by the American Marketing Association.

The marketing manager examines volume and profit produced per salesperson, per unit of advertising, and so forth. The determination of productivity is becoming more accurate as a result of combinations of market experimentation, more refined statistical techniques, and better input data.

Consumer satisfaction, the second level of productivity measurement, is more difficult, because it includes estimates of consumer behavior or attitudes on both input and output sides. For example, convenience food stores are less productive than supermarkets on an efficiency scale. Yet they are the fastest growing segment of the food retailing business, because consumers are not rating productivity in terms of store efficiency. They like the idea that they can buy in a convenience store when others are closed, and that they can save time making purchases.

Profitability remains a firm's basic measure of productivity, regardless of how the consumer affects the input/output ratio. But the ratio can serve as a tool for analyzing ways of improving total productivity.

The social satisfaction measure adds a third set of components to both the output and input sides. The social factor recognizes that the marketer and the consumer can both increase the productivity of their own systems by imposing costs on society—for example, in waste removal and pollution.

In the survey of top corporations referred to earlier, many executives held out dim hopes for a profitable future. They expressed the feeling that in order to produce enough profits to survive, the ultimate in strategic planning and integration of operations would be needed.

The amount of payoff from a given exchange is determined by the relationship:

$$payoff = benefits - cost$$

For example, a typical marketing decision is whether or not to use television advertising. In making such a decision, the marketing manager must identify systematically possible direct and indirect benefits and costs as they affect the producer, the consumer, and society.

Many other marketing activities can be evaluated in this way: the marketing of cigarettes, automobiles, pollution control equipment; lobbying activity to legalize abortion; political campaigns. Each such evaluation can lend new views on the unique problems of a situation. Table 27-4 illustrates a conceptual framework for such an evaluation.

Table 27-4
SUMMARY OF EVALUATION OF A TELEVISION ADVERTISEMENT

PARTICIPANTS	PAYOFFS	
	BENEFITS	COSTS
Producer	*DIRECT*	
	Product exposure, company image enhancement, specific information	Production costs of the advertisement, media time
	INDIRECT	
	Carryover effect to other products, goodwill derived from sponsoring a popular program, prestige of national name	Opportunity costs of a different campaign, damage to image from sponsoring unpopular program
Consumer	*DIRECT*	
	Product information, new or better uses for the product	Opportunity cost of time expended viewing the commercial
	INDIRECT	
	Entertainment or knowledge derived from the program	Advertising cost borne by products purchased, irritation with commercials and programs, misleading information
Society	*DIRECT*	
	Generation of jobs, incomes, taxes	Resources expended to produce and air commercial, time and energy consumed viewing
	INDIRECT	
	Increased expectations contributing to rising standards of living, entertainment, knowledge dissemination, contribution to social change	Inefficient allocation of resources, legal and economic consequences of deception, excess power over program content

From Richard E. Homans and Ben M. Enis, "A Guide for Appraising Marketing Activities," *Business Horizons* 16 (October 1973): 26. Copyright 1973 by the foundation for the School of Business at Indiana University. Reprinted by permission.

MANAGEMENT OF MARKETING

All businesses have access to more or less the same resources, except in the rare monopoly situation. What distinguishes one business from another is the quality of its management.

In recent years the focus of marketing activities has shifted from a "things first, people second" philosophy to "people first, things second." Proof is the fact that marketing is being applied to areas such as health services, politics, population control, charities, and recycling of waste materials. Corporate leaders are beginning to realize that the old ways of doing business don't work. And business has been affected by the traumatic events of the past decade, including the war in Vietnam, inflation, Watergate, and the oil crisis.

ROOM FOR MARKETING IMPROVEMENTS

Using marketing productivity as a yardstick is the best means for comparing management of different units within an enterprise and comparing management of different enterprises. Productivity is the first test of management's competence.

Procter & Gamble has enjoyed one of the greatest records in American marketing. They have defined the major factors in their success as "product quality, marketing experimentation and meticulous attention to detail—not unique services or in-house geniuses."[14]

P&G's marketing research suppliers frequently work for outside companies, and in general their marketing efforts are "open to the public." They feel that word gets around anyway, so a company might as well be open about its marketing efforts.

Thanks to advances in the behavioral and managerial sciences, management has more resources and tools available. The computer is having profound effects on the marketing world, making it possible for all marketing personnel to do a better job. And a growing number of analytical tools and procedures are available to managers.

One analyst has offered these steps to improving marketing productivity:[15]

1. Recognize that some natural resources are limited.

2. Increase technology, for example with an investment tax credit for scientific and marketing research.

3. Encourage expanded use of productive capital.

4. Provide recognition and dollar incentives to workers.

5. Encourage government to create a competitive environment for stimulating productivity, for example by requiring use of the metric system.

6. Maintain an aggressive, alert, and determined attitude.

RESHAPING MANAGERIAL MARKETING

In an era of rapid economic, political, and social change, the goal of greater marketing productivity will be difficult to attain. The big question becomes, Is the marketing concept up to the challenge?

Some marketing managers argue that the basis for successful marketing still rests on fundamental principles. As one top marketing executive put it, "go back to the marketing concept. Study consumer needs and build real benefits into your products or services—tailored to meet those needs. Then vigorously sell those benefits."[16]

This same executive points out that consumers today are demanding honesty, fairness, quality of performance, and quality of life. This means that marketing is faced with a greater opportunity and challenge than ever before.

Certainly, the marketing concept is evolving, and growth is healthy and necessary. A major reason for change is that the consumers are an enigma, and satisfying them means being more flexible than ever. They bring one set of values to the marketplace and perhaps quite another to their political decision making and social interests.

Certainly, the definition of marketing purpose has changed as a result of increasing pressure to recognize social responsibility. In the future, companies will be pressed to take active roles in defining and serving the public interest by offering a flow of goods and services. The new criterion of marketing effectiveness will include full accountability to the individual citizen.

Corporate social responsibility takes on new colors with this new view of marketing. Firms must make it their business to generate true social value in the marketplace, not just to redistribute profits. The basis of the consumer movement is to strengthen the role of business in a free-enterprise society.

A different marketing concept is consumer sovereignty, which holds that the essential purpose of a firm is to provide consumer satisfaction. Such a philosophy has inherent problems. Objectives of consumer satisfaction and corporate profits will come into conflict in the short run. The firm will face difficulties in determining which of the divergent needs of its customers should be considered. Also, the concept does not deal effectively with the entire consumption process.

ETHICS—THE TOUGH QUESTIONS

Should a nonsmoker refuse to work on a cigarette advertising account? Should an industrial product manager resign because he or she is convinced that a new tractor is not safe enough? Should a travel agent accept a large gift from an airline? These are some of the ethical questions that the marketing manager may have to deal with.

Figure 27-3   EXAMPLES OF MARKETING CAREER OPPORTUNITIES

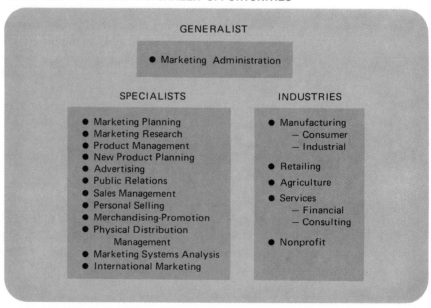

A survey of how more than 500 managers view the bribery of foreign officials is revealing.[17] Fifty percent were against bribes, but 48 percent thought bribes were all right if they were common practice in a particular country. Of those who accepted the practice, two-thirds considered it a cost of doing business in certain countries. Nearly two-thirds of those who would not pay bribes gave moral considerations as the reason.

The line between propriety and impropriety is often a very thin one in the business world. Society hands business accolades when it succeeds but brickbats when it uses unethical tactics. And between the poles of right and wrong there is a lot of gray territory.

Today's business person operates under a capitalist theory that allows a great deal of leeway in pursuing economic self-interest. Yet business also serves society. Some have suggested that if business people would bear in mind their social function, they might develop a sense of pride that would keep them from getting into trouble. They might also ask themselves how others would judge this practice if it became known to them.

MARKETING OPPORTUNITIES AND YOU

Even in the present low-growth economy, marketing survives and sometimes flourishes. Opportunities abound in the nonprofit sector—in welfare, religious, political, and charitable organizations.

Even if you feel that marketing is not for you as a career, this section can be relevant. First, you may change your mind. Second, since you may well come in contact with marketing people, you may find it very useful to understand more about their profession.

THE MARKETING PROFESSIONALS

Profit and nonprofit organizations are looking for marketing professionals of many descriptions, including product managers, personal salespeople, and retailers. Figure 27-3 illustrates examples of possible marketing careers. The generalist (marketing manager) and the specialists (planner, researcher, product manager, and so forth) may work in any of several industries (manufacturing, retailing, nonprofit, and so forth).

A large graduate school offers the following description of marketing career opportunities:[18]

1. *Product management.* Under this system of organization, each brand or product within a company is operated as a separate business. Each group plans, develops, and directs the consumer marketing effort for its product. Except for top corporate management, the members of the brand group are the only people who deal with all aspects of the company's business. Career opportunities exist in virtually all consumer goods companies and many industrial goods companies.

2. *Marketing research.* Entails collection of data from primary sources, usually employing a questionnaire applied during a field survey. The marketing researcher may be involved in decision making and in designing the research project. He or she will be concerned with data tabulation, analysis,

report preparation, and presentation of findings to management. Career opportunities exist within a variety of institutions, manufacturers, retailers, some wholesalers, trade and industry associations, and governmental and other public agencies.

3. *Advertising.* A combination of planning, fact-gathering, and creativity. Pay is comparable to that for other business executives, but opportunities for rapid advancement are usually greater. Careers exist in advertising agencies, large corporations, the media, management consulting, and market research.

4. *Marketing system analysis.* Individuals will tend to act as consultants to managers. Training required in management science, operations research, and systems analysis. The job will include demand measurement and forecasting, distribution policies, and field sales force problems. Career opportunities exist primarily within large marketing-oriented firms and in management consulting.

5. *International marketing.* Positions abroad usually go to people with some international marketing experience at headquarters. Starting jobs usually involve research, planning, or coordinating.

6. *Industrial marketing.* This includes in-stock and made-to-specification items. The specialist is concerned with application and installation and with sales of a product or a service. An engineering or scientific education is essential in some situations and helpful in others.

7. *Retailing management.* Retailing affords a person an early opportunity to use his or her professional knowledge to improve profits through maintenance of the best package of goods and services. Professional training is often part of preparation. Starting salary may be lower than in other marketing fields, but advancement may be more rapid.

WHAT YOU CAN EXPECT

The marketing graduate who chooses a company with an open and questioning environment will find substantial rewards. Dynamic companies are marketing oriented. They often provide thorough training, evaluation, and advancement for promising executives.

Marketing offers not only material rewards and personal challenge, but the opportunity for public service. As the backbone of private enterprise, marketing permits the nation's productive capacity to adapt to changing consumer requirements. The marketing manager's job is challenging and diversified.

A marketing career gives an individual a voice in the future. It is excellent preparation for the person who is interested in the "command" aspects of business, and who enjoys making decisions and taking action.

The financial rewards of a marketing career can be substantial but are seldom immediate. Specialists' salaries tend to level out somewhat below those that can be achieved by general marketing executives, such as product managers or marketing directors.

Certainly, the beginning pay in marketing is about as good as in many other fields recruiting college graduates. And the opportunities for advancement are greater. Few other fields offer such a direct relationship between

Table 27-5
PERCEPTIONS OF MARKETING FIELDS—AN ART OR A SCIENCE?

OPINION	RESPONSES OF 175 MARKETING EXECUTIVES			
	MARKETING RESEARCH	GENERAL MARKETING	ADVERTISING	PERSONAL SELLING
Primarily an art	2%	7%	24%	46%
An art which is slowly becoming a science	19	37	40	24
An art which is rapidly becoming a science	30	29	28	22
Primarily a science	49	27	8	8
TOTAL	100%	100%	100%	100%

Adapted from Jac L. Goldstucker, Barnett A. Greenberg, and Danny N. Bellenger, "How Scientific Is Marketing? What Do Marketing Executives Think?" *MSU Business Topics* 22 (Spring 1974): 40–41.

ability to produce and income. And in no other field are there so few restraints on progress.

Early promotions usually follow demonstration of ability to get along with others and to work with little regard for time expended. Later, promotions are usually related to the ability to take on more authority. The fact that individual ability can be easily recognized in marketing allows an element of independence. And marketing experience is invaluable for the person who wants his or her own business eventually.

WHAT IT WILL TAKE

Marketing is both an art and a science. It demands creativity, but at the same time requires application of the scientific method (see Table 27-5). Many marketing innovations arise from a creative approach. It is exciting to introduce a new product, beat out competition, witness public acceptance of a new campaign. A marketing job well done provides personal satisfaction as well as the knowledge that society is better off.

But marketing is also a science, where hypotheses are set up establishing criteria for success. Marketing is an applied discipline, like medicine or the law. The marketing manager must have a highly structured and logical approach to decision making.

The daily life of a marketing executive is full of challenge. A good executive seeks opportunity and meets it head on. And part of the challenge is that work must be carried on in uncertain conditions. Even the most carefully planned marketing strategy is at the mercy of changes in political, social, and economic areas. In fact, the ability to deal with change has been pinpointed as the most accurate test of the marketing executive's ability to succeed.

Many marketing success stories come from the ranks of specialists in one of the functional fields such as research, sales, or advertising and who also have a better than average knowledge of what is happening in other areas. The marketing executive today is involved in aspects of business formerly reserved for top management only, such as the financial impact of alternatives, the influence of government on product standards, and so forth.

Enthusiasm is the traditional hallmark of those entering marketing careers, and determination and self-assurance are necessary additions to that enthusiasm. The successful marketing executive must also be able to communicate with others, evaluate employees, use diplomacy and tact, digest and retain information, handle organizational problems skillfully, spot potential conflicts of interest, and be patient. And he or she must be able to keep abreast of new ideas in a rapidly changing world.

CONCLUSION

The challenges and opportunities of marketing are increasingly generated from outside. The marketing world is expanding conceptually, geographically, and functionally. This means that yesterday's approaches often don't work, and tradition and habit may even become barriers to success.

Marketing can play a major role in determining the extent to which American money will be channeled into material goods, as in the past, or into a better quality of life. A continuation of the traditional materialism may push the resources of society to the breaking point. Along with a new philosophy, marketing executives will have to develop a new ethic that makes legitimate their concerns for public, social, and ecological dimensions even when they are not consistent with the profit motive.

The future shapes up to be dynamic, if uncertain, and career opportunities in marketing will also offer dynamic possibilities. In the end, marketing is what we make of it. Like atomic power, it can be a destructive force or a constructive one. Marketing is not in itself good or bad, but becomes so depending on how it is used. In the future, marketing will clearly have to be used in a socially responsive context to survive as an economic system, to achieve organizational goals, and to provide meaningful career opportunities.

DISCUSSION QUESTIONS

1. What is your personal view on these critical issues in marketing's future:
   a. the type of "market system" that is best for society;
   b. the balance between productivity goals and social responsibilty goals;
   c. the nature of a revised marketing concept.
2. Considering marketing's role in society today, what is your evaluation of:
   a. its encouragement of materialism?
   b. its anticompetitive effects?
   c. its role in inhibiting consumer welfare?
3. What do you feel will be most different about the marketing system in 1985 in comparison with today? Most similar?
4. How can the automobile simultaneously be (a) the hallmark of society's high standard of living and (b) a serious threat to our quality of life? Do you see any way that society can reconcile these two views?
5. A 1970 *Wall Street Journal* news item ran: "Two 17,000-ton tankers collided

in heavy fog under the Golden Gate Bridge, spilling an estimated 500,000 gallons of tanker fuel into San Francisco Bay. There were no injuries." Do you agree with the last sentence? Assuming that one of the ships belonged to California Oil, is there any action you would recommend to it?

6. Analyze the marketing of cigarettes in terms of the cost–benefit matrix and the three measures of productivity.

7. In your opinion, are these marketing practices ethical or not?

   a. Products that cost relatively little to produce but sell for relatively high prices.

   b. Using the same part in two company products but selling them for a considerably different price for each.

   c. Promoting two products as differentiated although no significant differences exist.

8. What do you feel are the most promising marketing career opportunities for the future? Which of these interests you? Why?

NOTES

1. William Safire, "CB: Banding Together," *New York Times,* June 17, 1976, p. 35.

2. "Lazer Asks, 'Can Marketing Survive?' Replies, 'Yes, But . . .' " *Marketing News,* June 1, 1974, p. 1.

3. Thaddeus H. Spratlen, "Macromarketing Analysis of Aggregate Performance: Issues and Insights," *1975 Combined Proceedings* (Chicago: American Marketing Association, 1975), p. 564.

4. This section is based largely on Philip Kotler, *Marketing Management: Analysis, Planning, and Control,* 2d ed. (Englewood Cliffs, N.J.: Prentice-Hall, 1972) p. 813.

5. Grey Advertising Inc., *Grey Matter,* 46 (1976): 1.

6. C. Merle Crawford, *The Future Environment for Marketing* (Ann Arbor: University of Michigan, 1969), p. 113.

7. "Notable & Quotable," *Wall Street Journal,* November 18, 1975, p. 27.

8. Jon G. Udell, Gene R. Laczniak, and Robert F. Lusch, "The Business Environment of 1985," *Business Horizons* 19 (June 1976): 45.

9. Ibid., p. 51.

10. Edward M. Mazze, "Marketing in Turbulent Times: The Challenges and the Opportunities," *1975 Combined Proceedings* (Chicago:

American Marketing Association, 1975), p. xxvi.

11. William F. Martin and George Cabot Lodge, "Our Society in 1985—Business May Not Like It," *Harvard Business Review* 52 (November–December 1975): 143ff.

12. Louis P. Bucklin, "A Synthetic Index of Marketing Productivity," *1975 Combined Proceedings* (Chicago: American Marketing Association, 1975), p. 556.

13. Stephens Dietz, "How to Measure Productivity," *1973 Combined Proceedings* (Chicago: American Marketing Association, 1974), pp. 163–65.

14. Henry R. Bernstein, "P&G's Marketing Philosophy No Secret, Morgens Testifies," *Advertising Age,* June 2, p. 3.

15. Robert J. Eggert, "Productivity or Death," *Marketing News,* August 1, 1973, p. 3.

16. "Truth, Marketing Concept Are Answer to Consumerism," *Marketing News,* November 15, 1973, p. 5.

17. Fred T. Allen, "Corporate Morality: Is the Price Too High?" *Wall Street Journal,* Oct. 17, 1975, p. 16.

18. *Careers in Marketing,* Northwestern University Graduate School of Management brochure, 1975, p. 6ff.

MDS-EUROPE

In 1974, the overseas arm of Multinational Data Systems Corporation (MDS) produced, sold, leased, or serviced computer products in 112 nations around the world. MDS-Europe accounted for roughly 40 percent of the corporation's $6 billion in sales and $780 million in net income.

The bulk of these overseas operations take place in Western Europe. The European revenue represents 65 percent of all MDS revenue outside of the United States. MDS controls approximately 59 percent of the worldwide computer market and 52 percent of the European market.

Not surprisingly, political and industrial leaders in many European states are unhappy with this situation. They resent the dominance of an American firm in a rapidly expanding European computer market. One West German business leader predicts, "It's up to America to split up MDS. But if America doesn't, then it will be up to Europe to split up MDS-Europe."

MDS Strategy Alternatives in the European Marketing Environment

Julian A. Mydans, the president of MDS-Europe (based in Brussels), was faced with some difficult business problems. He had been sent internal MDS reports about the marketing environment for computer products in Western Europe. His superiors in the New York office of MDS were uneasy about growing demands that MDS-Europe be "split up." They wanted Mydans' opinions on the firm's European strategy alternatives of the period 1977 to 1987.

Mydans was increasingly irritated about talk of breaking up MDS-Europe. In calmer moments, he understood that this was the price of success in the international market: someone would always be talking about taking you over or breaking your firm into little pieces.

Unfortunately, he reflected, the threat of "trust-busting" was real. Even as he was preparing his report, attorneys in the Department of Justice were at work on an antitrust suit to break up the American operations of MDS. Mydans knew that any such action at home could only encourage similar moves by the governments of Common Market nations.

It was hard to argue with the facts. The European computer market was growing at an impressive 16 to 20 percent annual rate, compared with 10 to 12 percent within the United States. Meanwhile, MDS-Europe's subsidiaries in Britain, France, West Germany, and Italy had achieved combined revenues of over $2.3 billion in 1975. American firms were in control of an 80 percent share of the European computer market.

Mydans knew that this was a dangerous situation for MDS and other American firms. The Europeans were in a period of economic instability. Some sort of counterattack against MDS-Europe was almost inevitable. Indeed, there was already talk of combining the six major European computer firms into one giant transnational enterprise.

Many observers believed that this action would seriously weaken the MDS subsidiaries in Western Europe. But Julian Mydans had a different view.

If all of the European computer firms were joined into one larger unit, the "buy national" purchasing policies of many Common Market nations might be ended. MDS might end up with more European sales rather than less.

Mydans knew that his report would contain two basic conclusions. In the short run, MDS's position in Western Europe was virtually unchallenged. In the long run, there were intricate political problems to be faced. But, even so, MDS's future in Europe seemed bright. Mydans remembered with satisfaction a recent comment from a U.S. newspaper: "If all the computer makers in the world, much less all the Europeans, combined into one company, it still wouldn't enjoy the luxury of picking on someone its own size. MDS would still be bigger."

Questions
1. Analyze the threats to and opportunities for MDS-Europe posed by the European marketing environment in the short run and the long run.
2. What recommendations should Mydans make in his report regarding:
   a. MDS-Europe's marketing strategy;
   b. the relationship and organization of MDS in the U.S. and MDS in Europe.

THE KRAMER COMPANY

The Kramer Company is a manufacturer of golf clubs and other sporting equipment, located in Richmond, Virginia. As of 1976, the firm had only been involved in domestic sales. But in the summer of that year, it began considering its first overseas marketing. Golf had been booming in Japan, and Kramer decided to study the possibilities of selling its equipment there.

To help investigate the marketing of American consumer goods in Japan, Kramer turned to the federal government. Nicholas Karas, a marketing vice-president, met with Caroline Rawlins, a Department of Commerce official specializing in assisting American firms in their export activities.

Two Views of the Japanese Market

The meeting took place in Caroline Rawlins' office in the Department of Commerce. Nicholas Karas glanced out the window to get a view of downtown Washington, then sat down and began to speak:

"I've prepared very carefully for this meeting. At your suggestion, I've read a pile of studies from the Department of Commerce and from the Japan External Trade Organization (JETRO). I've boned up on business in Japan, the Japanese marketing system, the sporting goods market, and the problems of American export firms operating in Japan.

"Frankly, I'm very skeptical about this whole idea. If this were the early 1970s—when the Japanese gross national product was growing by 10 percent annually—I might be more enthusiastic. But, since 1973, Japan's economic situation has been lousy. Inflation, recession, low growth, the whole works!

"Just listen to these figures. In 1970 sales of American sports equipment in Japan were only $30 million. By 1973 this figure had skyrocketed to $145 million. But now we're back down to only $108 million. And I'm afraid it may get worse before it gets better."

Nicholas Karas started looking out the window again. "I realize that $108 million isn't small change. There's a market out there, *at the moment*, ready to be tapped. But will that market be there five years from now? The reports I've read leave me a little shaky about the future of luxury goods in Japan."

Caroline Rawlins had been listening intently to Karas' presentation. She shuffled a few papers on her desk, found the ones she had been looking for, and responded.

"Let's start with the present. We know that golf equipment is selling well in Japan. The American golf club is seen not only as a top-quality item, but as a symbol of status. My studies show this comment from a Japanese bank president to be typical: 'You have a little bit of prestige out on the course if you're carrying an American club.'

"A wide range of American firms in other fields are doing well in Japan. Some of the more recent exporters include Tiffany and Company, Alley Cat Fashions, and Whirlpool Corporation.

"The attitude of the Japanese government continues to be favorable. Since they revalued the yen in 1971, the government has encouraged many American manufacturers to begin exporting to Japan. Import tariffs have been lowered by as much as 20 percent. Laws have been changed so that American firms can package, warehouse, wholesale, and retail products in Japan.

"Finally, the market for consumer goods seems almost untapped. Only 3 percent of Japanese imports are nonfood consumer items like apparel or sporting goods. Trading companies such as Mitsubishi Industries are working hard to promote American products such as garden equipment and jewelry.

"I think there are a whole lot of reasons to consider exporting to Japan. I'm not saying that there aren't problems—there are—but I honestly believe that there's tremendous potential for a skillful American marketer."

Nicholas Karas looked unconvinced. "I know what you're saying. I've said the same thing myself in Kramer executive meetings, almost word for word. But our start-up costs will be very high, and our profits will be minimal for the first five to ten years. After that, we'll be in fine shape—*if* the Japanese market remains strong. But if there's further recession, people just won't be shelling out for our high-price golf clubs. And we'll be sunk!

Questions
1. What elements should Karas consider in whether Kramer Company should do business in Japan?
2. What organizational arrangement would be best to link Kramer with Japan?
3. Would you recommend that Kramer enter Japan? Why?

ELTON AND ROLAND COMPANY

Elton and Roland Company (E&R) is a five-store chain that was founded in 1898 in the Portland, Oregon metropolitan area. For the past ten years, E&R has been a division of a nation-wide retailing conglomerate. The store's 1976 sales figure of $65 million was the smallest of any division in the conglomerate; yet, interestingly, E&R has been one of the most profitable retailers despite its comparatively low sales.

The Social Responsibility Issue at E&R

Vernon O'Neil is a 23-year-old, lifelong Oregon resident. He was a marketing major in his undergraduate days at the University of Oregon at Eugene, and received his bachelor's degree in June, 1975. That summer, he began working as an assistant buyer in several ready-to-wear clothing departments at E&R. At the same time, he enrolled as a graduate student in an evening program at the University of Oregon at Portland. Vernon hopes to complete an M.B.A. program in the next three years.

In Vernon's marketing problems seminar he was asked to write a term paper on a marketing social responsibility issue. He chose to use his working situation at E&R as a "laboratory" for his studies, and began researching product safety and quality controls at Elton and Roland Company.

Here are some excerpts from Vernon O'Neil's term paper:

I began my research work quite naively. I assumed that all of the company executives at E&R would speak quite openly with someone who was both an assistant buyer and a marketing student. I learned differently. There were few E&R personnel who would speak freely about social responsibility questions. Members of the advertising and legal departments were particularly uncooperative.

The most informative—and shocking—interview was with Ms. Lilly Appell, a chemist who is in charge of testing facilities at E&R. In 1973, E&R basically abandoned a previously first-rate testing operation. As a result, there is virtually no internal testing of products for safety and quality today at E&R. Appell is currently spending most of her time on personnel matters, despite her official position as head of product testing.

Appell spoke quite forthrightly about why this change occurred. In her view, management has discouraged product testing because of the costs involved. They find it easier to satisfy the disgruntled customer— who they assume will be in a minority—than to guarantee a safe, top-quality product. Often management attempts to pass the costs of product replacement back to the manufacturer. . . .

I conducted a brief survey of care labeling in six ready-to-wear departments at E&R. Although state law explicitly requires content and care labeling for all merchandise that is subject to cleaning, many items for sale lacked any labeling information whatsoever. . . .

E&R has been on an "increased productivity" campaign for the past year. The goal is to maintain the chain's high profitability rating within the conglomerate. While it is difficult to speak definitively with such limited data in hand, it certainly appears that product safety and quality considerations have been disregarded by E&R management for the "greater goal" of high profits.

As one former commissioner of the Federal Trade Commission stated: "Competition and voluntary action of businessmen do not always suffice to safeguard the public interest. Competition does not always take the form of rivalry to produce the safest product. Indeed, the competitive struggle may sometimes lead to a shaving of the costs of manufacture involving some sacrifice of safety."

Personal Conflict— Ethic vs. Profits

Writing this term paper was a difficult experience for Vernon O'Neil. He began the project with enthusiasm, but the more he learned, the more his faith in business was shaken. By the end, he was well aware that he needed to sort out his values before deciding on future career choices.

O'Neil believed *before* he began the project—and still felt afterwards—that a firm like E&R had a perfect right, and a responsibility, to maintain profits and guarantee its survival. At the same time, his studies of consumer problems suggested that the public had a right to safe and high-quality products at a decent price. How could these rights be balanced? Could a firm spend the money for product testing and still make a profit? What if both were not possible at the same time?

These were the questions in Vernon O'Neil's mind at the end of his marketing problems course. He had no immediate answers, but he knew that he would have to resolve the internal conflict at some point if he hoped to continue working in firms like E&R.

Questions

1. Is there any conflict at E&R between increasing marketing productivity and recognizing social responsibility?
2. What might be O'Neil's recommendations in his term paper regarding the future of consumer protection at E&R?
3. If you were O'Neil, how would you evaluate the ethical dilemma? How would you evaluate E&R in terms of a future career?

Appendix

MARKETING ARITHMETIC

Quantitative data are a key tool of the marketing manager. As we saw in Chapter 25, they are a major factor in the marketing control process. As a result, the marketing manager must be familiar and comfortable with the basic concepts of business accounting. In this appendix, we will explore the terminology and arithmetic of the operating statement, operating ratios, and markup and markdown calculations.

THE OPERATING STATEMENT

The **operating statement**, also known as the **profit and loss statement**, is the most frequently used source of internal marketing information. It provides a detailed and meaningful answer to the question, "How are we doing?" As such, it is an important part of any situation analysis procedure. Simply stated, the operating statement is a financial summary of the sales, gross margin, expenses, and net profits or losses of an organization in a given period of time. This period is usually one month, three months, six months, or a year.

The critical task of the operating statement is to present the net profits or losses of the firm in the period under consideration. Table A-1 represents a short form of an operating statement that might be used by a wholesaler or a retailer. As the table shows, the Wellrun Company registered net sales of $700,000 during the year ending December 31, 1976. It sold from inventory

Table A-1
SHORT FORM OF AN OPERATING STATEMENT FOR THE WELL-RUN COMPANY FOR THE PERIOD ENDING DECEMBER 31, 1976

Net sales	$700,000
Less cost of goods sold	400,000
Gross margin	$300,000
Less total expenses	210,000
Net profit	$ 90,000

goods costing $400,000. The amount of net sales exceeded the costs of goods sold by a gross margin of $300,000. The firm's total expenses in the fiscal year, however, accounted for $200,000, which reduced the net profits to $100,000.

Let us examine in more detail the key elements of the operating statement: sales, cost of goods sold, gross margin, and expenses.

SALES   An operating statement begins with the firm's **gross sales**: the total amount of sales revenue received by the firm in the designated time period. But gross sales alone are not a true measure of sales revenue, since many goods are returned by customers, who may be given full or partial credit for the price. It may also be necessary to make allowances to customers for damaged goods, representing part of the purchase price. In order to determine final sales (called **net sales**), returns and other allowances must be subtracted from the gross sales figure. This net sales figure is also used in calculating operating ratios (see pp. 665–66).

The net sales figure by itself is not, of course, an accurate guide to the firm's financial state of health. It is, however, a commonly used yardstick for sales managers and other sales personnel. Increases in net sales are usually a primary goal of the sales department.

COST OF GOODS SOLD   An estimation of the **cost of goods sold** begins with the determination of the value of the goods on hand at the start of the period in question (in our example, this would be January 1, 1976). These goods are known as *beginning inventory*. Let us assume that the beginning inventory of Wellrun was $125,000. During the period in question (January 1–December 31, 1976), the company purchased $375,000 in goods. The company then took another inventory at the end of the period to determine the value of the goods left unsold during the year (*ending inventory*). This amounted to $100,000. Adding the value of goods purchased ($375,000) to the beginning inventory ($125,000) and then subtracting the ending inventory ($100,000), we can determine that the cost of goods sold was $400,000.

GROSS MARGIN   Gross margin, commonly called **gross profit**, is determined by subtracting the cost of goods sold from the net sales revenue. In other words, the company subtracts what it paid for the merchandise it sold from the revenue that the merchandise brought in. Calculation of the gross margin ratio is often used as a yardstick for comparing performance year by year and with that of the competition. In addition, the gross margin figure is used as a guideline for determining expense budgets.

EXPENSES In order to determine net profits, the organization must subtract its **expenses** (also called **operating expenses**) from the net sales figure. These expenses include salaries, supplies, accounting, bad debts, and many other categories. If the total of these expenses exceeds the gross margin, the organization is operating at a loss.

A detailed example of a profit and loss statement for Wellrun is illustrated in Table A-2.

Table A-2
OPERATING STATEMENT OF THE WELLRUN COMPANY
FOR THE PERIOD ENDING DECEMBER 31, 1976

			OPERATING RATIOS (percentage)
Gross sales	$725,000		
Less returns and allowances	25,000		
Net sales		$700,000	100
Cost of goods sold:			
Inventory Jan. 1, 1976	$125,000		
Purchases	375,000		
	500,000		
Less inventory Dec. 31, 1976	100,000		
Cost of goods sold		$400,000	57.0
Gross margin		$300,000	43.0
Operating expenses:			
Accounting and legal	3,500		.5
Advertising	31,500		4.5
Bad debts	3,500		.5
Delivery costs	7,000		1.0
Depreciation	7,000		1.0
Wages	87,500		12.5
Entertainment and travel	10,500		1.5
Insurance	2,100		.3
Interest	1,400		.2
Miscellaneous and repair	3,500		.5
Rent	31,500		4.5
Supplies	9,100		1.3
Taxes and licenses	8,400		1.2
Utilities and telephone	3,500		.5
Total expenses		$210,000	30.0
Net profit (before taxes)		$ 90,000	13.0

OPERATING RATIOS

As was indicated at the beginning of the Appendix, the critical question to be answered by the operating statement is, "How are we doing?" So far, we have answered this question in terms of *dollar amounts*. But the marketing manager will also want to know how these dollar amounts relate to the same calculations that were made last year and the year before that. To make these comparisons meaningful, the manager must calculate **operating ratios** (also called **control ratios**). These ratios are expressed in terms of a percentage of net sales (using the net sales amount as 100 percent). The most commonly calculated operating ratios are gross margin percentage, returns and allowances percentage, expense percentage, and net profit percentage.

GROSS MARGIN PERCENTAGE

The **gross margin percentage** is determined by dividing the gross margin by the net sales figure. In the case of Wellrun, the calculations would be:

$$\frac{\text{Gross margin (\$300,000)}}{\text{Net sales (\$700,000)}} = \text{Gross margin percentage (43\%)}$$

Taken by itself, a gross margin of 43 percent probably sounds as though Wellrun is doing very well. But we cannot make such a judgment until the gross margin percentage for 1976 is compared with that of 1975 and 1974 and with that of the competition, if known. Broadly speaking, gross margin percentages may be increased in three ways: by increasing sales, by decreasing costs, or by doing both.

RETURNS AND ALLOWANCES PERCENTAGE

It is, of course, impossible to please everyone, no matter what product or service is being sold. A certain number of returns are always to be expected. Calculating the **returns and allowances percentage** enables the marketing manager to spot potential problems relating to product quality. If the returns percentage begins to rise, the manager will want to investigate the possible sources of consumer dissatisfaction. In the case of Wellrun, the returns and allowances percentage would be:

$$\frac{\text{Returns and allowances (\$25,000)}}{\text{Net sales (\$700,000)}} = \text{Returns and allowances percentage (4\%)}$$

EXPENSE PERCENTAGE

As with the other ratios we have examined, the **expense percentage** is really only meaningful as a tool of comparison. In most cases, expenses as a percentage of net sales are compared within each company, rather than on an industry-wide basis. Different organizations place a different emphasis on expense items such as advertising or sales promotion, and so comparison of expenses may not necessarily be meaningful from company to company. In the case of Wellrun, the expense percentage would be:

$$\frac{\text{Expenses (\$210,000)}}{\text{Net sales (\$700,000)}} = \text{Expense percentage (30\%)}$$

NET PROFIT PERCENTAGE

The **net profit percentage** is actually made up of all the percentages we have previously analyzed. Taken by itself, this ratio provides an overall guide to the company's state of health and is commonly used as a convenient control measure. The other ratios we have analyzed must also be examined in detail by the manager if the source of problems is to be found. For Wellrun, the net profit percentage would be:

$$\frac{\text{Net profit (\$90,000)}}{\text{Net sales (\$700,000)}} = \text{Net profit percentage (13\%)}$$

MARKUP CALCULATIONS

As we saw in our consideration of pricing strategy in Chapters 14–16, **markup** is the amount added to the basic price of a product to return the seller a profit. Since the markup is used to cover expenses and generate a profit, the markup is closely related to the concept of gross margin. Markup may be calculated on the basis of cost or of selling price.

MARKUP BASED ON COST

For a retailer, a markup to be added to cost is usually somewhat greater than the gross margin, in order to cover costs of pilferage, breakage, and other damage that makes the goods unsaleable. In the case of Wellrun, whose gross margin we calculated as 43 percent, let us assume that the markup is 45 percent. Therefore, if an item costs Wellrun $20.00, the markup of 45 percent would translate into $9.00, for a retail price of $29.00.

MARKUP BASED ON PRICE

It is also possible to express markup as a percentage of the selling price. In the previous example, a $9.00 markup for an item with a retail price of $29.00 would be equivalent to 31 percent:

$$\frac{\text{Dollar markup (\$9.00)}}{\text{Retail price (\$29.00)}} = \text{Percentage markup (31\%)}$$

MARKDOWN CALCULATIONS

As we have already seen, prices sometimes have to be lowered. The amount by which they are lowered is known as **markdown**. Markdowns are expressed as a percentage of the price to which the item is marked down. If, for example, our $29.00 item is marked down $4.00 to sell for $25.00, the markdown is said to be 16 percent.

$$\frac{\text{Dollar markdown (\$4.00)}}{\text{Selling price (\$25.00)}} = \text{Percentage markdown (16\%)}$$

Markdowns may be used to establish prices during a sale. They may also be offered as an allowance to a customer who wishes to return an item because it is damaged or otherwise unsatisfactory.

Name Index

Subject Index